Dryland East Asia
Land Dynamics Amid Social and Climate Change

Editors:

Jiquan Chen, Shiqiang Wan,

Geoffrey Henebry,

Jiaguo Qi, Garik Gutman, Ge Sun,

Martin Kappas

Technical Editors:

Alona Gutman, Lisa Delp Taylor

高等教育出版社·北京

HIGHER EDUCATION PRESS   BEIJING

图书在版编目（C I P）数据

社会-气候交互变化中的东亚干旱与半干旱区生态系统研究 = Dryland East Asia : Land Dynamics Amid Social and Climate Change : 英文 /（美）陈吉泉等著.

—北京：高等教育出版社，2013. 8

（生态系统科学与应用）

ISBN 978-7-04-037819-1

Ⅰ. ①社… Ⅱ. ①陈… Ⅲ. ①干旱区-生态系-研究-东亚-英文 Ⅳ. ① P941.71 ② Q147

中国版本图书馆 CIP 数据核字（2013）第 154862 号

策划编辑	关 焱	责任编辑	关 焱	封面设计	张 楠	版式设计	杜微言
插图绘制	尹 莉	责任校对	刘丽娴	责任印制	朱学忠		

出版发行	高等教育出版社	咨询电话	400-810-0598
社　　址	北京市西城区德外大街4号	网　　址	http://www.hep.edu.cn
邮政编码	100120		http://www.hep.com.cn
印　　刷	北京信彩瑞禾印刷厂	网上订购	http://www.landraco.com
开　　本	787 mm × 1092 mm 1/16		http://www.landraco.com.cn
印　　张	31	版　　次	2013 年 8 月第 1 版
字　　数	400 千字	印　　次	2013 年 8 月第 1 次印刷
购书热线	010-58581118	定　　价	139.00 元

List of Contributors

Agrawal, Arun
School of Natural Resources and Environment, University of Michigan, Ann Arbor, MI, USA
arunagra@umich.edu

Ai, Likun
Chinese Academy of Sciences, Beijing, China
aili@mairs-essp.org

Batkhishig, Ochirbat
Institute of Geography, Mongolian Academy of Sciences, Ulaanbaatar, Mongolia
batkhishig@gmail.com

Becker, Richard H.
Department of Environmental Sciences, University of Toledo, Toledo, OH, USA
rbecker7@utnet.utoledo.edu

Brown, G. Daniel
School of Natural Resources and Environment, University of Michigan, Ann Arbor, MI, USA
danbrown@umich.edu

Chen, Jiquan
Landscape Ecology & Ecosystem Science (LEES) Lab, Department of Environmental Sciences, University of Toledo, Toledo, OH, USA
Jiquan.Chen@utoledo.edu

Chen, Liding
Research Center for Eco-Environmental Sciences, Chinese Academy of Sciences, Beijing, China
ldchen@rcees.ac.cn

Chen, Shiping
Institute of Botany, Chinese Academy of Sciences, Beijing, China
spchen@ibcas.ac.cn

Chen, Xi
Xinjiang Institute of Ecology and Geography, Chinese Academy of Sciences, Ürümqi, China
chenxi@ms.xjb.ac.cn

Chen, Yaning
Xinjiang Institute of Ecology and Geography, Chinese Academy of Sciences, Ürümqi, China
Chenyn@mx.xjb.ac.cn

Chuluun, Togtohyn
Dryland Sustainability Institute, Ulaanbaatar, Mongolia
chuluunjim@yahoo.com

Darmenova, Kremena
School of Earth and Atmospheric Sciences, Georgia Institute of Technology, Atlanta, GA, USA
kdarmenova@gatech.edu

de Beurs, Kirsten M.
Department of Geography and Environmental Sustainability, University of Oklahoma, Norman, OK, USA
kdebeurs@ou.edu

Fan, Peilei
Center for Global Change and Earth Observation, Michigan State University, East Lansing, MI, USA
fanpeile@msu.edu

Feng, Xiaoming
Research Center for Eco-Environmental Sciences, Chinese Academy of Sciences, Beijing, China
fengxm@rcees.ac.cn

Fu, Bojie
Research Center for Eco-Environmental Sciences, Chinese Academy of Sciences, Beijing, China
bfu@rcees.ac.cn

Gao, Liping
School of Forestry and Wildlife Sciences, Auburn University, AL, USA
lzg0005@tigermail.auburn.edu

Groisman, Pavel
NOAA National Climatic Data Center, Asheville, NC, USA
pasha.groisman@noaa.gov

Guo, Ke
Institute of Botany, Chinese Academy of Sciences, Beijing, China
guoke@ibcas.ac.cn

Gutman, Garik
NASA Land-Cover/Land-Use Change Program, Washington, DC, USA
garik.gutman@nasa.gov

Han, Guodong
Inner Mongolia Agricultural University, Hohhot, China
nmghanguodong@163.com

Havstad, Kris
USDA-ARS, Jornada Experimental Range, Las Cruces, NM, USA
khavstad@nmsu.edu

Henebry, Geoffrey M.
Geographic Information Science Center of Excellence, South Dakota State University, Brookings, SD, USA
Geoffrey.Henebry@sdstate.edu

Herrick, Jeffery E.
USDA-ARS, Jornada Experimental Range, Las Cruces, NM, USA
jherrick@ad.nmsu.edu

Huang, Huiqing
Center for Global Change and Earth Observation, East Lansing, MI, USA
Huiqingh@msu.edu

Huang, Jianping
College of Atmospheric Sciences, Lanzhou University, Lanzhou, China
hjp@lzu.edu.cn

John, Ranjeet
Landscape Ecology & Ecosystem Science (LEES) Lab, Department of Environmental Sciences, University of Toledo, Toledo, OH, USA
Ranjeet.John@utoledo.edu

Kalashnikova, Olga
Jet Propulsion Laboratory, California Institute of Technology, Pasadena, CA, USA
olga.kalashnikova@jpl.nasa.gov

Kappas, Martin
Institute of Geography, Georg-August University of Goettingen, Germany
mkappas@gwdg.de

Karnieli, Arnon
Jacob Blaustein Institutes for Desert Research, Ben Gurion University of the Negev, Israel
karnieli@bgu.ac.il

Kemp, David
Charles Sturt University, Orange, Australia
dkemp@csu.edu.au

Kurban, Alishir
Xinjiang Institute of Ecology and Geography, Chinese Academy of Sciences, Ürümqi, Xinjiang, China.
alishir@ms.xjb.ac.cn

Kurosaki, Yasunori
School of Earth and Atmospheric Sciences, Georgia Institute of Technology, Atlanta, GA, USA
kuro@alrc.tottori-u.ac.jp

Li, Fengmin
School of Life Sciences, Lanzhou University, Lanzhou, China
fmli@lzu.edu.cn

Li, Linghao
Institute of Botany, Chinese Academy of Sciences, Beijing, China
llinghao@ibcas.ac.cn

Li, Xue
Center for Global Change and Earth Observation, East Lansing, MI, USA
lixue@msu.edu

Li, Zhiguo
Inner Mongolia Agriculture University, Hohhot, China
nmndlzg@163.com

Lioubimtseva, Elena
Department of Geography and Planning, Grand Valley State University,
Allendale, MI, USA
lioubime@gvsu.edu

Liu, Tong
Inner Mongolia Agricultural University, Hohhot, China
h_liutong@yahoo.cn

Long, Ruijun
Engineering Research Centre for Arid Agriculture and Ecological Rehabilitation,
Lanzhou University, Lanzhou, China
longrj@gsau.edu.cn

Lu, Nan
Research Center for Eco-Environmental Sciences, Chinese Academy of Sciences,
Beijing, China
nanlv@rcees.ac.cn

Mátyás, Csaba
Institute of Environmental and Earth Sciences, University of West Hungary,
Hungary
cm@emk.nyme.hu

Messina, Joseph
Center for Global Change and Earth Observation, East Lansing, MI, USA
jpm@msu.edu

Niu, Shuli
Key Laboratory of Ecosystem Network Observation and Modeling, Institute
of Geographic Sciences and Natural Resources Research, Chinese Academy of
Sciences, Beijing, China
sniu@ou.edu

Ouyang, Zutao
Landscape Ecology & Ecosystem Science, University of Toledo, Toledo, OH, USA
Zutao.Yang@rockets.utoledo.edu

Ozdogan, Mutlu
Center for Sustainability and the Global Environment, University of Wisconsin,
Madison, WI, USA
ozdogan@wisc.edu

Piao, Shilong
College of Urban and Environmental Sciences, Peking University, Beijing, China
slpiao@pku.edu.cn

Propastin, Pavel
Institute of Geography, Georg-August University of Goettingen, Germany
ppropas@uni-goettingen.de

Qi, Jiaguo
Center for Global Change and Earth Observation, Michigan State University, East Lansing, MI, USA
qi@msu.edu

Qiao, Guanghua
College of Economics and Management, Inner Mongolia Agricultural University, Huhhot, China
qiao_imau@126.com

Reynolds, James F.
Nicholas School of the Environment, Duke University, Durham, NC, USA
james.f.reynolds@duke.edu

Reynolds, Julie A.
Department of Biology, Duke University, Durham, NC, USA
julie.a.reynolds@duke.edu

Shao, Changliang
Institute of Botany, Chinese Academy of Sciences, Beijing, China
zkyscl@ibcas.ac.cn

Shiklomanov, Alex
Institute for the Study of Earth, Oceans, and Space, University of New Hampshire, Durham, NH, USA
alex.shiklomanov@unh.edu

Sokolik, Irina N.
School of Earth and Atmospheric Sciences, Georgia Institute of Technology, Atlanta, GA, USA
isokolik@eas.gatech.edu

Sun, Ge
Eastern Forest Environmental Threat Assessment Center, Southern Research USDA Forest Service, Raleigh, NC, USA
gesun@fs.fed.us

Wan, Shiqiang
College of Life Sciences, Henan University, Kaifeng, Henan, China
swan@ibcas.ac.cn

Wang, Jun
School of Natural Resources and Environment, University of Michigan, Ann Arbor, MI, USA
junw@umich.edu

Wang, Xuhui
College of Urban and Environmental Sciences, Peking University, Beijing, China
wxh.pku@gmail.com

Wang, Shengping
Key Laboratory of Regional Energy System Optimization, North China Electric Power University, Beijing, China
wangshp418@yahoo.com.cn

Wang, Shuai
Research Center for Eco-Environmental Sciences, Chinese Academy of Sciences, Beijing, China
shuaiwangnmg@gmail.com

Wang, Zhongwu
Inner Mongolia Agricultural University, Hohhot, China
zhongwuwang1979@yahoo.com

Wright, Christopher K.
Geographic Information Science Center of Excellence, South Dakota State University, Brookings, SD, USA
Christopher.Wright@sdstate.edu

Wu, Jianguo
School of Life Sciences & School of Sustainability, Arizona State University, Tempe, AZ, USA
Jingle.Wu@asu.e

Xi, Xin
School of Earth and Atmospheric Sciences, Georgia Institute of Technology, Atlanta, GA, USA
xin.xi@eas.gatech.edu

Xia, Jianyang
Department of Microbiology and Plant Biology, University of Oklahoma, Norman, OK, USA
jxia@ou.edu

Xiao, Jingfeng
Earth Systems Research Center, Institute for the Study of Earth, Oceans, and Space, University of New Hampshire, Durham, NH, USA
j.xiao@unh.edu

Yan, Dong
Department of Geography and Environmental Sustainability, University of Oklahoma, Norman, OK, USA
Dong.Yan-1@ou.edu

Yan, Liming
School of Life Sciences, Fudan University, Shanghai, China
yanliming0108@gmail.com

Ye, Jiansheng
School of Life Sciences, Lanzhou University, Lanzhou, China
yejiansheng30@gmail.com

Yuan, Wenping
College of Global Change and Earth System Science, Beijing Normal University, Beijing, China
wyuan@bnu.edu.cn

Zhang, Li
Key Laboratory of Digital Earth Science, Institute of Remote Sensing and Digital Earth, Chinese Academy of Sciences, Beijing, China
lizhang@ceode.ac.cn

Zhang, Yaoqi
School of Forestry & Wildlife Sciences, Auburn University, AL, USA
yaoqi.zhang@auburn.edu

Zhang, Zhiqiang
College of Soil and Water Conservation, Beijing Forestry University, Beijing, China
zhqzhang@bjfu.edu.cn

Zhao, Mengli
Inner Mongolia Agriculture University, Hohhot, China
menglizhao@yahoo.com

Zmijewski, Kirk A.
Department of Environmental Sciences, University of Toledo, Toledo, OH, USA
kirk.zmijewski@rockets.utoledo.edu

Abbreviations

3Ns and YRB	Three North and the Yangtze River Basin
ADB	Asia Development Bank
AI	Aerosol Index
ANPP	Aboveground Net Prime Productivity
AO	Arctic Oscillation
AOD	Aerosol Optical Depth
AP	Annual Precipitation
AVHRR	Advanced Very High Resolution Radiometer
BII	Biodiversity Intactness Index
BNPP	Belowground Net Prime Productivity
BSC	Biological Soil Crusts
C	Carbon
CAI	Cellulose Absorption Index
CAS	Chinese Academy of Science
CBD	Convention on Biological Diversity
CBRM	Community-Based Resource Management
CCFP	Cropland Conversion to Forests Program
CMG	Climate Modeling Grid
CMS	Carbon Monitoring System
CNH	Coupled Natural and Human
CRU	Climatic Research Unit
CSDF	French Scientific Committee on Desertification
CST	Committee on Science and Technology
DC	Duolun Cropland
DCA	Drylands of Central Asia
DDP	Dryland Development Paradigm
DEA	Dryland East Asia
DLDD	Desertification/Land Degradation and Drought
DNA	Drylands of North America
DPSIR	Driving Force-Pressure-State-Impact-Response
DS	Duolun Steppe
DTR	Diurnal Temperature Range
DWG	Dryland Working Group
ECVs	Essential Climate Variables
EDN	European DesertNet
EEA	European Environment Agency

ENSO	El Niño-Southern Oscillation
EOS	Earth Observing System
ER	Ecosystem Respiration
EROS	Earth Resources Observation and Science
ESA	Ecosystem Science and Applications
ESIP	Earth Science Information Partner
ESS	Earth System Science
ESSP	Earth System Science Partnership
ET	Evapotranspiration
ETM	Enhanced Thematic Mapper
EVI	Enhanced Vegetation Index
FAO	Food and Agriculture Organization
FAPAR	Fraction of Absorbed Photosynthetically Active Radiation
FLAASH	Fast Line-of-Sight Atmospheric Analysis of Spectral Hypercubes
fPAR	Fraction of Photosynthetically Active Radiation
GMAO	Global Modeling and Assimilation Office
GCM	Global Climate Model
GCMs	Global Circulation Models
GCOS	Global Climate Observing System
GDOS	Global Drylands Observing System
GDP	Gross Domestic Product
GEP	Gross Ecosystem Productivity
GfGP	Grain for Green Program
GIMMS	Global Inventory Modeling and Mapping Studies
GMAO	Global Modeling and Assimilation Office
GPCC	Global Precipitation Climatology Centre
GPCP	Global Precipitation Climatology Project
GPP	Gross Primary Productivity
GS	Gansu Province
HDI	Human Development Index
H-E	Human-Environmental
HEC	Human-Environment-Climate
HPRS	Household Production Responsibility System
HS	Human System
HYDE	History Database of Global Environment
IGBP	International Geosphere-Bioshpere Programme
IGSNRR-CAS	Institute of Geographic Sciences and Natural Resources Research, CAS
IM	Inner Mongolia Autonomous Region
LAI	Leaf Area Index
LC	Land Cover
LCLU	Land Cover and Land Use
LCLUC	Land Cover and Land Use Change
LDA	Land Degradation Assessment
LDCM	Landsat Data Continuity Mission

LTK	Local Traditional Knowledge
LUE	Light Use Efficiency
LUR	Land Use Rights
LUT	Look Up Tables
MA	Millennium Assessment
MAIRS	Monsoon Asia Integrated Regional Study
MAT	Mean Annual Temperature
ME	Metabolisable Energy
MEA	Millennium Ecosystem Assessment
MERRA	Modern Era Retrospective-Analysis for Research and Applications
MG	Mongolia
MISR	Multi-angle Imaging Spectro-Radiometer
MODIS	Moderate Resolution Imaging Spectroradiometer
MSP	Medium Scale Project
MSS	Multispectral Scanner
N	Nitrogen
NAM	Northern Annular Mode
NAO	North Atlantic Oscillation
NARCM	Northern Aerosol Regional Climate Model
NASA	National Aeronautics and Space Administration
NBAR	Nadir BRDF-Adjusted Reflectance
NBSA	National Bureau of Statistics of China
NCAR	National Center For Atmospheric Research
NCEP	National Centers for Environmental Prediction
NDI	Normalized Difference Index
NDVI	Normalized Difference Vegetation Index
NEE	Net Ecosystem Exchange
NEESPI	Northern Eurasia Earth Science Partnership Initiative
NEP	Net Ecosystem Production
NFCP	Natural Forest Conservation Program
NFPP	Natural Forest Protection Program
NOAA	National Oceanic and Atmospheric Administration
NPP	Net Primary Production
NS	Natural System
NX	Ningxia Hui Autonomous Region
OLI	Operational Land Imager
OLS	Ordinary Least Squares
OMI	Ozone Monitoring Instrument
ORCHIDEE	Organizing Carbon and Hydrology in Dynamic Ecosystems
OS	Observation System
PAR	Photosynthetically Active Radiation
PES	Payment for Environmental Services
PPFD	Photosynthetic Photon Flux Density
PPP	Purchasing Power Parity
PRI	Photosynthetic Reflectance Index

PSR	Pressure-State-Response
PSURC	Pressure-State-Use-Response-Capacity
RAS	Russian Academy of Sciences
RCM	Regional Climate Model
RS	Remote Sensing
SACRI	Soil Adjusted Corn Residue Index
SAR	Synthetic Aperture Radar
SAVI	Soil-Adjusted Vegetation Index
SCP	Sand Control Program
SD	Standard Deviation
SeaWiFS	Sea-Viewing Wide Field-of-View Sensor
SK	Seasonal Kendall
SKFPs	State Key Forestry Programs
SLM	Sustainable Land Management
SMK	Seasonal Mann–Kendall
SOM	Soil Organic Matter
SRB	Surface Radiation Balance
SRTM	Shuttle Radar Topography Mission
SSC	Science Steering Committee
START	System for Analysis, Research and Training
START TEA	START Tropical East Asia
SWC	Soil Volumetric Water Content
TEA	Tropical East Asia
TIRS	Thermal Infrared Sensor
TM	Thematic Mapper
TNSFP	Three Norths Shelterbelt Forest Program
TOMS	Total Ozone Mapping Spectrometer
TPN	Thematic Program Network
UHDZ	Ürümqi High-tech Development Zone
UNCCD	United Nations Convention to Combat Desertification
UNFCCC	UN Framework Convention on Climate Change
USGS	U.S. Geological Survey
VI	Vegetation Index
VPD	Vapor Pressure Deficit
WAD	World Atlas of Desertification
WBM	Water Balance Model
WCDP	West China Development Program
WIST	Warehouse Inventory Search Tool
WMO	World Meteorological Organization
WRF	Weather Research and Forecast
XD	Xilinhot Degraded Steppe
XF	Xilinhot Fenced Steppe
XJ	Xinjiang Uygur Autonomous Region

Preface

Among many pressing challenges facing the world today, understanding global changes and their consequences to society have not been well-investigated at regional levels. Based on previous and active research conducted in the Dryland East Asia (DEA) region of Northern Eurasia, various teams have built rich databases on climate, socioeconomic changes, remote sensing products, direct measurements of vegetation, soil, carbon and water fluxes, and demography at county/prefecture levels. One of the greatest challenges in this context is to develop a full picture and synthesis on how dryland ecosystems respond to changes in climate, environment, and human activities. This volume is designed to summarize the accumulated knowledge thus far and to direct future efforts of investigations. A new paradigm—coupled natural and human (CNH) systems—has evolved in recent years as a unifying concept for interdisciplinary research toward the goal of a sustainable society and environment. We instructed the contributors to use the CNH concept in developing their chapters. Our longer-term goal is to develop a synthesis of the data and knowledge on the coupled DEA systems at multiple temporal and spatial scales. We are fully aware that highly variable and changing climatic conditions influence the land cover, land use, and land conditions dynamically and interactively. Likewise, socioeconomic pressures influence land change dynamics and have complex biogeophysical and biogeochemical consequences that cascade through the elements of CNH systems.

A workshop was organized at Henan University in Kaifeng, China during July 18–20, 2011 with co-sponsorship of the Land-Cover and Land-Use Change (LCLUC) Program of NASA, Henan University, and National Natural Science Foundation of China (NSFC). During the workshop, over 40 participants, all active researchers on DEA or other dryland ecosystems, brought up many stimulating questions and suggestions for forming a synthesis study. Two review papers and these book chapters involved 76 authors from 7 countries. These publications move the scientific community closer to understanding processes in DEA. One particular notification for this text is about the administrative boundaries used in almost all chapters. DEA happened to be a region that has experienced some changes in administrative boundaries at provincial, national, and international levels in recent years. Here, we define DEA as a scientific study area, rather than accurate political region; although, we attempted to get the most accurate information from various governments. Some maps were re-used from published literature where full citations are provided for the responsibility of the data sources.

Many students and researchers at the College of Life Sciences, Henan University provided excellent services that made the workshop a great success. The text of the 19 chapters in this book has been improved through the constructive contributions of both the editors and many reviewers, including Kirsten M. de Beurs, Peilei Fan, Xiaoming Feng, Pavel Groisman, Arnon Karnieli, Shilong Piao, Gabriel Senay, Andres Vina, and Ming Xu. Many others (Chenlu Zhang, Cancan Zhao, Yinzhan Liu, Tingjuan Wu, Lei Wang, Fude Shang, Rumin Gao and Weikai Bao, etc.) also helped with some technical parts of this volume. Dr. Li Zhang of the Chinese Academy of Sciences spent a great deal of time and assistance for the final illustrations—we owe her a sincere thank you. We owe much to Dr. Bingxiang Li of the Higher Education Press (HEP), who has been a long-time supporter of the research in DEA and the current volume. The careful managing editorial work of Yan Guan, Alona Gutman, and Lisa Delp Taylor were critical for the completion of this book. Stephanie Dawson of De Gruyer provided speedy support for the establishment of the book series and proposal reviews on Ecosystem Science and Applications (ESA).

The Editors

Contents

Part I

State and Changes in
Dryland East Asia

Chapter 1

State and Change of Dryland East Asia (DEA)

Jiquan Chen, Ranjeet John, Guanghua Qiao, Ochirbat Batkhishig, Wenping Yuan, Yaoqi Zhang, Changliang Shao, Zutao Ouyang, Linghao Li, Ke Guo, and Ge Sun

Summary: Dryland East Asia (DEA) refers to a region with 4.81 million square kilometers (km^2) and includes Mongolia and four provinces/regions in Northern China (hereafter called "administrative units"): Inner Mongolia, Gansu, Ningxia, and Xinjiang. This introduction chapter provides an overview of the DEA region from three perspectives: 1) geography, demography, and economics, 2) climate and land use changes, and 3) ecosystem production and evapotranspiration. Development of a sound adaptation plan, therefore, is becoming a necessity for the sustainable future of a region such as DEA. We emphasize the spatial and temporal variations of the major variables associated with each of the three topic areas. Finally, we discuss the scientific and societal challenges for developing adaptation plans based on the concept of coupled natural and human (CNH) systems.

1.1 Geography, Demography and Economics in DEA

Dryland East Asia (DEA) is defined in this book as a region that includes Mongolia (MG) and four provinces/regions in Northwestern China (hereafter, called "administrative units"): Inner Mongolia Autonomous Region (IM), Gansu Province (GS), Ningxia Hui Autonomous Region (NX), and Xinjiang Uygur Autonomous Region (XJ). The 4.81 million square kilometer region (Fig. 1.1) is approximately the half size of China or the USA, with XJ as the largest province

$(1.638\times10^6\ \mathrm{km}^2)$ and NX as the smallest province $(0.052\times10^6\ \mathrm{km}^2)$ (Table 1.1). DEA borders Russia and Kazakhstan to the north and Kyrgyzstan, Tajikistan, Afghanistan, and Kashmir to the west (Fig. 1.1). The biogeographic units of DEA (i.e., ecoregions), classified by the World Wildlife Fund (WWF), include eight biomes within the Palearctic Realm (Olson et al., 2001) and are dominated by deserts and xeric shrublands (47.3%), temperate grasslands (23.4%), and temperate forests (11.1%). DEA has the Pamir Plateau and the Tibetan Plateau

Table 1.1 Composition (%) of land cover types in the Dryland East Asia (DEA) region that includes four provinces in China and Mongolia. The five dominant cover types are shown in bold.

Cover Type	Regions					Overall
	IM	NX	GS	XJ	MG	
Region land area (million km²)	1.152	0.052	0.405	1.638	1.566	4.814
Evergreen needleleaf forest	0.08	0.07	0.62	0.31	0.62	0.38
Evergreen broadleaf forest	0.02	0.00	0.01	0.00	0.01	0.01
Deciduous needleleaf forest	1.08	0.00	0.02	0.07	0.55	0.47
Deciduous broadleaf forest	0.45	0.23	1.07	0.01	0.08	0.23
Mixed forests	**6.16**	**0.27**	**3.70**	**0.25**	**1.68**	**2.42**
Closed shrublands	0.07	1.56	0.57	0.07	0.08	0.13
Open shrublands	**9.85**	**43.03**	**13.28**	**10.64**	**9.14**	**10.52**
Woody savannas	2.50	0.16	0.92	0.37	0.98	1.12
Savannas	0.82	0.51	1.27	0.09	0.34	0.45
Grasslands	**41.21**	**40.19**	**28.12**	**12.66**	**54.66**	**34.77**
Permanent wetlands	0.03	0.01	0.01	0.00	0.02	0.01
Croplands	**13.11**	**8.73**	**7.83**	**3.04**	**1.58**	**5.42**
Urban and built-up	0.19	1.02	0.40	0.15	0.00	0.14
Croplands	0.36	0.27	0.39	0.18	0.06	0.20
Permanent snow and ice	0.00	0.00	0.02	0.70	0.00	0.26
Barrens	**23.59**	**3.51**	**41.70**	**71.00**	**29.24**	**42.87**
Water	0.48	0.42	0.08	0.45	0.95	0.59
Total (5 dominants)	**93.92**	**95.74**	**94.63**	**97.59**	**96.30**	**96.01**

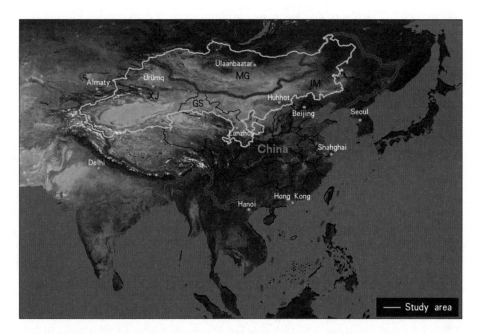

Fig. 1.1   The DEA region, with an elevation of −154 m–7,929 m asl, boarders the Tibetan Plateau in the southwest and is comprised of five administrative units, including four provinces/autonomous regions in China (Xinjiang, Gansu, Ningxia, and Inner Mongolia) and Mongolia. The Blue Marble Next Generation—a true-color earth dataset including seasonal dynamics from MODIS—is generated by combining MODIS NDVI with elevation derived from the three arc-second Shuttle Radar Topography Mission (SRTM) between 60°S and 60°N latitude (Stöckli et al., 2007).

in its southwest region and the Mongolian Plateau lies in the eastern portion of the region. The Tianshan and Kunlun Mountains lie at the western end of the DEA region, while the Qilian and Altay Mountains mark DEA's southern and northern boundaries, respectively. The Greater Xing'an Range runs from southwest to northeast in the northeastern part of DEA. The regional elevation varies from −154 m in the Lop Desert to 7,929 m in the Kunlun Mountains. These high-relief mountains are responsible for the existence of the 0.532×10^6 km^2 of temperate forest biomes and the relatively large amount of mountain grasslands and shrublands (17.1%). The Yellow River runs partially through the middle of the DEA region. Several major deserts (e.g., Gobi, Taklimakan, Junggar, Ordos, Lop, Badain Jaran and Maowusu) can be found within the region. The Taklimakan Desert is 337,000 km^2 with about 85% consisting of shifting sand dunes (i.e., the second-largest one next to the Sahara Desert) and is a major barrier along the Silk Road pathways. The Badain Jaran Desert, as another example, is home to the tallest stationary dunes on the earth (up to

500 m high). The increasing frequency and intensity of dust storms in East Asia have been attributed to these massive deserts and other degraded grasslands (Lu et al., 2009; Xuan et al., 2000).

In China, the region has special significance for national security and environmental concerns (e.g., the testing site for nuclear bombs in Lop Nur, the space flight center in Jiuquan, etc.). Mongolia itself is the 19th largest and most sparsely populated country in the world. It is also the world's second-largest landlocked country after Kazakhstan. The country contains very little arable land, as much of its area is covered by arid and unproductive steppes, with mountains to the north and west and the Gobi Desert to the southwest. Approximately 30% of the population is nomadic or semi-nomadic. For the Land Cover and Land Use Change (LCLUC) Program of the National Aeronautics and Space Administration (NASA), DEA is the continental extreme for the Monsoon Asia Integrated Regional Study (MAIRS) domain and the southern end of the Northern Eurasian Earth Science Partnership Initiative (NEESPI) domain (Groisman et al., 2009; Qi et al., 2012).

The population of all five administrative units has been steadily increasing, with an average annual rate of 2.19%, but varied from 1.14% in IM to 2.42% in NX (Fig. 1.2). The total population in DEA increased from 54.37 million in 1978 to 78.07 million in 2004. In 2008, the population density varied from $13.0/\text{km}^2$ in XJ to $118.1/\text{km}^2$ in NX, $21.3/\text{km}^2$ in IM, and $65.0/\text{km}^2$ in GS (Fig. 1.2a), which are all significantly lower than the Chinese national average of $139.6/\text{km}^2$. Mongolia remains sparsely occupied, with a population density of $1.6/\text{km}^2$ in 2004—an increase of 2.35%. Diverse ethnic groups such as Uygur, Mongol, Hui, Kazak, Man, and Zang (Tibetan) characterize all four administrative units in China. They are considered "Minority Regions" because of their diverse and numerous ethnic groups. Consequently, the region has been considered a focal area for government support (e.g., the Northwest Construction Program) since the early 1980s and for special policies set by the central governments such as college education, financial compensation, number of children per family, etc. However, the proportion of Han Chinese has been steadily increasing and becoming the majority in all four units. For example, Han Chinese comprises 79.1% of the population in IM, while Mongols account for 17.2%. In XJ, Uygur remains dominant (45%) over Han Chinese (41%). The major cities with large populations include Ürümqi (2.744 million) in XJ, Baotou (1.779 million) and Huhhot (2.867 million) in IM, Lanzhou (2.177 million) in GS, Yinchuan (1.290 million) in NX, and Ulaanbaatar (1.190 million) in MG (see Fan et al., this book). This accounts for 15.4% of the total population in the region. Further north, in Mongolia, 43.2% of its 2.6 million people can be found in its capital (Ulaanbaatar). Over the past decade, urbanization has continued to intensify due to the transition from a centralized economy to a market economy; this has resulted in an increase in urban population from 21.6% in 1956 to 63.3% in

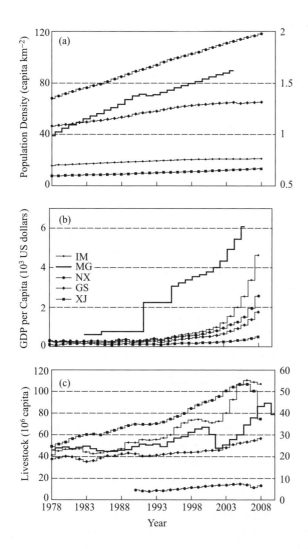

Fig. 1.2 Change in population density (a), gross domestic product (GDP) per capita (b), and livestock (c) in the five administrative units of the DEA region from 1978 through 2009. Note that the population density of Mongolia in (a) and livestock of MG, NX, GS, and XJ in (c) are marked by the second vertical axis on the right.

2006 (Ojima and Chuluun, 2008). The "Great Movement", started in 1990, will further aggregate land use in rural areas—a potential new land-use scenario for the future.

DEA has maintained a steady and high economic growth over the past three decades, with an earlier (since 1990) but slower takeoff in MG than those units in China (Fig. 1.2b). In MG, the transition from the centralized economy to the market economy started in 1990 after the collapse of former Soviet Union, with an average growth rate of about 2.8% in the 1990s and >6% in the recent decade.

The GDP per capita in MG was $611 in 1983 but jumped to $6,082 in 2006 — a tenfold increase over a 23-year period. In China, the "Open Economy Policy", implemented since 1979, promoted a miraculous growth of 9.7% between 1979 and 2006 at the national level. Interestingly, China was not affected by the global economic depression that began in 2008. However, because of its large population, the GDP per capita in the four DEA units of China was only $233 in 1983 and $1,373 in 2006, which were 38.1% and 22.8% of MG, respectively, for the two considered years, regardless of high GDP. Additionally, the economic growth was not evenly shared among the four units, with IM ranking first among China's 31 provinces, while XJ, GS, and NX had much smaller GDP growth. As a result, the GDP per capita in 2008 was $4,639 and $504 in IM and XJ, respectively. The lower-than-average economic growth and the significant differences among the units have been recognized by the government and are currently considered priority areas for development to address the regional disparity in upcoming years (i.e., China's 12th five-year plan, Qi et al., 2012).

Livestock has been widely used as a primary metric in dryland regions because of its importance in linking people, the economy and the environment. The livestock population in the DEA region doubled from 110.67×10^6 in 1978 to 222.38×10^6 in 2008 (Fig. 1.2c). An 88.7% increase was found in MG for the study period, while a 104.1% increase was found for the other four units within China. GS and XJ had the lowest increase, at ~50%, while IM and NX achieved 164.2% and 156.5% increases, respectively. The above differences in changes of livestock population among the four units in China may be partially due to the relatively high proportion of grasslands in IM (41.25) and NX (40.2%) and the low proportions in GS (28.2%) and XJ (12.7%) (Table 1.1). The large amount of livestock in IM (24.2% of DEA in 2008) made IM China's largest import base for dairy products (Sneath, 1998). Over time, the changes in livestock population seem to have had many more variables in IM and MG (i.e., on the Mongolian Plateau), but not in the other three units. We suspect that this may be related to the high sensitivity of the plateau to the changing climate because the Mongolian Plateau, with an elevation of 900–1,500 m, has been identified as one of the most sensitive regions in the world to the warming climate by IPCC (2007). For example, clear reductions in livestock population from 2000–2001 and 2008–2009 were recorded and both related to climate events such as low precipitation or drought (Fig. 1.3 and Fig. 1.4).

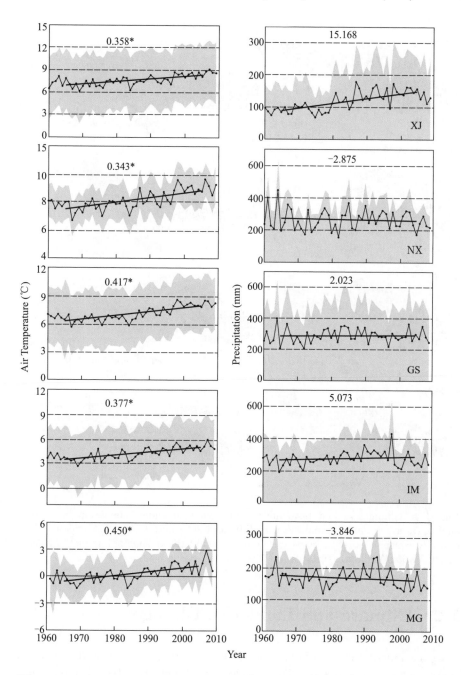

Fig. 1.3 Long-term changes of annual mean air temperature and precipitation between 1960 and 2009 in the five administrative units of DEA, showing a consistent
warming trend in all five units but a variable precipitation trend. The number in each
panel indicates the decadal change of temperature (°C) or precipitation (mm) and the
* indicates a significant level at 0.05.

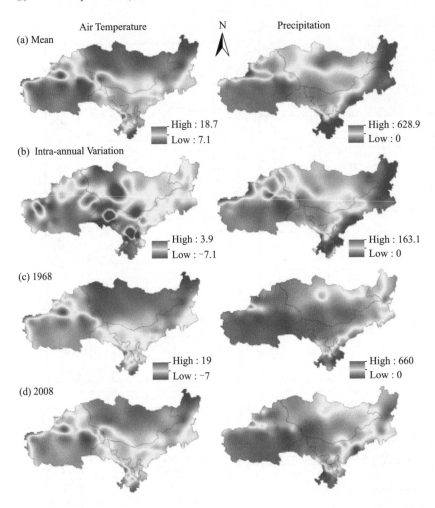

Fig. 1.4 Changes in long-term mean (1960–2009), standard deviation (i.e., intra-annual variation), and annual mean in 1996 and 2008 across the DEA region. These spatially continuous trend maps were created using the tension spline method based on 166 national climatic stations in China and Mongolia.

1.2 Climate and Land-Use Changes

Long-term *in situ* records of temperature and precipitation were used to quantify changes over time and across DEA landscapes (Lu et al., 2009). The daily meteorological data (1961–2009) from 149 weather stations was acquired from the China Meteorological Data Sharing Service System (http://cdc.cma.gov.cn/), while monthly mean temperature and precipitation at 17 national meteorological stations in Mongolia were provided by the Hydro-Meteorological Agency of

Mongolia for the same time period. The latitude, longitude, and elevation for each of the 166 stations were also included in the data, allowing us to analyze the spatial variation. We spatially interpolated the annual mean temperature and precipitation using a tension spline method (Franke, 1982; Mitas et al., 1988). The tension spline creates a less-smooth surface as compared to a regular spline, with values constrained closer to the sample range. This is especially true for the interpolated extreme values for annual temperature and precipitation. The tension spline was projected on a 5,600 m (i.e., 0.05 degree) to match the Climate Modeling Grid (CMG), with an Albers equal area projection.

There has been a significant increase in annual mean temperature, but variable, insignificant changes in precipitation for the study period from 1960–2009 (Fig. 1.3). The long-term changes in both temperature and precipitation are complicated by the high intra-annual variations as well as the complex topography (Fig. 1.1a). The decadal increase in annual temperature was higher in MG and GS (0.450 and 0.417 °C/10 yr, respectively) than in the three remaining units, with the lowest warming (0.343 °C/10 yr) in NX. As a result, the annual mean temperature in XJ, NX and IM has not been below zero since 1985. These increasing trends were previously reported for different biomes and spatial scales. Lu et al. (2009) reported that the warming is more affected by daily minimum temperature than daily maximum values (see also Zhai & Pan, 2003), suggesting that the warming trends reported here are likely less pronounced than when minimum daily temperature is used. They also reported that the grassland biome (+0.41 °C/10 yr) and desert biome (+0.39 °C/10 yr) experienced more increases in air temperature per decade than forest biomes (0.27 °C/10 yr). Precipitation at low elevations has been increasing; however, at high elevations, it has been decreasing. On a seasonal basis, the trend of temperature increases was higher in winter (0.42 °C/10 yr) than fall (0.34 °C/10 yr), spring (0.30 °C/10 yr), or summer (0.27 °C/10 yr). As for precipitation, we did not find a significant change for any unit from a linear regression analysis. However, NX and MG had an overall decreasing trend over the 50-year study period, compared to the increasing trends in the other three units (Fig. 1.3). XJ has the largest portion of deserts (71.0%, Table 1.1) and experienced the highest increase (15.2 mm/10 yr) in precipitation (Piao et al., 2005). The fact that arid biomes get more rain in DEA is different from other arid regions (e.g., North Africa and Australia), where a marked decrease in Sahelian rainfall and increased precipitation variability in arid Australia have been reported (Dai et al., 2004; Morton et al., 2011).

From the southwest to northeast, annual mean temperature decreases while precipitation increases (Fig. 1.4a). Warmer anomalies were found around the Lop and Taklimakan Deserts in XJ, while cold anomalies were found in Tianshan, the Greater Xing'an Range, and northern Mongolia. This spatial pattern of the surface air temperature in DEA does not match as well with the spatial distribution of precipitation in southeastern DEA as it does in southern GS, NX, and IM, where high annual means coincide with high precipitation. More importantly, there seem to be contrasting spatial patterns for the intra-annual variations (i.e., measured by the standard deviation of the climatic data from 1960 to 2009) for both variables (Fig. 1.4b). High intra-annual variations in temperature were found in southwest Tianshan, Yumen of GS (a.k.a., the west end of the Great Wall of China), Qilianshan, and the northern Gobi Desert. Precipitation variability, on the other hand, matches well with its spatial means—the higher mean values correspond to higher precipitation variances. To demonstrate the intra-annual variability of temperature and precipitation, we include the spatially interpolated distributions in an extreme cold and dry year (1968, Fig. 1.4c) and a warm and wet year (2008, Fig. 1.4d).

Current land cover types (MODIS-IGBP LC) following the IGBP classification system (Olson et al., 2001) in DEA are predominated by barrens and sparsely vegetated land (2.06×10^6 km^2, 42.9%), temperate grasslands (1.67×10^6 km^2, 34.8%), (0.51×10^6 km^2, 10.5%), and croplands (0.26×10^6 km^2, 5.42%) (Table 1.1, Fig. 1.5a). Croplands, open shrubland, and mixed coniferous forest account for >96% of the DEA region; urban land use occupies only 6.8×10^3 km^2 (0.2%), despite the high population in the region. From 1992 to 2004, there were significant increases in cropland, barren land, urban land, and grassland in IM, while MG had the smallest amount of croplands in the region. The average composition of land cover types is deviated for every unit, including ∼84% of MG as grasslands and barrens, 71.0% of XJ as barrens, and 43.0% NX as shrublands (Table 1.1).

DEA landscapes have also been undergoing dramatic changes. The grasslands fluctuated between 33.7% and 42.0% between 2001 and 2009, while barrens fluctuated between 43% and 47%. Urban growth, desertification and land conversion to agricultural systems are the three major land-use changes in recent decades. John et al. (2009) reported that the urban, crop, and barren lands in IM increased by 249%, 47%, and 151%, respectively, resulting in significant changes in species distribution (John et al., 2008) and increased water stress (Shao et al., 2008; Miao et al., 2009). Desertification normally results in an increase in both shrublands in semi-arid areas and deserts near the grassland-desert transitional zones (Figs. 1.5b and c). Herbaceous grass species native to the region are being replaced by deep-rooted invasive shrubs, which have less-efficient water use (Cheng et al., 2007). Based on the MODIS LU database, it seems that intensified land use changes are mostly within or around the transitional zones between the biomes (Figs. 1.5a and b). From a statistical point of view, however, the total land area for grasslands has increased (Fig. 1.5c). A careful study of the land-use changes (Fig. 1.5b) reveals that this is due to the large loss of forests in northern MG and northwest XJ. A surprising phenomenon is that the total cropland area has also been decreasing, which is likely related to the

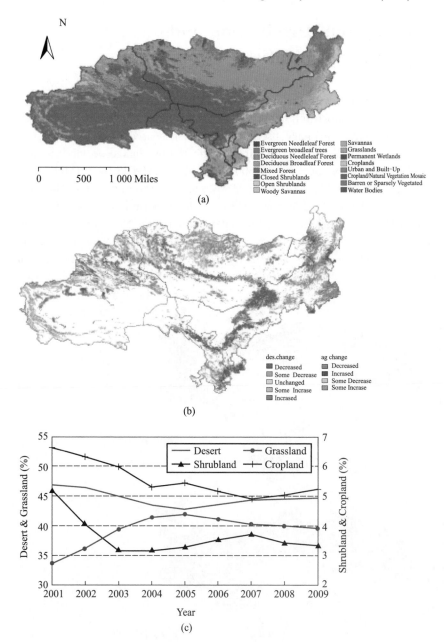

Fig. 1.5 Land use (a), land use changes between 2004 and 2009 (b), and the gradual changes of major land use types (c) in the DEA region. Data and maps are based on the MOD12Q1 land cover type (https://lpdaac.usgs.gov/products/modis_products_table).

major policy of "Restorations of Grasslands from Croplands", set by the Chinese Government for China's northwest region in the late 1990s.

1.3 Ecosystem Production and Evapotranspiration

Ecosystem production, evapotranspiration (ET), and their changes in time and space are among the most important functional variables to characterize ecosystem functions. Gross primary production (GPP) is used here for ecosystem production. Both GPP and ET are directly affected by changes in land use and climate. In this chapter, we used the 500 m resolution MODIS GPP (MOD17A2 /A3) and ET (MOD16A2/A3) from 2000 through 2009 to understand the state and changes of GPP and ET across DEA's spatiotemporal landscapes. Current MODIS GPP and ET products do not have estimates for the arid areas across the globe due to low vegetation cover for estimating leaf area, leading to unavailability of MODIS-derived LAI/fPAR (Mu et al., 2011). This restricted our analysis and discussion to within only about 55.7% of the DEA region (Fig. 1.6);

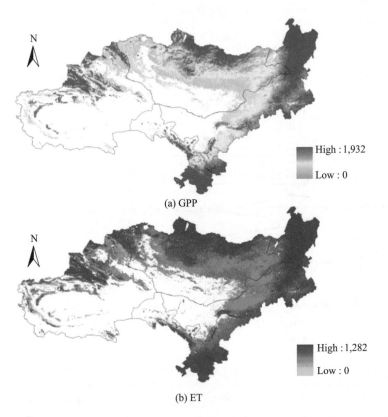

High : 1,932

Low : 0

(a) GPP

High : 1,282

Low : 0

(b) ET

Fig. 1.6 Decadal mean gross primary production (GPP, a) and evapotranspiration (ET, b) of the DEA region (2001–2009).
Data source: NASA's Earth Observing System (EOS) Clearinghouse (ECHO)-MOD17A3 with 500 m resolution (http://reverb.echo.nasa.gov/reverb/).

although the GPP and ET for the remaining 45.3% are near zero and, thus, negligible. Nevertheless, our discussion below is still possible and is based on the differences among the three ecoregion biomes (forest, grassland, and desert, Fig. 1.1) as well as among the five administrative units.

The mean (±standard deviation) GPP of the three dominant biomes for the study period (2000–2009) varied from 166.3 ± 96.0 g C m^{-2} yr^{-1} in the desert biome to 303.9 ± 151.9 and 508.5 ± 248.0 g C m^{-2} yr^{-1} in the grassland and forest biomes (Fig. 1.7). These results should be cautiously interpreted because a relatively large amount of area is treated as "no vegetation" by the MODIS team (i.e., no data) in barren areas. Yet, the total GPP for DEA is $(0.8243\pm0.3011)\times10^9$ g C yr^{-1} and the average ET is 276.1 ± 96.6 mm yr^{-1}. In addition to the three dominant biomes for the DEA region, we also obtained zonal statistics of GPP and ET in grassland, desert, and forest biomes at the provincial level. It is also clear that the intra-annual variations of the same biome in different administrative units were not always similar. IM and GS showed higher GPP at all three biomes than the other three administrative units. For example, GPP of the forest biome in GS was 736.0 ± 271.7 g C m^{-2} yr^{-1}, while

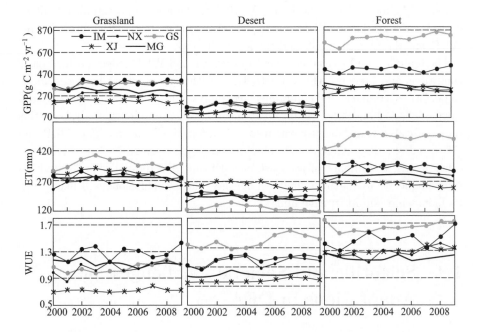

Fig. 1.7 Changes in GPP (g C m^{-2} yr^{-1}), ET (mm) and WUE of three dominant biomes in the five administrative units of the DEA region from 2000 to 2009, showing the nonparallel intra-annual variations among the biomes and provinces
Data source: same as in Fig. 1.6.

the forest biome in neighboring NX was about half of GS (51.7%) at 336.7±159.1 g C m^{-2} yr^{-1}. These differences are likely due to the favorable temperature and precipitation combination (Fig. 1.4) (see also Lu et al., 2011). ET of the forest biome (368.1±147.9 mm yr^{-1}) was expected to be higher than that at the grassland (267.1±96.5 mm yr^{-1}) or desert (194.5±45.5 mm yr^{-1}) biomes. However, these biome differences also varied among the five administrative units. The ET level in GS, for example, varied greatly among the three biomes at 182.4, 349.3, and 468.4 mm yr^{-1} for the desert, grassland, and forest biomes, respectively, while the biome differences in XJ seemed rather small (268.6–275.0 mm yr^{-1}), with ET of the grassland biome occasionally exceeding that of the forest biome. MG showed the smallest intra-annual variation of ET. When integrating GPP and ET into a concept of water-use efficiency (WUE=GPP/ET), there seemed to be different patterns among the biomes and administrative units. First, the clear-cut conclusion on WUE among the biomes is not very apparent. In GS and XJ, WUE of the forest and desert biomes was higher than that of the grassland biome, while the biome difference in NX was very small. Unlike GPP and ET, WUE differences among the units appeared independent of biomes. For the desert biome, WUE was lower in XJ and MG and the highest in GS. For the grassland biome, XJ has the lowest WUE but there were no significant differences for the grassland WUE among the other four units. For the forest biome, WUE was the highest in GS and the lowest in MG.

The temporal and spatial changes of GPP, ET and WUE reflect both climatic conditions and land use (Figs. 1.4 to 1.6). Although no effort has been made to perform systematic and comprehensive analyses on partitioning the contributions of climate and land use on GPP and ET, our preliminary analysis on this topic indicated that land use was responsible for 64.3% and 83.6% of GPP and ET variation, respectively, while climate explained only 26.8% and 14.5%. In other words, the impact of land use on GPP and ET dynamics is 2.4 and 5.8 times higher than that of climate. Logically, these conclusions will likely vary by biome and administrative unit.

1.4   Scientific and Societal Challenges for Adaptations in DEA

Global climatic change, human activities via various land-use practices and natural disturbances are considered the primary drivers for the ecosystem functions and services of any region. Development of a sound adaptation plan, therefore, is becoming a necessity for the sustainable future of a region such as DEA. One cannot develop a sound adaptation strategy without understanding the interactive changes between the natural and human systems on this "crowded planet" (Bulkeley, 2001; Palmer et al., 2004; Liu et al., 2008). Fortunately, many teams have extensively documented the similarities and differences in the past, present, and future of the DEA region (i.e., data and expertise availability). Accompanied by advanced technology (e.g., remote sensing products, models, available eddy-flux towers, etc.), we could reach out to these teams for a comprehensive analysis of the interactions between the human system (HS) and natural system (NS) toward science-based adaptation plans for the region (Fig. 1.8). Yet, this type of synthesis effort has not been made by any research team. Another research priority for the future of the DEA region is to examine and model the interactive changes of HS and NS at different temporal and spatial scales in order to develop sound adaptation plans for the changing climate and land use. Specifically, we need to understand how global climate change (including warming and climatic variability) and land-use change regulate both biophysical and socioeconomic functions through exploring the underlying processes and vulnerability analyses. Generally speaking, climate change and human stresses will place unequal pressure on each element of HS and NS matrices. Yet, because of the intra-connections among the elements and between the two matrices, one element of either matrix will have the potential to trigger the changes of the other elements. These changes, however, can be predicted when important un-

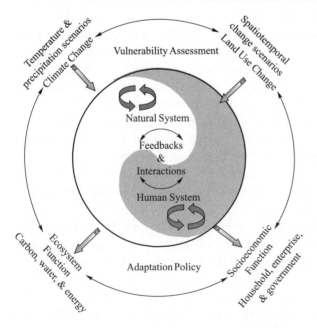

Fig. 1.8 Proposed conceptual framework for exploring the linkages between biophysical and socioeconomic parameters as well as their coupled effects on the interactions and feedbacks within and between the human system (HS) and natural system (NS).

derlying processes are understood and incorporated in a comprehensive model that includes both biophysical and socioeconomic influences.

A more pressing issue related to socioeconomic changes (e.g., population growth and institutional changes) impacts on ecosystem functions, which are often delineated by administrative boundaries (e.g., Zhen et al., 2010). These differences will likely yield different land-use intensities in each province and alter the function and dynamics of ecosystems, which, in turn, will have negative feedback on economic development and future policy. Using the livestock statistics of IM and MG as an example, major policy changes in both regions appear to be responsible for the shifts in livestock population (Fig. 1.2c; Qi et al., 2012). In IM, the substantial increase in livestock in the late 1980s was largely a result of livestock and grassland tenure reform, while the drop in livestock around 2000 was caused by grassland restoration policies enacted around 1998–1999. The substantial livestock increase since 2004 was likely caused by growing demand driven by fast economic growth and market reform. However, climatic extremes and episodic events (e.g., El Niño) complicated the dynamics of livestock populations (e.g., 18% mortality in MG due to the extreme snow and cold winter of 2009–2010). Recently, in southern DEA, the Chinese government announced several major policies (e.g., subsidy and reward program for the country's herdsmen over the coming years to reverse and prevent damage to grasslands, http://news.xinhuanet.com/english2010/china/2011-05/06/c_13862052. htm), while the Xinjiang Division of the National Development and Reform Commission disclosed that it will invest 1.8 billion RMB in sand prevention and control projects around the Tarim River Basin (http://english.peopledaily.com.cn/ 90001/90776/90882/7375561.html). These new policies will produce direct and immediate LCLUC in DEA. One caution associated with the coupled human and natural systems (CHN) is to realize that both the drivers and the dependent variables are hierarchically organized (i.e., county-prefecture-province-country) and have different spatial and temporal resolutions. Socioeconomic data are often collected at the county level annually by the national census program or at ten-year intervals, suggesting that our analysis will have to be conducted according to this hierarchy. In contrast, ecosystems are spatially organized by climate, soil, and/or land cover types.

The role of population and prices differ in the way they drive LCLUC. The local population growth may not cause LCLUC directly, but rather indirectly, through the market and price mechanism. Population and prices would also have different impacts on various land-use types via the markets. For built-up land uses (e.g., residential), local population changes would have a much stronger impact than other land-use types because foods and other products can be directly imported/exported from/to other regions, but the residential use cannot be solved by increasing more residential areas in other regions. Changes in land values resulting from relative price changes would significantly impact the population and economy. For example, a substantial rise in meat and milk prices driven by growing demands results in increased pastoral land values, wages and economic development in the region, attracting people to the region from the rest of the country.

Mongolians who maintain nomadic pastoral practices predominantly inhabit the Mongolian Plateau. However, the majority of the pastoral households in both MG and IM began settling around permanent towns or immigrated to large urban centers in recent decades because of rapid economic growth and new policies (Havstad et al., 2008). In 2007, the number of livestock in MG reached 40 million—an increase of 15.7% from 2006, resulting in >60% of the pastureland being overgrazed. These rapid changes in both climate and socioeconomic systems will place different levels of biophysical and anthropogenic stress on the ecosystems. Adaptive management plans and policies are therefore needed to maintain ecosystem resilience to the change (i.e., adaptation). IM and MG have developed contrasting political systems since 1979, with much more rapid changes in IM than in MG, producing distinct land cover changes between 1980 and the current decade (Sneath, 1998). As a consequence of the landcover changes, severe and frequent catastrophes (e.g., dust storms) have drastically increased in IM. The landuse changes are expected to escalate over the next two decades. Additionally, significant increases in air temperature since the 1950s have been observed due to global warming; the increases varied significantly and were non-parallel among ecosystems. In 2001, the total net primary production (NPP) of the Mongolian Plateau was 434 Tg C yr^{-1}, with IM and MG accounting for 48% and 52%, respectively. At the NEESPI meeting in Beijing in November, 2007, researchers of the Purdue Climate Change Center and Institute of Geographic Sciences and Natural Resources Research, CAS (IGSNRR-CAS) predicted that climate change on the Plateau during the 21st century will be higher than the global average (e.g., Lu et al., 2009). By 2100, the projected air temperature will increase by 4.6–8.3°C and the projected annual total precipitation will increase by 122 mm to 178 mm. NPP and net ecosystem production (NEP) will continuously increase during the 21st century, with NPP reaching 586–792 Tg C yr^{-1} (i.e., 24%–68% increase from 2001) and NEP reaching 57–113 Tg C yr^{-1} (280%–650% increase from 2001) by 2100. More importantly, MG, in this century, will contribute more NEP for the plateau—an increase from the current 48% to 61%. These preliminary projections provide a good start toward developing adaptation strategies on the Mongolian Plateau. Clearly, an urgent scientific synthesis, by including multiple countries and agencies, is needed toward the strategic preparation for future adaptations plans for the region.

Acknowledgements

Our study for this chapter has been partially supported by the LCLUC Program of NASA, the Natural Science Foundation of China, the Chinese Academy of Sciences, and Henan University. Many colleagues (e.g., Lisa Delp Taylor, Lin Zhen, Jian Ni, Nan Lu, Haitao Li, Pavel Groisman, Garik Gutman, and an anonymous reviewer) contributed data, thoughtful discussion, and directions for our research.

References

Bulkeley, H. (2001). No regrets? Economy and environment in Australia's domestic climate change policy. *Global Environmental Change*, 11, 155–169.

Cheng, X., An, S., Chen, J., Li, B., Liu, Y., and Liu, S. (2007). Spatial relationships among species, above-ground biomass, N, and P in degraded grasslands in Ordos Plateau, Northwestern China. *Journal of Arid Environments*, 68, 652–667.

Dai, A., Lamb, P. J., Trenberth, K. E., Hulme, M., Jones, P. D., and Xie, P. (2004). The recent Sahel drought is real. *International Journal of Climatology*, 24, 1323–1331.

Franke, R. (1982). Smooth interpolation of scattered data by local thin plate splines. *Computer and Mathematics with Applications*, 8, 273–281.

Groisman, P. Y., Clark, E. A., Kattsov, V. M., Lettenmaier, D. P., Sokolik, I. N., Aizen, V.B., et al. (2009). The Northern Eurasia earth science partnership: An example of science applied to societal needs. *Bulletin of the American Meteorological Society*, 5, 671–688.

Havstad, K. M., Herrick, J., and Tseelei, E. (2008). Mongolia's rangelands: Is livestock production the key to the future? *Frontiers in Ecology and the Environment*, 6, 386–391.

IPCC (2007). Summary for policy makers. In: Climate Change 2007: Impacts, Adaptation and Vulnerability, contribution of Working group II to the Fourth Assessment Report of the Inter-governmental Panel on Climate Change (IPCC). Cambridge, UK: Cambridge University Press.

John, R., Chen, J., Lu, N., Guo, K., Liang, C., Wei, Y., et al. (2008). Predicting plant diversity based on remote sensing products in the semi-arid region of Inner Mongolia. *Remote Sensing of Environment*, 112, 2018–2032.

John, R., Chen, J., Lu, N., and Wilske, B. (2009). Land cover/land use change and their ecological consequences. *Environmental Research Letters*, 4, 045010, doi: 10.1088/1748-9326/4/4/045010.

Liu, J., Li, S., Ouyang, Z., Tam, C., and Chen, X. (2008). Ecological and socioeconomic effects of China's policies for ecosystem services. *Proceedings of National Academy of Sciences*, 105, 9477–9482.

Lu, N., Chen, S., Wilske, B., Sun, G., and Chen, J. (2011). Evapotranspiration and soil water relationships in a range of disturbed and undisturbed ecosystems in the semi-arid Inner Mongolia, China. *Journal of Plant Ecology*, 4: 49–60.

Lu, N., Wilske, B., Ni, J., John, R., and Chen, J. (2009). Climate change in Inner Mongolia from 1955 through 2005. *Environmental Research Letters*, 4, 045006, doi: 10.1088/1748-9326/4/4/045006.

Lu, Y., Zhuang, Q., Zhou, G., Sirin, A., Melillo, J., and Kicklighter, D. (2009). Possible decline of the carbon sink in the Mongolian Plateau during the 21st century. *Environmental Research Letters*, 4, 045023. doi: 10.1088/1748-9326/4/4/045023.

Miao, H., Chen, S., Chen, J., Zhang, W., Zhang, P., Wei, L., et al. (2009). Cultivation and grazing altered evapotranspiration and dynamics in Inner Mongolia steppes. *Agricultural and Forest Meteorology*, 149, 1810–1819.

Mitas, L., and Mitasova, H. (1988). General variational approach to the interpolation problem. *Computer and Mathematics with Applications*, 16, 983–992.

Morton, S. R., Stafford Smith, D. M., Dickman, C. R., Dunkerley, D. L., Friedel, M.H., McAllister, R. R. J., et al. (2011). A fresh framework for the ecology of arid Australia. *Journal of Arid Environment*, 75, 31–329.

Mu, Q., Zhao, M., and Running, S. W. (2011). Improvements to a MODIS global terrestrial evapotranspiration algorithm. *Remote Sensing of Environment*, 115, 1781–1800.

Ojima, D., and Chuluun, T. (2008). Policy changes in Mongolia: Implications for land use and landscapes. In: Galvin, K. A., Reid, R. S., Behnke, R. H. and Hobbs, N. T. (Eds.). *Fragmentation in Semi-arid and Arid Landscapes: Consequences for Human and Natural Systems*. Springer, Dordrecht, The Netherlands: 179–193.

Olson, D. M., Dinerstein, E., Wikramanayake, E. D., Burgess, N. D., Powell, G. V. N., Underwood, E. C., et al. (2001). Terrestrial ecoregions of the world: A new map of life on Earth. *BioScience*, 51, 933–938.

Palmer, M., Bernhardt, E., Chornesky, E., Collins, S., Dobson, A., Duke, C., et al. (2004). Ecology for a crowded planet. *Science*, 304, 1251–1252.

Piao, S., Fang, J., Liu, H., and Zhu, B. (2005). NDVI-indicated decline in desertification in China in the past two decades. *Geophysical Research Letters*, 32, 10.1029/2004GL021764.

Qi, J., Chen, J., Wan, S., and Ai, L. (2012). Understanding the coupled natural and human systems in the Dryland East Asia. *Environmental Research Letters*, 7, 015202, doi:10.1088/1748-9326/7/1/015202.

Shao, C., Chen, J., Li, L., Xu, W., Chen, S., Tenney, G., et al. (2008). Spatial variability in soil heat flux at three Inner Mongolia steppe ecosystems. *Agricultural and Forest Meteorology*, 148, 1433–1443.

Sneath, D. (1998). Ecology: State policy and pasture degradation in inner Asia. *Science,* 281, 1147-1148.

Stöckli, R., Vidale, P. L., Boone, A., and Schär, C. (2007). Impact of scale and aggregation on the terrestrial water exchange: Integrating land surface models and Rhone catchment observations. *Journal of Hydrometeorology*, 8, 1002–1015, doi:10.1175/JHM613.1.

Xuan, J., Liu, G., and Du, K. (2000). Dust emission inventory in Northern China. *Atmospheric Environment*, 34, 4565–4570.

Zhai, P. and Pan, X. (2003). Trends in temperature extremes during 1951–1999 in China. *Geophysical Research Letters*, 30, 1913, doi:10.1029/2003GL018004.

Zhen, L., Ochirbat, B., Lv, Y., Wei, Y. J., Liu, X. L., Chen, J. Q., et al. (2010). Comparing patterns of ecosystem service consumption and perceptions of range management between ethnic herders in Inner Mongolia and Mongolia. *Environmental Research Letters*, 5, doi:10.1088/1748-9326/5/1/015001.

Authors Information

Jiquan Chen[1,6]*, Ranjeet John[1], Guanghua Qiao[2], Ochirbat Batkhishig[3], Wenping Yuan[4], Yaoqi Zhang[5], Changliang Shao[6,1], Zutao Ouyang[1], Linghao Li[6], Ke Guo[6], Ge Sun[7]

1. Landscape Ecology & Ecosystem Science (LEES) Lab, Department of Environmental Sciences, University of Toledo, Toledo, OH 43606-3390, USA
2. College of Economics and Management, Inner Mongolia Agricultural University, Huhhot 010019, P.R. China
3. Soil Science Department, Institute of Geography, Mongolian Academy of Sciences, Ulaanbaatar 210620, Mongolia
4. College of Global Change and Earth System Science, Beijing Normal University, Beijing 100875, P.R. China
5. School of Forestry & Wildlife Sciences, Auburn University, AL 36849-5418, USA
6. Institute of Botany, Chinese Academy of Sciences, Beijing 100093, P.R. China
7. Southern Global Change Program, USDA Forest Service, NH 03824, USA
* Corresponding author

Chapter 2

Dryland East Asia in Hemispheric Context

Geoffrey M. Henebry, Kirsten M. de Beurs, Christopher K. Wright, Ranjeet John, and Elena Lioubimtseva

Summary: This chapter aims to place dryland East Asia (DEA) into hemispheric context by contrasting recent patterns of variability and change observed within DEA with comparable dryland regions in Central Asia and North America. Key knowledge gaps in DEA include the impacts of climate variability and change on both biogeophysical and socio-physical processes (Qi et al., 2012). Water is the common limiting factor in all drylands. Thus, we focus on spatio-temporal patterns of three environmental variables related to water—the state of the vegetated land surface, land cover, and precipitation—to contextualize the recent land dynamics in the arid expanses of East Asia.

2.1 Study Regions

The region of focal interest in this book is the dryland (including deserts) of East Asia (DEA), which are delineated by five political entities: the country of Mongolia and four administrative units within China—Inner Mongolia Autonomous Region, Ningxia Hui Autonomous Region, Xinjiang Uygur Autonomous Region, and Gansu Province. The purpose of this chapter is to provide some broader context for the regional land dynamics found within DEA.

For comparison we will examine other drylands that occur globally within the latitudinal band from 35° N to 55° N. Rather than link these other drylands to political entities, we identify them using simple thresholds applied to total annual precipitation. We used the Global Precipitation Climatology Centre's precipitation normals at 0.25° resolution (Schneider et al., 2011) and applied three thresholds to average total annual precipitation to span an aridity gradient: 400 mm yr^{-1}, 350 mm yr^{-1}, and 250 mm yr^{-1} (Fig. 2.1).

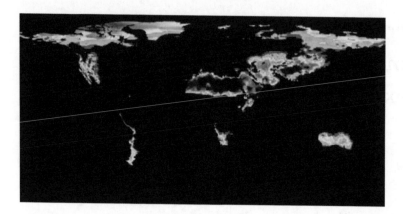

Fig. 2.1 Global dryland systems indicated by the Global Precipitation Climatology Centre (GPCC) precipitation normals at 0.25° (Schneider et al., 2011). Pinks, cyans, and blues highlight areas of 250 mm, 350 mm, and 400 mm annual precipitation, respectively.

In addition to DEA, the precipitation thresholds reveal two other large expanses of drylands in the latitudinal band: the drylands of Central Asia (DCA) and drylands of North America (DNA). The drylands of North America occur primarily in the western USA states including Arizona, California, Colorado, Idaho, Montana, New Mexico, Nevada, Oregon and Utah, and in the Canadian provinces including Alberta, British Columbia and Saskatchewan. The drylands of Central Asia occur primarily in Kazakhstan, Turkmenistan and Uzbekistan, along with smaller portions in eastern Kyrgyzstan and eastern Tajikistan (Fig. 2.2). In terms of areal extent, DEA > DCA > DNA and DEA has the largest proportion of the driest drylands (<250 mm yr^{-1}) at 76% versus 63% for DCA and only 25% for DNA (Table 2.1; Fig. 2.3).

Table 2.1 Major dryland systems occurring in the latitudinal band of 35° N–55° N.

Precipitation threshold (mm yr^{-1})	North America (DNA) (km^2)	Central Asia (DCA) (km^2)	East Asia (DEA) (km^2)
250	484,914	2,341,024	3,224,167
350	1,358,613	3,508,218	3,970,526
400	1,963,227	3,727,344	4,250,362

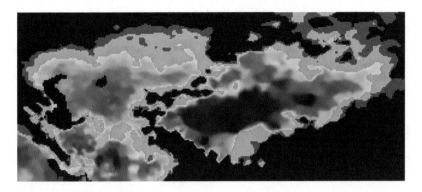

Fig. 2.2 Data from Fig. 2.1 focusing on the drylands of Central Asia and East Asia.

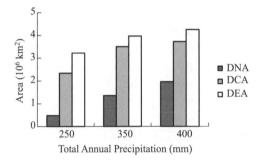

Fig. 2.3 Major dryland systems occurring in the latitudinal band of 35° N–55° N in North America (DNA), Central Asia (DCA) and East Asia (DEA).

2.2   Change Analysis of Vegetated Land Surface

To identify hotspots of change within the drylands, we applied a robust nonparametric change detection test—the Seasonal Kendall trend test—to two long-time series of Normalized Difference Vegetation Index (NDVI; Tucker, 1979) data: the AVHRR GIMMS dataset (Tucker et al., 2005) and the MODIS NBAR product (Gao et al., 2005).

The AVHRR GIMMS dataset features semi-monthly NDVI maximum value composites at a nominal spatial resolution of 8 km (Tucker et al., 2005). The MODIS NBAR (Nadir BRDF [Bidirectional Reflectance Distribution Function] Adjusted Reflectance) product provides top-of-canopy reflectance in 16-day composites at a nominal spatial resolution of 0.05 degrees ($\sim$ 5 km) from which NDVI can be calculated (Gao et al., 2005).

We have chosen to work at this coarser spatial resolution for two reasons. First, it is an appropriate scale for the coupling of the vegetated land surface and atmospheric boundary layer in the lower troposphere, which can be seen in mesoscale meteorological models (Stensrud, 2007). Second, the data needed to characterize the dynamics of the vegetated land surface in the 1980s only exist at coarser spatial resolutions (>1 km).

2.3 Retrospective Trend Analysis Reveals Areas of Significant Change

The Seasonal Kendall (SK) trend test corrected for first-order autocorrelation (Hirsch and Slack, 1984) is widely used in the climatology and hydrology communities (Lettenmaier et al., 1994; von Storch and Navarra, 1999; Adam and Lettenmaier, 2008), and it has been gaining ground over the past decade in the remote sensing community (de Beurs and Henebry, 2004b, 2005, 2010; Alcaraz-Segura et al., 2009, 2010; Sobrino and Julien, 2011; Gao et al., 2012; Pettorelli et al., 2012; Wright et al., 2012). Key advantages of the SK test include its parallel use of sub-annual time series to increase the power of the test, and its robustness to deviations from assumptions of classical linear regression, such as, random residuals identically distributed, normality and equal variance for all values of the independent variable.

What constitutes a "trend" and what does it mean to identify a trend statistically? In popular usage the word "trend" —either as a noun or a verb—usually connotes some causative association with time, e.g., "Jobless numbers continue to trend upward" or "The trend is toward cheaper but more functional tablets." The appropriate understanding of a statistical trend restricts any causative association to the past: a trend analysis can reveal that the accumulation of small, individually insignificant step-changes constitutes a significant change over time when reviewed retrospectively. The statistical trend analysis says nothing about the future, only about what has been witnessed in the past. Modeling how a past trend may evolve in the future is the role of forecasting and, indeed, a simple way to forecast is to project the trajectory of the recent past forward. But that projection is a conscious choice of model by the analyst. There is nothing intrinsic to a statistically identified trend that indicates that its application in a model of future behavior is appropriate, fitting or prudent.

For example, the slope parameter coefficient obtained through fitting a simple linear regression model to link dependent variable data with independent temporal data should not be interpreted as a concise summary of future dynamics. It is a snapshot of past dynamics that may be useful in forecasting future dynamics, but additional evidence and context are needed to establish the appropriateness of this model choice. Thus, the oft-directed criticism that "the time series is too short to establish a trend" muddles the important distinction between two different tasks: quantifying the past and forecasting the future. What we have sought to do here is the former—to detect and geo-locate significant trends in time series of environmental variables.

2.4   Vegetation Change in Three Epochs

We focused on three epochs using the two image time series: 1982–1991 (AVHRR GIMMS), 1992–2001 (AVHRR GIMMS), and 2001–2010 (MODIS NBAR). The first epoch includes the final years of the Soviet Union, the second spans the first decade of the Newly Independent States of Central Asia, and the third epoch captures an exceptional period of widespread drought in northern Eurasia.

Across the drylands changes in the vegetated land surface were not evenly distributed in space, time or direction (Fig. 2.4). The first epoch (1982–1991) was characterized by more than four times as many significant positive as negative changes, but the area of change (both positive and negative) across DNA, DCA, and DEA was less than 9% of the total drylands extent (Table 2.2). The large area of positive change in Canada has been attributed to changes in cultivation practices (Reed, 2006). The relative lack of negative changes across the dryland regions in this epoch is also remarkable, particularly in contrast to the subsequent epochs (Fig. 2.5).

The second epoch (1992–2001) was distinguished by fundamental institutional changes in Central Asia and, to a lesser extent, in East Asia. The disintegration of the Soviet Union at the end of 1991 led to manifold changes in the agricultural sectors of the Newly Independent States of Central Asia (Lerman et al., 2004). Some of these changes manifested as shifting land surface phenologies that were widespread in Kazakhstan (de Beurs and Henebry, 2004a, 2005) and limited to the intensely cultivated croplands of Uzbekistan and Turkmenistan (Henebry et al., 2005). The end of the epoch also includes the beginning of two important land conservation programs in China (Liu et al., 2008; de Beurs et al., 2013). However, the striking feature of the middle panel of Fig. 2.4 is the apparent dipole in Eurasia drylands: broadly distributed negative changes in DCA vs. positive changes in DEA. Significant changes occurred in nearly 24% of the drylands in DEA and DCA during the epoch from 1992–2001 (Table 2.2) with the areal proportion of negative changes in DCA exceeding positive changes in DEA (Fig. 2.5). In contrast, just 14% of DNA drylands saw significant changes with a virtual balance between positive and negative (Fig. 2.5, Table 2.2).

Table 2.2 Results of Seasonal Kendall analysis on NDVI time series across the drylands of North America, Central Asia and East Asia.

Epoch	Precipitation (mm yr^{-1})	DNA pos. (km^2)	DNA neg. (km^2)	DCA pos. (km^2)	DCA neg. (km^2)	DEA pos. (km^2)	DEA neg. (km^2)
1982–1991	250	36,084	30,079	130,458	15,643	175,246	83,445
1992–2001	250	58,307	34,512	63,182	583,280	554,063	82,155
2001–2010	250	9,432	26,247	10,602	800,160	117,408	768,925
1982–1991	350	161,002	49,608	202,740	16,759	222,187	86,641
1992–2001	350	108,644	100,171	83,236	961,736	630,893	115,916
2001–2010	350	55,331	78,018	12,858	1,490,263	151,964	850,117
1982–1991	400	263,080	62,853	221,557	16,758	240,579	89,670
1992–2001	400	143,045	133,898	89,341	1,014,855	657,361	124,778
2001–2010	400	77,335	134,991	13,187	1,567,635	182,885	928,262

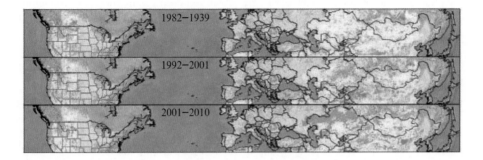

Fig. 2.4 Map of significant changes in the vegetated land surface over nearly three decades assessed using the Seasonal Kendall nonparametric trend test applied to AVHRR (8 km) and MODIS (0.05°) NDVI time series. Light yellow background delineates the precipitation region of 400 mm yr^{-1}. Orange [green] indicates a significant ($p < 0.01$) negative [positive] change over the specified period.

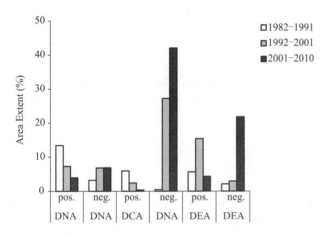

Fig. 2.5 Proportional area of significant ($p < 0.01$) positive (pos.) and negative (neg.) changes in NDVI during three epochs within the drylands delineated by precipitation normal of 400 mm yr^{-1}.

The hallmark of the third epoch (2001–2010) was a preponderance of significant negative changes across all three drylands regions, with particularly profound impacts in DCA, where most of northern and central Kazakhstan saw continued negative changes in the vegetated land surface (Fig. 2.4). Negative changes in the vegetated land surface affected more than one-third of the drylands in DEA and DCA—nearly 2.5 million km^2 (Table 2.2). Even in DNA the negative change area substantially exceeded positive change area, although the total area of change was less than 11% (Fig. 2.5, Table 2.2).

What are the proximate drivers of the observed changes in the vegetated land surface? We considered two types of environmental variables: land cover and precipitation.

2.5   Land Cover Variation and Change

Production of annual global land cover maps only became possible in the MODIS era. Classification results improved substantially with the inclusion of the early afternoon overpass of the Aqua MODIS to complement the late morning overpass of the Terra MODIS (Friedl et al., 2010). Accordingly, we evaluated recent land cover dynamics starting from 2003 using the International Geosphere-Biosphere Programme (IGBP) classification in the MODIS land cover product (MCD12C1 v5.1), with a particular attention to compositional changes at drylands peripheries. This MODIS product has a spatial resolution of 0.05 degrees and is generated from finer spatial resolution land cover products. A key feature of the coarser resolution product is the inclusion of percentage estimates for each land cover class at the grid cell level. For example, a cell with a single land cover class would have the value of 100 in the layer corresponding to that land cover class and values of zero in all other land cover layers. Likewise, a cell with tripartite representation would have values more than zero and less than 100 in each of three classes and zero in other classes.

We have taken seriously the producers' caveat not to interpret interannual changes in land cover area too strictly (Friedl et al., 2010). Rather than focus on interannual shifts among land cover categories, we sought to characterize land cover variation. We developed a simple scheme with two components: structured graphical display of mapped summary statistics and interpretive labeling of the resulting colors. For each land cover class of interest, we calculated the mean, maximum, minimum, and range (maximum minus minimum) of percentage composition over the eight year period 2003–2010. In the structured graphical display the red, green and blue plane present the percentage maximum, mean and range, respectively. Table 2.3 presents the interpretative labeling of the resulting colors. The scheme stresses three aspects of land cover variation—presence or absence; temporal stability (stable or unstable); and spatial centrality (core or periphery)—and yields five useful categories of land cover variability: absent, stable core, unstable core, unstable but persistent periphery, and unstable but ephemeral periphery (Table 2.3). The structure of the graphical display means that some color combinations are highly unlikely: reds (=high max + low mean + low range), greens (=low max + high mean + low range) and cyans (=low max + high mean + high range). Tonal variations are possible within four of the

Table 2.3 Interpretative legend for Figures 2.5 and 2.6 that display IGBP land cover (LC) variation from 2003–2010 at 0.05 degree resolution.

Color in LC Map	Red = Max% LC	Green = Mean% LC	Blue = Range% LC	Interpretation
Black	None	None	None	Land cover class absent
Blues	Low	Low	High	Unstable but ephemeral periphery; rare and erratic
Magentas	High	Low	High	Unstable but persistent periphery; sometimes high, but usually low
Whites	High	High	High	Unstable core; sometimes low, but usually high
Yellows	High	High	Low	Stable core of LC; always high so low range

useful categories since each summary statistic has a bounded range of possible values. Absences appear black.

We focused our analysis on the three main IGBP classes found in the drylands regions: grasslands (GRS=class 10), croplands (CRP=class 12), and barren and sparse vegetation (BSV=class 16). As the preponderance of yellow in the top panel of Figure 2.6 shows, grasslands constitute the dominant land cover across

Fig. 2.6 Land cover dynamics within the precipitation zone of 400 mm yr^{-1} as revealed by MODIS 0.05° land cover products 2003–2010. Top panel: grassland (IGBP class 10); middle panel: cropland (IGBP class 12); bottom panel: barren and sparse vegetation (IGBP class 16). Each panel displays a false color composite of land cover percentage for a specific IGBP land cover class: red=maximum percentage, green=mean percentage, and blue=range of percentages. Yellow indicates stable core area of the land cover with little or no interannual variation; white shows an unstable core area that displays substantial interannual variation; shades of magenta show unstable peripheral areas of the land cover; blue reveals areas with minimal presence of the land cover and high interannual variation; black indicates no occurrence of the land cover.

the 400 mm yr^{-1} precipitation normal that bound the drylands. The barren and sparse vegetation (bottom panel, Fig. 2.6) is the second ranked land cover in the drylands regions with croplands around the edges of grasslands or ribbons and patches of irrigated croplands amidst the sparsely vegetated landscapes (middle panel, Fig. 2.6).

A closer examination of these patterns is possible in Figure 2.7, which zooms into the area around the Aral Sea. This area is of particular interest due to the notorious decades-long desiccation of the Aral Sea (Micklin 1988, 2007). Across the area there has been much land cover variation, even over the relatively short period 2003–2010. Additionally, this area is masked out in the GPCC data and thus does not appear in Figure 2.6. In each structured graphical display panel,

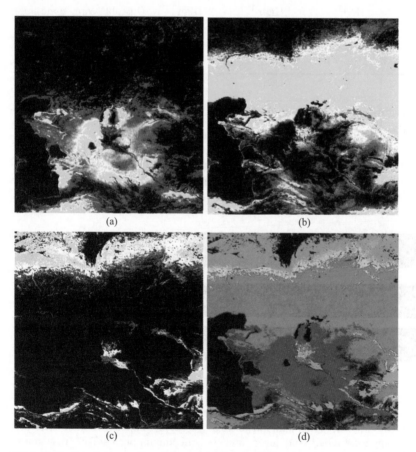

(a) (b)

(c) (d)

Fig. 2.7 Land cover dynamics near the Aral Sea revealed by MODIS land cover products 2003–2010. Interpretation of max-mean-range maps same as in Figure 6: (a) max-mean-range for percentage of barren and sparse vegetation (IGBP class 16); (b) max-mean-range for percentage of grassland (IGBP class 10); (c) max-mean-range for percentage of cropland (IGBP class 12); (d) percentage maxima of grassland (red), cropland (green) and barren/sparse vegetation (blue).

the full spectrum of land cover variation categories can be seen: black, blues, magentas, whites and yellows. The Amu Darya Delta in Karakalpakstan is the central feature of the cropland variation panel (Fig. 2.7, lower left). Bordered to the west by the arid Ustyurt Plateau, to the south by the Kara-Kum Desert, to the east by the Kyzl-Kum Desert, and to the north by the remains of the Aral Sea, the irrigated croplands of the Delta are a prominent "island" of vegetation. The maximum land cover percentage map (Fig. 2.7, lower right; Table 2.4) shows that the Delta is composed of both croplands and grasslands, the latter likely being former croplands that have been abandoned due to soil salinization (Micklin, 2007).

Table 2.4 Interpretative legend for lower right panel of Figure 2.6 that displays IGBP land cover (LC) percentage maxima from 2003–2010 at 0.05 degree resolution.

Color in LC Map	Red= Max% GRS	Green= Max% CRP	Blue= Max% BSV	Interpretation
Black	None	None	None	Absence of all three LC classes
Red	High	Low	Low	Dominated by grassland (GRS)
Green	Low	High	Low	Dominated by cropland (CRP)
Blue	Low	Low	High	Dominated by barren/ sparse vegetation (BSV)
Yellow	High	High	Low	Co-variation of grassland and cropland
*Cyan	Low	High	High	Co-variation of cropland and barren/sparse vegetation
Magenta	High	Low	High	Co-variation of grassland and barren/sparse vegetation
*White	High	High	High	Co-variation of all three LC classes

* This color does not appear in Figure 2.6.

Despite the fact that this analysis does not speak to land cover changes, it does identify areas of higher interannual variation that are land cover transition zones in which the land cover classification algorithm likely exhibits instability. The key lesson from this analysis of land cover variation is that there have not been large patches of land cover change which could explain the results of the NDVI trend analyses (Fig. 2.4), apart from recent variability in the barren/sparse vegetation class in the Ustyurt Plateau and new croplands in Turkmenistan along the Uzbekistan border (Lioubimtseva et al., 2013).

2.6 Precipitation Variation and Change

Drylands are characterized by moisture-limited ecosystems. A key component of the terrestrial water budget is precipitation. Thus, it is logical to look to precipitation as a contributory influence on observed changes in the vegetated land surface. We investigated the variation and change in precipitation across the drylands with two global gridded datasets at very different spatial resolutions and temporal depths: 1) the Full Data Reanalysis version 5 from GPCC which provides monthly precipitation totals interpolated from station data from 1901 through 2009 at a nominal spatial resolution of 0.5 degrees (Schneider et al., 2011); and 2) the version 2.2 of the Global Precipitation Climatology Project (GPCP) monthly dataset that merges multiple satellite data sources with station data at a coarser resolution of 2.5 degrees (Huffman et al., 2009; Huffman and Blovin, 2011).

The long temporal depth of GPCC offers both opportunities and challenges for change analysis. Since GPCC is station based, variations in the number and location of stations during the period of analysis have the potential to affect the results. The station data in the GPCC Full Reanalysis were not homogenized; thus, artifacts may appear in the data due to changes in reporting protocol or station location through time (Rudolf et al., 2010). Accordingly, any change analysis must be approached with caution (Wright et al., 2009). By applying the SK nonparametric test rather than simple linear regression to detect significant changes over time, we err on the side of caution. Temporal inhomogeneity is more likely to unduly influence parametric tests through extreme values and/or nonstationarity. Further, we apply the SK test on a series of overlapping 30-year (360 months) time series—from 1901 to 2009—to minimize the confounding effect of abrupt temporal boundaries. This approach has the consequence of "refocusing" the change detection away from interannual details to consider regional dynamics over longer periods.

The SK analysis of the GPCC data appears to reveal very little of consequence in DNA, where the maximal areal proportion of significant change (positive or negative) was less than 7% within the 400 mm yr^{-1} precipitation zone. In contrast, the SK analysis uncovers strong dipole dynamics between DCA and DEA across the mountain ranges of Central Asia (Fig. 2.8). A drier DCA and wetter DEA in the early part of the 20th century gradually shifted to a wetter DCA and drier DEA by mid-century and then back to drier DCA/wetter DEA at the end of the 20th century and beginning of the 21st century (Fig. 2.8). This quasi-periodicity becomes more evident in the relative trajectories of areal proportions of significant change across precipitation zones (Fig 2.9). There is not a simple inverse relationship between the areal extent of significant positive change in DCA and DEA; rather, there is a nearly identical progression across

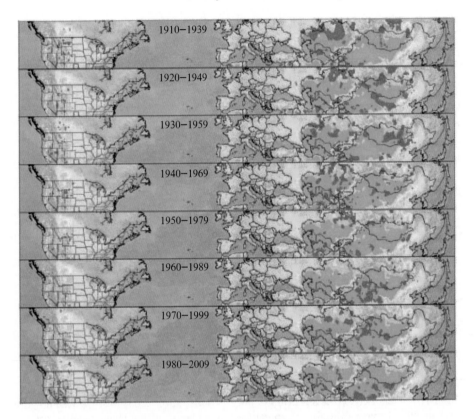

Fig. 2.8 Map of significant changes in precipitation over a century assessed using the Seasonal Kendall nonparametric trend test applied to GPCC Full Reanalysis V5 monthly time series at 0.5° resolution. Light yellow, light orange and dark orange backgrounds delineate the precipitation regions of 400, 350 and 250 mm yr^{-1}, respectively. Red (blue) indicates a significant ($p < 0.01$) negative (positive) change over the specified 30-year period.

the century of observations in the 350 and 400 mm yr^{-1} zones, with a distinct response in the more arid 250 mm yr^{-1} zone (top panel, Fig 2.9). A different but related progression is evident when linking significant negative areal proportion in DEA with significant positive areal proportion in DCA, in particular the trajectory of the most arid zone (bottom panel, Fig. 2.9).

The dipole precipitation dynamics of DCA and DEA are strong in the analysis of the GPCC data, but there also appear more subtle but intriguing links to the distant drylands of North America. The panels to the left in Figure 2.10 also show quasi-periodicity between significant negative areal proportions in DNA and significant positive areal proportions in DCA (top left), and negative DNA and positive DEA (bottom left), with the most arid zone showing the strongest response. The left panels of Figure 2.10 show the seven points of 30-year peri-

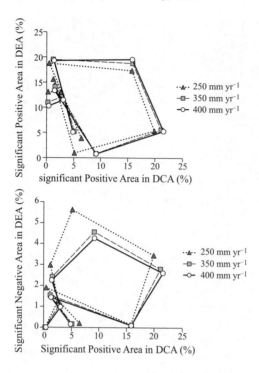

Fig. 2.9 Quasi-periodic dipole behavior in the drylands of Northern Eurasia (DCA and DEA) evaluated across a century of observations (1910–2009) in sequential 30-year periods with 10-year overlaps. Proportional areal extent of significant positive precipitation changes in DEA versus DCA at three aridity levels (top panel). Proportional areal extent of significant negative precipitation changes in DEA versus significant positive changes in DCA at three aridity levels (bottom panel).

ods from 1910–1999; the right panels reproduce the data in the left panels but add the eighth points of the 30-year period 1980–2009. These last points lie far outside of the dynamical manifold described in the previous 90 years. Clearly, something has changed over the 30-year period 1980–2009 to change the tele-connection dynamics between North America and Asia, but particularly over the final decade 2000–2009, since the earlier period (1970–1999) substantially overlaps the last period (1980–2009).

Can these patterns be confirmed by other data? Unfortunately, precipitation datasets are few in number and mostly too short in duration to reveal this kind of climate dynamics. The GPCP v2.2 dataset is one of the longer duration products that incorporate remote sensing datastreams. Despite a nominal length of 32 years, inclusion of microwave data starting in 1987 means the earlier eight years of data are distinctly different. We applied the SK analysis to the GPCP data in two periods: 1979–1986 and 1987–2010. The earlier series revealed very few areas of significant change over the land surface and none in the drylands of interest

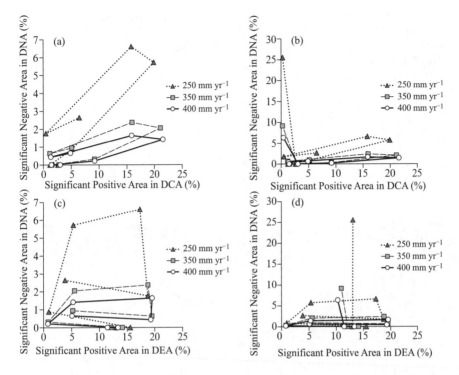

Fig. 2.10 Quasi-periodic dipole behavior between in the drylands of Northern Eurasia (DCA and DEA) and the drylands of North America (DNA) evaluated across a century of observations (1910–2009) in sequential 30-year periods with 10-year overlaps. Proportional areal extent of significant negative precipitation changes in DNA versus significant positive changes in DCA at three aridity levels for 1910–1999 (top left) and including 1980–2009 (top right). The proportional areal extent of significant negative precipitation changes in DNA versus significant positive changes in DEA at three aridity levels for 1910–1999 (bottom left) and including 1980–2009 (bottom right). Significant changes during 1980–2009 fall far outside the manifold described by the prior 90 years.

here (top panel, Fig. 2.11). This paucity of detected change is likely due to a shorter duration time series and coarse spatial resolution (2.5°). While there are many more areas of significant change in the later series, there are still very few within DCA and DEA and none in DNA (bottom panel, Fig. 2.11). However, there is support in the recent literature for a finding of recent significant changes in precipitation in DEA (Jiang et al., 2012; Li et al., 2012; Yang et al., 2012; Zhang et al., 2012a, b).

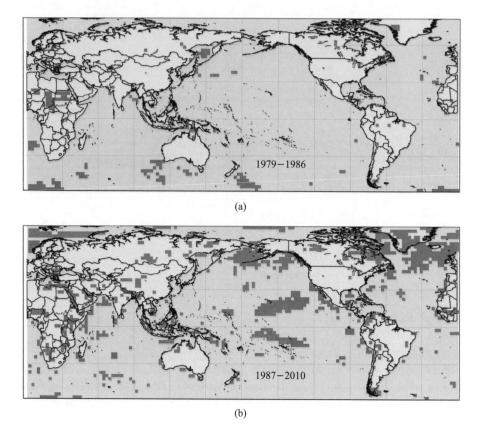

(a)

(b)

Fig. 2.11 Map of significant changes in precipitation over three decades assessed using the Seasonal Kendall nonparametric trend test applied to GPCP v2.2 monthly time series at 2.5° resolution. Red [blue] indicates a significant ($p < 0.01$) negative [positive] change over the specified period. Microwave data were included in the merged product starting in 1987.

2.7 Conclusion

The complexities and contingencies of the coupled bio-geophysical and socio-physical systems make the attribution of processes responsible for observed changes in the state of the vegetated land surface very difficult. Even in the more controlled setting of multi-model experiments, sensitivity evaluation and change attribution have been found challenging (Boisier et al., 2012; de Noblet-Ducoudré et al., 2012), due in large part to differences among models in how land surface states and processes are parameterized (Pitman et al., 2009).

Most of the time series we examined here had little temporal depth. Moreover, the spatial resolutions of data in our analyses were coarse relative to human settlements and activities, yet at an appropriate scale they were found to be appropriate to probe linkages to climatic forcings (de Beurs et al., 2009).

Stationary Rossby waves appear to have a major influence on warm season weather extremes across the northern hemisphere, including heat waves, drought, and deluges (Schubert et al., 2011). Atmospheric teleconnections may also be a contributor to the significant changes in temperature and precipitation extremes found at regional scales in a major analysis of Russia station data (Bulygina et al., 2007). A primary influence of the Northern Annular Mode (NAM)—as characterized through the North Atlantic Oscillation (NAO) and Arctic Oscillation (AO) indices—on growing season conditions is through modulation of the snow cover duration and thus temperature (de Beurs and Henebry, 2008). Changes in snow states across Northern Eurasia and North America indicate long-term decreasing trends in snow cover duration with significant regional differences poleward of 50° N (Bulygina et al., 2011; Callaghan et al., 2011). Winter NAO and AO indices have been linked to significant changes in land surface phenology in the circumpolar zone above 60° N (de Beurs and Henebry, 2010). However, the influence of winter AO on land surface phenology extends across Northern Eurasia well south of 60° N significantly affecting 18–25 Mha in dryland ecoregions (de Beurs and Henebry, 2008).

Drylands are characterized by extremes. Human settlements and livelihoods in drylands have always been precarious (Lioubimsteva and Henebry, 2009). Amidst the interannual variability and spatial heterogeneity induced by the action of climate modes, it is difficult to assess where and when climate variability grades into climate change. Yet, in the face of manifold uncertainties, the results presented here point not only to climatic drivers as the likely agents of the observed changes in the vegetated land surface, but also suggest that recent dynamics are qualitatively different from what has occurred before.

Acknowledgements

This research was supported in part by grants from the NASA Land Cover/Land Use Change program to GMH and KdB.

References

Adam, J., and Lettenmaier, D. P. (2008). Application of new precipitation and reconstructed steamflow products to streamflow trend attribution in Northern Eurasia.

Journal of Climate, 21, 1807–1828.

Alcaraz-Segura, D., Chuvieco, E., Epstien, H. E., Kasischke, E. S., and Trishchenko, A. (2010). Debating the greening vs. browning of the North American boreal forest: Differences between satellite datasets. *Global Change Biology*, 16, 760–770.

Alcaraz-Segura, D., Cabello, J., Paruelo, J. M., and Delibes, M. (2009). Use of descriptors of ecosystem functioning for monitoring a national park network: A remote sensing approach. *Environmental Management*, 43, 38–48.

Boisier, J. P., de Noblet-Ducoudré, N., Pitman, A. J., et al. (2012). Attributing the impacts of land-cover changes in temperate regions on surface temperature and heat fluxes to specific causes: Results from the first LUCID set of simulations. *Journal of Geophysical Research*, 117, D12116.

Bulygina, O. N., Razuvaev, V. N., Korshunova, N. N., and Groisman P. Y. (2007). Climate variations and changes in extreme climate events in Russia. *Environmental Research Letters*, 2, 045020.

Bulygina, O. N., Groisman, P. Y., Razuvaev, V. N., and Korshunova, N. N. (2011). Changes in snow cover characteristics over Northern Eurasia since 1966. *Environmental Research Letters*, 6, 045204.

Callaghan, T. V., Johansson, M., Brown, R. D., et al. (2011). The changing face of Arctic snow cover: A synthesis of observed and projected changes. *AMBIO*, 40, 17–31.

de Beurs, K. M., and Henebry, G. M. (2004a). Land surface phenology, climatic variation, and institutional change: Analyzing agricultural land cover change in Kazakhstan. *Remote Sensing of Environment*, 89, 497–509.

de Beurs, K. M., and Henebry, G. M. (2004b).Trend analysis of the Pathfinder AVHRR Land (PAL) NDVI data for the deserts of Central Asia. *IEEE Geoscience and Remote Sensing Letters*, 1, 282–286.

de Beurs, K. M., and Henebry, G. M. (2005). A statistical framework for the analysis of long image time series. *International Journal of Remote Sensing*, 26, 1551–1573.

de Beurs, K. M., and Henebry, G. M. (2008). Northern Annular Mode effects on the land surface phenologies of Northern Eurasia. *Journal of Climate*, 21, 4257–4279.

de Beurs, K. M, Wright, C. K., and Henebry, G. M. (2009). Dual scale trend analysis distinguishes climatic from anthropogenic effects on the vegetated land surface. *Environmental Research Letters*, 4, 045012.

de Beurs, K. M., and Henebry, G. M. (2010). A land surface phenology assessment of the northern polar regions using MODIS reflectance time series. *Canadian Journal of Remote Sensing* 36, S87–S110.

de Beurs, K. M., Yan, D., and Karnieli, A. (2013) The effect of largescale conservation programs on the vegetative development of China's Loess Plateau. Chapter 13 of this book.

de Noblet-Ducoudré, N., Boisier J.-P., Pitman, A., et al. (2012). Determining robust impacts of land-use-induced land cover changes on surface climate over North America and Eurasia: Results from the first set of LUCID experiments. *Journal of Climate*, 25, 3261-3281.

Friedl, M. A., Sulla-Menashe, D., Tan, B., et al. (2010). MODIS Collection 5 global landcover: Algorithm refinements and characterization of new datasets. *Remote Sensing of Environment*, 114, 168–182.

Gao, F., Schaaf, C., Strahler, A., Roesch, A., Lucht, W., and Dickinson, R. (2005). The MODIS BRDF/Albedo climate modeling grid products and the variability of albedo for major global vegetation types. *Journal of Geophysical Research*, 110, D01104.

Gao, J., Williams, M. W., Fu, X., Wang, G., and Gong, T. (2012). Spatiotemporal distribution of snow in eastern Tibet and the response to climate change. *Remote Sensing of Environment*, 121, 1–9.

Henebry, G. M., de Beurs, K. M., and Gitelson, A. A. (2005). Land surface phenologies of Uzbekistan and Turkmenistan between 1982 and 1999. *Arid Ecosystems*, 11, 25–32.

Hirsch, R. M., and Slack, J. R. (1984). A nonparametric trend test for seasonal data with serial dependence. *Water Resources Research*, 20, 727–732.

Huffman, G. J., Adler, R. F., Bolvin, D. T., and Gu, G. (2009). Improving the global precipitation record: GPCP Version 2.1. *Geophysical Research Letters*, 36, L17808.

Huffman, G. J., and Bolvin, D. T. (2011). GPCP Version 2.2 combined precipitation data set documentation. ftp://precip.gsfc.nasa.gov/pub/gpcp-v2.2/doc/V2.2_doc. pdf (accessed: 31 July 2012).

Jiang, F.-Q., Hu, R.-J., Wang, S.-P., Zhang, Y.-W., and Tong, L. (2012). Trends of precipitation extremes during 1960–2008 in Xinjiang, the Northwest China. *Theoretical and Applied Climatology*, doi: 10.1007/s00704-012-0657-3.

Lerman, Z., Csaki C., and Feder G. (2004). Agriculture in transition: Land policies and evolving farm structures in post-soviet countries. Lanham, MD: Lexington Books.

Lettenmaier, D.P., Wood, E.F., and Wallis, J.R. (1994). Hydro-climatological trends in the continental United States, 1948–1988. *Journal of Climate*, 7, 586–607.

Li, Q., Peng, J., and Shen, Y. (2012). Development of China homogenized monthly precipitation dataset during 1900–2009. *Journal of Geographical Sciences*, 22, 579–593.

Lioubimtseva, E., and Henebry, G. M. (2009). Climate and environmental change in arid Central Asia: Impacts, vulnerability, and adaptations. *Journal of Arid Environments*, 73, 963–977.

Lioubimtseva E., Kariyeva J., and Henebry, G. M. (2013). Climate change in Turkmenistan. In: Zonn, I. S., Kostianoy, A.G. (Eds). *The Turkmen Lake "Altyn Asyr" and Water Resources in Turkmenistan*. Springer.

Micklin, P. P. (1988). Desiccation of the Aral Sea: A water management disaster in the Soviet Union. *Science*, 241, 1170–1176.

Micklin, P. (2007). The Aral Sea disaster. *Annual Review of Earth and Planetary Sciences*, 35, 47–72.

Pitman, A. J., de Noblet-Ducoudré, N., Cruz, F. T., et al. (2009). Uncertainties in climate responses to past land cover change: First results from the LUCID intercomparison study. *Geophysical Research Letters*, 36, L14814.

Pettorelli, N., Chauvenet, A. L. M., Duffy, J. P., Cornforth, W. A., Meillere, A., and Baillie, J. E. M. (2012). Tracking the effect of climate change on ecosystem functioning using protected areas: Africa as a case study. *Ecological Indicators*, 20, 269–276.

Qi, J., Chen, J., Wan, S., and Ai, L. (2012). Understanding the coupled natural and human systems in Dryland East Asia. *Environmental Research Letters*, 7, 015202.

Reed, B. C. (2006). Trend analysis of time-series phenology of North America derived from satellite data. *GIScience and Remote Sensing*, 43, 24–38.

Rudolf, B., Becker, A., Schneider, U., Meyer-Christoffer, A., and Ziese, M. (2010). The new "GPCC Full Data Reanalysis Version 5" providing high-quality gridded monthly precipitation data for the global land-surface is public available since December 2010. http://www.dwd.de/bvbw/generator/DWDWWW/Content/Oeffe ntlichkeit/KU/KU4/KU42/en/Reports_Publications/GPCC_status_report_2010, templateId=raw,property=publicationFile.pdf/GPCC_status_report_2010.pdf (31JUL2012).

Schneider, U., Becker, A. Meyer-Christoffer, A., Ziese, M., and Rudolf, B. (2011). Global precipitation analysis products of GPCC. ftp://ftp-anon.dwd.de/pub/data/ gpcc/PDF/GPCC_intro_products_2008.pdf (31JUL2012).

Schubert, S. Wang, H., and Suarez, M. (2011). Warm season subseasonal variability and climate extremes in the northern hemisphere: The role of stationary Rossby waves. *Journal of Climate*, 24, 4773–4792.

Sobrino, J. A., and Julien, Y. (2011). Global trends in NDVI-derived parameters obtained from GIMMS data. *International Journal of Remote Sensing*, 32, 4267– 4279.

Stensrud, D. J. (2007). *Parameterization Schemes: Keys to Understanding Numerical Weather Prediction Models*. Cambridge, UK: Cambridge University Press.

Tucker, C. J. (1979). Red and photographic infrared linear combinations for monitoring vegetation. *Remote Sensing of Environment*, 8, 127–150.

Tucker, C. J., Pinzon, J. E., Brown, M. E., et al. (2005). An extended AVHRR 8- km NDVI dataset compatible with MODIS and SPOT VEGETATION NDVI data. *International Journal of Remote Sensing*, 26, 4485–4498.

von Storch, H., and Navarra, A. (1999). *Analysis of Climate Variability: Applications of Statistical Techniques*. Berlin, Germany: Springer-Verlag.

Wright, C. K., de Beurs, K. M., Akhmadiyeva, Z. K., Groisman, P. Y., and Henebry, G. M. (2009). Reanalysis data underestimate significant changes in growing season weather in Kazakhstan. *Environmental Research Letters*, 4, 045020.

Wright, C. K., de Beurs, K. M., and Henebry, G. M. (2012). Combined analysis of land cover change and NDVI trends in the Northern Eurasian grain belt. *Frontiers in Earth Science*, 6, 177–187.

Yang, Y., Chen, Y., Le, W., Yu, S., and Wang, M. (2012). Climatic change of inland river basin in an arid area: A case study in northern Xinjiang, China. *Theoretical and Applied Climatology*, 107, 143–154.

Zhang, Q., Li, J., Singh, V.P., and Xu, C.-Y. (2012a), Copula-based spatio-temporal patterns of precipitation extremes in China. *International Journal of Climatology*, doi: 10.1002/joc.3499.

Zhang, Q., Li, J., Singh, V.P., Xu, C.-Y., and Bai, Y. (2012b). Changing structure of the precipitation process during 1960–2005 in Xinjiang, China. *Theoretical and Applied Climatology*, doi: 10.1007/s00704-012-0611-4.

Authors Information

Geoffrey M. Henebry[1]*, Kirsten M. de Beurs[2], Christopher K. Wright[1], Ranjeet John[3], Elena Lioubimtseva[4]

1. Geographic Information Science Center of Excellence, South Dakota State University, Brookings, SD 57007, USA
2. Department of Geography and Environmental Sustainability, University of Oklahoma, Norman, OK 73019, USA
3. Department of Environmental Sciences, University of Toledo, Toledo, OH 43606, USA
4. Department of Geography, Grand Valley State University, Grand Rapids, MI 49401, USA
* Corresponding author

Chapter 3
NEESPI and MAIRS Programs in Dryland East Asia

Jiaguo Qi, Pavel Groisman, and Likun Ai

Summary: Dryland East Asia (DEA) lies within the geographic area involved in two regional programs: Northern Eurasia Earth Science Partnership Initiative (NEESPI) and Monsoon Asia Integrated Regional Study (MAIRS). The DEA region has been under a growing pressure of regional climate change and intensified anthropogenic exploitation. The lack of effective, balanced strategies makes it difficult to cope with increasing extreme climate events and social disturbances, which make the DEA region especially vulnerable to disturbances. To address the DEA environmental and socio-economic problems, NEESPI and MAIRS launched several research projects. Some of them were completed while others are still under way. The objective of this chapter is to introduce NEESPI and MAIRS research activities and primary findings. It is concluded that both Programs have been catalysts in regional research coordination, and have contributed to the understanding of climate change and its impact on both ecosystems and society in the region. Research teams have been established and basic infrastructure for research collaboration and coordination has been put in place for further development of local solutions to the DEA change problems.

3.1 Introduction

Dryland East Asia (DEA) refers to the region characterized by dry climate and vast extensive grasslands, agriculture, and sporadic urban settlements. This region lies within the geographic area indicated by two regional programs (Fig. 3.1): Northern Eurasia Earth Science Partnership Initiative (NEESPI) and Monsoon

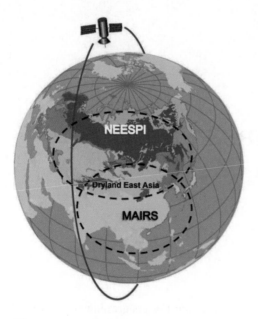

Fig. 3.1 Dryland East Asia is the overlap area involved in NEESPI and MAIRS program research domains.

Asia Integrated Regional Study (MAIRS). The geography of the region is described in Chapter 1 of this book. In general the majority of soils fall within the category of arid, highly erodible clay soils (Batjes, 2010) while precipitation and temperature vary considerably from west to east and from north to south. The dominant land-cover type is grassland, including desert-steppe (Groisman et al., 2009; John et al., 2009).

The DEA region has been under two major sources of pressure: regional climate changes and intensified anthropogenic exploitation, which have significantly impacted the livelihood and environment of the region, resulting in a gradual shift from extensive nomadic grazing systems to confined feeding and modern cropping systems (Sankey et al., 2009). Recent increases in energy demand have also escalated the commercial exploitation of natural resources, e.g., causing a spread of coal mining, resulting in unexpected socioeconomic and environmental consequences (Fortes, 1988).

The complexity of the coupled climate and human impacts on the grassland ecosystems and the livelihood of the locals makes the DEA region vulnerable to disturbances, as there is a lack of effective, balanced strategies to cope with increasing extreme climate events and social disturbances due to conflicting societal development (Higgins et al., 2002; Liu et al., 2007). To better understand the complexity of the interactive nature between grassland ecosystems, domesticated animals and climate, numerous research projects and programs have been carried out in this region, the latest of which are NEESPI and MAIRS. The objective of this chapter is to introduce these two programs, their research activities and primary findings, and thus illustrates how coordinated efforts through international programs can holistically address regional socio-environmental issues.

3.2   Contrast and Comparison

3.2.1   The Programs

NEESPI (http://neespi.org) is an interdisciplinary program of internationally-supported Earth systems and science research that addresses large-scale and long-term manifestations of climate and environmental change. The geographic area includes the former Soviet Union, Northern China, Mongolia, Fennoscandia, and Eastern Europe. The program started as a joint initiative between the National Aeronautics and Space Administration (NASA) and the Russian Academy of Sciences (RAS) in 2004 with an intended lifespan of 10 years. Its mission is comparable with that of the MAIRS Program (Table 3.1).

Table 3.1 Missions of NEESPI and MAIRS Programs.

NEESPI	MAIRS
– To capitalize on a variety of remote sensing and other tools and implement a general modeling framework linking socioeconomic factors, crop, pollution, land use, ecosystem and climate models with observational data to address key research questions within Northern Eurasia. – To provide information that empowers society and decision-makers to plan and react wisely, to mitigate the negative and to benefit from the positive consequences of environmental changes. – To establish educational activities for students, educators, and the general public.	– To better understand how human activities in the region are interacting with and altering natural variability of atmospheric, terrestrial and marine components of the monsoon system. – To contribute to the provision of a sound scientific basis for sustainable development of monsoon Asia. – To develop the predictive capacity of estimating changes in global-regional linkages in the Earth System and to project the future consequences of such changes.

MAIRS (http://mairs-espp.org) is an international research program, implemented by the System for Analysis, Research and Training (START), the START Tropical East Asia (TEA-RC) and Chinese donors under the Earth System Science Partnership (ESSP), focusing on monsoon system and society interactions. The entire geographic area is the area that the Asian Monsoon system affects, known as Monsoon Asia. The program was established in 2005 with the mission of addressing the coupled nature of monsoon climate and human activities in the region (Table 3.1).

3.2.2 Research Approaches

Both NEESPI and MAIRS take an interdisciplinary approach to addressing the regional social-environmental issues (Table 3.2). However, NEESPI primarily focuses on physical processes, modeling and understanding of climate and land surface processes such as hydrology and land cover changes, while MAIRS attempts to model the monsoon climate system and assesses its impacts on ecosystems (urban, mountain, and agro-pastoral systems).

Table 3.2 Research approaches and foci of the NEESPI and MAIRS Programs.

NEESPI	MAIRS

– Biophysical science on:
  ○ Large-scale and long-term manifestations of climate and environmental change.
  ○ Observations
	– Interface between climate and humans, focusing on:
	  ○ Coupled nature of human and environment systems
	  ○ Experiments and observations

– Interdisciplinary Approach focusing on boundaries of ecosystems':
  ○ Coastal zone
  ○ Mountains
  ○ Steppe-desert
  ○ Tundra-forest
  ○ Forest-steppe
	– Interdisciplinary Approach focusing on:
	  ○ Coastal Zone
	  ○ Mountain Zone
	  ○ Semi arid Zone
	  ○ Urban Zone

– Fundamental physical and ecological science questions focusing on
  ○ Climate
  ○ Hydrology
  ○ Biosphere
  ○ Land cover and land use change
	– Interdisciplinary science questions focusing on the interactions between environment and human systems:
	  ○ LCLUC
	  ○ Socioeconomics
	  ○ Climate
	  ○ Hydrology

3.2.3   Organization Structure

The organization and operations of NEESPI and MAIRS Programs are listed in Table 3.3.

Table 3.3 Organization and Operations of NEESPI and MAIRS Programs.

NEESPI	MAIRS
– Five affiliated Data and Science Centers	– Well linked to research programs of the region
– Topical and Regional Focus Research Centers spread across the region, West Europe and the United States	– Its own funding to support research activities
– Affiliated Projects	– An International Project Office for coordination
– Various funding agencies: primarily NASA in the US; primarily RAS in Russia	– Committed funding from the Chinese Academy of Sciences
– One "Project Scientist" to coordinate	– Coordination through regional workshops and working group meetings
– No funding commitment	
– Coordination through detailed Science Plan, scientific workshops, meetings and programmatic publications	

3.2.4   Major Research Activities

Dryland Working Group (DWG) of MAIRS was formed to specifically address the vulnerability, impacts and adaptation (VIA) of this area by developing a general framework in the dryland region with the following specific objectives: 1) to integrate existing monitoring systems of the region in order to better coordinate observational efforts, including both satellite systems and ground-based stations, in developing a database of key physical and social processes, 2) to coordinate a comparative analysis of existing regional climate models as well as land surface processes that are characteristic of the region, 3) to coordinate and develop cross-cutting studies for the assessment of dryland vulnerability and creation of adaptation/mitigation strategies, and 4) to develop and enhance Asian dryland research frameworks and capacity building. DWG makes specific recommendations to the Science Steering Committee (SSC) to set the future research agenda.

NEESPI's efforts in the dryland region have been directed to: 1) establish new studies in the region and surrounding mountain regions that supply water to it, 2) coordinate the new and the previous crop of studies via international workshops and conferences, 3) provide visitors' exchange programs, 4) stimulate joint publications, and 5) promote societal and international awareness about the environmental problems of the region and the urgent need to address its sustainable development.

3.3   Major Findings and Achievements

3.3.1   Understanding Climate Change

The paleoclimatic and historical evidence indicates dramatic changes over the DEA region. Lakes changed their levels by several meters. Oases shrank and were resurrected again with the prosperous agriculture population. Areas where numerous herdsmen found abundant grass for their horses became dry deserts that cannot support livestock, and thereafter the same areas returned to grassland again. The last century information for the period of instrumental observations also shows significant changes in the DEA region that include a gradual increase in the surface air temperature, regional drying and a more variable precipitation pattern that can cause alternating floods and droughts in the different parts of DEA (e.g., Dai et al., 1998).

There have been significant changes in the dryland region of East Asia in the form of global climate anomalies. From 1909 to 2009, the temperature anomalies, defined as a significant deviation from mean temperatures of the region, were concentrated in the DEA region and the northern part of the Northern Hemisphere (Lugina et al., 2006; Hansen et al., 2010). The climate anomalies also exhibited a very heterogeneous spatio-temporal pattern (Das and Parthasarathy, 2009; New et al., 2000; Dai et al., 2004), suggesting that climate impacts assessments and adaptation should be location specific. The frequency of extreme events increased by 5% over the past 30 years in some areas in comparison with the average from 1961–2010, manifested in the frequent occurrence of extreme low/high temperatures as well as high precipitation intensity and duration of extreme climate events such as drought and severe winter storms (Salinger et al., 2000; O'Brien and Leichenko, 2000; Groisman et al., 2009; Lu et al., 2009).

3.3.2   Understanding Societal Consequences

The increasing number of extreme climate events has caused major economic disasters, reflected in the loss of livestock (Shi et al., 2007; Qian and Lin, 2005) and crops (Deng et al., 2011, Qi et al., 2012a) in the region. For example, the loss of livestock closely coincided with the number of drought episodes or severe winter storms (Qi et al., 2012a, Retzer et al., 2006). However, the number of livestock animals maintained is increasing as a result of economic development to meet the growing demand for food production and also as a result of changing diet from grain to meat in the region (Li et al., 2007).

Similarly the climate impact on agricultural ecosystems makes the region very vulnerable, especially vulnerable to changes in precipitation, as the majority of the agricultural practices rely on rainfall. With the changing spatial and temporal rainfall pattern of the region, both ecosystems (grasslands and agriculture) and society became subject to greater risks due to climatic change.

The societal consequences were not just the result of regional climate change, as the local society also played a key role by creating a series of policy changes and initiatives. For example, during and shortly after the Cultural Revolution in the early 1970s in China and during the New Land Policy era that began in the late 1970s in Mongolia, the total number of livestock animals declined first and/or basically remained unchanged thereafter (e.g., Jiang, 2005). The

Fig. 3.2 Winter storm-related animal fatalities and drought-related impacts on crop productivity (Upper photo by Dr. Guodong Han, Inner Mongolia Agricultural University, China and lower photo by Dr. Jiaguo Qi, Michigan State University, USA).

economic reforms started in the late 1980s, particularly after the implementation of the livestock and grassland tenure system in China, and the new Free Market Policy in Mongolia, triggered a major growth in the total number of livestock animals. The growing economy for the livestock industry took a large blow in 2002 when the region had historical drought and cold winter storms (Fig.3.2), resulting in a major setback of the local economy. This was a tipping point for ranchers to switch from a nomadic grazing lifestyle to confined feeding with corn and other agricultural products as major feeding approach or as an adaptation strategy against extreme climate events (Chuluun and Ojima, 2002). The shift in land use in the region has increased water consumption (Fig. 3.3) by agricultural

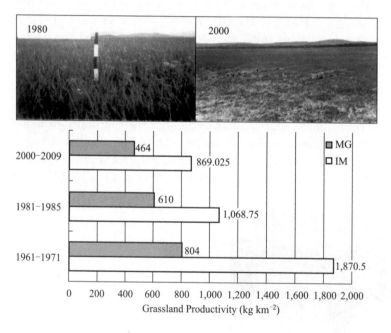

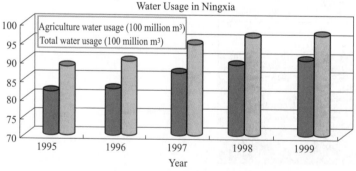

Fig. 3.3 Degradation of grassland productivity during three time periods from 1961–2009 and water use changes from 1995–1999.
Source: Xiangzheng DENG, CAS, China.

sector, which raises a question of the long-term sustainability of the changing economic development strategy.

However, continued climate change and environmental consequences associated with it, along with economic development opportunities, present new challenges to the local people in DEA (Mason, 2001; Angerer et al., 2008, Qi et al., 2012b). Recent energy crises worldwide and increasing energy consumption in China to support economic growth in particular have sparked new pressure on the grasslands in the region; increasingly grasslands are being converted to cash crops and coal mining, both of which have significant environmental consequences such as soil erosion and water pollution (Brogaard and Zhao, 2002). The key questions facing the local people are how to achieve a balance between economic development and ecological conservation and how to achieve further sustainable development of the region.

3.3.3 Understanding Ecosystem Impacts

Under the influence of both climate change and intensified human activities, the grassland ecosystems in the DEA region have been degraded and their productivities are declining (Fig. 3.3). Overall grassland productivity were 804 and 1,871 kg km^{-2} for Mongolia (MG) and Inner Mongolia Autonomous Region (IM), China respectively and declined by $\sim$43% for MG and 53% for IM from 1961 to 2009 (Brown, 2011). The grassland productivity reduction in IM was much faster in recent years as a result of overgrazing to meet the demand for meat production resulting from rapid economic development (Zhen et al., 2010). During the same period of time, the price of meat also almost tripled or quadrupled, which was believed by economists to be the major driver of grassland degradation (Waldron et al., 2010).

Existing grassland productivity has declined, while concurrently many acres of quality grasslands have given way to traditional croplands, urban development and coal mining operations (Jiang et al., 2006). The grassland conversion to croplands producing potato and corn occurred primarily along the traditional boundaries between agriculture and grazing lands (Williams, 1996). However, institutional engagement in land-use change, through environmental policies and economic incentives, has made the grasslands conversion an important subject of study. Although the total area of grasslands, by definition, was not significantly reduced, the quality grasslands have been reduced. Local herders and farmers in IM witnessed a rapid conversion of agricultural lands into urban lands. The agricultural lands, in order to meet the increasing urban demand for food production, particularly vegetables, were thereafter expanded to take over marginal grasslands, by adopting new irrigation technologies (Fig. 3.3). This conversion from nomadic grazing to intensified agricultural production systems also changed water consumption. Further, the land use conversion caused other environmental issues such as the tillage of thin layers of marginal soils which de-stabilizes the deeper soil layers and subjects them to wind and water erosion.

3.3.4 Institutional Responses to Environmental Change

Climate change, large-scale land-use conversion, intensified agricultural production and extensive grassland degradation, along with secondary environmental issues such as dust and sand storms in the DEA region, have caused major environmental and sustainability concerns. As a response to these environmental changes, the affected nations have taken measures to address these issues. For example, China implemented a series of environmental policies, including the "Three-north Shelterbelt Forest Program" initiated in 1978 and the "Sloping Land Conversion Program (also known as 'Grain for Green') Program " initiated in 1999 in the west of China. The effectiveness of these programs has been evaluated to be positive at the national level (e.g., Ojima and Chuluun, 2008; Xu et al., 2010; Liu et al., 2008), but at some local levels the responses have been less optimistic, as the long-term lifestyle for some ranchers and farmers has been altered (Liu et al., 2008). To balance environmental conservation and economic development needs, the Chinese government has taken further steps to limit ecological degradation of grasslands in Western China. For example, on June 15, 2011, the State Council of China introduced eight policy measures for the development of Inner Mongolia Autonomous Region (IM), the first of which is "to promote ecological construction and environmental protection" (Yin and Yin, 2010). At the same time, the IM government officially launched "the Inner Mongolia Grassland Ecological Protection Subsidiary Incentives Program", in which herders who have completed the mission of "non-grazing and pasture-animal balance" will receive compensation from the local government. These are the efforts composed at the national level, but their societal consequences are far-reaching and there has been no attempt to assess the intended and unintended consequences.

3.3.5 Understanding Challenges

Understanding the complexities and mitigating the negative consequences resulting from regional climate change and economic development in the region have been challenging. Current NEESPI and MAIRS Programs aim primarily at understanding the physical processes, regional climate variability, land-use and land-cover changes and associated carbon cycles in the region. There are few efforts to address the social processes, especially the development of mitigation and adaptation strategies. Therefore, research gaps and challenges remain as follows.

1. Insufficient data in the DEA region to holistically assess climate impacts on both grassland ecosystems and societal functions

Water is probably the most important issue in the region. However, there are a very limited number of water balance and hydrological stations in place to collect the fundamental data needed to understand the hydrological processes and water resources. Groundwater table data are too sparse to capture its spatial variability in the region and thus it is impossible to holistically assess precipitation impacts on grassland and agricultural productivity. The large forest plantation in DEA is the primary reason for land conversion from grassland to poplar plantations. Yet little is known about their impact on the regional water budget, as well as on the climate. Similarly, there is a lack of the dense network of long-term meteorological stations, particularly in Mongolia, and there is a need to develop and strengthen the networks of national meteorological stations. Data quality control is also recognized as a major challenge that needs to be addressed. There are no (or very limited) data on the social dimensions of the climate change and thus it is difficult and/or impossible to assess societal impacts of climate change, including, but not limited to, human health, gender disparity, age structure, education, cultural beliefs and other social and demographic aspects of the region, which are important in assessing societal impacts of climate change and policy effectiveness.

2. Key research priority areas have not yet been studied

The nature of future climate change in the region is unclear, as is its interaction with ecosystems and society. The consensus is that the DEA region became warmer and precipitation varied little over the past century, but the spatial and temporal climate variability in the future is unclear, as the simulations are significantly biased in the current General Circulation Models (GCMs) used by IPCC in the DEA region. This makes it difficult to develop potential risk assessments for planning purposes. The regional hydrological processes are not well understood. Glaciers are exceptionally important in providing water recharges in rivers and ground waters of the DEA region, but the role of the glaciers in the region is unclear under current and future climate changes (e.g., Immerzeel et al., 2010). Further, little is known about the total water resources in the region and the impact of dams' construction, reforestation, irrigation and inter-basin transfers on these resources. There is little knowledge about international water rights within the DEA region and total human consumption demands.

Considering the total land area, the total urban area within the DEA region may not be large enough to have significant environmental consequences. However, urban expansion and development played a key role in the livelihood changes for farmers and ranchers in the past. The majority of younger generations from rural areas migrated to urbanized settlements, leaving behind vacant or abandoned lands. How the shift in demography, particularly in the age distribution, affects the grassland ecosystems needs are to be further studied. Societal impacts of climate change have not been fully assessed, and are not yet understood. Little is known about how climate change has impacted the livelihoods of the rural communities of DEA in terms of food, health and water security. There is also a lack of research on adaptation solutions to climate change. There is very limited knowledge or even research about adaptation to future climate change, which will be necessary in order to maintain and improve human well-being in the region. Such research requires the quantification of key drivers of land degradation, including social, economic and biophysical drivers such as overgrazing, mining, and poor agricultural practices (irrigation). These issues necessitate further research and urge Programs such as NEESPI and MAIRS in order to initiate comprehensive studies of climatic, environmental and socio-economic problems of the DEA region in an integrated manner.

3. Coordination and communication among programs and projects in the region is important but lacking

Improved coordination is needed in order to effectively address the environmental issues in the region. There are many ongoing projects in the region funded by the US, the European Union and Japan, and many national projects in China. However, coordination and collaboration are limited. Some efforts are duplicative, although many are complementary. There are still barriers to sharing results, methods and data among different parties and researchers in the region. Engagement of stakeholders and decision-makers in the climate adaptation research process should be enhanced. The research results need to be presented in a format that is easily understood and applied by the local decision-makers.

3.4   Conclusions

The NEESPI and MAIRS Programs have been catalysts in regional research coordination, and have contributed to the understanding of climate change and its impact on both ecosystems and society in the region. Research teams have been established and basic infrastructure for research collaboration and coordination has been put in place. The research collaboration and coordination will continue to improve fundamental knowledge of the region and allow for the development of local solutions to the regional change problems.

The research activities, including regional workshops and meetings coordinated by the two Programs, have improved capacity-building in the region. Methods and tools developed by the international research community have been prototyped, applied and sometimes adapted to address region-specific environmental issues. Students and young researchers have been trained in various workshops organized by the two Programs to enhance the local capacity to independently conduct research and develop environmental solutions.

The NEESPI and MAIRS Programs have also drawn researchers from the region to collaborate among themselves in developing research programs and projects. As the two Programs continue to engage local scientists, decision-makers and the local community in research projects and regional workshops, the knowledge gaps identified above can be narrowed and eventually solved.

References

Angerer, J., Han, G., Fujisaki, I., and Havstad, K. (2008). Climate Change and Ecosystems of Asia With Emphasis on Inner Mongolia and Mongolia. *Rangelands*, 30, 46–51.

Batjes, N. H. (2010). A global framework of soil organic carbon stocks under native vegetation for use with the simple assessment option of the Carbon Benefits Project system. Report 2010/10, Carbon Benefits Project (CBP) and ISRIC—World Soil Information. Wageningen.

Brogaard, S., and Zhao, X. (2002). Rural reforms and changes in land management and attitudes: A case study from Inner Mongolia, China. *AMBIO: A Journal of the Human Environment*, 31, 219–225.

Brown, D., Wang J., and Agrawal, A. (2011). Governing Mongolian Grasslands Sustainably: Comparing Institutional, Market, and Ecological Changes in the Context of Climate Change in Mongolia and Inner Mongolia, China, Dryland Ecosystems in East Asia: State, Changes, Knowledge Gaps, and Future, Kaifeng, China, July 18–20, 2011.

Chen, X., Luo, G., Xia, J., Zhou, K., Lou, S., and Ye, M. (2005). Ecological response to the climate change on the northern slope of the Tianshan Mountains in Xinjiang. *Science in China Series D: Earth Sciences*, 48, 765–777.

Chuluun, T., and Ojima, D. (2002). Land use change and carbon cycle in arid and semi-arid lands of East and Central Asia. *Science in China Series C: Life Sciences*, 45, 48–44.

Dai, A., Trenberth, K., and Qian, T. (2004) A global dataset of Palmer drought severity index for 1870–2002: Relationship with soil moisture and effects of surface warming. *Journal of Hydrometeorology*, 5, 1117–1130.

Dai, A., Trenberth, K., and Karl, T. R. (1998). Global variations in droughts and wet spells: 1900–1995. *Geophysical Research Letters*, 25, 3367–3370.

Das, M., and Parthasarathy, S. (2009). Anomaly detection and spatio-temporal analysis of global climate system. In, *Proceedings of the Third International Workshop on Knowledge Discovery from Sensor Data*. Paris, France: ACM.

Fan, P., and Qi, J. (2010). Assessing the sustainability of major cities in China. *Sustainable Science*, 5, 51-68.

Fortes, M. D. (1988). Mangrove and seagrass beds of East Asia: Habitats under Stress. *AMBIO: A Journal of the Human Environment*, 17, 207–213.

Groisman, P. Y., Clark, E. A., Kattsov, V. M., Lettenmaier, D. P., Sokolik, I. N., Aizen, V. B., Cartus, O., Chen, J., Conard, S., Katzenberger, J., Krankina, O., Kukkonen, J., Machida, T., Maksyutov, S., Ojima, D., Qi, J., Romanovsky, V. E., Santoro, M., Schmullius, C., Shiklomanov, A. I., Shimoyama, K., Shugart, H. H., Shuman, J. K., Sofiev, M., Sukhinin, A. I., Vörösmarty, C., Walker, D., and Wood, E. F. (2009). The Northern Eurasia earth science partnership: An example of science applied to societal needs. *Bulletin of the American Meteorological Society*, 5, 671–688.

Hansen, J., Ruedy, R., Sato, M., and Lo, K. (2010). Global Surface Temperature Change. *Reviews of Geophysics*, 48, RG4004.

Higgins, P. A. T., Mastrandrea, M. D., and Schneider, S. H. (2002). Dynamics of climate and ecosystem coupling: Abrupt changes and multiple equilibria. *Philosophical Transactions of the Royal Society of London. Series B: Biological Sciences*, 357, 647–655.

Immerzeel, W. W., van Beek, L. P. H., and Bierkens, M. F. P. (2010). Climate change will affect the Asian water towers. *Science*, 328, 1382–1385.

Jiang, G., Han, X., and Wu, J. (2006). Restoration and management of the Inner Mongolia grassland require a sustainable strategy. *AMBIO: A Journal of the Human Environment*, 35, 269–270.

Jiang, H. (2005). Grassland management and views of nature in China since 1949: Regional policies and local changes in Uxin Ju, Inner Mongolia. *Geoforum*, 36, 641–653.

Jiang, H. (2006). Decentralization, ecological construction, and the environment in post-reform China: Case study from Uxin Banner, Inner Mongolia. *World Development*, 34, 1907–1921.

John, R., Chen, J., Lu, N., and Wilske, B. (2009). Land cover/land use change and their ecological consequences. *Environmental Research Letter*, 4, 045010. doi: 10.1088/1748-9326/4/4/045010.

Klein Tank, A. M. G., Peterson, T. C., Quadir, D. A., Dorji, S., Zou, X., Tang, H., Santhosh, K., Joshi, U. R., Jaswal, A. K., Kolli, R. K., Sikder, A. B., Deshpande, N. R., Revadekar, J. V., Yeleuova, K., Vandasheva, S., Faleyeva, M., Gomboluudev, P., Budhathoki, K. P., Hussain, A., Afzaal, M., Chandrapala, L., Anvar, H., Amanmurad, D., Asanova, V. S., Jones, P. D., New, M. G., and Spektorman, T. (2006). Changes in daily temperature and precipitation extremes in central and south Asia. *Journal of Geophysical Research*, 111, D16105.

Li, W. J., Ali, S. H., and Zhang, Q. (2007). Property rights and grassland degradation: A study of the Xilingol Pasture, Inner Mongolia, China. *Journal of Environmental Management*, 85, 461–470.

Liu, J., Dietz, T., Carpenter, S. R., Alberti, M., Folke, C., Moran, E., Pell, A. N., Deadman, P., Kratz, T., Lubchenco, J., Ostrom, E., Ouyang, Z., Provencher, W., Redman, C. L., Schneider, S. H., and Taylor, W. W. (2007). Complexity of coupled human and natural systems. *Science*, 317, 1513–1516.

Liu, B., Xu, M., Henderson, M., and Qi, Y. (2005). Observed trends of precipitation amount, frequency, and intensity in China, 1960–2000. *Journal of Geophysical Research*, 110, 08103. doi: 10.1029/2004JD004864.

Liu, J., Li, S., Ouyang, Z., Tam, C., and Chen, X. (2008). Ecological and socioeconomic effects of China's policies for ecosystem services. *Proceedings of the National Academy of Sciences*, 105, 9477–9482.

Lu, N., Wilske, B., Ni, J., John, R., and Chen, J. (2009). Climate change in Inner Mongolia from 1955 through 2005. *Environmental Research Letter*, 4, 045006. doi: 10.1088/1748-9326/4/4/045006.

Mason, A. (2001). Population change and economic development in East Asia: Challenges Met, Opportunities Seized. Stanford, CA: Stanford University Press.

New, M., Hulme, M., and Jones, P. (2000). Representing twentieth-century space-time climate variability. Part I: Development of a 1961–1990 mean monthly terrestrial climatology. *Journal of Climate*, 13, 2217–2238.

O'Brien, K. L., and Leichenko, R. M. (2000). Double exposure: Assessing the impacts of climate change within the context of economic globalization. *Global Environmental Change*, 10, 221–232.

Ojima, D., and Chuluun, T. (2008). Policy Changes in Mongolia: Implications for Land Use and Landscapes. In: Galvin, K. A., Reid, R. S., Jr, R. H. B., and Hobbs, N. T. (Eds.). *Fragmentation in Semi-Arid and Arid Landscapes*. Netherlands: Springer, 179–193.

Qi, J., Chen, J., Wan, S., and Ai, L. (2012a). Understanding the coupled natural and human systems in the dryland East Asia. *Environmental Research Letters*, 7, 015202. doi: 10.1088/1748-9326/7/1/015202.

Qi, J., Fan, P., and Chen, X. (2012b). The urban expansion and sustainability challenge in cities of China's West: The case of Ürümqi. In: Vojnovic (Ed.). *Urban Sustainability*. Michigan State University Press, 69–100.

Qian, W., and Lin, X. (2005). Regional trends in recent precipitation indices in China. *Meteorology and Atmospheric Physics*, 90, 193–207.

Retzer, V., Nadrowski, K., and Miehe, G. (2006). Variation of precipitation and its effect on phytomass production and consumption by livestock and large wild herbivores along an altitudinal gradient during a drought, South Gobi, Mongolia. *Journal of Arid Environments*, 66, 135–150.

Salinger, M. J., Stigter, C. J., and Das, H. P. (2000). Agrometeorological adaptation strategies to increasing climate variability and climate change. *Agricultural and Forest Meteorology*, 103, 167–184.

Sankey, T. T., Sankey, J. B., Weber, K. T., and Montagne, C. (2009). Geospatial assessment of grazing regime shifts and sociopolitical changes in a Mongolian rangeland. *Rangeland Ecology and Management*, 62, 522–530.

Shi, Y., Shen, Y., Kang, E., Li, D., Ding, Y., Zhang, G., and Hu, R. (2007). Recent and future climate change in Northwest China. *Climatic Change*, 80, 379–393.

Tan, K. S., and Khor, H. E. (2006). China's changing economic structure and implications for regional patterns of trade, production and integration. *China and World Economy*, 14, 1–19.

Waldron, S., Brown, C., and Longworth, J. (2010). Grassland degradation and livelihoods in China's western pastoral region: A framework for understanding and refining China's recent policy responses. *China Agricultural Economic Review*, 2, 298–320.

Williams, D. (1996). Grassland enclosures: Catalyst of land degradation in Inner Mongolia. *Human Organization*, 55, 307–313.

Xu, J., Tao, R., Xu, Z., and Bennett, M.T. (2010). China's sloping land conversion program: Does expansion equal success? *Land Economics*, 86, 219–244.

Yin, R., and Yin, G. (2010). China's primary programs of terrestrial ecosystem restoration: Initiation, implementation, and challenges. *Environmental Management*, 45, 429–441.

Ying, L. G. (1999). China's changing regional disparities during the reform period. *Economic Geography*, 75, 59–70.

Zhang, Q., Xu, C. Y., Zhang, Z., Chen, Y. D., and Liu, C. L. (2009). Spatial and temporal variability of precipitation over China, 1951–2005. *Theoretical and Applied Climatology*, 95, 1–2, 53–68.

Zhen, L., Ochirbat, B., Lv, Y., Wei, Y. J., Liu, X. L., Chen, J. Q., Yao, Z.J.M, and Li, F. (2010). Comparing patterns of ecosystem service consumption and perceptions of range management between ethnic herders in Inner Mongolia and Mongolia. *Environmental Research Letters*, 5, 015001.

Authors Information

Jiaguo Qi[1]*, Pavel Groisman[2], Likun Ai[3]
1. Department of Geography, Michigan State University, East Lansing, MI, USA
2. NOAA National Climatic Data Center, Asheville, NC, USA
3. Institute of Atmospheric Physics, Chinese Academy of Sciences, Beijing, China
* Corresponding author

Chapter 4

Land Use and Land Cover Change in Dryland East Asia

Richard H. Becker and Kirk A. Zmijewski

Summary: Land cover in the Dryland East Asia (DEA) region has undergone significant changes over the scale of centuries and decades, with changes accelerating through the 20th century. Analysis of long-term regional reconstructed datasets (HYDE 3.1, SAGE) and shorter-term field observations and satellite image records (MODIS, AVHRR, Landsat) reveals substantial land cover changes across the entire region.

Over the past 300 years there has been an increase of pastureland and cropland, a decrease in natural grasslands, and forested lands, and ultimately an increase in degraded pastureland. Since 1947, this has changed through accelerated urbanization, conversion of rangeland to cropland and increased sandy desertification (Liu and Tian, 2010). Most recently, there is an increase in reforestation and efforts at rangeland stabilization. Following the implementation of some of these changes, an increase in forest area and recovery of grasslands is noted. This recovery may be due to climate variability combined with reforestation/afforestation efforts and changed grazing policies (Cao, 2011; Liu and Tian, 2010; Squires and Zhang, 2009).

When compared with land-cover changes in recent years in another large dryland area, the Sahel in North Africa, which has experienced similar climate variability but different anthropogenic pressures, there are apparent similarities in trends. In both cases (Sahel and DEA), the percent coverage by grasslands increases by roughly the same extent, and barren lands experience a slight decrease. However, cropland and forest cover-have opposite trends between DEA and the Sahel (croplands increase and forest cover age decreases in the Sahel), possibly showing a measureable impact of the different land use policies between the two drylands regions, one of which has a centralized single policy covering a substantial portion of the drylands (DEA), and the other where the policy is set by far more countries with less political control (Sahel).

4.1   Introduction

Over the past millennia, humans have significantly modified the environment, including land use both on local and global scale. With increased population demands, this change has accelerated over recent centuries. Records of this land use change can be found in a wide variety of sources ranging from historical accounts and legers to maps of a variety of ages to more recently satellite derived land use classification maps. (Liu and Tian, 2010).

The Dryland East Asia (DEA) region (Fig. 4.1) consists of the country of Mongolia and four provinces in Northern China: Inner Mongolia Autonomous Region, Gansu Province, Ningxia Hui Autonomous Region, and Xinjiang Uygur Autonomous Region. This is an area of expansive deserts (e.g., Gobi, Taklimakan) and significant grasslands (e.g., Hulunbeier, Xilingol). As a result, the vast majority of this 4.8 million km^2 area ($\sim$77.5%) is made up of arid barren land and the semiarid grasslands. Smaller amounts of open shrublands, croplands and mixed forests make up most of the remaining land cover (Table 4.1). Almost 80% of the arid and semiarid areas in China are affected by degradation to some extent, with degradation being as high as 56% in some areas (Squires and Zhang, 2009).

Land cover in DEA has undergone significant changes over the past centuries (Lin et al., 2010). Over the past 300 years there has been an increase of pasturelands and croplands, a decrease in natural grasslands and forested lands, and ultimately an increase in degraded pasturelands (Liu and Tian, 2010; Ramankutty and Foley, 1999; Squires and Zhang, 2009) In the past 50 years, accelerated urbanization, conversion of rangeland to cropland and increased sandy desertification is noted (Liu and Tian, 2010; Squires and Zhang, 2009). More recently, some of these patterns have changed, as there is an increase in reforestation, causing an increase in forest area due to changes in land management policies (Liu and Tian, 2010) in many locations. MODIS derived land use classifications over the first decade of the 21st century indicate that there may also be a recovery in grasslands possibly due to climate variability and changed grazing policies in Inner Mongolia Autonomous Region, China.

This study summarizes the changes that have occurred over the time period that land cover data has both been reconstructed and directly measured. In this study, we incorporate change analysis of the HYDE 3.1 global land use databases for the past 12,000 years, providing a context for more recent land use change.

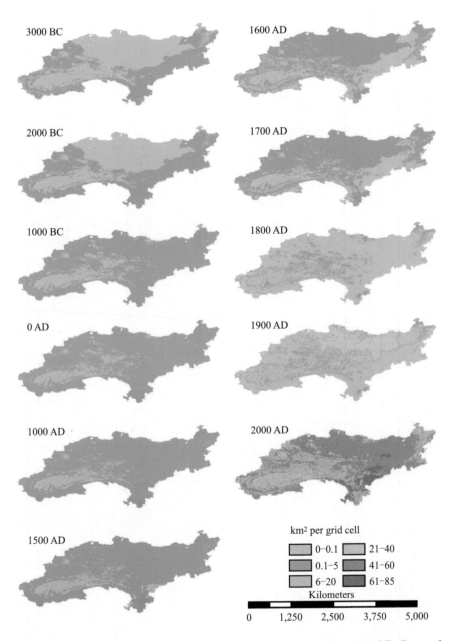

Fig. 4.1 Pastureland cover in the DEA region from 3000 BC to 2000 AD. Source from the HYDE 3.1 database.

Table 4.1 Land use in the DEA region in 2007 and Land use changes in the DEA region between 2001 and 2007 based on MODIS MOD12Q1 annual land cover image.

IGBP Classification	Land Cover Area (km^2)		Land Cover Area (%)		Change 2001–2009 (%)
	2001	2009	2001	2009	
Water	21,171	20,346	0.44%	0.42%	−3.90%
Forest	126,705	161,843	2.64%	3.37%	27.73%
Shrubland	68,829	74,180	1.43%	1.54%	7.77%
Woody savannas	49,782	27,728	1.04%	0.58%	−44.30%
Savannas	10,713	1,025	0.22%	0.02%	−90.44%
Grasslands	2,135,449	2,269,806	44.44%	47.24%	6.29%
Permanent wetlands	208	417	0.00%	0.01%	100.24%
Croplands	186,400	155,298	3.88%	3.23%	−16.69%
Urban and built-up	8,622	8,622	0.18%	0.18%	0.00%
Cropland/natural vegetation mosaic	56,076	51,978	1.17%	1.08%	−7.31%
Snow and ice	27,177	23,661	0.57%	0.49%	−12.94%
Barren or sparsely vegetated	2,114,057	2,010,287	44.00%	41.84%	−4.91%

This is complemented for the entire region by MODIS derived land use change trends for the DEA area during 2001–2009. These results are supplemented by published case studies of specific land cover changes, based on historical records, historical maps field studies and recent moderate to high resolution satellite or aerial photography derived land use classifications.

To provide context in a global environment, these changes are contrasted with changes in another drylands region, that of the Sahel, in Sub-Saharan Africa for 2001-2009, where cropland expansion and deforestation have a major role in land use and land cover changes.

4.2 Global Land Use Changes through Centuries

The HYDE 3.1 land-use database of human induced global change is a database of land use all over the globe. The time period covered is from 10,000 BC to 2000 AD, at a spatial resolution of 5' (Goldewijk et al., 2011). The HYDE database is generated using historical population information, cropland and pastures statistics, combined with satellite information and allocation algorithms which are used to create spatial maps for the time period. This database allows examination of changes in pasturelands and croplands globally. Examination of the global land uses data set HYDE 3.1 (Goldewijk et al., 2011) shows the slow steady increase in both pastureland and cropland until approximately 1700, followed by the rapid increase of rangeland and then cropland.

Because DEA encompasses portions of multiple countries and multiple administrative units inside each country over a broad spatial area, remote sensing techniques were used to determine the current land-cover characteristics of the region. Annual MODIS land cover products from 2001 through 2009 with 500m spatial resolution (MOD12Q1) were obtained from the EOS data gateway. The International Geosphere-Biosphere Programme (IGBP) land use classification was used to allow for easy inter-comparison with other studies. This classification scheme was then further generalized to forest, shrubland, savanna, grassland, wetland, cropland, urban, cropland/natural vegetation, barren and water following the techniques outlined in John et al. (2009). Land use types derived for this are listed in Table 4.1. These same techniques were completed on the MODIS 2001–2009 annual data sets to determine Land Cover and Land Use (LCLU) dataset for the Sahel region to assess recent changes to the Sahel drylands.

4.3 Long-Term Changes in Cropland and Pastureland in DEA

Figures 4.1 and 4.2 show the increase in both pastureland and cropland over the last 5000 years recorded in the HYDE 3.1 database (Goldewijk et al., 2011). From this it can be seen that starting by 3000 BC there is low density pastureland use over most of the southern DEA area. By 1000 BC, this has extended to low density pastureland distributed over the entire DEA with the exception of the Gobi Desert region. There is only a small increase in pasturelands for the next two and one half millennia. Starting around 1600, there is a notable increase in Inner Mongolia Autonomous Region (IM), China, and by 1800, this increase is evident across the entire region. By 1900, IM had surpassed the rest of DEA in pastureland extent, with most areas doubling the amount of pastureland between 1800 and 2000. Cropland has had far less land cover throughout this time period. For most of the first 4000 years between 3000BC and 1000 AD, cropland is limited to areas bordering the Gobi, and in IM. By 1000 AD, the small pockets of agriculture in Mongolia begin to expand. Starting around 1800 there is notable increase in land devoted to cropland. Most of the expansion through 1900 is in central Mongolia and the southern portion of IM. During the 20th century, however, significant expansion of cropland into the northeastern portion of IM and the north central Mongolia is noted. The changes noted in the HYDE land cover dataset for the past 300 years, showing expansion of cropland and urban area and reduction in natural cover are consistent with those of Liu and Tian (2010) for all of China, which supplement the Hyde database with historical archives, more recent satellite derived land cover from MODIS, Landsat and SPOT (Friedl et al., 2002; Liu et al., 2005), as well as slightly longer term AVHRR and model cropland cover from the SAGE croplands dataset (Ramankutty and Foley, 1999). For the North and Northwest regions of China which lie in the DEA region, Liu and Tian (2010) calculate a loss of 12.7 million ha of natural land cover (including forests, grasslands, tundra, desert, wetlands, shrub and woodlands), offset by an increase of 9.8 million ha of cropland, and 2.8 million ha of Urban land between 1700 and 2005. Though the baseline crop cover in 1700 varies from 13 million ha (HYDE) to 19 million ha (Liu and Tian, 2010) for these areas of China, both the Liu and the HYDE reconstruction show a large increase in cropland in this time period.

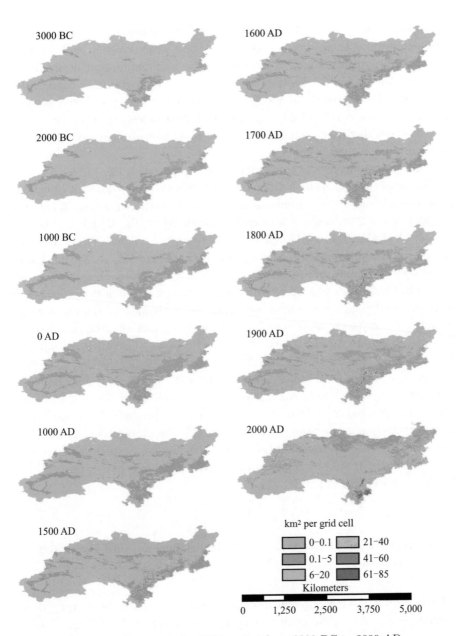

Fig. 4.2 Cropland Change in the DEA region from 3000 BC to 2000 AD. Source from the HYDE 3.1 database.

4.4 Recent Changes in Asian Drylands

In the past century in DEA, three major land use changes have shown to be most significant. These are: 1) the degradation, desertification and recovery of rangeland and abandoned croplands; 2) the reclamation and development of new cropland; and 3) deforestation and afforestation (Liu and Tian, 2010; Squires and Zhang, 2009). In addition to these major changes, there have also been less extensive yet notable changes, including depletion of surface water reservoirs resulting from increased irrigation in areas with increased croplands, urbanization and surface mining.

In the last two decades of the 20th century, cropland change varies by subregion inside of the region, with different case studies showing different directions in land use changes. For example, in examining the entire DEA area, if only the last part of the 20th century is examined (1980–2000), the HYDE 3.1 dataset (Goldewijk et al., 2011) would indicate an increase in croplands. Other datasets, limited to a smaller portion of DEA show little change (China NLCD; Liu et al., 2005) to a decrease of as much as 2.6 million ha in the North and Northwest regions in China (Liu and Tian, 2010). Case studies of individual provinces or autonomous regions show similar variability, even though for the same region there is not a complete agreement in magnitude. John et al. (2009) show an increase in croplands of 3,960,300 ha (3.43%) in IM based on AVHRR and MODIS derived LCLUC for the period 1992–2001, increasing further through 2004, for a total change between 1992–2004 of 6,614,600 ha (5.7%). For a similar period of 1990–2000, Liu et al. (2005) calculated an increase change of 973,000 ha in cropland in IM. Analysis of MODIS land cover data for the entire DEA shows that though there was an increase in cropland in IM, the overall effect in the DEA region is a decrease in cropland (Table 4.1), with cropland extent having peaked by 2004 and the trend beginning to reverse with croplands having decreased by 16.7% between 2001 and 2009.

4.4.1 Rangeland Degradation and Desertification and Increased Cropland

MODIS derived land use classification and change assessment by its very nature encompasses a very large area at a coarse resolution, and only for a limited recent time period. In order to investigate the different processes at locations in DEA, several studies are examined to highlight specific of many of these land use changes.

Studies throughout the Chinese portion of DEA, using historical records, field surveys and remote sensing data that show a consistent pattern in land degradation (Squires and Zhang, 2009). That pattern shows a trend starting in the 1950s of increased agricultural land cover, with resultant decreasing of the availability of pasture and rangeland combined with significant increase of livestock over this smaller rangeland. This increased grazing intensity leads to degraded rangeland and desertification through sand encroachment. Studies of the past decade show that there has been some abandonment of croplands (Dong et al., 2011) and either slowing of expansion or a significant recovery of these grasslands, particularly in regions of IM (Table 4.1, Fig. 4.3, Fig. 4.4) (Bagan et al., 2010; Li et al., 2009).

Lu et al. (2009) describe the degradation of rangeland in the Hulunbier sandy grasslands in the Northeastern section of IM. These lands are degrading from usable grasslands into sandy lands with 33% of the rangeland in Hulunbier clas-

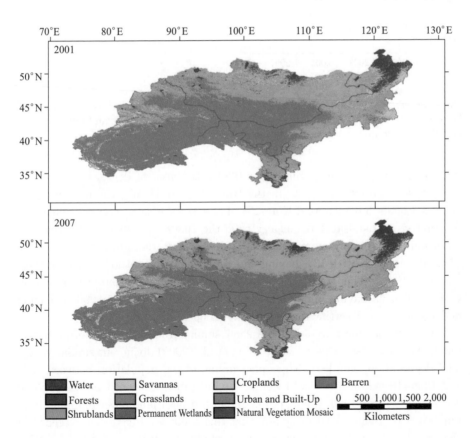

Fig. 4.3 MODIS MOD12Q1 annual land cover images for 2001 and 2007 showing changes in land cover in the DEA region.

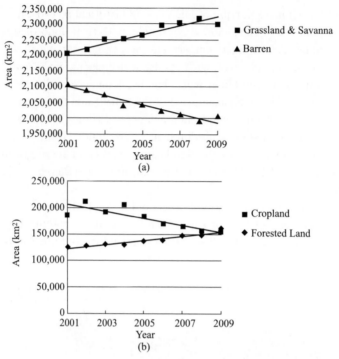

Fig. 4.4 Trends in land use in DEA from 2001 through 2009 derived from MODIS land use data for 2001–2009. These show the decrease in croplands and barren lands, and the accompanying increase in forest and savanna.

sified as severely degrade. Since the 1980's, the area of degraded grasslands has doubled (Lu et al., 2009). In the Hulunbier grasslands, the percentage of degraded lands has increased from 2% of the grasslands to greater than 18%. An analysis of Landsat TM imagery from the 1980s and 1990s shows that the grasslands have undergone an increased wind erosion (accounting for ∼43% of the grassland area, with 13% having undergone what the authors termed serious desertification). This translates in an area of slightly less than 10 million ha to 43 million ha having undergone some wind erosion, with 558,000 ha having undergone severe desertification (Lu et al., 2009).

Studies in the Horqin Sandy Land show similar trends. In the Horqin Sandy Land, the southeastern part of IM, Jiang et al. (2009) document similar rangeland degradation, coupled with a quadrupling of the population between 1947 and 1996. Based on historical records, the peak utilization of land as cropland was reached in the 1960s (Jiang et al., 2009), but later land cover mapping from Landsat TM (Bagan, 2010) suggests that this 1960s level has been exceeded in the first decade of the 21st century. An analysis of Landsat images from 1975–2007 shows both a rough doubling from croplands over this 30 year period (to 31.7% from 15.8%) and a reduction of rough half of grasslands and woodlands from 28.5% to 13.1%. In this time period, the most rapid desertification occurred between 1975 and 1987 (Bagan et al., 2010). This increase in cropland was also coupled with a decrease in surface water storage from 2.1% to 0.6% of the land cover, partially attributed to increased water usage for irrigation of these newly expanded croplands. The resultant reduction in rangeland led to overgrazing as the rangeland now carries a higher livestock load.

The Xilingol grassland, west of the Horqin sandy lands, has undergone even more extensive desertification (Huang et al., 2009). In the 1980s, approximately 49% of the rangeland was degraded, and by the 1990s, this had increased to between 70% and 80%. The Xilingol is approximately 97% grasslands, with the predominant use of those grasslands being pasture/rangeland. Between 1950 and 1999, the density of domesticated livestock increased dramatically. For example, the density of sheep increased from 1 sheep/6 ha to 1 sheep/0.7 ha (an increase from 3 million to 24 million sheep in the area) (Huang et al., 2009).

The MuUs sandy lands on the Ordos Plateau have experienced similar rangeland degradation due to high amounts of grazing and encroachment of sand dunes throughout the area. From the 1950s through the 1970s, much like the other portions of IM, the use of rangeland for grazing intensified. Through the 1970s rangeland degradation increased to 70% of the total rangeland having experienced degradation (Zheng, 2009). Studies based on NDVI from AVHRR during 1982 to 1993 show an increase in NDVI in the MuUs region, with a significant increase in NDVI in the areas undergoing land reclamation from agriculture, with grasslands showing only a very slight increase on average (Runnstrom, 2000). Though the average is slightly positive with respect to NDVI for grasslands, there are still large areas showing a decrease in NDVI, and significant degradation through the study period of 1987–1997. The grassland areas that show increase in NDVI suggest that some of the land stabilization techniques in this area have assisted in slowing the pace of desertification in the areas where they were implemented (Runnstrom, 2000).

Field and remote sensing studies have found similar trends in rangeland degradation in the Chinese area of DEA, such as GS, IM (> 60% degraded) (Li and Squires, 2009), Alshan (Li, 2009), to Qinghai (18% of land characterized by sandy desertification, 70% of rangeland degraded) (Long et al., 2009), to Siziwang (Lin et al., 2010). In all these cases, degradation over the second half of the 20th century (1947–~2000) is attributed to a sizable increase in overgrazing, due to increasing livestock number and decreasing rangeland area caused by agricultural expansion into former rangeland.

In areas of the Mongolian Plateau in Mongolia, similar trends are evident. In a study utilizing both remote sensing and field sampling, Sternberg (2011) found a 16% decrease in plant density in the Overhangai province, based on field measurements at 33 grasslands sites, combined with SPOT derived NDVI measurements.

4.4.2 Grassland Recovery

During the first decade of the 21st century, these trends have been to some extent reversed. Figure 4.3 shows the trend of increasing grasslands. This trend is highly visible in MODIS derived land cover maps over IM, showing the recovery of the grasslands between 2001 and 2007 (Fig. 4.4). This figure shows the recovery of grasslands in large portions of IM and also on the Mongolian Plateau. This recovery is not limited by international boundaries, suggesting that regional weather patterns may play a substantial role, as the effects are not limited to one side of the border. In addition, this image shows that the grassland recovery has replaced both barren and shrublands.

Even though during the first decade of the 20th century, grassland expansion has dominated over desertification. However, this change is not a one-way process. In the Western Qinghai region, MODIS derived land cover change maps show increased amounts of barren land (Fig. 4.4). Though this change does not cover as large an area as the grassland recovery shown in Figure 4.5, there is still evidence that the local climate policy does play a role in the grasslands/barrenlands shift.

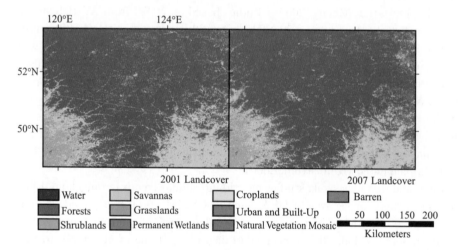

Fig. 4.5 MODIS MOD12Q1 Annual land cover images for the Hulunbeir area of DEA for 2001 and 2007 showing effects of reforestation.

4.4.3 Reforestation/Afforestation

The Natural Forest Conservation Program (NFCP) and Grain for Green Project (GGP) have been implemented in all of the Chinese provinces in the DEA region, in an effort to stem loss of forested land. This afforestation and reforestation was brought about partially to mitigate water runoff, soil erosion, flooding and biodiversity loss (Liu et al., 2008). In some areas, these projects have increased vegetation cover by as much as 2% per year (Cao, 2011).

In the Horqin Sandy Land, in the Northeastern portion of DEA, afforestation has been used as an effective method of controlling desertification (Hu et al., 2008; Su et al., 2010). In one example, since the 1950s Mongolian pine have been planted and used for afforestation in the region (Zeng et al., 1996). The long-term effectiveness of this type afforestation has been questioned, as in many cases the trees are not from appropriately selected species, and as few as 15% survival (Cao, 2011).

The MODIS land cover maps also show the recovery and expansion in the first decade of the 20 th century of forested land in the Hulunbier region of IM. In the MODIS land cover data from 2001, Figure 4.6 shows the presence of many agricultural areas in the forested region of Hulunbeir. MODIS land cover maps between 2001 and 2007 show an increase in forested land cover, and in 2007, the MODIS land cover map shows noticeably less cropland, and more forested land distributed in the middle of the forest. At the same time, to the southwest of the forested mountain region, the croplands expand into the grassland region between 2001 and 2007. This shows that a shift of abandoning croplands is one region, replacing with potentially more suitable cropland further in nearby areas 200-400 km away.

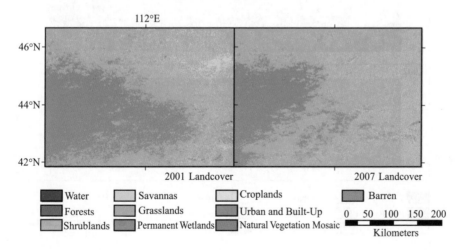

Fig. 4.6 MODIS MOD12Q1 Annual land cover images of the Horquin sandy lands in central IM for 2001 and 2007 showing the recovery of grassland land cover type.

4.5 Sahel Land Use Change

The Sahel region in Africa, like DEA, is also an extensive area of dry grasslands, bordering the barren lands of the Sahara desert. The area stretches across the African continent (Fig. 4.7). This area has undergone similar pressures to land utilization as DEA. Land use and climate variability have led to degradation of rangeland, with some recent recovery with increased rainfall. Over the past two centuries, the most significant influence on the Sahel region has been the decrease in rainfall in semi-arid west Africa (Nicholson, 2001). This system has been noted to be impacted by protracted aridity causing a decrease in both crop yield and grassland vegetation (Eklundh and Olsson, 2003; Nicholson, 2001). A strong increase in vegetation recorded in the AVHRR NDVI datasets during 1982–1999 was noted as precipitation returned to values closer to long-term normal (Dai, 2011; Eklundh and Olsson, 2003). As precipitation returns to a longer term average, following the lows in the 1970s and early 1980s, we can begin to see the effects of increased crop and rangeland demands on the land use patterns.

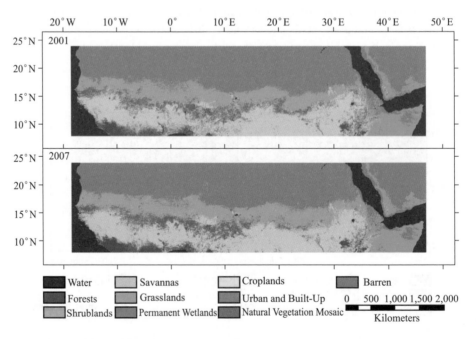

Fig. 4.7 MODIS MOD12Q1 Annual land cover images for 2001 and 2007 showing changes in the Sahel region in Africa.

Over the period 2001–2009, MODIS derived land cover data show a substantial increase in irrigated croplands area (Fig. 4.8, Table 4.2). At the same time, there has been an increase in grasslands, a transition from savanna to woody savanna, and an increase in shrubland area, even though grasslands displaced a large amount of shrubland (Fig. 4.9, Table 4.2). In addition, there was a sizable decrease in the forested land. The trends in cropland and forested land are the opposite of what is seen at the same time in the DEA region. At the same time, land classified as grasslands increased in both areas by similar percentages in both the Sahel and the DEA region.

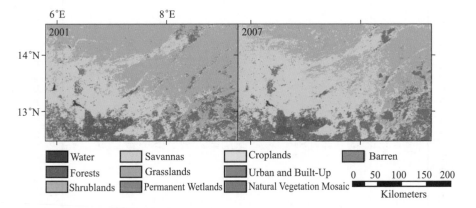

Fig. 4.8 MODIS MOD12Q1 Annual land cover images for 2001 and 2007 showing cropland expansion in the eastern portion of the Sahel.

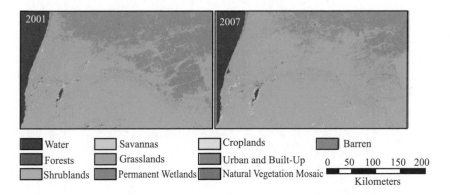

Fig. 4.9 Detail of land cover changes shown in MODIS MOD12Q1 Annual land cover images for 2001 and 2007 showing expansion of grasslands in the near-coastal regions of the Sahel.

The recovery of grasslands in the Sahel seen in the MODIS images is noted as a "greening" which was also evident through the 1990's (Eklundh and Olsson, 2003). Hickler et al. (2005) showed that precipitation was the primary driver of this increasing greenness in the grasslands. Miehe et al. (2010) interpret the degradation of rangeland in the Sahel not as a function of overgrazing, but note

Table 4.2 Land use in the Sahel between 2001 and 2007 based on MODIS MOD12Q1 Annual land cover images.

IGBP Classification	Land Cover Area (km^2)		Land Cover Area (%)		Change 2001–2007 (%)
	2001	2009	2001	2009	
Forest	132,152	117,320	0.99	0.88	−11.22
Shrubland	518,907	532,672	3.90	4.00	2.65
Woody savannas	661,681	519,874	4.97	3.91	−21.43
Savannas	1,502,982	1,324,959	11.29	9.95	−11.84
Grasslands	1,332,572	1,447,574	10.01	10.88	8.63
Permanent wetlands	25,648	24,054	0.19	0.18	−6.21
Croplands	446,304	718,114	3.35	5.40	60.90
Urban and built-up	10,438	10,439	0.08	0.08	0.01
Cropland/natural vegetation mosaic	1,275,370	1,342,638	9.58	10.09	5.27
Snow and ice	70	30	0.00	0.00	−56.99
Barren or sparsely vegetated	7,383,984	7,255,096	55.47	54.51	−1.75

The MODIS MCD12Q1 data were obtained through the online Data Pool at the NASA Land Processes Distributed Active Archive Center (LP DAAC), USGS/Earth Resources Observation and Science (EROS) Center, Sioux Falls, South Dakota (http://lpdaac.usgs.gov/get_data).

that it exhibits a far better correlation with weather variations observed in the precipitation record during their 27 year study than with overall trend of increasing grazing pressures.

Nevertheless, in examining the 2001–2007 period, several locations are noted where there is a distinct increase in croplands at the expense of grassland (Fig. 4.8). At the same time the grasslands have recovered into the lands formerly classified as barren (Fig. 4.9). If the recovery of the grasslands is indeed due to short-term variation weather, this suggests that in future periods of increased drought, the shift to higher cropland abundance combined with a reversion of grasslands to barren will cause significant stresses on the rangeland, being pinched out by booth climate driven and human driven land cover change.

A second difference between DEA and the Sahel is seen in changes in forest cover. Unlike in China, where the Three-norths Shelter belt Forest Project and the Grain for Green Project have focused on rangeland stabilization and reforestation, no equivalent large scale efforts have been undertaken in the Sahel (Fig. 4.10). In spite of the imperfect nature of the afforestation efforts in the Chinese provinces (Cao, 2011), they have had a measurably different effect than is seen in the Sahel region, where deforestation is still going on.

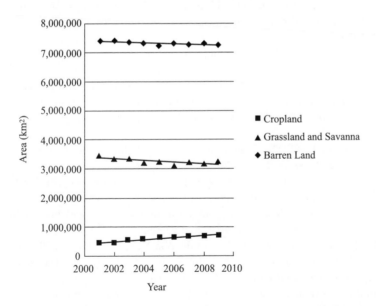

Fig. 4.10 Trends in land use from 2001 through 2009 derived from MODIS land use data for 2001–2009 in the Sahel. These show the increase in croplands small decrease in barren lands.

Both DEA and the Sahel are seen to exhibit changes in land use which are regional, crossing both internal and international borders, as a result of extending across areas where multiple policies influence the human impacts on land use.

In both cases, though the effect of human actions can be seen (for example, in increasing afforestation in specific regions in DEA, or in increased cropland in the Sahel), the effects on vegetation on short-term trends in weather and long-term trends trends in precipitation are noted to be important. The strong influence of precipitation on the variability of vegetation health in the long term (Eklundh and Olsson, 2003; Nicholson, 2001) on such dryland systems should be noted, as the impact of potential climate shifts or anomalously dry weather periods could negatively impact the DEA region in similar ways.

References

Bagan, H., Takeuchi, W., Kinoshita, T., Bao, Y., and Yamagata, Y. (2010). Land cover classification and change analysis in the Horqin Sandy Land from 1975 to 2007. *IEEE Journal of Selected Topics in Applied Earth Observations and Remote Sensing*, 3, 168–177.

Cao, S. (2011). Impact of China's large-scale ecological restoration program on the environment and society in arid and semiarid areas of China: Achievements, problems, synthesis, and applications. *Critical Reviews in Environmental Science and Technology*, 41, 317–335.

Dai, A. (2011). Drought under global warming: A review. *Wiley Interdisciplinary Reviews—Climate Change*, 2, 45–65.

Dong, J., Liu, J., Yan, H., Tao, F., and Kuang, W. (2011). Spatio-temporal pattern and rationality of land reclamation and cropland abandonment in mid-eastern Inner Mongolia of China in 1990–2005. *Environmental Monitoring and Assessment*, 179, 137–153.

Eklundh, L., and Olsson, L. (2003). Vegetation index trends for the African Sahel 1982–1999. *Geophysical Research Letters*, 30.

Friedl, M. A., McIver, D. K., Hodges, J. C. F., Zhang, X. Y., Muchoney, D., Strahler, A. H., Woodcock, C. E., Gopal, S., Schneider, A., Cooper, A., Baccini, A., Gao, F., and Schaaf, C. (2002). Global land cover mapping from MODIS: Algorithms and early results. *Remote Sensing of Environment*, 83, 287–302.

Goldewijk, K. K., Beusen, A., van Drecht, G., and de Vos, M. (2011). The HYDE 3.1 spatially explicit database of human-induced global land-use change over the past 12,000 years. *Global Ecology and Biogeography*, 20, 73–86.

Hickler, T., Eklundh, L., Seaquist, J. W., Smith, B., Ardö, J., Olsson, L., Sykes, M. T., and Sjöström, M. (2005). Precipitation controls Sahel greening trend. *Geophysical Research Letters*, 32, L21415.

Hu, Y. L., Zeng, D. H., Fan, Z. P., Chen, G. S., Zhao, Q., and Pepper, D. (2008). Changes in ecosystem carbon stocks following grassland afforestation of semiarid sandy soil in the southeastern Keerqin Sandy Lands, China. *Journal of Arid Environments*, 72, 2193–2200.

Huang, J., Bai, Y., and Jiang, Y. (2009). Case Study 3: Xilingol grassland, Inner

Mongolia. In: Squires, V. R., Lu X. S., Lu, Q., Wang, T., and Yang, Y. L. (Eds.). *Rangeland Degradation and Recovery in China's Pastoral Lands*, CAB International, Wallingford, UK, 120–135.

Jiang, D. M., Kou, Z. W., Li, X. H., and Li, M. (2009). Case Study 2: Horqin Sandy Land, Inner Mongolia. In: Squires, V. R., Lu X. S., Lu, Q., Wang, T., and Yang, Y. L. (Eds.). *Rangeland Degradation and Recovery in China's Pastoral Lands*. CAB International, Wallingford, UK, 103–119.

John, R., Chen, J., Lu, N., and Wilske, B. (2009). Land cover/land use change in semi-arid Inner Mongolia: 1992–2004. *Environmental Research Letters*, 4.

Li, Q. (2009). Case Study 6: Alashan plateau, Inner Mongolia. In: Squires, V. R., Lu X. S., Lu, Q., Wang, T., and Yang, Y. L. (Eds.). *Rangeland Degradation and Recovery in China's Pastoral Lands*. CAB International, Wallingford, UK, 171–183.

Li, Y., Cui, J., Zhang, T., Okuro, T., and Drake, S. (2009). Effectiveness of sand-fixing measures on desert land restoration in Kerqin Sandy Land, Northern China. *Ecological Engineering*, 35, 118–127.

Li, Y., and Squires, V. R. (2009). Case Study 5: Hexi Corridor, Gansu. In: Squires, V. R., Lu X. S., Lu, Q., Wang, T., and Yang, Y. L. (Eds.), *Rangeland Degradation and Recovery in China's Pastoral Lands*. CAB International. Wallingford, UK, 151–170.

Lin, Y., Han, G., Zhao, M., and Chang, S. X. (2010). Spatial vegetation patterns as early signs of desertification: A case study of a desert steppe in Inner Mongolia, China. *Landscape Ecology*, 25, 1519–1527.

Liu, J., Li, S., Ouyang, Z., Tam, C., and Chen, X. (2008). Ecological and socioeconomic effects of China's policies for ecosystem services. *Proceedings of the National Academy of Sciences*, 105, 9477–9482.

Liu, J. Y., Liu, M. L., Tian, H. Q., Zhuang, D. F., Zhang, Z. X., Zhang, W., Tang, X. M., and Deng, X. Z. (2005). Spatial and temporal patterns of China's cropland during 1990-2000: An analysis based on Landsat TM data. *Remote Sensing of Environment*, 98, 442–456.

Liu, M., and Tian, H. (2010). China's land cover and land use change from 1700 to 2005: Estimations from high-resolution satellite data and historical archives. *Global Biogeochemical Cycles*, 24.

Long, R., Shang, Z., Guo, X., and Ding, L. (2009). Case Study 7: Qinghai-Tibetan Plateau Rangelands. In: Squires, V. R., Lu X. S., Lu, Q., Wang, T., and Yang, Y. L. (Eds.). *Rangeland Degradation and Recovery in China's Pastoral Lands*. CAB International, Wallingford, UK, 184–196.

Lu, X., Ai, L., and Lv, S. (2009). Case Study 1: Hulunbier Grassland, Inner Mongolia. In: Squires, V. R., Lu X. S., Lu, Q., Wang, T., and Yang, Y. L. (Eds.). *Rangeland Degradation and Recovery in China's Pastoral Lands*. CAB International, Wallingford, UK, 91–102.

Miehe, S., Kluge, J., Von Wehrden, H., and Retzer, V. (2010). Long-term degradation of Sahelian rangeland detected by 27 years of field study in Senegal. *Journal of Applied Ecology*, 47, 692–700.

Nicholson, S. E. (2001). Climatic and environmental change in Africa during the last two centuries. *Climate Research*, 17, 123–144.

Ramankutty, N., and Foley, J. A. (1999). Estimating historical changes in global land cover: Croplands from 1700 to 1992. *Global Biogeochemical Cycles*, 13, 997–1027.

Runnstrom, M. C. (2000). Is Northern China winning the battle against desertification? Satellite remote sensing as a tool to study biomass trends on the Ordos Plateau in semiarid China. *AMBIO*, 29, 468–476.

Squires, V. R., and Zhang, K. (2009). The context for the study of rangeland degradation and recovery in China's pastoral lands. In: Squires, V. R., Lu, X. S., Lu, Q. Wang, T., and Yang Y. L. (Eds.). *Rangeland Degradation and Recovery in China's Pastoral Lands*. CAB International, Wallingford, UK, 3–14.

Sternberg, T., Tsolmon, R., Middleton, N., and Thomas, D. (2011). Tracking desertification on the Mongolian steppe through NDVI and field-survey data. *International Journal of Digital Earth*, 4, 50–64.

Su, Y. Z., Wang, X. F., Yang, R., and Lee, J. (2010). Effects of sandy desertified land rehabilitation on soil carbon sequestration and aggregation in an arid region in China. *Journal of Environmental Management*, 91, 2109–2116.

Zeng, D., Jiang, F., and Fan, Z. (1996). Stability of Mongolian pine plantations on sandy land. *Chinese Journal of Applied Ecology*, 7, 337–343.

Authors Information

Richard H. Becker*, Kirk A. Zmijewski
Department of Environmental Sciences, University of Toledo, Toledo, OH 43606-3390, USA
* Corresponding author

Chapter 5

Urban Expansion and Environment Change in Dryland East Asia

Peilei Fan, Jiaguo Qi, Xi Chen, Joseph Messina, Huiqing Huang, and Xue Li

Summary: Large-scale urban developments have increasingly occurred in traditionally resource-limited and environmentally vulnerable regions in developing countries, such as the arid zone in East Asia, resulting in serious environmental consequences. This chapter assesses the urban expansion and environment change in Dryland East Asia (DEA) from the 1990s to 2010 by focusing on the experiences of several large urban areas in the region, including Ürümqi, Lanzhou, Yinchuan, Hohhot, and Ulaanbaatar in Northwest China and Mongolia, respectively. We further provide a detailed case of Ürümqi by evaluating its urban sprawl and spatial transformation from the 1960s to 2000s and concomitant environment change in recent years. We found that the impact of urban sprawl on the environment in DEA is directly reflected by the loss of surrounding grazing and agriculture lands and the deterioration of water and air quality.

5.1 Introduction

The exponential growth of urban populations in recent decades has led to a renewed interest in the study of urban systems. The urbanization process exerts tremendous pressure on social, economic and environmental sustainability (Pickett et al., 2001). The world's urban population has grown 16.5-fold from 200 million in 1900 to about 3.3 billion in 2007 (United Nations, 2007), and is currently over 7 billion according to United States Census Bureau (2012). Corresponding to the astonishing growth in urban population, the urban sprawl has become a global-scale phenomenon (Clark, 2001). Although currently accounting for a mere 3% of the Earth's surface, urban areas host half of the world population (UN-Habitat, 2010) and the ecologic footprint associated with urbanization has enormous environmental consequences (Moore et al., 2001; Varis and Somlyódy, 1997; Turner et al., 2004). The most rapid urban expansions tend to occur in coastal and well-developed regions across the globe. Nevertheless, in recent decades we have witnessed large-scale urban developments in traditionally resource-limited and environmentally vulnerable regions, such as the dryland region in East Asia and the Mediterranean region (Qi et al., 2012; Portnov and Safriel, 2004).

Despite the severe environment impact of urbanization and the extreme vulnerability of urban environment in arid regions, only a few studies (e.g., Dong et al., 2007; Dong and Zhang, 2010; Luo et al., 2010; Zhen et al., 2007; Amarbayasgalan, 2008; Amarsaikhan et al., 2011; Badamdorj, 2004; Bolormaa, 2011) have examined the urban expansion and its environmental changes in major cities in Northwest China and Mongolia, mainly due to access and data availability issues. Although some Chinese scholars have examined limited aspects of urbanization, such as land use change, ecological impact, and formation of urban heat island and other urban islands for Ürümqi (Dong et al., 2006; Hang and Chang, 2006; Xiong et al., 2010), Lanzhou (Bai et al., 2008; Dong et al., 2005; Huang and Zhang, 2009; Liang et al., 2010; Wang et al., 2007; Zhang et al., 2005; Ren et al., 2006), Yinchuan (Chen and Gao, 2007; Du, 2007; Zhu and Zhang, 2010; Li and Tan, 2009), and Hohhot (Du, 2003; Li et al., 2008; Sheng, 2004; Zhang et al., 2008), they have not made an integrated and comparative analysis on the urban expansion and environmental challenges that are faced with the cities.

This chapter assesses the urban expansion and environment change in Dryland East Asia (DEA), defined as a region, including Mongolia (MG) and four provinces in Northwestern China: Inner Mongolia Autonomous Region (IM), Gansu Province (GS), Ningxia Hui Autonomous Region (NX), and Xinjiang Uygur Autonomous Region (XJ) (Chen et al., Chapter 1 of this book). It will focus on the experiences of provincial/national capital cities in the region, i.e., Ürümqi, Lanzhou, Yinchuan, Hohhot in Northwest China, and Ulaanbaatar in Mongolia. We aim to address the following specific research questions: 1) What are the spatial and temporal dynamics of the urban expansion in major cities in Northwest China and Mongolia over the past two decades? 2) What kind of urban environmental challenges have these cities confronted due to their rapid urban expansion?

The rest of this chapter is organized as follows: after the introduction, we describe the study area, data and our methodology in section 5.2. We present our findings on the urban land expansion and urban environment of Lanzhou, Yinchuan, Hohhot, and Ulaanbaatar in section 5.3. In section 5.4, we provide a detailed case of Ürümqi by evaluating its urban sprawl and spatial transformation from 1960s to 2000s and environment change in recent years. In Section 5.5, we discuss 1) the main characteristics of environmental impact of urbanization in arid regions and 2) major factors driving the urban expansion in Ürümqi, Hohhot, Lanzhou, Yinchuan and Ulaanbaatar. We then summarize the findings and explore potential policy implications in section 5.6.

5.2   Study Area, Data, and Methodology

5.2.1   Study Area

Located in the arid region of Northwest China and Mongolia, Ürümqi, Lanzhou, Yinchuan and Hohhot are provincial capitals of XJ, GS, NX and IM, respectively; Ulaanbaatar is the capital city of MG (Table 5.1). Most of the cities developed along rivers and surrounded by mountains, as typical river valley cities in arid regions. The cities feature semi-arid climates, with low annual temperature and precipitation and long cold winter (except Lanzhou); while Yinchuan and Hohhot have hot and humid summers, Ürümqi has hot, dry summers and Ulaanbaatar has brief and warm summers. As the provincial or national capitals, they play important roles in economic development, and political and cultural activities of their respective regions/countries. Having a population range between one and three million (Table 5.1), they all have experienced rapid urbanization and vast urban sprawl in the recent decades. Characteristic land use changes are the expansion of urban land at the cost of agricultural land and the conversion of other types of lands for agricultural usage.

Table 5.1 Major cities in Northwest China and Mongolia.

	Total Population (Urban Population) (1995, million)	Total Population (Urban Population) (2010, million)	GDP per Capita (1995) (US$)	GDP per Capita (2009) (US$)
Ürümqi	1.44 (1.18)	3.11 (2.30)	1413	6646
Lanzhou	2.71 (1.43)	3.62 (2.18)	1629	4187
Yinchuan	0.89 (0.48)	1.99 (1.29)	1126	5416
Hohhot	1.78 (0.79)	2.87 (1.98)	850	10598
Ulaanbaatar	0.83[a]	1.07[b]	630	2250

Source: For Ürümqi, Lanzhou, Yinchuan and Hohhot, the figures are from NBS (1996 and 2010) and 2010 China Census. For Ulaanbaatar, the figures of population in 2002 and 2008 are from Bolormaa (2011). We use GDP per capita of Mongolia (World Bank, 2011) for that of Ulaanbaatar.

Note: US$ 1 = RMB 8.351 in 1995 and US$ 1 = RMB 6.831 in 2009.

a: 2002's figure; b: 2008's figure.

Ürümqi (43°48'N, 87°35'E) literally "the beautiful pasture land" in the ancient Mongolian, is located at the north slope of Tianshan Mountains, and the south edge of the Junggar Basin in the central north part of XJ. Lying between mountains at the southwest and northeast sides, the city is composed of the Chaiwopu-Dabancheng Valley in the south and the alluvial plains of Ürümqi and Toutan rivers in the north. With 2,500 km (1,400 miles) from the nearest coastline, Ürümqi is also the most remote city from any sea in the world. Ürümqi has a semi-arid climate, with precipitation of 286 millimeters (11.4 in) and 2523 sunshine hours in an average year. Its hot summer (average temperature around 30°C in July) is in direct contrast with its cold winter (average temperature −7.4°C in January), with slightly wetter climate in summer than in winter. With a population of 3.11 million (2.30 million urban) in 2010, Ürümqi has 49 ethnic groups and the non-Han ethnicity population is 25% of the total population. Multiethnic groups live in compact, mixed communities consisting of primarily Uygur, Han, Hui, Kazak, Mongolian, Kirgiz and Xibe ethnicities. The city was once an important town on the northern route of the Silk Road, essential to Sino-foreign economic and cultural exchanges.

Lanzhou (36°02'N, 103°48'E) is located in the upper course of the Yellow River and bounded by mountains on the south and north sides. Due to its unique geography, Lanzhou has developed in a "dumb-bell" shape. The distance between the west and the east of the city is about 35 km whereas the distances from the north to the south vary dramatically from 2 km to 8 km. It has a total area of 14,620 km², with the urban built-up area of 1,631.6 km². In 2010, the total population reached 3.62 million and 2.18 million of them lived in city. Belonging to the middle temperate zone and with the average altitude 1,520 m, Lanzhou has a moderate climate with an annual average temperature of 11.2°C, without freezing winter or hot summer. Like other cities in Northwest of China, Lanzhou is dry with an annual precipitation of 327 mm, primarily occurring from June to September. Although daily temperature varies widely, it has plenty of sunshine with sunlight hours of 2,446 and more than 180 frost-free days per year. As one of the oldest industrial bases of China, Lanzhou is the largest industrial city in the upper stream of the Yellow River and an important base of the raw material industry in China's West. At the intersection of the inland China, Northwest of China and Tibet Plateau, Lanzhou is the transportation center of Northwestern China with four of China's main railway lines and six national highways converging here.

Yinchuan (38°28'N, 106°16'E) is located in the middle of the Yinchua Plain, with the Helan Mountain to its west and the Yellow River running through the · city from southwest to northeast. With a desert climate and an annual average temperature of 9.0°C, Yinchuan's winters are cold, windy and dry whereas summers are hot and humid. Yinchuan has a long history of development, especially agricultural and commercial activities. Irrigation systems in Yinchuan were developed during the Han Dynasty to improve wheat and rice production (Chen and Gao, 2007). Yinchuan's urbanization accelerated after 1949 when the P.R. China was established: the total population grew from 200,000 in 1949 to nearly 1.99 million by 2010, with a non-agriculture population increasing from about 30,000 to 1.29 million. The city is also a center for the Muslim (Hui) minority people that account for 25% to 30% of Yinchuan's population.

Hohhot (40°49'N, 111° 39'E) the "green city" in Mongolian, is located on the Tumochuan Plain, the south central part of IM, surrounded by Daqing Mountain to its north and the Yellow River and Hetao Plateau to its south. Hohhot had a population of 2.87 million (1.98 million urban population) in 2010. It has a cold semi-arid climate with a low annual average temperature of 6.7°C and the annual precipitation of 400mm. The city has long, cold and very dry winters and hot, somewhat humid summers, with strong winds especially in springs. Although most residents are Han Chinese (87.2%), Hohhot has a significant presence of ethnical minorities, especially Mongolian (8.6%) and Hui (1.6%). Founded by Mongol ruler Altan Khan in the late 16th century, the city has a rich cultural background. Serving as the region's administrative, economic and cultural centre, it is also called the "Dairy Capital of China" due to two giant dairy producers headquartered in the city—Mengniu and Yili.

Ulaanbaatar (47°55'N 106°55'E) meaning "Red Hero" in Mongolian, is located in the north central part of MG, in a valley on the Tuul River at the foot of the mountain Bogd Khan Uul. Ulaanbaatar is the coldest national capital in the world, due to its high elevation, relatively high latitude location, hundreds of kilometers from any coast, and the effects of the Siberian anticyclone. It has a monsoon-influenced, cold semi-arid climate featuring long, cold and dry winters and brief, warm summers. As the capital of the country, Ulaanbaatar is the largest city in MG and it hosted a population of over one million in 2008, one third of the total population of MG (Bolormaa, 2010). Apart from the political importance of Ulaanbaatar, the city contributes 48% of the national industry output, 52% of construction, 41% of trade, 75% of hotel and restaurant service as well as 56% of transportation and communication in MG (Herro et al., 2003). Ulaanbaatar's urban development is concentrated along the Tuul River valley, with an east-west built-up area of approximately 24 km long.

5.2.2 Data and Methodology

Satellite images, including sources of Enhanced Thematic Mapper (ETM), Thematic Mapper (TM), Landsat Multispectral Scanner (MSS), were downloaded from the USGS data pool. The administrative boundary datasets of China and MG were downloaded from the geographical information center of China and the

GADM organization (Available at http://gadm.org), respectively. The supervised classification and unsupervised classification are used in the processing of TM and ETM images while the visual interpretation is adopted to identify the urbanized areas in MSS images (Richards and Jia, 1999). Due to the qualities of the satellite images of Yinchuan city, we were able to conduct the supervised classification with maximum likelihood algorithm for the city. Post-classification processes, such as recode, clump and eliminate processes (in ERDAS Image 9.3), were applied to refine the resultant maps. However, the atmospheric condition and terrains made the task of automatically extracting the urban information for other cities difficult. Therefore, visual interpretation, conducted at 1 : 30, 000 scale, is used in the identification of urbanized areas, including large townships or villages in suburban areas and concrete surfaces in the cities for Ürümqi, Lanzhou, Hohhot and Ulaanbaatar. For Ürümqi, besides satellite images, an aerial photo (1965) was used and processed based on visual interpretation. We found that the machine-classified result may result in lower accuracy in this study as it may include more non-urban areas due to the wrong classification. We conducted the accuracy assessment for 2010's urban land maps, based on independent literatures and Google Earth high-resolution images. We consider our classification sufficiently accurate as the kappa coefficients range from 0.87 to 0.93 and producer/user accuracies of all cities are over 0.9. Yinchuan, as expected, has slight lower values of kappa coefficient and producer/user accuracies than others.

Other data, particularly economic statistics, population, environment and pollution indicators are from data sources such as the China Statistical Yearbook, Statistical Yearbook of the cities and planning and government policy documents (NBS, 1996 and 2010; Xinjiang Bureau of Statistics, 1996 and 2010; Gansu Bureau of Statistics, 1996 and 2010; Ningxia Bureau of Statistics, 1996 and 2010; Inner Mongolia Bureau of Statistics, 1996 and 2010; Mongolia Bureau of Statistics, 2011). To have a deeper understanding of environmental challenges of major cities in dryland regions, we use Ürümqi as a case to review the environmental characteristics, summarize the environment consequences of urban expansion, and assess the current environment condition and the recent trend.

5.3   Findings

This section presents our findings on urban expansion and environmental challenges of the five cities.

5.3.1 Urban Expansion

We found that our selected cities have experienced extensive urbanization since the 1990s, as their urban land has expanded over or about two times within two decades (Table 5.2). Our results are consistent with findings of other researchers on these individual cities mentioned in our introduction.

Table 5.2 Urbanized area (km^2) of Ürümqi, Lanzhou, Yinchuan, Hohhot and Ulaanbaatar.

City	1980	1990	1995	2000	2005	2010
Ürümqi	–	208.54	–	262.22	–	381.42
Lanzhou	60.61	78.90	94.57	–	128.09	169.55
Yinchuan	–	46.53	103.50	–	155.03	239.74
Hohhot	–	–	104.89	116.53	182.54	228.91
Ulaanbaatar	–	81.62	–	93.87	108.12	142.31

Source: calculated by the authors from our classification of urban land data.

The urbanized area of Lanzhou grew almost three times from 1980 to 2010 (Fig. 5.1), mostly occurring between the existing urban built-up areas and the northern bank of the Yellow River. The city experienced the fastest expansion in the last decade, especially from 2005 to 2010.

Among the five cities, Yinchuan experienced the most dramatic expansion. The urban area only occupied 46.53 km^2 in 1990, yet grew to 239.74 km^2 in 2010. Two of its major urban districts, Xixia and Xingqing separated by farmland in 1990, became connected over time (Fig. 5.2).

The rate of urban expansion in Hohhot increased after 2000 with an annual area increase of close to 10 km^2 yr^{-1} (Fig. 5.3). While the city grew mostly in the east urban fringe area from 1995 to 2005, urban built-up lands were added to the rest of the urban periphery area from 2005 to 2010.

Although Ulaanbaatar fell behind the other major cities in China's Northwest in overall urbanized area and the speed of urban expansion, it nevertheless expanded noticeably from 81.62 km^2 in 1990 to 142.31 km^2 in 2010 (Fig. 5.4), especially after 2005. Examining the high-resolution Google Earth images, we found that the settlement areas in the northern hilly areas accounted for most of Ulaanbaatar's urban expansion. This echoes Amarsaikhan (2011) that the newly added urban built up areas concentrated in the original agricultural lands along the Tuul River and the mountainous areas in the north and mainly consisted of the Ger areas, settlements of small private houses and traditional "Gers", round and cone-shaped tents. The Ger areas emerged as a result of rapid immigration

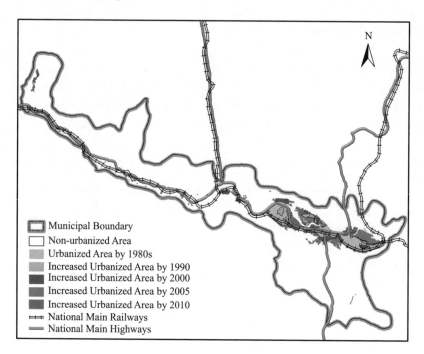

Fig. 5.1 Urban expansion of Lanzhou, 1980–2010.

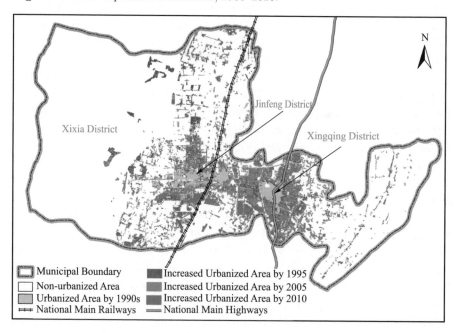

Fig. 5.2 Urban expansion of Yinchuan, 1990–2010.

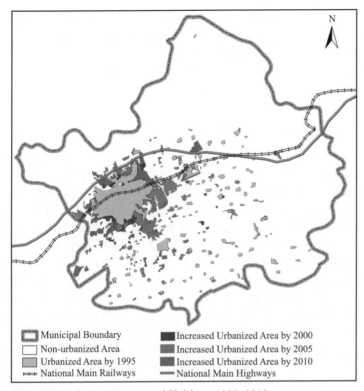

Fig. 5.3 Urban expansion of Hohhot, 1995–2010.

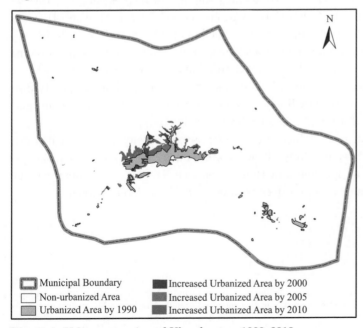

Fig. 5.4 Urban expansion of Ulaanbaatar, 1990–2010.

to the city of Ulaanbaatar, accommodating over half of the city's whole population. According to the official registration, up to 700 m^2 of land plot is allocated for each household (Amarbayasgalan, 2011). Further, satellite towns emerged in response to the high living cost of the city center (Amarsaikhan, 2011).

5.3.2 Environment Impact

Not only the impact of urban sprawl on the environment is directly reflected by the loss of surrounding grazing and agriculture lands to urban built-up area, the deterioration of soil, water and air quality over the past decades have become common for the selected cities in arid region of East Asia. We obtained the environmental indicators related to the air quality of selected cities from national statistics (Table 5.3). We found that while some cities (Lanzhou, Ürümqi) had serious air pollution, others managed to keep the air relatively clean. Overall, the air quality improved for Lanzhou, Yinchuan and Hohhot, but deteriorated for Ürümqi and Ulaanbaatar over the past decades. We compared indicators of urban air pollution, PM_{10}, SO_2, NO_2 and days of air quality equal to or above Grade II [1] in Ürümqi, Lanzhou, Yinchuan, Hohhot, and Ulaanbaatar with China's national average. In general, Yinchuan and Hohhot fared well in terms of urban environment quality, as most indicators scored better than China's national averages. Lanzhou and Ürümqi, routinely reported as the two most polluted cities in China (NBS, various years), show much worse than the national average for pollution indicators in China (Table 5.3). Similar to China's other major cities, urban environment measured by air quality seem to be improved for the periods of 1998 to 2003 and 2003 to 2010 for all of the selected Chinese cities except Ürümqi, which shows a trend of degrading air quality from 2003 to 2010. In particular, Hohhot made a noticeable improvement in air quality from 2003 to 2010 in all measures except SO_2.

Ulaanbaatar, in general, had a much better urban air environment as its available indicators (SO_2 and NO_2) demonstrated much better values than those of Ürümqi, Lanzhou, Yinchan and Hohhot, as well as China's national average. Nevertheless, Ulaanbaatar's values became worse from 2005 to 2008.

---

1 In China, the government uses an air pollution index to indicate the air quality. The calculation of the air pollution index was based on the concentration of SO_2, NO_2 and PM_{10}. Currently, based on the value of the air pollution index, a city's air quality can be evaluated into one of the five grades. While Grades I and II refer to excellent and fine air quality, Grades III, IV and V represent a light, medium and heavy degree of air pollution.

Table 5.3 Environmental indicators for selected cities.

	Ürümqi	Lanzhou	Yinchuan	Hohhot	Ulaanbaatar	China Average
Particulate Matter (PM_{10}) (10^{-9} mg m^{-3})						
1999	0.504	0.632	n.a.	n.a.	n.a.	n.a.
2003	0.127	0.174	0.132	0.116	n.a.	0.118
2009	0.14	0.150	0.09	0.074	n.a.	0.095
Sulphur Dioxide (SO_2) (10^{-9} mg m^{-3})						
1998	0.104	n.a.	0.083	n.a.	n.a.	n.a.
2003	0.096	0.086	0.063	0.039	0.013 (2005)	0.056
2010	0.093	0.059	0.044	0.049	0.017 (2008)	0.043
Nitrogen Dioxide (NO_2) (10^{-9} mg m^{-3})						
1999	0.087	0.065	n.a.	n.a.	n.a.	n.a.
2003	0.054	0.050	0.037	0.046	0.030 (2005)	0.042
2009	0.068	0.043	0.031	0.040	0.033 (2008)	0.040
Days of Air Quality equal to or above Grade II (days) (% of the total year)						
2003	282 (77%)	207 (57%)	291 (80%)	286 (82%)	n.a.	288 (78%)
2009	262 (72%)	236 (65%)	328 (90%)	346 (94%)	n.a.	321 (88%)

Source: For Ürümqi, Lanzhou, Yinchuan and Hohhot, the figures are from NBS (2010, 2004 and 2000). For Ulaanbaatar, the figures are from Bolormaa (2010).

Note: China average refers to the average of China's major cities, i.e. provincial capitals.

5.4 Case of Ürümqi[1]

We present the case of Ürümqi here to provide more details about urban sprawl and spatial transformations from the 1960s to 2000s of this dryland city and to illustrate the typical environment challenges that cities in dryland regions have to face.

5.4.1 Spatio-Temporal Change in Ürümqi

Figure 5.5 illustrates the spatially asymmetric urban development of Ürümqi, as it has expanded towards north and northeast from its original city center from the 1960s to 2010. A slightly rotated (towards west) T-shape features the current urban built-up of Ürümqi, with wide area in the north and narrow stripe in the south, respectively. Both natural factors and administrative boundary constraints have contributed to the current urban landscape of Ürümqi. Due to the geographic and geological constraints of a river valley city, the initial settlement settled along the old river bed (Hetan, in Chinese) that runs southeast to northwest and later development drastically expanded the city to the northwest and southeast along the valley. Some of the oasis ecosystems, which were cultivated during and shortly after China's civil war that ended in 1949 (officially), were converted into impervious urban lands. However, the administrative boundary of Ürümqi city also constrained its urban expansion as Miquan, and Changji are closely bordered Ürümqi. Finally, the urban expansion in the late 1990s along the major transportation routes was believed to be a result of the rapid development of public transportation and increased use of private vehicles. We plotted the urban area as a function of year and found that the regression has impressive coefficient of determination of 0.97 (Fig. 5.6).

Similar to the spatial pattern of Ürümqi's urban expansion, its temporal rate of expansion is also asymmetric, with a sharp increase in urban area from 1963 to 1975 followed by another relatively quick expansion from 1990 to 1999 (the lower part of Fig. 5.5). These two time periods corresponded, respectively, to the large migration from the inland in the 1960s and the later stage of the economic reform. The overall rate of urban sprawl in Ürümqi is substantial (Fig. 5.5 b), on average about 7.31 km^2 per year. The urban area increased over 10 times from 1963 to 2010. Such a rate of urban expansion is of major concern for long-term sustainability of the city. This concern is even more warranted in light of recent changes in the region's climate (Lioubimtseva et al., 2005; Schmidhuber

---

[1] Part of the material of Section 5.4 "Case of Ürümqi" is summarized and updated from Fan and Qi (2010) and Qi et al. (forthcoming).

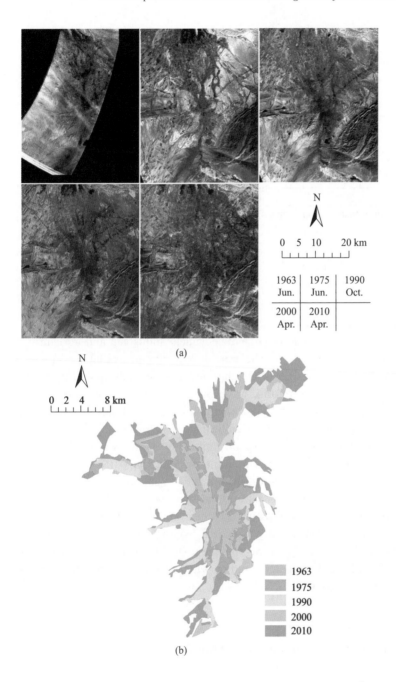

Fig. 5.5 Remote sensing images (a) and urban expansion (b) of Ürümqi, 1963–2010.

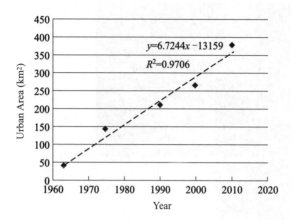

Fig. 5.6 Ürümqi's urban expansion (1963–2010).

and Tubiello, 2007). Despite the water scarcity due to the arid climate of the region and the primary water resource of snowmelt, industrial and agricultural activities place high demands on the water. In Ürümqi, available water per capita is only 489 m^3, a quarter of the national average and one tenth of XJ's average. Since the economic reform, water supply of Ürümqi increased almost five times from 1978 to 2000 and the over-exploitation of underground water has lowered the underground water level significantly (Chen, 2008).

Ürümqi's urban expansion used to be limited by the city's administrative boundary. To solve the shortage of the available land, the Wuchang (Ürümqi+ Changji) Economic Region was established in 2004 to support a holistic regional development plan to take into account these two areas together. Thus more space along the northern alluvial plains became available for Ürümqi to expand, and the less-developed Changji area benefited from the economic prosperity of Ürümqi. One product of this plan was the merging of Miquan from Changji into Ürümqi in 2007, which offered more land on which Ürümqi to expand and more stress to the oasis ecosystem.

5.4.2 Environment Challenges of Ürümqi

Although Ürümqi is a rather small city compared to other major cities in China, its economic development surpassed many major cities even on the east coast (Fan and Qi, 2010). However, its declining urban environment stands in stark contrast to its rising economy. From 1978 to present, as the city developed rapidly, several major urban environment problems emerged: the significantly decreased agricultural land due to the expansion of urban built-up area, air pollution mainly caused by industrial discharges, and the water shortages due to the conflict between the swelling population and limited water resources of the region (Fan and Qi, 2010).

In 1998, Ürümqi was identified as one of the ten most polluted cities in the world (Blacksmith Institute, 2007). Its air quality was still worse than that of all major cities in China except Lanzhou in 2009. Unfavorable geographic characteristics and winter heating based on coal have aggravated soot and dust air pollution (Fan and Qi, 2010). In the past decade, as the industries developed in the city, a total of 3,052 ha of land was acquired for urban usage, and 26% on the limited arable land. The residential usage and industrial mining claimed almost 2,000 ha during the period (Ürümqi Land Resource Bureau, 2008). Despite the water shortage due to resource scarcity, the city's scarce water resources have been contaminated because of the garbage disposal near sources and industrial wastes leaking from factories along the Ürümqi River. For instance, in 2006, only 78% of industrial waste water in Ürümqi met discharge standards, whereas the national average was 90%. Likewise, only 66% of industrial solid waste was utilized in Ürümqi in comparison with the national average of 81%. Soil pollution is another problem, contributed by agriculture, industry and transportation (Liu et al., 2007). Low precipitation in this arid region makes it even more difficult for soil to be naturally cleaned, as there is not enough water to dilute or transport the pollutants.

Established in 1992, the Ürümqi High-tech Development Zone (UHDZ) has been the growth engine of the city with five main sectors: biomedicine, electronic machinery, new energy, new materials and petro-chemicals. The "cleaner" high-tech industries located in the zone may bring less environmental pollution than the traditional industries. However, the industries based on XJ's unique energy resources, such as coal and petroleum, threaten Ürümqi's urban environment. A few gigantic energy enterprises such as the Shenhua Group, Petro China Company and the China Petroleum and Chemical Corporation (Sinopec) are located in UHDZ. Although the rapid development of these industries quickly brought economic benefits to the city, maintaining the lax environmental standards for these enterprises will likely further deteriorate the quality of air, water and soil. (Qi et al., forthcoming)

5.5 Discussion

5.5.1 Characteristics of Urbanization in Arid Regions

Although we have conducted only a preliminary assessment of urban land expansion of our selected cities in this chapter and we have not established any land conversion matrix, literature review on selected cities indicates that cities in arid regions share common trends of urbanization and land conversion. We will discuss these trends in details here: 1) the increase of urban land at the cost of other land, 2) a typical land conversion pattern of "grass land → agricultural land → urban land", and 3) the reverse trend to increase forest land mainly through government intervention.

First, our findings confirmed other studies on the rapid urban land expansion from the 1980s to the 2010s for our selected cities, at the cost of other types of non-urban land. Second, while urban land expanded mostly at the cost of the loss of agricultural land, agricultural land further takes in land converted from other types of land, especially grassland or forest land, as shown by situations in Ürümqi (Chen et al., 2010), Lanzhou (Dong et al., 2005; Huang and Zhang, 2009; Zhang et al., 2005; Zhen et al., 2007), Yinchuan (Chen and Gao, 2007; Du, 2007; Zhu and Zhang, 2010), Hohhot (Du, 2003; Li et al., 2008; Sheng, 2004; Zhang et al., 2008), and Ulaanbaatar (Amarsaikhan et al., 2011). The study of Chen and Gao (2007) on urban land conversion from 1996 to 2003 in Yinchuan illustrated that urban built-up land increased fastest and took large areas of existing agricultural land whereas agricultural land did not decrease as it expanded and took other types of land such as graze land and forest land. Further, the research of Chen et al. (2010) on Ürümqi from 1990–2005 indicated that agricultural land increased dramatically in XJ, including Ürümqi Metro area, during the period, with forest land and graze land as main contributors. Third, nevertheless, government policies on converting agricultural land back to forest land have a significant impact on the increase of forest land for Lanzhou (Huang and Zhang, 2009), Yinchuan (Chen and Gao, 2007; Du, 2007), Hohhot (Sun et al., 2010; Zhang et al., 2008), and Ulaanbaatar (Amarsaikhan et al., 2011). As Kirsten M. de Beurs et al. (Chapter 13 of this book) found in their analysis, vegetation conservation programs, such as the Natural Forest Conservation Program (NFCP) in 1998 and the Grain for Green Program (GfGP) in 1999 launched by the Chinese government to mitigate the degraded vegetation condition, has had a significant impact on vegetation dynamics in Loess Plateau, where Lanzhou and Yinchuan are located. For instance, from 1990 to 2006, forest land gained most area in Lanzhou, mainly due to the conversion from graze land and agricultural land, under the proactive land management and investment of the Lanzhou municipal government. It is also interesting to note that the observed changes of vegetation are highly dependent on the type of anthrome and population density as irrigated villages reveal far fewer significant changes than other anthromes whereas the most populated rangelands reveal the most change (de Beurs et al., Chapter 13 of this book).

It is worth mentioning that the geographic locations of our selected cities have contributed to certain characteristics of the urban expansion and environment challenges. These arid region cities exemplify four urban island phenomena: heat island, rain island, dry island and dark island (Ren et al., 2006; Li and Tan, 2009). Due to the constraints of surrounding mountains and other geographic factors such as location of rivers, elevation and soil types, most development options are spatially restricted. Further, most of the cities experience severe ambient air pollution, especially during the winter months when coal-generated pollutants are trapped in the city's air by surrounding mountains and atmospheric inversions. Another distinguishing environmental challenge shared by the cities is the aggravation of scarce water resources. The case cities have the temperate continental climate with little rainfall and a high evaporation rate, causing the scarcity of water resources, as exemplified by Ürümqi.

5.5.2   Socio-Economic Factors Driving Urbanization

We would like to highlight three distinct socio-economic factors that have played significant roles in the urban expansion and development in dryland regions of East Asia. First, economic growth, especially industrialization, is the most distinguishing factor behind the rapid urban expansion of our selected cities and highly associated with the pollution loads of the cities. In our field visit to Ürümqi, we witnessed the large-scale conversion of agricultural or grazing land to urban land along the urban fringe, mostly for industrial uses. Other cities followed the same trajectory (Liang et al., 2010; Li et al., 2008). The intensification of three major air pollutants, i.e. particulate matter, sulfur dioxide and nitrogen dioxide, in our selected cities indicated the linkage between industrialization, urbanization and urban environment degradation. As the wealth of city residents increased, life style changes and social infrastructure upgrading has become another major cause of urban land conversion (to urban residential land), air pollution (due to automobile usage) and water shortages (due to increased per capita usage as well as increase of urban population).

Second, institutional factors at multiple scales have affected the urban development of our selected cities. Here we would like to focus on the national development policy and urban land/property market in China, as well as planning and development in MG after the market reform. The rapid urban sprawl of major cities in China's Northwest has to be considered in the context of China's national development policies. The West China Development Program (WCDP) set forth by the central government in 2000 had a great influence on the development of our selected cities and their respective regions at large. One of the central goals of WCDP was to decrease the inequality of regional development as the first two decades of China's economic reform mainly benefited east coast areas, and the western region fell far behind the national average in GDP per capita. For instance, two of WCDP's projects, Xi Dian Dong Song (sending electricity from the west to the east) and Xi Qi Dong Shu (sending natural gas from the west to the east), had a direct impact on XJ and Ürümqi because of the coal and natural resources in XJ. Before WCDP, from 1996 to 1999, Ürümqi's GDP per capita grew at a slow rate of 2.6%. However, after WCDP, the city's economy took off, and its GDP per capita grew at a rate of 14.5% from 2000 to 2006, higher than the national average.

In the reform era, China set up a new type of urban land tenure system whereby the government retains the ownership of land but sells land use rights (LUR) through a market mechanism (Chan, 1999; Li et al., 2000; Liu, 1997). Nevertheless, a dual-track land-use system exists in which both administrative land allocation and market LUR transfers are utilized simultaneously. Furthermore, China started to transit into a market-based urban housing system in 1993 (Chen et al., 1996; Lim and Lee, 1993; Tong and Hays, 1996). The changing land/property market became an important driver for urban sprawl in China, expanding urban boundaries at an accelerating rate. Large-scale private or quasi-private investments were particularly favored by local authorities due to the potential revenue that such land transactions bring to local governments (Zhang and Fang, 2004). All major cities in China have experienced rapid urban expansion and the astonishing rise of real estate prices, including provincial capitals, in China's arid region.

Similarly, Ulaanbaatar's urban development and environment conditions have been significantly shaped by institutional factors, especially the market economy. The political change in 1990 promoted the market economy and completely changed the urban development process in MG. While before 1990, the urban development in Ulaanbaatar as well as other Mongolian cities was entirely planned, owned and controlled by the government, after 1990, many urban developments occurred without any control and the private sectors became significantly involved, leading to the increased commercialization of the city's center and inner city region, urban expansion in formal and informal Ger areas, the formation of satellite towns around Ulaanbaatar and the quickened suburbanization featured by single family houses (Amarsaikhan et al., 2011). In particular, Ger areas, appearing after 1990, have become a major consequence for Ulaanbaatar, housing 58% of its urban residents and occupying 70% of the geographic area of Ulaanbaatar (Amarsaikhan et al., 2011; Amarbayasgalan, 2008). Most Ger areas are built with insufficient or without necessary infrastructures such as heating, pipe water, sewage, solid waste collection and public transit, and Ger areas have become the major source of urban environment pollutions and the *de facto* slums (Herro et al., 2003; ADB, 2008; Guttikunda, 2007).

Finally, the urban development of our selected cities should be examined through a social lens, because of their unique historic, ethnic and cultural characteristics. Ürümqi, Yinchuan and Hohhot are provincial capitals of China's ethnic autonomous regions with high concentration of ethnic minorities such as Uygur, Hui and Mongol. The recent tragic ethnic clash in 2009 between the Han majority and Uygur minority attracted national and international attention. The Chinese government's ability of effectively building harmonious ethnic relationships in XJ and other regions of Northwest, either through economic development, migration strategy, policy incentives or a combination of all three measures, will be critical to the sustainability of these cities.

5.6   Conclusions

Large-scale urban developments have increasingly occurred in traditionally resource-limited and environmentally vulnerable regions in developing countries, such as the arid region in East Asia, leading to serious environmental consequences. We assessed the urban expansion in Dryland East Asia by examining histories of several large urban areas in the region, i.e., Ürümqi, Lanzhou, Yinchuan, Hohhot, and Ulaanbaatar, in Northwest China and Mongolia, respectively. We compared the urban expansion based on data obtained from satellite images. We also evaluated the environments changes of these cities in recent years. We provided a detailed case of Ürümqi by evaluating its urban sprawl and spatial transformation from 1960s to 2000s and environment changes in recent years. We found that the impact of the urban sprawl on the environment is directly reflected by the loss of surrounding grazing and agriculture lands and the deterioration of water and air quality over the past decades. Land conversions in this arid region share the common trends of: 1) the increase of urban land at the cost of other land, 2) a typical land conversion pattern of "grass land → agricultural land → urban land," and 3) the reverse trend to increase forest land mainly through government intervention. Moreover, the geographic characteristics of the locations of the cities caused the cities to have similar environmental challenges including the ambient air pollution and the scarcity of water resource. In addition to economic industrialization drivers, we highlighted institutional factors at multiple scales and social factors that have affected and can affect the urban development of cities in the arid region of East Asia.

Acknowledgements

Our study for this chapter has been partially supported by the National Aeronautics and Space Administration (NASA)'s Land Cover and Land Use Program through the grant to Michigan State University (NNX09AI32G) and "Urbanization in Asia" Project at the Asia Development Bank (ADB). We also thank Nathan Moore, Peter Verburg, Jianjun Ge, Yaowen Xie, and Yinchun Yang for their supports to this research, data sharing and insights on urban land development. Any opinions, findings, and conclusions or recommendations expressed in this chapter are those of the authors and do not necessarily reflect the views of NASA or ADB.

References

Amarbayasgalan, A. (2008). Applications of GIS for urban development and housing in Ulaanbaatar city, Mongolia. Manuscript. Available at rdarc.itakura.toyo.ac.jp/webdav/ask/public/ACP2010/1.pdf.

Amarsaikhan, D., Chinbat, B. Ganzorig, M., Battsengel, V., Bulgan, G., Nergui, B., Egshiglen, E., and Gantuya R. (2011). Applications of remote sensing (RS) and geographical information system (GIS) for urban land use change study in Ulaanbaatar City, Mongolia. *Journal of Geography and Regional Planning*, 4(8), 471–481.

Asian Development Bank (ADB), Operations Evaluation Department. (2008). *Mongolia: Urban Development Sector*. Manila: Asian Development Bank.

Badamdorj, C. (2004). Changes in the internal structure of Ulaanbaatar, Mongolia. *The Scientific Annual of Korea Mongolian Economic Association*, 14 (June 2004).

Bai, Y., Shang, Z., and Niu, D. (2008). Study on landuse-structure and driving factors in Lanzhou. *Journal of Huaihai Institute of Technology (Natural Science)*, 17(4), 81–84.

Blacksmith Institute. (2007). *World's worst polluted places* 2007. New York: Blacksmith Institute.

Bolormaa, T. S. (2011). From vulnerability to sustainability: Environment and human development, environmental challenges of urbanization and city growth. Background paper for Human development report of Mongolia 2010. Available at http://www.docstoc.com/docs/92773455/ENVIRONMENTAL-CHALLENGES-OF-URBANIZATION-AND-CITY-.

Chan, N. (1999). Land-use rights in mainland China: Problems and recommendations for improvement. *Journal of Real Estate Literature*, 7(1), 53–63.

Chen, H., and Gao, Y. (2007). A preliminary study on land use/cover change of Yinchuan city. *Research of soil and water conservation*, 14(4), 95–99.

Chen, H., Wu, S., and Feng, X. (2010). The temporal-spatial characteristics of land reclamation in Xinjiang in recent 15a. *Journal of Arid Land Resources and Environment*, 24(9), 16–21.

Chen, J. J., and Wills, D. (1996). Urban housing reform in China—Policies and performance. *Building Research and Information*, 24(5), 311–317.

Chen, X. 2008. *Land Use/Cover Change in Arid Areas in China*. Beijing: Science Publication House. (in Chinese)

Clark, D. (2003). Global patterns and perspectives, In: Clark, D. (Ed.). *Urban World/Global City*. London: Routledge, 1–17.

Dong, W., and Zhang X. (2010). City profile: Ürümqi. *Cities*, 28, 115–125.

Dong, W., Zhang X., Wang, B., and Duan, Z. (2007). Expansion of Ürümqi urban area and its spatial differentiation. *Science in China Series D: Earth Sciences*, 50, 159–168.

Dong, W., Zhang, X., Wang, B., and Duan, Z. (2006). Analysis of landuse expansion and spatial differentiation of Ürümqi. *China Science D: Geography Science*, 36 (Supplementary II), 148–156.

Dong, X., Liu, L., Zhang, B., and Wang, J. (2005). Study on land use change based on RS and GIS in the metropolitan coordinating region of Lanzhou. *Journal of Lanzhou University (Natural Science)*, 41 (1), 8–11.

Du, G. (2003). Analysis of Hohhot's land use change. *Science and Economics in Inner Mongolia*, 1, 87–89.

Du, L. (2007). Land use /cover change in Yinchuan city based on RS technology. *Arid land geography*, 30 (4), 585–589.

Fan, P., and Qi, J. (2010). Assessing the sustainability of major cities in China. *Sustainability Science Journal*, 5 (1), 51–68.

Gansu Bureau of Statistics. (1996 and 2010). *Gansu Statistical Yearbook*. Lanzhou: Gansu Bureau of Statistics.

Guttikunda, S. (2007). Urban air pollution analysis for Ulaanbaatar. *The world bank consultant report*. Washington DC: The World Bank.

Hang, F., and Chang, T. (2006). Research into urban land expanding change and its driving force in Ürümqi. *Journal of Chongqing Technology Business University (West Forum)*, 16(1), 47–49.

Herro, M., Naidan, O., Erdene, M., Lkhagva, A., Shagdarsuren, S., Samdantsoodol, S., Chimidhisig, M., Jadamba, U., Tumurbaatar, O., and Lookhondorj, T. (2008). *Ulaanbaatar Rapid Needs Assessment*. Ulaanbaatar: USAID/CHF Growing Entrepreneurship Rapidly Initiative: "The GER Initiative".

Huang, H., and Zhang, Q. (2009). Land-use change and ecological environmental impact in Lanzhou, a study based on RS and GIS. *Soil and Water Conservation in China*, 9, 57–59.

Inner MongoliaBureau of Statistics. (1996 and 2010). *Inner Mongolia Statistical Yearbook*. Hohhot: Inner Mongolia Bureau of Statistics.

Li, F., and Tan, H. (2009). Analysis of temperature contrast and observation between urban and outskirt areas of Yongning county. *Ningxia engineering technology*, 8(4), 303–309. (in Chinese)

Li, L. H., McKinnell, K., and Walker, A. (2000). Convergence of the land tenure systems of China, Hong Kong and Taiwan. *Journal of Property Research*, 17(4), 1–14.

Li, X., Zhang, Q., and Fu, X. (2008). Studies on driving forces of land utilizing changes in Hohhot city. *Anhui Agriculture Science Bulletin*, 14(9), 61–63.

Liang, X., Cao, Y., and Zhou, W. (2010). Analysis on change in land use and its driving forces in Lanzhou city. *Resource development and market*, 26(10), 876–879.

Lim, G.-C., and Lee, M.-H. (1993). Housing consumption in urban China. *Journal of Real Estate Finance and Economics*, 6, 89–102.

Lioubimtseva, E., Cole, R., Adams, J. M., and Kapustin, G. (2005). Impacts of climate and land-cover changes lands in arid lands of Central Asia. *Journal of Arid Environments*, 62, 285–308.

Liu, W. (1997). Hong Kong's impact on Shenzhen real property law. *Hong Kong Law Journal*, 27, 356–373.

Liu, Y., Liu, M., and Liu, H. (2007). Heavy metal content and its influence mechanisms to urban soils at Ürümqi City. *Arid Land Geography*, 30 (4), 552–556.

Luo, G., Feng, Y., Zhang, B., and Cheng, W. (2010). Sustainable land-use patterns for arid lands: A case study in the northern slope areas of the Tianshan Mountains. *Journal of Geographic Science*, 20(4), 510–524.

MongoliaBureau of Statistics. (2011). *Mongolia Statistical Yearbook*. Ulaanbaatar: Mongolia Bureau of Statistics.

Moore, M., Gould, P., and Keary, B. S. (2001). Global urbanization and impact on health. *International Journal of Hygiene and Environmental Health*, 206, 269–278.

National Bureau of Statistics (NBS). (1996). *China Statistical Yearbook*. Beijing: National Bureau of Statistics.

National Bureau of Statistics (NBS). (2000). *China Statistical Yearbook*. Beijing: National Bureau of Statistics.

National Bureau of Statistics (NBS). (2004). *China Statistical Yearbook*. Beijing: National Bureau of Statistics.

National Bureau of Statistics (NBS). (2010). *China Statistical Yearbook*. Beijing: National Bureau of Statistics.

Ningxia Bureau of Statistics. (1996 and 2010). *Ningxia Statistical Yearbook*. Yinchuan: Ningxia Bureau of Statistics.

Pickett, S. T. A., Cadenasso, M. L., Grove, J. M., Nilon, C. H., Pouyat, R. V., Zipperer, W. C., and Constanza, R. (2001). Urban ecological systems: Linking terrestrial ecological, physical, and socioeconomic components of metropolitan areas. *Annual Review of Ecology and Systematics*, 32, 127–157.

Portnov, B. A., and Safriel, U. N. (2004). Combating desertification in the Negev: Dryland agriculture vs. dryland urbanization. *Journal of Arid Environments*, 56, 659–680.

Qi, J., Chen, J., Wan, S., and Ai., L. (2012). Understanding the coupled natural and human systems in Dryland East Asia. *Environmental Research Letters*, 7, doi:10.1088/1748-9326/7/1/015202.

Qi, J., Fan, P., and Chen, X. (Forthcoming). The urban expansion and sustainability challenge of cities in China's west: The case of Ürümqi. In: Igor Vojnovic (Ed.). *Sustainability: A Global Urban Context*. East Lansing, MI: Michigan State University Press.

Ren, C., Wu., D., and Dong, S. (2006). The influence of urbanization on the urban climate environment in Northwest China. *Geographical Research*, 25(2), 233–241.

Richards, J. A., and Jia, X. (1999). *Remote sensing digital image analysis: An in-troduction* (Third, revised and enlarged edition). Germany: Springer-Verlag Berlin Heidelberg.

Schmidhuber, J., and Tubiello, F. N. (2007). Global food security under climate change. *PNAS (Proceedings of National Academy of Sciences)*, 104(50), 19703–19708.

Sheng, Y. (2004). Characteristics of the timing and spatial change and analysis on driving factors in land use of Hohhot. *Journal of Inner Mongolia Normal University (Natural Science Edition)*, 33(3), 313–316.

Sun, X., Zhang, X., and Zhang, Y. (2010). Regional disparity analysis of land use efficiency in Hohhot. *Economic Forum*, 475(3), 111–114.

The United Nations Human Settlements Programme (UN-Habitat). (2010). *State of the World's Cities 2010/2011*. Nairobi, Kenya: UN-Habitat.

Tong, Z., and Hays, A. R. (1996). The transformation of the urban housing system in China. *Urban Affairs Review*, 31, 5, 625–58.

Turner, W. R., Nakamura, T., and Dinetti, M. (2004). Global urbanization and the separation of humans from nature. *BioScience*, 54 (6), 585–590.

United Nations. (2007). *Urban Agglomerations 2007*. New York: United Nations, Department of Economic and Social Affairs, Population Division.

United States Census Bureau (USCB). (2012). *World POPClock Projection*. Washington D.C.: USCB. Available at http://www.census.gov/population/popclockworld.html.

United Nations Human Settlements Programme (UN-Habitat). 2010. *State of the world's cities 2010/2011*. Nairobi, Kenya: UN-Habitat.

Ürümqi Bureau of Statistics. (2001 and 2010). *Ürümqi Statistical Yearbook*. Ürümqi: Ürümqi Bureau of Statistics.

Ürümqi Land Resource Bureau. (2008). *Land Use and Planning of Ürümqi*. Official document. Available at http://www.Ürümqiland.gov.cn/.

Varis, O., and Somlyody, L. (1997). Global urbanization and urban water: can sustainability be afforded? *Water Science and Technology*, 35 (9), 21–32.

Wang, L., Chen X., Pang, F., and Pang, J. (2007). Research on the process and social driving forces of land use change in Lanzhou city. *Journal of Northwest Normal University (Natural Science)*, 43(2), 88–92.

World Bank. (2011). *World Development Indicator 2011*. Washington D.C.: The World Bank.

Xiong, H., Zou, G., and Cui, J. (2010). Evolution of urban land spatial structure in Ürümqi based on GIS. *Geography Science*, 30 (1), 86–91.

Zhang, J., Chang, X., Li, J., and Cai, M. (2008). Land use change and its ecological effect in Hohhot city based on 3S technology. *Chinese Journal of Ecology*, 27 (12), 2184–2187.

Zhang, Q., Ma, J., and Zhao, C. (2005). The change of land use and its progress in Lanzhou based on GIS and RS. *Journal of Arid Land Resources and Environment*, 19 (1), 96–100.

Zhang, Y., and Fang, K. (2004). Is history repeating itself?: From urban renewal in the United States to inner-city redevelopment in China. *Journal of Planning Education and Research*, 23 (3), 286–298.

Zhen, Y., Niu, S. Liu, H., and Li, G. (2007). Study on mechanism of landuse conversion in metropolitan area: a case study of Lanzhou metropolitan area, China. *IEEE International, Geoscience and Remote Sensing Symposium.* IGARSS 2007, 2170–2173.

Zhu, Z., and Zhang, X. (2010). Study on the land use temporal dynamics in Yinchuan city. *Journal of Anhui Agricultural Science*, 38(13), 6796–6799.

Authors Information

Peilei Fan[1,2]*, Jiaguo Qi[1,3], Xi Chen[4], Joseph Messina[1,3], Huiqing Huang[1,3], Xue Li[1,3]

1. Center for Global Change and Earth Observation, Michigan State University, 218 Many Miles Building, 1405 S. Harrison Road, East Lansing, MI 48823, USA
2. School of Planning, Design and Construction, Michigan State University, 102A Human Ecology Building, 552 West Circle Drive, East Lansing, MI 48823, USA
3. Department of Geography, Michigan State University, 673 Auditorium Road, East Lansing, MI 48823, USA
4. Xinjiang Institute of Ecology and Geography, Chinese Academy of Sciences, 818 South Beijing Road, Ürümqi 830011, P. R. China
* Corresponding author

Chapter 6

Ecosystem Carbon Cycle under Changing Atmosphere, Climate and Land Use in Dryland East Asia

Jianyang Xia, Shuli Niu, Xuhui Wang, Shilong Piao, Liming Yan, and Shiqiang Wan

Summary: Dryland ecosystems cover a large area of the earth's land surface and contain a huge amount of soil organic and inorganic carbon (C). Because of the rapid climate change and various land use types in Dryland East Asia (DEA), it is important to study the responses of ecosystem C cycling to both climate and land use changes in this region. In this chapter, we first used a process-oriented terrestrial biosphere (Organizing Carbon and Hydrology in Dynamic Ecosystems, ORCHIDEE) to simulate the carbon and water cycles in DEA. Then, we synthesized the response patterns and mechanisms of ecosystem C cycling to changes in atmospheric (CO_2 and nitrogen) and climatic (precipitation and temperature) conditions as well as land use. Both the current simulation and previous findings show the environmental changes in this area have greatly impacted ecosystem C cycling and will play an important role in the future regional C budgets. This chapter highlights the urgent needs of improving ecosystem management to enhance the contribution of DEA in mitigating the regional and global climate change.

6.1 Introduction

Human activities, such as land use and fossil-fuel burning, have resulted in rapid changes in external environment conditions for terrestrial ecosystems. The environmental changes include buildup of atmospheric CO_2 concentration, accelerating of global nitrogen cycling, rising air temperature and shifting precipitation regimes (IPCC, 2007). Such environmental changes have been observed in Dryland East Asia (DEA). For example, a significant increase in annual mean temperature and various trends of precipitation among regions have been observed during 1960–2009 in DEA (see details in Chapter 1). Changes in these multiple environmental factors will profoundly influence ecosystem carbon (C) cycling in DEA.

In the past few decades, a growing body of research efforts, including gradient observations (Bai et al., 2008), manipulative experiments (Xia et al., 2009a, b), remote sensing (Piao et al., 2011) and ecological modeling (Piao et al., 2009), have been made to study C responses in DEA to atmospheric (CO_2 and nitrogen), climatic (precipitation and temperature) and land use changes. These studies have found various response patterns of DEA ecosystem to those environmental changes. Within the typical temperate steppe in DEA, for example, a positive dependence of the rain-use efficiency upon the annual precipitation was found by a large-scale investigation (Bai et al., 2008), whereas a negative relationship was detected by a manipulative experiment (Niu et al., 2010). Thus, a comprehensive synthesis of the previous findings is helpful for a better understanding of the C cycle under future environmental changes in DEA.

In this chapter, we first simulate the carbon and water cycles in this region by a common used process-oriented terrestrial biosphere model (Organizing Carbon and Hydrology in Dynamic Ecosystems, ORCHIDEE), and show how climate has changed and related to ecosystem productivity during 1951–2006 in DEA. Then we reviewed and synthesized responses of C cycle in DEA to atmospheric (CO_2 and nitrogen), climatic (precipitation and temperature) and land use changes. We focus on key terms of C fluxes, including gross primary productivity (GPP), soil respiration and ecosystem respiration, and net ecosystem productivity (NEP).

6.2 Simulated Ecosystem Carbon Patterns in DEA

A process-oriented terrestrial biosphere model (ORCHIDEE) was used in this study to simulate the dynamics of ecosystem C fluxes in the past decades. A detailed description of the model structure and its applications can be found in previous studies (Krinner et al., 2005, Piao et al., 2011). Global atmospheric CO_2 concentration (Keeling and Whorf, 2005) and monthly climate dataset from Climatic Research Unit (CRU TS2.1) was used to drive the model and in the following analyses. The CRU TS2.1 dataset has a spatial resolution of $0.5° \times 0.5°$ spanning from 1901 to 2006. Details of the dataset could be found in Mitchell and Jones (2005). Since climate data earlier than 1950s is more uncertain due to sparse climate station distribution than the data afterwards (Mitchell and Jones, 2005), our analyses focus on C cycle dynamics from 1951–2006.

Ecosystem C cycle in DEA showed significantly spatial variations during the period of 1951–2006. The spatial distribution of GPP and Net Primary Production (NPP) (Fig. 6.1c and d) showed a clear west-to-east gradient, similar to that of precipitation (Fig. 6.1b). For instance, in Taklimakan Desert and Tarim Basin, the vegetation density varies from very low to negligible with GPP less than 30 g C m^{-2} yr^{-1} and NPP less than 20 g C m^{-2} yr^{-1}. This was likely due to the extremely low precipitation (< 50 mm yr^{-1}) and higher evaporation demand due to relative high temperature (mean annual temperature > 10 °C, Fig. 6.1a). The surrounding alpine area (e.g., Tianshan and Altay Mountains)

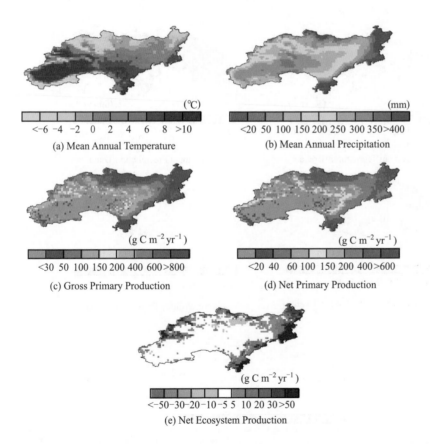

(°C)

<-6 -4 -2 0 2 4 6 8 >10

(a) Mean Annual Temperature

(mm)

<20 50 100 150 200 250 300 350>400

(b) Mean Annual Precipitation

(g C m^{-2} yr^{-1})

<30 50 100 150 200 400 600>800

(c) Gross Primary Production

(g C m^{-2} yr^{-1})

<20 40 60 100 150 200 400>600

(d) Net Primary Production

(g C m^{-2} yr^{-1})

<-50-30-20-10-5 5 10 20 30>50

(e) Net Ecosystem Production

Fig. 6.1 Spatial distribution of mean GPP, NPP and NEP during the period of 1951–2006 estimated by ORCHIDEE. Positive values of NEP indicate C sink and negative values of NEP indicate C source.

showed higher GPP and NPP than the deserts but still lower than the eastern and southern parts of the region where annual precipitation is as much as 400 mm. The spatial distribution of NEP (Fig. 6.1e) was different from GPP and NPP. Although the entire DEA was a weak C sink, most area of the region was approximately C neutral with mean annual NEP ranging from -0.5 to 0.5 g C m^{-2} yr^{-1}, even in southern Mongolia (MG) and some areas in central Inner Mongolia Autonomous Region (IM) of China where GPP could exceed 200 g C m^{-2} yr^{-1}. Some areas in northern MG were estimated to be a weak C source. Large C sinks in DEA were found to be in the northeastern IM, southern Gansu Province (GS) and Ningxia Hui Autonomous Region (NX), and alpine area in northern Xinjiang Uygur Autonomous Region (XJ) of China. Although alpine area showed smaller GPP and NPP than the eastern and southern areas, their C sink densities were comparable.

During the period of 1951–2006, the changing trend of ecosystem C cycle

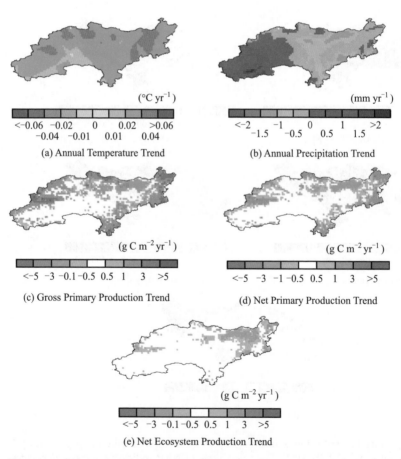

Fig. 6.2 Spatial distribution of ORCHIDEE derived trend in GPP, NPP and NEP from 1951 to 2006. The trends were calculated using least square linear regression.

showed spatial variations in DEA (Fig. 6.2). For GPP, most area (58%) showed an increasing trend, and the magnitude of increasing GPP in some areas like Tianshan Mountains, northeastern IM and southern GS could be larger than 3 g C m^{-2} yr^{-1}. However, in a belt from central MG to central IM, GPP decreased mostly from -3 g C m^{-2} yr^{-1} to -1 g C m^{-2} yr^{-1}, with an exception of a small area in northeastern MG showing a larger decrease than -3 g C m^{-2} yr^{-1} (Fig. 6.2c). The spatial distribution of NPP trend (Fig. 6.3d) was similar to the spatial distribution of GPP trend but with smaller magnitude. Similarly, NEP trend also showed a resembled pattern to GPP trend, but with much less magnitude that 76% of the area shows a small NEP trend (between -0.5 g C m^{-2} yr^{-1} and 0.5 g C m^{-2} yr^{-1}), and 14% area particularly in eastern MG and central IM shows decreasing NEP larger than -0.5 g C m^{-2} yr^{-1}. Such spatial variations of GPP and NPP changes were probably associated with spatial patterns of the

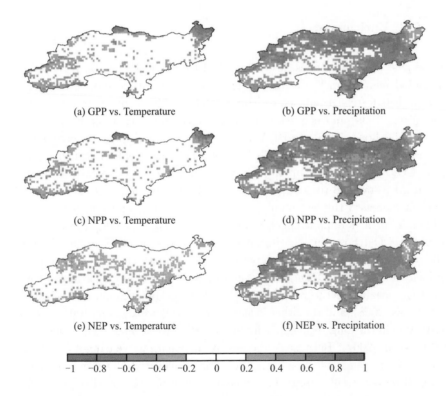

(a) GPP vs. Temperature   (b) GPP vs. Precipitation

(c) NPP vs. Temperature   (d) NPP vs. Precipitation

(e) NEP vs. Temperature   (f) NEP vs. Precipitation

-1 -0.8 -0.6 -0.4 -0.2 0   0.2   0.4   0.6   0.8   1

Fig. 6.3 Spatial distribution of correlation coefficient between climate (temperature and precipitation) and C fluxes (GPP, NPP and NEP). correlation (a) between GPP and mean annual temperature (MAT), (b) between GPP and annual precipitation (AP), (c) between NPP and MAT, (d) between NPP and AP, (e) between NEP and MAT, and (f) between NEP and AP.

precipitation change (Fig. 6.1b). The correlation analyses between GPP and temperature/precipitation (Fig. 6.3a and b) also suggested a strong influence of precipitation on GPP in most vegetated areas, while the temperature only positively affected GPP in northeastern MG, alpine area in XJ and a small area in north MG. The variations in spatial and temporal responses of ecosystem C processes to climate changes indicate that both biotic and abiotic factors could strongly influence the C processes and pools state in the dryland of Northeast Asia.

6.3 Responses of Ecosystem Carbon Cycling to Atmospheric Change

6.3.1 CO_2 Enrichment

Over the past several decades, a great deal of the evidence has been reported about global increase in the atmospheric CO_2 concentration and its resultant increase in leaf water-use efficiency (Hungate et al., 1997), plant growth (Curtis and Wang, 1998) and ecosystem primary productivity (Nowak et al., 2004, Ainsworth and Long, 2005). In DEA, the evidence of the response of ecosystem C cycling to CO_2 enrichment is still lacking. The only field experiment with elevated CO_2, as we known up to now, was conducted in a typical temperate steppe in IM from 2006 to 2008 (Zhang et al., 2010). In that experiment, CO_2 enrichment increased the leaf number, leaf photosynthesis and both shoot and root biomass of a dominant species (*Leymus chinensis*). Under the elevated atmospheric CO_2, however, the initial increase of the plant C assimilation is usually not sustained over long-term periods because of at least two mechanisms (Aranjuelo et al., 2011). One is the acclimation of plant photosynthesis at elevated CO_2 because of the reducing in the photosynthetic apparatus (Gruber and Galloway, 2008), and the other is the progressively nitrogen limitation on C sequestration in the long-term exposure of ecosystem to elevated CO_2 concentration (Luo et al., 2004). Because of the lack of information, we cannot draw out the long-term response of ecosystem C cycling to elevated CO_2 concentration in DEA. However, results from some recent studies in other arid or semi-arid ecosystems provided us important implications about the dynamics of ecosystem C cycling under the elevated CO_2 concentration in the DEA region. For example, Nevada Desert maintained its photosynthetic capacities via expansion of existing storage capacity and developing new C sinks under eight-year elevated CO_2. Also in that experiment, the CO_2 elevation did not influence the fine standing stop, production, loss, turnover, persistence and depth distribution of fine root (Ferguson and Nowak, 2011). The responses of C cycling to the elevated CO_2 concentration could be different in DEA from other terrestrial ecosystems. More studies dealing with ecosystem C responses to the CO_2 enrichment are needed to improve our understanding of the future C dynamics in DEA.

6.3.2 Nitrogen Deposition and Its Impact on DEA Ecosystems

As one of the preliminary abiotic factors constraining plant growth, nitrogen (N) is recognized as the most widely limiting factor to terrestrial primary productivity (Xia and Wan, 2008). Many studies in DEA (Bai et al., 2010b, Zhang et al., 2010) have supported the positive dependence of ecosystem C uptake on N availability. Some recent studies have reported that N addition can stimulate those C loss processes, such as litter decomposition (Liu et al., 2006) and soil respiration (Yan et al., 2010). Yan et al. (2010) even found that the two components of soil respiration, autotrophic and heterotrophic respiration, showed different responses to N addition. All these results suggest N response of NEP may not necessarily be positive in DEA, and could be mediated by many other environmental factors.

At ecosystem scale, recent studies in DEA using field manipulative experiments revealed some patterns and mechanisms of the ecosystem C exchange to N enrichment. For example, Niu et al. (2010) reported the response of net ecosystem CO_2 exchange (NEE) to four years N addition in a temperate steppe in IM. The results showed the magnitude of N stimulation on NEE declined over time, with significant increases in 2005 (+60%) and 2006 (+21%) but no effect on 2007 or 2008. In the same study site, Xia et al. (2009b) reported that N addition enhanced NEE both in a wet and an extremely dry growing seasons. Both of these two studies found out that N-induced shifts in plant species composition could be an important mechanism in regulating the direct N effects on C sequestration in this region. Bai et al. (2010b) suggested a threshold as 1.75 g N m^{-2} yr^{-1} above which the N enrichment will trigger plant species loss, and a N addition rate of about 10.5 g N m^{-2} yr^{-1} for saturating aboveground biomass, species richness and plant functional group composition. For soil microbial biomass and functional diversity, an optimum N input between 16-32 g N m^{-2} yr^{-1} was suggested in this region (Zhang et al., 2008a). These studies have greatly improved our understanding of the ecosystem C cycling in response to N addition in DEA.

6.4 Responses of Ecosystem Carbon Cycling to Climate Change

6.4.1 Responses to Precipitation Changes

Previous studies in dryland regions have suggested that both the intensity and frequency of precipitation are critical in determining species survivorship and composition, and therefore plant growth and ecosystem functions (Dodd et al., 1998). The long-term meteorology record shows increasing trends of the proportions of both the heavy and light precipitation events in the arid and semi-arid areas of Northern China (Liu et al., 2005), which indicates an increase in precipitation variability in DEA (see Chapter 1).

In arid ecosystems, the increasing precipitation can enhance both ecosystem C uptake via stimulating plant photosynthesis (Huxman et al., 2004, Patrick et al., 2007) and C release through respiration (Patrick et al., 2007, Wan et al., 2007). In the temperate steppe in Northern China, previous studies have reported that the increased precipitation amount enhances the gross ecosystem productivity (GEP) more than ecosystem respiration (ER) and lead to the resultant enhanced NEE (Niu et al., 2009). To date, most of the published findings about precipitation changes and ecosystem C cycling in DEA are short-term results (Chen et al., 2009, Niu et al., 2009). In the long-term (1951–2006) stimulation in this study, a negative relationship between NEP and annual precipitation was found in northeastern IM (approximately 60°N; Fig. 6.3f). The reason is unclear, but possibly the precipitation increase may lead to a decrease of downward solar radiation, which should be a limiting factor to the high latitude vegetation growth (Nemani et al., 2003). We suggest that further studies are needed to explicit the mechanisms behind this phenomenon.

In arid and semi-arid regions, plants of differential life forms usually have differential soil water use strategies (Schwinning and Ehleringer, 2001, Schenk and Jackson, 2002), e.g., herbs usually compete for resources in the upper soil layers whereas shrubs and trees takes more deep soil (Schenk and Jackson, 2002). As a consequence, precipitation regime shifts would influence the ecosystem C cycling through reshaping the plant community structure in DEA. In a 6-year manipulative experiment from a temperate steppe in IM, Yang et al. (2011a, 2011b) reported that the soil water availability is the predominant factor in regulating the community structure and composition in response to climate changes. The precipitation pulse and its effects on soil respiration is another process enhancing the uncertainty of response ecosystem C cycling to precipitation changes in arid and semi-arid regions (Huxman et al., 2004). Cheng et al. (2006) reported differential rainwater utilization patterns of three dominant desert plants to the rain pulse in a desertified grassland in DEA. A threshold as 10 mm–25 mm of the rain pulse size above which rainfall favored C sequestration was detected in a temperate steppe in IM (Chen et al., 2009). Since responses of ecosystem C processes to precipitation changes are usually non-linear (Zhou et al., 2008), there are still great uncertainties in predicting the ecosystem C cycling under future precipitation regimes in DEA. To reduce such uncertainties, we need more research efforts not only focus on the precipitation intensity but also the temporal distributions of precipitation events with a long time scale.

6.4.2   Responses to Temperature Changes

Temperature influences all biological processes and affects almost all ecosystem C processes. In DEA, some recent studies have reported warming effects on NEE and its two components, GEP and ecosystem respiration (ER) (Niu et al., 2008, Xia et al., 2009b). Those results generally showed a negative effect of climate warming on net ecosystem C uptake, which was primarily determined by the reduction in water availability under climate warming (Niu et al., 2008, Xia et al., 2009b). The simulation with the ORCHIDEE model in this study showed similar results. Unlike GPP and NPP, the negative correlation between NEP and temperature (Fig. 6.3e) was found in more than 20% of the DEA region, from northern XJ to southern IM and southern GS and NX. In consistent with the responses of NEP, the global warming was also found to reduce the species richness and community coverage from 2006 to 2009 in IM (Yang et al., 2011b).

One aspect of the global warming is that the temperature increase is greater at night than during daytime (Easterling et al., 1997). A field study conducted with both day and night warming in a temperate steppe in IM found that night, but not day, warming enhanced ecosystem C sequestration via increasing plant photosynthesis during daytime (Wan et al., 2009). In addition, the summed effects of day and night warming on ecosystem C processes were not equal to the diurnal warming effects (Xia et al., 2009a). These results suggest differential impacts of day and night warming on ecosystem C cycling in DEA. Given that the diurnal change in temperature varies greatly among different regions, these results provide us strong evidence that future projections of the ecosystem C cycling should consider the diurnal patterns of temperature change in this region.

6.5 Responses of Ecosystem Carbon Cycling to Land Use and Land Cover Changes

During the 20th century, dramatic land use/cover changes occurred in DEA due to the high growth rate of human population and economic development. These changes contain grassland degradation, desertification and the conversion of grasslands or forests into croplands, etc. Changes in land use can remarkably influence the ecosystem C cycling and sequestration.

The over-grazing is one of the most primary reasons for grassland degradation. For example, in IM, the livestock numbers doubled from 1994 to 2006 (Zhang et al., 2008b), and one third of the Xilinguole rangeland has been degraded as a result of over-grazing. The light grazing could maintain a high species diversity and NPP (Zhao et al., 2004) and have a slight effect on the ecosystem C balance (Li et al., 2005). However, the over-grazing could result in considerable decreases in species diversity and NPP. Results of a grazing experiment which conducted at a sandy grassland in DEA showed that the over-grazing caused a large loss of plant productivity after two years of treatment (Zhao et al., 2004). Another mowing manipulative experiment in DEA showed that four years mowing has little effect on GPP, ER, or NEP (Niu et al., 2010). This could be partly due to that mowing was treated in the late growing season when plants began to senescence, and thus had little effect on plant growth and ecosystem C fluxes. Moreover, the possible negative clipping effects on the upper canopy species might have been compensated by the stimulated growth of the lower-canopy species due to the improved light condition after clipping (Niu et al., 2010). This suggests that appropriate management of the grassland in DEA may not destructively destroy ecosystem carbon storages in this region.

The grazing effects on the grassland ecosystem C cycling may vary due to different vegetations and managements. For example, Zhou et al. (2002b) investigated C balance along the Northeast China transect, and they found that the grazing led to increased CO_2 efflux in *Stipa grandis* grassland and decreased that in *Leymus chinensis* grassland. Many studies have showed that aboveground net primary production (ANPP), belowground net primary production (BNPP) and live root biomass would decrease with the grazing intensity in DEA (Gao et al., 2008, Han et al., 2008, Schonbach et al., 2011). The grazing could lead to a loss in soil coverage, increase the possibility of soil erosion (Schonbach et al., 2011) and decrease soil organic carbon and soil quality (Han et al., 2008). Thus, these changes could induce more emission of CO_2 to the atmosphere. The grassland under mowing has lower ANPP than the ungrazed one, but its C storage in roots and soils is equal to the ungrazed grassland (Zhou et al., 2002a, Zhou et al., 2007).

The land cover and vegetation change have affected the ecosystem C dynamics in this region as well. From 1992 to 2004, the proportion of shrub cover increased in the grassland of IM (John et al., 2009). The conversion of grassland into shrub dominated ecosystem is one form of desertification (Grover and Musick, 1990). A research at the Ordos Plateau in DEA showed that desert shrub had higher aboveground biomass and NPP and lower soil respiration compared to grassland. However, the change of soil environment should be paid more attention, as the soil in the desert shrub ecosystem had been transformed into eolian sand soil, which is more fragile and sensitive to human activities and climate change (Jin et al., 2010).

The conversion of grassland into cropland caused C loss in DEA. Although the cropland has higher ANPP than grassland, its C storage in litter, roots and soils is lower than that of grassland (Zhou et al., 2007, Wang et al., 2008). Besides, most of the cropland biomass is removed from the ecosystem and returned to the atmosphere through human utilization. In the agriculture-pasture transition region in southeast IM, researchers measured the C fluxes of a typical steppe and a crop field by two eddy-covariance flux towers. They found that the cropland ecosystem had higher GPP and lower ecosystem respiration than steppe, and acted as a strong sink in July. However, 76% of the cropland biomass was removed via harvesting, so that the C sequestration strength of cropland was greatly reduced. In contrast, the steppe was a week C sink or nearly in balance during the growing season (Zhan et al., 2007). Another study in IM indicated that when grassland converted to spring wheat field, soil respiration markedly enhanced and C storage in the surface soil reduced (Dong et al., 2007).

Previous studies showed that the Northeast China was a net C source owing to overharvesting and degradation of forest during the 1980s and 1990s (Piao et al., 2009). With the new policy of restoration of degraded or decertified lands, the land use change has had a positive effect on ecosystem restoration and C storage in recent years. Documents have showed that the semi-arid region in IM was nearly in balance or a week C sink even under extremely arid conditions (Zhang et al., 2009).

6.6 Interactions among Environmental Changes

6.6.1 Limitation of Nitrogen Availability on CO_2 Impacts

Elevated CO_2 could stimulate plant photosynthesis and growth, subsequently enhance NPP of ecosystem. But the response of plant growth to elevated CO_2 may be limited when the nutrient (N in particular) is limiting. Nevertheless, a study which was on a *Leymus chinensis* steppe in IM concluded that the effect of elevated CO_2 on photosynthetic rate of *Leymus chinensis* was independent on N levels (Zhang et al., 2010). However, the authors only measured the dominant species and the plants were grown in pots which would constrain plant roots and depress the response of plant growth to elevated CO_2 and N addition. Further research is needed to investigate the responses of communities and ecosystems to elevated CO_2 under N limited in this region.

6.6.2   Dependence of Nitrogen Effects on Water Status (Precipitation Regimes)

It is well known that NEP in DEA is both water and nutrient limited (Hooper and Johnson, 1999). So, concurrent changes in precipitation and N deposition may potentially trigger complex interactive influences on ecosystem C cycling. As water availability increases, plant growth is expected to be more limited by N than by water (Hooper and Johnson, 1999). In IM, water and N are tightly coupled and both can significantly affect ANPP. The study of Bai et al. (2008) showed that ANPP responded to N addition more strongly in wet than dry years. Besides, the net N mineralization rates in soil are positively correlated with mean annual precipitation in several sites of IM grassland. These results conclusively prove the dependence of N effects on water in this region. The interactive effect of water and N addition was also detected in other experiments in this region (Lü and Han, 2010; Lü et al., 2010). However, a multi-factor global change experiment in the temperate steppe in Northern China showed that there are non-additive effects of water and N addition on ecosystem C cycling (Niu et al., 2010). Increases in ecosystem C fluxes were smaller than that could be expected if the resources acted additively. Thus the effect of N addition was lower in the watered than unwatered subplot, and the effect of water addition was lower in the fertilized than unfertilized plots. The non-additive effects of N and water additions on ecosystem C fluxes was due to the shifts in species composition. Lower canopy species were stimulated by water addition while the upper canopy species were stimulated by N addition. The shading effect of upper species on lower species caused the non-additive effect of water and N addition.

6.6.3   Interaction between Temperature (Warming) and Water Availability (Precipitation)

Water may be the primary factor controlling ecosystem C fluxes in DEA where water is lacking (Niu et al., 2009). Soil water availability can regulate the effects of elevated temperature and precipitation on ecosystem C fluxes. However, global warming could stimulate evaporation and plant transpiration, leading to increased water loss from soil (Wan et al., 2002). Therefore, lower soil water availability associated with global warming will exacerbate water limitation in this region.

The results of a manipulative experiment which set up in a temperate steppe in southeast IM showed that the lower soil water availability caused by warming exacerbated the negative warming effect on net ecosystem CO_2 exchange, soil respiration, and microbial biomass C and N (Niu et al., 2008, Liu et al., 2009). Although there was no significant interaction between warming and increased precipitation on ecosystem C fluxes, the interaction between the two treatments significantly affected root productivity, mortality and standing crops. Warming had a positive effect on root production, mortality and standing crop under ambient precipitation while it had negative effects on these variables under the increased precipitation treatment (Bai et al., 2010a). The underlying mechanisms of the non-additive effect of warming and the increased precipitation in affecting root variables could be partly explained by changes in belowground/aboveground C allocation in this experiment. Similar to root parameters, BNPP/ANPP ratio exhibited significant responses to interactions of warming and increased precipitation (Bai et al., 2010a).

6.6.4 Relationship and Interactions between Land Use and Climate Changes on Ecosystem Carbon Cycling

Both the land use change and climate change can dramatically affect the ecosystem C cycling in DEA. These changes co-occur in many ecosystems. Understanding how ecosystem C cycling responds to the simultaneous environmental changes is a key point to predict transformation of the ecosystem structure and function in the future. For example, the grassland under different land use practices would respond differently to precipitation. Previous studies in this region have shown that although the grassland aboveground biomass all had a linear relationship with precipitation under three land use practices (grazing, mowing and fencing), the plant species number, soil C and N under the three land use practices had different relationships with precipitation. Under fencing and mowing, plant species number, soil C and N had linear relationships with precipitation, but under grazing the relationships were non-linear (Zhou et al., 2002a). Another manipulative experiment which has been conducted for five years in IM showed that there was no significant interaction between mowing and nutrient addition (N, P and N plus P addition) on ecosystem carbon fluxes (Niu et al., 2010).

6.7 Carbon Sequestration Potential and Human Adaption to Climate Change

Drylands have the potential to play a big role in mitigating climate change. Effective dryland management practices can lead to greater carbon (C) sequestration. Although the C storage potential of dryland ecosystem per unit area basis is lower than the moist tropical systems, the large area of drylands means that overall they have significant scope for sequestration (see Chapter 1). Studies on the steppe in central MG or IM showed that the grassland in northeast Asia was nearly in balance or a weak carbon sink (Li et al., 2005, Zhang et al., 2009). However, the soil C storage which accounts for most of total C in grassland would decrease substantially with grassland degradation (He et al., 2008). Thus, the potential of C sequestration in DEA depends on changes in management policies. The practices such as excluding grazing, fencing and fertilizer applications could improve the C sequestration of degraded grassland. On non-degraded grassland, the grazing intensity and frequency should be considered to improve C storage.

DEA has a large potential of C sequestration. In the semi-arid areas, soil C sequestration through conversion to restoration land use was 200 kg C ha^{-1} yr^{-1} (Lal, 2009). Many strategies can be taken to increase the stock of C in this ecosystem, such as change croplands to grasslands or forests, water and nutrients addition, exclusion of grazing on grasslands and so on. Establishing a vigorous vegetation cover is an effective strategy for C sequestration in soil and vegetation. Thus, restoration of desertified and degraded soils will enhance the terrestrial C pool, lending to increases in both vegetation and soil C pools. Further research is required to demonstrate the feasibility of large area measurement schemes.

Acknowledgements

The authors thank Drs. Jiaguo Qi and Jiquan Chen for their constructive comments on the manuscript.

References

Ainsworth, E. A., and Long, S. P. (2005). What have we learned from 15 years of free-air CO$_2$ enrichment (FACE)? A meta-analytic review of the responses of photosynthesis, canopy. *New Phytologist*, 165, 351–371.

Aranjuelo, I., Ebbets, A., Evans, R. Dave, Tissue, D., Nogués, S., van Gestel, N., Payton, P., Ebbert, V., Adams, W. III, Nowak, R., and Smith, S. (2011). Maintenance of C sinks sustains enhanced C assimilation during long-term exposure to elevated [CO_2] in Mojave Desert shrubs. *Oecologia*, 1–16.

Bai, W. M., Wan, S. Q., Niu, S. L., Liu, W. X., Chen, Q. S., Wang, Q. B., Zhang, W. H., Han, X. G., and Li, L. H. (2010a). Increased temperature and precipitation interact to affect root production, mortality, and turnover in a temperate steppe: implications for ecosystem C cycling. *Global Change Biology*, 16, 1306–1316.

Bai, Y. F., Wu, J. G., Clark, C. M., Naeem, S., Pan, Q. M., Huang, J. H., Zhang, L. X., and Han, X. G. (2010b). Tradeoffs and thresholds in the effects of nitrogen addition on biodiversity and ecosystem functioning: Evidence from Inner Mongolia Grasslands. *Global Change Biology*, 16, 358–372.

Bai, Y. F., Wu, J. G., Xing, Q., Pan, Q. M., Huang, J. H., Yang, D. L., and Han, X. G.. (2008). Primary production and rain use efficiency across a precipitation gradient on the Mongolia plateau. *Ecology*, 89, 2140–2153.

Chen, S. P., G. H. Lin, J. H. Huang, and G. D. Jenerette. (2009). Dependence of carbon sequestration on the differential responses of ecosystem photosynthesis and respiration to rain pulses in a semi-arid steppe. *Global Change Biology*, 15, 2450–2461.

Cheng, X. L., An, S. Q., Li, B., Chen, J. Q., Lin, G. H., Liu, Y. H., Luo, Y. Q., and Liu, S. R. (2006). Summer rain pulse size and rainwater uptake by three dominant desert plants in a desertified grassland ecosystem in Northwestern China. *Plant Ecology*, 184, 1–12.

Curtis, P. S., and Wang X. Z. (1998). A meta-analysis of elevated CO_2 effects on woody plant mass, form, and physiology. *Oecologia*, 113, 299–313.

Dodd, M. B., Lauenroth, W. K., and Welker, J. M. (1998). Differential water resource use by herbaceous and woody plant life-forms in a shortgrass steppe community. *Oecologia*, 117, 504–512.

Dong, Y. S., Qi, Y. C., Liu, J. Y., Domroes, M., Geng, Y. B., Liu, L. X., Liu, X. R., and Yang, X. H. (2007). Effect of the conversion of grassland to spring wheat field on the CO_2 emission characteristics in Inner Mongolia, China. *Soil and Tillage Research*, 94, 310–320.

Easterling, D. R., Horton, B., Jones, P. D., Peterson, T. C., Karl, T. R., Parker, D. E., Salinger, M. J., Razuvayev, V., Plummer, N., Jamason, P., and Folland, C. K. (1997). Maximum and minimum temperature trends for the globe. *Science*, 277, 364–367.

Ferguson, S. D., and Nowak, R. S. (2011). Transitory effects of elevated atmospheric CO_2 on fine root dynamics in an arid ecosystem do not increase long-term soil carbon input from fine root litter. *New Phytologist*, 190, 953–967.

Gao, Y. Z., Giese, M., Lin, S., Sattelmacher, B., Zhao, Y., and Brueck, H. (2008). Belowground net primary productivity and biomass allocation of a grassland in Inner Mongolia is affected by grazing intensity. *Plant and Soil*, 307, 41–50.

Grover, H. D., and Musick, H. B. (1990). Shrubland encroachment in southern New-Mexico, USA—Analysis of desertification processes in the American Southwest. *Climatic Change*, 17, 305–330.

Gruber, N., and Galloway, J. N. (2008). An Earth-system perspective of the global nitrogen cycle. *Nature*, 451, 293–296.

Han, G., Hao, X., Zhao, M., Wang, M., Ellert, B. H., Willms, W., and Wang, M.. (2008). Effect of grazing intensity on carbon and nitrogen in soil and vegetation in a meadow steppe in Inner Mongolia. *Agriculture Ecosystems and Environment*, 125, 21–32.

He, N. P., Yu, Q., Wu, L., Wang, Y. S., and Han, X. G. (2008). Carbon and nitrogen store and storage potential as affected by land-use in a Leymus chinensis grassland of Northern China. *Soil Biology and Biochemistry*, 40, 2952–2959.

Hooper, D. U. and Johnson L. (1999). Nitrogen limitation in dryland ecosystems: Response to geographical and temporal variation in preciptation. *Biogeochemistry*, 46, 247–293.

Hungate, B. A., Holland, E. A., Jackson, R. B., Chapin, F. S., Mooney, H. A., and Field, C. B. (1997). The fate of carbon in grasslands under carbon dioxide enrichment. *Nature*, 388, 576–579.

Huxman, T. E., Smith, M. D., Fay, P. A., Knapp, A. K., Shaw, M. R., Loik, M. E., Smith, S. D., Tissue, D. T., Zak, J. C., Weltzin, J. F., Pockman, W. T., Sala, O. E., Haddad, B. M., Harte, J., Koch, G. W., Schwinning, S., Small, E. E., and Williams, D. G. (2004). Convergence across biomes to a common rain-use efficiency. *Nature*, 429, 651–654.

IPCC. (2007). *Climate Change 2007: The Physical Science Basis*. Cambridge, UK: Cambridge University Press.

Jin, Z., Dong, Y. S., Qi, Y. C., and An, Z. S. (2010). Soil respiration and net primary productivity in perennial grass and desert shrub ecosystems at the Ordos Plateau of Inner Mongolia, China. *Journal of Arid Environments*, 74, 1248–1256.

John, R., Chen, J. Q., Lu, N., and Wilske, B. (2009). Land cover/land use change in semi-arid Inner Mongolia: 1992–2004. *Environmental Research Letters*, 4, 45010–45019.

Keeling, C. D. and T. P. Whorf. (2005). Trends: A compendium of data on global change. In: T. A. Boden, D. P. Kaiser, et al. (Eds.). *Carbon Dioxide Information Analysis Center*. Oak Ridge National Laboratory, US Department of Energy, Oak Ridge, TN.

Krinner, G., Viovy, N., de Noblet-Ducoudre, N., Ogee, J., Polcher, J., Friedlingstein, P., Ciais, P., Sitch, S., and Prentice, I. C. (2005). A dynamic global vegetation model for studies of the coupled atmosphere-biosphere system. *Global Biogeochemical Cycles*, 19, GB1015, doi:10.1029/2003GB002199.

Lal, R. (2009). Sequestering carbon in soils of arid ecosystems. *Land Degradation and Development*, 20, 441–454.

Li, S. G., Asanuma, J., Eugster, W., Kotani, A., Liu, J. J., Urano, T., Oikawa, T., Davaa, G., Oyunbaatar, D., and Sugita, M. (2005). Net ecosystem carbon dioxide exchange over grazed steppe in central Mongolia. *Global Change Biology*, 11, 1941–1955.

Liu, B. H., Xu, M., Henderson, M., and Qi, Y. (2005). Observed trends of precipitation amount, frequency, and intensity in China, 1960–2000. *Journal of Geophysical Research-Atmospheres*, 110, D08103, doi:10.1029/2004JD004864.

Liu, P., Huang, J. H., Han, X. G., Sun, O. J., and Zhou, Z. (2006). Differential responses of litter decomposition to increased soil nutrients and water between two contrasting grassland plant species of Inner Mongolia, China. *Applied Soil Ecology*, 34, 266–275.

Liu, W. X., Zhang, Z., and Wan, S. Q. (2009). Predominant role of water in regulating soil and microbial respiration and their responses to climate change in a semiarid grassland. *Global Change Biology*, 15, 184–195.

Lü, X. T., and Han, X. G. (2010). Nutrient resorption responses to water and nitrogen amendment in semi-arid grassland of Inner Mongolia, China. *Plant and Soil*, 327, 481–491.

Lü, X. T., Wei, C. Z., Cui, Q., Zhang, Y. H., and Han, X. G. (2010). Interactive effects of soil nitrogen and water availability on leaf mass loss in a temperate steppe. *Plant and Soil*, 331, 497–504.

Luo, Y., Su, B., Currie, W. S., Dukes, J. S., Finzi, A. C., Hartwig, U., Hungate, B., McMurtrie, R. E., Oren, R., Parton, W. J., Pataki, D. E., Shaw, M. R., Zak, D. R., and Field, C. B. (2004). Progressive nitrogen limitation of ecosystem responses to rising atmospheric carbon dioxide. *Bioscience*, 54, 731–739.

Mitchell, T. D. and Jones, P. D. (2005). An improved method of constructing a database of monthly climate observations and associated high-resolution grids. *International Journal of Climatology*, 25, 693–712.

Nemani, R. R., Keeling C. D., Hashimoto, H., Jolly, W. M., Piper, S. C., Tucker, C. J., Myneni, R. B., and Running, S. W. (2003). Climate-driven increases in global terrestrial net primary production from 1982 to 1999. *Science*, 300, 1560–1563.

Niu, S. L., Wu, M. Y., Han, Y., Xia, J. Y., Li, L. H., and Wan, S. Q. (2008). Water-mediated responses of ecosystem carbon fluxes to climatic change in a temperate steppe. *New Phytologist*, 177, 209–219.

Niu, S. L., Wu, M. Y., Han, Y., Xia, J. Y., Zhang, Z., Yang, H. J., and Wan, S. Q. (2010). Nitrogen effects on net ecosystem carbon exchange in a temperate steppe. *Global Change Biology*, 16, 144–155.

Niu, S. L., Yang, H. J., Zhang, Z., Wu, M. Y., Lu, Q., Li, L. H., Han, X. G., and Wan, S. Q. (2009). Non-additive effects of water and nitrogen addition on ecosystem carbon exchange in a temperate steppe. *Ecosystems*, 12, 915–926.

Nowak, R. S., Ellsworth, D. S., and Smith, S. D. (2004). Functional responses of plants to elevated atmospheric CO_2—do photosynthetic and productivity data from FACE experiments support early predictions? *New Phytologist*, 162, 253–280.

Patrick, L., Cable, J., Potts, D., Ignace, D., Barron-Gafford, G., Griffith, A., Alpert, H., Van Gestel, N., Robertson, T., Huxman, T. E., Zak, J., Loik, M. E., and Tissue, D. (2007). Effects of an increase in summer precipitation on leaf, soil, and ecosystem fluxes of CO_2 and H_2O in a sotol grassland in Big Bend National Park, Texas. *Oecologia*, 151, 704–718.

Piao, S., Wang, X., Ciais, P., Zhu, B., Wang, T., and Liu, J. (2011). Changes in satellite-derived vegetation growth trend in temperate and boreal Eurasia from 1982 to 2006. *Global Change Biology*, 17, 3228–3239.

Piao, S. L., Fang, J. Y., Ciais, P., Peylin, P., Huang, Y., Sitch, S., and Wang, T. (2009). The carbon balance of terrestrial ecosystems in China. *Nature*, 458, 1009–1082.

Schenk, H. J., and Jackson, R. B. (2002). Rooting depths, lateral root spreads and below-ground/above-ground allometries of plants in water-limited ecosystems. *Jour-

nal of Ecology, 90, 480–494.

Schonbach, P., Wan, H. W., Gierus, M., Bai, Y. F., Muller, K., Lin, L. J., Susenbeth, A., and Taube, F. (2011). Grassland responses to grazing: Effects of grazing intensity and management system in an Inner Mongolian steppe ecosystem. *Plant and Soil*, 340, 103–115.

Schwinning, S., and Ehleringer, J. R. (2001). Water use trade-offs and optimal adaptations to pulse-driven arid ecosystems. *Journal of Ecology*, 89, 464–480.

Wan, S., Luo, Y., and Wallace, L. L. (2002). Changes in microclimate induced by experimental warming and clipping in tallgrass prairie. *Global Change Biology*, 8, 754–768.

Wan, S., Norby, R. J., Ledford, J., and Weltzin, J. F. (2007). Responses of soil respiration to elevated CO_2, air warming, and changing soil water availability in a model old-field grassland. *Global Change Biology*, 13, 2411–2424.

Wan, S. Q., Xia, J. Y., Liu, W. X., and Niu, S. L. (2009). Photosynthetic overcompensation under nocturnal warming enhances grassland carbon sequestration. *Ecology*, 90, 2700–2710.

Wang, Z. P., Han, X. G., and Li, L. H. (2008). Effects of grassland conversion to croplands on soil organic carbon in the temperate Inner Mongolia. *Journal of Environmental Management*, 86, 529–534.

Xia, J., Han, Y., Zhang, Z., and Wan, S. (2009a). Effects of diurnal warming on soil respiration are not equal to the summed effects of day and night warming in a temperate steppe. *Biogeosciences*, 6, 1361–1370.

Xia, J. Y., Niu, S. L., and Wan, S. Q. (2009b). Response of ecosystem carbon exchange to warming and nitrogen addition during two hydrologically contrasting growing seasons in a temperate steppe. *Global Change Biology*, 15, 1544–1556.

Xia, J. Y., and Wan, S. Q. (2008). Global response patterns of terrestrial plant species to nitrogen addition. *New Phytologist*, 179, 428–439.

Yan, L. M., Chen, S. P., Huang, J. H., and Lin, G. H. (2010). Differential responses of auto- and heterotrophic soil respiration to water and nitrogen addition in a semiarid temperate steppe. *Global Change Biology*, 16, 2345–2357.

Yang, H. J., Li, Y., Wu, M. Y., Zhang, Z., Li, L. H., and Wan, S. Q. (2011a). Plant community responses to nitrogen addition and increased precipitation: the importance of water availability and species traits. *Global Change Biology*, 17, 2936–2944.

Yang, H. J., Wu, M. Y., Liu, W. X., Zhang, Z., Zhang, N. L., and Wan, S. Q. (2011b). Community structure and composition in response to climate change in a temperate steppe. *Global Change Biology*, 17, 452–465.

Zhan, W. L., Chen, S. P., Chen, J., Wei, L., Han, X. G., and Lin, G. H. (2007). Biophysical regulations of carbon fluxes of a steppe and a cultivated cropland in semiarid Inner Mongolia. *Agricultural and Forest Meteorology*, 146, 216–229.

Zhang, L., Yang, Y. X., Zhan, X. Y., Zhang, C. J., Zhou, S. X., and Wu, D. X. (2010). Responses of a dominant temperate grassland plant (*Leymus chinensis*) to elevated carbon dioxide and nitrogen addition in China. *Journal of Environmental Quality*, 39, 251–259.

Zhang, N., Zhao, Y. S., and Yu, G. R. (2009). Simulated annual carbon fluxes of grassland ecosystems in extremely arid conditions. *Ecological Research*, 24, 185–206.

Zhang, N. L., Wan, S. Q., Li, L. H., Bi, J., Zhao, M. M., and Ma, K. P. (2008a). Impacts of urea N addition on soil microbial community in a semi-arid temperate steppe in Northern China. *Plant and Soil*, 311, 19–28.

Zhang, Y. J., Han, J. G., Wang, C. J., Bai, W. M., Wang, Y. R., Han, G. D., and Li, L. H. (2008b). Rangeland degradation and restoration management in China. *Rangeland Journal*, 30, 233–239.

Zhao, H. L., Li, S. G., Zhang, T. H., Ohkuro, T., and Zhou, R. L. (2004). Sheep gain and species diversity: In sandy grassland, Inner Mongolia. *Journal of Range Management*, 57, 187–190.

Zhou, G., Wang, Y., and Wang, S. (2002a). Responses of grassland ecosystems to precipitation and land use along the Northeast China Transect. *Journal of Vegetation Science*, 13, 361–368.

Zhou, G. S., Wang, Y. H., Jiang, Y. L., and Xu, Z. Z. (2002b). Carbon balance along the Northeast China Transect (NECT-IGBP). *Science in China Series C: Life Sciences*, 45,18–29.

Zhou, X. H., Weng, E. S., and Luo, Y. Q. (2008). Modeling patterns of nonlinearity in ecosystem responses to temperature, CO_2, and precipitation changes. *Ecological Applications*, 18, 453–466.

Zhou, Z. Y., Sun, O. J., Huang, J. H., Li, L. H., Liu, P., and Han, X. G. (2007). Soil carbon and nitrogen stores and storage potential as affected by land-use in an agro-pastoral ecotone of Northern China. *Biogeochemistry*, 82, 127–138.

Authors Information

Jianyang Xia[1]*, Shuli Niu[2], Xuhui Wang[3], Shilong Piao[3], Liming Yan[4], Shiqiang Wan[5]

1. Department of Microbiology and Plant Biology, University of Oklahoma, Norman, OK 73072, USA

2. Key Laboratory of Ecosystem Network Observation and Modeling, Institute of Geographic Sciences and Natural Resources Research, Chinese Academy of Sciences, Beijing 100101, P. R. China

3. College of Urban and Environmental Sciences, Peking University, Beijing 100080, P. R. China

4. School of Life Sciences, Fudan University, Shanghai 200433, China

5. College of Life Sciences, Henan University, Kaifeng, Henan 475004, P. R. China

* Corresponding author

Chapter 7

Dynamics of Vegetation Productivity in Dryland East Asia from 1982 to 2010

Jingfeng Xiao, Li Zhang, Jiquan Chen, and Ranjeet John

Summary: We use the satellite-derived normalized difference vegetation index (NDVI) to examine the trends of vegetation productivity in the Dryland East Asia (DEA) region over the period from 1982 to 2010. Our results show that, overall, vegetation productivity significantly increased in the DEA region over the study period. Vegetation productivity shows increasing trends for all broad vegetation types except forests. Increasing trends were observed for many areas of the region, particularly western Mongolia, central Inner Mongolia Autonomous Region of China, and western Xinjiang Uygur Autonomous Region of China. Temperature is the dominant climatic factor of increasing productivity in the region. Warmer temperatures in spring and fall increased the growing season length and productivity. Other factors such as the increases in the area and/or yield of crops and grass, changes in land cover/land use, irrigation projects, and changes in agricultural practices (e.g., increased use of chemical fertilizers) also enhanced plant productivity in the region. MODIS NDVI data complement AVHRR NDVI data and extend the AVHRR record to the present. Future inter-calibration and seamless integration of these two NDVI records will provide continuity for analysis of vegetation productivity over a longer and continuous time period from 1982 to the present.

7.1 Introduction

The global average land surface air temperature has been systematically increasing since the industrial revolution, particularly during the last three decades

(IPCC, 2007). The northern middle and high latitudes have warmed more rapidly than the tropics (Hansen et al., 1999). Warmer temperatures are accompanied by changes in precipitation. Global land precipitation increased by ∼2% during the 20th century (Jones and Hulme, 1996; Hulme et al., 1998). Precipitation exhibits substantial spatial and temporal variability (Karl and Knight, 1998; Doherty et al., 1999; Mekis and Hogg, 1999; Zhai et al., 1999). Moreover, global average land surface temperature is projected to continue to rise during the 21st century under different emission scenarios (IPCC, 2007). Warmer temperatures and wetter conditions may increase vegetation productivity by lengthening the growing season length (Nemani et al., 2002), enhancing photosynthesis (Keeling et al., 1996), and changing nutrient availability by accelerating decomposition or mineralization (Melillo et al., 1993).

Numerous studies have used long-term satellite records to examine the changes in vegetation productivity over the last two decades of the 20th century at regional to global scales (e.g., Myneni et al., 1997; Tucker et al., 2001; Zhou et al., 2001; Bogaert et al., 2002; Xiao et al., 2004a, 2005; Beck and Goetz, 2011). These studies were mainly based on the normalized difference vegetation index (NDVI) derived from the Advanced Very High Resolution Radiometer (AVHRR) instrument onboard the National Oceanic and Atmospheric Administration (NOAA) series of meteorological satellites. Many studies identified increasing trends in vegetation productivity (or vegetation greening trends) in the northern middle and high latitudes, especially in Eurasia (e.g., Zhou et al., 2001; Xiao et al., 2005). The greening trends correspond to the pronounced warming and are consistent with ground-based phenological observations (Colombo, 1998; Cayan et al., 2001; Fitter and Fitter, 2002). The rising temperature is believed to be the leading climatic factor controlling the greening trends (Tucker et al., 2001; Zhou et al., 2001; Xiao et al., 2005). Precipitation plays a minor role in increasing vegetation activity (Ichii et al., 2002; Xiao et al., 2005). Other factors such as forest regrowth, forestry plantations, and trends in agricultural practices can also significantly contribute to the increasing trends in plant productivity (Xiao et al., 2004a).

Many studies have explicitly examined the dynamics of vegetation productivity in eastern Asia or China. For instance, Ma et al. (2003) assessed vegetation dynamics in the Northwestern China from 1981 to 2001 using AVHRR NDVI data. Xiao et al. (2004a) used AVHRR-derived leaf area index (LAI) to analyze the trends of vegetation productivity in China and their climatic correlates over the period from 1982 to 1998. Brogaard et al. (2005) examined primary production of Inner Mongolia Autonomous Region of China between 1982 and 1999. Park and Sohn (2010) investigated the trends in vegetation changes over East Asia from 1982 to 2006 using NDVI data. These studies identified the trends of vegetation productivity and their geographical patterns at regional to national scales.

Here, we use satellite-derived NDVI observations to examine the trends of vegetation productivity in the Dryland East Asia (DEA) region over the period from 1982 to 2010. The DEA region includes Mongolia (MG) and four provinces/autonomous regions—Xinjiang (XJ), Inner Mongolia (IM), Gansu (GS) and Ningxia (NX) in Northern China. Ecosystems in this semi-arid and arid region are sensitive to climate change. Rising temperature and changes in precipitation patterns may alter plant productivity in the region. Trends in agricultural practices, such as increased use of high-yield crops and applications of chemical fertilizers, along with land-use changes such as urbanization, afforestation, and reforestation may also significantly affect ecosystem dynamics and plant productivity. The objectives of this chapter are to examine the trends of vegetation productivity in the DEA region from 1982 to 2010 using satellite observations and to analyze the drivers of these trends. We use satellite observations from AVHRR and Moderate Resolution Imaging Spectroradiometer (MODIS), climate reanalysis data, and agricultural statistics, and present an analysis of the linear trends of vegetation activity and their associations with climate variability and other factors in the region.

7.2   Data and Methods

7.2.1   AVHRR NDVI

The normalized difference vegetation index (NDVI) captures the contrast between the visible-red and near-infrared reflectance of vegetation canopies. NDVI is defined as:

$$NDVI = \frac{\rho_{nir} - \rho_{red}}{\rho_{red} + \rho_{nir}} \tag{7.1}$$

where ρ_{red} and ρ_{nir} are the visible-red and near-infrared reflectances, respectively. NDVI is scaled between -1.0 and $+1.0$. NDVI typically varies from -0.2 to 0.1 for snow, inland water bodies, deserts, and bare soils, and increases from about 0.1 to 0.75 for progressively increasing amounts of vegetation (Tucker et al., 1986).

NDVI has been widely used to characterize plant productivity (e.g., Asrar et al., 1984; Tucker et al., 2001; Zhou et al., 2001; Xiao and Moody, 2004a, 2005). NDVI is closely related to the fraction of photosynthetically active radiation radiation (fPAR) absorbed by vegetation canopies, and is indicative of the abundance and activity of chlorophyll pigments (Asrar et al., 1984; Myneni et al., 1995). NDVI has been used as a proxy for plant productivity or greenness at various spatial scales ranging from landscape to the globe. Although NDVI only approximates vegetation activity and there are various sources of uncertainty, NDVI time series derived from AVHRR provide perhaps the best empirical device for examining spatial and temporal patterns of vegetation productivity at large scales and over decadal time scales (Xiao and Moody, 2005).

We use NDVI data from the Global Inventory Modeling and Mapping Studies (GIMMS) (Tucker et al., 2004, 2005; Pinzon et al., 2005). This data set consists of global NDVI data for a 25-year period from 1982 to 2006. The GIMMS data set has a spatial resolution of 8 km, and consists of two 15-day composites for each month. The data set is derived from observations from the AVHRR instrument onboard the National Oceanic and Atmospheric Administration (NOAA) satellite series 7, 9, 11, 14, 16, and 17 (Tucker et al., 2004). This NDVI data set has been corrected for effects that are not related to vegetation change including calibration, view geometry, volcanic aerosols, and other effects (Tucker et al., 2004). Specifically, this data set has been corrected for the following effects: 1) residual sensor degradation and sensor intercalibration differences, 2) distortion caused by persistent cloud cover, 3) solar zenith angle and viewing angle effects due to satellite drift, 4) volcanic aerosols, 5) missing data due to high solar zenith angles, and 6) low signal-to-noise ratio due to subpixel cloud contamination and water vapor (Tucker et al., 2004).

7.2.2 MODIS NDVI

MODIS is a key instrument on board the National Aeronautics and Space Administration's (NASA) Terra and Aqua satellites. The Terra MODIS and Aqua MODIS provide observations of the entire Earth's surface with 36 spectral bands and with spatial resolutions of 250 m, 500 m, and 1 km. A series of vegetation index products with various spatial resolutions have been derived from MODIS observations. These products are derived from atmospherically corrected bidirectional surface reflectances. MODIS NDVI is referred to as the "continuity index" to the existing NDVI time series derived from AVHRR (Huete et al., 2002). MODIS NDVI extends the AVHRR NDVI record and provides a longer-term data record and continuity for historical studies of vegetation productivity (Huete et al., 2002).

We use the vegetation indices product (MOD13Q1; Collection 5) for the period 2000–2010 from NASA's Warehouse Inventory Search Tool (WIST; https://wist. echo. nasa.gov). The spatial resolution of this product is 250 m, and the temporal resolution is 16 days. For each variable, we determined the quality of the value of each pixel using the quality assurance (QA) flags and replaced the bad value using neighboring values with good quality (Xiao et al., 2008).

7.2.3 Land Cover Map

We also obtained the MODIS land cover map (MCD12Q1) with the University of Maryland (UMD) classification scheme (Friedl et al., 2002) from NASA's WIST. This land cover map was developed from various MODIS data streams using a regression tree approach (Friedl et al., 2002). This map was used to identify the land cover type of each pixel across the DEA region. We aggregated the vegetation types of the map to the following five broad vegetation types in our study: forests, shrublands, savannas, grasslands, and croplands (Table 7.1). About 51.5% of the DEA region is vegetated, and 47.8% of the region is barren. Grasslands account for 65.5% of the vegetated area in the DEA region; croplands and shrublands account for 14.6% and 10.5%, respectively; forests (7.0%) and savannas (2.4%) only account for small portions of the region.

7.2.4 MERRA Reanalysis Data

We use the air temperature and precipitation data from the Modern Era Retrospective-Analysis for Research and Applications (MERRA) reanalysis data set. The MERRA time period covers the modern era of remotely sensed data from 1979 through the present. MERRA makes use of observations from NASA's Earth Observing System satellites and reduce the uncertainty in precipitation and interannual variability by improving the representation of the water cycle in reanalyses (Rienecker et al., 2011). We obtained MERRA data from the Global Modeling and Assimilation Office (GMAO; http://gmao.gsfc.nasa.gov/).

We calculated total precipitation and mean air temperature at both annual and seasonal scales for each year over the period from 1982 to 2010 from the daily MERRA data. These climate data were then used to examine the trends of temperature and precipitation and the correlations with NDVI.

7.2.5 Agricultural Statistics

We obtained provincial statistics on the cropland area and annual grain yield for XJ, IM, GS, and NX from the National Bureau of Statistics of China (NBSA, http://www.stats. gov.cn). The grassland area and yield were also obtained for IM from NBSA and these data were not available for XJ, GS and NX. We also obtained annual statistics on the cropland area/yield and grassland area for MG from the Food and Agriculture Organization of the United Nations (FAO) Statistical Database (FAOSTAT; http://faostat.fao. org/).

Table 7.1 The five broad vegetation types used in the study and the corresponding UMD vegetation classes. The area of each broad vegetation type and its percentage of the vegetated area over the DEA region are given.

Vegetation Type	UMD Classes	Definition*	Area (10^3 km^2)	Percentage (%)
Forests	Evergreen forests, deciduous forests, mixed forests	Tree canopy cover > 60% and tree height > 2 m	172.70	6.99
Shrublands	Closed shrublands, open shrublands	Shrub canopy cover > 10% (10%–60% for open shrublands, >60% for closed shrublands) and height < 2 m	258.27	10.46
Savannas	Woody savannas, savannas	Forest canopy cover between 10%–60% (30%–60% for woody savannas, 10%–30% for savannas) and height > 2 m	60.13	2.44
Grasslands	Grasslands	Herbaceous cover. Woody cover < 10%	1618.53	65.54
Croplands	Croplands	Temporary crops followed by harvest and a bare soil period	359.74	14.57

* Belward and Loveland (1996).

7.2.6   Statistical Analysis

We extracted AVHRR NDVI, MODIS NDVI, and MERRA data for the DEA region. For each pixel, we calculated annual NDVI by integrating biweekly AVHRR or 16-day MODIS NDVI data throughout the year. Negative NDVI values were indicative of non-vegetation, and were thus not included in the summation. Similarly, we calculated seasonal NDVI by integrating biweekly AVHRR or 16-day MODIS NDVI data for each season.

We then produced spatially averaged time series of annual NDVI, annual mean temperature, and annual precipitation for all vegetated pixels and for each broad vegetation type within the region. The linear trends of spatially averaged NDVI were then determined by linearly regressing NDVI as a function of time over the period from 1982 to 2006. Similarly, we analyzed the trends of annual mean temperature and annual precipitation. We also examined the trends of NDVI for each season: spring (March-May), summer (June-August), fall (September–November), and winter (December-February).

The trends of spatially averaged NDVI may hide the geographical variability of NDVI trends over space (Xiao and Moody, 2005). We thus also analyzed the spatial patterns of NDVI trends at both annual and seasonal scales. Similarly, the linear trend of annual or seasonal NDVI was determined by linearly regressing NDVI as a function of time for each pixel.

To confirm and explain the trends of vegetation productivity, we also used agricultural statistics including the cropland area, crop yield, grassland area and grass yield. We analyzed the trends of the crop yield, cropland area, grass yield and grassland area, and also examined the relationships between these variables with NDVI.

7.3   Results and Discussion

7.3.1   Trends of Spatially-Averaged NDVI

We examined the trends of spatially averaged time series of annual NDVI for the DEA region over the period 1982–2006 (Fig. 7.1). For all vegetated pixels, annual NDVI exhibits a statistically significant upward trend (Fig. 7.1a). Annual NDVI increased by 5.8% over the 25-year period. This shows that, overall, vegetation productivity has been increasing in the region during this period. This is generally consistent with the findings of previous studies that vegetation productivity in the northern middle latitudes had been increasing over the last two decades of the 20th century (e.g., Zhou et al., 2001; Xiao et al., 2004a, 2005).

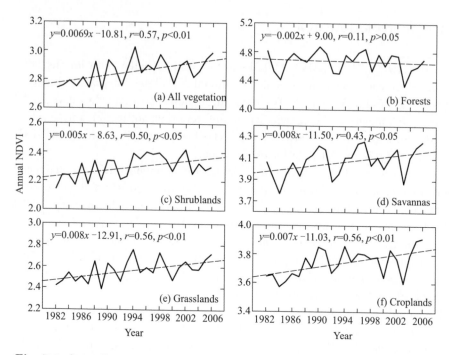

Fig. 7.1 Spatially averaged time series of annual NDVI over the DEA region during the period 1982–2006: (a) all vegetation, (b) forests, (c) shrublands, (d) savannas, (e) grasslands, and (f) croplands. The heavy, solid lines stand for annual NDVI, and the light, dashed lines are the linear trend lines.

We also examined the trends of annual NDVI for each broad vegetation type (Fig. 7.1b–f). Our results show that annual NDVI exhibits significant upward trends for all broad vegetation types except forests. Annual NDVI increased by 9.4%, 4.4%, 6.5%, and 5.9% for shrublands, savannas, grasslands, and croplands, respectively. The downward trend of forests does not switch the direction of NDVI changes over the entire DEA region because forests only account for a small portion (7.0%) of the vegetated areas.

We also examined the trends of vegetation productivity over the period 2001–2010 using MODIS NDVI data (Fig. 7.2). The spatially averaged time series of annual NDVI for all vegetated areas also exhibits an upward trend. This trend is not statistically significant likely due to the relatively short period of time and the large decrease in NDVI in 2009 and 2010. As with AVHRR record, annual MODIS NDVI also exhibits an upward trend for shrublands, savannas, grasslands, and croplands from 2001 to 2010. Similarly, these linear trends are also statistically insignificant.

In addition to annual trends, we also examined the trends of seasonal NDVI over the period 1982–2006 (Fig. 7.3). For all vegetated areas, the spatially averaged time series of spring and fall NDVI had significant increasing trends over

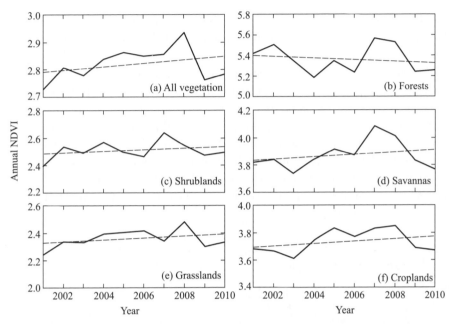

Fig. 7.2 Spatially averaged time series of annual NDVI over the DEA region during the period 2001–2010: (a) all vegetation, (b) forests, (c) shrublands, (d) savannas, (e) grasslands, and (f) croplands. The heavy and solid lines stand for annual NDVI, and the light and dashed lines are the linear trend lines.

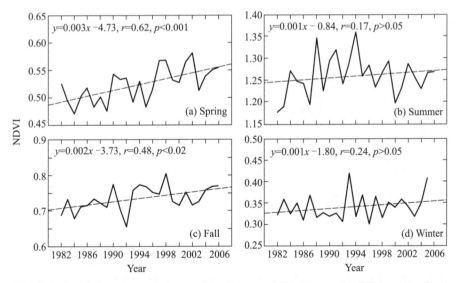

Fig. 7.3 Spatially averaged time series of seasonal NDVI over the DEA region during the period 1982–2006: (a) spring (March–May), (b) summer (June–August), (c) fall (September–November), and (d) winter (December–February). The heavy and solid lines stand for seasonal NDVI, and the light and dashed lines are the linear trend lines.

the 25-year period. Summer and winter NDVI also exhibits upward trends but they are not statistically significant. Spring and fall NDVI increased by 5.9% and 7.5% from 1982 to 2006, respectively.

We then examined the trends of spring and fall NDVI for each broad vegetation type. For spring, NDVI shows an upward trend for each broad vegetation type, but only the trend of grasslands is statistically significant (Fig. 7.4a). Spring NDVI increased by 17.5% for grasslands. For fall, grasslands and croplands exhibit significant increasing trends in NDVI (Figs. 7.4b and c). Fall NDVI increased by 8.4% and 7.5% for grasslands and croplands, respectively. We are not able to examine the trend of the cropland NDVI for each crop type due to the lack of a crop type map over the region. The trend of the cropland NDVI may vary with crop type.

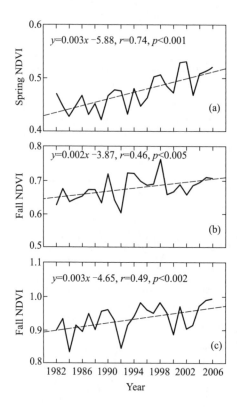

Fig. 7.4 Spatially averaged time series of seasonal NDVI over the DEA region during the period 1982–2006: (a) grasslands (spring), (b) grasslands (fall), and (c) croplands (fall). The heavy and solid lines stand for seasonal NDVI, and the light and dashed lines are the linear trend lines.

7.3.2　Spatial Patterns of NDVI Trends

Spatially averaging of NDVI over the entire region conceals the variability of NDVI trends over space. Thus, we evaluated the spatial patterns of annual NDVI trends for all the vegetated pixels (Fig. 7.5). Increasing trends were observed for many areas of the region, particularly western MG, central IM, and western XJ. The increases in annual NDVI were as high as 30%.

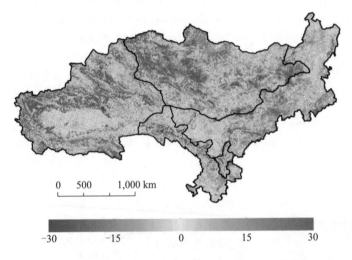

Fig. 7.5 Linear trends of annual NDVI across the DEA region over the period 1982–2006. The trends are given in percentages (%).

Previous studies also examined the trends in vegetation activity in parts of the DEA region. For instance, several studies showed increasing trends in IM. Zhang et al. (2008) showed an increasing trend in annual net primary production (NPP) of the typical steppe in IM over the period from 1982 to 2002. Broggard et al. (2005) showed also positive trends in gross primary productivity (GPP) in central IM. Yan et al. (2009) also showed that NPP exhibited increasing trends in central IM over the period 1960–2004. Several studies also showed greening trends in XJ. Ma et al. (2003) found the increasing vegetation cover in western and northern XJ over the period from 1981 to 2001. Dan et al. (2007) showed increasing trends for NPP in western and northern XJ over the period 1982–1998. Xin et al. (2009) showed increases in biomass in western and northern XJ and central IM over the period 1983–2003. Chen et al. (2008) showed that vegetation activity increased in NX from 1982 to 2003 using NDVI. Li et al. (2011) examined the dynamics of vegetation cover in central and southern NX over the period 1982–2006, and found that vegetation cover increased in the region.

Despite the overall increasing trend of the region, some areas also show decreasing trends in annual NDVI, such as southeastern MG, northeastern IM, and parts of XJ and GS (Fig. 7.5). Several previous studies also showed decreasing trends in vegetation productivity in parts of the DEA region. For instance, Chen et al. (2007) showed that vegetation cover declined in eastern NX, and increased in central NX from 1981 to 2004. Broggard et al. (2005) showed negative trends in GPP in the northeastern IM. Ma et al. (2003) also showed that vegetation cover declined in most parts of GS. Angerer et al. (2008) suggested that rangeland productivity in grazing exclosures has decreased by 20%–30% during the last 40 years in MG and rangeland productivity has also substantially declined in meadow steppe, typical steppe and desert steppe grassland areas in IM.

The spatial patterns of NDVI trends vary with season (Fig. 7.6). Larger areas exhibit greening trends for spring and winter than for summer and fall. The majority of MG exhibits greening trends in spring and winter. Northern XJ and northeastern IM show decreases in winter NDVI. Our results show increasing trends for spring, summer, and fall in central IM, which are consistent with the results of Yan et al. (2009).

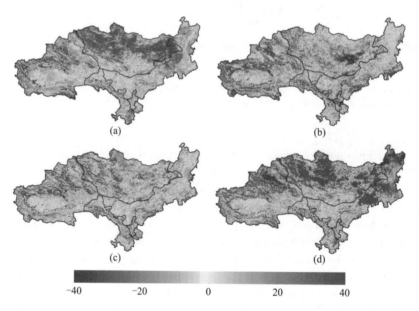

Fig. 7.6 Linear trends of seasonal NDVI across the DEA region over the period 1982–2006: (a) spring (March–May), (b) summer (June–August), (c) fall (September–November), and (d) winter (December–February). The trends are given in percentages (%).

7.3.3 Climatic Drivers

We examined the trends of annual mean air temperature and precipitation from 1982 to 2010 (Fig. 7.7). The annual mean temperature exhibits a significant increasing trend, with an increase of 5.6% over the 29-year period. The increasing trend of temperature coincides with the overall increasing trend in NDVI in the region. A decreasing trend is observed for annual precipitation but the trend is not statistically significant. These trends are consistent with the trends based on individual weather stations (Liu et al., 2005; Han et al., 2010; Xin et al., 2009; Yan et al., 2009).

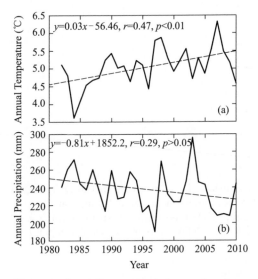

Fig. 7.7 Spatially averaged time series of annual mean air temperature (a) and annual precipitation (b) over the DEA region during the period 1982–2010. The heavy and solid line stands for temperature or precipitation, and the light and dashed lines are the linear trend lines.

We then analyzed the relationships between annual NDVI and climatic variables. Annual NDVI is significantly correlated with mean annual temperature (Fig. 7.8a), but not with annual precipitation. This suggests that the trends of annual NDVI can be partly attributed to elevated air temperature. At seasonal scales, NDVI is significantly correlated with temperature for spring and fall (Figs. 7.8b and c). Our results show that the trends of vegetation productivity can be partly attributed to elevated air temperature in spring and fall and the resulting lengthening of the growing season length. Zhang et al. (2008) also showed that the increasing trend of NPP in IM over the period 1982–2002 was mainly caused by the lengthening of the growing season. Yan et al. (2009) argued that NPP increases in central IM were mainly due to warmer tempera-

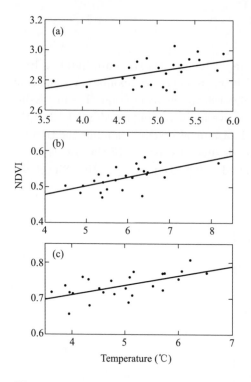

Fig. 7.8 Correlation between NDVI and mean air temperature in the DEA region over the period 1982–2006: (a) annual NDVI versus mean annual temperature ($y = 0.078x + 2.47, r = 0.45, p < 0.05$); (b) spring NDVI versus mean spring temperature ($y = 0.024x + 0.38, r = 0.60, p < 0.01$); (c) fall NDVI versus mean fall temperature ($y = 0.026x + 0.61, r = 0.61, p < 0.01$).

tures and CO_2 enrichment, and the enhancement effect of these factors partly offset the negative effect of decreasing precipitation. Dan et al. (2007) suggested that elevated temperature significantly contributed to the increases in vegetation productivity in western and northern XJ, and precipitation only made a minor contribution. Tao et al. (2003) investigated the changes of NPP in China during the 1980s and 1990s, and suggested that precipitation is the dominant factor controlling the interannual variability of NPP in Northwestern China. Our results were in agreement with Dan et al. (2007) and were not consistent with Tao et al. (2003).

Our results do not show significant relationship between changes in vegetation productivity and changes in precipitation for the DEA region. Precipitation is thought to be the dominant climatic factor controlling plant productivity in northern and Northwestern China (e.g., Li et al., 2008). Using carbon fluxes and micrometeorological data measured using the eddy covariance technique, Li et al. (2008) analyzed the controlling factors of GPP for an arid steppe ecosystem in MG and showed that soil moisture availability, especially water availability in the upper 20-cm soil layer, is the most important controlling factor. Our results show that although precipitation controls the spatial patterns of productivity, air temperature is the dominant climatic factor enhancing vegetation productivity during last three decades. The decreases in vegetation productivity in northeastern IM, however, are likely due to decreases in rainfall (Broggard et al., 2005). Han et al. (2010) showed a decline trend in precipitation in northeastern IM suggesting that the decline in precipitation is likely responsible for the decreases in vegetation productivity in the region.

7.3.4 Other Drivers

Climatic factors only explain a portion of the variance of NDVI trends in the DEA region. Other factors also contribute to the increases in vegetation productivity. For instance, warmer temperatures in spring can lead to advances in snowmelt, which in turn can lead to advances in greenup and the lengthening of the growing season. In the meanwhile, snow cover's NDVI value $(-0.2 - 1)$ is typically lower than that of green vegetation. Rising air temperatures can thus increase the NDVI value of a given pixel by reducing snow cover.

We analyzed the trends in the area and yield of crops and grass for the region (Fig. 7.9; Table 7.2). The cropland area exhibits a significant increasing trend

Table 7.2 Linear trends of crop area, crop yield, grassland area, and grass yield in the DEA region.

Variable	Region	Equation	r	p
Crop area (10^6 ha)	IM	y=0.091x−176.3	+0.94	< 0.001
	XJ	y=0.052x−101.4	+0.88	< 0.001
	GS	y=0.013x−22.32	+0.84	< 0.001
	NX	y=0.016.9x−30.12	+0.97	< 0.001
	MG	y=−0.02x+44.14	−0.85	< 0.001
Crop yield (10^6 t)	IM	y=0.54x−1065.0	+0.95	< 0.001
	XJ	y=0.19x−367.8	+0.94	< 0.001
	GS	y=0.14x−270.6	+0.92	< 0.001
	NX	y=0.08x−152.3	+0.97	< 0.001
	MG	y=−0.04x+71.6	−0.85	< 0.001
Grass area (10^6 ha)	IM	y=0.63x−1179.0	+0.87	< 0.001
	MG	y=−0.29x+695.5	−0.47	< 0.001
Grass yield (10^6 t)	IM	y=0.33x−643.4	+0.81	< 0.001

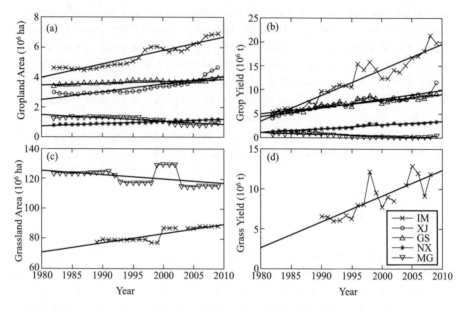

Fig. 7.9 Trends in the area and yield of crops and grass in the DEA region: (a) cropland area; (b) crop yield; (c) grassland area; (d) grass yield. The units of area are 10^6 ha, and the units of yield are 10^6 tons. The solid line with symbols stand for grass or crop area (or yield), and the light and dashed lines are the linear trend lines.

for IM, XJ, GS and NX, and a decreasing trend for MG (Fig. 7.9a). The crop yield also significantly increased for IM, XJ, GS and NX, and significantly decreased for MG (Fig. 7.9b). We observed the significant increasing trend for the grassland area for IM and a decreasing trend for MG (Fig. 7.9c). The grass yield significantly increased for IM (Fig. 7.9d).

We also examined the relationship between NDVI and yield for croplands and grasslands (Fig. 7.10). There is a significant positive relationship between annual NDVI and crop yield for IM, XJ and GS. Annual NDVI is not significantly related to crop yield for NX. For MG, annual NDVI is negatively related to crop yield. This relationship is weak and mainly driven by three data points; moreover, the vegetation signal is low as the annually integrated NDVI is typically lower than 1.0. There is also a significant positive relationship between annual NDVI and grass yield for IM. Our results show that the increases in NDVI for croplands and grasslands in the DEA region are partly due to the increases in the area and/or yield of these vegetation types, particularly for IM, XJ and GS.

Land-cover/land-use change can also lead to increasing or decreasing trends in vegetation productivity. For instance, Wei et al. (2008) showed that croplands and forests had significantly decreased, and grasslands had degraded despite its insignificant change in total area in Mongolia. Grasslands in Northern China,

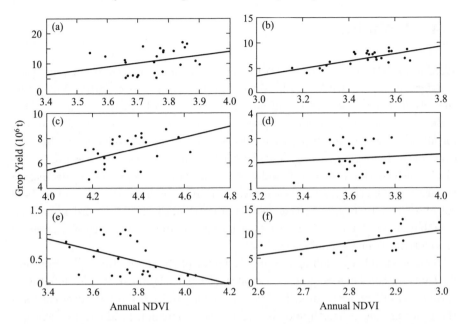

Fig. 7.10 Relationships between yield and annual NDVI for crops and grass in the DEA region: (a) crop yield versus annual NDVI for IM ($y = 12.79x - 37.11$, $p > 0.05$); (b) crop yield versus annual NDVI for XJ ($y = 7.24x - 18.15$, $r = 0.71$, $p < 0.001$); (c) crop yield versus annual NDVI for GS ($y = 4.36x - 11.96$, $r = 0.51$, $p < 0.01$); (d) crop yield versus annual NDVI for NX ($y = 0.41x + 0.70$, $p > 0.05$); (e) crop yield versus annual NDVI for MG ($y = -1.15x + 4.82$, $r = 0.47$, $p < 0.05$); (f) grass yield versus annual NDVI for IM ($y = 12.20x - 26.08$, $r = 0.54$, $p < 0.05$).

particularly Xinjiang and Inner Mongolia are subject to degradation (e.g., Zhou et al., 2003). Wang et al. (2002) used Landsat data to examine the changes in land use/land cover from 1996 to 2000, and found that the forest area in IM significantly decreased over the five-year period. The lost forest land was mainly converted to croplands and grasslands (Wang et al., 2002). Despite the degradation, NDVI exhibited an increasing trend in IM because of the conversion of forest lands to grasslands.

The dynamics of vegetation productivity can also be attributed to management practices and irrigation projects. For instance, Chen et al. (2007) and Li et al. (2011) suggested that improved management practices (e.g., forest reservations and afforestation, and "grain for green") during the last decade have led continued increases in the vegetation cover in central and southern NX. Li et al. (2011) suggested that several agricultural irrigation projects along the Yellow River since the 1980s led to the increase in the vegetation cover in central and southern NX. In addition, the increased use of chemical fertilizers and the substitution of high-yield crops for low-yield crops may also have enhanced the productivity of croplands (Xiao and Moody, 2004a).

7.4 Conclusions

We use AVHRR and MODIS NDVI records to examine the trends of vegetation productivity in the DEA region over the period from 1982 to 2010. Our results show that, overall, vegetation productivity significantly increased in the DEA region over the study period. Vegetation productivity shows increasing trends for all broad vegetation types except forests. Changes in productivity also vary over space. Increasing trends were observed for many areas of the region, particularly western MG, central IM, and western XJ. Some areas also show decreasing trends in productivity, such as southeastern MG, northeastern IM, and parts of XJ and GS. Our results further demonstrate that the NDVI record provides a valuable device for examining the spatial and temporal patterns of vegetation productivity over regional scales.

Temperature is the dominant climatic factor of the increasing vegetation productivity in the DEA region. Seasonally, NDVI is significantly correlated with spring and fall temperature. The rises in spring and fall temperature increased the growing season length and thus increased vegetation productivity. Precipitation slightly declined over the study period, and is not significantly related to NDVI. Temperature, however, can explain only a portion of the variance ($\sim$20%–36%). Other factors such as the increases in the area and/or yield of crops and grass, changes in land cover/land use, irrigation projects, and changes in agricultural practices (e.g., increased use of chemical fertilizers) also contribute to the increases in vegetation productivity in the region.

MODIS NDVI data complement AVHRR NDVI data and extend the AVHRR record to the present, providing continuity for analysis of vegetation productivity. However, the NDVI of these two data sets are derived from different sensors, and careful calibration is needed for the seamless integration of AVHRR and MODIS data in time series analysis. We examined the trends of AVHRR NDVI and MODIS NDVI respectively as these two data sets were not calibrated. Future work should calibrate and integrate these two NDVI records seamlessly and examine the trends of vegetation productivity over a longer and continuous time period from 1982 to the present.

Acknowledgements

This work is supported by the National Aeronautics and Space Administration (NASA) through the Carbon Monitoring System (CMS) under grant number NNX11AL32G (J. Xiao). J. Chen is partly supported by NASA (NN-H-04-Z-YS-005-N). We thank the Global Land Cover Facility at the University of Maryland,

NASA's Warehouse Inventory Search Tool, and NASA's Global Modeling and Assimilation Office for making the GIMMS data set, MODIS data streams, and MERRA data available, respectively. We thank the anonymous reviewer for constructive comments on the manuscript.

References

Angerer, J., Han, G., Fujisaki, I., and Havstad, K. (2008). Climate change and ecosystems of Asia with emphasis on Inner Mongolia and Mongolia. *Rangelands*, 30, 46–51.

Asrar, G., Fuchs, M., Kanemasu, E. T., and Hatfield, J. L. (1984). Estimating of absorbed photosynthesis radiation and leaf area index from spectral reflectance in wheat. *Agronomy Journal*, 76, 300–306.

Beck, P. S., and Goetz, S. J. (2011). Satellite observations of high northern latitude vegetation productivity changes between 1982 and 2008: Ecological variability and regional differences. *Environmental Research Letters*, 6, 045501, doi:10.1088/1748-9326/6/4/045501.

Belward, A., and Loveland, T. (1996). The DIS 1 km land cover data set. Global Change. *The IGBP Newsletter*, 27.

Bogaert, J., Zhou, L., Tucker, C. J., Myneni, R. B., and Ceulemans, R. (2002). Evidence for a persistent and extensive greening trend in Eurasia inferred from satellite vegetation index data. *Journal of Geophysical Research*, 107(D11), 4119, doi:10.1029/2001JD001075.

Broggard, S., Runnstrom, M., and Seaquist, J. W. (2005). Primary production of Inner Mongolia, China, between 1982 and 1999 estimated by a satellite data-driven light use efficiency model. *Global and Planetary Change*, 45, 313–332.

Cayan, R. C., Kammerdiener, S. A., Dettinger, M. D., Caprio, J. M., and Peterson, D. H. (2001). Changes in the onset of spring in the western United States. *Bulletin of the American Meteorological Society*, 82, 399–415.

Chen, X., Li, J., Han, Y., Li, Z., and Chen, B. (2007). Vegetation coverage and its relationships with temperature and precipitation in Ningxia in 1981–2004. *Chinese Journal of Ecology*, 26, 1375–1383.

Chen, Y., Chen, N., Zheng, G., Mu, J., Ma, S., Na, L., and Shao, J. (2008). Change of temperature, precipitation and NDVI in recent 45 years in Ningxia. *Journal of Natural Resources*, 23, 626–634.

Colombo, S. J. (1998). Climatic warming and its effect on bud burst and risk of frost damage to white spruce in Canada. *Forestry Chronicle*, 74, 567–577.

Dan, L, Ji, J., and Ma, Z. (2007). The variation of net primary production and leaf area index over Xinjiang Autonomous Region and its response to climate change. *Acta Ecologica Sinica*, 27, 3582–3592.

Doherty, R. M., Hulme, M., and Jones, C. G. (1999). A gridded reconstruction of land and ocean precipitation for the extended Tropics from 1974–1994. *International Journal of Climatology*, 19, 119–142.

Fitter, A. H., and Fitter, R. S. R. (2002). Rapid changes in flowering time in British plants. *Science*, 296, 1689–1691.

Friedl, M. A., McIver, D. K., Hodges, J. C. F., Zhang, X. Y., Muchoney, D., Strahler, A. H., et al. (2002). Global land cover mapping from MODIS: Algorithms and early results. *Remote Sensing of Environment*, 83, 287–302.

Han, F., Niu, J., Liu, P., Narisu, Zhang, Y., and Wang, H. (2010). Impact of climate change on forage potential climatic productivity in desert steppe in Inner Mongolia. *Chinese Journal of Grassland*, 32, 57–65.

Hansen, J., Ruedy, R., Glascoe, J., and Sato, M. (1999). GISS analysis of surface temperature change. *Journal of Geophysical Research*, 104, 30997–31022.

Huete, A., Didan, K., Miura, T., Rodriguez, E. P., Gao, X., and Ferreira, L. G. (2002). Overview of the radiometric and biophysical performance of the MODIS vegetation indices. *Remote Sensing of Environment*, 83, 195–213.

Hulme, M., Osborn, T. J., and Johns, T. C. (1998). Precipitation sensitivity to global warming: Comparison of observations with HadCM2 simulations. *Geophysical Research Letters*, 25, 3379–3382.

Ichii, K., Kawabata, A., and Yamaguchi, Y. (2002). Global correlation analysis for NDVI and climatic variables and NDVI trends: 1982–1990. *International Journal of Remote Sensing*, 23, 3873–3878.

Intergovernmental Panel on Climate Change, Climate Change (2007). The Physical Science Basis, 2007. *Contribution of Working Group I to the Fourth Assessment Report of the IPCC*. Cambridge University Press, New York.

IPCC. (2007). Summary for policy makers. In: Contribution of Working Group II to the fourth Assessment Report of the Inter-government Panel on Climate Change (IPCC). Climate Change 2007: Impacts, Adaptation and Vulnerability. Cambridge, UK: Cambridge University Press.

Jiao, C., Zheng, G., and Sun, D. (2008). Spatial-temporal change of the terrestrial net primary production (NPP) in Shaanxi Province. *Journal of Anhui Agricultural Sciences*, 36, 9684–9685.

Jones, P. D., and Hulme, M. (1996). Calculating regional climatic time series for temperature and precipitation: Methods and illustrations. *International Journal of Climatology*, 16, 361–377.

Karl, T. R., and Knight, R. W. (1998). Secular trends of precipitation amount, frequency, and intensity in the USA. *Bulletin of the American Meteorological Society*, 79, 231–241.

Kawabata, A., Ichii, K. and Yamaguchi, Y. (2001). Global monitoring of interannual changes in vegetation activities using NDVI and its relationships to temperature and precipitation. *International Journal of Remote Sensing*, 22, 1377–1382.

Keeling, C. D., Chin, J. F. S., and Whorf, T. P. (1996). Increased activity of northern vegetation inferred from atmospheric CO_2 measurements. *Nature*, 382, 146–149.

Li, J., Wang, L., Li, Q., and Li, J. (2011). Features of vegetation change in the Middle South of Ningxia and its relationship with climatic factors over the past 25 years. *Chinese Agricultural Science Bulletin*, 27, 284–289.

Li, S.-G., Eugster, W., Asanuma, J., Kotani, A., Davaa, G., Oyunbaatar, D., and Sugita, M. (2008). Response of gross ecosystem productivity, light use efficiency, and water use efficiency of Mongolian steppe to seasonal variations in soil moisture.

Journal of Geophysical Research, 113, G01019, doi:10.1029/2006JG000349.

Liu, B., Xu, M., Henderson, M., and Qi, Y. (2005). Observed trends of precipitation amount, frequency, and intensity in China, 1960–2000. *Journal of Geophysical Research*, 110, D08103, doi:10.1029/2004JD004864.

Ma, M., Dong, L., and Wang, X. (2003). Study on the dynamically monitoring and simulating the vegetation cover in Northwest China in the past 21 years. *Journal of Glaciology and Georyology*, 25, 232–236.

Mekis, E., and Hogg, W.D. (1999). Rehabilitation and analysis of Canadian daily precipitation time series. *Atmosphere*, 37, 53–85.

Melillo, J. M., McGuire, A. D., Kicklighter, D. W., Moore, B., Vorosmarty, C. J., and Schloss, A.L. (1993). Global climate change and terrestrial net primary production. *Nature*, 363, 234–240.

Myneni, R. B., Hall, F. G., Sellers, P. J., and Marshak, A. L. (1995). The interpretation of spectral vegetation indexes. *IEEE Transactions on Geoscience and Remote Sensing*, 33, 481–486.

Myneni, R. B., Keeling, C. D., Tucker, C. J., Asrar, G., and Nemani, R. R. (1997). Increased plant growth in the northern high latitudes from 1981 to 1991. *Nature*, 386, 698–702.

Nemani, R., White, M., Thornton, P., Nishida, K., Reddy, S., Jenkins, J., and Running, S. (2002). Recent trends in hydrologic balance have enhanced the terrestrial carbon sink in the United States. *Geophysical Research Letters*, 29, doi: 10.1029/2002GL014867.

Park, H. S., and Sohn, B. J. (2010). Recent trends in changes of vegetation over East Asia coupled with temperature and rainfall variations. *Journal of Geophysical Research*, 115, D14101, doi:10.1029/2009JD012752.

Pinzon, J., Brown, M. E., and Tucker, C. J. (2005). Satellite time series correction of orbital drift artifacts using empirical mode decomposition. In: N. Huang (Ed.). *Hilbert-Huang Transform: Introduction and Applications*. Singapore: World Scientific Publishing, 167–186.

Rienecker, M. M., Suarez, M. J., Gelaro, R., Todling, R., Bacmeister, J., Liu, E. et al. (2011). MERRA—NASA's Modern-Era Retrospective Analysis for Research and Applications. *Journal of Climate*, 24, 3624–3648, doi: 10.1175/JCLI-D-11-00015.1.

Tao, B., Li, K., Shao, X., and Cao, M. (2003). Temporal and spatial pattern of net primary production of terrestrial ecosystems in China. *Acta Geographica Sinica*, 58, 372–380.

Tucker, C. J., Fung, I. Y., Keeling, C. D., and Gammon, R. H. (1986). Relationship between atmospheric CO_2 variations and a satellite-derived vegetation index. *Nature*, 319, 195–199.

Tucker, C. J., Slayback, D. A., Pinzon, J. E., Los, S. O., Myneni, R. B., and Taylor, M. G. (2001). Higher northern latitude normalized difference vegetation index and growing season trends from 1982 to 1999. *International Journal of Biometeorology*, 45,184–190.

Tucker, C. J., Pinzon, J. E., and Brown, M. E. (2004). Global Inventory Modeling and Mapping Studies, NA94apr15b.n11-VIg, 2.0, Global Land Cover Facility, University of Maryland, College Park, Maryland, 04/15/1994.

Tucker, C. J., Pinzon, J. E., Brown, M. E., Slayback, D., Pak, E. W., Mahoney, R., et al. (2005). An Extended AVHRR 8-km NDVI Data Set Compatible with MODIS and SPOT Vegetation NDVI Data. *International Journal of Remote Sensing*, 26, 4485–5598.

Wang, S., Zhang, Z., Zhou, Q., Zhao, X., and Zhang, Z. (2002). Dynamic change of forest land and grassland based on remote sensing and GIS. *Resources Science*, 24, 64–69.

Wei, Y., Zhen, L., and Liu, X. (2008). Land use change and its driving factors in Mongolia from 1992 to 2005. *Chinese Journal of Applied Ecology*, 19, 1995–2002.

Xiao, J., and Moody, A. (2004a). Trends in vegetation activity and their climatic correlates: China 1982 to 1998. *International Journal of Remote Sensing*, 25, 5669–5689.

Xiao, J., and Moody, A. (2004b). Photosynthetic activity of US biomes: responses to the spatial variability and seasonality of precipitation and temperature. *Global Change Biology*, 10, 437–451.

Xiao, J., and Moody, A. (2005). Geographic distribution of global greening trends and their climatic correlates: 1982–1998. *International Journal of Remote Sensing*, 26, 2371–2390.

Xiao, J., Zhuang, Q., Baldocchi, D. D., Law, B. E., Richardson, A. D., Chen, J., et al. (2008). Estimation of net ecosystem carbon exchange of the conterminous United States by combining MODIS and AmeriFlux data. *Agricultural and Forest Meteorology*, 148, 1827–1847, doi:10.1016/j.agrformet.2008.06.015.

Xin, X., Zhang, B., Li, G., Zhang, H., Chen, B., and Yang, G. (2009). Variation in spatial pattern of grassland biomass in China from 1982 to 2003. *Journal of Natural Resources*, 24, 1583–1592.

Yan, W., Chen, S., Wulan B., Wei, Y., and Yang, L. (2009). Net primary production in response to climate changes in Inner Mongolia steppe. *Journal of Natural Resources*, 24, 1625–1634.

Zhai, P. M., Sun, A., Ren, F., Liu, X., Gao B., and Zhang Q. (1999). Changes of climate extremes in China. *Climatic Change*, 42, 203–218.

Zhang, F., Zhou, G., and Wang, Y. (2008). Dynamics simulation of net primary productivity by a satellite data-driven CASA model in Inner Mongolia typical steppe, China. *Journal of Plant Ecology*, 32, 786–797.

Zhou, L., Tucker, C. J., Kaufmann, R. K., Slayback, D., Shabanov, N. V., and Myneni, R. B. (2001). Variations in northern vegetation activity inferred from satellite data of vegetation index during 1981 to 1999. *Journal of Geophysical Research*, 106, 20069–20083.

Zhou, Y., Zhang, Z., Zhou, Q., and Zhao, X. (2003). Land use change dynamics spatial patterns in ecotone between agriculture and animal husbandry and its driving force analysis. *Journal of Natural Resources*, 18, 222–227.

Authors Information

Jingfeng Xiao[1]*, Li Zhang[2], Jiquan Chen[3], Ranjeet John[3]
1. Earth Systems Research Center, Institute for the Study of Earth, Oceans, and Space, University of New Hampshire, Durham, NH 03824, USA
2. Key Laboratory of Digital Earth Science, Institute of Remote Sensing and Digital Earth, Chinese Academy of Sciences, Beijing 100094, P. R. China
3. Department of Environmental Sciences, University of Toledo, Toledo, OH 43606, USA
* Corresponding author

Summary I: Contexts of Change

Geoffrey M. Henebry and Jiagou Qi

The chapters comprising the first section offer different perspectives on characterizing and contextualizing the myriad of biogeophysical dynamics found within Dryland East Asia (DEA). Chapter 1 provides the geographic and socio-economic settings found in DEA and recent terrestrial ecosystem dynamics. Projected large increases in Net Ecosystem Production in the Mongolian Plateau by the end of the century, resulting from projected regional warming, pose significant opportunities and challenges. The authors argue for planning approaches that attend to the coupled natural-human environmental system in the face of changing climatic and socio-economic conditions. Chapter 2 compares DEA with two other drylands found in central Asia and North America in the latitudinal band from 35°–55°N. Within this broader spatio-temporal context, using spaceborne sensor observations of vegetation dynamics, the authors find widespread increases in vegetation status in DEA prior to 2001 and a mixed picture thereafter. Moreover, the widespread drying was particularly evident for the drylands of central Asia in the past two decades and only in the past decade in DEA. They also find some evidence for teleconnections linking precipitation dynamics between the three dryland regions resulting in quasi-periodic dipoles and the suggestion of a qualitative change in precipitation dynamics having occurred in the past three decades.

The programmatic contexts for the recent multilateral, multi-year scientific research campaigns—MAIRS and NEESPI—are described in Chapter 3. The authors identify major challenges for addressing ongoing and projected future environmental changes. Principal among these are the gaps in knowledge about the interactivity of key processes and a lack of coordination among national efforts, including the sharing of data, methods and results.

Chapters 4 and 5 each deal with land-cover dynamics at different spatial and temporal scales. Chapter 4 takes a longer temporal perspective and compares land change in DEA with the Sahel in Africa. The author speculates that some of the recent land change, particularly afforestation, may be attributable to the institutional factors: a single strong, the central authority versus multiple, weak nation-states. Urbanization in DEA is the theme of Chapter 5. The authors compare recent urbanization in four cities in Northwest China and one in Mongolia and they focus on the case of Ürümqi, which has seen, over past few decades, urban sprawl resulting in a loss of agricultural land uses and significant increases in air and water pollution. They detect a particular sequence of land-use change in the periphery of dryland cities: grazed grasslands give way to croplands and then eventually to urban land uses, whether residential, commercial or industrial. Moreover, environmental degradation increases with increasing urban land use intensity.

The cycling and sequestration of carbon in DEA is the focus of Chapter 6. Through reviewing simulations and manipulative experiments, the authors identify the factors affecting carbon sequestration potential in DEA. Regional carbon loss has been associated with the overgrazing of native grasslands and subsequent conversion from grasslands to croplands or, alternatively, to depauperate desertified lands. Experimental manipulations suggest that proper land management practices could enhance the carbon sequestration of DEA under projected climate scenarios.

Chapter 7 analyzes synoptic sensor data from DEA since the early 1980s to detect linear associations between time, climatic drivers and indicators of the vegetated land surface.Averaging across large areas at annual resolution over the study period, the authors detect a strong temperature signal region-wide but only localized precipitation signals. The coarser spatio-temporal scale of analysis employed in Chapter 7 likely masks the dynamic complexity revealed in Chapter 2. The apparent disparity of results points to the underlying complexity of DEA.

Authors Information

Geoffrey M. Henebry[1]*, Jiagou Qi[2]
1. Geographic Information Science Center of Excellence, South Dakota State University, Brookings, SD, 57007, USA
2. Department of Geography, Michigan State University, East Lansing, MI, 48823, USA
* Corresponding author

Part II
Consequences

Chapter 8

Impacts of Global Change on Water Resources in Dryland East Asia

Ge Sun, Xiaoming Feng, Jingfeng Xiao, Alex Shiklomanov, Shengping Wang, Zhiqiang Zhang, Nan Lu, Shuai Wang, Liding Chen, Bojie Fu, Yaning Chen, and Jiquan Chen

Summary: The vast Dryland East Asia (DEA) area consists of several large geographic regions including the Qinghai-Tibet Plateau, Loess Plateau, and Mongolia Plateau. The region is of great importance to the functioning of the earth system under a changing climate. In the past three decades, due to the unprecedented land use/land cover change, urbanization, industrialization and climate change, water stress in many areas in DEA have reached a dangerous level that threatened the sustainability of the region. In addition to reviewing literature for the causes of the water crisis observed in the region, as case studies, we examined water balances at a basin and regional scale using multiple modeling techniques, including a remote sensing-based EC-MOD model, a watershed water balance model (WBMPlus), and an evapotranspiration model calibrated for the Loess Plateau region. Our synthesis study suggests that land use change and human water withdrawal account for most of the observed water resource declines in the study region. However, climate change will have profound impacts on areas where local water supply and ecosystem services rely on melting glaciers. The current large-scale soil conservation practices and vegetation-based ecological restoration activities such as reforestation should be comprehensively evaluated to assess their broad impacts on water resources such as groundwater recharge and water yield downstream. Much uncertainty remains to predict future water availability in DEA due to the uncertainty in predicting climate change patterns. Facing the large uncertainty of climate change and socioeconomic changes in DEA, decision-making processes and institutions must adopt a robust and adaptive framework to achieve long-term sustainability.

8.1 Introduction

Globally, about 20% of the human population live in drylands, which cover approximately 50% of the Earth's surface. Depending on local moisture and heat conditions, a variety of ecosystems with high biodiversity is found in drylands, primarily including woodlands, savannas, irrigated croplands, and deserts (e.g., John et al., 2008). Dryland East Asia (DEA) consists of several large geographic regions including the Qinghai-Tibet Plateau, Loess Plateau, and Mongolia Plateau, which are of great importance to the functioning of the earth system (Fig. 8.1) (Groisman et al., 2007, 2009; Qi et al., 2012).

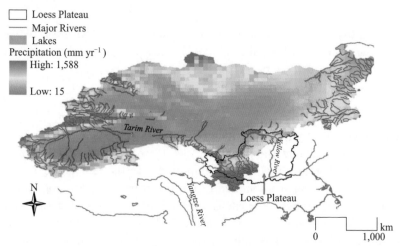

Fig. 8.1 Major river systems and precipitation regime in Dryland East Asia.

In China, about 33% of the land is in arid to semi-arid regions and about 27% of the land is considered to be susceptible to desertification. Desertification is currently expanding at a rate of 2,460 km^2 per year, resulting in serious environmental problems such as soil erosion and sandstorms (Kurosaki et al., 2011). The total DEA area (Fig. 8.1) in the Xinjiang Uygur Autonomous Region (XJ), western Gansu Province(GS), western Qinghai Province(QH), and western Inner Mongolia Autonomous Region (IM) is approximately 2.16 million km^2. The management of the area is important for combating desertification and sandstorms. The major environmental threat of the area is the lack of water resources. Sandstorms occur frequently and some oases have already deteriorated or disappeared. The Hexi corridor in GS is one of the severest desertification areas in China. The Qilian Mountains, located between GS and QH, is a major ecological conservation area for natural grasslands, forests and sources of rivers.

The DEA region is dominated by summer and winter monsoon climate systems, but influenced by land surface conditions of the massive Eurasian continent. The region contains the headwaters of many important river systems (i.e., Yellow River) that provide critical wildlife habitats and sustain stream flow for downstream water use. Dryland ecosystems and socioeconomic vitality are mainly constrained by water availability. The DEA region in China produces a significant part of the country's total production of grain (i.e., winter wheat, maize), vegetables, fruit, dairy products and meat. To produce the food, many of the Northern China croplands are irrigated (Siebert et al., 2005) and water withdrawals are in excess of sustainable water use. A global synthesis on groundwater recharge in DEA suggests that recharge rates vary from 10 to 485 mm per year, representing only 1%–25% of irrigation plus precipitation, resulting in long-term groundwater mining in groundwater-fed irrigated areas (Scanlon et al., 2006).

The drastic changes in land use and land cover (i.e., increase in irrigated croplands and urbanization), industrialization and climate warming have resulted in dramatic degradation of water quantity and quality in the arid region, as evidenced by many of the regional severe water resource problems, such as shortages for drinking water, water pollution, loss of wetlands, lakes and rivers, soil sanitization, and dust storms. Other drivers of environmental changes include woody plant extraction, overgrazing, modification of fire regimes, and urban expansion, contributing to the current ecological crisis. Land degradation, soil erosion (both wind- and water-induced), woody plant encroachment and domination by invasive species, and water shortages are the common phenomena (Wilcox et al., 2006). For example, major rivers in North China, including the mighty Yellow River, have run dry during part of the year (e.g., Yang et al., 2004; Liu and Xia, 2004) and groundwater levels in the North China Plain are dropping rapidly (Liu and Yu, 2001). Water stress in Beijing and the surrounding regions has reached a dangerous level. To alleviate the situation, a major South to North Water Diversion project is currently under construction (central and eastern routes) and in planning (western route) to divert ~45 km^3 yr^{-1} (~10% of China's surface water resources) from the Yangtze Basin to the Yellow River and North China Plain (Cheng et al., 2009). In inland river basins in Northwest China, excessive water use is leading to desertification and severe challenges for food production (e.g., Kang et al., 2008). Irrigation in northern and Western China relies, in part, on runoff from high elevations, including the Tibet-Qinghai Plateau, for a significant fraction of its sustainable irrigation water. Industrial water use in Northern China is expected to increase by >50% and domestic water demand by ~80% by 2050 (JBIC, 2004). Ecological restoration that aims at reducing soil erosion and land degradation has been challenging in DEA in large part due to the delicate relationship between water and human influences on the vegetation's consumptive water use (Sun et al., 2006; Cao, 2008; Cao et al., 2011). Recent emphasis on bioenergy production and biological carbon sequestration causes further concerns about their water impacts and promotes renewed scientific debate on the effects of vegetation on water and other ecosystem services (Jackson et al., 2005; Ellison et al., 2011).

Climate change and variability have direct impacts on water resources in DEA (IPCC, 2007). Small changes in precipitation would result in large changes in runoff. The rising air temperature is especially of concern to watersheds where streamflow is generated from snow melt. The cryosphere (snow and ice) of the Qinghai-Tibet Plateau is a major water source area for intensively developing DEA. The Qinghai-Tibet Plateau has warmed ~0.25°C per decade over 40 years while precipitation has declined 5–10 mm per decade (Yang et al., 2003). Many glaciers are found on the Qinghai-Tibet Plateau. For example, there are 15,953 glaciers in the whole Tianshan Mountains range with a total area of 15,416 km^2 and an ice volume of 1,048 km^3, supplying the majority of the river flows in XJ. However, like other glaciers in the Himalaya-Tibet Plateau, which drains to South Asia (Bagla, 2009; Barnett et al., 2009; Yang et al., 2003; Xu et al., 2009), the glaciers in XJ have been retreating rapidly in the past few decades. For example, the Tianshan glaciers retreated as much as 3 km from the 1860s to 2003 (Aizen et al., 2007). During the past 60 years, the total area of the Tianshan glaciers reduced by 14.2% due to an increase in summer air temperatures, especially since the 1970s (Aizen et al., 2007). The Qinghai-Tibet Plateau permafrost is thawing and this may be contributing to the reduced water volume and deteriorating eco-environments in the source region of major rivers in the QH region of the Qinghai-Tibet Plateau (Cheng and Wu, 2007). A recent national study on China's lakes concludes that, overall, hydrological functions (i.e., flooding mitigation) and water quality (i.e., eutrophication) are degrading. Lake water levels in arid northern and Northwestern China have dropped significantly and salinity has increased dramatically while lake water resources in the Qinghai-Tibet Plateau show large annual variability. Ecosystem functions in DEA are extremely responsive to soil moisture dynamics that are directly linked to climatic variability. For example, the remote sensing monitoring data show that vegetation evolutions are particularly sensitive to changes in air temperature and precipitation in arid and semi-arid regions in China (Cao et al., 2012).

This study focuses on drylands in Northern China. We use published literature and regional water balance, Precipitation minus Evapotranspiration modeling to answer the following questions:

- What are the key water resource issues and driving factors?
- How has land use/land cover change affected water quantity and water quality?
- How has climate change impacted the chronic water shortage in DEA?
- What are the potential options to mitigate negative impacts of climate change and to adapt to future environmental conditions with higher water stress?

Integrated watershed management practices that focus on balancing watershed services and healthy socioeconomic development could provide the best solutions to water problems and environmental sustainability for the DEA region.

8.2   Key Water Resource Challenges

Due to low precipitation (<400 mm per year, in most places) and large differences in air temperature between the growing season and non-growing season, the DEA region is dominated by grasslands and deserts that are sensitive to both natural climate variation (Cao et al., 2012) and human disturbances. The DEA region has several important river systems, notably the Yellow River and several inland rivers such as the Tarim River (Fig. 8.1). Sources of water supply include glaciers (Sorg et al., 2012) and stream flow generated from mountainous upland areas that receive relatively higher precipitation than the lowlands. Deep groundwater is another important water source that supports productive agriculture in a dry environment. Similar to other arid regions in the world, DEA is considered one of the most water-stressed regions where water supply has increasingly fallen behind water demand due to human population growth, exhaustion of groundwater resources, and climate changes. For example, the 1,321 km Tarim River, China's largest inland river that supports eight million people living in oases clustered along its banks and in an alluvial plain downstream, has been seriously impacted (Chen and Xu, 2005) and major associated lakes have been drying up for decades due to excessive water use for irrigation and random land reclamation upstream.

8.2.1   Distribution of Water Balances across DEA and Historical Changes

We use the annual water balance equation (Water Yield = Precipitation − Evapotranspiration) to examine the spatial variation of water yield. Precipitation data were derived from the Modern Era Retrospective-Analysis for Research and Applications (MERRA) reanalysis data set. MERRA makes use of observations from NASA's Earth Observing System satellites and reduces the uncertainty in precipitation and interannual variability by improving the representation of the water cycle (Rienecker et al., 2011). The MERRA data (1/2 degrees latitude × 2/3 degrees longitude) were obtained from the Global Modeling and Assimilation Office (GMAO). We calculated mean annual precipitation over the period of 2001–2010. We extracted evapotranspiration (ET) estimates for the DEA region from a global flux dataset (Jingfeng Xiao, unpublished) produced by the EC-MOD model. The EC-MOD dataset consists of gridded estimates of carbon fluxes and ET with 0.05 degree spatial resolution and eight-day time step over the period from 2000 to 2010. This dataset was developed from FLUXNET observations and MODIS data streams using a data-driven approach (Xiao et al., 2008). The MODIS land cover map (MCD12Q1) with the University of Maryland (UMD) classification scheme (Friedl et al., 2002) was used to estimate ET by land-cover type. Obtained from the NASA's Warehouse Inventory Search Tool, the land cover map was developed from various MODIS data streams using a regression tree approach. We aggregated the vegetation types of the map to the following five broad vegetation types: forests, shrublands, savannas, grasslands and croplands.

Vegetation cover, land use, hydrologic fluxes (ET, mean water yield defined as precipitation minus ET) and human settlement in the DEA region are largely controlled by surface and groundwater availability (Fig. 8.2). Precipitation varies greatly across the DEA region with a steep gradient, resulting in large spatial and temporal variability in ET rates and water yield. In this study, ET rates for areas classified as non-vegetated barren lands (Fig. 8.2 a) are not mapped (Fig. 8.2 c)

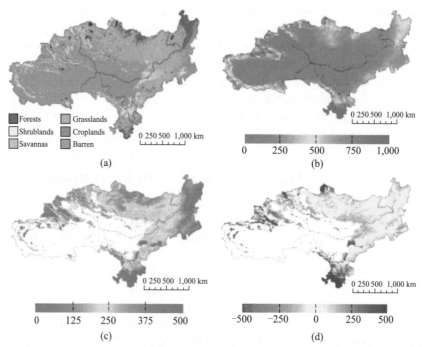

Fig. 8.2 Distribution of land cover (a), annual mean precipitation (mm yr^{-1}) (b), evapotranspiration (mm yr^{-1}) (c), and water yield (mm yr^{-1}) (d) in DEA during the period of 2001–2010.

Source: Jingfeng Xiao, unpublished data.

and are presumably similar to precipitation, which is rather low (<100 mm
yr^{-1}) (Fig. 8.2b). The areas mapped with high precipitation rates ($>\sim750$ mm
yr^{-1}) show high water yield, representing the source areas for local river systems
(Fig. 8.2d). Large areas show negative values, indicating that local precipitation
does not meet ET demands. This might be especially true for the cropland
areas where irrigation is used (Liu et al., 2012). These areas are identified in
northwest NX, central IM and northwest XJ (Fig. 8.2 d), where grasslands have
been converted to highly productive croplands. Groundwater overuse is a major
water crisis for these areas, as it is in other agriculture-dominated regions in
Northern China. Because ET is estimated independently from precipitation, the
negative values of water yield can be partially caused by data or modeling errors.
However, the general patterns suggest that the major renewable sources of water
supply in the region are concentrated in southern GS (Qilian Mountain Range),
central XJ (Tianshan Mountain Range) and northern Mongolia, which are high-
elevation mountainous areas with relatively high precipitation and glaciers.

Analysis of historic changes in the runoff over 2001–2010 versus 1979–2000
across Northern China and IM was made using meteorological data from the
NASA's MERRA (Rienecker et al., 2011) and a water balance model (WBMPlus)
(Wisser et al., 2008) (Fig. 8.3). Runoff in most of the DEA region showed an
upward trend except for a few wet areas. Northeastern China, the Northern
China Plain, and northern Mongolia showed a decline in water availability during
the past decade. Although the MERRA-driven runoff simulation had better
agreement with runoff observations in Eurasia than other reanalysis products

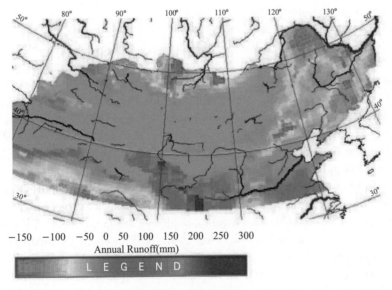

Fig. 8.3 Simulated deviation of average annual runoff during the 2001–2010 period
from the mean over the 1979–2000 time period (Wisser et al., 2008).

(Shiklomanov et al., 2013), the regional modeling results showed large variability and uncertainty in predicting mean annual runoff.

8.2.2 Land Use/ Land Cover Change

In DEA, land use change is driven by several forces such as agricultural development (i.e., land conversion from forests or grasslands to croplands), intensive grazing, urbanization, and soil conservation practices. Previous global studies show that water balances in DEA can be greatly influenced by land use/land cover change (Zhang et al., 2001; Andreassian, 2004; Brown et al., 2005; Foley et al., 2005; Jackson et al., 2005; Scanlon et al., 2006). For example, deforestation generally increased river flow because of reduced total ET. Similarly, conversion of native vegetation to cropland in semi-arid regions can increase the recharge into underlying aquifers and lead to secondary impacts, such as water-table rise and salinization (Allison et al., 1990; Leduc et al., 2001; Scanlon et al., 2006), and changes from natural grasslands and shrublands to dryland (rain-fed) agriculture-altered systems from discharge (ET) to recharge in the southwest US. In Niger, the impact of land use change was much greater than that of climate variability, where replacement of savanna by crops increased groundwater recharge by about an order of magnitude even during severe droughts (Scanlon et al., 2006). A theoretical analysis on hydrologic data from Northern China suggests that annual vegetation cover dynamics affect regional water balances in the non-humid region (Yang et al., 2009).

Land use and land cover change directly alter the hydrologic processes including ET (Zhang et al., 2001; Huang et al., 2003a, 2003b; Sun et al., 2011; Yang et al., 2009; Wang, Y. et al., 2011; Wang S. et al., 2011), soil infiltration and groundwater recharge (Gates et al., 2008), and soil moisture dynamics (Lu et al., 2011). Diverting surface water or mining groundwater for cropland irrigation (Liu and Yu, 2001) are major causes of wetland losses in DEA. Land use changes may also modify land surface energy and water balances (Zhang et al., 2012) and thus alter regional climate patterns through land surface-climate feedback mechanisms (Liu et al., 2008).

The effects of land use change, land management, and climatic variability on water balances have been studied across DEA in China such as the Loess Plateau and Mongolia Plateau that span a complex physiographic gradient. Techniques used include stable isotope tracers (Gates et al., 2008), weighing lysimeter (Ohte et al., 2003; Wang, X. et al., 2004), eddy-covariance flux measurement (Miao et al., 2009; Chen et al., 2009; Wilske et al., 2009), plot or small watershed vegetation manipulations (Wang, Y. et al., 2008; Zhang, et al., 2008a, 2008b; Wang, S. et al., 2008), remote sensing techniques (John et al., 2009; Cao et al.,

2012), and watershed ecosystem modeling (Zhang et al., 2008).

Lu et al. (2011) found that, compared to the undisturbed grasslands, the mean ET/P ratios of croplands and grazed grasslands were significantly lower. The observed lower surface soil moisture content in the grazed and fallowed croplands was part of the reason for the measured lower ET/P. The widely planted and fast-growing poplar trees in Northern China, albeit in their early growing stages, used more water (a higher ET/P) than the undisturbed shrubland, presumably because of its ability to access groundwater by deep roots. Lu et al. (2011) concluded that ecosystem ET was mainly controlled by soil moisture in the semi-arid region unless groundwater was available and accessible. This study indicates that land cover and land use can have different sources of water for ET due to altered soil physical properties and root distributions. Water balance studies in the Tengger Desert (IM) by Wang et al. (2004) showed that re-vegetating shifting dunes used all available soil water. Similar findings were reported that planting trees in some dry areas (precipitation <400 mm per year) on the Loess Plateau can result in soil moisture desiccation and increase compaction (Chen et al., 2010; Jin et al., 2011), thus causing a decrease in infiltration, promoting overland flow and reducing groundwater recharge. Studies with stable isotope tracers also suggest that mature trees and shrub plantations can prevent deep drainage in the Loess Plateau.

Wang, Y. et al. (2008, 2011) examined how the soil erosion control measures, such as reforestation, the affected water yield at the watershed scale in the semi-arid Loess Plateau region in Northwestern China. Multi-year water balances were constructed to estimate the respective long-term mean annual ET and runoff for the forestlands and non-forestlands of 57 basins. They reported that the overall annual runoff and corresponding runoff/precipitation ratio were low, with a mean of 33 mm (7%) ranging from 10 mm (2%) to 56 mm (15%). The average of annual precipitation was 463 mm for all basins. The corresponding averages of annual ET and runoff were 447 and 16 mm for forestlands and 424 and 39 mm for non-forestlands, respectively. Although the absolute difference in the grand average of annual runoff was only 23 mm, it represents a large difference in relative terms, representing 58% of annual runoff from non-forestlands. Similar findings were reported in a synthesis study that aimed at detecting forests' roles in influencing annual water yield across Northern China (Wang, S. et al., 2011). The authors concluded that stream flow amount and runoff/precipitation ratios for watersheds on the Loess Plateau were negatively correlated to the percentage of forest covers. However, the relationships between forest cover percentage and stream flow were not as obvious and consistent in two other relatively wetter regions in northwestern (XJ/GS) and Northeastern China (Fig. 8.4). Air temperature regime, snow/glacier distribution, and forest cover types might have masked the true forest-water relationships (Wang, S et al., 2011) found in the semi-arid Loess Plateau region or other regions in the

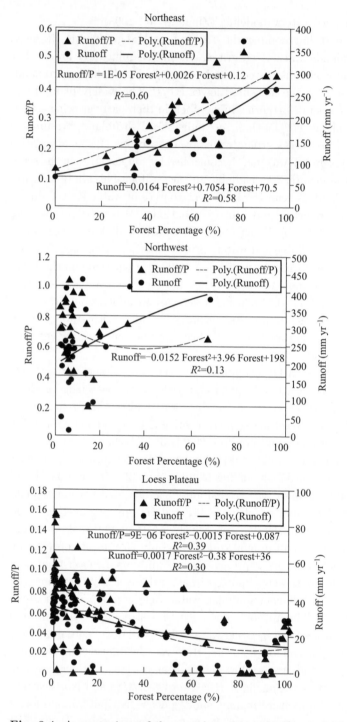

Fig. 8.4 A comparison of the complex relationships between forest cover rates and observed stream flow in three regions in Northern China (Wang et al., 2011).

world (Andreassian, 2004). These studies suggest that large-scale forestation may have serious consequences for water management and sustainable development in the dry regions because of the potential stream flow reduction, especially during low-flow periods (Brown et al., 2005). Soil conservation practices such as reservoir construction can increase or decrease base flow depending operation schemes (Huang and Zhang, 2004; Zhang et al., 2008b). It is important to quantitatively evaluate how land cover change may affect the water balances in arid environments. Soil conservation measures that include both biological (reforestation) and engineering approaches (check dams, terracing, etc.) have been implemented in arid Northern China, particularly in the Loess Plateau region, since the 1950s to reduce soil erosion and sediment loading to the Yellow River, which increases crop productivity and improves the harsh environments.

8.2.3 Agricultural Irrigation and Industrialization

It was estimated that China has 141.1 million ha cropland, about 25% of which is paddy lands and 75% dry farmlands (Liu et al., 2005). More than 30% of farmlands rely on irrigation that accounts for a large portion of all water use, especially for the dry north (Lu et al., 2012). Irrigation is essential for growing winter wheat and maize in the Northern China Plain and for producing cash crops (e.g., cotton, vegetables or fruit trees) in the DEA region. During 1990–2000, the northeast and northwest regions of China gained cropland areas by converting grasslands, wetlands, and through deforestation, while the north and southeast regions showed a loss of high-quality croplands due to urbanization. The newly created croplands in the dry regions in China most likely need irrigation to achieve profitability, causing emerging environmental concerns.

In the Northern China Plain, groundwater is the major source for irrigation because surface water is not sufficient to meet the high ET demand from May to September under the monsoon climate, in which most precipitation occurs from June to September. In some areas in the Northern China Plain, pumping groundwater for irrigation has resulted in water table declines of 20–30 m over the past 30 years and large reductions in stream flow (Jin et al., 2009; Foster et al., 2004; Liu and Xia, 2004). A groundwater monitoring well in the Daxing District, 90 km outside of downtown Beijing, showed that the water table level of the surficial aquifer has declined at a rate of 1.4 meter per year in the last decade (Fig. 8.5). In this area, large groundwater withdrawal occurred during spring and summer seasons as a result of irrigation but water table decline recovers as a result of groundwater recharge during fall and winter seasons when water use by agriculture subsides. Similarly, rapid groundwater level declines are common in the Heilongjiang Province and surrounding regions, Northeastern

China, where agriculture accounts for 84% of water use (Liu and Xia, 2004). Observed monthly streamflow and rainfall data over a period of 35 years (1961–1966, 1973–2001) from the Chao-Bai River in Hebei Province that provides much of the water supply for Beijing show that human activities had bigger impacts on streamflow than climate (Wang et al., 2009) (Fig. 8.6). It was estimated that human activities (i.e., forest cover change, human water withdrawal, siltation dam and reservoir constructions) and precipitation decreases contributed to 70% and 30% of the observed decrease in runoff, respectively. Similar findings are

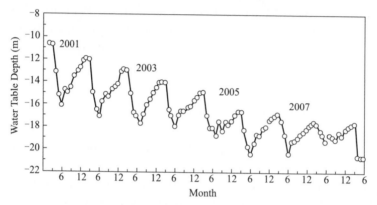

Fig. 8.5 Water table level declines during 2001–2009 measured by a well in the Daxing District, suburban Beijing (Zhang, Y. et al., 2012).

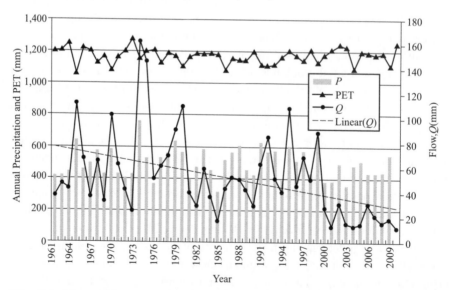

Fig. 8.6 Observed long-term (1961–2009) trend of streamflow change in the Chao-Bai River of Hebei Province, showing a sharp decline in surface water resources since the early 2000s due to human water use. Both precipitation and potential evapotranspiration variables have no significant trend.

reported by Zheng et al. (2009) to explain the observed streamflow decline in the headwaters of the Yellow River Basin. The lower reach of the Yellow River had similar water shortage crisis due to increased water consumption for irrigation. Irrigation accounts for about 90% of water consumption in the Yellow River basin (Chen et al., 2003; Xia et al., 2004). With the rapid industrialization, water demand by other economic sectors increased rapidly as well in the Yellow River Basin (Xu, 2005).

8.2.4 Climate Change

Climate change is hydrologic change, which has profound impacts on all aspects of water resources. The water-limited drylands are especially sensitive to climate change, precipitation in particular (Ma et al., 2008) because surface and groundwater resources are scarce and the hydrologic balances are dominated by precipitation variability (Zheng et al., 2009).

China's climate is warming up by 1.1°C over the past 50 years, faster than the global average of 0.74 °C (1906–2005) (IPCC, 2007) or even that of the Northern Hemisphere for the same period (Dong et al., 2009). The warming has been accelerating since the mid-1980s, particularly in Northern China. The rise of air temperature is particularly significant in winter. The air temperature in the Yellow River basin has increased 0.29 °C per decade since 1989. The largest warming is found in Northeast China, with a trend of 0.36 °C per decade, and in IM with 0.4°C per decade (Piao et al., 2010). The air temperature in XJ increased 1.01 °C during 1881–2001 (Xia et al., 2011). Precipitation is increasing in southern and some western regions and decreasing in the north and northeast (Tao et al., 2003). In the Tarim river basin, the temperature experienced a significant monotonic 1°C rise, and annual precipitation showed a significant decrease in the 1970s, and a Significant increase in the1980s and 1990s at a rate of 6.8 mm per decade. A step change occurred in both temperature and precipitation time series around 1986 due to global climate change (Chen and Xu, 2005). The climate records of IM suggested a warmer and drier trend from 1955 to 2005 (Lu et al., 2009). The annual daily mean, daily maximum and daily minimum temperature increased whereas the diurnal temperature range (DTR) decreased. The decreasing trend of annual precipitation was not statistically significant. However, the vapor pressure deficit (VPD) increased significantly. By biome region, climate in the grassland and the desert biomes had more pronounced change than in the forest biome. DTR and VPD showed the largest inter-biome gradient from the lowest rate of change in the forest biome to the highest rate of change in the desert biome, suggesting drier regions were experiencing more changes.

China experienced a series of severe extended droughts (1920–1930, 1939–1940, 1956–1958, 1960–1963, 1965–1968, 1978–1980 and 1999–2002) during the 20th century (Xiao et al., 2009). Future projections for China's climate are uncertain (Piao et al., 2010), but most studies show climate change will have serious impacts on water supply in the drylands in Northern China. Climate change will likely have a larger impact on water supply in light of projected widespread summer drying in mid-latitude regions during the 21st century (IPCC, 2007). Two major water resources issues related to climate change are summarized below.

1. Glacier retreat

There are about 46,000 glaciers covering an area of 59,000 km^2 in the Qinghai-Tibetan Plateau region, Western China (Xia et al., 2011). Glaciers play a key role in providing water for the dryland rivers and recharging local groundwater systems. There are serious concerns about the short- and long-term hydrologic impacts of glacier retreat on freshwater supply, irrigation and hydropower potential (Immerzeel et al., 2010; Sorg et al., 2012).

It was estimated that roughly 1,400 km^2 of glaciers has been lost in Western China in the past 50 years (Xia et al., 2011). Since 1985 alone, glacier storage in the dryland areas in Western China has decreased by 15%, resulting in 5%–32% increase in annual streamflow. Consequently, the Tarim River basin in central XJ saw a significant rise in the water levels of glacier lakes and an record floods down streams in the 1990s (Chen and Xu, 2005; Xia et al., 2011; Sorg et al., 2012). Piao et al. (2010) summarized observed changes in glaciers at 22 monitoring stations in Western China. They reported that the some glaciers have shrunk as high as 50% in the Tianshan Mountains over the past 30–40 years. Tianshan Mountains, known as the "water tower of Central Asia", has had shifts of seasonal runoff maxima in some rivers (Immerzeel et al., 2010; Sorg et al., 2012). The increasing trend in glacial runoff, especially in spring and early summer, may result in reduced water availability in late summer and fall and in a water shortage in the long run. Over the next 50 years, small glaciers (<1 km^2) may disappear. Overall, 5%–27% of the glacial area is projected to disappear by 2050 and 10%–67% by 2100. Glacier melt runoff may increase in the next few decades and peak around 2030–2050 and could gradually decline afterwards (Piao et al., 2010). Other studies suggested that, by 2030, the total area of glaciers in China will shrink 5.6%–8.5% and storage will decrease by 6.1%–9.3%; consequently, total river flow will increase by 9.6%–15%. Long-term exhaustion of glacial water supply will have a considerable impact on the availability of water for both agricultural and human consumption in the region.

2. Surface water and groundwater availability

An increase in air temperature and decrease in precipitation partially contribute to the general drying trend in Northern China (Xia et al., 2011). Compared to the time period of 1956–1979, total water resources decreased by about 25% during 1980–2000 in the four major rivers (Yellow River, Huaihe, Haihe, Liaohe) in Northern China. An increase in air temperature will increase water used for irrigation. A 1°C temperature rise will increase the demand for irrigation by 6%–10% (Cruz et al., 2007). In the past 30 years, stream flow of the Yellow River (recorded at Huayuankou Hydrologic Station at middle reach) has decreased by 22%. During 1972–1999, the Yellow River was found to be dried up for 22 years of the 28-year record. In 1997, the river stopped running for 226 days with over 88% of the river channel being dried up. Sediment loading has decreased from 1.4 billion tons per year in the 1950s to only less than 0.4 billion tons in the early 2000s. Climate change (decrease in precipitation and rise of air temperature), soil conservation activities, and water withdrawal upstream for irrigation all contributed to the hydrologic and sediment dynamics (Xia et al., 2011). Li et al. (2009) reported that the large climate variability during 1981–2000 influenced surface hydrology more significantly than the minor land use change in an agriculture-dominated basin in GS. Overall, climate fluctuations and massive land-use changes are the root causes of the water shortages of the Yellow River Basin (Yang et al., 2004; Xu, 2005). It appears that the disturbance magnitude and forms of land use changes determine the relative influences of climate change vs. land use change for one particular basin.

According to several Global Circulation Models (GCMs), droughts will likely continue to dominate the Northern China Plain, but precipitation in Northwestern China may increase in the next 40 years. Water stress in the Yellow River Basin will likely increase due to a rise of water demand (Wilske et al., 2009). Headwater regions of the Yellow River will see rapid soil thawing that affects wetland resources and water balances (Sato et al., 2008). There are also concerns that an increase of precipitation and intensified rain storms will cause large flooding and sediment movement events in sections of the river where the channel beds are already high due to chronic sediment deposition (Xia et al., 2011).

8.3 Water Resources under Environmental Changes: Case Studies

8.3.1 Loess Plateau

The Loess Plateau, approximately 640,000 km^2 in land area, is dominated by grasslands, dry farmlands, and shrublands in a semi-arid, continental monsoon climate in Northern China. Annual precipitation rates vary from less than 200 mm per year in the desert to more than 750 mm in the mountains. The region is well-known for its high rate of soil erosion and sediment loading to the upper and middle reaches of the Yellow River (Fu, 1989; Lal, 2003). The Loess Plateau is one of the most severely eroded areas in the world as a consequence of the loose loess soils, steep slopes, high rainfall intensity, and poor vegetation conditions as a consequence of intensive human disturbances (Li et al., 2009).

In the past three decades, large-scale soil conservation efforts that involve structural approaches (i.e., terracing, check dams) and vegetation approaches (i.e., reforestation) have been devoted to reducing soil erosion and improve the local people's well-being in this traditionally economically disadvantaged region (Fu et al., 2011). The regional ecological effects of these long-term efforts are being evaluated (Chen et al., 2010; Fu et al., 2011; Jin et al., 2011). Numerous studies are available in the literature that describe the combined impacts of climate change and land use change on water resources at different spatial scales (Huang et al., 2003a, b; Huang and Zhang, 2004; Zhang et al., 2008a, b; Rustomji et al., 2008; Li et al., 2009; Wang et al., 2011).

We conducted a case study that aimed at understanding the hydrologic effects of a recent reforestation campaign: the Grain-for-Green (GFG) project. Specific objectives were to: 1) detect the individual and combined roles of climate and land cover in affecting evapotranspiration and water yield across the Loess Plateau region, 2) understand how climate variability may enhance or mask the effects of land cover change across the Loess Plateau region, and 3) examine the spatial and temporal hydrologic responses to vegetation in the Loess Plateau region so that we can provide recommendations to land planners at the regional scale. Empirical evapotranspiration models are developed from global eddy flux measurements and local watershed hydrological monitoring data. Remote sensing data such as vegetation cover type and leaf area index (LAI) derived from MODIS products are integrated with models to extrapolate site-level hydrologic measurements to the regional scale and are used for model validations (i.e., ET validation). Research methods are illustrated in Fig. 8.7 to demonstrate the processes of model development, validation and application. Details of this study can be found in Feng et al. (2012).

The land cover change considered in the study was mostly a result of the government-funded GFG project that involved converting croplands and abandoned farmlands into forests and pasture lands. Vegetation covers in some areas have improved greatly since the project was implemented at the end of 1999. For example, total vegetation cover in northern Shaanxi Province (combined for planted forest and herbaceous vegetation, i.e., grasses, forbs, herbs) increased from 30% in 1998 to 42% in 2005 as a result of the GFG project (Cao et al., 2009). Although it is generally accepted that reforestation and soil conservation practices can result in reduced water yield and sediment (see review in McVicar

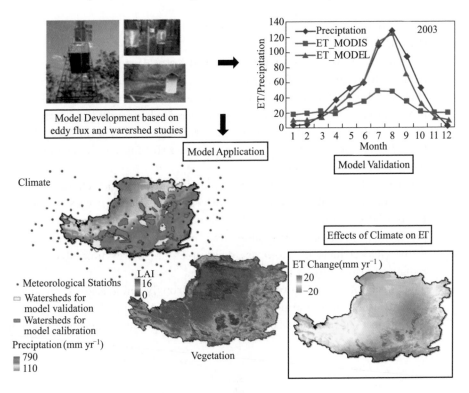

Fig. 8.7 Illustration of the method to model regional evapotranspiration and water yield across the Loess Plateau region.

et al., 2007; Wang Y. et al., 2011), few studies have been conducted to examine the relationship between observed vegetation change, climate variability, and hydrological responses at a regional scale for the Loess Plateau. Such types of studies are surely needed to explain regional change patterns in ecosystem functions such as water availability and soil erosion control (Fu et al., 2011). For example, the observed land cover change toward more productive states in the 1990s is perhaps an indication of vegetation recovery due to human intervention, but the contribution of climate variability in the region cannot be excluded (Fang et al., 2003).

This case study focuses on the time period from 1999 to 2007 in which year 1999 is designated as the "baseline" period and 2000 to 2007 as the "treatment" period that has different land cover and climatic conditions from the baseline period. Changes in ET (treatment period—baseline) at both annual and monthly scales are examined. If precipitation is assumed not to be affected by vegetation cover change, the effect of land cover on water yield is considered to be equivalent to changes in ET. A summary of findings for this regional modeling study follows.

- Water yield had large spatial and temporal variability in the study region (Fig. 8.8a).
- In general, the vegetation-based ecological restoration effort, GFG project, resulted in an increase of water loss through evapotranspiration (Fig. 8.8c). However, the actual impacts on water yield depended on the variability of precipitation. Simulation showed that increased precipitation during the project implementation period masked the water yield reduction effects; the GFG project might have aggravated water shortages in some areas that received reduced precipitation.
- Due to the large spatial variability in climate and vegetation characteristics, the magnitude of hydrologic effects of vegetation change varies across the Loess Plateau (Figs. 8.8b and c). The forested areas that received more precipitation had higher responses than the drier areas in terms of absolute water yield reduction. However, drier areas are more vulnerable to flow reduction, especially in the growing season.
- The effects of ecological restoration were strongly influenced by precipitation variability in the arid region. The current regional vegetation restoration projects have variable effects on local water resources across the region

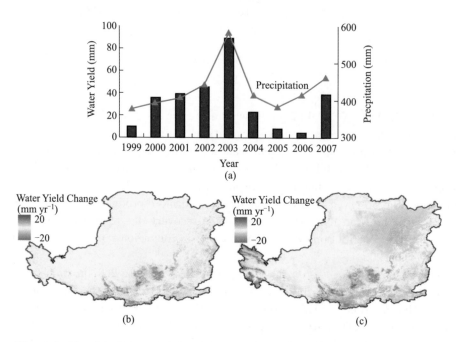

Fig. 8.8 Simulated mean annual water yield across the Loess Plateau region during 1999–2007 (a), effects of land use change only (b), and land use change + climate variability (c) over 2000–2007 when compared to year 1999. Positive values indicate an increase and otherwise a decrease in water yield (Feng et al., 2012).

that had a large precipitation gradient. The future climate change in the study region is likely to alter the water balances due to both air warming and changes in precipitation patterns. Land management planning must consider the influences of spatial climate variability and long-term climate change on water yield and ecosystem structures.

8.3.2 Impacts of Future Climate Change on Runoff across DEA

Global Circulation Models (GCMs) can more or less adequately reproduce the annual variability of air temperature and precipitation; however, they have large uncertainties in runoff simulation due to the simplified representation of land surface processes, lack of runoff routing computation and neglected local human impacts (i.e., reservoirs). To eliminate these shortcomings, we analyzed future runoff changes modeled by a modified version of the water balance model (WBMPlus) (Wisser et al., 2008; Shiklomanov et al., 2013) driven by several AO GCMs under the IPCC SRES A1B emission scenario (Table 8.1).

Table 8.1 Description of Eight IPCC AO GCMs.

GCM Models	Country	Spatial Resolution
ECHAM5/MPI-OM	Germany	$1.9°\times1.9°$
CGCM3.1(T63)	Canada	$2.8°\times2.8°$
UKMO-HadCM3	Great Britain	$1.25°\times1.875°$
BCCR-BCM2	Norway	$2.8°\times2.8°$
NCAR_CCSM3	USA	$1.4°\times1.4°$
INM-CM3 RAS	Russia	$3.0°\times4.0°$
GFDL-CM2.1	USA	$2.0°\times2.5°$
MIROC3.2(medres)	Japan	$2.8°\times2.8°$

WBM is a global-scale, gridded model that simulates both the vertical exchange of water between the ground and the atmosphere, and the horizontal transport of water through runoff and stream networks. The used version of the model also has the capability to model the impact of large reservoirs on stream flow and the role of irrigation on the vertical exchange of water. To analyze future changes in regional hydrology, we ran WBMPlus with 30×30 min spatial resolution and monthly time steps using future climate scenarios generated from eight AO GCMs (Table 8.1) (http://neespi.sr.unh.edu/maps/).

Results indicate a tendency toward decreases in river runoff across DEA, although the projected changes are not spatially uniform. Figure 8.9 shows changes in annual river runoff across DEA by 2040–2060 from the long-term

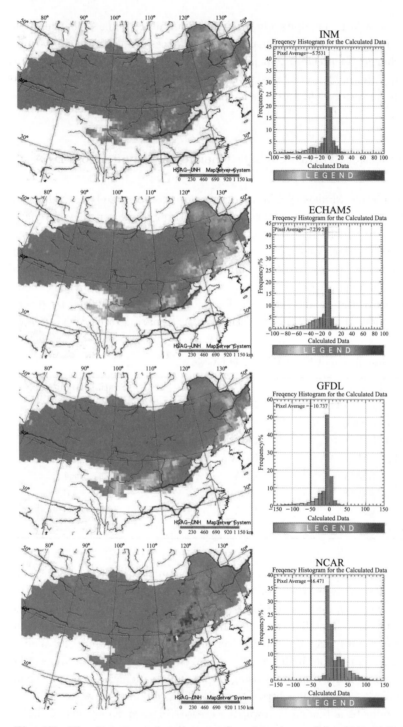

Fig. 8.9 The deviations of mean annual projected runoff for 2040–2060 from mean contemporary runoff over 1959–1999 under 20c3m scenario simulated with WBMplus using different AO GCMs (IPCC, 2007; Shiklomanov et al., 2013).

average (1959–1999) for GFDL-CM2.1, INM-CM3 RAS, MPI ECHAM5 and NCAR CCSM3 AO GCMs. The DEA region, in the future, will be drier with a decline in annual river runoff aggregated for the entire domain in the range from −5 mm to −11 mm (Fig. 8.9). However, NCAR CCSM3, with the best spatial resolution and the most sophisticated representation of land surface processes, projects completely different future climates with higher annual precipitation and thus increased annual runoff by 16 mm by 2040–2060 (Fig. 8.9). Thus, there is a great uncertainty in future runoff projections because of a great uncertainty of future climate among different IPCC AO GCMs.

There is also a large uncertainty in the projection of changes in monthly and annual river discharge for the large regional rivers, such as the Yellow River. Simulations for the same location are presented in Figures 8.10 and 8.11. Large discrepancies among models were found for the fall season. According to the most AO GCM (except NCAR), increases in river discharge are projected during winter and spring months and decreases during summer-fall when water use by ecosystems and humans is highest.

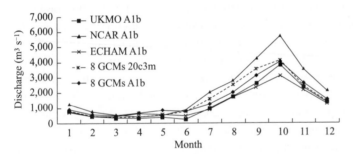

Fig. 8.10 Mean monthly discharge simulated with the WBMplus model for the Yellow River for 2040–2060 (IPCC A1B emission scenario) and 1959–1999 (for 20th century IPCC AR4 20c3m scenario) from different GCMs.

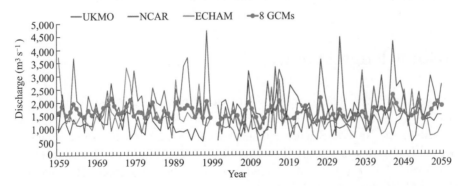

Fig. 8.11 Mean annual discharge variability for the Yellow River simulated with the WBMplus model for different GCMs using the 20c3m scenario until 1999 and SRES A1B since 2001.

8.4 Conclusions

This review found that both climate change (e.g., glacier melting due to global warming) and land use change (e.g., conservation, irrigation) have severely impacted stream flow in many areas in DEA. The region is facing an unprecedented water shortage that has caused serious concerns for the sustainability of the region as a whole. Dramatic land use changes driven by population growth, urbanization, industrialization, and poorly guided ecological restoration are the root causes for this water crisis. Global climate warming has altered the normal local hydrologic cycles and ecosystem functions in some key regions by melting glaciers, thawing frozen soils, and elevating water demand for agricultural irrigation and human use. Continued climate change will have profound impacts on DEA and will likely aggravate the current water problems characterized as diminishing surface water, groundwater depletion, increased water pollution and expansion of soil erosion/desertification.

Solving the water resource issues in DEA cannot be achieved by looking at the water sector alone. In fact, single-handed soil and water conservation practices such as reforestation in Northern China have resulted in unintended environmental consequences. An ecosystem approach is needed to manage the trade-offs between all ecosystem services (i.e., soil erosion control, water supply, groundwater recharge, carbon sequestration, and climate moderation). Integrated watershed management that considers all watershed service needs by humans and natural ecosystems should be promoted. Water conservation practices that promote increasing water use efficiency and implementing demand-based water allocation management in agricultural irrigation and industry water use may have immediate effects in the face of rapid economic transformation in Northern China. Facing the large uncertainty of climate change and socioeconomic changes in DEA, decision-making processes and institutions must adopt a robust and adaptive framework to achieve long-term sustainability in DEA (Lu et al., 2012).

Acknowledgements

Major funding for this synthesis comes from the USDA Forest Service Eastern Forest Environmental Threat Assessment Center, the LCLUC Program of NASA, the Natural Science Foundation of China, the Chinese Academy of Sciences, the Research Priorities Programme of China (No. 2009CB421104), the National Natural Science Foundation of China (No. 40801070), and the CAS/SAFEA International Partnership Programme for Innovation Research Teams of "Ecosystem Processes and Services". GIMMS AVHRR-NDVI data and SPOT VEGETATION data were provided from the Environmental and Ecological Science Data Center for West China (http://westdc.westgis.ac.cn). Also, we would like to thank two anonymous reviewers for their comments and suggestions that helped to improve the quality of this chapter.

References

Aizen, V. B., Kuzmichenok, V. A., Surazakov, A. B., and Aizen, E. M. (2007). Glacier changes in the Tien Shan as determined from topographic and remotely sensed data. *Global and Planetary Changes, Special NEESPI Program Issue*, 56, 3–4, 328–340.

Allison, G. B., Cook, P. G., Barnett, S. R., Walker, G. R., Jolly, I. D., and Hughes, M. W. (1990). Land clearance and river salinisation in the western Murray Basin, Australia. *Journal of Hydrology*, 119, 1–20.

Andreassian, V. (2004). Waters and forests: From historical controversy to scientific debate. *Journal of Hydrology*, 291, 1–27.

Barnett, T. P., Adam, J. C., and Lettenmaier, D. P. (2009). Potential impacts of a warming climate on water availability in snow-dominated regions. *Nature*, 438, doi:10.1038.

Brown, A. E., Zhang, L., McMahon, T. A., Western, A. W., and Vertessy, R. A. (2005). A review of paired catchment studies for determining changes in water yield resulting from alterations in vegetation. *Journal of Hydrology*, 310, 28–61.

Cao, S. (2008). Why large-scale afforestation efforts in China have failed to solve the desertification problem. *Environmental Science and Technology*, 42, 1826–1831.

Cao, S., Chen, L., and Yu, X. (2009). Impact of China's Grain for Green Project on the landscape of vulnerable arid and semi-arid agricultural regions: A case study in northern Shaanxi Province. *Journal of Applied Ecology*, 46, 536–543.

Cao, S., Sun, G., Zhang, Z., Chen, L., Feng, Q., Fu, B., McNulty, S. G., Shankman, D., Tang, J., Wang, Y., and Wei, X. (2011). Greening China Naturally. *AMBIO*, doi: 10.1007/s13280-011-0150-8.

Cao, L., Xu, J., Chen, Y., Li, W., Yang, Y., Hong, Y. and Li, Z. (2012). Understanding the dynamic coupling between vegetation cover and climatic factors in a semiarid region—A case study of Inner Mongolia, China. *Ecohydrology*, doi: 10.1002/eco.1245.

Chen, Y., and Xu, Z. (2005). Plausible impact of global climate change on water resources in the Tarim River Basin. *Science in China Series D*, 48, 65–73.

Chen, L., Wang, J., Wei, W., Fu, B., and Wu, D. (2010). Effects of landscape restoration on soil water storage and water use in the Loess Plateau Region, China. *Forest Ecology and Management*, 259, 7,1291–1298.

Chen, S., Chen, J., Lin, G., Zhang, W., Miao, H., Wei, L., Huang, J., and Han, X. (2009). Energy balance and partition in Inner Mongolia steppe ecosystems with different land use types. *Agricultural and Forest Meteorology*, 149, 1800–1809.

Chen, J., He, D., and Cui, S. (2003). The response of river water quality and quantity to the development of irrigated agriculture in the last four decades in the Yellow

River Basin, China. *Water Resources Research*, 39, 1047.

Cheng, G., and Wu, T. (2007). Responses of permafrost to climate change and their environmental significance, Qinghai-Tibet Plateau. *Journal of Geophysical Research*, 112, F02S03.

Cheng, H., Hu, Y., and Zhao, J. (2009). Meeting China's water shortage crisis: Current practices and challenges. *Environmental Science and Technology*, 43, 240–244.

Cruz, R. V., Harasawa. H., Lal, M., Wu, S., Anokhin, Y., Punsalmaa, B., Honda, Y., Jafari, M., Li, C., and Ninh, N. H. (2007). Asia. In: Parry, M.L., Canziani, O. F., Palutikof, P. J. (Ed.). *Climate Change 2007: Impacts, Adaptation and Vulnerability*. Cambridge, UK: Cambridge University Press, 469–506.

Dong, J., Liu, J., Tao, F., Xu, X., and Wang, J. (2009). Spatio-temporal changes in annual accumulated temperature in China and the effects on cropping systems, 1980s to 2000. *Climate Research*, 40, 37–48.

Ellison, D., N. Futter, M., and Bishop, K. (2011). On the forest cover-water yield debate: from demand- to supply-side thinking. *Global Change Biology*, doi: 10.1111/j.1365-2486.2011.02589.x.

Fang, J., Piao, S., Field, C. B., Pan, Y., Guo, Q., Zhou, L., Peng, C., and Tao, S. (2003). Increasing net primary production in China from 1982 to 1999. *Frontiers in Ecology and the Environment*, 1,6, 293–29.

Feng, X., Sun, G., Fu, B., Su, C., Liu, Y., and Lamparski, H. (2012). Regional effects of vegetation restoration on water yield across the Loess Plateau, China. *Hydrology and Earth System Sciences*, doi:10.5194/hess-16-2617-2012.

Foley, J. A., DeFries, R., Asner, G. P., Barford, C., Bonan, G., Carpenter, S. R., Chapin, F. S., Coe, M. T., Daily, G. C., Gibbs, H. K., Helkowski, J. H., Holloway, T., Howard, E. A., Kucharik, C. J., Monfreda, C., Patz, J. A., Prentice, I. C., Ramankutty, N., and Snyder, P. K. (2005). Global consequences of land use. *Science*, 309, 570–574.

Foster, S., Garduno, H., Evans, R., Olson, D., Tian, Y., Zhang, W., and Han, Z. (2004). Quaternary aquifer of the North China Plain—assessing and achieving groundwater resource sustainability. *Hydrogeology Journal*, 12, 81–93.

Friedl, M. A., McIver, D. K., Hodges, J. C. F., Zhang, X. Y., Muchoney, D., Strahler, A. H., et al. (2002). Global land cover mapping from MODIS: algorithms and early results. *Remote Sensing of Environment*, 83, 287–302.

Fu, B. (1989). Soil erosion and its control in the Loess Plateau of China. *Soil Use Management*, 5, 76–82.

Fu, B., Liu, Y., Lü, Y., He, C., Zeng, Y., and Wu, B. (2011). Assessing the soil erosion control service of ecosystems change in the Loess Plateau of China. *Ecological Complexity*, 8, 4, 284–293.

Gates, J. B., Edmunds, W. M., Ma, J. Z., and Scanlon, B. R. (2008). Estimating groundwater recharge in a cold desert environment in Northern China using chloride. *Hydrogeology Journal*, 16, 893–910.

Groisman, P. Y. , Sokolik, I., Hibbard, K., Brasseur, G., and Katzenberger, J. (2007). Northern Eurasia in the global Earth system. *Transactions American Geophysical Union*, 88, 4–6, 487.

Groisman, P. Y., Clark, E. A., Kattsov, V. M., Lettenmaier, D. P., Sokolik, I. N., Aizen, V. B., Cartus, O., Chen, J., Conard, S., Katzenberger, J., Krankina, O.,

Kukkonen, J., Machida, T., Maksyutov, S., Ojima, D., Qi, J., Romanovsky, V. E., Santoro, M., Schmullius, C., Shiklomanov, A. I., Shimoyama, K., Shugart, H.H., Shuman, J. K., Sofiev, M., Sukhinin, A. I., Vörösmarty, C., Walker, D., and Wood, E. F. (2009). The Northern Eurasia earth science partnership: An example of science applied to societal needs. *Bulletin of the American Meteorological Society*, 5, 671–688.

Huang, M., Gallichand, J., and Zhang, P. (2003a). Runoff and sediment responses to conservation practices: Loess Plateau of China. *Journal of American Water Resources Association*, 39, 1197–1207.

Huang, M., Zhang, L., and Gallichand, J. (2003b). Runoff responses to afforestation in a watershed of the Loess Plateau, China. *Hydrological Processes*, 17, 2599–2609.

Huang, M., and Zhang, L. (2004). Hydrological responses to conservation practices in a catchment of the Loess Plateau, China. *Hydrological Processes*, 18, 1885–1898.

Immerzeel, W. W., van Beek, L. P. H., Bierkens, M. F. P. (2010). Climate change will affect the asian water towers. *Science*, 328, 5984, 1382–1385.

Intergovernmental Panel on Climate Change (IPCC). (2007). Climate Change 2007— The Physical Science Basis. Contribution of Working Group I to the Fourth Assessment Report of the IPCC. Cambridge University Press, New York.

JBIC (Japan Bank for International Cooperation). (2004). Issues and challenges for water resources in North China: Case of the Yellow River Basin. *JBICI Research Paper*, 28.

Jackson, R. B., Jobbagy, E. G., Avissar, R., Roy, S. B,, Barrett, D. J., Cook, C. W., Farley, K. A., Le Maitre, D. C., McCarl, B. A., and Murray, B. C. (2005). Trading water for carbon with biological carbon sequestration. *Science*, 310, 1944–1947.

Jin, T., Fu, B., Liu, G., and Wang, Z. (2011). Hydrologic feasibility of artificial forestation in the semi-arid Loess Plateau of China. *Hydrology and Earth System Sciences Discussions*, 15, 2519–2530.

Jin, H., He, R., Cheng, G., Wu, Q., Wang, S., Lu, L., and Chang, X. (2009). Changes in frozen ground in the source area of the Yellow River on the Qinghai-Tibet Plateau, China, and their eco-environmental impacts. *Environmental. Research Letters*, doi:10.1088/1748-9326/4/4/045206.

John, R., Chen, J., Lu, N., Guo, K., Liang, C., Wei, Y., Noormets, A., Ma, K., and Han, X. (2008). Predicting plant diversity based on remote sensing products in the semi-arid region of Inner Mongolia. *Remote Sensing of Environment*, 112, 2018–2032.

John, R., Chen, J., Lu, N., and Wilske, B. (2009). Land cover/land use change and their ecological consequences: Lessons from Inner Mongolia. *Environmental Research Letters*, doi:10.1088/1748-9326/4/4/045010.

Kang, S., Su, X., Tong, L., Zhang, J., Zhang, L., and Davies, W.J. (2008). A warning from an ancient oasis: Intensive human activities are leading to potential ecological and social catastrophe. *The International Journal of Sustainable Development and World Ecology*, 15, 440–447.

Kurosaki, Y., Shinoda, M., and Mikami, M. (2011). What caused a recent increase in dust outbreaks over East Asia? *Geophysical Research Letters*, 38, L11702.

Lal, R. (2003). Soil erosion and the global carbon budget. *Environmental International*, 29(4), 437–450.

Leduc C., Favreau, G., and Schroeter, P. (2001). Long-term rise in a Sahelian water-table: the continental terminal in south-west Niger. *Journal of Hydrology*, 243, 43–54.

Li, Z., Liu, W., Zhang, X., and Zheng, F. (2009). Impacts of land use change and climate variability on hydrology in an agricultural catchment on the Loess Plateau of China. *Journal of Hydrology*, 377, 35–42.

Liu, M., Tian, H., Lu C., Xu X., Chen G., and Ren, W. (2012). Effects of multiple environment stresses on evapotranspiration and runoff over the Eastern China. *Journal of Hydrology*, 426-427, 39–54.

Liu, C. M., and Xia, J. (2004). Water problems and hydrological research in the Yellow River and the Huai and Hai River basins of China. *Hydrological Processes*, 18, 2197–2210.

Liu, C., and Yu. J. (2001). Groundwater exploitation and its impact on the environment in the North China Plain. *Water International*, 26, 265–272.

Liu, J., Liu, M., Tian, H. Q., Zhuang, D., Zhang, Z., Zhang, W., Tang, X., and Deng, X. (2005). Spatial and temporal patterns of China's cropland during 1990–2000: An analysis based on Landsat TM data. *Remote Sensing of Environment*, 98, 442–456.

Liu, Y., Stanturf, J., and Lu, H. (2008). Modeling the potential of the Northern China forest shelterbelt in improving hydroclimate conditions. *Journal of American Water Resources Association*, 44, 5, 1–17.

Lu, N., Wilske, B., Ni, J., John, R., and Chen, J. (2009). Climate change in Inner Mongolia from 1955 through 2005. *Environmental Research Letters*, 4, 045006.

Lu, N., S. Chen; B. Wilske; G. Sun, and Chen, J. (2011). Evapotranspiration and soil water relationships in a range of disturbed and undisturbed ecosystems in the semi-arid Inner Mongolia, China. *Journal of Plant Ecology*, 4, 49–60.

Lu, Y., Fu, B., Feng, X., Zeng, Y., Liu, Y., et al. (2012). A Policy-Driven Large Scale Ecological Restoration: Quantifying Ecosystem Services Changes in the Loess Plateau of China. *PLoS ONE*, 7(2), e31782.

Ma, Z., Kang, S., Zhang, L., Tong, L., and Su, X. (2008). Analysis of impacts of climate variability and human activity on streamflow for a river basin in arid region of northwest 430 China. *Journal of Hydrology*, 352, 239–249.

McVicar, T. R., Li, C. T., Van Niel, T. G., Zhang, L., Li, R., Yang, Q. K., Zhang, X. P., Mu, X. M; Wen, Z. M., Liu, W. Z., Zhao, Y. A., Liu, Z. H., Gao, P. (2007). Developing a decision support tool for China's re-vegetation program: Simulating regional impacts of afforestation on average annual streamflow in the Loess Plateau. *Forest Ecology Management*, 251, 65–81.

Miao, H., Chen, S., Chen, J., Zhang, W., Zhang, P., Wei, L., Han, X., and Lin, G. (2009). Cultivation and grazing altered evapotranspiration and dynamics in Inner Mongolia steppes. *Agricultural and Forest Meteorology*, 149, 1810–1819.

Ohte, N., Koba, K., Yoshikawa, K., Sugimoto, A., Matsuo, N., Kabeya, N., and Wang, L. (2003). Water utilization of natural and planted trees in the semiarid desert of Inner Mongolia, China. *Ecological Applications*, 13, 337–351.

Piao, S., Ciais, P., Huang, Y., Shen, Z., Peng, S., Li, J., Zhou, L., Liu, H., Ma, Y., Ding, Y., Friedlingstein, P., Liu, C., Tan, K., Yu, Y., Zhang, T., and Fang, J. (2010). The impacts of climate change on water resources and agriculture in China. *Nature*, 467, 43–51.

Qi, J., Chen, J., Wan, S., and Ai, L. (2012). Understanding the Coupled Natural and Human Systems in the Dryland East Asia. *Environmental Research Letters*, 7, 015202, doi:10.1088/1748-9326/7/1/015202

Rienecker, M. M., Suarez, M. J., Gelaro, R., Todling, R., Bacmeister, J., Liu, E., et al. (2011). MERRA—NASA's Modern-Era Retrospective Analysis for Research and Applications. *Journal of Climate*, 24, 3624–3648.

Rustomji, P., Zhang, X., Hairsine, P., Zhang, L., and Zhao, J. (2008). River sediment load and concentration responses to changes in hydrology and catchment management in the Loess Plateau region of China. *Water Resourource Research*, 44, W00A04.

Sato, Y., Ma, X., Xu, J., Matsuoka, M., Zheng, H., Liu, C., and Fukushima, Y. (2008). Analysis of long-term water balance in the source area of the Yellow River basin. *Hydrological Processes*, 22, 1618–1629.

Scanlon, B. R., Keese, K. E., Flint, A. L., Flint, L. E., Gaye, C. B., Edmunds, W. M., and Simmers, I. (2006). Global synthesis of groundwater recharge in semiarid and arid regions. *Hydrological Processes*, 20, 3335–3370.

Shiklomanov, A. I., Lammers, R. B., Lettenmaier, D., Polischuk, Y., Savichev, O., and Smith, L. C. (2012). Hydrological changes: historical analysis, contemporary status and future projections. In: Gutman P.Y. and Groisman, G (Eds.). *Regional Environmental Changes in Siberia and Their Global Consequences*. Springer, 111–155.

Siebert, S., Döll, P., Hoogeveen, J., Faures, J. M., Frenken, K., and Feick, S. (2005). Development and validation of the global map of irrigated areas. *Hydrology and Earth System Science*, 9, 535–547.

Sorg, A., Bolch, T., Stoffel, M., Solomina, O., and Beniston, M. (2012). Climate change impacts on glaciers and runoff in Tien Shan (Central Asia). *Nature Climate Change*, doi:10.1038/nclimate1592.

Sun, G., Zhou, G., Zhang, Z., Wei, X., McNulty, S. G., and Vose, J. M. (2006). Potential water yield reduction due to forestation across China. *Journal of Hydrology*, 328, 548–558.

Sun, G., Alstad, K., Chen, J., Chen, S., Ford, C. R., Lin, G., Liu, C., Lu N., McNulty, S. G., Miao, H., Noormets, A., Vose, J. M., Wilske, B., Zeppel, M., Zhang, Y., and Zhang, Z. (2011). A general predictive model for estimating monthly ecosystem evapotranspiration. *Ecohydrology*, 4, 245–255.

Tao, F., Yokozawa, M., Hayashi, Y., and Lin, E. (2003). Changes in agricultural water demands and soil moisture in China over the last half-century and their effects on agricultural production. *Agriculture and Forest Meteorology*, 118, 251–261.

Wang, G., Xia, J., and Chen, J. (2009). Quantification of effects of climate variations and human activities on runoff by a monthly water balance model: A case study of the Chaobai River basin in Northern China. *Water Resource. Research*, 45, W00A11.

Wang, S., B. Fu, C.-S. He, G. Sun, G.Y. Gao. (2011). A comparative analysis of forest cover and catchment water yield relationships in Northern China. *Forest Ecol. Manage.* doi:10.1016/j.foreco.2011.06.013.

Wang, S. P., Zhang, Z., Sun, G., McNulty, S. G., Zhang, H., Li, J., and Zhang, M. (2008). Long-term streamflow response to climatic variability in the Loess Plateau, China. *Journal of the American Water Resources Association*, 44, 5, 1098–1107.

Wang, X., Brown-Mitic, C., Kang, E., Zhang, J., and Li, X. (2004). Evapotranspiration of *Caragana korshinskii* communities in a revegetated desert area: Tengger Desert, China. *Hydrological Processes*, 18, 3293–3303.

Wang, Y., Yu, P., Xiong, W., Shen, Z., Guo, M., Shi, Z., Du, A., and Wang, L. (2008). Water yield reduction after afforestation and related processes in the semi-arid Liupan Mountains, Northwest China. *Journal of the American Water Resources Association*, 44, 5, 1086–1097.

Wang, Y., Yu, P., Feger, K., Wei, X., Sun, G., Bonell, M., Xiong, W., Zhang, S., and Xu, L. (2011). Annual runoff and evapotranspiration of forestlands and non-forestlands in selected basins of the Loess Plateau of China. *Ecohydrology*, 4, 277–287.

Wilske, B., Lu, N., Wei, L., Chen, S., Zha, T., Liu, C., Xu, W., Noormets, A., Huang, J., Wei, Y., Chen, J., Zhang, A., Ni, J., Sun, G., Guo, K., McNulty, S., John, J., Chen, J., Han, X., and Lin, G. (2009). Poplar plantation has the potential to alter water balance in semiarid Inner Mongolia. *Journal of Environmental Management*, 90, 2762–2770.

Wisser, D., Frolking S., Douglas E. M., Fekete B. M., Vörösmarty C. J., and Schumann A. H. (2008). Global irrigation water demand: Variability and uncertainties arising from agricultural and climate data sets. *Geophysical Research Letters*, 35, L24408.

Wilcox, B. P., and Thurow, T. L. (2006). Emerging issues in rangeland ecohydrology: Vegetation change and the water cycle. *Rangeland Ecology and Management*, 59, 220–224.

Xia, J., Wang, Z., Wang, G., and Tan, G. (2004). The renewability of water resources and its quantification in the Yellow River basin, China. *Hydrological Processes*, 18, 2327–2236.

Xia, J., Liu, C., Ding, Y., Jia, S., and Lin, Z. (2011). *Water Issues: Vision in China.* Beijing: Science Press.

Xiao, J., Zhuang, Q., Baldocchi, D. D., Law, B. E., Richardson, A. D., Chen, J., et al. (2008). Estimation of net ecosystem carbon exchange of the conterminous United States by combining MODIS and AmeriFlux data. *Agricultural and Forest Meteorology*, 148, 1827–1847.

Xiao, J., Zhuang, Q., Liang, E., McGuire, A. D., Moody, A., Kicklighter, D. W., and Melillo, J. M. (2009). Twentieth century droughts and their impacts on terrestrial carbon cycling in China. *Earth Interactions*, 13, 010, 1–31.

Xu, J. X. (2005). Temporal variation of river flow renewability in the middle Yellow River and the influencing factors. *Hydrological Processes*, 19, 1871–1882.

Xu, J., Grumbine, E., Shrestha, A., Eriksson, M., Yang, X., Wang, Y., and Wilkes, A. (2009). The melting Himalyas: Cascading effects of climate change on water, biodiversity and livelihoods. *Conservation Biology*, 23, 520–530.

Yang, J. P., Ding, Y. J., Chen, R. S., Liu, S. Y., and Lu, A. X. (2003). Causes of glacier change in the source regions of the Yangtze and Yellow Rivers on the Tibetan Plateau. *Journal of Glaciology*, 49, 539–546.

Yang, D., Li, C., Hu, H., Lei, Z., Yang, S., Kusuda, T., Koike, T., and Musiake, K. (2004). Analysis of water resources variability in the Yellow River of China during the last half century using historical data. *Water Resources Research*, 40, W06502.

Yang, D., Shao, W., Yeh, P. J., Yang, H., Kanae, S., and Oki, T. (2009). Impact of vegetation coverage on regional water balance in the nonhumid regions of China. *Water Resources Research*, 45, W00A14.

Zhang, Z., Wang, S., Sun, G., McNulty, S. G., Zhang, H., Li, J., Zhang, M., Klaghofer, E., and Strauss, P. (2008). Evaluation of the MIKE SHE Model for Application in the Loess Plateau, China. *Journal of the American Water Resources Association*, 44, 5,1108–1120.

Zhang, L., Dawes, W. R., and Walker, G. R. (2001). Response of mean annual evapotranspiration to vegetation changes at catchment scale. *Water Resource Research*, 37(3), 701–708.

Zhang, X. P., Zhang, L., McVicar, T. R., Van Niel, T. G., Li, L., Li, R., Yang, Q., and Liang, W. (2008a). Modeling the impact of afforestation on mean annual streamflow in the Loess Plateau, China. *Hydrological Processes*, 22, 1996–2004.

Zhang, X. P., Zhang, L., Zhao, J., Rustomji, P., and Hairsine, P. (2008b). Responses of streamflow to changes in climate and land use/cover in the Loess Plateau, China. *Water Resources Research*, 44, W00A07.

Zhang, Y., Zhang, Z., Sun, G., Zha, T., Noormets, A., Chen, J., McNulty, S., and Chen, L. (2012). Water balance of a poplar plantation forest in suburb Beijing, China. *Environmental Management* (in review).

Zheng, H., Zhang, L., Zhu, R., Liu, C., Sato, Y., and Fukushima, Y. (2009). Responses of streamflow to climate and land surface change in the headwaters of the Yellow River Basin. *Water Resource Research*, 45, W00A19.

Authors Information

Ge Sun[1]*, Xiaoming Feng[2], Jingfeng Xiao[3], Alex Shiklomanov[3], Shengping Wang[4], Zhiqiang Zhang[5], Nan Lu[2], Shuai Wang[2], Liding Chen[2], Bojie Fu[2], Yaning Chen[6], Jiquan Chen[7]

1. Eastern Forest Environmental Threat Assessment Center, Southern Research Station, USDA Forest Service, Raleigh, NC 27606, USA
2. Research Center for Eco-Environmental Sciences, Chinese Academy of Sciences, Beijing 100085, P.R. China
3. Earth Systems Research Center, Institute for the Study of Earth, Oceans, and Space, University of New Hampshire, Durham, NH 03824, USA
4. Key Laboratory of Regional Energy System Optimization, North China Electric Power University, Beijing 102206, P.R. China
5. College of Soil and Water Conservation, Beijing Forestry University, Beijing 100083, P.R. China
6. Xinjiang Institute of Ecology and Geography, Chinese Academy of Science, Ürümqi 830011, P.R. China
7. Department of Environmental Sciences, University of Toledo, Toledo, OH 43606-3390, USA
*   Corresponding author

Chapter 9

Examining Changes in Land Cover and Land Use, Regional Climate and Dust in Dryland East Asia and Their Linkages within the Earth System

Irina N. Sokolik, Kremena Darmenova, Jianping Huang, Olga Kalashnikova, Yasunori Kurosaki, and Xin Xi

Summary: The goal of the chapter is to examine the changes that have occurred in dust aerosols, land cover and land use and regional climate in Dryland East Asia (DEA), the major processes governing these changes, including coupling and feedbacks, and implications for the human-environment-climate systems. Comparison to drylands in Central Asia is provided to facilitate discussion of common features and regional specifics of the world's drylands. The chapter starts by documenting the major historical changes in land cover and land use (LCLU) that have occurred in the region during past decades (since the 1950s). These changes are explored in the context of variations and changes in regional and global climate and human activities, including socio-economic transformations specific to the region. The main emphasis is on LCLU changes and climate variables that affect the production of wind-blown dust. Dust emission assessment is presented on the basis of integrative analyses of historical LCLU maps, climatological data and the regional coupled dust modeling system WRF-Chem-DuMo. The intensity and frequency of dust events are examined by using historical data of visibility and weather types provided by meteorological stations. Analysis also includes multi-satellite, multi-sensor records of atmospheric aerosols for the past decade. Building on observational data and modeling results, the interactions among LCLU, climate, and dust are addressed across the broad range of spatial and temporal scales and implications of the dust impacts for the human-environment-climate systems are explored.

9.1 Introduction

Vulnerability of terrestrial ecosystems, food security, water resources, air quality and human health in a changing climate are becoming the most pressing problems of the 21st century. These problems are especially severe in the drylands that cover over 40% of the Earth's land surface, and are home to more than a third of the world's population. Facing harsh climatic conditions, these regions are particularly prone to climate and environmental changes, as well as human perturbations. Understanding the vulnerability and resilience of human-environment-climate (HEC) systems is a major scientific challenge (IPCC, 2007).

In recent decades, the dramatic increase in the human population has had a crucial impact on Earth's drylands. Overcultivation of poor soils, inappropriate irrigation practices, human-induced wind erosion, severe trampling and heavy grazing, deforestation, urbanization, building and road construction, off-road vehicle use, and tourism are among the anthropogenic drivers affecting drylands in complex ways and at multiple scales. Resulting changes in landscapes as well as climate change are thought to have a particularly significant impact on atmospheric dust aerosol by altering the areal extent of dust sources, and promoting or suppressing dust emission. These effects have regional and global consequences that have been receiving increasing interest in recent years, as awareness about the significance of the multiple roles dust plays in the HEC systems grows (Ravi et al., 2011; Shao et al., 2011).

Wind erosion and massive dust storms have been a long-standing problem in China and Mongolia. There have been numerous national and international efforts to combat desertified and degraded lands prone to dust emission. The so-called "Green Wall" project in China, which involved planning approximately 9 million acres of trees in an effort to prevent dust erosion, has been one of the largest ecological restoration efforts in history. The impacts of Asian dust are not only regional, but may also affect areas thousands of kilometers from the dust source, making interactions between climate, land and Asian dust relevant globally. The most recent IPCC (2007) report identifies LCLU change (via surface albedo) and atmospheric dust as two of the most important climate forcing drivers, yet these were considered as two independent factors. The need to study the linkages between LCLU change, climate and atmospheric dust by treating them as part of the coupled HEC system has been previously highlighted (Ravi et al., 2011; Shao et al., 2011). At the same time, there has been a growing recognition of the complexities associated with the various processes and feedbacks involved in LCLU-dust-climate interactions that necessitates the integration of historical records, satellite data, and models to address these issues.

The focus of this chapter is on the linkages between LCLU, atmospheric dust, and climate in drylands of East Asia (DEA). There have been numerous studies of atmospheric dust in this region (e.g., Zou and Zhai, 2004; Zhao et al., 2006; Lee and Sohn, 2011), with some addressing connections to climate, meteorology, and LCLU. Collectively, these studies establish a general understanding of major dust sources, seasonality of dust events, their long-term frequency, and their inter-annual variability. At the climate-relevant scales, practically all research is based on long-term data records that have been provided by meteorological stations in China since the 1950s (Wang et al., 2008b) and in Mongolia since the 1930s (Natsagdorj et al., 2003). In the past two decades or so, satellite data offer a unique tool for studying land characteristics, dust aerosol, and meteorology/climate at the larger regional scale. There have also been various improvements in the regional and global models for representing dust-related processes (Gong et al., 2006; Uno et al., 2006; Darmenova et al., 2009). Building on research conducted by the authors as part of the Northern Eurasia Earth Science Partnership Initiativel (NEESPI) and Monsoon Asia Integrated Regional Study (MAIRS) programs, this chapter concentrates on addressing the LCLU-dust-climate linkages in DEA with an emphasis on the decadal time scale, starting in the 1950s. Organization of the chapter is as follows. Section 9.2 presents new estimates of decadal dust emission performed with the regional coupled dust modeling system WRF-Chem-DuMo based on reconstructed LCLU changes and climatological reanalysis data. Section 9.3 discusses observation-based climatology of atmospheric dust in the context of LCLU and regional climate changes. Section 9.4 provides a satellite perspective for the past decade, and Section 9.5 explores the impacts of Asian dust on the HEC systems.

9.2 Assessment of Decadal Dust Emission Based on Historical LCLU, Regional Climate and the Regional Coupled Dust Modeling System WRF-Chem-DuMo

Measurements of emission and entrainment of dust aerosols into the atmosphere are extremely limited and hard to obtain. Various simplified modeling approaches have been proposed over the years, largely as part of wind erosion estimates, i.e., saltation, the horizontal movement of soil particles. Some of these were applied to the DEA region. For instance, Xuan and Sokolik (2002) and Xuan et al. (2004) estimated the multi-year mean dust emission rates in Northern China and southern Mongolia employing a formula developed by the U.S. Environmental Protection Agency for fugitive dust. More recently, there have been significant efforts directed towards the development of a dedicated dust emission parameterization to simulate atmospheric dust for use in regional and global models (Marticorena and Bergametti, 1995; Shao et al., 1996). To date, practically all Global Climate Models (GCM), Regional Climate Models (RCM) and numerical weather prediction models treat dust aerosols. Despite this progress, the majority of regional models and all GCMs still rely on the so-called "simple" type of dust emission scheme which uses a fixed value of threshold friction velocity regardless of land surface properties. This is despite the fact that the threshold friction velocity, the minimum friction velocity necessary to set soil particles in motion, is a function of land surface characteristics such as soil particle sizes, aeolian roughness, soil moisture, soil mineralogical composition, vegetation coverage and its type, among others. The LCLU changes can affect these land surface properties in multiple ways and across a broad range of spatiotemporal scales, with implications for dust emission.

Two state-of-the-art physically-based dust emission schemes have been developed recently that are capable of treating both the land surface properties and meteorology: Marticorena and Bergametti (1995) and Shao et al. (1996) with some recent improvements (e.g., Shao et al., 2011). These schemes were incorporated into the mesoscale National Center for Atmospheric Research (NCAR) Weather Research and Forecast (WRF) model as part of the development of the coupled regional dust modeling system WRF-Chem-DuMo targeted at the drylands in Asia (Darmenova et al., 2009, Darmenova and Sokolik, 2012). Dust emission schemes are fully coupled with the Noah land surface model and meteorological fields within WRF-Chem-DuMo, providing an advanced modeling capability for examining the linkages and coupling between the LCLU changes, climate and dust in Central and East Asia.

Addressing these linkages with WRF-Chem-DuMo necessitates the reconstruction of the historical LCLU changes and the use of climatological reanalysis data for targeted time periods of interest. Although a great amount of effort has been devoted to documenting LCLU changes in DEA, as well as at the large continental scale and globally, this effort, to a large degree, has been concentrated on providing information in support of carbon cycle-climate studies, as part of Intergovernmental Panel on Climate Change (IPCC) assessments, for example. Quantifying the influence of LCLU changes on dust emission, however, requires a special kind of LCLU analysis aimed at the potential dust sources such as natural deserts, gobi, sand lands, sparsely vegetated areas, shrublands, desert steppe, grassland, and agricultural fields. In addition to gridded LCLU data, several datasets such as aeolian roughness and undisturbed soil grain size distribution that are specific to physically-based dust emission schemes are needed (Darmenova et al., 2009). To support the WRF-Chem-DuMo modeling, a new dedicated database was developed as part of the Asian Dust Databank.

Figure 9.1 shows the dryland regions in Northern China and southern Mongolia that have experienced the most extensive LCLU changes since the 1950s and are of relevance to dust emission. The land cover is shown with the USGS

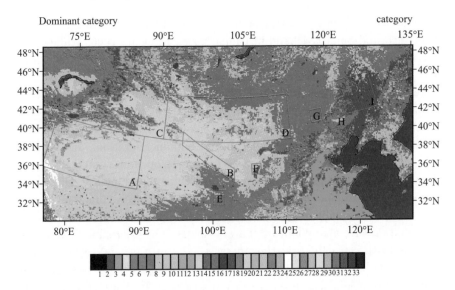

Fig. 9.1 East Asian regions that experienced extensive land-cover change during the 1950–2000 period: A) Tarim Basin, B) Hexi Corridor, C) Junggar Basin, D) Mongolian grassland and Gobi, E) Gonghe Basin, F) northern Ningxia, G) Xilin River Basin, H) Horqin Sandy Land, and I) western part of Northeast China.

Classification categories (1-33): 1—Urban and Built-Up Land, 2—Dryland Cropland and Pasture, 3—Irrigated Cropland and Pasture, 4—Mixed Dryland/Irrigated Cropland and Pasture, 5—Cropland/Grassland Mosaic, 6—Cropland/Woodland Mosaic, 7—Grassland, 8—Shrubland, 9—Mixed Shrubland/Grassland, 10—Savanna, 11—Deciduous Broadleaf Forest, 12—Deciduous Needleleaf Forest, 13—Evergreen Broadleaf Forest, 14—Evergreen Needleleaf Forest, 15—Mixed Forest, 16—Water Bodies, and 17—Herbaceous Wetland, 18—Wooded Wetland, 19—Barren or Sparsely Vegetated, 20—Herbaceous Tundra, 21—Wooded Tundra, 22—Mixed Tundra, 23—Bare Ground Tundra, 24—Snow or Ice, 25—Playa, 26—Lava, 27—White Sand, 28-30 — Unassigned, 31—Low Intensity Residential, 32—High Intensity Residential, and 33—Industrial or Commercial.

33-category land classification, which is incorporated into the WRF model by default. This data set was created from the 1-km AVHRR data collected during 1992–1993 (Eidenshink and Faundeen, 1994). Thus, it represents the LCLU state in the 1990s and is referred to hereafter as the default land cover. The land cover representative of other decades was reconstructed by changing the default land cover assignment to a certain category based on analyses of the historical LCLU changes.

Global LCLU datasets, various publications and reports, and historical records and maps were utilized for historical LCLU reconstructions. The global data include, for instance, History Database of Global Environment (HYDE) (Klein, 2001), historical cropland datasets (Ramankutty and Foley, 1999), EOS-WEBSTER Earth Science Information Partner (ESIP) datasets (http://eos-webster.sr.unh.edu/), and the dataset of annual cropland and pasture fractions developed under the ongoing Land Use Harmonization project (http://luh.sr.unh.edu/).

In addition, we have gathered various literature on LCLU in China (e.g., Atlas of Desertified and Sandified Land in China, 2008, Ta et al., 2006; Wang et al., 2008a; Wang et al., 2004; Zhang et al., 2002; Liu et al., 2005; Liu et al., 2010; Yang et al., 2005; 2010), as well as available national surveys and reports.

There have been many significant LCLU changes in DEA in response to diverse political, socioeconomic and climatic changes occurring in the region. Since the mid-20th century China experienced large-scale agricultural development that has resulted in intense land reclamation and human migration. In the early 1950s, the national land policy encouraged farmers to open up wastelands, which resulted in a sharp increase in cultivated lands (Huang et al., 2004). During the "Great Leap Forward" period (1958–1959) harmful agricultural practices in combination with unfavorable climate conditions (droughts and locust infestation) resulted in a massive abandonment of arable lands. The drier climate and lower crop yields in the late 1950s further increased the rate of land reclamation in the early 1960s (Huang et al., 2004). Since the mid-1970s to the 2000s the area of cultivated land has been steadily increasing. In contrast, the natural pastures, grasslands and steppes have been steadily decreasing as a result of over-grazing, uncontrolled land reclamation, and urbanization. Much desertification associated with sandification (i.e., sandy desertification) occurred as a blistering process on rangeland, which was climatically steppe but through sandification become covered with mass mobile sand dunes (Chen and Tang, 2005). Although natural vegetation is well adapted to its climate, human interventions make the land system more vulnerable to climatic variability. Reclamation of grassland is thought to be the most important human cause of desertification in the DEA.

Mongolian agriculture developed at a slower rate compared to the Chinese. Development of virgin lands (steppes and grasslands) was responsible for most of the expansion of arable lands. Land reclamation started in the late 1950s and the early 1960s, when 530,000 ha were developed, and continued to increase steadily throughout each five-year plan (Worden and Savada, 1989). Overgrazing has been widely blamed for grassland deterioration in the region. Cultivation of grassland has destroyed soil structure, increased soil erosion, and triggered desertification, as well as dust storm activity. The increase of sandy areas was the ultimate consequence of land degradation.

In the literature, changes that occurred in natural deserts are broadly divided into three categories: progressing, potential and other deserts (Gong et al., 2004; Yang et al., 2010). Other deserts represent the original deserts in the 1950s, while progressing and potential deserts are the main desertification areas created since then. According to a survey by the Chinese Academy of Sciences (1998), desertification has increased barren sandy lands by 144,000 km^2 and 175,000 km^2 as the progressing and potential desertification areas in China, respectively, accounting for about 15% and 19% of the current desert areas of 930,000 km^2, which includes about 850,000 km^2 of deserts in the 1950s and 80,000 km^2 of new deserts. The cause of this rapid desertification is rather complex and it could be a result of both anthropogenic and natural factors (Yang et al., 2010).

Below we briefly summarize the major historical LCLU transformations and how they were represented in terms of the WRF-Chem-DuMo land cover categories in order to model dust emission. The Tarim Basin (region A in Fig. 9.1) is located in the Xinjiang Uygur Autonomous Region (XJ) in Western China. The Taklimakan Desert, the largest mobile sandy desert in China and one of the largest sandy deserts in the world, covers much of the basin. Although it is an extremely dry region, the Tarim River Basin supports a variety of oases and arable lands. The basin produces one sixth of China's cotton, as well as grains and fruits. During the 1950s, about 3,838 km^2 of land was desertified as a result of intense land reclamation (Ta et al., 2006). In the period 1961–1962, reclamation activities ceased, resulting in abandonment of arable lands; however, they started increasing again in 1964–1967. In the default land cover, the arable land and oases around the Taklimakan are represented by a mixture of grasslands, shrublands and irrigated croplands, and pasture. To account for the increased land cultivation in 1950–1970, we replaced natural shrublands and grasslands in the default land cover with drylands, cropland and pasture categories. During the period 1970–2000, we kept the default land cover. The net expansion rate of the Taklimakan Desert is relatively low 0.009% per year (Yang et al., 2010).

In the 1950s, XJ had 52 lakes but the lake area has declined sharply by the late 1970s. The most famous example is the Lop Nor Lake. The lake was used for nuclear testing in the 1960s and it vanished completely in 1972 due to the regional precipitation deficit. We used historical maps to reconstruct the lake waterbodies in the 1950s.

The Hexi Corridor (region B in Fig. 9.1) is a well-known active dust source. According to Ta et al. (2006), land reclamation in the 1950s peaked around 1954, followed by a relatively steady decrease until 1961. Ta et al. (2006) suggested that in the Hexi Corridor, the number of dust storm days positively correlated with annual land reclamation areas in the period 1954–1961. The land-cover categories in the Hexi Corridor include bare and sparsely vegetated land, grasslands, and shrublands. To reconstruct the extensive land reclamation in the 1950s, grasslands and shrublands in the default land cover were converted to dryland cropland and pasture categories.

The Junggar Basin (region C in Fig. 9.1) is a largely steppe and semi-desert basin bordered by the Tianshan Mountains to the south and the Altay Mountains to the north. The Gurbantonggut Desert occupies a large part of the Junggar Basin. According to the HYDE database, from the 1970s to the 1990s, the grasslands/steppes surrounding the Gurbantonggut were converted to marginal croplands used for grazing. To represent the natural grasslands in the 1950s and 1960s, shrublands in the default land cover were replaced by grasslands. For the 1970s and 1980s, grasslands in the default land cover were partially replaced by shrublands to capture the land degradation and transformation from steppe to open shrublands. The Gurbantonggut Desert expands at an annual rate of 0.91% (Yang et al., 2010).

Extensive grasslands and desert steppes (region D in Fig. 9.1) cover approximately 80% of Mongolia (Erdenetuya and Khudulmur, 2002). These are extremely fragile ecosystems, easily affected by overgrazing, which can result in land degradation and desertification. According to the HYDE database, Mongolian grasslands experienced large-scale changes from 1950–1990. For this period, HYDE indicates transformation of marginal croplands to open shrubland, glassland and steppe, and intensive cropland. To reproduce the natural land cover conditions in the 1950s and 1960s, shrublands in the default land cover were replaced by the grassland category, and bare and sparsely vegetated surfaces were replaced by shrublands. For the 1970s and 1980s, shrublands and sparsely vegetated areas were expanded by decreasing grassland areas to reproduce land degradation and desertification. This region also includes the Gobi Desert, which expands into Inner Mongolia Autonomous Region (IM), China. The Gobi and Taklimakan are the major dust source regions in East Asia. In IM the annual rate of land sandification (i.e., sandy desertification) is 0.86% (Yang et al., 2010), the largest in Northern China.

The Gonghe Basin (region E in Fig. 9.1) is located in the upper reaches of the Yellow River in the northeast Qinghai-Tibetan Plateau. Land cover consists of extensive grasslands that suffered from overgrazing from the 1950s to the 1980s. Zeng et al. (2003) showed that between 1987 and 1996, moderately covered grasslands were transformed to sandy areas, while farmlands increased as a result of cultivation of densely covered grasslands. Assuming a continuous decrease in grasslands/shrublands in this region during the 1950s–1980s, we replaced this category with grassland.

The northern Ningxia Hui Autonomous Region (region F in Fig. 9.1) is an arid and semi-arid region that includes parts of the Helan Mountains and the Yinchuan Plain. Using Landsat data, Wu and Zhang (2003) showed that the region experienced extensive farmland expansion from 1987 to 1999. Land cover changes were extrapolated back to the 1950s by assuming gradual land degradation and desertification in this region. For the 1950s–1970s, we replaced dryland cropland and pasture with grasslands, while for the 1980s–1990s the default land cover remained.

The Xilin River Basin (region G in Fig. 9.1) is a semi-arid region located on the eastern Inner Mongolia Plateau. The basin has experienced grassland degradation during the time period 1987–2000 (Chen et al., 2004; Liu et al., 2010). Dense grasslands were converted to fragmented and sparse grasslands. For the 1980s and 1990s, the dominant grassland land-cover type was kept unchanged because the U.S. Geological Survey (USGS) classification does not have a separate category for fragmented/dense/sparse grasslands; however, a constant decrease in grasslands was applied for the last 50 years.

The Horqin Sandy Land (region H in Fig. 9.1) is a semi-arid region located in Northeast China. Brogaard and Prieler (1998) found an improvement in grassland conditions during 1975–1989. A more recent analysis by Li et al. (2011) also indicated long-term vegetation increase from 1982 to 2006 in a large portion of IM. About 17% of the region showed a significant increasing trend. To reflect the improved grassland cover in the 1980s, we replaced the shrublands with mixed grassland/shrublands, keeping the default shrubland land cover in the 1990s.

The western part of Northeast China (region I in Fig. 9.1) is a semi-arid region that occupies part of the Songnen and Horqin grasslands. Huang et al. (2004) reported on the complex dynamics of the land cover in this region, identifying two peak periods in cultivated land area—the early 1950s and the late 1970s. As a result of the local policy of pasture conservation and the grassland responsibility system, grasslands increased in the early 1980s. During 1986–2000, grasslands and forestlands gradually declined. The HYDE database shows the conversion of grassland/steppes to marginal croplands from 1950–1970. A steady decrease of woodland and grassland and an increase in croplands from 1954 to 2000 was reported in the literature. The default cropland/grassland was changed to grasslands for the 1950s and 1960s to represent these LCLU changes.

Figure 9.2a–e presents the historical reconstruction of land-cover and land-use patterns discussed above. Figure 9.2f–j also presents, as an example, monthly mean (April) vertical fluxes of emitted atmospheric dust in a selected year for each decade (1955, 1964, 1975, 1988 and 1998). Dust fluxes were computed at 10 km resolution with WRF-Chem-DuMo driven by National Centers for Environmental Prediction (NCEP) reanalysis data of respective years. Spatiotemporal patterns of dust fluxes, therefore, depend on both a given state of LCLU and year-specific meteorology. Modeled dust emission fields show a high degree of spatial heterogeneity across the DEA region. In the Taklimakan, the largest amount of dust emission is seen at the edges of the desert where the most human activities occur. Simulated dust emission is particularly prominent in southern Mongolia, Alxa Plateau, and Hexi Corridor. Smaller and patchier emission spots occur in Northeastern China.

To our knowledge, our study is the first attempt to incorporate LCLU historical dynamics into assessments of atmospheric dust fluxes within a coupled mesoscale model. Although we employ the state-of-art physically-based dust emission schemes to account for land surface properties in response to LCLU changes, still there are many assumptions involved and some critical input data (e.g., aeolian roughness and undisturbed soil grain size distribution) are not available at the required spatiotemporal resolution in the historical context (Darmenova and Sokolik, 2012). One critical weakness is that the model does not

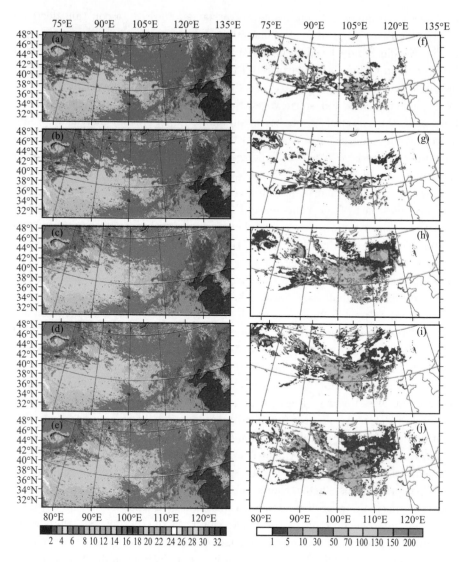

Fig. 9.2 (a–e) Reconstrucred historical LCLU (per decade) and (f–g) simulated dust monthly mean (April) emission fluxes $(\mathrm{g\,km^{-2}\,s^{-1}})$.

simulate the vegetation lifecycle (growth and decay), which limits its applicability in studies of the vegetation–dust emission interactions at all relevant scales. A recent review by Shinoda et al. (2011) provides a comprehensive analysis of the major issues involved in the modeling of dust emission from vegetated surfaces such as temperate grasslands in DEA, and highlights the needs for further research.

The only other studies that have modeled the long-term atmospheric dust emission in East Asia are Hara et al. (2006) and Zhang et al. (2003). The latter study was followed by climatological analyses of atmospheric dust loading (Zhao et al., 2006) and trans-Pacific transport (Gong et al., 2006). None of these studies considered the historical dynamics of LCLU, so dust sources were not changed with time in the models. A study by Zhang et al. (2003), however, made some adjustments to dust sources in order to reflect the expansion of deserts. In turn, Hara et al. (2006) used the simple type of dust emission parameterization with a fixed value of threshold friction velocity which does not depend on LCLU and surface properties.

Zhao et al. (2006) and Gong et al. (2006) used the Northern Aerosol Regional Climate Model (NARCM) to produce a simulated 44-year dust climatology for the spring season from 1960–2003. The model was run at a horizontal resolution of 100 km, which is much coarser than our study with WRF-Chem-DuMo at 10 km resolution. These studies revealed significant interannual variability in dust emission and atmospheric dust load, concluding that meteorological and climatic variations play a major role in explaining the dynamics of dust emission and storm frequencies. El Niño and La Niña, the two opposite phases of the El Niño-Southern Oscillation (ENSO) cycle, were found to affect the dust emission and the transport of Asian dust across the Pacific. In particular, Asian dust emission from the major source regions was found to be lower in El Niño years (negative Southern Oscillation Index). Gong et al. (2006) further showed that the anomalies of dust loading for eight typical El Niño and eight La Niña years from the 44-year averaged values exhibited contrasting behavior in most parts of China, with a sharp negative anomaly for El Niño years and a positive anomaly for La Niña years.

Several studies have attempted to predict changes in Asian dust emission in the future in response to global-scale climate variability and/or changes in the mesoscale meteorology of the region (e.g., cyclonic activity). For instance, Zhu et al. (2008) suggested that the warming trend around Lake Baikal induces a weakening of the westerly jet stream and the atmospheric baroclinicity in Northern China and Mongolia, which in turn suppress the frequency of occurrence and the intensity of the Mongolian cyclones and thus result in decreasing dust occurrence in this region. They suggested that this mechanism will likely further reduce spring dust events in the future global warming scenario. Tsunematsu et al. (2011) reached similar conclusions in a study based on numerical experiments comparing the modeled future climate (2091–2100) and the recent climate (1991–2000), although potential changes in vegetation were not considered. On the other hand, studies that considered future changes in vegetation associated with CO_2 fertilization in a warming climate (e.g., Mahowald and Luo, 2003) also suggested a decrease in the future Asian dust activity. However, these hypotheses seem to be in conflict with increasing dust trends in IM and Mongolia occurring concurrently with increasing temperature in the region as discussed below (see Section 9.3).

Combined past studies and our research demonstrate the complex relationships between the changes in LCLU and climate and associated changes in spatiotemporal patterns of dust emission, indicating that the relative importance of LCLU varies from source to source across the DEA region. The influence of LCLU changes on dust emission is strongly modulated by changes in winds caused by climate variability or climate change. There appears to be little change in the seasonal cycle of dust emission in DEA, with the spring season being a highest dust emission period. In contrast, significant variability of dust emission occurred at the interannual and decadal scales.

9.3　Observation-based Dust Climatology and Its Relationship to LCLU and Regional Climate

Modeling and long-term observations of visibility and dust-related weather types recorded at meteorological stations in China and Mongolia are the only sources of information available for establishing an observation-based dust climatology in the DEA region. Despite the region-wide influence of climatological factors (e.g., El Niño or La Niña years) and ongoing warming, there have been distinct differences in the spatial distribution of dust event occurrence across DEA. The heterogeneous patterns of the dust event frequency seem to be a common feature in East Asia and Central Asia, reflecting a complex interplay between meteorology and LCLU in controlling the emission, transport and removal of dust. Figure 9.3 shows spatial and temporal changes in atmospheric dust in Central and East Asia in terms of decadal frequencies of by World Meteorological Organization (WMO) dust present weather in spring (March–May). For this analysis, dust events were defined on the basis of WMO present weather codes 06–09, 30–35, and 98 from 1,456 weather stations located in the study domain for the time period from 1950 to present. The spatial and temporal distribution of dust events exhibits a complex pattern, showing multiple differences between East and Central Asian regions, as well as variation from station to station within the same region. For instance, dust weather frequencies increased at several stations along the Syr Dariya River, but decreased at most stations in Central Asia. In addition, our analysis of 50-year ground-based visibility data revealed a decreasing tendency in dust storm frequency (defined as the number of dust events with visibility below 1 km) in the Aral Sea region (see Fig. 8 in Groisman et al., 2009). This result demonstrates that the formation of a new large dust source, in this case resulting from the desiccation of the Aral Sea, does not necessarily

WMO Dust Weather Frequency March–May

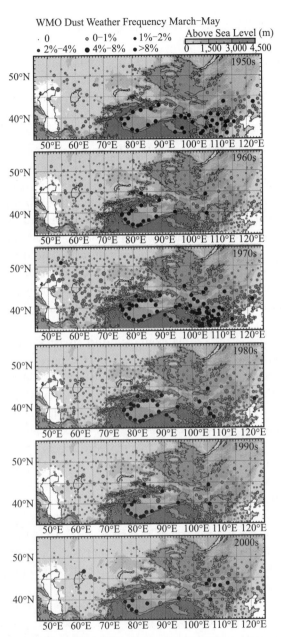

Fig. 9.3 Spatial and temporal changes in atmospheric dust in Central and East Asia shown in terms of decadal frequencies of WMO dust present weather (see text for further details).

lead to increased frequency of dust storms in the region. Decreased near-surface wind speeds over steppe regions of southern Russia and Kazakhstan caused by changes in atmospheric circulation counterbalanced the increase in dust source extent (Darmenova and Sokolik, 2007), conversely increasing trends in moderate dust outbreaks (visibility < 10 km) were found.

Furthermore, our analysis revealed that changes in LCLU and climatic factors affect not only frequency of dust events but also their onset, duration and intensity. To illustrate, Figure 9.4 presents the duration of total dust events and dust storms at two stations: Aralskoe More, Central Asia (top panel), and Ejin Qi, IM (bottom panel). Total dust events are defined here as the sum of dust storms, blowing dust events, and suspended dust events. The upper plot in each panel shows accumulated hours of dust events and dust storms which were calculated based on the combined visibility and dust weather criterion. Color bars in Figure 9.4 show the number of days of dust events (green) and dust storms (red) with different total accumulated hours represented by corresponding rows. Three-hour duration is considered as a single dust event due to the three-hour observation frequency. Figure 9.4 shows various differences in duration and dust event frequency at two compared stations. This suggests that establishing a new metric for developing the dust climatology, going beyond dust event frequencies alone, will be useful for obtaining more comprehensive characterization of dust events.

A more recent study by Kurosaki et al. (2011) examined dust weather data (from meteorological stations shown in Fig. 9.5) with an attempt to delineate the effects of meteorology and surface conditions in atmospheric dust trends. They showed that in the past decade the frequency of dust weather increased in Mongolia, eastern IM, and Northeastern China (see Fig. 9.5), while the frequency of high-speed winds showed no change or decreased. This suggests that changes in land-surface conditions were the likely factor causing increased dust emission. To explain this result, Kurosaki et al. (2011) hypothesized that decreased precipitation in summer caused a reduction in the amount of vegetation, resulting in a decreased amount of dead-brown leaves in spring of the following year, and therefore exposing more land surfaces prone to dust emission. However, this hypothesis cannot explain all differences in dust trends observed across the DEA region. Other factors such as snow cover, soil freeze/thaw and soil moisture in spring could play a role, as well as human activities such as cultivation and grazing.

The increasing tendency of dust events in eastern DEA is also supported by other independent studies. Lee and Sohn (2011) reported trends in dust events over China and Mongolia based on an analysis of 34 years (1974–2007) of visibility data and 10 years (1998–2007) of WMO dust weather type data. Dust occurrences in Mongolia and northern IM increased over the 1998–2007 period, while most dust source regions in China experienced a continuous decrease over the 34-year data period. They suggested that increased dust occurrences in Mongolia and in IM was caused by degraded surface vegetation and reduced soil moisture associated with intensified drought conditions after the mid-1990s.

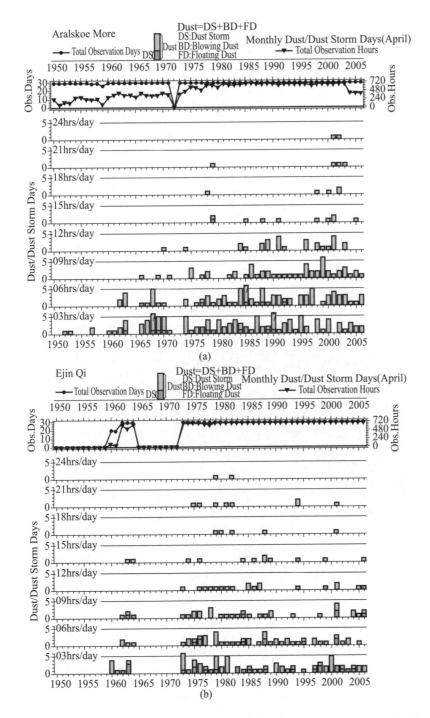

Fig. 9.4 Duration (in hours) of dust events and dust storms at station Aralskoe More in Central Asia (a) and station Ejin Qi in IM (b).

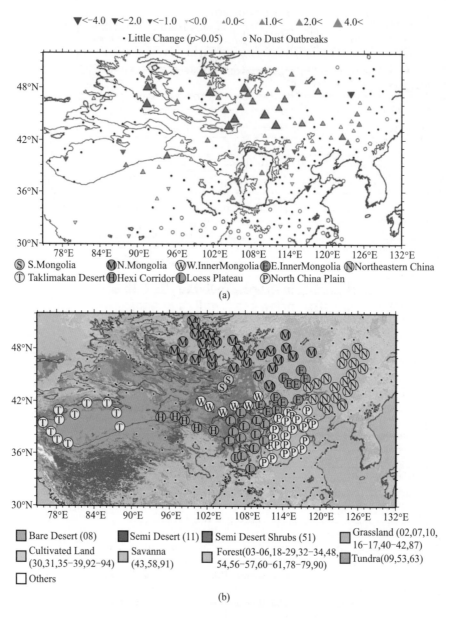

Fig. 9.5 (a) Change in dust outbreak frequency for April from the 1990s to the 2000s, which is the difference between frequency for 1990–1999 and that for 2000–2009. Inverted triangles and triangles denote statistically significant frequency decreases and increases, respectively. Dots denote statistically insignificant changes. (b) Distribution of meteorological stations (denoted by symbols indicating geographical regions) used for analysis (modified from Kurosaki et al., 2011).

These results suggest that recent increases in dust events over Korea and Japan are most likely linked to increased dust occurrences in Mongolia and IM.

In South Korea, an increasing trend of dust events has been observed since the 1980s (Kim, 2008). This long-term increasing tendency in South Korea differs from the trend of dust occurrence days reported for Northern China (e.g., Zou and Zhai, 2004; Zhu et al., 2008) and Mongolia (Natsagdorj et al., 2003) but is in agreement with Kurosaki et al.(2011) and Lee and Sohn (2011). The difference in the long-term trend estimates between the studies may be attributed to regional differences in dust occurrence and transport. In addition, differences in the definition of a dust event and the non-standardized methods of observing atmospheric dust in these countries may also be responsible for the different trends reported in the literature. Although introducing a unified methodology may resolve these issues, the sparsity of meteorological stations, especially in active dust source regions, poses a significant problem in characterizing the spatiotemporal dust distribution and trends; therefore, increasing attention has been given to satellite-based aerosol products.

9.4   A Satellite Perspective on the Last Decade

A measurement-based characterization of dust aerosols on regional to global scales can be achieved only through satellite remote sensing due to the large spatial and temporal heterogeneities of aerosol distribution (Sokolik, 2003). Given the fact that available satellite aerosol data have about a decade-long record, our study and several other recent studies (Guo et al., 2011; Hsu et al., 2012) have attempted to establish a satellite-based dust climatology in dust sources in China and Mongolia using the aerosol optical depth and/or aerosol index retrieved from satellite observations. Several sensors onboard NASA satellites have provided aerosol optical depth (AOD) over the extended time period, including Total Ozone Mapping Spectrometer (TOMS), Ozone Monitoring Instrument (OMI), Sea-viewing Wide Field-of-view Sensor (SeaWiFS), Moderate Resolution Imaging Spectroradiometer (MODIS), and Multi-angle Imaging Spectro-Radiometer (MISR). In addition, TOMS and OMI provide UV-absorbing aerosol index (AI), which is commonly used for dust detection (e.g., Darmenova et al., 2005).

A combination of multi-satellite, multi-sensor products enables the examination of the spatiotemporal behavior of AOD and AI across the DEA region which can be interpreted in terms of the dust spatiotemporal distribution. Figure 9.6 shows the satellite-based aerosol climatology computed from multi-annual monthly mean aerosol products for March, April and May from MISR, OMI and MODIS. The MODIS instrument flies onboard two NASA Earth Observing System (EOS) satellites: Terra and Aqua. Both sensors have near-global coverage daily. The MODIS Deep Blue retrieval technique (Hsu et al., 2004) uses the MODIS blue channels, where surface reflectance is low, to retrieve AOD over arid and semi-arid regions. The 7-year (2003–2009) AOD record from MODIS-Terra and the five-year (2005–2009) AOD from MODIS-Aqua were used to generate mean values shown in Fig. 9.6.

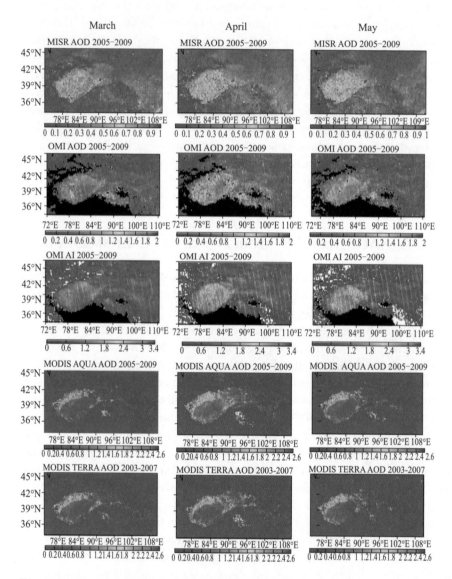

Fig. 9.6 Satellite perspective on the dust climatology: multi-annual mean AOD for March, April and May from MISR, OMI and MODIS.

The MISR sensor flies onboard the Terra satellite together with MODIS. MISR benefits from its multi-angle capability to perform simultaneous retrievals of aerosol and surface properties over arid and semi-arid regions with high reflectivity (Kalashnikova et al., 2011). The MISR instrument has a relatively narrow swath (400 km), providing full coverage over mid-latitudes in 6–7 days. The MISR climatology data in Figure 9.6 was computed with MISR AOD (558 nm) from the latest version (V22) of the standard MISR Level 2 aerosol product, gridded to $0.25° \times 0.25°$.

OMI is a push-broom imaging spectrometer that measures backscattered solar radiation in the spectral range of 270–500 nm. The 2,600-km wide swath provides global coverage on a daily basis. The OMI pixel size is 13 km $\times$ 24 km in the nadir direction. OMI AOD (500 nm) and AI Level 2 products were gridded to $0.25° \times 0.25°$ and averaged to monthly products in order to compute the multi-annual mean shown in Figure 9.6.

Figure 9.6 presents several important features in the spatial pattern of multi-year mean monthly AOD in spring (March, April and May). All satellite sensors show higher AOD and AI values over the Taklimakan, which are indicative of the presence of atmospheric dust. Higher AOD values caused by dust are also seen in the Gobi and Northeastern China. At the same time, there exist apparent differences in values and spatial pattern of AOD between different sensors. For instance, MISR consistently shows lower AOD values compared to MODIS Deep Blue AOD due to lower sensitivity of MISR to high dust load and infrequent MISR sampling (Kalashnikova et al., 2011). MODIS Deep Blue AODs have highest values in the northwestern part of the Tarim Basin, while MISR AODs are more distributed across the basin. In turn, OMI AOD and AI are the largest in the northeastern part of the Taklimakan. Differences seen in satellite data can be caused by a number of factors such as radiometric calibration, differences within the retrieval algorithms, and differences in spatial sampling, cloud contamination and correction of the surface effect.

Among the three spring months, the largest differences between the sensors are found in the Taklimakan in April, the month of highest dust activity. Over the Gobi, all sensors are in relatively good agreement in summer (not shown). Also in the summer, all sensors exhibit more uniform distribution of AODs over the Taklimakan. Summer AOD values are generally more consistent between sensors, with all showing lower values compared to spring. Summer AODs in Northeastern China are much lower than in the Taklimakan; this result is in good agreement with the seasonality of dust events established from ground-based observations that show low dust activity in non-spring months in Northeastern China (e.g., Wang et al., 2008b).

Comparing multi-annual mean AODs (e.g., shown in Fig. 9.6) to the dust event climatology created from ground-based observations reveals various similarities but there are also some significant differences. For instance, Figure 1 of

Wang et al. (2008b) presents the spatial pattern of multi-annual mean surface observed occurrence days of spring dust storms, blowing dust, and floating dust. There is general agreement on the location of "hot spots" but the patterns are not identical, nor should they be expected to be identical (Darmenova et al., 2005). The relationship between the frequency (or number) of dust events and AOD is not straightforward. Frequent floating dust events, for instance, may result in low AOD values, while the infrequent strong dust events generated by high winds may result in very high AOD and have a larger areal extent. The residence time of dust in the atmosphere is generally longer than the duration of individual dust outbreaks, so satellite sensors most likely capture atmospheric dust originating from several events. Actual dust emission occurs at even shorter time scale. Given these differences in scales, an integrative framework will need to leverage the synergy between ground-based and satellite-based observations for characterizing the spatiotemporal dynamics of atmospheric dust. Integrative analysis has been demonstrated in a case study (e.g., analysis of spring 2001 dust events by Darmenova et al., 2005), but applying this type of analysis to long-term data records poses a significant challenge.

Although the satellite aerosol data record is relatively short, it is of interest to examine interannual variability and tendencies. Our analysis of all available MODIS, MISR, SeaWiFS, and OMI data records did not reveal any statistically significant trends in AOD in either the Tarim Basin or IM and southern Mongolia. This result is in agreement with an independent satellite data study by Guo et al. (2011). They analyzed TOMS AOD(500 nm) from 1980–2001 and MODIS AOD(550 nm) data from 2000–2008 in order to investigate spatial and temporal variations and trends in eight regions in China. One of their studied regions lies in the Taklimakan Desert, and another in the Gobi ($\sim$88°E–103°E, 36°N–46°N). No significant trends were detected in either region. However, some decreasing tendencies in AOD from TOMS (1980–1992) and MODIS were found over both the Taklimakan and the considered Gobi region, although TOMS AOD increased from 1996–2001 (Guo et al., 2011). Apparently, increasing frequency of dust events reported from ground-based observations (see Section 9.3) is only partly supported by satellite data. An important related issue is how trends in the Asian dust sources will affect the amount of dust transported over large distances, including mid- and long-range, as well as intercontinental transport. Ultimately, better linkages between varying dust sources and atmospheric dust load will need to be established to develop the reliable climatology of Asian dust which is required for assessment of the various impacts of dust on the HEC systems at the local, regional and global scales.

9.5 Impacts of Dust on Human-Environment-Climate Systems

Dust directly affects natural and human environments in multiple ways and across a broad range of scales. In addition, there has been a growing recognition of importance of indirect effects of dust and feedbacks involving dust within the HEC systems. Regarding the direct impact on the physical climate system, atmospheric dust exerts the direct radiative forcing through interactions with solar and longwave radiation (Sokolik et al., 2001). Dust-induced perturbations to the radiative energy distribution have a significant impact on the surface energy balance and the planetary (global) energy balance, with implications for the regional and global climate (Sokolik, 2008; IPCC, 2007). Our research and other studies demonstrated that Asian dust reduces the solar irradiance reaching the surface and increases longwave radiation by a lesser amount, so the net surface radiative balance decreases (Xi and Sokolik, 2012; Huang et al., 2006a). At the top-of-the-atmosphere, dust direct radiative forcing is positive (leading to warming) in some locations and negative (leading to cooling) in others (Sokolik and Toon, 1996; IPCC, 2007). Thus the presence of dust may enhance greenhouse warming in some regions and oppose in others. Whether the presence of dust leads to heating or to cooling depends to the large extent on the ability of dust to absorb sunlight as well as atmospheric conditions and surface reflectance.

The most important indirect effect of dust on the energy balance proceeds through dust-induced changes in the properties, amount and lifetime of clouds (Huang et al., 2006 a, 2006 b; Su et al., 2008). By affecting clouds, dust may also influence precipitation. Because clouds are a sustainable water resource for arid and semi-arid regions, small variability or changes in clouds can have a significant impact on the surface energy balance, precipitation, and the hydrological cycle over these regions. Additional influence of dust on the energy and hydrological cycle proceeds through dust deposition on snow-covered surfaces, resulting in decreased surface reflectivity while promoting snow-melt (Huang et al., 2011).

Our recent study examined the dust aerosol effect on clouds in the semi-arid region of Northwest China and the U.S. using multiple years of A-Train satellite-retrieved and surface-observed data during the most active dust event seasons (Huang et al., 2010). These regions have similar climatic conditions, but more aerosols are present in the atmosphere over China. Results show that dust aerosols can significantly reduce water cloud drop size, optical depth, and liquid water path. Asian dust is hypothesized to provide a positive feedback to drought by altering clouds and suppressing precipitation, supporting the persistence of drought in arid and semi-arid regions that may result in more dust emission (Huang et al., 2006a, 2006b). The study of aerosol-cloud-radiation-precipitation processes over semi-arid regions is climatically important and possibly more urgently needed for these areas than for others. Knowledge of these processes, however, is still very limited.

Dust-induced changes in the water and energy cycles will in turn affect the carbon cycle and the functioning of ecosystems in general. Figure 9.7, a modified version of Fig. 1 from Shao et al. (2011), illustrates the pathways of the dust aerosol lifecycle and the linkages with the energy (E-cycle), carbon (C-cycle), and water (W-cycle). The important linkage with the C-cycle involves deposition of dust which provides iron supply into oceans (Mahowald et al., 2011). In addition, by altering the photosynthetically active radiation (PAR, 400 nm–700 nm), dust affects the terrestrial vegetation functioning, with implications for the C-cycle (Xi and Sokolik, 2012).

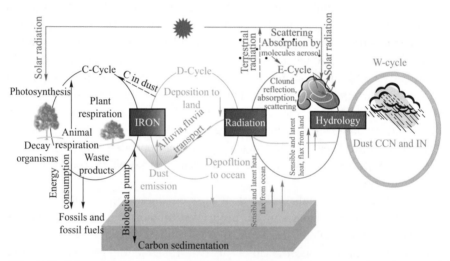

Fig. 9.7 Schematic illustration of the linkages between dust aerosol and energy (E-cycle), carbon (C-cycle) and water (W-cycle) in the Earth system (modified from Shao et al., 2011).

Light is a vital factor governing plant photosynthetic activities, and changes in PAR caused by dust aerosols may therefore influence the plant-air carbon/water exchange processes. In addition, dust-induced changes in the land surface radiation balance (SRB) are important because they may affect the surface evapotranspiration, sensible and latent heat, soil temperature and moisture, and major land-atmosphere exchange processes that along with light availability are critically important to ecosystems. Xi and Sokolik (2012) found that dust-induced changes in SRB and PAR exhibit large variations over the dryland ecosystems in East Asia, depending on the dust optical properties, vegetation types, and surface albedo. While dust aerosols reduce the total PAR, they may enhance the diffuse fraction of PAR, leading to a higher gross photosynthetic rate. The underlying mechanism (known as the "diffuse radiation fertilization" effect) is believed to be due to the redistribution of light between sunlit and shaded leaves within the plant canopy: aerosol absorption and scattering causes a reduction in PAR received by the sunlit leaves with no change or some reduction in the photosynthesis, while more diffuse PAR becomes available to the majority of light-limited shaded leaves, such that the gross photosynthetic rate increases. Based on the light use efficiency (LUE) models for several types of crops (wheat, soybean and corn), Xi and Sokolik (2012) estimated the influence of dust-induced changes in PAR on plant photosynthesis. The plant photosynthetic rate was enhanced under a low dust loading, but decreased when dust loading exceeded a certain optimal level. The dust influence varies between C3 and C4 plants and also depends on leaf area index (LAI). Lower LAI indicates a lesser effect of the dust-enhanced diffuse radiation. Wohlfahrt et al. (2008) provided the observational evidence showing that temperate mountain grassland is less sensitive to the diffuse radiation when LAI is low. They suggested that biomes with LAI < 2 such as desert shrublands exhibit low sensitivity to diffuse PAR. Jing et al. (2010) also show that semi-arid grassland exhibits no fertilization effect associated with aerosol-enhanced diffuse PAR. However, Asian dust can be transported downwind for thousands of kilometers, affecting large regions with vegetation that have higher LAI values. It is important to stress that in addition to dust-induced PAR changes, there are a number of important factors that can significantly influence vegetation functioning by affecting photosynthesis, respiration, and transpiration processes. Under aerosol-laden conditions, concurrent variations in leaf/soil temperature and humidity may occur that will amplify the diffuse PAR effect. Specifically, due to less incoming solar radiation, decreased leaf/soil temperature could depress leaf/soil respiration, while a lower vapor pressure deficit tends to enhance stomatal conductance and leaf-air exchanges. These environmental changes can exert either significant or negligible effects on the canopy photosynthesis and need to be considered synergistically within the Earth system framework.

Within active dust sources, wind erosion and associated mobilization (saltation) of soil and dust grains are thought to have an adverse impact on ecosystems (Ravi et al., 2011). This includes loss of topsoil, reduction of soil fertility and soil water storage capacity, and reduction of the capacity of soils to sustain a certain vegetation community, causing vegetation successional changes with implications for biodiversity. The soil erosion-ecosystem interactions and feedbacks, however, will vary significantly between different landscape settings, vegetation types and climatic conditions. Despite this complexity, intensive dust storms have been long recognized as a significant environmental hazard. They pose substantial hazards to the ecosystems and human health. Dust outbreaks disrupt socioeconomic activities, such as transportation, aviation, construction, and trade. A single dust storm in April 2000 in Beijing has caused a shutdown of nearly 60 million m^2 of construction sites, delayed 129 flights, and caused an increase in road accidents by 20%–30% (Guo et al., 2008). A study by Ai and Polenske (2008) attempted to evaluate the economic impact of this dust storm by integrating regional economic analysis models with environmental-economic evaluation techniques. Their results demonstrated that the costs of delayed effects of dust storms can be higher than those of the immediate effects. At the same time, their study stressed that comprehensive socioeconomic impact evaluations of dust storms have not been undertaken. Ultimately, the improved understanding of how dust sources in East Asia respond to and impact upon climate, land cover and land use, and the role of humans will be required to develop new modeling capabilities which are able to deal with the complexity involved and to represent the major processes operating in the HEC systems.

Acknowledgements

We would like to thank Drs. Marticorena, Bergametti and Shao for providing the dust emission parameterizations and helpful discussion. This work was funded by NASA LCLUC program.

References

Ai, N., and Polenske, K. R. (2008). Socioeconomic impact analysis of Yellow-dust storms: An approach and case study for Beijing. *Economic Systems Research*, 20 (2): 187–203.

Brogaard, S., and Prieler, S. (1998). Land cover in the Horqin Grasslands, North China. Detecting changes between 1975 and 1990 by means of remote sensing. Interim report IR-98-044/July. International Institute for Applied Systems Analysis, 26.

Chen, Y., and Tang, H. (2005). Desertification in North China: Background, anthropogenic impacts and failures in combating it. *Land Degrad. Develop.*, 16, 367–376.

Chen, S., Liu, J., Zhuang, D., Xiao, X., Yu, X., and Chen, H. (2004). Analyzing the degradation sequence of the meadow grassland in Xilin River Basin, Inner Mongolia, using multi-temporal Landsat TM/ETM+ sensor data. *Proceedings of SPIE*, 5544, doi: 10.1117/12.559293.

Darmenova K., Sokolik, I. N., and Darmenov, A. (2005). Characterization of East Asian dust outbreaks in Spring of 2001 using ground-based and satellite data. *Journal of Geophysical Research*, 110, D02204, doi:10.1029/2004JD004842.

Darmenova, K., and Sokolik, I. N. (2007). Assessing uncertainties in dust emission in the Aral Sea region caused by meteorological fields predicted with a mesoscale model. *Global and Planetary Change*, 56, 297–310.

Darmenova, K., Sokolik, I. N., Shao, Y., Marticorena, B., and Bergametti, G. (2009). Development of a physically-based dust emission module within the Weather Research and Forecasting (WRF) model: Assessment of dust emission parameterizations and input parameters for source regions in Central and East Asia. *Journal of Geophysical Research*, 114, D14201, doi:10.1029/2008JD011236.

Darmenova, K., and Sokolik, I. N. (2012). The influence of model horizontal resolution on simulated intensity and spatiotemporal pattern of dust aerosol emission. *Advances in Meteorology*, (Submitted).

Eidenshink, J. C., and Faundeen, J. L. (1994). The 1km AVHRR global land data set: First stages in implementation. *International Journal of Remote Sensing*, 15, 3443–3462.

Gong, S. L., Zhang, X. Y., Zhao, T. L., and Barrie, L. A. (2004). Sensitivity of Asian dust storm to natural and anthropogenic factors. *Geophysical Research Letters*, 31, L07210, doi:10.1029/2004GL019502.

Gong, S. L., Zhang, X. Y., Zhao, T. L., Zhang, X. B., Barrie, L. A., McKendry, I.G., and Zhao, C.S. (2006). A Simulated climatology of Asian dust aerosol and its trans-Pacific transport. Part Ⅱ: Interannual variability and climate connections. *Journal of Climate*, 19, 104–122.

Groisman, P. Ya., Clark, E. A., Kattsov, V. M., Lettenmaier, D. P., Sokolik, I. N., et al. (2009). The Northern Eurasia Earth Science Partnership: An example of science applied to societal needs. *Bulletin of American Meteorological Society*, 5, 671–688.

Guo, Z., Ai, N., and Polenske, K. R. (2008). Evaluating environmental and economic benefits of Yellow dust storm-related policies in North China. *International Journal of Sustainable Development and World Ecology*, 15, 5, 457–470.

Guo, J.P., Zhang, X.Y., Wu, Ye.R., Zhaxi, Y., Che, H.Z., La, B., Wang, W., and Li, X.W. (2011). Spatio-temporal variation trends of satellite-based aerosol optical depth in China during 1980–2008. *Atmospheric Environment*, 45, 37, 6802–6811.

Hara Y., Uno, I., and Wang, Z. (2006). Long-term variation of Asian dust and related climate factors. *Atmospheric Environment*, 40, 35, 6730–6740.

Huang, J., Deng, X., and Rozelle, S. (2004). Cultivated land conversion and bioproductivity in China. *Proceedings of SPIE*, 5544, 135–148.

Huang, J., Minnis, P., Lin, B., Wang, T., Yi, Y., Hu, Y., Sun-Mack, S., and Ayers, K. (2006a). Possible influences of Asian dust aerosols on cloud properties and radiative forcing observed from MODIS and CERES. *Geophysical Research Letters*, 33, L06824, doi:10.1029/2005GL024724.

Huang, J., Lin, B., Minnis, P., Wang, T., Wang, X., Hu, Y., Yi, Y., and Ayers, J.R. (2006b). Satellite-based assessment of possible dust aerosols semi-direct effect on cloud water path over East Asia. *Geophysical Research Letters*, 33, doi:10.1029/2006GL026561.

Huang, J., Minnis, P., Yan, H., Yi, Y., Chen, B., Zhang, L., and Ayers, J. K. (2010). Dust aerosol effect on semi-arid climate over Northwest China detected from A-Train satellite measurements. *Atmospheric Chemistry and Physics*, 10, 6863–6872.

Huang, J., Fu, Q., Zhang, W., Wang, X., Zhang, R., Ye, H., and Warren, S.G. (2011). Dust and black carbon in seasonal snow across Northern China. *Bulletin of the*

American Meteorological Society, 92, 175–181.

Hsu, N. C., Tsay, S.-C., King, M. D., and Herman, J. R. (2004). Aerosol properties over bright-reflecting source regions. *IEEE Transactions on Geoscience and Remote Sensing*, 42, 557–569.

Hsu, N. C., Gautam, R., Sayer, A. M., Bettenhausen, C., Li, C., Jeong, M. J., Tsay, S.-C., and Holben, B. N. (2012). Global and regional trends of aerosol optical depth over land and ocean using SeaWiFS measurements from 1997 to 2010. *Atmospheric Chemistry and Physics*, 12, 8465–8501.

IPCC, Intergovernmental Panel on Climate Change (2007). *Radiative Forcing of Climate Change*. In: Houghton, J. T., et al. (Eds.). *Climate Change: The Scientific Basis*. New York: Cambridge University Press.

Jing, X., Huang, J., and Wang, G., et al. (2010). The effects of clouds and aerosols on net ecosystem CO_2 exchange over semi-arid loess plateau of Northwest China. *Atmospheric Chemistry and Physics*, 10, 17, 8205–8218.

Kalashnikova, O. V., Garay, M. J., Sokolik, I. N., Diner, D. J., Kahn, R. A., Martonchik, J. V., Davis, A. B., Lee, J. N., Torres, O., Marshak, A., Goetz, M., Kassabian, S., and Chodas, M. (2011). Capabilities and limitations of MISR aerosol products in dust-laden conditions for dust study applications. *Proceedings of SPIE-Remote Sensing*, doi:10.1117/12.897773.

Kim, J. (2008). Transport routes and source regions of Asian dust observed in Korea during the past 40 years (1965–2004). *Atmospheric Environment*, 42, 19, 4778–4789.

Klein Goldewijk, K. (2001). Estimating global land use change over the past 300 years: The HYDE database. *Global Biogeochemical Cycles*, 15, 417–433.

Kurosaki, Y., Shinoda, M., and Mikami, M. (2011). What caused a recent increase in dust outbreaks over East Asia? *Geophysical Research Letters*, 38, L11702, doi:10.1029/2011GL047494.

Lee, E., and Sohn, B. (2011). Recent increasing trend in dust frequency over Mongolia and Inner Mongolia regions and its association with climate and surface condition change. *Atmosphere Environment*, 45, 27, 4611.

Li, B., Yu, W., and Wang, J. (2011). An analysis of vegetation change trends and their causes in Inner Mongolia, China from 1982 to 2006. *Advances in Meteorology*, 1–8, doi:10.1155/2011/367854.

Liu, S., Wang, T., Guo, J., Qu, J., and An, P. (2010). Vegetation change based on SPOT-VGT data from 1998 to 2007, Northern China. *Environmental Earth Sciences*, 60, 7, 1459–1466.

Liu, J., Tian, H., Liu, M., Zhuang, D., Melillo, J. M., and Zhang, Z. (2005). China's changing landscape during the 1990s: Large-scale land transformations estimated with satellite data. *Geophysical Research Letters*, 32, L02405, doi:10.1029/2004GL021649.

Mahowald, N. M., and Luo, C. (2003). A less dusty future? *Geophysical Research Letters*, 30, 1903, doi: 1910.1029/2003GRL017880.

Mahowald, N., Ward, D., Kloster, S., Flanner, M., Heald, C., Heavens, N., Hess, P., Lamarque, J.-F., and Chuang, P. (2011). Aerosol impacts on climate and biogeochemistry. *Annual Reviews of Environment and Resources*, 36, 45–74.

Marticorena, B., and Bergametti, G. (1995). Modeling the atmospheric dust cycle: 1. Design of a soil-derived dust emission scheme. *Journal of Geophysical Research*,

100, D8, 16, 415–16, 430.

Natsagdorj, L., Jugder, D., and Chung, Y. S. (2003). Analysis of dust storms observed in Mongolia during 1937–1999. *Atmospheric Environment*, 37, 1401–1411.

Ramankutty, N., and Foley, J. A. (1999). Estimating historical changes in global land cover: Croplands from 1700 to 1992. *Global Biogeochemical Cycles*, 13, 997–1027.

Ravi, S., et al. (2011). Aeolian processes and the biosphere. *Reviews of Geophysics*, 49, RG3001, doi:10.1029/2010RG000328.

Shao, Y., Raupach, M. R., and Leys, J. F. (1996). A model for predicting Aeolian sand drift and dust entrainment on scales from paddock to region. *Australian Journal of Soil Research*, 34, 309–342.

Shao, Y., and Dong, C. H. (2006). A review on East Asian dust storm climate, modelling and monitoring. *Global Planetary Change*, 52, 1–22.

Shao, Y., Ishizuka, M., Mikami, M., and Leys, J. F. (2011). Parameterization of size-resolved dust emission and validation with measurements. *Journal of Geophysical Research*, 116, D08203, doi:10.1029/2010JD014527.

Shinoda, M., Gillies, J. A., Mikami, M., and Shao, Y. (2011). Temperate grasslands as a dust source: Knowledge, uncertainties, and challenges. *Aeolian Research*, 3, 3, 271–293.

Sokolik, I. N. and Toon O. B. (1996). Direct radiative forcing by anthropogenic airborne mineral aerosols. *Nature*, 381, 681–683.

Sokolik, I. N., Winker, D., Bergametti, G., Gillette, D., Carmichael, G., Kaufman, Y., Gomes, L., Schuetz, L., and Penner, J. (2001). Introduction to special section on mineral dust: outstanding problems in quantifying the radiative impact of mineral dust. *Journal of Geophysical Research*, 106, 18, 015–18,028.

Sokolik, I. N. (2003). Dust. In: Holton, J., Pyle, J., and Curry, J. (Eds.). *Encyclopedia of Atmospheric Sciences*. Academic Press, London, 668–672.

Sokolik, I. N. (2008). Global radiation balance. In: E. Jorgensen (Ed.). *Encyclopedia of Ecology*. Elsevier.

Su, J., Huang, J., Fu, Q., Minnis, P., Ge, J., and Bi, J. (2008). Estimation of Asian dust aerosol effect on cloud radiation forcing using Fu-Liou radiative model and CERES measurements. *Atmospheric Chemistry and Physics*, 8, 2763–2771.

Ta, W. Q., Dong, Z. B., and Sanzhi, C. D. (2006). Effect of the 1950s large-scale migration for land reclamation on spring dust storms in Northwest China. *Atmospheric Environment*, 40, 30, 5815–5823

Tsunematsu, N., Kuze, H., Sato, T., Hayasaki, M., Cui, F., and Kondoh, A. (2011). Potential impact of spatial patterns of future atmospheric warming on Asian dust emission. *Atmospheric Environment*, 45, 37, 6682–6695.

Uno, I., et al. (2006). Dust model intercomparison (DMIP) study over Asia: Overview. *Journal of Geophysical Research*, 111, D12213, doi:10.1029/2005JD006575.

Wang, T., Wu, W., Xue, X., Sun, Q., and Chen, G. (2004). Study of spatial distribution of sandy desertification in North China in recent 10 years. *Science in China Series D: Earth Sciences*, 47, Supp. I, 78–88.

Wang, X., Chen, F., Hasi, E., and Li, J. (2008a). Desertification in China: An assessment. *Earth-Science Reviews*, 88, 3–4, 188–206.

Wang, X., Huang, J., Jia, M., and Kaz, H. (2008b). Variability of East Asia dust events and their long-term trend. *Atmospheric Environment*, 42, 3156–3165.

Wohlfahrt, G., Hammerle, A., Haslwanter, A., Bahn, M., Tappeiner, U., and Cernusca, A. (2008). Disentangling leaf area and environmental effects on the response of the net ecosystem CO_2 exchange to diffuse radiation. *Geophysical Research Letters*, 35, L16805, doi:10.1029/2008GL035090.

Worden, R.L., and Savada A.M. (1989). *Mongolia: A Country Study*. Washington: GPO for the Library of Congress.

Wu, W., and Zhang W. (2003). Present land use and cover patterns and their development potential in North Ningxia, China. *Journal of Geographical Sciences*, 13, 1, 54–62.

Xi, X., and Sokolik I. N. (2012). Impact of Asian dust aerosol and surface albedo on photosynthetically active radiation and surface radiative balance in dryland ecosystems. *Advances in Meteorology*, 1–15, doi:10.1155/2012/276207.

Xuan, J., and Sokolik I. N. (2002). Characterization of sources and emission rates of mineral dust in Northern China. *Atmospheric Environment*, 36, 4863–4876.

Xuan J., Sokolik, I. N., Hao, J., Guo, F., Mao, H., and Yang, G. (2004). Identification and characterization of sources of atmospheric mineral dust in east Asia. *Atmospheric Environment*, 38, 6239–6252.

Yang, X., Jia, B., Ci, L., and Zhang, K. (2005). Desertification assessment in China: An overview. *Journal of Arid Environments*, 63, 517–531.

Yang, X., Zhou, H., Li, S., and Zhnag, K. (2010). Sandy deserts, gobi, sandlands and sandified land in dryland. In: Ci, L. and Yang, X. (Eds.). *Desertification and its control in China*. Springer, Germany.

Zeng, Y., Zhaodong, F., and Guangchao, G. (2003). Land cover change and its environmental impact in the upper reaches of the Yellow River, Northeast Qinghai-Tibetan Plateau. *Mountain Research and Development*, 23, 4, 353–361.

Zhang, G., Liu, J., Zhang, Z., Zhao, X., and Zhou, Q. (2002). Spatial changes of wind erosion-caused landscapes and their relation with wind field in China. *Journal of Geographical Sciences*, 12, 2, 153–162.

Zhang, X. Y., Gong, S. L., Zhao, T. L., Arimoto, R., and Wang, Y. Q. (2003). Sources of Asian dust and role of climate change versus desertification in Asian dust emission. *Geophysical Research Letters*, 30, 2272, doi:10.1029/2003GL018206.

Zhao, T. L., Gong, S. L., Zhang, X. Y., Blanchet, J.-P., McKendry, I. G., and Zhou, Z. J. (2006). A simulated climatology of Asian dust aerosol and its trans-Pacific transport. Part I: Mean climate and validation. *Journal of Climate*, 19, 88–103.

Zou, X. K., and Zhai, P. M. (2004). Relationship between vegetation coverage and spring dust storms over Northern China. *Journal of Geophysical Research*, 109, D03104, doi:10.1029/2003JD003913.

Zhu, C., Wang, B., and Qian, W. (2008). Why do dust storms decrease in Northern China concurrently with the recent global warming? *Geophysical Research Letters*, 35, L18702, doi:10.1029/2008GL034886.

Authors Information

Irina N. Sokolik[1]*, Kremena Darmenova[1,2], Jianping Huang[3], Olga Kalashnikova[4], Yasunori Kurosaki[1,5], Xin Xi[1]

1. School of Earth and Atmospheric Sciences, Georgia Institute of Technology, Atlanta, GA 30332, USA
2. Current affiliation: Energy and Environment Department, Northrop Grumman Corporation, Chantilly, VA 20151, USA
3. College of Atmospheric Sciences, Lanzhou University, Lanzhou 730000, P.R. China
4. Jet Propulsion Laboratory, California Institute of Technology, Pasadena, CA 91109, USA
5. Current affiliation: Arid Land Research Center (ALRC), Tottori University, Tottori 680-0001, Japan
* Corresponding author

Chapter 10

Biophysical Regulations of Grassland Ecosystem Carbon and Water Fluxes in DEA

Changliang Shao, Shiping Chen, Jiquan Chen, and Linghao Li

Summary: Coupling the land use and climate changes would complicate the underlying mechanisms responsible for ecosystem functions such as carbon production and evapotranspiration. This chapter was designed to address the biophysical regulations of ecosystem carbon and water fluxes and their links to anthropogenic disturbances and climate variability through open-path eddy-covariance measurements in the Mongolian Plateau of Dryland East Asia (DEA) over four sites with different land use types. Two common types of grassland use changes were emphasized in the analysis. One is grazed and ungrazed grassland and the other is grassland and the cultivated cropland. The result may contribute to grassland sustainability management and to model the future changes of carbon and water cycles.

10.1 Brief Introduction of Abiotic and Biotic Factors in Relation to Carbon and Water Fluxes in DEA

The Photosynthetically active radiation (PAR) refers to radiation with a wavelength between 400 and 700 nm, which is the wavelength range that chlorophyll can absorb. It is synonymous with photosynthetic photon flux density (PPFD). Its basic unit is $\mu mol\ m^{-2}\ s^{-1}$, which can be converted into $W\ m^{-2}$. As we know, the productivity of plants depends on the efficiency of the photosynthetic process; therefore, the availability of PAR as well as the ambient temperature and the rates of supply of moisture and carbon dioxide to the photosynthesizing plants are factors that control overall plant productivity. The diurnal variation that integrated the whole-year data of PAR is approximately unimodal in shape for 2006 for the Duolun site and the Inner Mongolian steppe located in the DEA area (Fig. 10.1a). The annual PAR pattern is similar to the diurnal one but has many drops because of the cloudy or rainy days. The whole-year data showed that the PAR is smallest in December with about 20 mol m^{-2} d^{-1}, while largest in May with about 60 mol m^{-2} d^{-1}. Therefore, the PAR in summer is three times that of winter and the long-day C$_3$ plants are active in this area (Fig. 10.1b).

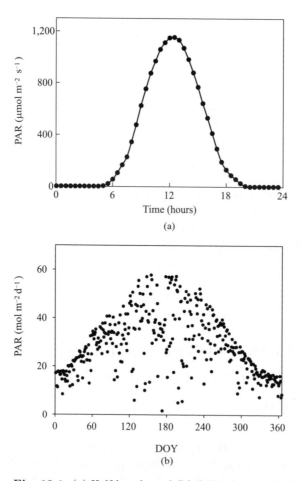

Fig. 10.1 (a) Half-hourly and (b) daily photosynthetically active radiation (PAR) in 2006 in the Duolun site, Mongolian Plateau (Lat: 42°02′N, Long: 116°17′E). Data of the two figures were derived from the whole year's record.

Environmental temperature is one of the most important factors in determining living organism activities. Temperature strongly influences the rates of all metabolic processes in living organisms and, therefore, affects almost all aspects of the growth and development of an organism. Figures 10.2 and 10.3 show a typical range for diurnal temperature variation with depth in soil and the air temperature at the time in a typical grassland in the Inner Mongolia Autonomous Region (IM), China. The features to note are that the temperature extremes occur at the surface, where radiant exchange occurs, and that the diurnal variation decreases rapidly with depth in the soil.

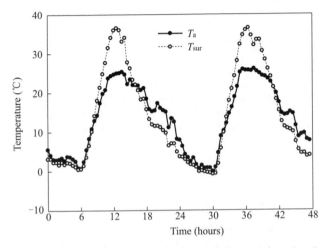

Fig. 10.2 Half-hourly air temperature (T_a, 2 m) and soil surface temperature (T_{sur}) from September 22–23, 2006 at the Dongwu typical steppe on the Mongolian Plateau (Lat: 45° 33′N, Long: 116° 59′E).

The diurnal variation of soil temperature is approximately sinusoidal, the amplitude decreases rapidly with depth in the soil, and the times of the maximum and minimum shifts with depth. At the surface, the time of maximum temperature is around 14:00 hours, as it is in the air. At deeper depths, the times of the maxima and minima lag solar noon even farther and at 0.22 m, the maximum is about seven hours after the maximum at the surface. The typical minimum temperature occurs around predawn as the decrease in soil heat flux is during the night (Fig. 10.3).

When the surface temperature is known, we can use this equation to model the temperature in the soil. This model assumes uniform soil properties throughout the soil profile and a sinusoidally varying surface temperature. Given these assumptions, the following equation gives the temperature as a function of depth and time (Gaylon and John, 1998):

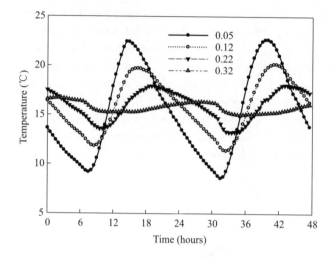

Fig. 10.3 Half-hourly soil temperature at four depths showing the attenuation of diurnal variations and the shift in maxima and minima with depth on September 22–23, 2006 at the Dongwu typical steppe of the Mongolian Plateau (Lat: 45°33′N, Long: 116°59′E).

$$T_{(z,t)} = T_{\text{avg}} + A_{(0)} \exp(-z/D) \sin[\omega(t-8) - z/D] \qquad (10.1)$$

where T_{avg} is the mean daily soil surface temperature, ω is $\pi/12$, $A_{(0)}$ is the amplitude of temperature fluctuations at the surface (half of the peak-to-peak variation), and D is the damping depth. The "−8" in the sine function is a phase adjustment to the time variable so that when $t = 8$, the sine of the quantity in brackets is zero at the surface ($z = 0$). D has a value around 0.1 m for moist mineral soils and 0.03 to 0.06 m for dry mineral soils and organic soils. This relationship has limitations because the thermal properties do vary with depth and the temperature variations are not necessarily sinusoidal. In spite of these limitations, however, a lot can be learned from this simple model.

Figure.10.4 shows soil temperature variations in a fenced steppe (FS) and a grazed steppe (GS) [1] by integrating all the monthly half-hour data to one day in August, 2010. At both ecosystems, the diurnal variation is approximately sinusoidal. The times of maximum temperature are around 14:30 hours while the minimum temperature is around 6:30 hours in August.

Variation of soil temperature in FS was less than that in GS. With grazing, the soil temperature increased during day but decreased at night. The maximum of soil temperature was 2.5 °C higher at midday and 2.0 °C lower at predawn for GS as compared to the values for FS. Daytime averages (6:30–18:00 h) were

1 The acronym is used in this chapter only.

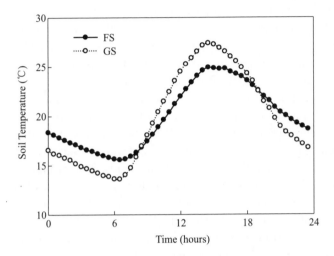

Fig. 10.4 Half-hourly soil (5 cm depth) temperatures (points) bin-average for all of August, 2010 data at grazed steppe (GS) and ungrazed fenced steppe (FS) ecosystems on the Mongolian Plateau (Lat: 41°48′N, Long: 111°54′E). The curve is to interpolate daily maximum and minimum temperatures to obtain half-hourly estimates.

21.2 °C and 22.5 °C while nighttime (18:30–6:00 h) averages were 18.6 °C and 17.1 °C for FS and GS, respectively. As a result, the diurnal temperature range (DTR; the difference between daily maximum and minimum temperature) also became higher in the grazed plots, with increases by 4.4 °C in GS over that of FS.

The annual soil temperature pattern is similar to the diurnal one modeled, with the maximum temperature in summer and the minimum temperature in winter. The modeling equation can also be used to describe the annual variation, but D is 2 m and ω is $2\pi/365$.

The diurnal soil volumetric water content (SWC) pattern is similar to the temperature, with the maximum at midday while the minimum is at predawn. This is because the soil moisture moves as a result of temperature gradients (Gaylon and John, 1998). The water in the soil is in thermal equilibrium with the soil metric at the same depth. We know that liquid or vapor flows from areas where its kinetic energy is high to areas where it is low; that is, from warm to cold. Therefore, the temperature profile may influence the patterns of moisture distribution in the soil. The complication is SWC between the fenced steppe and the grazed steppe, with various patterns being observed. Some studies showed higher SWC in a grazed steppe and some showed it in a fenced steppe, while some showed no difference. In fact, all of the aspects above exist. The reason is the difference in evapotranspiration (ET) in different measurement periods caused by the differences in weather conditions, disturbed intensities, vegetation characteristics, and soil physical properties (Miao et al., 2009). The variances of ET between disturbed (e.g., grazing/mowing) and undisturbed locations also showed with some studies, supporting that a decrease in aboveground biomass reduced seasonal ET (Bremer et al., 2001; Frank, 2003), with some demonstrating an increase in seasonal ET (Ewers et al., 2000) and others reporting no significant effect (Stewart and Verma, 1992). As a result, different conclusions can be drawn. Vapor pressure deficit (VPD) is the deficit between the amount of moisture in the air and how much moisture the air can hold when it is saturated. Once air becomes saturated, water will condense to form clouds, dew, or films of water over leaves. It is this last instance, water films on leaves, that makes VPD important for greenhouse regulation. If a film of water forms on a plant leaf, it becomes far more susceptible to rot. On the other hand, as VPD increases, the plant needs to draw more water from its roots (and if it is a cutting, it will dry out and die). For this reason, the ideal range for VPD in a greenhouse is from 0.45 kPa to 1.25 kPa, ideally sitting at around 0.85 kPa. As a general rule, most plants grow well at VPDs from 0.8 to 0.95 kPa. In ecology, it is the difference between the actual water vapor pressure and the saturation water vapor pressure at a particular temperature. Unlike relative humidity, VPD has a simple, nearly straight-line relationship to the rate of ET and other measures of evaporation. Figure 10.5 shows the daily VPD of a fenced steppe and cultivated cropland in the Duolun site. There were little variances or differences in VPD in the non-growing season. However, VPD in both ecosystems varied dramatically during the growing season, with a relatively high level from May to early July.

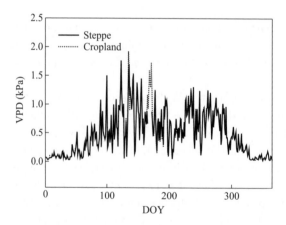

Fig. 10.5 Daily vapor pressure deficit (VPD) of a fenced steppe and cultivated cropland in the Duolun site in the Mongolian Plateau in 2006 (Lat: 42°02′N, Long: 116°17′E).

Vegetation, as an intermediary, plays a central role in buffering the mass and energy exchanges of land surfaces and the atmosphere (Baldocchi et al. 1988; Beringer et al., 2005). Any change in vegetation composition or structure would bring significant influences on the CO_2, heat and water regimes, and budgets (Hernandez-Ramirez et al., 2010; Li et al., 2000). The biotic indicating factors include aboveground net prime productivity (ANPP), belowground net prime productivity (BNPP), leaf area index (LAI), cover, litter, dead standing, and so on.

In the DEA area, rainfall is the first limited factor to control the community characteristics above. An investigation was conducted under three mowing treatments (intended to mimic the grazing) where the steppe was trimmed once a year to heights of 2 cm (R_2), 10 cm (R_{10}), or had no mowing (i.e., control R_c) in a *S. krylovii* typical steppe. Changes in ANPP with mowing intensity showed clear seasonal patterns were highly consistent with that in the accumulated rainfall, and showed that with the increase in mowing intensity, there was a decrease in ANPP during the whole measurement growing season (Fig. 10.6). Other investigations showed that the total vegetation coverage was comparable among the three mowing treatments. However, the percent of cover of different individual species differed greatly in response to the mowing treatments. The total LAI decreased with mowing intensity and was significantly higher ($P <$ 0.05) in the R_c plots than in the mowed plots. Litter weight in the mowed plots was consistently lower than that in the unmowed plots (R_c), with litter coverage

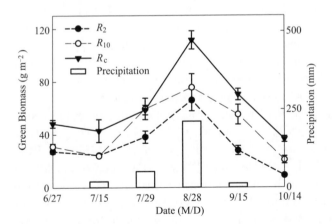

Fig. 10.6 Seasonal variations in green biomass and precipitation under two mowing treatments plus control in 2007 in a semi-arid typical steppe ecosystem of Northern China. R_2, R_{10} and R_c represent three mowing treatments where the steppe was trimmed once a year to a height of 2 cm, 10 cm, or with no mowing (i.e., control), respectively.

at least 4 cm thicker in the R_c plots. Dead stand and stem weight were also significantly lower in the mowed plots than in the reference plots, with weights nine times higher in R_c than in R_2 or R_{10}.

10.2 Biophysical Regulations of Carbon Fluxes between Grazed and Ungrazed Grasslands

10.2.1 Responses of Daytime Net Ecosystem Exchange to Biotic/Abiotic Factors

In order to examine the dependence of the daytime NEE-PAR response on abiotic variables with the continuously half-hour EC data, we usually select the non-gap-filled NEE data that fits the quality criterion (e.g., u^*, no raining days, non-stability, etc.). NEE can be examined for its relationship with PAR under different T_a, SWC, and VPD conditions. Falge et al. (2001) used the rectangular hyperbola Michaelis-Menten light response model with an embedded dynamic (soil or air) temperature response function for ecosystem respiration (Michaelis and Menten, 1913):

$$\text{NEE} = \text{Re}_{\text{day}} + [(\alpha \times \text{PAR} \times \text{NEE}_{\text{max}})/(\alpha \times \text{PAR} + \text{NEE}_{\text{max}}) \qquad (10.2)$$

where α (μmol CO_2 μmol^{-1} PAR) is apparent quantum yield or the initial slope of the light response curve, PAR (μmol quanta m^{-2} s^{-1}) is photosynthetic active radiation, NEE_{max} (μmol CO_2 m^{-2} s^{-1}) is the maximum apparent photosynthetic capacity of the canopy, and Re_{day} (μmol CO_2 m^{-2} s^{-1}) is the bulk Re during the daytime derived from the relationship between temperature and nighttime NEE. Li et al. (2005) used this light response model to study the dependence of the daytime NEE-PAR response on abiotic variables and provided a kind of class with respect to T_a ($T_a \leqslant 15$ °C, 15 °C $< T_a \leqslant 25$ °C, and $T_a >$ 25 °C), SWC (SWC $\leqslant 10\%$, $10\% <$ SWC $\leqslant 14\%$, and SWC $> 14\%$), and VPD (VPD $\leqslant 1$ kPa, 1 kPa $<$ VPD $\leqslant 2$ kPa, and VPD > 2 kPa) in grassland studies of the DEA area. For each of the aforementioned levels, the NEE values were usually grouped by PAR at 100 μmol m^{-2} s^{-1} intervals ranging from 0 to over 2000 μmol m^{-2} s^{-1}. Some studies considered the depression of NEE when PAR was over 1600 μmol m^{-2} s^{-1}; thus, the maximum PAR was limited to 1600 μmol m^{-2} s^{-1} (Li et al., 2005). NEE was then averaged for each PAR level. Statistically, these grouped data help to reduce or offset the errors associated with the measurements. Zhang et al. (2007) also used this method to study the NEE-PAR response on abiotic variables in a typical steppe and a nearby cropland in the DEA area.

By using the same method mentioned above from our recent study, the daytime NEE is examined for its relationship with PAR under different T_a, SWC, and VPD conditions (Fig. 10.7, Table 10.1) in FS and GS during the whole growing season with non-gap-filled eddy-covariance data. Overall, NEE increased with PAR but leveled off or decreased as PAR exceeded the saturation point (i.e., NEE_{max}, carbon assimilation ability) at approximately 1,200–1,400 μmol m^{-2} s^{-1}. For example, the saturation PAR level was ~1,400 μmol m^{-2} s^{-1} when SWC > 14%, ~1,200 μmol m^{-2} s^{-1} at 1 kPa < VPD $\leqslant$ 2 kPa for both sites and ~1,300 and 1,200 μmol m^{-2} s^{-1} at 15 °C < $T_a \leqslant$ 25 °C for FS and

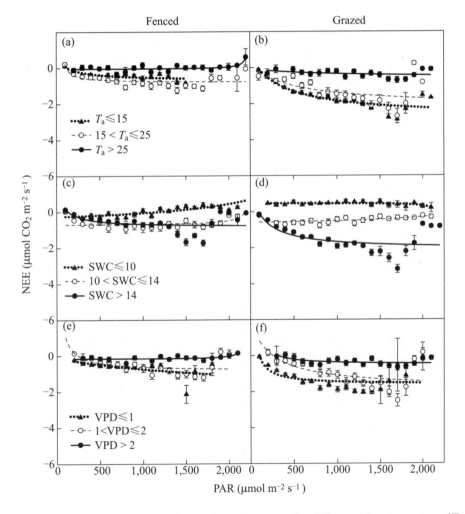

Fig. 10.7 Daytime NEE light response curves under different air temperature (T_a, °C), volumetric soil water content (SWC, %), and vapor pressure deficit (VPD, kPa) in 2010 at the fenced and grazed steppes.

Table 10.1 Values of the parameters describing features of the rectangular hyperbolic responses of daytime NEE to incident PAR [Eq. (10.2)] under different SWC, T_a and VPD levels in the fenced steppe (FS) and grazed steppe (GS).

Varible	NEE_{max} ($\mu mol\ CO_2\ m^{-2}s^{-1}$)		Re_{day} ($\mu mol\ CO_2\ m^{-2}s^{-1}$)		α ($\mu mol\ \mu mol^{-1}$)		r^2	
	FS	GS	FS	GS	FS	GS	FS	GS
$T_a \leqslant 15°C$	-4.77 ± 0.28	-7.41 ± 0.33	1.18 ± 0.35	1.31 ± 0.34	-0.012 ± 0.002	-0.016 ± 0.003	0.98	0.99
$15< T_a \leqslant 25°C$	-4.99 ± 1.65	-6.96 ± 0.99	2.34 ± 1.94	2.28 ± 1.39	-0.025 ± 0.009	-0.017 ± 0.004	0.71	0.80
$T_a >25°C$	-3.42 ± 0.42	-4.25 ± 0.46	1.07 ± 0.49	0.78 ± 0.57	-0.016 ± 0.005	-0.013 ± 0.003	0.21	0.18
$SWC\leqslant10\%$	-0.4 ± 0.45	—	-0.88 ± 0.28	—	0.0002 ± 0.001	—	0.55	—
$10\%<SWC\leqslant14\%$	-4.41 ± 2.86	-2.92 ± 2.16	2.55 ± 3.01	1.04 ± 2.51	-0.0473 ± 0.026	-0.025 ± 0.01	0.70	0.63
$SWC>14\%$	-5.16 ± 1.02	-6.44 ± 0.49	1.92 ± 1.35	1.75 ± 0.67	-0.0175 ± 0.004	-0.017 ± 0.004	0.78	0.94
$VPD\leqslant1kPa$	-4.79 ± 0.43	-7.38 ± 0.49	1.68 ± 0.81	1.51 ± 0.71	-0.019 ± 0.004	-0.018 ± 0.003	0.96	0.96
$1kPa<VPD\leqslant2kPa$	-3.51 ± 0.35	-4.50 ± 0.40	1.03 ± 0.42	0.74 ± 0.51	-0.014 ± 0.004	-0.012 ± 0.003	0.25	0.22
$VPD>2kPa$	-3.92 ± 2.26	-5.75 ± 1.14	1.97 ± 2.57	1.21 ± 0.61	-0.017 ± 0.007	-0.005 ± 0.001	0.68	0.88

GS, respectively. The mean light saturation point was $\sim$1,150 μmol m^{-2} s^{-1} for FS and 1,300 μmol m^{-2} s^{-1} for GS; NEE$_{max}$ was -2.11 and -3.07 μmol CO$_2$ m^{-2} s^{-1}, respectively.

NEE$_{max}$ in FS was higher when $T_a < 25\ ^{\circ}$C than that of $T_a > 25\ ^{\circ}$C. Interestingly, NEE$_{max}$ in GS was nearly 50% higher than that in FS when $T_a < 25\ ^{\circ}$C. SWC also had notable effects on NEE$_{max}$. Absolute values of NEE$_{max}$ increased with increasing SWC, with no record of SWC $< 10\%$ in GS. In FS, NEE$_{max}$ under SWC $> 14\%$ condition was much higher than that when SWC $\leqslant 10\%$. With SWC $> 14\%$, NEE$_{max}$ of GS was 20% higher than that of FS. Separated by 1 kPa, NEE$_{max}$ of both ecosystems decreased with increasing VPD but kept stable when VPD < 2 kPa. NEE$_{max}$ of both ecosystems under low VPD ($\leqslant 1$ kPa) were 25% more than those at high VPD (> 2 kPa). NEE$_{max}$ in GS was 50% higher than that of FS under VPD < 1 kPa. Apparent quantum yield at the ecosystem level (α) also showed differences in both ecosystems. α and the bulk daytime ecosystem respiration (Re$_{day}$) of the two sites at optimum temperature ($15\ ^{\circ}$C $< T_a \leqslant 25\ ^{\circ}$C) were high. When T_a increased to $> 25\ ^{\circ}$C, NEE$_{max}$ and α were depressed.

Water is the most critical environmental limiting factor for plant growth of the semi-arid desert steppe in the DEA area due to the vegetation characteristics and irregular rainfall patterns. These can substantially change plant physiology and therefore impact CO$_2$ uptake (Hunt et al., 2002). Drought usually causes a decline in the net CO$_2$ uptake and leads to decreases in leaf internal CO$_2$ concentrations through adjusting to closed-leaf stomata (Farquhar et al. 1980). NEE$_{max}$ showed a decrease with decreasing SWC/precipitation at our sites (Fig. 10.7 and Table 10.1), which was consistent with results from other studies in the typical steppe on the Mongolian Plateau (Li et al., 2005; Wang et al., 2010; Zhang et al., 2007). Compared to FS, GS had a higher NEE$_{max}$ and light saturation point in relatively higher soil moisture ($> 14\%$), which might be related to its more physiologically active leaves and single-leaf photosynthetic capacity because its GNPP (green aboveground NPP) and LAI were less. Owensby et al. (2006) also reported that grazing need not reduce canopy photosynthesis or grassland NEE as greatly as biomass in a tallgrass prairie. In our study, the growing season mean value of the dead standing plants of the fenced steppe was near three times that of GS. The more open structural characteristics of vegetation canopies determine the amount of radiant energy absorbed and reflected by the GS canopy, thus directly improving rates of photosynthesis (Zhang et al., 2007).

Grazing also indirectly affected carbon fluxes by increasing soil temperature (Polley et al., 2008). Growing season averages of daytime (6:30–18:00 LT) and daily (24 h) soil temperature were greater in GS than in FS by 0.91 and 0.43 $^{\circ}$C, respectively, because grazing reduced the biomass of litter and dead standing caused the increase in soil heat flux, which is a dominant energy flux in the area

(Shao et al., 2008). The severe drought at the earlier growing stage caused the amount of dead standing on the soil surface and within plant canopies in FS. This reduces the amount of solar radiation that reaches the soil, resulting in cooler soil (Klein et al., 2005; Wan et al., 2002). Re increased partly because soil temperature was greater on the grazed steppe than ungrazed one. The better light penetration and suitable microclimate (LeCain et al., 2000) near the soil surface in GS compared to FS was a reason to increase gross ecosystem productivity (GEP). As a result, NEE increased in GS.

Temperature influences photosynthesis and respiration of plants primarily via temperature-dependent enzyme activity, especially Rubisco (Farquhar et al., 1980). In our study, the optimum temperature for NEE_{max} appeared to be between 15 °C and 25 °C (Fig. 10.7 and Table 10.1). A significant reduction in carbon assimilation was found when T_a was > 25 °C in both ecosystems (similar to those reported by Zhang et al., 2007). NEE_{max} of FS shared the maximum value when 15 °C $< T_a \leqslant 25$ °C, while of GS when $T_a \leqslant 15$ °C. GS showing relatively greater CO_2 uptake under low air temperature conditions might be the result of an open canopy with more sun shining in GS. This means that there was longer CO_2 uptake time in GS during the day than in FS.

Separated by 2 kPa, NEE_{max} of both ecosystems decreased with increasing VPD. At higher VPD, there was a reduction in NEE because of stomatal closure under drought conditions (Farquhar et al., 1980). When VPD was greater than 2 kPa, NEE_{max} of FS and GS ecosystems showed a similar reduction, suggesting a similar threshold on both ecosystems. Although it is difficult to identify the independent effects of VPD and T_a on NEE because of their close association, increasing VPD and T_a affect the fluxes by different mechanisms (i.e., a substantial increase in VPD may primarily result in stomatal closure, whereas higher temperatures may favor respiration, Zhang et al., 2007). Despite the complication, the obvious difference showed that the CO_2 uptake capacity in GS was higher than in FS when VPD < 2.

10.2.2 Response of Nighttime NEE (Re) to T and SWC

The nighttime NEE (i.e., nighttime ecosystem respiration, Re) was parameterized with traditional Q_{10} (the respiration temperature sensitivity coefficient) model using only the nighttime good data (here, nighttime conditions are defined by PAR < 4 μmol m^{-2} s^{-1} and time $<$ sunrise time or time $>$ sunset time) to fit the corresponding half-hourly air temperature at 2 m height following Lloyd and Taylor (1994) and Falge et al. (2001):

$$NEE_{nighttime} = R_0 \times e^{b \times T_s} \tag{10.3}$$

where R_0 and b are the regression coefficients and R_0 is the respiration rate at a temperature of 0 °C, which is also written as A or a in other studies. Q_{10} was determined as:

$$Q_{10} = e^{10 \times b} \tag{10.4}$$

The relationships as exponential functions of air temperature were examined for the two ecosystems based on the data collected in darkness. Because this studied semi-arid desert steppe shows a large monthly variation in precipitation and canopy growth, we determined the temperature sensitivity of Re for selected periods where the LAI and soil moisture were similar (Fig. 10.8). The exponential function described the relationships between Re and soil temperature very well in most of the months in both FS and GS. In the growing season, high Q_{10} values were observed in growth initial and mid-later stages (May and October), whereas low Q_{10} values were mostly in dry months when grass was less active (June and July). Obviously, different patterns were shown between drought and non-drought periods. In droughts of June and July, Re was stable with the air temperature increasing, with similar Q_{10} between the two ecosystems. While in other non-drought months, the Re were exponentially increasing when air temperature increased. Q_{10} was estimated to be 1–4 in the growing period, with higher Q_{10} in GS than in FS.

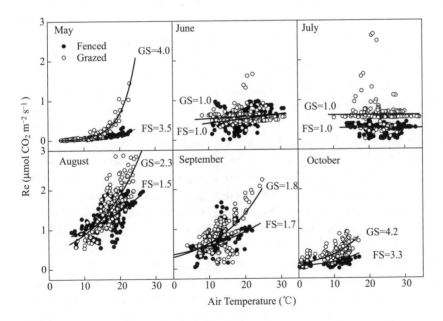

Fig. 10.8 Response of nighttime ecosystem respiration (Re) to changes in air temperature at 2 m height in each month during the growing season. Numbers showed the Q_{10} values of the fenced (FS) and grazed (GS) desert steppes.

Re is a composite flux comprising aboveground respiration by foliage and stem tissues and belowground respiration by roots (autotrophic respiration, R_a), soil organisms (heterotrophic respiration, R_h) (Janssens et al., 2001), etc. and Re is a function of temperature. However, the temperature sensitivity of Re is affected by variations in soil moisture and substrate availability (Davidson et al. 2006). In the growth season, high Q_{10} values were observed in growth initial and mid-later stages (May and October), whereas low Q_{10} values were mostly in dry months when the grass was less active, a reflection of the different temperature sensitivities for R_a and R_h and the turnover times of the multiple carbon pools. This also indicates that only when SWC was higher, Re increased. Qi et al. (2002) referred that ecosystem respiration by roots and soil microbials requires adequate moisture as well as temperature and the reduced soil moisture in the semi-arid steppe will also decrease the temperature sensitivity of Re. At a given site, root respiration will increase with temperature because root biomass typically peaks in summer and specific root respiration rates increase with temperature. Thus, in the absence of drought stress, temperature would exert dominant control over R_a (Janssens et al., 2001).

A wider variation in Q_{10} values has been occurring in grasslands. Flanagan and Johnson (2005) reported Q_{10} values varying from about 1.5 to 2.5 in the northern temperate grassland. Yet, Xu and Baldocchi (2004) estimated a narrower variation in Q_{10} values, ranging from 2.1 to 2.5 during the season of 2000–2001 in a Mediterranean C_3 grassland. Similar to this study, reductions in Q_{10} related to decreases in soil moisture were documented for other typical steppes in IM, which decreased from more than 3.3 at > 10% of SWC to 2.9 in dry soil (Zhang et al., 2007). Zhao et al. (2006) also reported high Q_{10} values near 4.5 in the growth initial stage, whereas, in contrast to our results, low Q_{10} values were mostly in wet months when the grass was very active over an alpine shrubland ecosystem. These results might also be caused by the contributions of different compositions to Re. It also indicated that the temperature sensitivity of Re depended not only on the soil water conditions but also on the biome type and the phenological stage of plant growth and development (DeForest et al., 2006).

Re of both FS and GS followed an exponential relationship with T_s, consistent with previous studies (Lloyd and Taylor, 1994). The profound differences in the capacity of photosynthesis between the two ecosystems also lead to the different response of Re to temperature since respiration is also effectively limited by the supply of carbohydrates fixed through photosynthesis (Fu et al., 2006). Grazing maintained higher carbohydrates. In addition, it maintained higher soil water levels during most of the growing season, which likely sustained microbial action for a longer period, which would increase soil CO_2 flux (Bremer et al., 2001). Also, comparison of the two ecosystems suggests that GS was more sensitive to the change of temperature than FS, probably because of the contributions of different compositions to Re, with different temperature sensitivities for autotrophic and heterotrophic respiration. Heterotrophic respiration was nearly correlated with T_s, which means that GS enhanced Re through an increase in heterotrophic respiration. Grazing disturbed soil structure and accelerated the decomposition of soil organic matter (especially with moderate soil water levels), which could increase heterotrophic respiration rates (Lindroth et al., 1998) and result in a higher contribution to Re. It is demonstrated that only about 24% of soil CO_2 flux was due to root respiration in the steppe (Li et al., 2002). Thus, the Q_{10} value of Re in the GS was high during the peak growing season without water stress.

10.3 Ecosystem Carbon Fluxes between Grassland and Cultivated Cropland

10.3.1 Responses of Daytime NEE to Biotic/Abiotic Factors

As in the grassland ecosystems, the Michaelis-Menten model [Eq.(10.2)] is also an appropriate model for modeling daytime NEE in cultivated cropland ecosystems under different microclimates. Zhang et al. (2007) used this model to study the NEE-PAR response on abiotic variables in a typical steppe and a nearby cropland. The results showed that NEE increased with PAR at low to intermediate levels of PAR, but as PAR exceeded the light saturation point (1,000 μmol m^{-2} s^{-1} at SWC $\leqslant$ 10% for both ecosystems; ~1,200 and 1,600 μmol m^{-2} s^{-1} at SWC > 10% for the steppe and cropland, respectively), NEE began to decline. Light-saturated rates of net photosynthetic assimilation (NEE_{max}) of the two ecosystems were greatly affected by SWC, T_a, and VPD. NEE_{max} increased with increasing SWC (Table 10.2). In the steppe, NEE_{max}, when SWC > 14%, was twice that when SWC $\leqslant$ 10%. When SWC dropped to lower than 10% in the cropland, NEE_{max} was only 20%–25% of that recorded when SWC was > 10%. T_a also had notable effects on NEE_{max}. NEE_{max} in the two ecosystems was highest when T_a varied from 15 °C to 25 °C (Table 10.2). At these intermediate temperatures, NEE_{max} in the cropland was nearly 50% higher than in the steppe. NEE_{max} declined with increasing VPD. NEE_{max} of both ecosystems at the lowest VPD ($\leqslant$ 1 kPa) were more than twice those at the highest VPD (> 2 kPa). NEE_{max} in the cropland was 38% higher than in the steppe under VPD less than 1 kPa.

Apparent quantum yield at the ecosystem level (α) also showed clear differences in both ecosystems (Table 10.2). α of both ecosystems at low VPD ($\leqslant$1 kPa) was more than twice α at high VPD (> 2 kPa). At the optimum temperature and SWC, NEE_{max} and α of both ecosystems decreased with increasing

Table 10.2 Values of the parameters describing features of the rectangular hyperbolic responses of daytime NEE to incident PAR [Eq. (10.2)] under different SWC, T_a, and VPD levels in the fenced steppe and cropland.

Variable	NEE_{max} (μmol CO_2 m^{-2}s^{-1})		Re_{day} (μmol CO_2 m^{-2}s^{-1})		α (μmol μmol^{-1})		r^2	
	Steppe	Cropland	Steppe	Cropland	Steppe	Cropland	Steppe	Cropland
SWC≤10%	−2.9±0.4	−1.8±0.5	0.9±0.1	0.7±0.5	−0.007±0.001	−0.004±0.002	0.53	0.37
10%<SWC≤14%	−3.9±0.5	−9.5±3.1	0.3±0.5	0.9±1.1	−0.005±0.001	−0.010±0.005	0.63	0.89
SWC>14%	−5.8±1.2	−8.3±0.9	1.0±1.1	0.3±0.7	−0.008±0.004	−0.009±0.002	0.95	0.77
T_a ≤15°C	−3.4±0.7	−1.5±1.3	0.2±0.1	0.3±1.3	−0.006±0.003	−0.007±0.008	0.35	0.66
15°C< T_a ≤25°C	−4.4±0.1	−8.2±2.7	0.8±0.1	1.0±1.4	−0.007±0.001	−0.010±0.007	0.81	0.92
T_a >25°C	−2.8±1.5	−5.6±1.0	0.6±1.3	0.03±0.9	−0.005±0.007	−0.005±0.001	0.74	0.36
VPD≤1kPa	−4.9±1.4	−8.1±0.8	0.1±1.4	0.4±0.7	−0.006±0.004	−0.008±0.001	0.41	0.45
1kPa<VPD≤2kPa	−4.5±0.5	−7.8±0.5	0.8±0.4	0.7±0.4	−0.005±0.001	−0.005±0.001	0.61	0.79
VPD>2kPa	−2.0±0.3	−4.0±0.9	0.1±0.3	0.3±0.7	−0.002±0.001	−0.004±0.001	0.43	0.26

VPD. When VPD was less than 1 kPa and T_a was less than 15 °C, NEE_{max} in the steppe was higher than that in the cropland. The changes of NEE_{max} in the steppe with temperature when VPD < 1 kPa was much smaller than that in the cropland under the same VPD conditions. At 1 kPa $<$ VPD $\leqslant 2$ kPa, NEE_{max} and α of the steppe were depressed a lot while those of cropland changed a little when T_a was over 25 °C. When VPD was over 2 kPa, NEE_{max} and α of the two ecosystems were depressed.

Compared to the steppe ecosystem, the cropland had a higher NEE_{max} and light saturation point than the steppe in relatively higher soil moisture (SWC $> 10\%$), which might be related to its higher LAI, ANPP, and single-leaf photosynthetic capacity. The structural characteristics of vegetation canopies, in particular, leaf area and light interception capacity, determine the amount of radiant energy absorbed and reflected by the canopy, thus directly affecting the rates of photosynthesis (Ogren, 1993). A study on a *Stipa kryloii* grassland in Mongolia demonstrated that NEE responded to LAI in a linear manner and 26% of the variance in NEE could be explained by the variation in LAI (Li et al., 2005). Dugas et al. (1999) showed that daytime NEE of a sorghum field exceeded that of bermudagrass and prairie due to greater LAI. The peak value of ANPP of the cropland ecosystem was more than three times that of the steppe, which suggested a higher leaf area for photosynthesis and efficient utilization of radiation. Thus, the cropland had a higher carbon assimilation ability, light saturation point, and apparent quantum yield (α) in higher soil moisture conditions (SWC $> 10\%$).

Although higher carbon assimilation ability and light use efficiency appeared in the cropland ecosystem in relatively moderate soil moisture conditions (SWC $> 10\%$), the steppe showed higher NEE_{max} and α in drought conditions (SWC $< 10\%$), suggesting that plant species in the steppe ecosystem had higher tolerance to drought stress. The data clearly showed that when SWC $< 10\%$, NEE_{max} and α in the steppe was nearly 60% and 75% higher than in the cropland, respectively. Different trends were showed to that when SWC $> 10\%$. The tolerance of plant species to drought is a very frequent phenomenon in arid and semi-arid regions (e.g., Chen et al., 2006); plants with high drought tolerance possess adaptations that compensate for the effects of reduced water availability and provide a substantial advantage over non-drought-tolerant plants in arid environments (Ni and Pallardy, 1991).

In this study, the optimum temperature for NEE_{max} appeared to be between 15 °C and 25 °C. Significant reduction in carbon assimilation was found when T_a was > 25 °C in both ecosystems (similar to those reported by Li et al., 2005). NEE_{max} and α of both ecosystems decreased with an increase in VPD because of the physical cohesiveness between temperature and VPD, which influences photosynthesis and respiration of plants primarily via stomatal aperture (Farquhar et al., 1980) and due to the fact that high temperatures are often accompanied by low relative humidity in this region. The changes of NEE_{max} in the steppe with temperature when VPD < 1 kPa was much smaller than that in the cropland under the same VPD conditions, suggesting a stronger temperature dependence of the crops. At 1 kPa < VPD $\leqslant$ 2 kPa, NEE_{max} and α of the steppe were more severely reduced than those of the cropland when T_a was over 25 °C. An important conclusion drawn by this study was that the steppe performed better (i.e., higher NEE) at low temperatures while the crops performed better under higher temperatures. When VPD was greater than 2 kPa, NEE_{max} and α of the two ecosystems showed a similar reduction, suggesting a similar threshold on both ecosystems.

As a conclusion, the results indicated that soil water content and temperature were the main factors controlling grassland and cropland ecosystem carbon assimilation in an arid region. The cropland ecosystem had a stronger ability to uptake carbon than the native steppe ecosystem under optimal soil water and temperature conditions due to species and management. The steppe showed relatively greater carbon uptake under drought stress and low air temperature conditions, which might be the result of evolutionary adaptations of steppe species to local stressful environments.

10.3.2 Response of Nighttime NEE (Re) to T and SWC

The effects of both temperature and moisture on Q_{10} are of critical importance in assessing the impacts of the changing climate and land use on ecosystem carbon fluxes (Betts, 2000; Chen et al., 2004; Wen et al., 2006). Therefore, Zhang et al. (2007) also determined that Re was an exponential function of T_a under different SWC levels. The results showed that in both grassland and cropland ecosystems, Re was, in fact, an exponential function of air temperature under different SWC levels. An obvious difference between these two ecosystems is that with increasing SWC, R_0 of Equation (10.3) in cropland ecosystems also increased, but no changes occurred in the steppe. Q_{10} at low SWC ($\leqslant 10\%$) was 2.64 and 2.87 in the steppe and cropland, respectively. Q_{10} in the steppe (3.31) was much higher than in the cropland (1.73) when SWC increased to more than 10%.

Flanagan and Johnson (2005) reported that Q_{10} declined with reductions in soil moisture. However, there was an abnormal relationship between Q_{10} and SWC in our study. No difference in Q_{10} was seen between the two ecosystems in the early or late growing season when SWC was less than 10%. During the peak growing season, SWC was higher than 10% most of the time due to frequent rain events and Q_{10} values in the steppe increasing to 3.77 while those in the cropland decreased to 1.73. These results might be caused by the contributions of different compositions to Re. Soil respiration is generally the largest flux contributing to Re. Dugas et al. (1999) demonstrated that up to 90% of soil CO_2 flux was due to root respiration in the prairie. The belowground biomass of the steppe in August was much higher than that of the cropland ($P < 0.01$), which could explain its higher Q_{10} value during the peak growing season. Moreover, organic matter pools in the undisturbed soils of the steppe contributed less to soil respiration than organic matter in the cropland, where plowing disturbed soil structure and accelerated decomposition of soil organic matter (especially with moderate soil water levels), which increased heterotrophic respiration rates (Lindroth et al., 1998) and resulted in a higher contribution to Re. Compared with R_a, R_h had a relatively lower Q_{10} value. Thus, the Q_{10} value of Re in the cropland was low during the peak growing season without water stress. However, Tang et al. (2005) reported a lower Q_{10} for root respiration than soil heterotrophic respiration in a ponderosa pine plantation. Obviously, there is little agreement on the temperature sensitivity of R_a and R_h. More empirical data are needed to confirm these patterns. It further indicated that the temperature sensitivity of Re depended not only on the soil water conditions but also on the biome type and the phenological stage of plant growth and development.

As an integration conclusion through the paired comparison under the same weather conditions between the grazed and intact steppes and between the cultivated and intact steppes, we found that:

–   Soil water content and temperature were the main factors controlling grassland (grazed and intact) and cropland ecosystem carbon assimilation in this semi-arid to arid DEA region. The cropland ecosystem had a stronger ability to uptake carbon than the native steppe ecosystem under optimal soil water and temperature conditions due to species and management. The steppe showed relatively greater carbon uptake under drought stress and low air temperature conditions, which might be the result of evolutionary adaptations of steppe species to local stressful environments. It seemed that the grazed steppe showed relatively greater CO_2 uptake under low air temperature conditions than the fenced steppe.

–   Although higher carbon assimilation ability and light use efficiency appeared in the grazed steppe and cropland ecosystems in relatively moderate soil moisture conditions (e.g., SWC > 10%), both intact steppes showed higher NEE_{max} and α under drought conditions (e.g., SWC < 10%), suggesting that plant species in the intact steppe ecosystems had higher drought tolerance, possess adaptations that compensate for the effects of reduced water availability, and provide substantial advantages over non-drought-tolerant plants in arid environments. It showed that the absence of disturbance might alleviate the stress of high temperature and drought during the hot and dry periods, leading to a high resistance of vegetation to environmental changes.

10.4 Biophysical Regulations of Water and Energy Fluxes

10.4.1 Energy Partitioning and Its Response to Abiotic/Biotic Factors

We developed a mobile energy system to quantify the energy partitioning at three EC measurement sites in Duolun, Xilinhot, and Dongwu of IM in DEA. The system was rotated during the growing season of 2006; site I was sampled from July 9–29, site II from July 31–August 20, and site III from August 21 to September 15.

The diurnal changes of the surface energy balance components (net radiation Rn, sensible heat flux H, lateat heat flux LE, and soil heat flux G) varied greatly with soil moisture content; however, they were distinct among the three study sites (Fig. 10.9). The average soil volumetric water content (θ) in the top 150 mm of the soil profile were 18.1, 6.8, and 7.9%, respectively. The daytime peaks of Rn, H, LE, and G were near 550, 100, 320, and 130 W m^{-2} at site I, 450, 300, 55, and 95 W m^{-2} at site II, and 350, 200, 40, and 95 W m^{-2} at site III, respectively. LE was much higher than H at site I but was clearly lower at sites II and III. The variations in LE, H, and Rn were different among the three sites during the day but similar at night. The daily EF was 0.76, 0.15, and 0.14, the daily sensible heat flux fraction (H/Rn) was 0.24, 0.85, and 0.78, and the daily β was 0.18, 4.55, and 3.25 for sites I, II, and III, respectively. With decreases in θ, LE decreased and H increased across the three sites.

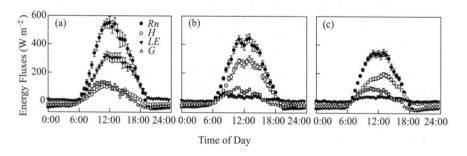

Fig. 10.9 Diurnal trends of net radiation (Rn), sensible heat flux (H), latent heat flux (LE), and soil heat flux (G). Vertical bars indicate standard errors among different days. Beijing standard time is used. Sites I (a), II (b), III (c).

Under high θ conditions (Fig. 10.9a), H, LE, and G showed trends similar to those observed for Rn—increasing during the morning and reaching maximum values by 11:00–11:30 h. LE exceeded both H and G during the day and decreased during the late afternoon and early evening. At night, H and G dropped below zero and the negative Rn was accounted for by the release of heat from the soil. However, the energy partitioning under dry conditions (Figs. 10.9b and c) was distinct from those described above. G reached a maximum value ~ 100 W m^{-2} at 10:30–11:00 h, which was earlier than at site I, and then gradually declined throughout the afternoon. The LE values at sites II and III varied little throughout the day. At these two sites, the daytime H dropped later than at site I, with delayed G, and increased gradually throughout the morning, reaching a maximum in the early afternoon (13:00), whereas a maximum at site I occurred at 11:00. G was larger than H for site I and larger than LE for sites II and III. The percentages of G/Rn were 26%, 24%, and 30% at the G maximum times at sites I, II, and III, respectively, with negative correlation with the plant cover ($r = -0.964$, $P = 0.086$, one-tailed test).

Soil moisture played a critical role in partitioning the energy flux. Under wet and high-LE conditions (Fig. 10.9a), all of the energy fluxes either increased or decreased consistently. Under dry conditions (Figs. 10.9b and c), however, Rn was typically dissipated by means of G and H rather than by LE. At the two drier sites, for example, peak G reached nearly 30% of Rn at corresponding times at mid-morning and then dropped rapidly to negative values, whereas H increased throughout the morning until early afternoon. At these three sites, G plays an important role in energy partitioning and is higher than H at site I (Fig. 10.9a) and higher than LE at sites II and III (Fig. 10.9b and c) during the majority of the day, agreeing with the studies of Bastable et al. (1993) and Heusinkveld et al. (2004). G/Rn was 70% at night (20:00–4:00) and 20% during the day (9:00–16:00). Our findings on G were similar to 25% of Rn found for North American grasslands at midday during drought conditions (Meyers, 2001). We also found that G was overwhelmingly dominant at night, similar to the findings by Li et al. (2006). The nighttime partitioning was similar at sites I and III, which were both slightly larger than site II, likely because site II had a thicker litter cover where a part of the heat storage term was not included in this study.

10.4.2   Ecosystem Water and Energy Fluxes between Grazed and Ungrazed Grasslands and between Grassland and Cultivated Cropland

Chen et al. (2009) examined the changes in energy balance and partitioning and their biophysical regulations as a result of land use change in four steppe ecosystems (two are the steppe and cropland in Duolun and the other two are the fenced steppe and degraded steppe in Xilinhot) in IM of DEA.

1. Energy balance and partitioning in the different land use type ecosystems

The results showed that the seasonal patterns of energy fluxes of Rn among LE, H, and G of the four sites were very low (near zero for LE and H and negative values for Rn and G) during the non-growing season. For both sites, at the beginning of March, Rn went up to a positive value and continued to increase, reaching a maximum in July, and then gradually decreased. The annual variation of LE showed a similar one-peak curve with the change of Rn, while LE was relatively low in the early spring and started to rapidly increase after May. The maximum value of LE appeared in mid-July for the Duolun sites (13.96 and 14.64 MJ m^{-2} d^{-1} for the Duolun steppe (DS) and the Duolun cropland (DC) and June for the Xilinhot sites (9.04 and 8.59 MJ m^{-2} d^{-1} for the Xilinhot degraded steppe (XD) and the Xilinhot fenced steppe (XF). LE obviously decreased after mid-August and became extremely low when the soil froze in late October. The seasonal pattern of H was different from that of LE. H significantly increased with the increase of Rn from late March but began to decrease in May, even though Rn kept increasing. H started to increase again in August and reached the second peak in about late August.

More than 85% of Rn was partitioned as H and LE, whereas the contribution of G and S_{soil} (heat flux in the upper above the soil heat flux plate) was very small at all of the sites (Table 10.3). LE/Rn values remained low during the non-growing season, with mean values of 0.25, 0.30, 0.25, and 0.18 for DS, DC, XD, and XF, respectively. Over the growing season, the LE/Rn increased and peaked in July at Duolun and in June at Xilinhot. The seasonal changes in H/Rn were reversed to that of LE/Rn at all four sites, as expected. The lowest value of H/Rn was observed during the growing season when LE/Rn was the highest, while H/Rn began increasing in late September as LE/Rn rapidly decreased. Rapid and extreme seasonal changes in the Bowen ratio (β, H/LE) were also observed at all four sites, which corresponded to the same periods of shifting dominance in LE and H. Low LE and high H during severe drought periods resulted in a dramatic increase in the mean daytime β. The summertime β values were consistently lower compared to those during the wintertime, possibly due to high LE and low H fluxes.

The seasonal changes of LE flux (i.e., evapotranspiration) are often affected by the seasonal changes in the air as well as soil temperature, radiation, soil moisture, and LAI. The temperature and precipitation increases, along with vegetation development, were the primary reasons for LE increases during the summer period. The significantly lower LE flux and fraction (LE/Rn) in the Xilinhot sites suggested that the partitioning of the surface energy was very sensitive to the change in precipitation in those semi-arid ecosystems in IM of the DEA region. On one hand, limited precipitation could cause a decrease in

Table 10.3 Daily means of solar radiation, energy balance components, and major biological and meteorological factors of different sites in IM (Chen et al. 2009).

	Non-growing Season (Oct.–Apr.)				Growing Season (May–Sept.)				Whole Year			
	DS	DC	XD	XF*	DS	DC	XD	XF	DS	DC	XD	XF*
T_a (°C)	−6.21	−6.21	−8.64	−8.68	15.11	15.12	15.57	15.48	2.73	2.73	1.51	1.45
T_s (°C)	−2.65	−2.30	−4.92	−6.04	17.17	17.66	18.44	16.34	5.66	6.07	5.26	3.72
VWC (%)	6.11	5.51	7.60	8.79	15.68	11.31	11.84	13.67	10.12	7.91	9.45	10.92
VPD (kPa)	0.30	0.30	0.24	0.23	0.78	0.78	0.94	0.94	0.50	0.50	0.53	0.53
Rainfall (mm)	30	30	18	18	394	394	184	184	424	424	202	202
LAI	–	–	–	–	0.47	1.20	0.25	0.26	–	–	–	–
Rn (MJ m^{-2} d^{-1})	2.67	2.68	1.87	3.15	9.48	9.48	8.82	9.86	5.52	5.53	4.79	5.96
LE (MJ m^{-2} d^{-1})	0.91	1.01	0.91	0.70	5.70	4.74	3.23	3.71	2.91	2.65	1.89	3.01
H (MJ m^{-2} d^{-1})	2.56	2.04	1.03	1.76	3.01	3.16	3.91	5.51	2.75	2.65	2.24	4.63
G (MJ m^{-2} d^{-1})	−0.13	−0.35	−0.15	−0.29	1.06	0.81	0.88	0.69	0.37	0.16	0.28	0.46
S (MJ m^{-2} d^{-1})	0.003	0.004	0.006	−0.009	0.002	0.003	0.003	0.003	0.003	0.004	0.004	0.001
LE/Rn	0.25	0.30	0.25	0.18	0.61	0.51	0.37	0.41	0.41	0.40	0.31	0.35

(Continued)

	Non-growing Season (Oct.–Apr.)				Growing Season (May–Sept.)				Whole Year			
	DS	DC	XD	XF*	DS	DC	XD	XF	DS	DC	XD	XF*
H/Rn	0.84	0.73	0.66	0.75	0.32	0.35	0.45	0.61	0.61	0.56	0.57	0.60
G/Rn	0.04	0.03	−0.01	0.07	0.07	0.06	0.06	0.05	0.05	0.04	0.02	0.06
S/Rn	−0.01	−0.01	−0.01	0.01	−0.005	−0.004	−0.008	0.01	−0.01	−0.01	−0.08	0.02
BER	1.24	0.95	0.94	0.71	1.04	0.91	0.90	1.01	1.10	0.93	0.91	0.98
Bowen ratio	7.96	6.63	4.58	6.59	1.19	2.10	3.21	3.21	5.19	4.70	3.97	3.98
LE/LE_{eq}	0.49	0.45	0.47	0.20	0.71	0.56	0.42	0.41	0.58	0.50	0.44	0.36
g_c(mm s^{-1})	3.07	3.77	2.88	1.77	5.54	4.42	2.23	2.66	4.19	4.04	2.54	2.46
Omega	0.18	0.24	0.18	0.13	0.44	0.34	0.25	0.22	0.29	0.28	0.21	0.20

T_a—daily air temperature; T_s—daily soil temperature at 5 cm depth; VWC—daily soil volumetric water content at 10cm depth; VPD—daily vapor pressure deficit; LAI—leaf area index; Rn—daily net radiation; LE—daily latent heat flux; H—daily sensible heat flux; G—daily soil heat flux; S_{soil}—daily soil heat storage; BER—energy balance ratio; Bowen ratio—midday Bowen ratio; LE_{eq}—equilibrium evapotranspiration; g_c—midday canopy surface conductance; Omega—midday decoupling factor. Midday was defined as 10:00 am through 15:00 pm local standard time. DS—Duolun steppe; DC—Duolun cropland; XD—Xilinhot degraded steppe; XF—Xilinhot fenced steppe.
* The data from December 2005 to April 2006 in the XF site were not available.

soil moisture and limit the refilling of dry soil, which will decrease the evaporation component of LE. On the other hand, higher daily vapor pressure deficit (VPD) together with high temperatures and radiation could drive a reduction in the stomatal conductance of the foliage and canopy and, therefore, transpiration.

The seasonal changes in H/Rn were generally reverse those of LE/Rn at all four of the sites (Table 10.3), as expected from the energy budget equation. Studies showed that the pattern of the partition of available energy into sensible heat flux and latent heat flux in grasslands was apparently affected by management practices (e.g., grazing intensity), although the magnitude of management impacts was also intertwined with and dependent upon other environmental factors such as soil moisture and plant phenology (Li et al., 2000). The evaporative fraction of the available energy tends to decrease with the increasing intensity of grazing due to the reduction of vegetation cover. Consequently, sensible heat fraction tends to increase. The available energy of XF was about 13% higher than that of XD in Xilinhot. However, there was only 3% higher LE/Rn at the fenced steppe site than at the degraded site, while another 10% of the available energy was partitioned to H. There was no difference in β between these two sites. This might be attributed to the dramatic drought stress in Xilinhot. In the Duolun site, the steppe showed a significantly higher latent heat fraction and a lower β value than the cropland, although the cropland had about three times greater LAI during the growing season than that of the steppe. In practice, crops are planted in late May, germinated in early June, and harvested in early September, while the growing season for native grasses extends from late April to late September in IM. Apparently, agricultural activities could result in a rapid shift between LE and H and largely decrease the latent heat fraction because of a shortened plant growing period. In addition, lower soil moisture may also be a reason for a higher β value in a cropland ecosystem.

2. Climatic and biological control of energy partitioning

LE/LE_{eq}, defined as the ratio of midday LE to LE_{eq} (the equilibrium latent heat flux), appeared < 1 through the whole year at all four sites, except in the case of several exceptionally high values (about 1.2) that occurred in the early spring in XD. The lowest LE/LE_{eq} values (< 0.2) occurred in May and late autumn (September to November), while the highest values (> 1) were recorded in early spring and mid-summer (June to July). The mean LE/LE_{eq} during the non-growing season ranged from 0.45 to 0.49. At the Duolun sites, the maximum LE/LE_{eq} (1.06 at DS and 0.97 at DC) in the growing season approached 1. Throughout the whole growing season, the mean LE/LE_{eq} were 0.71, 0.56, 0.42, and 0.41 in DS, DC, XD, and XF, respectively (Table 10.3). Partitioning available energy to sensible and latent heat fluxes is dependent on both the biological and climatological conditions of an ecosystem. The LE/LE_{eq} is often used as a measure for comparison studies on the control of daily evaporation by atmospheric and physiological factors among sites, because this ratio normalizes site LE values against equilibrium rates (LE_{eq}) determined primarily by net radiation (Wilson et al., 2002). Wet ecosystems, which have an unlimited supply of water, have high LE/LE_{eq} ratios (> 1.26), while dry ecosystems with low potential evaporation rates have a characteristically low LE/LE_{eq} ratio (< 1) (Chen et al., 2009). During the growing season, DS showed higher LE/LE_{eq} than DC in Duolun, especially during the periods from late May to mid-June and from mid-August to September, indicating that crop cultivation and agricultural management (such as plowing, seeding, and harvesting) may decrease the latent heat fraction and the evapotranspiration of the ecosystem in this semi-arid area. The LE/LE_{eq} values of the Xilinhot sites were significantly lower than those of the Duolun sites and there was no obvious difference in LE/LE_{eq} between the fenced and degraded steppe sites in Xilinhot. Meyers (2001) reported that the LE/LE_{eq} ratio was between 0.6 and 0.7 for grassland sites during the non-drought years, which dramatically dropped to 0.39 during the drought year. LE/LE_{eq} values similar to the Xilinhot values were reported by Li et al. (2007) for a Mongolian steppe site during the growing season (LE/LE_{eq} values ranging from 0.04 to 0.70). These low LE/LE_{eq} values indicated the restriction of the water supply for LE and evapotranspiration at both of these semi-arid steppe ecosystems and evidently showed an insignificant effect from grazing on the latent heat fraction in a drought year.

Canopy surface conductance (g_c) is the aggregate conductance of leaves (transpiration through stomates), soil, and within-canopy turbulent transport. The seasonal changes of midday mean g_c for the rain-free periods appeared to have obvious differences in g_c among the four sites during the growing season, with seasonal means of 5.54, 4.42, 2.23, and 2.66 mm s^{-1} for DS, DC, XD, and XF, respectively (Table 10.3). There was a significantly positive relationship between LAI and g_c at all four sites. Significantly positive relationships were also found between g_c and LE/LE_{eq} in all four sites. The slope of the steppe was larger than that of the cropland in Duolun; however, the fenced steppe and the degraded steppe in Xilinhot showed similar slope values. The g_c value reflects the biological control of evapotranspiration (i.e., latent heat fraction). Wilson and Baldocchi (2000) pointed out that g_c responded primarily to two different biological phenomena during the growing season: changes in leaf area and changes in leaf-level stomatal conductance. The latter response can occur due to changes in photosynthetic capacity or to changes in humidity deficits, soil water content, and solar radiation. A significantly positive relationship between LAI and g_c suggested that the increased g_c values were associated with the increased leaf area. The g_c values at the Xilinhot sites seemed lower during summertime. The lasting drought conditions at these Xilinhot sites might be the reason for the stomatal closure that reduced the photosynthetic activity of the ecosystems. The significantly positive relationships between g_c and LE/LE_{eq} indicated that the lack of precipitation coupled with high VPD resulted in the decrease of stomatal conductance that limited the latent heat partitioning of energy. The smaller slope of regression curves in the Xilinhot site further indicated that LE/LE_{eq} at these sites was less sensitive to changes of g_c and more dependent on the ambient humidity deficit.

The decoupling coefficient (Omega), an index for separating the effect of VPD on the LE from that of Rn, showed similar seasonal changes with g_c. Midday mean Omega values at these study sites ranged from 0.44 to 0.22 during the growing season. The Omega values only reached values of > 0.5 at the Duolun sites in July. Following its peak, the Omega value rapidly decreased and approached a similar level to those in the Xilinhot sites in late August. Both crop cultivation and large animal grazing decreased g_c and Omega values. In this study, the difference between the surfaces in relation to the relative effect of the radiation and specific humidity deficit on transpiration were analyzed by the Omega factor (V). Overall, small values of V indicate that LE (therefore, evapotranspiration) is highly sensitive to surface conductance and the ambient humidity deficit, while high values of V indicate that LE or evapotranspiration is more sensitive to net radiation (Jarvis et al., 1986). The lower seasonally averaged V values of the cropland than the steppe site in Duolun indicated that the LE fraction and evapotranspiration coupled more with the air-specific humidity deficit than with net radiation, which was consistent with the lower soil water content in the cropland than the steppe. Thus, non-irrigated agricultural management carried out in the semi-arid IM steppe would exacerbate drought and increase the sensibility of evapotranspiration to water restrictions. Similar to LE/LE_{eq}, the V values of the two sites in Xilinhot were remarkably lower than those in Duolun and no significant differences in the V values existed between the degraded and fenced sites. Those results showed that the dependence of the LE fraction on the water deficit and canopy conductance will remarkably increase in a drought year.

From the above whole year of eddy-covariance energy flux measurements over four sites with different land use types (steppe and cropland in Duolun; fenced and degraded steppes in Xilinhot) in the IM steppe showed that more than 85% of Rn was partitioned as H and LE. The seasonal changes of energy fluxes (Rn, LE, H, and G) at the four sites were similar, with very low values during the snow-cover period (December to February) and increases and peaks in the growing season. A reverse seasonal change was found in partitioning available energy into LE and H, which resulted in the significant seasonal changes in the Bowen ratio (β). The summertime β values (1.19–3.21) were low due to high LE and low H fluxes, while the wintertime β values (4.58–7.96) were relatively high due to very low LE. Human agricultural activities in the cropland ecosystems resulted in a rapid shift in energy partitioning between LE and H and dramatically decreased the latent heat fraction due to the shortening of the growth period for row crops compared with native plant species. The substantial suppression of LE in the Xilinhot sites in July indicated that precipitation might be the most important factor regulating the energy partition in those semi-arid ecosystems in IM. The significantly positive relationships between g_c and LE/LE_{eq} of all of the sites suggested that a lack of precipitation in conjunction with high VPD might result in a large decrease in stomatal conductance, hence hampering the latent heat partitioning of available energy in semi-arid ecosystems in IM. Decreases in both g_c and V at the cropland and the degraded steppe showed that land use change would reduce the latent flux fraction and increase its sensibility to air and soil drought. In conclusion, cultivation significantly decreased the LE fraction and changed the seasonal pattern of energy partitioning between LE and H in a wet year, while grazing did not show significant effects on the energy partition in a dry year. The results showed that the effects of land use change on the energy partition might be relative to drought and especially to precipitation change in the semi-arid steppe region (Chen et al., 2009).

Acknowledgements

Our study for this chapter has been partially supported by the Natural Science Foundation of China (No.31170454, No.30928002), the Knowledge Innovation Program of the Chinese Academy of Sciences (No.KZCX2-YW-Q1-06), LCLUC Program of NASA, the State Key Basic Research Development Program of China (No.2007CB106800). The author gratefully acknowledges the support of K. C. Wong Education Foundation, Hong Kong, and the USCCC. Many colleagues (e.g., Wenli Zhang, Lisa Delp Taylor, Haixia Miao, Jianfeng Liu, Long Wei, Ping Zhang, Tingting Ren) contributed data, thoughtful discussion, and language edit.

References

Baldocchi, D. D., Hincks, B. B., and Meyers, T. P. (1988). Measuring biosphere-atmosphere exchanges of biologically related gases with micrometeorological methods. *Ecology*, 69, 1331–1340.

Bastable, H. G., Shuttleworth, W. J., Dallarosa, R. L. G., Fisch, G., and Nobre, C. A. (1993). Observations of climate, albedo, and surface radiation over cleared and undisturbed amazonian forest. *International Journal of Climatology*, 13, 783–796.

Beringer, J., Chapin, F. S., Thompson, C. C., and McGuire, A. D. (2005). Surface energy exchanges along a tundra-forest transition and feedbacks to climate. *Agri-*

cultural and Forest Meteorology, 131, 143–161.

Betts, R. A. (2000). Offset of the potential carbon sink from boreal forestation by decreases in surface albedo. *Nature*, 408, 187–190.

Bremer, D. J., Auen, L. M., Ham, J. M., and Owensby, C. E. (2001). Evapotranspiration in a prairie ecosystem: Effects of grazing by cattle. *Agronomy Journal*, 93, 338–348.

Chen, J. Q., Paw, U., Ustin, S. L., Suchanek, T. H., Bond, B. J., Brosofske, K. D., and Falk, M. (2004). Net ecosystem exchanges of carbon, water, and energy in young and old-growth Douglas-fir forests. *Ecosystems*, 7, 534–544.

Chen, S., Chen, J., Lin, G., Zhang, W., Miao, H., Wei, L., Huang, J., and Han, X. (2009). Energy balance and partition in Inner Mongolia steppe ecosystems with different land use types. *Agricultural and Forest Meteorology*, 149, 1800–1809.

Chen, Y., Li, W., and Xu, C. (2006). Characterization of photosynthesis of Populus euphratica grown in the arid region. *Photosynthetica*, 44, 622–626.

Davidson, E. A., Janssens, I. A., and Luo, Y. Q. (2006). On the variability of respiration in terrestrial ecosystems: moving beyond Q(10). *Global Change Biology*, 12, 154–164.

DeForest, J. L., Noormets, A., McNulty, S. G., Sun, G., Tenney, G., and Chen, J. Q. (2006). Phenophases alter the soil respiration-temperature relationship in an oak-dominated forest. *International Journal of Biometeorology*, 51, 135–144.

Dugas, W. A., Heuer, M. L., and Mayeux, H. S. (1999). Carbon dioxide fluxes over bermudagrass, native prairie, and sorghum. *Agricultural and Forest Meteorology*, 93, 121–139.

Ewers, B. E., Oren, R., and Sperry, J. S. (2000). Influence of nutrient versus water supply on hydraulic architecture and water balance in Pinus taeda. *Plant Cell and Environment*, 23, 1055–1066.

Falge, E., Baldocchi, D., Olson, R., Anthoni, P., Aubinet, M., Bernhofer, C., Burba, G., Ceulemans, R., Clement, R., and Dolman, H. (2001). Gap filling strategies for defensible annual sums of net ecosystem exchange. *Agricultural and Forest Meteorology*, 107, 43–69.

Farquhar, G. D., Schulze, E. D., and Kuppers, M. (1980). Responses to humidity by stomata of Nicotiana-glauca L and Corylus-avellana L are consistent with the optimization of carbon-dioxide uptake with respect to water-loss. *Australian Journal of Plant Physiology*, 7, 315–327.

Flanagan, L. B., and Johnson, B. G. (2005). Interacting effects of temperature, soil moisture and plant biomass production on ecosystem respiration in a northern temperate grassland. *Agricultural and Forest Meteorology*, 130, 237–253.

Frank, A. B. (2003). Evapotranspiration from northern semiarid grasslands. *Agronomy Journal*, 95, 1504–1509.

Fu, Y. L., Yu, G. R., Sun, X. M., Li, Y. N., Wen, X. F., Zhang, L. M., Li, Z. Q., Zhao, L., and Hao, Y. B. (2006). Depression of net ecosystem CO_2 exchange in semi-arid Leymus chinensis steppe and alpine shrub. *Agricultural and Forest Meteorology*, 137, 234–244.

Gaylon, S. C. and John, M. N. (1998a). Liquid water in organisms and their environment. In: *An Introduction to Environmental Biophysics*. Spring, 53–61.

Gaylon, S. C. and John, M. N. (1998b). Temperature. In: *An introduction to Envi-*

ronmental Biophysics. Spring, 15–35.

Hernandez-Ramirez, G., Hatfield, J. L., Prueger, J. H., and Sauer, T. J. (2010). Energy balance and turbulent flux partitioning in a corn-soybean rotation in the Midwestern US. *Theoretical and Applied Climatology,* 100, 79–92.

Heusinkveld, B. G., Jacobs, A. F. G., Holtslag, A. A. M., and Berkowicz, S. M. (2004). Surface energy balance closure in an arid region: role of soil heat flux. *Agricultural and Forest Meteorology,* 122, 21–37.

Hunt, J. E., Kelliher, F. M., McSeveny, T. M., and Byers, J. N. (2002). Evaporation and carbon dioxide exchange between the atmosphere and a tussock grassland during a summer drought. *Agricultural and Forest Meteorology,* 111, 65–82.

Janssens, I. A., Lankreijer, H., Matteucci, G., Kowalski, A. S., Buchmann, N., Epron, D., Pilegaard, K., Kutsch, W., Longdoz, B., Grunwald, T., Montagnani, L., Dore, S., Rebmann, C., Moors, E.J., Grelle, A., Rannik, U., Morgenstern, K., Oltchev, S., Clement, R., Gudmundsson, J., Minerbi, S., Berbigier, P., Ibrom, A., Moncrieff, J., Aubinet, M., Bernhofer, C., Jensen, N.O., Vesala, T., Granier, A., Schulze, E. D., Lindroth, A., Dolman, A.J., Jarvis, P. G., Ceulemans, R., and Valentini, R. (2001). Productivity overshadows temperature in determining soil and ecosystem respiration across European forests. *Global Change Biology,* 7, 269–278.

Jarvis, P. G., McNaughton, K. G., MacFadyen, A., and Ford, E. D. (1986). Stomatal control of transpiration: Scaling up from leaf to region. In: *Advances in Ecological Research.* Academic Press, 1–49.

Klein, J. A., Harte, J., and Zhao, X. Q. (2005). Dynamic and complex microclimate responses to warming and grazing manipulations. *Global Change Biology,* 11, 1440–1451.

LeCain, D. R., Morgan, J. A., Schuman, G. E., Reeder, J. D., and Hart, R. H. (2000). Carbon exchange rates in grazed and ungrazed pastures of Wyoming. *Journal of Range Management,* 53, 199–206.

Li, L. H., Han, X. G., Wang, Q. B., Chen, Q. S., Zhang, Y., Yang, J., Bai, W. M., Song, S. H., Xing, X. R., and Zhang, S. M. (2002). Seperating root and soil microbial contributions to total soil respiration in a grazed grasslang in the Xilin River Basin. *Acta Phytoecologica Sinica,* 26, 29–32.

Li, S. G., Asanuma, J., Eugster, W., Kotani, A., Liu, J. J., Urano, T., Oikawa, T., Davaa, G., Oyunbaatar, D., and Sugita, M. (2005). Net ecosystem carbon dioxide exchange over grazed steppe in central Mongolia. *Global Change Biology,* 11, 1941–1955.

Li, S. G., Asanuma, J., Kotani, A., Davaa, G., and Oyunbaatar, D. (2007). Evapotranspiration from a Mongolian steppe under grazing and its environmental constraints. *Journal of Hydrology,* 333, 133–143.

Li, S. G., Eugster, W., Asanuma, J., Kotani, A., Davaa, G., Oyunbaatar, D., and Sugita, M. (2006). Energy partitioning and its biophysical controls above a grazing steppe in central Mongolia. *Agricultural and Forest Meteorology,* 137, 89–106.

Li, S. G., Harazono, Y., Oikawa, T., Zhao, H. L., He, Z. Y., and Chang, X. L. (2000). Grassland desertification by grazing and the resulting micrometeorological changes in Inner Mongolia. *Agricultural and Forest Meteorology,* 102, 125–137.

Lindroth, A., Grelle, A., and Morén, A. S. (1998). Long-term measurements of boreal forest carbon balance reveal large temperature sensitivity. *Global Change Biology,*

4, 443–450.

Lloyd, J., and Taylor, J. A. (1994). On the temperature-dependence of soil respiration. *Functional Ecology*, 8, 315–323.

Meyers, T. P. (2001). A comparison of summertime water and CO_2 fluxes over rangeland for well watered and drought conditions. *Agricultural and Forest Meteorology*, 106, 205–214.

Miao, H., Chen, S., Chen, J., Zhang, W., Zhang, P., Wei, L., Han, X., and Lin, G. (2009). Cultivation and grazing altered evapotranspiration and dynamics in Inner Mongolia steppes. *Agricultural and Forest Meteorology*, 149, 1810–1819.

Michaelis, L., and Menten, M.L. (1913). Die Kinetik der Invertinwirkung. *Biochem. Z.*, 49, 333–369.

Ni, B. R., and Pallardy, S.G. (1991). Response of gas exchange to water stress in seedlings of woody angiosperms. *Tree Physiology*, 8, 1–9.

Ogren, E. (1993). Convexity of the photosynthetic light-response curve in relation to intensity and direction of light during growth. *Plant Physiology*, 101, 1013–1019.

Owensby, C. E., Ham, J. M., and Auen, L. M. (2006). Fluxes of CO_2 from grazed and ungrazed tallgrass prairie. *Rangeland Ecology & Management*, 59, 111–127.

Polley, H. W., Frank, A. B., Sanabria, J., and Phillips, R. L. (2008). Interannual variability in carbon dioxide fluxes and flux-climate relationships on grazed and ungrazed northern mixed-grass prairie. *Global Change Biology*, 14, 1620–1632.

Qi, Y., Xu, M., and Wu, J.G. (2002). Temperature sensitivity of soil respiration and its effects on ecosystem carbon budget: nonlinearity begets surprises. *Ecological Modelling*, 153, 131–142.

Shao, C. L., Chen, J. Q., Li, L. H., Xu, W. T., Chen, S. P., Gwen, T., Xu, J. Y., and Zhang, W. L. (2008). Spatial variability in soil heat flux at three Inner Mongolia steppe ecosystems. *Agricultural and Forest Meteorology*, 148, 1433–1443.

Stewart, J. B., and Verma, S. B. (1992). Comparison of surface fluxes and conductances at 2 contrasting sites within the FIFE area. *Journal of Geophysical Research-Atmospheres*, 97, 18623–18628.

Tang, J., Misson, L., Gershenson, A., Cheng, W., and Goldstein, A. H. (2005). Continuous measurements of soil respiration with and without roots in a ponderosa pine plantation in the Sierra Nevada Mountains. *Agricultural and Forest Meteorology*, 132, 212–227.

Wan, S., Luo, Y., and Wallace, L. L. (2002). Changes in microclimate induced by experimental warming and clipping in tallgrass prairie. *Global Change Biology*, 8, 754–768.

Wang, Z., Xiao, X., and Yan, X. (2010). Modeling gross primary production of maize cropland and degraded grassland in Northeastern China. *Agricultural and Forest Meteorology*, 150(9), 1160–1167.

Wen, X. F., Yu, G. R., Sun, X. M., Li, Q. K., Liu, Y. F., Zhang, L. M., Ren, C. Y., Fu, Y. L., and Li, Z. Q. (2006). Soil moisture effect on the temperature dependence of ecosystem respiration in a subtropical Pinus plantation of Southeastern China. *Agricultural and Forest Meteorology*, 137, 166–175.

Wilson, K. B., and Baldocchi, D.D. (2000). Seasonal and interannual variability of energy fluxes over a broadleaved temperate deciduous forest in North America. *Agricultural and Forest Meteorology*, 100, 1–18.

Wilson, K. B., Baldocchi, D. D., Aubinet, M., Berbigier, P., Bernhofer, C., Dolman, H., Falge, E., Field, C., Goldstein, A., Granier, A., Grelle, A., Halldor, T., Hollinger, D., Katul, G., Law, B. E., Lindroth, A., Meyers, T., Moncrieff, J., Monson, R., Oechel, W., Tenhunen, J., Valentini, R., Verma, S., Vesala, T., and Wofsy, S. (2002). Energy partitioning between latent and sensible heat flux during the warm season at FLUXNET sites. *Water Resources Research*, 38, 1294–1304.

Xu, L.K., and Baldocchi, D.D. (2004). Seasonal variation in carbon dioxide exchange over a Mediterranean annual grassland in California. *Agricultural and Forest Meteorology*, 123, 79–96.

Zhang, W. L., Chen, S. P., Chen, J., Wei, L., Han, X. G., and Lin, G. H. (2007). Biophysical regulations of carbon fluxes of a steppe and a cultivated cropland in semiarid Inner Mongolia. *Agricultural and Forest Meteorology*, 146, 216–229.

Zhao, L., Li, Y. N., Xu, S. X., Zhou, H. K., Gu, S., Yu, G. R., and Zhao, X. Q. (2006). Diurnal, seasonal and annual variation in net ecosystem CO_2 exchange of an alpine shrubland on Qinghai-Tibetan Plateau. *Global Change Biology*, 12, 1940–1953.

Authors Information

Changliang Shao[1,2]*, Shiping Chen[1], Jiquan Chen[2], Linghao Li[1]

1. State Key Laboratory of Vegetation and Environmental Change, Institute of Botany, the Chinese Academy of Sciences, Beijing 100093, P.R. China
2. Department of Environmental Sciences, University of Toledo, Toledo, OH 43606, USA
* Corresponding author

Chapter 11

Afforestation and Forests at the Dryland Edges: Lessons Learned and Future Outlooks

Csaba Mátyás, Ge Sun, and Yaoqi Zhang

Summary: In the Drylands of Northern China, such as the Loess Plateau region, a buffer zone of planted forests—a "Green Great Wall"—has been created in the last five decades. These government programs have often generated unintended environmental consequences, and have failed to achieve the desired benefits. Planted forests withhold erosion, dust storms and silting of streams but may reduce stream flow due to higher water use with serious consequences for water management. In spite of contrary expectations, afforestations improve regional climate conditions only insignificantly in the temperate zone. Cost-effective, ecologically useful forest policy in the Drylands requires the consideration of local conditions, and of alternatives such as restoration of grasslands and shrublands. The negative impact of expected rising temperatures on vitality and survival of forests needs to be taken into account as well.

11.1 Introduction

Forests provide many ecosystem services and benefits to society such as regulating water resources and soil protection. In the DEA region, forests are scarce (see Table 4.1 in Chapter 4 of this book). Forest restoration plays an important role in rehabilitating of degraded and over-exploited lands. China has invested great efforts in country-wide afforestation and forest conservation in order to stabilize water supply and reduce soil erosion and desertification.

Recent studies suggest that the effects of afforestation are ambivalent in the drought-threatened drylands. Water consumption of man-made forests may contribute to water scarcity and aridification, and may not achieve the goals of environmental protection (Jackson et al., 2005; Sun et al., 2006; Andréassian, 2004; Brown et al., 2005; Wang, Y. et al., 2008). Projected changes in global climate pose a further challenge on dryland ecosystems, as relatively small changes in the moisture balance may lead to considerable ecological shifts. Forests may even become a factor of increasing climate forcing (Drüszler et al., 2010; Gálos et al., 2011; Mátyás et al., 2009).

At the potentially retreating xeric limits of forests in the meeting zone of steppe and woodland, afforestation and restoration of natural conditions should be carefully considered. Especially concerns about hydrology and climate should be weighed when making decisions about land use changes (Cao, 2008; Cao et al., 2011; Mátyás, 2010b).

In order to put the issue into a wider perspective, the chapter introduces also examples from other countries where ecological conditions are comparable to the DEA drylands, such as from the United States, and from the forest steppes in Russia and Hungary, without the intention to comprehensively survey and assess the global situation of dryland afforestation.

11.2 Vegetation Zonation and Climate

Precipitation and temperature are the ultimate drivers of vegetation distribution on earth. Globally, zonal forests are generally found in areas where annual precipitation exceeds evapotranspiration, and thus forests are sources of surface water resources. For example it is estimated that 50% of US water supply comes from forest lands (Brown et al., 2008). Water use by temperate forests is generally less than 700 mm during the growing season, suggesting that ecosystem water use (tree transpiration + evaporation) is limited by energy and water availability (Fig. 11.2) (Sun et al., 2011a). Analyzing temperate grassland and forest sites in the USA, Sun et al. (2011a) found that in the warm-temperate zone forests require at least 400 mm of precipitation in the growing season to sustain desired functions, and grassland and scrub lands are found at sites where growing season precipitation is below 400 mm (Fig. 11.1). Interestingly, atmospheric precipitation was barely sufficient for most ecosystems among the 16 sites in the USA, with only one exception in the humid subtropical region (in Fig. 11.1).

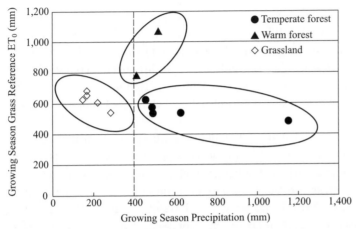

Fig. 11.1 Growing season precipitation and grass reference evapotranspiration (i.e., P-ET) are major drivers for zonal vegetation distribution. Data are derived from an ecohydrological study with sites in the United States, China, and Australia. The figure shows grassland sites (cold steppes and milder-climate shrublands), poplar plantations where precipitation exceeds 400 mm (warm forests), respectively temperate forest sites (Sun et al., 2011a).

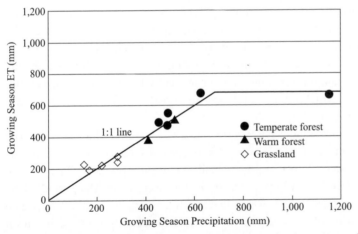

Fig. 11.2 Water use (growing season evapotranspiration vs. precipitation) of grasslands and forests across ecohydrologic study sites.

11.3   Climate Forcing Effect of Forests: Ambiguous Conditions at the Dryland Edges

Climate model simulations prove that land cover, i.e., vegetation, has an important role in climate regulation. Due to their higher leaf area, forests display a high photosynthetic activity and transpiration. Leaf area index (LAI) of deciduous forests exceed that of croplands by a factor of approximately 1.4–1.7 (Breuer et al., 2003). Forest cover modifies the hydrological cycle, albedo and turbulent fluxes above land surface. Thus, forests have both a direct and indirect effect on factors contributing to both natural and also to anthropogenic climate forcing (land use change, forest destruction or afforestation). Half a century of land use changes may be enough to cause significant regional changes of climate (Drüszler et al., 2010).

Although it is generally believed that planting forests may mitigate climate change impacts and slow down the aridification process, current views on the role of temperate forests are contradictory and fragmentary. Some scientists even state that—contrary to the tropics—afforestation in the temperate zone may have climatically "little to no benefits" (Bala et al., 2007; Bonan, 2008). Forests have a lower albedo than crops (e.g., coniferous forests: 0.14 vs. crops: 0.24; Breuer et al., 2003), which is compounded by the fact that evergreen (coniferous) forest canopy masks highly reflective winter snow cover. The lower albedo of forest cover may cause somewhat higher summer and winter temperatures, thus worsening drought. Contradicting investigations at the Canadian prairie-woodland border (Hogg and Price, 2000) indicate, however, that forest cover may have a positive effect. Summer temperatures were significantly lower where deciduous woodland cover remained. The deciduous forest mainly causes anomalies in summer; temperatures were cooler, mean precipitation was higher and length of growing season increased. It seems that the balance between albedo and actual evapotranspiration determines whether there is a cooling or warming effect. The surface roughness of the forest crown layer leads to different aerodynamic conductance, which alters cloudiness and creates additional atmospheric feedback (Drüszler et al., 2010).

Applying the climate model REMO [1], Gálos et al. (2011) have studied the regional feedback effect of afforestation for projected climatic scenarios in the transition zone between forest and grassland climate in Hungary. The climate of the recent past (1961–1990) was compared to projections for the period 2070–2100, when precipitation is expected to decline by 24% (Gálos et al., 2007). The effect of transpiration of the additionally planted forests (d_{Tr}) on precipitation increase (d_P) was investigated for a realistic, 7% increase of 20% of the present forest cover, and also for an extreme scenario, where all available agricultural land would have been afforested, resulting in 92% of forest cover (Fig. 11.3).

The mitigating effect of higher evapotranspiration on decreasing precipitation appeared relatively modest. Even the unrealistic maximum afforestation could lower the projected precipitation decrease by one quarter only (<6% in Fig. 11.3). It may be suspected that part of the precipitation feedback is carried into neighboring regions by westerly winds.

---

1 REMO is a climate model developed at the Max Planck Institute for Meteorology, Hamburg, Germany.

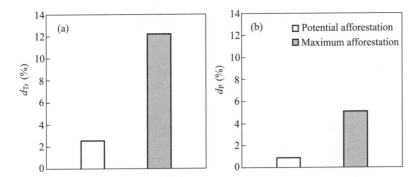

Fig. 11.3 Feedback of planned afforestation on future climate conditions in Hungary. (a) projected transpiration increase (d_{Tr}); (b) projected precipitation increase (d_P), for a realistic (light columns) and an extreme scenario (dark columns). Explanation is in the text (Gálos et al., 2011).

The impact of energy balance on climate due to past land use changes has also been investigated in Hungary. Lower albedo, as well as changed sensible/latent heat ratios resulted in a rise of summer temperature in the last century in afforested regions. The increase remained however relatively modest, compared to the overall anthropogenic rise of temperature (Drüszler et al., 2010).

When planning and assessing afforestation in semi-arid conditions, the projected climate of the far future has to be carefully considered because of the extreme long-term character of forest management. Stability and growth of forests depend on available water resources and temperature conditions of the future. Across the temperate zone, a relatively rapid increase of annual mean temperature has been observed in recent decades, and the dryland zone in China and Mongolia is no exception. In the last half century, both average temperatures and climatic extremes increased (Qi et al., 2012). For instance, average temperatures in Mongolia increased by more than 2 °C since 1940 and nine out of the ten warmest years occurred after 1990 (Lu et al., 2009). In North China, frequency of droughts intensified during the past several decades, leading to an unprecedented increase of dry areas (Piao et al., 2010). Growing season anomalies have been generally increasing in China in the 2000s: drought events got significantly stronger in North China and soil moisture declined (Zhao and Running, 2010).

At the same time, analyses of impacts on forests in dry regions are limited or sporadic. For instance, Food and Agriculture Organization of the United Nations (FAO) global statistics do not yet calculate with the effect of forest cover loss due to aridification (FAO, 2010). There are reports from western North America (Allen et al., 2010; Hogg and Price, 2000), while impacts in Eastern Europe, Central Asia and the Chinese drylands are less known (Zhang et al., 2008b; Piao et al., 2010; Mátyás, 2010a). Experiments on growth and yield confirm the negative impact of rising temperatures on vitality and survival (Mátyás et al., 2010; Fig. 11.4).

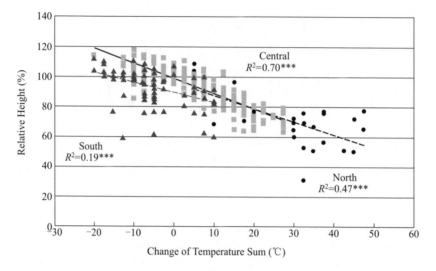

Fig. 11.4 Growth response of geographically transferred Scots pine (*Pinus sylvestris*) populations (provenances) to simulated warming. The increase of annual temperature sum (in °C degree-days) resulted in a decline of relative height irrespective of origin (central, northern or southern populations). Re-analyzed data of six Russian experiments (Mátyás et al., 2010).

11.3.1 Low Elevation Xeric Limits: Vulnerable Forest-Grassland Transition

Xeric (or rear, trailing[1]) limits are at the low latitude, low altitude end of distribution ranges of temperate forests, where presence/absence of species is determined by climatic aridity (Mátyás et al., 2009). Xeric limits appear in semi-arid zones along the foothills of mountain ranges, and at the edges of dry basins such as in Central Asia or in the DEA region (for maps, see Chapter 4 in this book). Xeric limits follow the southern edge of closed forests westwards through Russia and the Ukraine as far as Hungary. Temperate xeric limits exist also on other continents, along the edge of the Prairies of North America, notably from the southwest states of the USA northward into Alberta (Canada). At the xeric limit, the closed forest belt forms a transition zone or ecotone toward the open woodland or forest steppe, which dissolves with decreasing precipitation

---

1 The terms in brackets refer to events of postglacial migration, where xeric limits represent the "rear" end of shifting vegetation zones, triggered by gradual warming.

into the true steppe or grassland. The forest/grassland ecotone is dependent on a volatile minimum of rainfall and is therefore sensitive to prolonged droughts. The physical characteristics of the land surface (e.g., albedo, evapotranspiration, roughness etc.) as well as carbon cycle and ecological services are strongly affected by land use policy and changes in this transition zone.

The forest-grassland transition zone is especially vulnerable to expected climatic changes in flat lands because of the magnitude of the *latitudinal lapse rate*. It is generally known that the altitudinal lapse rate for temperature (i.e., the rate of change with increasing elevation) is 5.0–6.5°C/1,000 m. The latitudinal (south to north) lapse rate is less recognized. In the temperate zone its mean value is around 6.9°C/1,000 km—a difference of three magnitudes. This means that predicted changes of temperature affect disproportionately larger tracts of plains as compared to mountainous regions. A temperature increase of only +1°C causes a shift upwards along a mountain slope of approximately 170 m. On a plain, the same change triggers a shift of close to 150 km (Jump et al., 2009). This explains the much greater vulnerability of rain-dependent vegetation on plains.

11.3.2 Management of Forests—Plantations vs. Close to Nature Ecosystems

In most temperate zone countries, returning to close-to-nature forest management seems to be the general trend to mitigate impacts of environmental change. The concept is based on the hypothesis that stability and persistence of forest ecosystems are warranted by plant communities evolved during the past millennia, and enhancing the naturalness of forests will also enhance their stability. The hypothesis is challenged at the xeric limits by numerous constraints, such as

- Long-lasting human interference and land use have caused a partial or total loss of natural (woody) plant cover;
- Number of native species expected to tolerate potential environmental changes is usually low;
- Functioning of close-to-natural systems is disturbed by indirect human effects (e.g., grazing, air pollution) and by the expected climatic changes and extreme events.

These constraints necessitate a revision of the commitment to naturalness, first of all in regions of high drought risk. Across the DEA region, plantation forest have been generally introduced. Recent changes in forest policy support a return to close-to-nature conditions in China (Xu, 2011). It is believed, however, that the carefully planned and active human interference is unavoidable in dry lands because a long-term adaptation to environmental changes has to be considered, especially at the xeric limits.

11.4 Effects of Forest Management on Forest Hydrological Balances in Dry Regions: A Comparison of China and the United States

Compared to grasslands or short-cycle crops, forests have large above-ground biomass and deeper roots. Therefore forests can use more water (Wang, Y. et al., 2011) and can capture larger amounts of carbon through photosynthesis as carbon and water cycles are highly coupled (Law et al., 2002; Sun et al., 2011b). World-wide vegetation manipulation experiments show that forest removals reduce water use, i.e., evapotranspiration (ET), and thus increase watershed stream flow. On the other hand, reforestation or afforestation on watersheds previously covered by native grassland can reduce stream flow due to an increase in ET (Andréassian, 2004). Forests have higher ET than harvested sites or croplands, so groundwater table levels are generally lower under forests (Sun et al., 2000). Figure 11.5 demonstrates one such case in the forest steppe

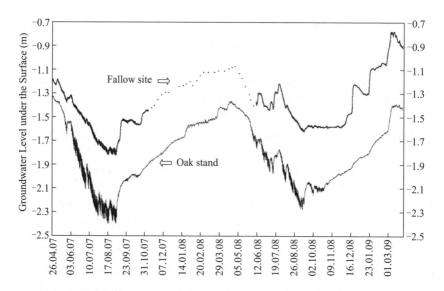

Fig. 11.5 Water table fluctuation in the course of one year under an oak forest (*Quercus robur*) and a neighboring grassland (fallow) site in the forest steppe zone of Hungary.
Source: Móricz et al. (2012).

region of Hungary where the forest stand's ET was 30% higher than that of neighboring grassland.

Earlier long-term forest hydrologic studies focused on deforestation effects, floods and sedimentation (Alila et al., 2009). Hydrologic studies on the consequences of forestation have emerged in the past decade (Scott et al., 2005; Sun et al., 2006; Wang, Y. et al., 2011). In particular, evaluation of worldwide reforestation campaigns has shown that human intervention requires a closer look at the unexpected consequences. An emerging question is how reforestation in different climatic regimes affects watershed functions such as water yield (Sun et al., 2006). The potential water yield reduction following afforestation for bioenergy development, ecological restoration, respectively for climate change mitigation, has drawn renewed attention to the relations between forests and water resources in watersheds (Calder, 2002; Brown et al., 2005; Jackson et al., 2005; Trabucco et al., 2008; Malmer et al., 2009) and on a regional scale (Ellison et al., 2011). The hot debate on "planting" or "not planting" policies is especially relevant in arid regions or regions with scarce water resources (Greeff, 2010).

11.4.1   China

The comprehensive forest hydrological studies that address forest-water relations did not start until the 1990s. Important findings emerged rapidly in the past two decades (Wei et al., 2008). In dry Northern China, such as the Loess Plateau region, empirical and modeling studies confirm that that forest vegetation and associated soil conservation engineering had a significant influence on watershed stream flow (Zhang et al., 2008a, 2008b; Wang, Y. et al., 2011; Wang, S. et al., 2011).

Recent forest hydrology studies have detected that land cover and land use changes played a substantial role in stream flow reduction downstream (Zhang et al., 2008a). A water balance modeling study suggests that if 5.8% and 10.1% of the study area on the Loess Plateau is planted with trees, stream flow will decrease by 5.5% and 9.2%, respectively. The rate of stream flow reduction decreased from dry to wet area in the Loess Plateau region (Zhang et al., 2008a). In another 40-year retrospective study (1959–1999), Zhang et al. (2008b) examined stream flow and climate data from 11 catchments in the Loess Plateau to investigate the response of stream flow to land use/cover changes. They found that all catchments had significant reductions in annual stream flow of -0.13 mm to -1.58 mm per year between 1971 and 1985. Land use/cover changes accounted for over 50% of the reduction in mean annual stream flow in 8 out of the 11 catchments, while in the remaining three watersheds precipitation and potential evaporation were more important. Among the soil conservation measures, construction of sediment-trapping dams and reservoirs, and the diversion for irrigation appeared to be the main cause of reduced stream flow.

To understand the effects of vegetation on stream flow in the Loess Plateau region, Wang, Y. et al. (2011) constructed multi-annual water balances for 57 basins to estimate annual evapotranspiration (ET) and runoff for forest lands and non-forest lands. Mean annual precipitation was 463 mm and the corresponding averages of annual ET and runoff were 447 mm and 16 mm for forest lands, and 424 mm and 39 mm for non-forest lands. Although the difference in annual runoff was only 23 mm, this is a large difference in relative terms, being equivalent to nearly 60% of annual runoff from non-forest lands. The authors argue that large-scale afforestation may have serious consequences for water management and sustainable development in dry regions because of runoff reduction.

11.4.2   United States

Since the late 1930s, numerous "paired watershed" studies have been conducted in the United States to examine forest management effects (harvesting with various intensities, species conversion, farming as an alternative), on water quality and yield across various climatic and topographic conditions (Ice and Stednick, 2004). In general, humid areas with high precipitation have higher hydrologic response in absolute terms, but dry areas with low water flow can have a higher relative response. For example, clear-cutting a deciduous forest in the humid south-eastern USA, with an annual precipitation >1,800 mm, can result in an increase in stream flow of 130–410 mm per year, which is 15%–40% of undisturbed control watersheds, while the same management practice in the drier area of northern Arizona with an annual precipitation of 500–600 mm may result in a water yield increase of 60 mm or >40% of undisturbed control watersheds. Zou et al. (2009) summarized century-long vegetation manipulation experiment studies in the Colorado River Basin that provide a bounty of knowledge about effects of change in forest vegetation on stream flow in water-deficit areas. The watershed is situated at the headwaters of streams and rivers that supply much of the water to downstream users in the western United States. The authors found that vegetation can be managed to enhance annual water yields while still providing other ecological services. The effects of vegetation manipulation on stream flow are associated with the precipitation/elevation gradient and, therefore with vegetation type. An annual water yield increase between 25 mm and 100 mm could be achieved by implementing vegetation manipulation in the high elevation subalpine and mixed conifer forests, the lower ponderosa pine forests and portions of the low elevation chaparral scrublands. The annual precipitation was generally above 500 mm in areas where a 100 mm increase in stream flow was achieved. Negligible or small increases in water yield were observed from treating sagebrush, pinyon-juniper woodlands and desert scrubs, with an annual precipitation below 500 mm. This study suggests that reforestation is likely to cause relatively larger hydrologic effect in areas where precipitation is roughly balanced by evapotranspiration demand, i.e., above 500 mm.

11.5   Past and Future of Forest Policy in Dryland Regions of China

11.5.1   Causes and Consequences of Expanding Desertification

In China, deserts and semi-desert lands cover an estimated 150 million ha, while another 140 million ha of pastures and croplands are threatened by desertification, mainly because of human activities such as deforestation and overgrazing (Fullen and Mitchell, 1994). One third of the desertification is attributed to over-harvesting of forests (Liu et al., 2008); although droughts and climate change contribute as well. As a consequence, the Gobi desert is expanding by an estimated rate of 246 thousand ha per year (Ratliff, 2003). In the most seriously threatened Loess Plateau region of China, 43 million ha are affected by desertification. In addition, 99 million ha of land is subject to salinization and alkalization (MOF, 1995; see also Chapter 13 and Chapter 4 in this book). Soil erosion causes heavy sediment loads and deposition in river beds especially on the Loess Plateau. There is general agreement that increasing flood damages are partly caused by soil erosion that clog drainage channels and reduce the holding capacity of many reservoirs.

11.5.2   Shelterbelt Development and Sand Control Programs in China

Soil conservation practices were initiated in the 1950s and were aimed at reducing upland soil erosion and sedimentation of rivers (e.g., on the Yellow River). Therefore, vegetation restoration, especially afforestation, has been encouraged as an effective measure for controlling soil erosion, to alleviate flash floods, increase forest productivity and diversify rural incomes. Furthermore, afforestation is increasingly viewed as an effective measure of carbon sequestration to partially offset CO_2 emissions. This policy has brought about an extensive conversion of grassland, shrubland and slope farmland into forest plantations (Wang, Y. et al., 2011).

To combat environmental deterioration, a buffer zone called as "Green Great Wall" has been envisaged along the transition from the humid farming region to the arid and semi-arid grazing zone to block expanding desertification. Since the green belt stretches across Northeast, North and Northwest China, it has been named "Three-north Shelterbelt Forest Program". The program was launched in 1978 and aimed to green a total of 23.74 million ha by 2010 (CFA, 2007; see also Chapter 13 in this book).

The program has progressed in several phases. During the first phase (1979–1985), more than 11.2 million ha were planted, out of which over 6 million ha were successful. In the second phase (1986–1995), about 10.6 million ha were planted, resulting in 6.8 million ha of fully stocked forest. On the whole, between 1978 and 1995, 10% of the desert land was restored, 13 million ha of agricultural land were protected by the planted forest, and 10 million ha of pasture land were converted to forest. During this period about 10 million US dollars from the central government budget and about 40 million US dollars were locally provided annually to finance this program.

In the third phase (1995–2000), the work continued with priority in the regions of Liaoning, Jilin, Heilongjiang, Beijing, Hebei, the Kerqin Desert, the Mu Us Desert, the Loess Plateau north of Wei River, the southern part of Luliang Mountains and the Hexi Corridor, etc. (Zhang et al., 1999). Apparently, some corrections have been made after problems with planted trees had been reported. The use of native species and of more shrubs in the restoration programs has been encouraged by both academic scholars and governmental officials. For example, in the plan made in 2000, 40% of an estimated 9.5 million ha potential afforestation area was foreseen to be planted with shrubs (SFA, 2000). To supplement the Three-north Shelterbelt Forest Program in order to establish a second belt to block sand/dust storms was launched in 2000. The program is often called as the Sandstorm Control Program for Areas in the Vicinity of Beijing and Tianjin). The objective to control 6.12 million ha of land at risk of desertification was achieved and 101,200 persons have been reallocated (CFA, 2007).

11.5.3 Debates and Critics about the Achievements of the Past Programs

The initiative of greening the three regions of the North started in the 1960s, and resumed and intensified after the country suffered from a big flood in 1998 and from frequent sand storms in North China, including Beijing. While the achievements had been widely acclaimed, the projects increasingly stirred criticism and were debated. It was pointed out that afforestation often generated unintended environmental, ecological, and socioeconomic consequences, and has failed to achieve the desired ecological benefits (Cao, 2008; Cao et al., 2011; Xu, 2011; see also Chapter 13, in this book).

It has been argued that the arid and semi-arid regions are mostly not suitable for tree growth which requires a lot of water and makes the land even drier, leading to more severe soil erosion and desertification. The majority of the vegetation restoration programs—including the Three-north Shelter Forest Program and the Regional Sandstorm Control Programs—involve planting trees in areas where annual precipitation is less than 400 mm. As a result, water yields have dropped by 30%–50% and vegetation cover has decreased by 6.1% on the semi-arid Loess Plateau (Sun et al., 2006). In the whole DEA region, although forest cover increased by 22 tsd. km^2 between 2001 and 2007 but the total area of woody savannas and shrublands decreased nearly five-fold (91 tsd. km^2) according to IGPB's classification (Chapter 4 in this volume)

In the government plans, trees were over-planted while subsequent care was disregarded, and unsuitable species were used. For example, aspen (*Populus tremula*) which is excessively water-demanding, accounts for almost half of China's reforestation (Liu et al., 2008). Exotic tree species were being planted in arid and semi-arid conditions, where perennial grasses with their extensive root systems would better protect the topsoil (Xu, 2011). Other experts (e.g., Yang and Ci, 2008) argue that afforestation is not equivalent to forestry or tree planting, and is closer to the term of "greening" as a large part of restoration was executed with shrubs (CFA, 2007). This could be true at the later stage when the problem was discovered.

Economy is another aspect of the debate. Critics contend that the massive tree planting efforts are expensive—the Green Great Wall being an expensive band aid on a century-old wound. At the turn of the century the central government made a strategic realignment of the former afforestation projects in the whole country, and integrated them into the State Key Forestry Programs (SKFPs), including the Natural Forest Protection Program (NFPP), the Cropland Conversion to Forests Program (CCFP), the Key Shelterbelt Development Programs for the Three North and the Yangtze River Basin (3Ns and YRB), and the Sand Control Program for the Beijing and Tianjin area (SCP). For the SKFPs, China has invested a total of 183.5 billion RMB (ca. US $22 billion) from 1998 to 2006 (Wang, G. et al., 2008). A majority of the programs are concentrated in the arid and semi-arid zones of the North and Northwest.

Such huge investments raise the question of economic efficiency. Many studies have been conducted to assess the results. Efficiency is however not the only goal. The afforestation projects also aim to alleviate poverty, improvement of food supply and population reallocation. Local studies (e.g., Zhi et al., 2004; Kong,

2004) are insufficient to evaluate the benefits of the whole program. To assess the ecological, economic and social impacts of the programs in their complexity remains a challenging task.

11.5.4   Lessons Learned from Past

As a result of mixed experiences with the past programs and due to increasing criticism, China's forest and environmental policy has been changing in the recent times. It was recommended to shift from political solutions to economic solutions, e.g., paying farmers to reduce livestock, raising water prices to encourage conservation, and temporarily relocating local inhabitants away from arid areas to allow recovery (Williams, 2002). The emphasis has been shifted from tree plantations to natural ecosystem restoration, and an engineering approach has been replaced with a more comprehensive socio-economic and ecological attitude which is usually more cost-effective. Shrub and grassland restoration has been qualified as equally important as the forest restoration according to the "Green for Grain" policy initiated in the early 2000s. A more social approach has been increasingly adopted like providing economic incentives for farmers to reduce livestock and relocation to other areas or cities (Ratliff, 2003).

The updated policy recommendations may be summarized as follows. The objective is greening or vegetation restoration instead of just afforestation. Greening should be tailored to local environmental conditions and the right plant species or species composition should be used, considering also alternatives such as shrubland and grassland restoration. The emphasis should be placed on the results achieved rather than on efforts invested. Long-term monitoring must be implemented to provide the data needed to develop a cost-effective, scientifically based restoration policy (Cao et al., 2011).

11.6   Conclusions

Current views and experiences about the role of forests at dryland edges are contradictory. Although forests may provide multiple ecological benefits, reforestation or afforestation on watersheds previously covered by native grassland can reduce stream flow due to higher water use. Therefore large-scale afforestation may have serious consequences for water management and sustainable development because of runoff reduction. In the drylands of Northern China, such as the Loess Plateau region, studies confirm results achieved in other parts of the world that forest management and associated soil conservation engineering have a significant influence on watershed stream flow.

Forests directly influence atmospheric climate forcing. Therefore it is believed that forests mitigate climate change impacts such as warming and aridification. According to some investigations, the forest cover at dryland edges has a positive effect on lowering summer temperatures. Detailed studies indicate that in spite of increased evapotranspiration, precipitation changes only insignificantly in afforested regions. At the same time, the lower albedo of forests may cause a moderate temperature rise.

In China, deserts have been expanding, mainly because of deforestation and overgrazing. Huge efforts have been invested in the arid and semi-arid regions to combat desertification and soil erosion and to control the environmental deterioration. A buffer zone of planted forests—a "Green Great Wall"—has been created in the last five decades in the areas where annual precipitation is often less than 400 mm. The politically directed afforestation programs had often generated unintended environmental, ecological and socioeconomic consequences, and had failed to achieve the desired benefits. Due to mechanistic implementation of projects, planting of forests has often led to more severe soil erosion and desertification. To consider the relation of expenditures to benefits achieved is essential, but afforestation projects are intended not only to improve ecological conditions but also to play an important socioeconomic role.

A cost-effective, scientifically based forest policy in the drylands requires the consideration of local environmental conditions, of alternatives such as restoration of grasslands and scrublands, and the use of the proper technology. Experiences from the United States confirm that vegetation can be successfully managed to enhance annual water yields while still providing other ecological benefits. Carefully planned human interference is therefore essential in dry lands, to achieve a policy of restoration and of adaptation to the long-term effects of expected environmental changes.

References

Alila, Y., Kuras, P. K., Schnorbus, M., and Hudson, R. (2009). Forests and floods: A new paradigm sheds light on age-old controversies. *Water Resources Research*, 45, W08416, doi:10.1029/2008WR007207.

Allen, C. D., Macalady, A. K., Chenchouni, H., Bachelet, D., McDowell, N., Vennetier, M., Kizberger, T., et al. (2010). A global overview of drought and heat-induced tree mortality reveals emerging climate change risks of forests. *Forest Ecology and Management*, 259, 4, 660–684.

Andréassian, V. (2004). Waters and forests: From historical controversy to scientific debate. *Journal of Hydrology*, 291, 1–27.

Bala G., Caldeira K., Wickett, M., Phillips, T. J., Lobell, D. B., Delire, C., et al.

(2007). Combined climate and carbon-cycle effects of large-scale deforestation. *Proceedings of the National Academy of Sciences*, 104, 6550–6555.

Bonan, G. B. (2008). Forests and climate change: Forcings, feedbacks, and the climate benefits of forests. *Science*, 320, 1444–1449.

Breuer, L., Eckhardt, K., and Frede, H.G. (2003). Plant parameter values for models in temperate climates. *Forest Ecology and Management*, 169, 237–293.

Brown, A. E., Zhang, L., McMahon, T. A., Western, A. W., and Vertessy, R. A. (2005). A review of paired catchment studies for determining changes in water yield resulting from alterations in vegetation. *Journal of Hydrology*, 310, 28–61.

Brown, T. C., Hobbins, M. T., and Ramirez, J. A. (2008). Spatial distribution of water supply in the coterminous United States. *Journal of the American Water Resources Association*, 44, 6, 1474-1487.

Calder, I. R. (2002). Forests and hydrological services: reconciling public and science perceptions. *Land Use and Water Resources Research*, 2, 1–12.

Cao, S. (2008). Why large-scale afforestation efforts in China have failed to solve the desertification problem. *Environmental Science and Technology*, 42, 1826–1831.

Cao, S., Sun, G., Zhang, S., Chen, L., Feng, Q., Fu, B., McNulty, S., et al. (2011). Greening China naturally. *AMBIO*, 40, 7, 828–831.

CFA. (2007). Forestry Development in China. Accessed Nov. 2, 2011, at http://www.china.org.cn/e-news/news071204-1.htm.

Drüszler, Á., Csirmaz, K., Vig, P., and Mika, J. (2010). Effects of documented land use changes on temperature and humidity regime in Hungary. In: Saikia, S. P. (Ed.). *Climate Change*. Int. Book Distr., Dehra Dun, Uttarakhand, India, 394–418.

Ellison, D., N. Futter, M., and Bishop, K. (2011). On the forest cover-water yield debate: From demand- to supply-side thinking. *Global Change Biology*, doi: 10.1111/j.1365-2486.2011.02589.x.

FAO. (2010). Global Forest Resources Assessment 2010. Main report. FAO Forestry Paper, 163, Rome.

Fullen, M. A., and Mitchell, D. J. (1994). *Desertification and Reclamation in North-Central China*. *AMBIO*, 23, 2, 131–135.

Gálos, B., Jacob, D., and Mátyás, C. (2011). Effects of simulated forest cover change on projected climate change—A case study of Hungary. *Acta Silvatica et Lignaria Hungarica*, 7, 49–62.

Gálos, B., Lorenz, P., and Jacob, D. (2007). Will dry events occur more often in Hungary in the future? *Environmental Research Letters*, doi: 10.1088/1748-9326/2/3/034006.

Greeff, L. (2010). Thirsty tree plantations, no water left and climate confusion: what version of sustainable development are we leaving our children? *EcoDoc Africa*, 39.

Hogg, E. H., and Price, D. T. (2000). Postulated feedbacks of deciduous forest phenology on seasonal climate patterns in the Western Canadian Interior. *Journal of Climate*, 13, 4229–4243.

Ice, G. G., and Stednick, J. D. (2004). *A century of forest and wildland watershed lessons*. Society of American Foresters, Bethesda, Maryland, 287.

Jackson, R. B., Jobbágy, E. B., Avissar, R., Roy, S. B., Barrett, D. J., Cook, C. J., et al. (2005). Trading water for carbon and with biological carbon sequestration. *Science*, 310, 1944–1947.

Jump, A., Mátyás, C., and Penuelas, J. (2009). The paradox of altitude-for-latitude comparisons in species' range retractions. *Trends in Ecology and Evolution*, 24, 12, 694–700.

Kong, F. (2004). Analysis of policy question and optimizing proposal about converting cropland to forest and grassland project. *Scientia Silvae Sinicae*, 40, 5, 62–70.

Law, B. E., Falge, E., Gu, L., Baldocchi, D. D., Bakwin, P., Berbigier, P., Davis, K., et al. (2002). Environmental controls over carbon dioxide and water vapor exchange of terrestrial vegetation. *Agricultural and Forest Meteorology*, 113, 97–120.

Liu, J., Li, S., Ouyang, Z., Tam, C., and Chen, X. (2008). Ecological and socioeconomic effects of China's policies for ecosystem services. *Proceedings of the National Academy of* Sciences, 105, 9477–9482.

Lu N., Wilske, B., Ni, J., John, R., and Chen J. (2009). Climate change in Inner Mongolia from 1955 through 2005. *Environmental Research Letters*, 4, 045006.

Malmer, A., Murdiyarso, D., Bruijnzeel, L. A., and Ilstedt, U. (2009). Carbon sequestration in tropical forests and water: A critical look at the basis for commonly used generalizations. *Global Change Biology*, 16, 1–6.

Mátyás, C. (2010a). Forests and Climate Change in Eastern Europe and Central Asia. Forests and Climate Change. W. Pap. Nr. 8, Rome, FAO, 189.

Mátyás, C. (2010b). Forecasts needed for retreating forests (Opinion). *Nature*, 464, 1271.

Mátyás, C., Vendramin, G. G., and Fady, B. (2009). Forests at the limit: Evolutionary-genetic consequences of environmental changes at the receding (xeric) edge of distribution. *Annals of Forest Science*, 66, 800–803.

Mátyás, C., Nagy, L., and Ujvári-Jármay, É. (2010). Genetically set response of trees to climatic change, with special regard to the xeric (retreating) limits. *Forstarchiv* (Hannover), 81, 130–141.

MOF–Ministry of Forestry. (1995). *China's 21 st Century Agenda: The Forestry Action Plan*. Beijing: Forestry Publishing House of China.

Móricz, N., Mátyás, C., Berki, I., Rasztovits, E., Vekerdy, Z., Gribovszki, Z. (2012). Comparative water balance study of forest and fallow plots. *iForest*, 5: 188–196.

Piao, S. L., Ciais, P., Huang, Y., Shen, Z. H., Peng, S. S., Li, J. S., et al. (2010). The impacts of climate change on water resources and agriculture in China. *Nature*, 467, 43–51.

Qi, J., Chen, J., Wan, S., and Ai, L. (2012). Understanding the coupled natural and human systems in Dryland East Asia. *Environmental Research Letters*, 7, 015202.

Ratliff, E. (2003). The Green Wall of China. *WIRED Mag.* Accessed Nov. 2, 2011 at http://www.wired.com/wired/archive/11.04/greenwall.html.

Scott, D. F., Bruijnzeel, L. A., and Mackensen, J. (2005). The hydrologic and soil impacts of reforestation in the tropics. In: Bonell, M. and Bruijnzeel, L.A. (Eds.). *Forests, Water and People in the Humid Tropics*. Cambridge, UK: Cambridge University Press, 622–651.

SFA (2000). *The General Plan for the Fourth Stage of the Three Norths Shelter Forest System Project*. Beijing: State Forestry Administration.

Shapiro, J. (2001). Mao's War against Nature: Politics and the Environment in Revolutionary China. Cambridge, UK: Cambridge University Press.

Sun, G., Zhou, G. Y., Zhang, Z. Q., Wei, X. H., McNulty, S. G., and Vose, J. M.

(2006). Potential water yield reduction due to forestation across China. *Journal of Hydrology*, 328, 548–558.

Sun, G., Alstad, K., Chen, J., Chen, S., Ford, C. R., Lin, G., et al. (2011a). A general predictive model for estimating monthly ecosystem evapotranspiration. *Ecohydrology*, 4, 245–255.

Sun, G., Caldwell, P., Noormets, A., Cohen, E., McNulty, S. G., Treasure, E., et al. (2011b). Upscaling key ecosystem functions across the conterminous United States by a water-centric ecosystem model. *Journal of Geophysical Research*, 116, G00J05, doi:10.1029/2010JG001573.

Sun, G., Riekerk, H., and Kornak, L. V. (2000). Groundwater table rise after forest harvesting on cypress-pine flatwoods in Florida. *Wetlands*, 20, 1, 101–112.

Trabucco, A., Zomer, R. J., Bossio, D. A., van Straaten, O., and Verchot, L. V. (2008). Climate change mitigation through afforestation/reforestation: a global analysis of hydrologic impacts with four case studies. *Agricultural Ecosystems and Environment*, 126, 81–97.

Wang, G., Innes, J. L., Lei, J., Dai, S., and Wu, S. (2008). China's forestry reforms. *Science*, 318, 1556–1557.

Wang, Y., Yu, P., Xiong, W., Shen, Z., Guo, M., Shi, Z., et al. (2008). Water yield reduction after afforestation and related processes in the semiarid Liupan Mountains, Northwest China. *Journal of the American Water Resources Association*, 44,5, 1086–1097.

Wang, S., Fu, B., He, C.S., Sun, G., and Gao., G.Y. (2011). A comparative analysis of forest cover and catchment water yield relationships in Northern China. *Forest Ecology and Management*, 262, 7, 1189–1198.

Wang, Y., Yu, P., Feger, K.-H., Wei, X., Sun, G., Bonell, M., et al. (2011). Annual runoff and evapotranspiration of forestlands and non-forestlands in selected basins of the Loess Plateau of China. *Ecohydrology*, 4, 277–287.

Wei, X., Sun, G., Liu, S., Hong, J., Zhou, G., and Dai, L. (2008). The forest, streamflow relationship in China: A 40-year retrospect. *Journal of American Water Resources Association*, 44, 5, 1076–1085.

Williams, D. (2002). *Beyond Great Walls: Environment, Identity, and Development on the Chinese Grasslands of Inner Mongolia*. Stanford University Press.

Xu, J. (2011). China's new forests aren't so green as they seem. *Nature,* 477, 371.

Yang, X., and Ci, L. (2008). Comment on "why large-scale afforestation efforts in China have failed to solve the desertification problem". *Environmental Science and Technology*, 42, 20, 7723.

Zhang, X. P., Zhang, L., McVicar, T. R., van Niel, T. G., Li, L. T., Li, R., et al. (2008a). Modeling the impact of afforestation on mean annual stream flow in the Loess Plateau, China. *Hydrological Proceedings*, 22, 1996–2004.

Zhang, X. P., Zhang, L., Shao, J., Rustomji, P., and Hairsine, P. (2008b). Responses of stream flow to changes in climate and land use/cover in the Loess Plateau, China. *Water Resources Research*, 44, W00A07, doi:10.1029/2007WR006711.

Zhang, Y., Dai, G., Huang, H., Kong, F., Tian, Z., Wang, X., et al. (1999). The forest sector in China: Towards a market economy. In: Palo, M. and Uusivuori, J. (Eds.). *World Forests, Society and Environment*. Berlin, New York: Springer Verlag, 35–45.

Zhi, L., Li, N., Tian, Z., and Wang, J. (2004). Evaluation of social impacts of the project of conversing cropland to forestland in the Western China. *Scientia Silvae Sinicae*, 40, 3, 2–9.

Zhao, M. S., and Running, S. W. (2010). Drought induced reduction in global terrestrial net primary production from 2000 through 2009. *Science*, 329, 940–943

Zou, B. C., Ffolliott, P. F., and Wine, M. (2009). Stream flow responses to vegetation manipulations along a gradient of precipitation in the Colorado River Basin. *Forest Ecology and Management*, 259, 7, 1268–1276.

Authors Information

Csaba Mátyás[1]*, Ge Sun[2], Yaoqi Zhang[3]

1. Institute of Environmental and Earth Sciences, University of West Hungary, 9401 Sopron, Hungary
2. Eastern Forest Environmental Threat Assessment Center, Southern Research Station, USDA Forest Service, Raleigh, NC 27606, USA
3. School of Forestry & Wildlife Sciences, Auburn University, AL 36849-5418, USA

* Corresponding author

Chapter 12

Human Impact and Land Degradation in Mongolia

Ochirbat Batkhishig

Summary: Climate warming and human actions both have negative impacts on the land cover of Mongolia, and are accelerating land degradation. Anthropogenic factors which intensify the land degradation process include mining, road erosion, overgrazing, agriculture soil erosion, and soil pollution, which all have direct impacts on the environment. In 2009–2010, eroded mining land in Mongolia increased by 3,984.46 ha, with an expansion in surrounding road erosion. By rough estimation, transportation eroded 1.5 million ha of land. This area is nearly equal to the total amount of agricultural land in Mongolia. Road erosion reduces pastureland capacity and furthermore creates gullies, a very severe result of soil erosion. Overgrazing is one of the main reasons for land degradation in Mongolia. Pastureland in the vicinity of water bodies, settlements, lakes, and along livestock driving roads has severely degraded. Sand movement and free sand cover is becoming one main indicator of overgrazing and desertification. The 145 settlement areas in the Gobi desert steppe region of Mongolia are affected by sand problems. Agricultural soil loss is another big issue. Research results show about 46.9% of total arable land was eroded, and of that 33.7% of the land has experienced moderate to severe erosion. The shallow soil, sparse vegetation cover, and extra-continental climate are additional factors for soil erosion. To determine soil erosion intensity in the Mongolian steppe areas, we used fallout radionuclide techniques—Cs-137. In the study catchment of Baga Boor valley of central Mongolian steppe areas, soil erosion rates varied from 0.93 to 23.83 t ha^{-1}yr^{-1} and average erosion was 5.613 t ha^{-1}yr^{-1}. The soil sedimentation and accumulation patterns were complicated due to the combination of water and wind erosion. The agricultural soil erosion rates in the case of Selenge aimag Nomgon soum and Central aimag Sumber soum are 32.6 and 49.6 t ha^{-1}yr^{-1}. This is 5.5–8.8 times more than the rate found in the pasture area.

The soil erosion in agricultural fields of Mongolia is thus significant. Land conservation policy and adequate land management practice is therefore currently very important in Mongolia.

12.1 Introduction

Climate warming and human actions both have negative impacts on the land cover of Mongolia, accelerating land degradation and desertification. However, it is difficult to distinguish the exact contribution of each of these factors. In Mongolia, where there is a vast territory occupied by pastureland, the climate warming impact on land cover may be very serious. But most researchers argue for the domination of human impacts over climate warming (Qi and Kulmatov, 2008, Dorjgotov et al. 2002), suggesting that anthropogenic factors are the main causes for land degradation in Mongolia.

The economic growth and mining development in Mongolia over the last decades has accelerated land degradation. Loss of productivity in arid regions has created the major environmental constraints for sustainable development. Land degradation due to mining, road erosion, overgrazing, agricultural soil erosion and settlement area pollution are the major environmental problems of the country. Soil degradation is also recognized as a serious and widespread problem (Bridges and Oldeman, 1999). Many peoples' lives are affected by soil degradation; they may suffer directly from a shortage of food and decreased environmental quality. Creating scientifically accurate assessments and precise estimation of soil degradation in Mongolia are challenging issues. The mining land degradation assessment data are comparatively accurate, but side effects of mining are not clear. In addition, overgrazing and desertification assessment data are very uncertain. Researchers have used different methods and approaches for the study of land degradation, but more comprehensive methods and approaches are still needed.

This Chapter attempts to review land degradation data for Mongolia and presents soil erosion case study results using fallout radionuclide methods.

12.2 Land Degradation Overview

There are several different sources for statistics about land degradation in Mongolia. One of most reliable data sources are the "Land use inventory reports" of the Mongolian Administration of Land Affairs, Geodesy and Cartography. However, some of these data are not very reliable, thus requiring the development of more advanced methods and technologies for accurate estimating. Dregne (2002) noted the uncertainty of world land degradation datasets and the lack of good research data. Table 12.1 presents severe degraded land statistics (Land use inventory report of Mongolia, 2010).

Table 12.1 Severe degraded land of Mongolia, 2010.

Land degradation activities	Area (ha)
Mining exploration	16,061.5
Mining investigation	1,904.5
Road construction	1,206.4
Former military activities	25,483.0
Building construction, pipeline establishment work	255.6
Total	44,911.5

Estimation of pastureland degradation, desertification and road erosion is very complicated, and researchers have used different methods and approaches. Since 2000, environment investigation has been operating using remote sensing, ground observation and monitoring. Research data have become more accurate and realistic. The total area affected by severe degradation has been found at about 44,911.5 ha (Table 12.1). Former military activity degraded a large area of occupied land. Since 1990, army activities have been drastically reduced, with military-affected land naturally recovering for more than 20 years. Mining eroded land increased after 1995 due to gold fever. In 2008, a campaign for mining eroded land reclamation was initiated, but a large area still needs to recover.

Anthropogenic factors that intensify the land degradation process include human activities such as overgrazing, soil erosion of arable land, deforestation, mining, soil pollution, and road erosion, which all have a direct impact on the environment

12.2.1   Mining Land Degradation

Currently, the mining industry in Mongolia is booming. GDP growth for the country in 2011 was about 17%, largely due to mining. However, the negative environmental impact from mining has become a serious problem, especially resulting from gold mining. Anthropogenic land degradation occurs near mining areas and adjacent road networks for transportation. On-site effects of these features have a significant impact: dusting, pasture degradation, water shortage and pollution.

In total, 38.5 million ha or 24.6% of the territory of Mongolia is covered by 4,728 mining licenses (Mijiddorj, 2011). According to the "Land use inventory report of Mongolia 2010", 16,061.5 ha of land was destroyed due to mining explorations and 1,904.5 ha of land was destroyed due to mining investigation.

Mining and inadequate waste management are also significant factors for land degradation. The development of strip mines, as well as the deposition of overburden spoils and tailings all degrade land resources (Batjargal, 1997). A Ministry of Nature Environment report noted that "in 2009–2010 mining eroded land increased by 3,984.46 ha".

In 2009, the Mongolian government adopted laws to stop gold mining activities in upstream river and forested areas. These administrative activities resulted in a decrease of mining land degradation. Mining land reclamation started in 2000, and more areas are incorporated every year.

Illegal gold diggers caused land degradation without any reclamation. In 2006, 66,179 illegal gold diggers were counted, while government activities have resulted in a reduction in the number of gold diggers at the present time. 66,179, 53,959 and 35,000 illegal gold diggers were counted in 2007, 2008, and 2009, respectively (Report of Mining Department, 2010).

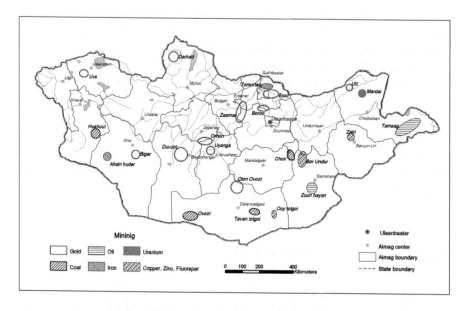

Fig. 12.1 Land degradation surrounding area of mining in Mongolia. All of these mining sites have been developed since 1995.

Table 12.2 Mining land degradation by aimags (province).*

Aimag (province)	Area (ha)
Central	6,645.4
Selenga	3,021.0
Uvurkhangai	2,174.9
Orkhon	2,152.0
Khentii	1,709.0
Umnugobi	1,093.7
Others	1,170.0
Total	17,966.0

* Land use inventory report of Mongolia, 2010.

Table 12.3 Mining land reclamation (ha).*

Year	Technical reclamation	Biological reclamation
2008	898.8	807.9
2009	494.84	280.6
2010	688.1	389.75

* Report of Mining Department, 2010.

The peak period of mining land degradation occurred from 1995 until 2008. After 2008, government control increased and land reclamation work become better. But off site effects of mining land degradation such as road erosion, dusting, and water resource shortage expanded.

12.2.2 Land Degradation by Road

Road erosion is one of biggest contributors to land degradation in Mongolia. There are not exact data for road erosion. By rough estimation, about 1 million ha of land have been covered with vehicle tracks (Sarantuya, 2000). Road erosion is directly related to the number of vehicles, which is drastically increasing. In 2011, the number of vehicles in Mongolia increased 6–7 times as compared to the 1990s.

Heavy machineries used for mining are most destructive by way of soil erosion. From Tavan tolgoi coal mining to the Chinese boundary Zagaan Khad, 240 km of road were heavily degraded by tracks and 3000 ha of soil were eroded.

According to official statistics, the total amount of road in Mongolia is 49,249.9 km, of which only 3,174.8 km is hard covered road, while 3,704.7 km is improved gravel road and 42,370.4 km is soil road (Mongolian Department of Road report, 2010). In reality, however, every single well, spring and "ger" (Mongolian traditional nomadic living tent) is connected by roads. It is therefore difficult to measure the total amount of roads in Mongolia.

Road erosion in Mongolia is increasing due to an increase in vehicles and mining activities. By rough estimation, 1.5 million ha of land have been eroded by transportation. This area is nearly equal to the total amount of agricultural land in Mongolia. Road erosion reduces pastureland capacity and furthermore creates gullies, a very severe form of soil erosion (Fig. 12.2).

Fig. 12.2 Coal transportation in Gobi desert of Mongolia is one of the major causes of soil erosion and dusting. Coal track road in Tavan tolgoi-Zagaan Khad, 2010. Photo: Batkhishig.

12.2.3 Pastureland Degradation and Desertification

Overgrazing is one of main reasons of pastureland degradation (Qi and Kulmatov, 2008). For thousands of years over the history of the Mongolian pasture system, there was some level of equilibrium between the number of livestock and the existing vegetation coverage. A small increase in animal populations or changes in land-use patterns may therefore result in localized degradation. According to the Mongolian Ministry of Nature environmental report, 73.87% (115,525.9 thousand ha) of the country's territory is suitable for agricultural and pastoral livestock production (Nature environment condition report of Mongolia, 2011). Grassland conversion to cropland and the degradation of grassland are largely due to increasing human population and political reforms of pastoral systems (Chuluun and Ojima, 2002).

For many centuries, the amount of livestock in Mongolia was around 20 million, and did not exceed 30 million (Batkhishig, 2000). After the privatizations of the 1990s, the number of livestock rose, and reached 44.8 million in the year 2009 (Fig. 12.3). The number of goats increased due to the high price of cashmere. In 2009, the number of goats was 20.0 million or 44.5% of total livestock. Goats are the animals that are most destructive to pasture and soil, because they eat grass with the roots. As a result of the increase of livestock, pasture pressure rose, which instigated the pasture and soil cover degradation process. According to the reported statistics, 6.8 million ha of pastureland was degraded (Land use inventory report of Mongolia, 2010). Vegetation species gradually changed due to overgrazing, reducing some native species (*Stipa baicalenses, Festuca sibirica etc.*), dominated *Leymus chinensis, Carex duriuscula* and *Artemisia adamsii* (Bazha et al., 2010). Long-term remote sensing data from NOAA/NDVI indicate 69% pasture degradation due to global warming and overgrazing (Erdenetsetseg and Erdenetuya, 2010).

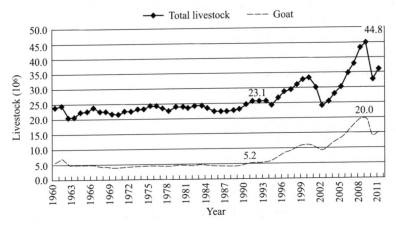

Fig. 12.3 Number of total livestock and goats in Mongolia.

A case study examining the impact of overgrazing on soil cover in the Eastern Hovsgol lake area indicated that soil humus content decreased by 30%–50% in overgrazed areas. Soil temperature increases and moisture content decreases as a result of overgrazing. Topsoil becomes more dense and compact as a result of animal pressure on the soil surface (Batkhishig, 2006).

Pastureland in the vicinity of water bodies, settlements and lakes, and along livestock driving roads, has severely degraded. Water resources have decreased and rivers and springs are desiccating due to aridity, overgrazing and the centralization of settlements. Areas of degraded vegetation have been formed around population centers and wells. By rough estimation, the size of degraded rangelands around these centers totals 200 thousand ha In addition, another 400,000 ha of degraded rangelands are located around numerous desert wells (Kharin et al., 1999).

Researchers and scientists have estimated that 90% of Mongolian territory is vulnerable to desertification and 72% of territory is already affected by desertification (National Program Combating Desertification in Mongolia, 2010). Sand movement and free sand cover are becoming one of the main indicators of desertification, with the 145 settlement areas in the Gobi desert steppe region of the country affected by sand problems. A recent Mongolian report estimates that 5% of desertificated area is very severely affected by land degradation and desertification; 18% is severely affected, 26% is moderately affected and 23% is slightly affected (National Program Combating Desertification in Mongolia. 2010).

Desertification in arid areas seems to depend mostly on precipitation and air temperature. Summer 2011 in Mongolia was very rainy, especially in the month of June. Nearly 80% of the territory of Mongolia had very good grass growth for the first time since 2000. Local peoples of the Gobi desert region claimed as a result "desertification disappeared". There still needs to be a more careful and comprehensive assessment of desertification in this region.

Livestock pressure on pastureland and negative impacts on land cover are increasing. There is a need to improve pasture management and land use policies to prevent pastureland degradation.

12.2.4 Soil Erosion of Arable Land

Cultivated land occupies 1.331 thousand ha of the total land area. Over 57% of total arable land is located in the north-central aimags (provinces) of Tov and Selenge and the northeastern aimag of Dornod in Mongolia.

Since the second half of the 1960s, the agricultural industry has been developed as an individual part of agriculture, and has satisfied all of Mongolia's vegetable needs. The decrease of crop yields, notably affecting the vegetative industry, is primarily related to arable land erosion and degradation. The shallow soil, sparse vegetation cover, and extra-continental climate are additional factors contributing to soil erosion. In its early years, the agricultural industry did not pay any attention to the issue of soil conservation. In 1999, about 60% of total arable land was abandoned (Avaadorj et al., 2000). Research on soil in central and eastern agricultural regions identified that 46.9% of total arable land was eroded, and of this, 33.7% had experienced moderate or severe erosion (Nyamsambuu, 2007).

In topsoil at a depth of 0–20 cm, arable soil humus content loss within 20 years (1970–1990) was about 30.4%; at a depth of 0–10 cm, topsoil had humus loss of 40.3% (Dobrovolskii et al., 2000). Soil erosion of agricultural land was very intensive over the period 1965–1990.

Mongolia implements a short rotation system for use in agriculture named fallow-crop/fallow-crop-crop, and it may be the main cause of soil deterioration. In the past 40 years, due to the conversion from the traditional method, which has been used only for pastoral rangeland, the ecological condition of agricultural land has deteriorated.

In the 1990s, Mongolia's agricultural sector was drastically reduced due to the country's transition to a market economy (Fig. 12.4). Over the last 20 years, most agricultural soil was in the process of naturally recovering its organic resources and fertility. However, most of the 200,000 ha of fertile agricultural land were utilized intensively, without any fertilizers. Between 1999 and 2008, a period of hot, dry climate dominated Mongolia, and the agricultural sector declined. The Mongolian government launched the agriculture-expanding program "Atar-3" in 2008; agriculture is now increasing, and wet, rainy years have followed the dry period. However, not many soil conservation measures have been practiced. Soil erosion, nutrient depletion, and loss of productivity are threatening agricultural land.

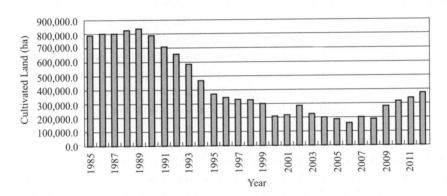

Fig. 12.4 Cultivated land of Mongolia.

12.2.5   Deforestation

In Mongolia, 12,917.5 thousand ha of land are covered by forest; this represents 8.26% of the country's total territory (Nature environment report of Mongolia, 2011). Mongolia is one of the most poor forest resource countries in the world. The forest area includes 140 species of trees and bushes, and is mainly dominated by coniferous and deciduous trees. Due to climate warming and negative human impact, the frequency and probability of occurrence of forest fires is increasing. In the last 30 years, forest area has decreased by 210.3 thousand ha, and 757.4 thousand ha of forestland has been damaged by forest fires and cutting (Dorjsuren, 2009).

Most timber harvesting is carried out by clear-cutting. Deforested areas, as well as vehicle tracks, which are generally located on sloped or steep terrain, are particularly subject to water erosion. Forests are cut for commercial and household purposes, and saxaul (desert tree—*Haloxylon ammodendron*) and bushes are cut for household purposes as well.

In the period of 1990–2005, human impact on forestland increased. Forest conservation policies have improved in the last few years. Forest cutting and forest fires are decreasing.

12.2.6   Soil Pollution

Soil and water pollution in big cities, especially in Ulaanbaatar, the capital city of Mongolia, is a major environmental problem. Urban and settlement areas occupy 620.6 thousand ha or 0.39% of the total territory. The population of urban areas is continuously increasing; currently about 63.3% of the population is living in cities (Statistical Yearbook of Mongolia, 2010).

Domestic and industrial waste is currently deposited on the soil surface in unnecessarily large and designated dumping sites on the outskirts of cities and towns. Each year, 780–800 thousand tons of solid waste are disposed in 321 open waste dumps in rural areas and at 11 open waste points in Ulaanbaatar city, causing severe health problems and environmental pollution (Nature environment report of Mongolia, 2011).

Ulaanbaatar (UB) city's environmental conditions have been drastically declining for the last few years, threatening the normal living conditions of the local population. According to results from 2011 research, a nearby leather-processing factory contaminated soil with up to 637–555 ppm of chromium, exceeding the standard level by 3–4 times. Due to an increase in transportation and the use of unleaded gasoline, soil was contaminated by lead (Pb). The average lead content in UB city soil is 47.3 ppm, twice as high as the 1995 level (Batkhishig et al., 2011). The soil, air and water pollution situation in Ulaanbaatar city is currently very serious, and city governors are trying to address these problems.

12.3   Use of Fallout Radionuclide Methods for Soil Erosion Study

Soil erosion in Mongolia is becoming a very serious problem. It is therefore necessary to obtain accurate estimations of the soil erosion and sedimentation rates.

In the 1990s, N. Norov of the Nuclear Center of the National University of Mongolia measured cesium-137 isotopes in the soils of Mongolia, but this was not significantly connected with soil erosion rates (Norov et al., 1998). In 2000, Japanese researchers studied soil erosion in the areas of Kherlen Bayaan Ulaan and Baganuur, using Cs-137 (Kato et al., 2006). They concluded that the "long-term soil erosion is very significant, and deposition areas were detected at the down slope of the catchment". Since 2007, we have been involved in the IAEA project "Implementation of the Fallout Radionuclide Technique for Erosion Measurement, MON/ 5015". Some results of our investigation are presented here.

Objective of the study. To establish a soil erosion sedimentation rate in the steppe region of Mongolia, using fallout radionuclides methodology Cs-137 (Fig. 12.5).

–   Identification of local reference value.
–   Soil erosion rate in pasture and abandoned crop field area in steppe region of Mongolia in the case of Argalant.

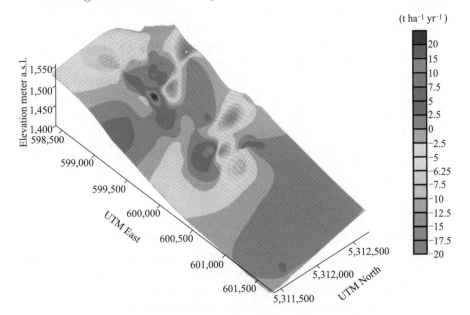

Fig. 12.5 The spatial distribution of Cs-137 inventories in the Baga Boor valley of Central Mongolia, steppe pasture conditions.

Specifics of Mongolian conditions. In the Mongolian steppe areas, soil erosion is caused by both water and wind. It is difficult to distinguish the dominant erosion factors. Fallout radionuclide techniques for wind soil erosion are not sufficiently developed. The use of Cs-137 in wind erosion studies is less common (Pennock and Appleby, 2002). Therefore, there were some difficulties in sampling methods, especially when choosing reference sites in wind and water erosion conditions.

Study area. Typical steppe of central Mongolia, with hillocks, small mountains, and valleys. The soil erosion and deposition rates were studied in small valleys and hillock fields in steppe area.

Administratively, this land belongs to Argalant Soum of Central Aimag, central Mongolia. Average elevation ranges from 1,400–1,600 m above sea level. This land is used for grazing purposes, while in the northern plains, abandoned agricultural fields are distributed. Our study field is the small valley of Baga Boor, which is oriented towards the southeast with 3 km long and 2 km wide. The highest point in the valley is the upstream mountaintop, which reaches an elevation of 1,563 m above sea level. The southern mountaintop of Doloon Undur reaches an elevation of 1,545.1 m above sea level. The lowest point in the valley is 1,420 m above sea level. The area has a relative height of about 140–150 m, with an average slope inclination of $6°–10°$. The area of the valley is about 250 ha

Methods. In the study catchment area of Baga Boor, sampling points were selected according to relief elements. In total, 120 soil samples were analyzed to determine Cs-137 activities in 2007. Core sampling methods with depth of 15 cm were used, with a depth of 20 cm for the valley bottom area. Transformation of measured Cs-137 inventories of soil movement used *Profile distribution model,* and for agricultural soil used *Mass balance model-2* (Walling et al., 2002).

Reference inventory. The tops of small hillocks were selected as the local reference inventory site. The soil samples taken along the northwest to southeast wind directions oriented transects of Zagaan hutul. In 2007, scraper plate methods were used at the reference sites for soil sampling, at 2 cm intervals. In the next year, 2008, 2 mm intervals were incorporated for scraper plate method soil sampling.

Results. At the top of the hillocks, the Cs-137 reference inventory range was $1,558–1,778$ Bq m^{-2}, with an average of 1,668 Bq m^{-2}. We used this value for our calculations. In the mid slopes, soil Cs-137 activities ranged from 561–1,349 Bq m^{-2}, lower than the reference value, while in the southeast-facing lower shaded slopes, a higher value of 1,980 Bq m^{-2} was found. Lower slopes showed significant soil accumulation, especially notable in the lower shaded slopes. Accumulation of sediments was caused mostly by water erosion, while wind blowing concentrated materials at the lower slopes. Plant coverage was thicker and denser in shaded lower slopes than on wind-facing lower slopes. Upper slopes indicated a more significant loss of sediments. In the study catchment area of Baga Boor, soil erosion rates varied from 0.93 to 23.83 t ha^{-1}yr, and average erosion was 5.613 t ha^{-1} yr, or 0.37 mm of soil loss per year. Deposition rates varied from 0.01 to 32.187 t ha^{-1}yr, and average deposition was 4.43 t ha^{-1} yr, or 0.47 mm of soil accumulation per year. The soil sedimentation and accumulation patterns were complicated due to the combination of water and wind erosion. Water erosion dominated mountainous hillocky areas, with soil loss at steeper slopes and deposition of sediments at the lower slopes. The northwest- and southeast-facing slopes were more affected by wind erosion.

Soil erosion and soil organic content were significantly correlated (Correlation coefficient=0.559, n=124). Eroded soil had less organic content and less fertility than non-eroded soils (Fig. 12.6).

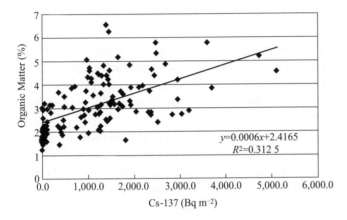

Fig. 12.6 Soil organic content and erosion.

South-facing slopes were more affected by erosion than north-facing slopes. North-facing slopes were less dry and had more vegetation cover. Due to less erosion activity, north-facing slopes were usually steeper than south-facing slopes.

In the lower plains of Baga Boor area, there are abandoned agricultural fields. The agriculture mostly consists of wheat produced from 1970 until 1990. In the last 20 years, this area was used as grazing land. A total of five core points were sampled at a depth of 30 cm. *Mass balance model-2* was used to determine soil erosion. Agricultural soil erosion rate is 3.403 t $ha^{-1}yr^{-1}$; if compared with nearby grazing land soil erosion rates, the agriculture soil erosion rate increased to 5.178 t $ha^{-1}yr^{-1}$. Soil organic content decreased by 34.9% compared to non-agricultural fields.

Beryllium-7 methods were used for short-term erosion events. Zagaan hutul hillocks were selected as the study area, the same as the Cs-137 reference site. The main scope of the study was concerned with soil wind erosion specifics. The sampling was made on July 2, 2008 using the scraper plate method with 2 mm depth intervals from the top 2 cm of soil. A total of 10 sites were selected along the northwest to southeast directions transect, following the dominant wind direction.

The Beryliium-7 activity was only found in the top 2 mm; below this, depths were not counted or had a zero value. Also, the top 2 mm of some soil profiles had a zero value. Wind-facing upper slopes, and wind-shaded lower slopes had no value, or more erosion. Accumulation marked lower wind-facing slopes, upper shaded slopes, and plain sections. According to Davaat station (100 km northwest from study site), the weather before the sampling period was rainy; May–June of 2007 experienced 121.7 mm rain, with especially high precipitation at the end of June.

Using the profile distribution model in the steppe pasture catchment of Baga Boor study area, the average soil erosion rate was found to be 5.613 t ha^{-1}yr, the net erosion rate was 0.8 t ha^{-1}yr^{-1}, and the sediment delivery ration was 31%.

A study of short-term soil erosion events in steppe area using Beryllium-7 methods shows that there is more soil erosion on the wind-facing upper slopes, with accumulation on the upper part of wind shaded slopes and the lower part of wind-facing slopes. This indicated the influence of both water and wind erosion on soil.

A study on agricultural soil erosion was conducted in the northern Mongolian Nomgon soum of Selenge aimag and Sumber soum of Central aimag. In the study area, dark Kastanozem soils with loess-like silt texture are distributed. Agriculture practices beginning in the 1970s have involved planting mostly wheat. For soil erosion calculation, we used *Mass balance model-2* (MBM2). The results of the study show significant loss of topsoil, mostly by wind erosion.

Agricultural soil erosion rates in the case of Selenge aimag Nomgon soum and Central aimag Sumber soum using MBM2 were found to be 32.6 and 49.6 t ha^{-1}yr^{-1}. This is 5.5–8.8 times more than pasture area. The soil erosion in agriculture fields in Mongolia is therefore significant. In Mongolian agriculture, soil conservation practices are rarely used.

12.4   Conclusions

Anthropogenic land degradation in Mongolia is increasing. Mining land degradation, road erosion, overgrazing, agriculture soil erosion and settlement area pollution are currently major environmental issues in Mongolia. There are different statistics about the land degradation of Mongolia. The estimation of Pastureland degradation, desertification and road erosion is very complicated and researchers used different methods and approaches. Since 2000, environmental investigation has been accomplished using remote sensing, ground observation and monitoring. The peak period of mining land degradation continued from 1995 until 2008. After 2008, government control increased, and land reclamation work improved. However, there were off-site effects of mining land degradation expanding, such as road erosion, dusting and water resource shortage. Road erosion increased in Mongolia due to an increase in vehicles and mining activities. By rough estimation, 1.5 million ha of land was eroded by transportation. Overgrazing and desertification are two of the biggest environmental issues in Mongolia. Desertification in arid areas seems to mostly depend on precipitation. Summer of 2011 in Mongolia was very rainy, especially in the month of June. Nearly 80% of the territory of Mongolia had a very high level of grass growth for the first time in the last ten years since 2000. Locals of the Gobi desert region claimed that "desertification disappeared". More careful and comprehensive assessment of desertification is necessary. Since 2008, agriculture in Mongolia has expanded. However, soil conservation measures are rarely practiced. Soil erosion, nutrient depletion, and loss of productivity are threatening food security in the country. We used fallout radionuclide methods for soil erosion rate estimation. The average soil erosion rate for one year in the steppe pasture catchment of the Baga Boor study area of central Mongolia is 5.613 t ha^{-1}yr^{-1} In the cases of Selenge aimag Nomgon soum and Central aimag Sumber soum, agricultural soil erosion rates were 32.6 and 49.6 t ha^{-1}yr^{-1}, respectively. This is 5.5–8.8 times more than pasture area. Arable land soil organic content decreased by 34.9%, compared to non-agricultural fields. Therefore, soil erosion in agricultural fields in Mongolia was found to be significant. It is thus necessary to improve pasture management and land use policies in order to reduce land degradation.

Acknowledgements

This work was partially supported by the Institute Geography—Mongolian Academy of Sciences, LCLUC Program of NASA, and TC project of IAEA. Thanks for profs. Jiaguo Qi, and Jiquan Chen for their help and assistance with preparation of the manuscript.

References

Avaadorj, D. Nyamsambuu, N. and Baasandorj, Ya. (2000). The ecological and economical assessment of cultivated land Mongolia. State and Dynamics of Geosciences and Human Geography of Mongolia (Extended abstracts of the international symposium). Berlin, 194–197.

Batjargal, Z. (1997). Desertification in Mongolia. Rala report No 200. Iceland, 107–113.

Batkhishig, O. (2000). Influence of overgrazing for the soils cover in Mongolia. Extended Abstracts of International Congress on the State and Dynamic of Geoscience and Human Geography of Mongolia. FU, Berlin, 126–131.

Batkhishig, O. (2006). Specifics of soil cover and soil property changes in Eastern Hovsgol lake area. In: *Changes in Climate, Ecology and Patterns of Pastoral Nomadism in Lake Hovsgol National Park, Mongolia.* Ulaanbaatar, Mongolia, 12–14.

Batkhishig, O., Burmaa, B., Nyamsambuu, N., Nyamdavaa, B., Davaadorj, D., and Enkhbat, N. (2010). Soil erosion study using fallout radionuclides in Mongolia. *Proceedings of the Eight Mongolia.* Korea Joint Seminars on Environmental Changes of North East Asia. April 27–30, Ulaanbaatar, Mongolia, 12–14.

Batkhishig, O. Dorjgotov, D., Nyamsambuu, N, et al. (2011). Ulaanbaatar city soil pollution and ecogeochemical assessment report. Ministry of Nature Environment of Mongolia, UB, 136–140. (in Mongolian)

Batkhishig, O., and Lehmkuhl, F. (2003). Degradation und Desertification in der Mongolei. *Petermanns Geographische Miiteilungen,* 147, 2003/5, 48–49. (in Germany)

Bazha, S.N., Gunin, P. D., Danzhalova, E. V., Kazantseva, T. I., Bayasgalan, D., and Drobyshev Yu. I., (2010). Contemporary processes of degrdadation of pastoral steppe ecosystems in Mongolia. *Proceedings of International conferense, Ecological consequences of Biosphere provess in the ecotone zone of southern Siberia and Central Asia.* Ulaanbaatar, Mongolia, 1, 59–63. (in Russian)

Bridges, E. M. and Oldeman, L. R. 1999. Global assessment of human-induced soil degradation. *Arid Soil Res. Rehabil.,* 13, 319–325.

Chuluun, T., and Ojima, D. (2002). Land use change and carbon cycle in arid and semi-arid lands of East and Central Asia. *Science in China Series C,* 45 (Supp), 48–53.

Dobrovolskii, G. V., Dorjgotov, D., Balabco., P, N., and Vostokova, L, B. (2000). Problem of soil degradation of Mongolian ecosystem. International Conference "Central Asian ecosystem–2000". Proceeding of abstracts. Ulaanbaatar, 239–242. (in Russian)

Dorjgotov, D. Batkhishig, O. and Nyamsambuu, N. (2002). Land degradation and desertification problem in Mongolia. Extended abstracts of Mongolia and Korea First joint Seminar on "Environmental changes of North East Asia". Ulaanbaatar, Monglolia, 17–20.

Dorjsuren, Ch. 2009. Anthropogenic succession of larch forest of Mongolia. *Biological recourse and nature condition of Mongolia,* 50, 209. (in Russian)

Dregne, N. E. (2002). Land Degradation in the Drylands. *Arid Land Research and Management.* 16, 99–132.

Erdenetsetseg, B. and Erdenetyua, M. (2010). The remote sensing and ground measurement approaches of Mongolian pasture recourses. *Natural Resources and Sustainable Development in Surrounding Regions of the Mongolian Plateau.* 6th International Conference. Ulaanbaatar, Mongolia, 23–30.

Kato, H., Onda, Y., Tanaka, Y., Tsujimura, M., Davaa, G., and Oyunbaatar, D. (2006). Evaluating soil erosion history using fallout radionuclides in semi-arid grassland, Mongolia. *Geophysical Research Abstracts,* 8.

Kharin, N., Tateishi, R., Haranshen, H. (1999). *Degradation of the Drylands of Asia.* Chiba University, Japan, 60.

Land use inventory report of Mongolia (2010). *Administration of Land affairs and Geodesy and Cartography.* Ulaanbaatar, Mongolia. (in Mongolian)

Mijiddorj, R. (2011). Mining activities and environment problem. *Ecology—Sustainable Development*, 11, 50. (in Mongolian)

Mongolian Department of Road Report. (2010). (in Mongolian)

National Atlas of Mongolia. (2009). Institute Geography Mongolia Academy of Sciences. Ulaanbaatar, 20–21. (in Mongolian)

National Program Combating Desertification in Mongolia. (2010). Ulaanbaatar. (in Mongolian)

Ministry of Nature Environment and Tourism of Mongolia. (2011). Nature environment condition report of Mongolia, 2008–2010. Ulaanbaatar, 78.

Norov, N., Davaa, S., and Shagjjamba, D. (1998). Studies on the soil radioactivity in some city using gamma-ray spectrometer. Mongolian National University. *Physical Electronical School*, 5, 138, 19–26.

Nyamsambuu, N. (2007). Degraded agriculture soil fertility change. *Geographical review of Mongolia*, 5, 85–94. (in Mongolian)

Pennock, D,J., and Appleby, P.G. (2002). Site selection and sampling design. In: Zapata, F., IAEA (Eds.). *Handbook for the Assessment of Soil Erosion and Sedimentation Using Environmental Radionucludes.* IAEA. Vienna, Austria, 16.

Qi, J., and Kulmatov, R. (2008). An overview of environmental issues in Central Asia. In: Qi, J.G and Evered, K.T. (Eds.). *Environmental Problems of Central Asia and Their Economic, Social and their Economic, Social and Security Impacts.* NATO Science for Peace and Security Series-C. Environmental Security, 3–13.

Report of Mining Department. 2010. Ulaanbaatar. (in Mongolian)

Sarantyua, N. (2000). Status of desertification in Mongolia. *Proceedings of Abstracts International Conference Central Asian ecosystems.* Ulaanbaatar, Mongolia, 128.

Statistical Yearbook of Mongolia. (2010). (in Mongolian)

Walling, D. E., He, Q. and Apleby, P. G. (2002). Conversion models for use in soil-erosion, soil redistribution and sedimentation investigations. In: Zapata, F. (Ed.). *Handbook for the Assessment of Soil Erosion and Sedimentation Using Environmental Radionucludes.* IAEA. Vienna, Austria, 111–164.

Authors Information

Ochirbat Batkhishig
Institute of Geography, Mongolian Academy of Sciences, Sukhbaatar duureg, 11-r horoolol, PO 20, Ulaanbaatar 14192, Mongolia

Chapter 13

The Effect of Large-Scale Conservation Programs on the Vegetative Development of China's Loess Plateau

Kirsten M. de Beurs, Dong Yan, and Arnon Karnieli

Summary: The Natural Forest Conservation Program (NFCP) in 1998 and the Grain for Green Program (GfGP) in 1999 were launched by the Chinese government to mitigate the degraded vegetation condition of China. In this study, we applied MODIS time series data to analyze the impacts of land cover change as a result of vegetation conservation programs on vegetation dynamics in the Chinese Loess Plateau from 2001 through 2009. We applied the seasonal Mann-Kendall trend test to the Normalized Difference Vegetation Index (NDVI) time series calculated based on the Nadir BRDF-Adjusted Reflectance data at 500 m (MCD43A4). In addition, to identify the changes at multiple scales, we also applied the seasonal Mann-Kendall trend test to the global Albedo product and NDVI calculated based on the Nadir BRDF-Adjusted Reflectance data at 0.05 deg CMG (MCD43C3 and MCD43C4). To understand the effect of grazing changes in grasslands we selected data from three separate Landsat tiles and two different years and calculated both NDVI and the Enhanced Vegetation Index (EVI). We show that the observed changes are the most widespread when observed with NDVI data at 0.05° resolution and the least widespread when observed with albedo data. The data at the higher spatial resolution of 500 m revealed that the rainfed croplands are changing (i.e., 69% exhibiting change) while the irrigated croplands remain stable (just 11% reveal change). This change appears consistent with the effect of GfGP. Both the counties with increased and degreased grazing reveal an increase in 500 m NDVI data. Thus, grazing analyses are more complicated for these areas.

13.1 Introduction

The Loess Plateau in China is suffering the world's most serious soil erosion, losing 2,000–2,500 t km^{-2} annually (Hu et al., 2006; Shi and Shao, 2000). Some even estimate the annual soil erosion to reach as high as 5,000–10,000 t km^{-2} (Fu and Chen, 2000). The Loess Plateau is located in Northern China in the southern part of the drylands East Asia (DEA). The Loess Plateau completely overlaps Ningxia Hui Autonomous Region and Shanxi Province. In addition, large areas of Shaanxi and Gansu Provinces are also part of the Loess Plateau. The severe environmental problems in the Loess Plateau are the result of degraded vegetation conditions due to intensified agriculture and expansion of built-up areas (Zhou et al., 2009).

Starting in 1978 with the Three-north Shelterbelt Forest Program (TNSFP) and intensifying in 1998 and 1999 with the Natural Forest Conservation Program and the Grain for Green Program, the Loess Plateau was subjected to several large governmental conservation programs. The Chinese government has spent tremendous efforts to halt desertification and soil erosion, and improve environmental quality. These three conservation programs, further described below, mainly aim to increase forest and grassland cover in favor of croplands and barren lands. However, while increases in vegetation as a result of afforestation programs have been reported, some argue that the large-scale forest conservation programs cause significant damage to the fragile ecosystems in arid and semi-arid areas (Cao et al., 2010a; 2010b). Many studies investigating the GfGP indicate that the program is not effective and missed the program's objective (Cao et al., 2009b; Chen et al., 2007). They indicate that the trees that are planted are the wrong species (Chen et al., 2007; Xu et al., 2004a) and that tree survival is very low (Xu et al., 2004a). One study using GIMMS NDVI data between 1982 and 2003 concluded that there has been no greening of Northern China (Wang et al., 2010). In addition, some report that the conservation programs were not efficient in suppressing dust (Wang et al., 2010).

Nevertheless, many other studies using satellite images have revealed significant vegetation increases in the Loess Plateau during the past twenty to thirty years (Song and Ma, 2007; Xin et al., 2008; Yang et al., 2002). For example, Yang et al. (2002), using the Advanced Very High Resolution Radiometer (AVHRR) Pathfinder Normalized Difference Vegetation Index (NDVI) data, detected a significant increase in vegetation cover in the northern and western part of the Loess Plateau from 1982 through 1999, with an average annual increase up to 3.8%. Song and Ma (2007) employed 1 km SPOT VEGETATION NDVI to estimate the vegetation trend across five northwestern provinces of China between 1998 and 2004, and they only observed significant vegetation increase in the Loess Plateau. The observed vegetation increase has been attributed to a variety of potential causes such as afforestation (Yang et al., 2002), increased precipitation during the growing season (Sun et al., 2001) and significant temperature increases (since 1980) (Xin et al., 2008).

In this study we apply a multi-resolution change analysis based on the popular vegetation indices NDVI and EVI and less commonly used broadband albedo data. We will first provide an overview of the general trends in NDVI and albedo that are found within the Loess Plateau at a spatial resolution of 0.05° (or ∼ 5.6 km). We will then step down and evaluate NDVI trends at 500 m resolution. In the last step we will evaluate changes in NDVI and EVI for specific target regions based on Landsat TM/ETM+ data. The ultimate goal is to determine if, where, and in what way large governmental conservation programs are responsible for the observed increase in vegetation. Since humans have such an extraordinary impact on the land surface of the Loess Plateau we will use anthropogenic biomes (anthromes) to filter our change results. Anthromes represent the global ecological patterns created by sustained direct human interactions with ecosystems (Ellis et al., 2010; Ellis and Ramankutty, 2008).

13.2   Conservation Programs

Three large conservation programs have been implemented in the Loess Plateau: 1) the Three-north Shelterbelt Forest Program (TNFSP); 2) the Natural Forest Conservation Program (NFCP); and 3) the Grain for Green Program (GfGP). These programs are also described in more detail in Mátyás et al. (2012) and Becker (2012). The main goal of the TNSFP was to diminish desertification and dust storms by increasing forest cover by 5%–15% in arid and semi-arid areas in China. Efficient afforestation practices for TNSFP began in 1978 (Wang et al., 2010) and the program is supposed to run until 2050. The key goal of TNSFP was to increase vegetation cover in sandy regions by artificial planting (Wang et al., 2010).

NFCP was created to restore natural forests in ecologically sensitive areas, plant forests for soil and water protection, increase timber production in plantation forests and protect existing natural forests (Liu et al., 2008; Zhang et al., 2000). Implementation of NFCP was planned to consist of multiple stages. The short-term goals (1998–2000) were to reduce timber production in natural forests (Liu et al., 2008) and offer reeducation and training for laid-off foresters to get different jobs (Zhang et al., 2000). The medium-term goals were to increase timber production from planation forests (2001–2010) (Liu et al., 2008). The final goal of NFCP (2011–2050) is to develop the planation forests as the major source of timber supply for domestic demand (Liu et al., 2008, Zhang et al., 2000). NFCP targeted so called the first and second priority areas, with the entire Loess Plateau being part of the first priority area, except for Shanxi province that was part of the second priority area. In the year 2000 alone nearly half a million ha of cropland were converted to forests (Zhang et al., 2000) and by 2005, NFCP had closed mountains or created forests in almost 11 million ha (Liu et al., 2008).

In 1999, the Loess Plateau became a target area of a third conservation program, which is indicated as one of the world's largest conservation programs, GfGP program or Sloping Land Conversion Program (Xu et al., 2004b). GfGP is managed by the Chinese Bureau of Forestry and had two major goals. The first goal was to reduce soil erosion by converting agriculture on steep slopes ($\geqslant 15°$ in Northwestern China and $\geqslant 25°$ elsewhere) (Uchida et al., 2005) to permanent vegetation such as forests and grassland (Hu et al., 2006). The second goal of the program was to change croplands to grazing land or to perennial forage crops (Brown et al., 2009). Gansu and Shaanxi Provinces were included among the three provinces to initiate the program in 1999. Other regions were incorporated by the end of 2002. The ultimate goal was to increase vegetative cover by 32 million ha by 2010 (Liu et al., 2008), 14.7 million ha was supposed to come from converted cropland and the remainder from afforestation of barren lands. According to the Chinese State Forestry Administration, more than eight million ha of croplands and almost 12 million ha of barren lands were converted to forests between 1999 and 2008. Both NFCP and GfGP include grazing bans (Cao et al., 2009a; 2010b).

13.3   Study Region

13.3.1   Loess Plateau

China's Loess Plateau is about 626,287 km^2 large and is bounded by the Yanshan Mountains in the north and the Qinling Mountains in the south (Fig. 13.1). Ningxia Hui Autonomous Region and Shanxi Province fall entirely within the Loess Plateau and large areas of Shaanxi and Gansu Provinces are also part of the Loess Plateau. There are several major cities located on the Loess Plateau: Baotou and Taiyuan in the north, Xi'an in the south and Yinchuan and Lanzhou in the southwest. The total population of the Loess Plateau is approximately 50 million people (Jiang, 1997).

The annual precipitation in the Loess Plateau ranges between 200 mm in the North and 650 mm in the South and varies greatly by season, with higher amounts in the summer than in the winter. The average temperature varies from

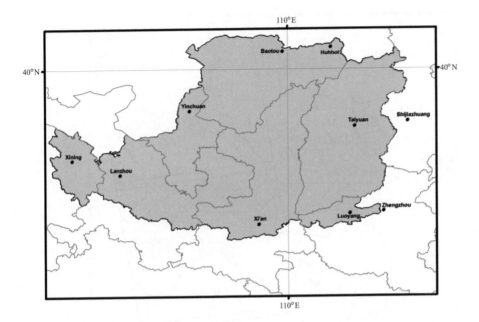

Fig. 13.1 Overview of the Loess Plateau.
The Loess Plateau outline was provided by Dr. Qinke Yang at the Institute of Soil and Water Conservation, Chinese Academy of Science. Boundary shapefiles were acquired from the Data Sharing Infrastructure of Earth System Science of China (http://www.geodata.cn/Portal/aboutWebsite/aboutus.jsp).

20°C in summer to −5°C in winter. There is a north-south climate gradient in the Loess Plateau. The southern part of the Loess Plateau is mainly covered by forests and croplands while grasslands and barren lands dominate the land cover in the north.

13.3.2   Subset for Fine Scale Analysis

A subset of the Loess Plateau was investigated in more detail with fine-scale analysis to further understand the effect of changes in grazing patterns (Fig. 13.2). This subset consists of nine counties administered by the districts of Yan'an and Yulin, in northern Shaanxi Province. The region covers an area of about 28,000 km² with an average elevation of 1100 m. The study area lies in the agro-pastoral transitional zone of China. The land use in this region is characterized by semi-arid pastoral in the north (Qi et al., 2012) and temperate agriculture in the south (Li and Ren, 2011).

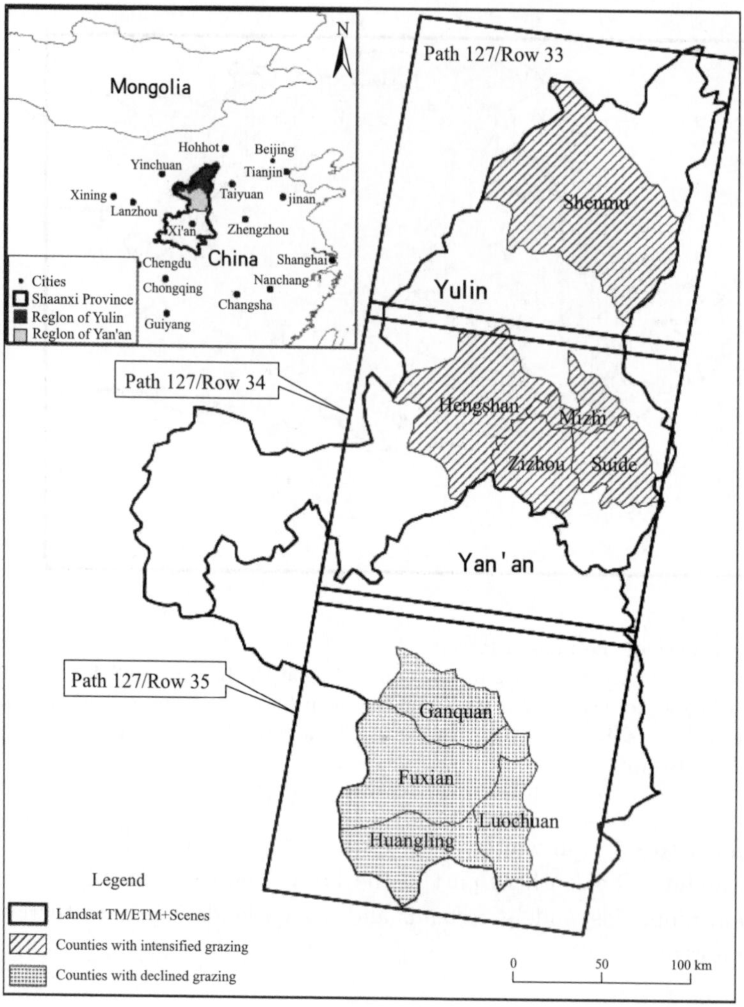

Fig. 13.2 Overview of the study regions subset for fine scale analysis.

13.4 Data

13.4.1 MODIS Data

In this study we used the Nadir BRDF-Adjusted Reflectance (NBAR) data at 500 m and 0.05° spatial resolution (MCD43A4 and MCD43C4, respectively).

Both products consist of 16-day composites. The MODIS NBAR product is created with the use of a bidirectional reflectance distribution function that models reflectance to a nadir view (Lucht et al., 2000). We downloaded all available images between January, 2001 and December, 2009. We used NBAR data to calculate NDVI (Tucker, 1979) and EVI (Huete et al., 2002, 1994) as proxies of vegetation condition. NDVI and EVI calculations are shown in Equations (13.1) and (13.2)

$$\text{NDVI} = \frac{\rho_{\text{NIR}} - \rho_{\text{RED}}}{\rho_{\text{NIR}} + \rho_{\text{RED}}} \tag{13.1}$$

$$\text{EVI} = 2.5 \times \frac{\rho_{\text{NIR}} - \rho_{\text{RED}}}{\rho_{\text{NIR}} + 6\rho_{\text{RED}} - 7.5\rho_{\text{BLUE}} + 1} \tag{13.2}$$

Besides the NBAR reflectance product, we use the MODIS albedo product (MCD43C3) at 0.05° spatial resolution. We used the broadband white sky albedo for three broad bands (0.3–0.7 μm, 0.7–5.0 μm, and 0.3–5.0 μm). Land surface albedo is an important parameter in climate simulation models and is important in understanding the feedback mechanisms between the radiation balance and its influence on vegetation dynamics (Zhang et al., 2010). Increases in vegetation density typically result in reduced albedo, due to the strong absorption of photosynthetically active radiation (Bounoua et al., 2000). Thus, albedo values are typically lower for multilayer canopies such as forests and higher for grasslands and croplands (Zhang et al., 2010). However, despite the fact that land surface albedo is influenced significantly by vegetation cover, it is not simply a variation of NDVI (Zhang et al., 2010). Few studies have been conducted to determine the changes in albedo over time (Zhang et al., 2010).

The last MODIS product we used in this study is the MODIS Land Cover product from the year 2000 at 500 m resolution. We used the data from year 2000 to correspond to the last year that the Anthromes dataset (Section 13.4.4) was available.

13.4.2   Landsat Data

We downloaded six Landsat TM/ETM+ images from the USGS Global Visualization Viewer (GLOVIS) portal (http://glovis.usgs.gov/). We select two images for each path/row (127/33, 127/34, 127/35, Fig. 13.2) and to avoid bias caused by phenological variation in the comparison of NDVI and EVI between years. We chose anniversary Landsat TM/ETM+ images. The available anniversary Landsat TM/ETM+ images covering the 9 counties which are part of the fine scale analysis are shown in Table 13.1. Note that for each path/row the earliest image was acquired by the ETM+ sensor while the latest image came from the TM sensor.

Table 13.1 Downloaded Landsat TM/ETM+ Scenes.

Scene	Acquisition Date	Sensor
Path 127/ Row 33	August 06, 2002	ETM+
Path 127/ Row 33	August 12, 2007	TM
Path 127/ Row 34	August 06, 2002	ETM+
Path 127/ Row 34	August 12, 2007	TM
Path 127/ Row 35	June 29, 2000	ETM+
Path 127/ Row 35	June 30, 2009	TM

The Landsat TM/ETM+ scenes were Level 1T data that had been systematically corrected for radiometric and geometric errors and topographical effects (Landsat Product Type Descriptions, U.S. Geological Survey). However, Landsat Level 1T data still suffer from atmospheric contamination. In order to retrieve surface reflectance using Landsat data, we further atmospherically corrected the Level 1T data using Fast Line-of-Sight Atmospheric Analysis of Spectral Hypercubes (FLAASH) available in ENVI 4.8. FLAASH is a first-principles atmospheric correction tool that corrects wavelengths in the visible through near-infrared and shortwave infrared regions and incorporates the MOD-TRAN4 radiation transfer code. We calculated NDVI and EVI as described in Equations (13.1) and (13.2) above.

13.4.3 Grazing Statistics

We employed the total number of livestock (including: Horse, Cattle, Donkey, Mule, and Goat) documented by official statistical yearbooks of Yan'an and Yulin as an indicator of grazing intensity. The official statistical year books of Yan'an and Yulin were archived in the Database of Statistics in Socio-Economic Development of China, which is available at http://tongji.cnki.net/kns55/Navi/NaviDefault.aspx. Based on statistical data availability, we investigated the change in the total number of livestock in Yulin and Yan'an from 1999 to 2006 (excluding 2003 for Yan'an), respectively. The counties were further divided into two groups; those with a significant increase and decrease in the total number of livestock across the study years.

13.4.4 Anthromes

Humans are directly interacting with ecosystems surrounding them, making a profound impact on how the ecosystems are altered. In this study we use the anthromes dataset as described in Ellis and Ramankutty (2008). Anthromes are defined as human biomes and describe the terrestrial biosphere in its contemporary form. Estimated population density plays an important role in the delineation of the anthromes. We downloaded the dataset from Anthromes v.2.0 from http://ecotope.org/anthromes/v2/data/ and used the data for the year 2000 which was the latest year that the Anthrome data was available. Figure 13.3 gives the anthromes for the Loess Plateau. The spatial resolution of the data is 0.083° lat/lon. Table 13.2 provides the six largest anthromes in the Loess Plateau, which are the anthromes that we incorporated in this study. These six anthromes combined cover 86% of the total study region. There are no other anthromes available that cover more than 10% of the study area.

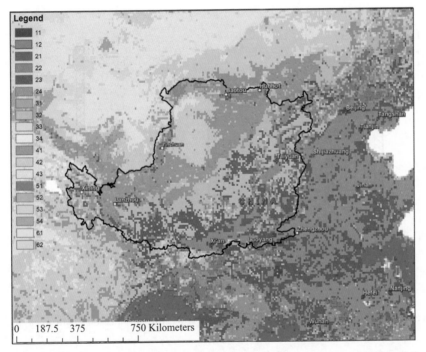

Fig. 13.3 Anthromes v.2.0 from http://ecotope.org/anthromes/v2/data/ from the year 2000. The spatial resolution of the data is 0.083° lat/lon. See Table 13.2 for the definitions of the major anthromes belonging to the legend.

The Loess Plateau outline was provided by Dr. Qinke Yang at the Institute of Soil and Water Conservation, Chinese Academy of Science. Boundary shapefiles were acquired from the Data Sharing Infrastructure of Earth System Science of China (http://www.geodata.cn/Portal/aboutWebsite/aboutus.jsp).

We used the MODIS IGBP classification to determine the dominant land cover classes (i.e., grasslands, croplands, and barren lands) within each anthrome (Fig. 13.4). Grasslands (class 10) are the largest class in the rainfed villages, and

Table 13.2 Six largest anthromes in the Loess Plateau ordered from the anthrome with the highest proportion to the lowest proportion.

#	Anthromes	Loess Plateau (%)	Population Density (persons km^{-2})
41	Residential rangeland	20	10–100
32	Residential rainfed croplands	17	10–100
42	Populated rangelands	15	1–10
23	Rainfed villages	14	100
22	Irrigated villages	10	100
43	Remote rangelands	10	< 1

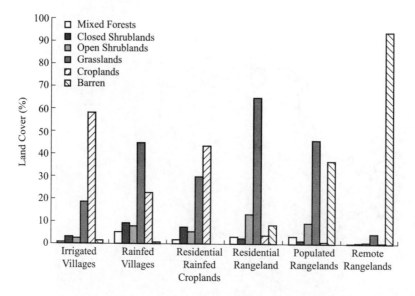

Fig. 13.4 Percentage of pixels in each IGBP class within the selected anthromes.

the residential and populated rangelands. Cropland is the largest land cover class in both the residential rainfed croplands, and irrigated villages. Barren land is the largest land cover class in the remote rangelands (94.2%) and the second largest for populated rangelands (37.2%). The percentage of barren in the rangelands is negatively related with population decrease; we found 8.6% barren in the residential rangelands but 37.2% barren in the populated rangelands and 94.2% barren in the remote rangelands.

13.5 Methods

To detect the changes in the land surface greenness and land surface brightness as observed by the MODIS NDVI/EVI data and the albedo data, we apply the seasonal Mann-Kendall trend test. This test is a non-parametric alternative to ordinary least squares (OLS) regression for trend estimation in image time series (de Beurs and Henebry, 2004, 2005). We applied the seasonal Mann-Kendall (SMK) trend test to estimate vegetation index and albedo change from all image composites between 2001 and 2009. If a pixel revealed a positive SMK test statistic and a p-value lower than or equal to 0.01, we counted the pixel as showing a positive change. Pixels with negative SMK trend statistics and p-values lower than 0.01 were counted as showing negative change. If more than 40% of the observations were missing from the pixel time series we did not investigate the change. We analyzed the changes in the 0.05° data by anthromes and the changes in the 500 m data by anthrome and land cover class.

13.6 Results and Discussion

13.6.1 Vegetation Index and Albedo Changes

More than half of the Loess Plateau reveals a significant change ($p < 0.01$) and the majority of the pixels that reveal change show an increase in NDVI and EVI. NDVI reveals a positive change in 59.4% (372,015 km²) of the Loess Plateau and EVI reveals a positive change in 55.6% (348,216 km²) of the Loess Plateau (Fig. 13.5). Only 1% of the pixels reveal a negative change. Table 13.3 shows that the percentage of pixels with significant changes in NDVI and EVI varies widely by anthromes.

More than two thirds of the pixels in rainfed villages (72.9%) and residential rainfed croplands (68.1%) reveal significant increases in NDVI and EVI as opposed to only 28.1% of the pixels in irrigated villages and 19.6% of the pixels in remote rangelands. It appears that irrigated areas and areas with low population density do not show as much change as the rainfed croplands and more populated rangelands. The change in the rangelands reveals an increase with population density. The most changes can be found (50% in NDVI) in the residential rangelands, followed by 32% of the pixels changing in the populated rangelands and just 19.6% in the remote rangelands. The EVI reveals similar changes although slightly fewer pixels changed significantly.

With vegetation increase, NDVI and EVI are increasing and albedo is decreasing (Fig. 13.5). The broad band albedo time series reveal a similar discrepancy of changes between rainfed villages and irrigated villages and remote rangelands

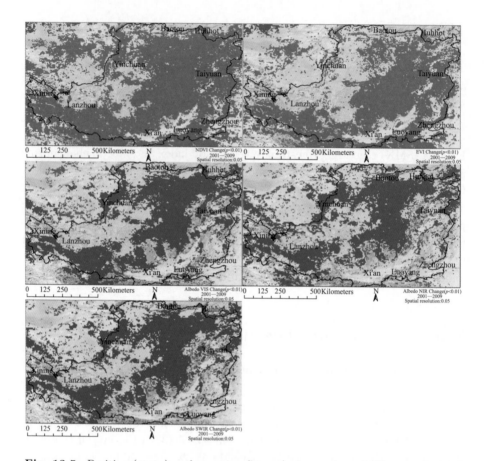

Fig. 13.5 Positive (green) and negative (brown) change ($p < 0.01$) over the study region based on 0.05° albedo and vegetation index data.

The Loess Plateau outline was provided by Dr. Qinke Yang at the Institute of Soil and Water Conservation, Chinese Academy of Science. Boundary shapefiles were acquired from the Data Sharing Infrastructure of Earth System Science of China (http://www.geodata.cn/Portal/aboutWebsite/aboutus.jsp).

for near-infrared (NIR) and shortwave infrared (Table 13.4). However, in general fewer pixels reveal significant changes for the broad band albedo time series than for the vegetation indices, e.g., in rainfed villages just 53.4% for the NIR albedo change as opposed to 72.9% for the NDVI in rainfed villages (Table 13.4).

The order is different for the visible broadband albedo data. For the remote rangelands, we found a significant decline in the visible albedo (46.9%). The visible light albedo is the only dataset in which we found a significant change in a large part of that anthrome. All other data, NIR and shortwave albedo as well as NDVI and EVI, reveal change in less than 20% of the pixels in the remote rangelands.

Table 13.3 Percentage of pixels with significant positive and negative changes in NDVI and EVI sorted from the anthromes with the most changes to the anthromes with the least changes.

#	Anthrome	NDVI		EVI	
		+	−	+	−
32	Rainfed Villages	72.9	0.0	73.3	0.4
23	Residential Rainfed Croplands	68.1	0.7	65.1	0.6
41	Residential Rangeland	50.0	0.3	43.9	0.5
42	Populated Rangelands	32.1	0.8	25.8	1.3
22	Irrigated Villages	28.1	2.0	23.1	3.2
43	Remote Rangelands	19.6	1.8	15.4	6.8
	Loess Plateau	59.4	0.6	55.6	1.0

$p < 0.01$.

Table 13.4 Percentage of pixels with significant positive and negative changes in broadband albedo sorted by NIR.

#	Anthrome	VIS		NIR		SW	
		+	−	+	−	+	−
32	Rainfed Villages	0.4	60.7	2.2	53.4	1.7	54.9
41	Residential Rangeland	0.9	45.7	1.6	50.9	1.6	47.6
42	Populated Rangelands	3.8	28.4	1.5	37.5	2.0	33.0
23	Residential Rainfed Croplands	0.5	54.6	2.4	36.3	1.1	45.0
22	Irrigated Villages	1.0	23.2	2.3	19.8	0.9	21.6
43	Remote Rangelands	8.0	46.9	3.0	14.2	4.6	9.5
	Loess Plateau	0.6	51.2	2.4	46.6	1.9	47.9

$p < 0.01$.

13.6.2 500 m NDVI Changes

The 500 m NDVI data reveal a significant ($p < 0.01$) positive change for 304,179 km^2 or 48.7% of the Loess Plateau (Fig. 13.6). Increasing the spatial resolution from 0.05° (or $\sim$ 5.6 km) to 500 m led to the decline of significant changes for 67,836 km^2, which corresponds with a decline of 22% in the total area with significant positive change.

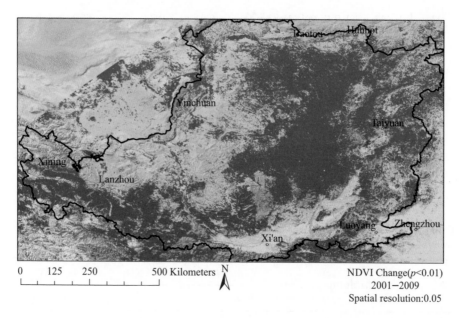

Fig. 13.6 Positive (green) and negative (brown) NDVI change over the study region between 2001 and 2009 based on 500 m NDVI data.
The Loess Plateau outline was provided by Dr. Qinke Yang at the Institute of Soil and Water Conservation, Chinese Academy of Science. Boundary shapefiles were acquired from the Data Sharing Infrastructure of Earth System Science of China (http://www.geodata.cn/Portal/aboutWebsite/aboutus.jsp).

We found a similar difference in changes between the two spatial resolutions in a previous study in Russia and Kazakhstan (de Beurs et al., 2009). However, in that study we found that some changes that were visible with the 500 m data disappeared in the 0.05° analyses. Changes at the coarser resolution are likely the result of aggregated patches of significant changes detectable only at finer resolutions. It is important to note that the rescaling of change results is not straightforward due to 1) high spatial heterogeneity at the finer scale, 2) the nonlinearity of vegetation indices, and 3) the thresholding effect of specific significance levels. Furthermore, the coarser scale of the MODIS CMG (0.05° or 5.6 km) is relevant to atmospheric boundary layer processes and, indeed, is at the effective resolution limit of current regional climate and mesoscale meteorological models. The finer scale analysis typically reveals changes that are more relevant to human decision-making and regional economics (de Beurs et al., 2009). The dual scale of the trend analysis enables a partitioning of change attribution that would be very difficult at a single scale.

Interesting patterns became visible when we analyzed the positive NDVI changes found in the 500 m time series by land cover class within anthromes (Table 13.5). We focused only on the positive vegetation changes since the majority of the changing pixels revealed a NDVI increase. We found that, between 40% and 49% of the mixed forests are changing within the rainfed villages (#32), residential rangelands (#41) and residential rainfed croplands (#23). However, just 12.9% of the mixed forests in the populated rangelands are changing. A similar pattern can be deciphered for the closed shrublands where just 14.5% of the closed shrublands reveal a significant change in the populated rangelands, while for the other anthromes at least 30% of the closed shrublands are changing. Changes in the open shrublands are mainly found in the rainfed villages (77%) and the residential rainfed croplands (79.9%). Only about 22% of the open shrublands in the rangelands (#41 and #42) are changing. Both rainfed villages and populated rangelands consist of approximately 45% grasslands. However, 58.6% of the grasslands are changing within the rainfed villages, while only 31% of the grasslands are changing within the populated rangelands. The residential rangelands reveal that 48% of the grasslands are changing. The most change in the grasslands is found in the residential rainfed croplands, with a little over 62% of the grasslands changing. Most croplands can be found in the irrigated villages (58.4%), but these croplands reveal the least change (11%). Most changes in the croplands can be found in the rainfed villages (69.7%).

Table 13.5 Percentage of pixels with positive NDVI change (500 m) by class and anthromes.

	Rainfed Villages	Residential Rangelands	Populated Rangelands	Residential Rainfed Croplands	Irrigated Villages	Remote Rangelands
Mix forests	40.3	40.2	12.9	48.8	NA	NA
C. shrubl.	34.0	50.8	14.5	54.2	30.1	NA
O. shrubl.	77.0	21.9	22.0	79.9	30.5	NA
Grasslands	58.6	48.0	31.0	62.3	36.4	7.3
Cropland	69.7	55.5	NA	45.9	11.0	NA
Barren	NA	32.9	23.6	NA	29.9	25.4

C. shrubl.: closed shrubland; O.shrubl.: open shrubland.

We find that the changes in NDVI are highly dependent upon the type of anthrome and its population density. For example, irrigated croplands are likely more profitable than rainfed croplands. We find many more significant changes in rainfed croplands and villages than in their irrigated counterparts. We believe that this is the effect of large-scale conservation programs which target the less productive croplands and change them into forests and grasslands that have no fallow periods and hence reveal increased vegetation indices. In addition, the more populated the rangelands, the more significant vegetation changes we find. We also believe that this is the result of large-scale conservation programs that target barren lands for conversion to grasslands and forests. A certain population density is required to effectively change barren lands into forest because it takes manual labor to make the conversion happen. We believe that it is less likely that the observed changes are a result of large-scale weather effects because the effect of the weather would result in a more homogenous increase in vegetation indices.

13.6.3   Grazing Intensity Change

To understand the effect of grazing intensity changes we investigated in detail four counties in the greater district of Yan'an, Shannxi Province of China. These four counties saw a decline in grazing pressure from between 22 and 72 animals per km^2 to less than 10 animals per km^2 (Fig. 13.7a). We also investigated five counties in the greater district of Yulin, Shannxi Province of China, that reveal an increase in grazing pressure from between 43 and 66 animals per km^2 to between 83 and 166 animals per km^2 (Fig. 13.7b).

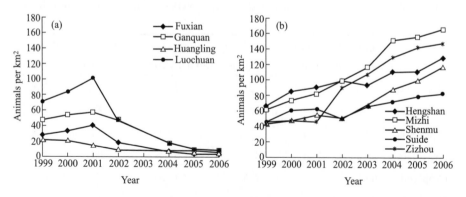

Fig. 13.7 Change in the number of animals / km^2 for the counties in Yan'an (a) and Yulin (b).

Figure 13.8a shows the MODIS land cover classification for the counties in the district of Yan'an, which is the district that revealed grazing declines. There is

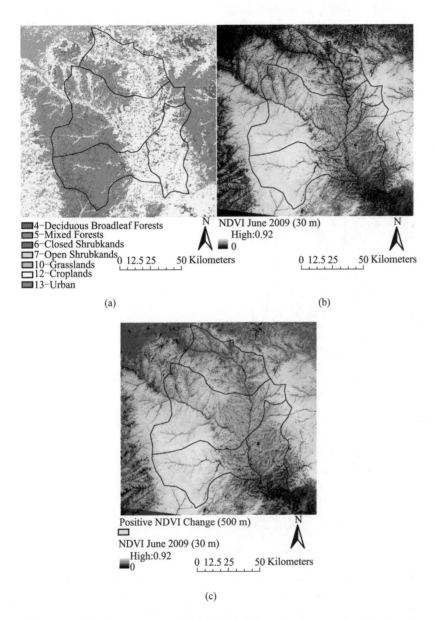

(a)

(b)

(c)

Fig. 13.8 Yan'an counties. (a) MODIS 500 m land cover classification from 2000. (b) Landsat NDVI June 2009. The forested areas stand out as very bright and have high NDVI values. (c) Landsat NDVI from June 2009 with the MODIS 500 m NDVI change areas overlaid. Change is predominantly occurring in non-forests (lower NDVI) areas. These areas are dominated by grasslands, croplands, and shrublands.

a relatively large amount of forests in these four counties. The corresponding NDVI image based on Landsat data confirms the forest land cover as an area with much higher NDVI. In Figure 13.8c the area with significant change as found in the 500 m MODIS time series is overlaid. The changes in the 500 m MODIS NDVI data appear to be limited to the agricultural and rangeland areas while the forested areas remain stable and do not reveal a significant NDVI change.

Figure 13.9a reveals that the land cover of the area with increased grazing consists mainly of shrublands and grasslands. The 500 m MODIS data reveals an increase in NDVI for the entire region (Fig. 13.6). Figure 13.9b, reveals the difference image based on the Landsat images from August 2002 and August 2007. Landsat EVI data revealed a similar change (not shown).

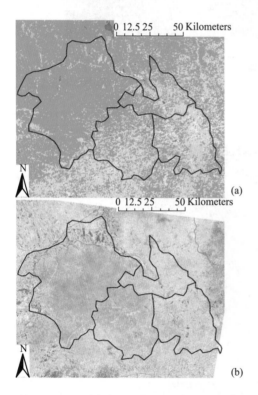

Fig. 13.9 (a) MODIS IGBP 500m land cover classification for Yulin region, (b) Landsat NDVI difference between August 2002 and August 2007 with brown areas showing negative changes and green areas showing vegetation index increases.

While the MODIS NDVI time series revealed ongoing NDVI increase, the Landsat based difference image revealed a decline in NDVI in the majority of the four counties in Yulin. To understand this discrepancy we plotted both the MODIS NDVI values for the two MODIS composites overlapping August and the Landsat NDVI values from one county (Hengshan) in Figure 13.10b. In addition we plotted the amount of precipitation in July in Figure 13.10c (the Landsat imagery is from the first week of August). Figure 13.10c reveals that July 2002 was wetter than July 2007. Thus we conclude that the NDVI decrease as observed with the Landsat imagery is most likely a result of a high amount of precipitation in July 2002 that increased the vegetation in that year and subsequently led to an apparent vegetation decline in July 2007, and not a result of grazing changes. This example illustrates the power of image time series analysis as opposed to discrete change analysis as done with the Landsat imagery.

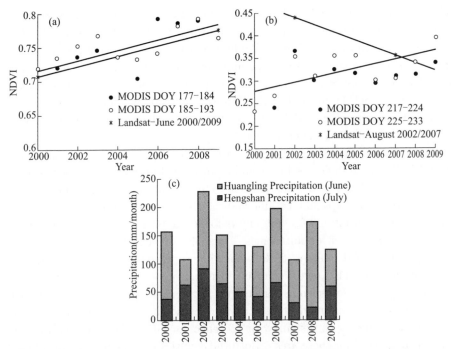

Fig. 13.10 MODIS and Landsat NDVI for Huangling county in Yan'an region (a) and Hengshan county in Yulin region (b). (c) shows the monthly precipitation for June in Huanling and July in Hengshan that are the months immediately preceding the Landsat images.

Livestock density is generally high in Western China resulting in increasing cover of less palatable and poisonous plant species (Harris, 2010). Karnieli et al. (2012) used Landsat data and showed that EVI is higher for grazed areas in Mongolia than for ungrazed areas as a result of the different vegetation structure of these less palatable plants (Karnieli et al., 2012). Both GfGP and NFCP support enclosure of degraded grasslands from livestock grazing. However, when looking over a time period we find an increase in both NDVI and EVI both in the areas with increased grazing pressure (Yulin) and the areas with decreased grazing pressure (Yan'an). The EVI and NDVI increase was generally more widespread in the shrub and grass dominated regions of Yulin and localized to just grasslands and shrublands in Yan'an. Unfortunately, the Landsat image analysis could not improve our understanding because the anniversary date imagery came from two years with drastically different precipitation regimes (Fig. 13.10).

13.7   Conclusions

This chapter evaluated NDVI, EVI, and broad-band albedo changes at 0.05° resolution by anthrome. In addition, we evaluate NDVI changes at a spatial resolution 100 times finer, 500 m. We find that the observed changes are highly dependent on the type of anthrome and population density. Irrigated villages reveal far fewer significant changes than other anthromes and the most populated rangelands reveal the most change. This work extends previous work by others who only incorporated NDVI data at coarse spatial resolution (1 km, 8 km) (Song and Ma, 2007; Yang et al., 2002).

We show that the observed changes are the most widespread when observed with NDVI data at 0.05° resolution and the least widespread when observed with albedo data. While NDVI is most sensitive to vegetation changes, climate simulation models that typically use albedo data will not reveal as much change. The higher spatial resolution of 500 m allows for a more accurate division of change by land cover type within anthromes. These data reveal that the croplands are changing in rainfed villages (69%) while the croplands in irrigated villages remain stable (just 11% reveal change). The conversion of rainfed croplands to permanent vegetation such as forests and grasslands would result in increased NDVI values since permanent vegetation does not have fallow periods. Thus, this change appears consistent with the effect of GfGP. Grazing analyses are more complicated for these areas. Both the counties with increased grazing and the counties with decreased grazing reveal an increase in 500 m NDVI data.

Acknowledgements

We would like to thank P. de Beurs for the application development that allowed us to estimate the land surface phenology data efficiently. We would like to thank two anonymous reviewers for the comments on an earlier version of this manuscript. We would also like to thank NASA and Jiquan Chen for the invitation to attend the NASA workshop on Drylands of East Asia.

References

Becker, R., Zmijewski, K.A. (2013). Land use and land cover change in drylands of East Asia. In: Chen, J., S. Wan, G.M., Henebry, J. Qi, G. Gutman, G. Sun, M. Kappas. (Eds.) *Dyland East Asia (DEA): Land dynamics Amid Social and Climate Change*. HEP-De Gruyer.

Bounoua, L., Collatz, G.J., Los, S.O., Sellers, P.J., Dazlich, D.A., Tucker, C.J., and Randall, D.A. (2000). Sensitivity of climate to changes in NDVI. *Journal of Climate*, 13, 2277–2292.

Brown, G.G., Waldron, S.A., and Longworth, J.W. (2009). *Sustainable Development in Western China: Managing People, Livestock and Grasslands in Pastoral Areas*. Cheltenham, UK: Edward Elgar Publishing.

Cao, S., Chen, L., and Liu, Z. (2009a). An investigation of Chinese attitudes toward the environment: Case study using the Grain for Green Project. *AMBIO: A Journal of the Human Environment*, 38, 55–64.

Cao, S., Chen, L., and Yu, X. (2009b). Impact of China's Grain for Green Project on the landscape of vulnerable arid and semi-arid agricultural regions: a case study in northern Shaanxi Province. *Journal of Applied Ecology*, 46, 536–543.

Cao, S., Chen, L., and Zhu, Q. (2010a). Remembering the ultimate goal of environmental protection: including protection of impoverished citizens in China's environmental policy. *AMBIO: A Journal of the Human Environment*, 39, 439–442.

Cao, S., Tian, T., Chen, L., Dong, X., Yu, X., and Wang, G. (2010b). Damage caused to the environment by reforestation policies in arid and semi-arid areas of China. *AMBIO: A Journal of the Human Environment*, 39, 279–283.

Chen, L.D., Wei, W., Fu, B.J., and Lu, Y.H. (2007). Soil and water conservation on the Loess Plateau in China: review and perspective. *Progress in Physical Geography*, 31, 389–403.

de Beurs, K.M., and Henebry, G.M. (2004). Trend analysis of the Pathfinder AVHRR Land (PAL) NDVI data for the deserts of Central Asia. *Geoscience and Remote Sensing Letters*, 1, 282–286.

de Beurs, K.M., and Henebry, G.M. (2005). A statistical framework for the analysis of long image time series. *International Journal of Remote Sensing*, 26, 151–1573.

de Beurs, K.M., Wright, C.K., and Henebry, G.M. (2009). Dual scale trend analysis distinguishes climatic from anthropogenic effects on the vegetated land surface *Environmental Research Letters*, 4, 045012.

Ellis, E.C., Klein Goldewijk, K., Siebert, S., Lightman, D., and Ramankutty, N. (2010). Anthropogenic transformation of the biomes, 1700 to 2000. *Global Ecology and Biogeography*, 19, 589–606.

Ellis, E.C., and Ramankutty, N. (2008). Putting people in the map: anthropogenic biomes of the world. *Frontiers in Ecology and the Environment*, 6, 439–447.

Fu, B.J., and Chen, L.D. (2000). Agricultural landscape spatial pattern analysis in the semi-arid hill area of the Loess Plateau. *China Journal of Arid Environment*, 44, 291–303. (in Chinese)

Harris, R.B. (2010). Rangeland degradation on the Qinghai-Tibetan plateau: A review of the evidence of its magnitude and causes. *Journal of Arid Environments*, 74, 291–

303.

Hu, C.X., Fu, B.J., Chen, L.D., and Gulinck, H. (2006). Farmer's attitudes towards the Grain-for-Green programme in the Loess hilly area, China: A case study in two small catchments. *International Journal of Sustainable Development and World Ecology*, 13, 211–220.

Huete, A., Didan, K., Miura, T., Rodriguez, E.P., Gao, X., and Ferreira, L.G. (2002). Overview of the radiometric and biophysical performance of the MODIS vegetation indices. *Remote Sensing of Environment*, 83, 195–213.

Huete, A., Justice, C.O., and Liu, H. (1994). Development of vegetation and soil indices for MODIS-EOS. *Remote Sensing of Environment*, 49, 224–234.

Jiang, D.S. (1997). *Soil erosion and its controlling patterns on the Loess Plateau in China*. Beijing: China's Water Resources and Hydropower Press.

Karnieli, A., Bayarjargal, Y., Bayasgalan, M., Mandakh, B., Dugarjavc, C., Burgheimera, J., Khudulmurb, S., Bazhad, S.N., and Gunind, P.D. (2012). Do vegetation indices provide reliable indication of vegetation degradation? A case study in the Mongolian pastures. *International Journal of Remote Sensing*, Accepted.

Li, J., and Ren, Z.Y. (2011). Variations in ecosystem service value in response to land use changes in the Loess Plateau in northern Shaanxi Province, China. *International Journal of Environmental Research*, 5, 109–118.

Liu, J.G., Li, S.X., Ouyang, Z.Y., Tam, C., and Chen, X.D. (2008). Ecological and socioeconomic effects of China's policies for ecosystem services. *Proceedings of the National Academy of Sciences of the United States of America*, 105, 9477–9482.

Lucht, W., Schaaf, C.B., and Strahler, A.H. (2000). An algorithm for retrieval of albedo from space using semiemperical BRDF models. *IEEE Transactions of Geoscience and Remote Sensing*, 38, 977–998.

Mátyás, C., G.Sun, Y. Zhang (2012). Afforestation and forests at the dryland edges: Lessons learned and future outlooks. In: Chen, J., S. Wan, G.M., Henebry, J.Qi, G. Gutman, G. Sun, M. Kappas (Eds.). *Dryland East Asia (DEA): Land Dynamics Amid Social and Climate Change*. HEP-De Gruyer.

Qi, Y.B., Chang, Q.R., Jia, K.L., Liu, M.Y., and Chen, T. (2012). Temporal-spatial variability of desertification in an agro-pastoral transitional zone of northern Shaanxi Province, China. *Catena*, 88, 37–45.

Shi, H., and Shao, M. (2000). Soil and water loss from the Loess Plateau in China. *Journal of Arid Environments*, 45, 9–20.

Song, Y., and Ma, M.G. (2007). Study on vegetation cover change in Northwest China based on SPOT VEGETATION data. *Journal of Desert Research*, 27, 89–93.

Sun, R., Liu, C.M., and Zhu, Q.J. (2001). Relationship between the fractional vegetation cover change and rainfall in the Yellow River basin. *Acta Geographica Sinica*, 56, 667–672. (in Chinese with English abstract)

Tucker, C.J. (1979). Red and photographic infrared linear combinations for monitoring vegetation. *Remote Sensing of Environment*, 8, 127–150.

Uchida, E., Xu, J., and Rozelle, S. (2005). Grain for green: Cost-effectiveness and sustainability of China's conservation set-aside program. *Land Economics*, 81, 247–264.

Wang, X.M., Zhang, C.X., Hasi, E., and Dong, Z.B. (2010). Has the Three Norths Forest Shelterbelt Program solved the desertification and dust storm problems in arid and semiarid China? *Journal of Arid Environments*, 74, 13–22.

Xin, Z.B., Xu, J.X., and Zheng, W. (2008). Spatiotemporal variations of vegetation cover on the Chinese Loess Plateau (1981–2006): Impacts of climate changes on human activities. *Science in China Series D: Earth Sciences*, 67–78.

Xu, X.Z., Zhang, H.W., and Zhang, O. (2004a). Development of check-dam systems in gullies on the Loess Plateau, China. *Environmental Science and Policy*, 7, 79–86.

Xu, Z., Bennett, M.T., Tao, R., and Xu, J. (2004b). China's sloping land conversion programme four years on: Current situation, pending issues. *International Forestry Review*, 6, 317–326.

Yang, S.T., Liu, C.M., and Sun, R. (2002). The vegetation cover over last 20 years in Yellow River Basic. *Acta Geographica Sinica*, (in Chinese with English abstract) 57, 679–684.

Zhang, P.C., Shao, G.F., Zhao, G., Le Master, D.C., Parker, G.R., Dunning, J.B., and Li, Q.L. (2000). Ecology—China's forest policy for the 21st century. *Science*, 288, 2135–2136.

Zhang, X.T., Liang, S.L., Wang, K.C., Li, L., and Gui, S. (2010). Analysis of global land surface shortwave broadband albedo from multiple data sources. *IEEE Journal of Selected Topics in Applied Earth Observations and Remote Sensing*, 3, 296–305.

Zhou, H.J., Van Rompaey, A., and Wang, J.A. (2009). Detecting the impact of the "Grain for Green" program on the mean annual vegetation cover in Shaanxi Province, China using SPOT-VGT NDVI data. *Land Use Policy*, 26, 954–960.

Authors Information

Kirsten M. de Beurs[1]*, Dong Yan[1], Arnon Karnieli[2]

1. Department of Geography and Environmental Sustainability, University of Oklahoma, Norman, OK, USA
2. The Remote Sensing Laboratory, Jacob Blaustein Institutes for Desert Research, Ben Gurion University of the Negev, Israel

* Corresponding author

Summary II: Consequences

Ge Sun and Shiqiang Wan

The authors of Chapters 8–13 aim at quantifying the impacts of historic and future environmental and socioeconomic changes in the DEA region. These studies examine a wide range of stresses including climate change, landuse/land cover dynamics, socioeconomic growth, and the interactions of these stresses.

The DEA region represents one of the most water-stressed regions in the world. Water availability is the single most important factor that controls ecosystem processes and socioeconomic development in DEA. In Chapter 8, Sun et al. review water resource issues facing the entire DEA region and provide a modeling case study on the hydrologic impacts of land use change on the Loess Plateau. The authors report that above-global-average climate warming rates in the DEA region have resulted in the accelerated melting of glaciers in the Xinjiang Uygur Autonomous Region of China, causing concerns of a shift of watershed hydrology in the short term and water shortages in the long term in the Tarim Basin. Even though there is a large uncertainty about the future predictions in precipitation regimes by various General Circulation Models (GCMs), regional water balance modeling results suggest that the DEA region is likely to see a drier future during this century. During the late 1990s, the Chinese government launched several large-scale vegetation restoration projects, such as the Natural Forest Conservation Program (NFCP) and the Grain for Green Program (GfGP). These projects all aim at reducing soil erosion and improving the general environment in Western China. In Chapter 13, using time series MODIS and Landsat remote sensing data and trend analyses, de Beurs et al. systematically evaluate the land cover changes and grazing patterns in the Loess Plateau region during 2001–2009 when the large-scale vegetation restoration projects were implemented. The study shows that the rain-fed croplands are changing toward forests or grasslands while the irrigated croplands remain stable.de Beurs et al. conclude that these changes are consistent with the goals of the GfGP program. Sun et al. (Chapter 8) argue that the large ecological restoration efforts and the land use changes detected by de Beurs et al. are likely to reduce stream flow; however, climate change and variability may mask the hydrologic effects of land cover change. The hydrologic and climatic effects of reforestation in the dryland edges in China, Hungary, and the U.S. are further discussed by Mátyás et al. (Chapter 11), who conclude that planted forests can be beneficial in erosion control and dust storm mitigation but have often generated unintended consequences such as reducing groundwater storage and stream flow due to higher water use by trees. Cost-effective and ecologically sound forest policy in DEA requires the consideration of local environmental conditions and the projected negative impact of climate warming on the vitality and survival of plantation forests.

Climate warming and human actions both contribute to land degradation and desertification in DEA. Clearly, understanding the processes of how climate and land cover change affect ecosystem functions such as carbon and water balances become important to detangle the coupled effects. Based on this need, Shao et al. (Chapter 10) compared carbon and water fluxes measured at four research sites representing grazed grasslands,ungrazed grasslands, and cultivated croplands in the Inner Mongolia Autonomous Region of China. The authors conclude that the effects of land use change on the solar energy partition might be related to precipitation change in the semi-arid steppe region. As expected, soil water content and temperature are found to be the main factors controlling grassland and cropland ecosystem carbon assimilation in the dry region. Shao et al. (Chapter 10) also suggest that the absence of disturbances might alleviate the stress of high temperature and drought during the hot and dry periods, leading to a high resistance of vegetation to environmental changes. At a large scale, with a high magnitude of disturbance,Batkhishig (Chapter 12) suggests that anthropogenic activities such as mining, road construction, erosion, overgrazing, agriculture soil erosion, and soil pollution are the major factors that directly impact the environment. Thus, sound land conservation policy and land management practices to address human influences are needed to curb the current land degradation trend in Mongolia.

In addition to water shortage and soil erosion, another major environmental concern in DEA is the rising dust aerosols that have negative impacts on the tightly coupled human-environment-climate systems beyond territory boundaries. Sokolik et al. (Chapter 9) examine the linkages among the trend of dust aerosols (onset, duration, intensity), land cover and land use change,ecosystem processes and functions, and the regional climate in DEA using a meso-scale physically based climate-dust emission model (WRF-Chem-DuMo) coupled with land use dynamics. The authors indicate that the recent increases in dust events over Korea and Japan are most likely linked to increased dust occurrences in Mongolia and Inner Mongolia of China.

Part III
Solutions/Adaptations

Chapter 14

Monitoring and Assessment of Dryland Ecosystems with Remote Sensing

Martin Kappas and Pavel Propastin

Summary: The Millennium Ecosystem Assessment (MEA) underlined the lack of an adequate monitoring and assessment of land degradation and desertification in drylands. MEA (2005) asserted that "without a scientifically robust and consistent baseline of desertification, identifying priorities and monitoring the consequences of actions are seriously constrained". Furthermore the science community declared that long-term monitoring is necessary in order to separate between the effects of human influence and climate variability on vegetation development (Propastin et al., 2008a). Glenn et al. (1998) and Verón et al. (2006) stated that the missing of an objective database and monitoring program on which policy decisions are based is the main constraint for large-scale investments in anti-desertification actions. Referring to the United Nations Convention to Combat Desertification (UNCCD) "Parties agree, according to their respective capabilities, to integrate and coordinate the collection, analysis and exchange of relevant short-term and long-term data and information to ensure systematic observation of land degradation..." (UNCCD, Article 18, 1994). In general, monitoring and assessing the current state of the land is of interest for many groups of the society (land users and managers, policy makers, local land owners). Therefore, this chapter looks at the challenges to the implementation of monitoring and assessment systems in the Dryland East Asia (DEA) region considering the complexity of land degradation in this region.

Monitoring and assessment (M&A) has conventionally been focused more on land degradation and desertification than on the sustainable management of land resources (including soil, water, animals and plants). Extensive research efforts have assessed land degradation—often focusing exclusively on soil degradation—in the field (Schilch et al., 2011). This chapter provides a comprehensive overview of remote sensing approaches for future sustainable land management and is structured into five sections.

The main objectives of the chapter are:

- To rethink our current understanding of monitoring and assessment of drylands choosing an adapted framework, the Driving Force-Pressure-State-Impact-Response (DPSIR).
- To rethink data and monitoring needs for a more ecological and sustainable land management (SLM).
- To review indicators of land degradation and desertification, as well as to discuss possibilities and perspectives of their detection by remote sensing (RS).
- To review available remotely sensed data over DEA with respect to their use for monitoring and assessment of dryland degradation and desertification.
- To introduce case studies on remote sensing based monitoring and assessment of drylands in Central Asia.
- To provide recommendations for establishment of a DEA Observation System (DEA-OS) (take-home messages for decision makers) for land degradation and ecosystem assessment.

These objectives were achieved through an extensive literature review and a case study demonstrating how the rethinking framework can address emerging challenges in the new paradigm of ecosystem assessment with remotely sensed data and information.

14.1 Problems of Land Degradation and Desertification in Drylands: Current Challenges and Perspectives

Research after the Sahel droughts of the 1970s and attendant food crises has shown that desertification is functionally dependent on a lot of factors, including rainfall variation. Desertification today is seen as a broad phenomenon of environmental degradation and its interaction with human populations. The United Nations Convertion to Combat Desertification (UNCCD) defined desertification as "land degradation in arid, semi-arid and dry sub-humid areas resulting from various factors, including climatic variations and human activities", whereby land degradation is defined with regard to the Millennium Ecosystem Assessment (MEA) report (Adeel et al., 2005). In this sense the definition of land degradation means the loss of biological or economic productivity and is based on the framework of ecosystems services. The latest revision defining desertification, land degradation and drought is coming from UNCCD 1st Scientific

Conference COP 9 (UNCCD, 2009c) and is widely accepted in the research community:

"Desertification, land degradation and drought as defined by the UNCCD results from dynamic, interconnected, human-environment interactions in land systems, where land includes water, soil, vegetation and humans—requiring a rigorous scientific framework for monitoring and assessment, which has heretofore been lacking"...The text of UNCCD puts humans "at the center of concerns to combat desertification and mitigate the effects of drought". It notes that desertification/land degradation and drought (DLDD) "is caused by complex interactions among physical, biological, political, social, cultural and economic factors", and is interrelated with "social problems such as poverty, poor health and nutrition, and lack of food security".

On closer inspection of this definition, one central consequence is the need for a causality-based conceptual framework as a baseline for monitoring and assessment of DLDD. Several stress and response frameworks have been developed and implemented for environmental assessment. These frameworks strengthen the causal relationships between forces acting on the environment and their consequences, and societal response through a set of interlinked indicators. Well-known examples are the Pressure-State-Response (PSR) framework OECD (1993) or the Driving Force-Pressure-State-Impact-Response (DPSIR) framework by the European Environment Agency (EEA, 2005). Inside other conventions similar frameworks were buildup such as the Pressure-State-Use-Response-Capacity (PSURC) framework verbalized by the Convention on Biological Diversity (CBD, 2003). All of these frameworks have in common that they tackle both the origins and consequences of issues, but they differ in their individual structuring of the causal chain (Niemeijer, 2008a).

As conceptual framework for deriving desertification indicators for assessment and monitoring the DPSIR approach is chosen (DPSIR after Smeets and Weterings, 1999): that of drivers, pressures, states, impacts and responses (Fig. 14.1). DPSIR has been chosen by most of the research groups working to develop indicators of desertification, and its mitigation through sustainable land management (SLM). Ongoing approaches to derive desertification indicators that use the DPSIR conceptual framework are:

– The GEF-UNDP KM: Land "Ensuring Impacts from SLM—Development of a Global Indicator System" medium scale project (MSP).
– The Land Degradation Assessment (LADA) in Drylands indicator toolbox development.
– The desertification monitoring and assessment Thematic Program Network (TPN) for the Asia Region (TPN-1).
– The benchmarks and indicators for the Latin America and Caribbean RAC (TPN-1).
– The joint French Scientific Committee on Desertification (Comité Scientifique

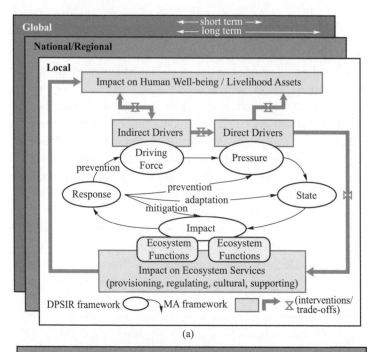

(a)

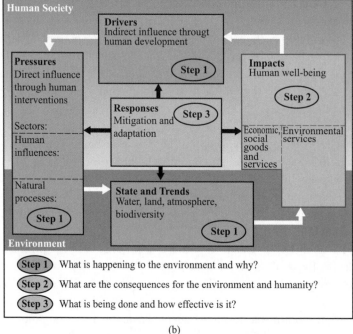

(b)

Fig. 14.1 (a) Amended DPSIR-approach as a combination of DPSIR and ecosystem services approaches (source: after GEF KM: Land, 2010 and FAO LADA, 2009); (b) Processing steps 1 to 3 where monitoring and assessment is embedded (e.g., step 1).

Francais de la Désertification, CSDF) — European DesertNet (EDN) indicator development effort.

- The Sahara and Sahel Observatory's Long-term Ecological Monitoring Observatories Network (Réseau d'Observatories de Surveillance Ecologique á Long Terme/Observatories du Sahara et du sahel (ROSELT/OSS)) local environments indicator development effort.
- The UNDP Global Environment Facility (UNDP-GEF) Carbon Benefits Project.
- The World Atlas of Desertification (WAD) project.

Box 1: A side note to DPSIR framework in Figure 14.1a and b

Driving forces: are indirect factors that produce pressures that vice versa create changes in the state (quality and quantity) of the resources. Drivers can determine both anthropogenic (e.g., demographic change) and natural forces. Human activities can be changed by socio-economic factors, which boost or diminish pressures on the environment. Human based drivers can be altered by policy and societal influences or societal responses. Natural based drivers (e.g., climate variability) cannot be controlled by people directly, but must be considered for future land management (policy related).

Pressures: are direct stresses, which are caused by human activities acting on the environment. These stresses (e.g., land use pressure) can provoke soil or vegetation loss and degradation. Pressure indicators are normally linkable to specific drivers: population increase (driving force) activates land use change in form of land fragmentation (pressure) and this pressure leads to habitat/biotope change, which is a change in system state.

State: variables of state are indicators of the condition of the system (including biophysical and socio-economic factors/processes). State variables often possess trends, which are seen in relation to environmental change. Furthermore interrelations exist between state variables, where a change in one variable may influence the state of the other.

Impact: is the measurement of the implication on human life and the environment resulting from state changes. For example impacts are the consequences of environmental degradation and are measured in relation to possible risks emerging when system boundaries are exceeded (reduction of ecosystem services).

Responses: are answers of people and societies that are chosen in reaction (feedback) to experienced impacts. In land degradation/desertification, mitigation is the response to impact, while prevention is the response to drivers and pressures, and adaptation is the response to changes in status.

Inside this framework, land degradation forms an important component for the welfare of affected populations, strengthening the integral role of social and ecological systems in DEA. With the Dryland Development Paradigm (DDP) (Reynolds et al., 2007), a new focus has been set on desertification as a problem of linked social-ecological systems. DDP highlights five factors which describe drylands as areas with high climate variability, low fertility, sparse population, remoteness and distant voice. Inside the DPP drylands, ecosystems are seen as dynamical systems possibly switching between alternative states (Holling, 1973) with an inherent potential for resilience. Over the past years, this approach has been largely embraced, showing a development away from single discipline perspective of soil degradation (e.g., GLASOD, Oldeman et al., 1991), towards acceptance of multiple interacting agents (Geist and Lambin, 2004). Moreover the behavior of non-linearity inside the ecological systems is accepted and the growing importance of adaptation need of local populations in the face of rapid global changes is acclaimed. Figure 14.1 shows the combination of DPSIR and ecosystem services approaches and contents the different spatial-temporal scales of concern. This framework is chosen to rethink the conceptualization of a possible indicator set for assessment and monitoring over the DEA area. Inside the side note box below, explanations about DPSIR are given.

Starting with the focus on current understanding of the state of DEA in general and its influence on land degradation and desertification in DEA (see also Chapter 1 in this book), the driving forces for degradation of arid ecosystems and controlling factors will be shortly displayed (Fig. 14.2). In respect to climate change over the DEA area in general a relative lack of down-scaled, precise data and attendant modeling of drivers for impacts of the future climate variability and drought exists. While in science, there is a widespread agreement that global climate change will increase temperature in DEA, for changing climate variability the impacts are less evident. Compared to the theoretical framework of drivers, pressures, state, impacts and response in Figure 14.1, the dominant interactions among climate and human activities that affect functioning of drylands in the DEA region are diagramed in Figure 14.2.

The interactions in Figure 14.2 reveal that for a comprehensive assessment of DLDD, a conceptual background for integrating biophysical and socio-economic data is needed. In this chapter we focus on a more general aspect of deriving biophysical parameters by remote sensing that are linked to desertification processes. The subsequent integration of biophysical and socio-economic data is one of the most important issues in the context of drylands desertification.

Corresponding to the above-mentioned global initiatives (LADA, GEF KM: Land etc.) that request standardized information for regional to continental scale, the subsequent sections 14.2 and 14.3 introduce indicators, data archives and sensors suitable for such tasks, and investigate methodologies to extract meaningful information for the assessment and monitoring of DLDD.

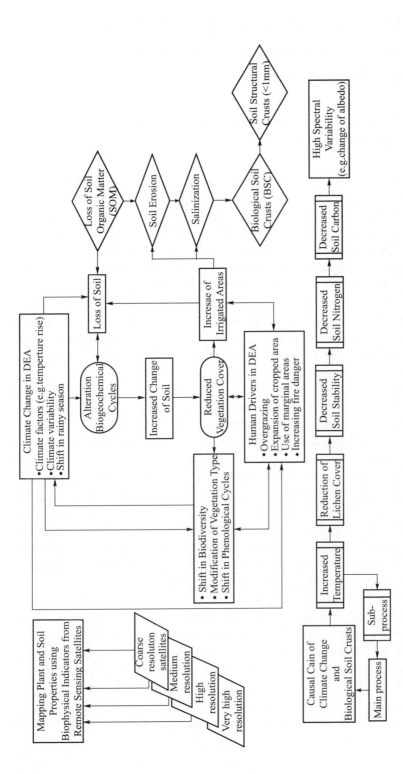

Fig. 14.2 Possible interactions among climate and human activities in DEA that affect functioning of drylands and give a hint for reasonable indicators for assessment and monitoring of landscape degradation by Remote Sensing (RS). At the bottom an example of a feasible causal chain of temperature rise (as cause of climate change) and the formation of biological soil crusts and their influence on surface albedo (decisive for RS-based analysis) is given.

14.2 Indicators of Land Degradation/ Desertification and Their Detection by Remote Sensing

14.2.1 History of Degradation/Desertification Indicator Development in Recent Decades

The origin of degradation/desertification indicator development can be traced back to the work of Berry and Ford (1977) and Reining (1978). Twenty years later UNCCD (1997, 1998) addressed the challenge of indicator development and selection at the Conference of the Parties in Beijing, China. Since that time, subsequent work has been carried out by numerous subgroups of scientists that were appointed by the Committee on Science and Technology (CST) of UNCCD as experts working towards a set of national/global indicators for DLDD. Most of this work is summarized in reports and peer-reviewed publications (e.g., Abraham et al., 2006; Grainger, 2009; Verstraete et al., 2009). This progress persists today (e.g., 2011 a special issue of the journal *Land Degradation and Development* focused on indicators: http://onlinelibrary.wiley.com/journal/10.1002/%28ISSN%291099-145X/earlyview.%20E.g).

The magnitude of degradation over the DEA area is estimated using various measurable quantities, called indicators. An indicator is defined as a measurable variable representing an operational attribute inside a given system (Gallopin, 1997). A feasible indicator is "representative, scientifically valid, simple and easy to interpret, shows trends over time, gives early warning about irreversible trends, is sensitive to changes, based on data that are readily available, adequately documented and of known quality, and capable of being updated at regular intervals" (DOE, 1996). Besides single indicators, so called indicator systems exist, which comprise sets of indicators or combine these to build up composite indices. Table 14.1 summarizes eleven important impact indicators for the assessment and monitoring of land degradation/desertification, which are partly available over the DEA area and presented in the book.

As seen from Table 14.1, the mentioned indicators can be distinguished in non-RS-based indicators (population statistics, ground measurements) and RS-based indicators (e.g., NPP via NDVI). Prior to looking at RS-based indicators (Section 14.2.2) attention is drawn on several parallel, synergistic approaches such as the indicator development work of the UN Convention on Biological Diversity (CBD) (Biodiversity Indicator partnership 2010, CBD 2010), the UN Framework Convention on Climate Change (UNFCCC) Essential Climate Variables (ECV) (GCOS, 2010; GOSIC, 2010; Kappas, 2009), the GEF-UNDP KM: Land

Table 14.1 Recommended indicators from the UNCCD "minimum list of impact indicators", adapted from Berry et al. (1977) and Zucca and Biancalani (2010).

Provisional Impact Indicators	Stated Purpose	Metric/Proxy/Definition
I . Water availability per capita in affected areas	Monitor the progress in the access of the population to improved water resources	Population with water stress—UN Sustainable Development Indicators (%)
II . Change in land use	Highlight changes in the productive or protective uses of the land resource	Proportion of change of each land use category to another per a unit of time (%)
III . Proportion of the population in affected areas living above the poverty line	Monitor poverty as the most important defining characteristic of underdevelopment and as a root-cause and consequence of desertification	The percentage of affected population with a standard living above the poverty line (%)
IV . Childhood malnutrition and/ or food consumption/calorie intake per capita in affected areas	Measure long-term nutritional imbalance and malnutrition. Nutritional status is the best global indicator of well-being in children and an indicator of the availability of ecosystem services	Percentage of underweight (weight-for-age below -2 standard deviation (SD) of the WHO Child Growth Standards median) among children under five years of age; percentage of stunting (height-for-age below -2 SD of the WHO Child Growth Standards median) among children under five years of age; and percentage of overweight (weight-for-height above $+2$SD of the WHO Child Growth Standards median) among children under five years of age. [Percent (%)]
V . The Human Development Index (HDI) as defined by UNDP	Approximate the status and change in the well-being of populations. Applied in affected areas it will be an effective surrogate for the impact of the efforts to combat desertification on the livelihood of peoples	UNDP's HDI, based on 4 basic indicators: – life expectancy at birth; – adult literacy; – combined gross enrolment in primary, secondary and tertiary level education; – gross domestic product (GDP) per capita in Purchasing Power Parity US dollars (PPP US$) (Parametric index)

(Continued)

Provisional Impact Indicators	Stated Purpose	Metric/Proxy/Definition
VI. Level of land degradation (including salinization, water and wind erosion, etc.)	Measure the extent of land Degradation at the national level. It also measures the impact of agreements and programs to address land degradation and to reclaim degraded lands.	The amount of land affected by degradation and its proportion of national Territory, LADA . [Area (km^2) and Percent (%) of land area affected]
VII. Plant and animal biodiversity	Approximate overall biodiversity condition of a region relative to a "pristine" state. The current condition in protected areas is used as a surrogate measure of this pristine state.	Biodiversity intactness index (BII) [Rate of change of BII in percentage (%)]
VIII. Aridity index	Use as base indicator for characterizing sensitive and desertification-affected areas.	UNEP Aridity Index (Bioclimatic Index), defined as the ratio between mean annual precipitation (P) and mean annual evapotranspiration: (ETP) $Ia=Pa/Eto$ (Indicative value of the ratio Pa/Eto)
IX. Land cover status	Monitor land degradation in terms of long-term loss of ecosystem primary productivity and taking into account effects of rainfall on NPP	GLADA—Land cover status—in both cultivated and non-cultivated lands—based on NPP and RUE trends as obtained through long term series NDVI data. [kg C ha^{-1} yr^{-1} -1% (NPP) and mm^{-1} (RUE)]
X. Carbon stocks above and below ground	Encourage countries to monitor their carbon stocks and to record changes in above and below ground stocks as a global benefit.	Indicator to be developed in conjunction with IPCC process (t ha^{-1})
XI. Land under SLM	Land under Sustainable Land Management (SLM) is an important surrogate for a number of global benefits	Area of land under SLM (World Bank) (ha)

"Ensuring Impacts from SLM—Development of a Global Indicator System" medium scale project (MSP) (GEF KM: Land 2010), the Land Degradation Assessment in Drylands (LADA) indicator toolbox development effort (FAO-LADA, 2009), a joint French Scientific Committee on Desertification (CSFD)—European DesertNet (EDN) indicator development effort (CSFD-EDN. 2009), and the work of Réseau d'Observatoires de Surveillance Ecologique à Long Terme/Observatoire du Sahara et du Sahel (ROSELT/OSS) (OSS 2008), the World Atlas on Desertification (WAD) (JRC, 2010), and efforts to promote a Global Drylands Observing System (GDOS) (Verstraete et al., 2011).

The current and ongoing approaches have a huge impact for the future assessment and monitoring of landscape degradation/desertification in the DEA area concerning SLM which is considered as the sustainable response to the drivers, pressures and states of degradation in the DEA area (Table 14.2).

Table 14.2 Selection of current and ongoing approaches for assessment and monitoring of landscape degradation/desertification.

GLASOD: Global Assessment of Soil Degradation produced the first global map of soil degradation (Oldeman et al., 1991)	**WOCAT:** The World Overview of Conservation Approaches and Technologies (2007)
LADA: UNEP and FAO launched the Land Degradation Assessment in Drylands Project in 2001, with the financial support of the Global Environment Facility (GEF); initially it focused on land degradation, but the collaboration with WOCAT strengthened the SLM component of LADA.	**DESIRE:** The DESIRE project (2007–2012, http://www.desire-project.eu) is developing and testing alternative strategies for desertification vulnerable areas. Like WOCAT, DESIRE advocates an SLM approach based on inventories of local knowledge.

Once a set of indicators has been selected, judgments are needed on how to quantify them. One possibility would be to use scientifically credible methods to ensure the assessment of DLDD. Mostly a multi-scalar and multi-source measurement approach that combines remote sensing data, ground observations and official statistics is chosen. Easily accessible monitoring and assessment methods are based on simple soil and vegetation indicators whose interconnections are outlined in Figure 14.2. The possible interactions of climate and human activities can be captured by "fast" variables (rainfall or grass growth per season) and "slow" variables (e.g., shrub encroachment or cropland expansion). In the last years there is a growing acceptance that a small number of the slow variables explain changes in the human-environment system best. Contrary to this, the inherent noise of the fast variables often masks any signal from the slow variables. Consequently there is a pressing demand for long-time series of observations to isolate the slow trends from the short-term fluctuations of the fast variables. One general outcome of various place-based researches on desertification is that desertification is driven by a limited collection of recurrent core variables, which are identifiable by regional patterns (Geist and Lambin, 2004). In the following, we concentrate on remote sensing based assessment and monitoring of biophysical indicators for land degradation and desertification, focusing of which the RS-based indicators are best for monitoring and assessment.

14.2.2 Retrieving Biophysical Spectral Information with Remote Sensing for DLDD

This section reviews biophysical indicators for the assessment and monitoring of ecosystem desertification. Additionally a brief look will be drawn on remote sensing-based methods for recognition of desertification indicators. Advantages and constrains of remote sensing based on optical sensors for detection of desertification indicators will be shortly discussed.

A well-structured remote sensing survey, assisted by ground truth data collection, can reduce the time taken to undertake a Baseline Survey of land degradation over a large area such as the DEA region. Carrying out regular surveys thereafter will detect changes in the intensity and extent of degradation in different areas. But first of all the creation of a baseline survey is a prerequisite for all further steps to estimate land desertification (see Box 2). Remote Sensing data provide an efficient method to deliver biophysical indicators about the status of the landscape. In the following, the spectral characteristics of vegetation and soils that are detectable using optical sensors and methods to quantify characteristics with capabilities for assessment and monitoring of desertification are reviewed.

Box 2: A side note on the need of Baseline Surveys

A *baseline survey* is a starting point for monitoring that provides a comprehensive characterization of a phenomenon in a specific year so that later changes in its attributes can be measured. It identifies not a potential hazard, but the actual *status* of the extent and degree of desertification in a given *baseline year*, to provide a marker with which the status in future years can be compared (going back and forwards). Important "status-variables" are for instance LAI and FAPAR and their spatial patterns.

Moderate spatial resolution sensors (100–300 m) such as MODIS/MERIS with frequent (daily to weekly) or coarse resolution sensors (1,000 m) such as NOAA AVHRR, SPOT Vegetation or SEASAT with their sensitive and unbiased observations of vegetation properties such as the Fraction of Absorbed Photosynthetically Active Radiation (FAPAR) or Leaf Area Index (LAI) deliver fundamental indicators for environmental assessments and have already been recognized as "Essential Climate Variables" (ECVs) by the Global Climate Observing System (GCOS, 2010; Kappas, 2009). These measurements derive the quantitative information about the environment and are useful for assessments. Indicators such as FAPAR or LAI (Kappas et al., 2012) replace dimensionless indices such as the Normalized Difference Vegetation Index (NDVI). Vegetation indexes are little sensible at low leaf area development and fractional cover of the vegetation, primarily when the soil background owns a high diversity. Secondary, dry plant material (e.g., litter accumulated over years) challenges the correct measurement of the soil surface. The overlapping of soil and vegetation spectral characteristics makes it difficult to detect biogeochemical constituents.

NDVI has been widely criticized because of its sensitivity to a wide range of effects (e.g., atmospheric composition, soil moisture, surface anisotropy) unrelated to vegetation. Today long-term trends in NDVI derivatives are seen as maladjusted indicators of land degradation and improvement in drylands. Nevertheless NDVI is still an important indicator and widely used. Another problem is the missing of baseline surveys in many drylands so that a starting point for subsequent change analysis is missing. Despite this constraint to measure vegetation and soil properties precisely, the loss of vegetation cover is widely recognized as a primary driver of desertification and many RS-based indicators focus on vegetation. Generally the life forms of vegetation in drylands shift in relation to the variability of precipitation. A higher predictability of precipitation normally enables an occurrence of grasses and a more irregular precipitation pattern enables a shift to shrub lands. This tendency is often accompanied by limited nutrients in soil, particularly nitrogen is rare. Where nitrogen availability is higher, vegetation growth is positively influenced and vegetation attributes such as species composition, plant height and growth and phenological patterns could change. Frequently a fragmentation in areas of higher and lower nutrient content and vegetation fertility is observed. Schlesinger et al. (1990) documented a progressive pattern of desertification during the transformation from grassland to shrub land accompanied by a higher diversity of soil nutrients in space. This inhomogeneous nutrient distribution results in islands of higher vegetation density inside a surrounding area of unproductive barren soil. Both variables, vegetation and soil surface properties that build up a mosaic and are characteristic for drylands can provide key indicators of desertification. In the case of soil properties the upper centimeters of the soil are most fertile and most prone to rainfall and water and wind erosion. Only these first centimeters of soil are detectable by optical sensors. In particular soil chemistry can deliver key indicators of desertification (see Table 14.3). For instance, distribution of soil organic matter (SOM) and secondary clay influence the range of vegetation and soil responses in drylands

Table 14.3 Soil Indexes and their explanation.

Soil Index	Equation/Formula	Explanation	Source
RI	$RI=TM3^2/(TM1 \times TM2)$	Hematite Content	a
	$RI = XS2^2 / XS1^3$		b
	$RI = XS2^2 / XS1^4$		c
CI	$CI = (TM3 - TM2) / (TM3 + TM2)$	Hematite/Goethite ratio	d
	$CI = (XS2 - XS1) / (XS2 + XS1)$		b, d
HI	$HI = (2 \times TM3 - TM2 - TM1) / (TM2 - TM1)$	Hue index	e
SI	$SI = (TM3 - TM1) / (TM3 + TM1)$	Spectral Slope	e
BI	$BI = SQRT(TM1^2 + TM2^2 + TM3^2 / 3)$	Average soil reflectance	c
NDI	$BI = SQRT(XS1^2 + XS2^2 /2)$	Discriminates soil and	a
	$NDI = (L_{840} - L_{1650})/(L_{840} + L_{1650})$	dry matter	

Source: a: McNairn and Protz (1993); b: Madeira et al. (1997); c: Mathieu et al. (1998); d: Escadafal and Huete (1991); e: Escadafal et al. (1994).
RI: Redness Index, CI: Coloration Index, HI: Hue Index—dominant wavelength, SI: Saturation Index—spectral slope, BI: Brightness Index—average soil reflectance, NDI: Normalized Index; TM from Landsat Thematic Mapper and XS from Spot HRV.

under stress (e.g., climate change or depletion). Measuring clay and SOM will contribute to understand impacts coming from altered rainfall patterns and accompanied deposition of pollutants. From the point of view of climate change and desertification, the formation and dissolution of soil inorganic carbon is of specific concern, because climate change will cause changing hydrologic processes that have a direct impact on the inorganic carbon pool of drylands ecosystems. Figure 14.3 shows the different processes of land degradation and their relations that influence the entire status of a landscape.

Summarizing the complex interconnectedness of atmosphere (particularly temperature and rainfall patterns over drylands), hydrology, soil and vegetation, we can retrieve important biophysical spectral information from different sources in the landscape:

- Biophysical properties of living vegetation.
- Biophysical properties of dead or dry vegetation.
- Biophysical properties of soil in general and from biological and structural crusts.

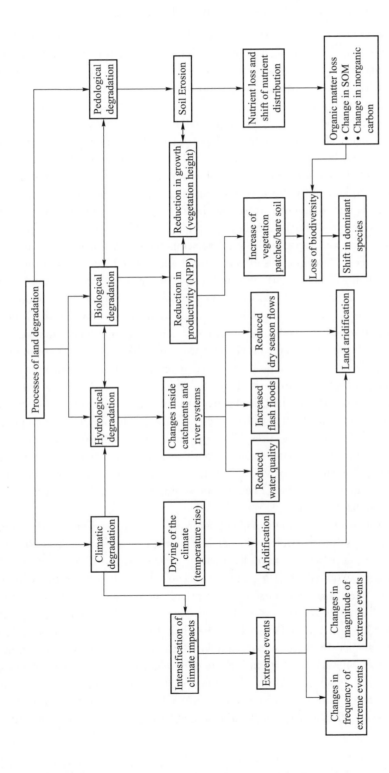

Fig. 14.3 Main physical processes of landscape degradation in DEA and their interconnectedness.

1. Mapping biophysical indicators from living vegetation

Plants in drylands have developed similar adaptation strategies over time. They have similar leaf structures and their growth forms are mostly grasses or shrubs. The vegetation cover is contracted (often terrain dependent) or fragmented and normally with a dominance or cover ratio under 20%. Nevertheless vegetation cover is the most important indication of rainfall amount and soil moisture condition in a landscape. Plenty of research studies proved a linear relation between vegetation cover, biomass amount and leaf area index with reference to water availability (Beatley, 1980). In general, the reflectance and transmittance of drylands plant leaves are response to the concentration of light absorbing constituents (dry plant matter, water, chlorophyll, etc.) and the surface scattering of light that is not completely absorbed. Leaf characteristics of drylands species are thick leaves with a thick cuticle, pubescence (small hairs on the leaf) reduced stomata function accompanied by small mesophyll cells with thick cell walls and small air spaces. Pubescence and waxes on the leaves reduce leaves absorbance potential. The leaf characteristics produce wavelength specific absorption and scattering which can be tracked as diagnostic patterns of vegetation conditions. Today there is a strong interest in the absorption of light by photosynthetic pigments (chlorophylls, xantophylls, anthocyanins, carotenoids) dominating the green leaves characteristics in the visible spectrum (VIS: 400–700 nm, minimum at 550 nm). Research about photosynthetic efficiency and its variation is ongoing and might best be summarized by the development of the Photosynthetic Reflectance Index (PRI) which is sensitive to varying photosynthetic pigments and offers a normalized ratio (Garnon et al., 1997). Rethinking the changing influence of different photosynthetic compounds (e.g., response to higher stress caused by rising temperatures), their identification might become an indicator for the physiological state of vegetation in the future, but is up to the present restricted to laboratory based investigations and far away from operational use for large area assessment.

Apart from the VIS range of the spectrum, the near-infrared (NIR: 700–1,100 nm) range has restricted biochemical absorption features. The NIR absorption characteristics are more designed by dry leaves and their cellulose content or other carbohydrates (e.g., lignin). The interior leaf structure with its proportions of air spaces and air-water interfaces is influencing the resulting reflectance. Normally, reflectance and albedo decline in NIR in contrast to VIS. The transmittance and reflectance in the shortwave infra-red (SWIR: 1,100–2,500 nm) is ruled by water absorption with primary water absorption features at 1,450nm, 1,940nm, and 2,500nm. Secondary water absorptions are detectable at 980 nm and 1,240 nm. Many plants and surface soil molecules have similar chemical composition and mixture (e.g., similar C-N-, C-O- or N-O-bonds) and produce overlapping absorption/reflection features that make it hard to differentiate them. Overall the spectral behavior of biochemical constituents is very complex in the SWIR and challenges specific identification.

Plenty of methods (plate models, N-flux models, compact spherical particle models, radiative transfer models, stochastic models, ray tracing models, etc.) are already developed to estimate structural and biochemical properties (Rotondi et al., 2003, Ustin et al., 2009). Most prominent are leaf inversion models (e.g., PROSPECT, Jacquemoud and Baret, 1990). PROSPECT is an improved radiative transfer model based on Allen's generalized "plate model" (Allen et al., 1969, 1970) that represents the optical properties of plant leaves from 400 nm to 2,500 nm.

However until today, the overlapping wavelengths of different absorption features make a distinct identification of constituents challenging and most of the described methods are restricted to work under laboratory conditions and do not allow monitoring and assessment of larger areas.

2. Mapping biophysical indicators from dead or dry vegetation

Reflectance and transmittance of dry leaves or dry plant materials are caused by carbon-based constituents like lignin, cellulose and sugars, as well as proteins and enzymes. The portion of dry vegetation is called non-photosynthetic vegetation and constitutes of dry leaves, branches, bark and wood (all non-green plant parts). The reflectance behavior builds up a more monotonic spectral curve between 400 nm and 1,500 nm which normally is lacking any red-edge features. The red-edge is a small spectral area between 700–725 nm at the long-wavelength of the chlorophyll absorption trait. The red-edge is totally absent in soils, rocks and most of the dry plant mass. Therefore the red-edge is chosen as a decisive bio-signature of green vegetation and at the same time the red-edge is an indicator for the detection of trace quantities of green vegetation (cover <10%). As mentioned before Lignin and cellulose are present in plant residues and have characteristic absorption features in the SWIR (between 2,000 nm and 2,500 nm). Additionally Lignin has strong absorption in the ultraviolet at 280 nm with an absorption area across the VIS and NIR. This specific absorption feature of lignin is detectable when the leaf pigments are degraded (hint for dry and matured vegetation). During the decomposition process, lignin is more imperishable as cellulose and thus lignin is enriched in plant residues. This gives rise to a more distinct ultraviolet absorption feature caused by lignin. Because reflectance behavior changes during the decomposition process, the separation of litter and soil is possible. One approved example is the Cellulose Absorption Index (CAI) exploiting the feature at 2,100 nm, where soils normally do not absorb but plant residues do (Nagler et al., 2000). Many multispectral residue indexes consider the different absorption behavior of dry plant residues and soils. Generally the reflectance of plant residues increases from 400 nm to 1,300 nm and decline strongly at longer wavelength. In contrast soil reflectance continues to raise up to 1,750 nm and declines then slowly. The reflectance behavior of plant residues and soil is supplementary influenced by varying moisture. Investigations of crop residues showed a higher reflectance of plant residues on wet soils than on dry soils. One outcome of these considerations is the development of the Normalized Difference Index (NDI) that distinguishes dry plant matter from soil (see Table 14.3). NDI was revised to the Soil Adjusted Corn Residue Index (SACRI, Biard and Baret, 1997) that strengthened the index against the influence of soil texture. Apart the identification of plant matter, SACRI is used as a potential erosion index discriminating areas with a lower plant residues cover of 15%–20% (Threshold of critical plant matter cover for soil erosion assessment is around 15% in drylands). But for the development of applicable indicators of land degradation the identification of non-photosynthetic vegetation at diverse levels of decomposition and cover is still challenging and only feasible for high resolution sensors.

3. Mapping biophysical indicators from soil

The environment for soil formation in drylands is made up of irregular rainfall, slow soil development (resulting in shallow soils) and sparse vegetation cover accompanied by small infiltration capacity and high runoff events. Dissolution of salts and high evaporation rates cause the formation of crusts and hardpans. Additionally structural (caliche layers) and biological crusts influence the spectral properties of soils in drylands. On the other hand, soils show smaller spectral variations comparing to dry plant matter. As soil is a mixture of various minerals, the organic matter soil spectra vary only little with time. Most of the soils differ only in brightness in the red and NIR range which form a linear relationship, the soil brightness vector or soil line. The main problem for dry areas is to define a unique soil line caused by high soil heterogeneity. Today many sophisticated methods exist to derive information about mineral absorption features of soils. One of the most used methods is normalization depending on the background continuum. Instead of going into details of soil analysis methods, we like to concentrate on issues that change the temporal variability of soil reflectance and could be used for deriving indicators of land degradation. Soil moisture is one of these issues that change reflectance behavior of soils and give hint about the status of the landscape. Soil moisture was successfully modeled making use of the 1,450 nm and 1,900 nm bands (Liu et al., 2002). Another important soil parameter is soil organic matter (SOM) that is directly related to soil quality and therefore an indicator of vegetation status and other biogeochemical processes. Low contents of SOM are typical for dry areas and the amount of SOM can be used to stratify a landscape into different quality zones and levels of degradation. For instance, SOM quality under degraded shrub areas is lower as under non-degraded shrub areas. This causality suggests that degraded vegetation is causing soil degradation and vice versa. Another important issue is soil salinity which is also a consequence of soil degradation. Soil salinity alters the soil structure (clay dispersion and decrease in infiltration) and influences vegetation development (most plants are salt intolerant). The most important salts (calcium, carbonate, sodium sulfate, gypsum) have a high reflectance in the VIS-NIR domain and show clear absorption features in the SWIR domain. Most of the salt surfaces have a high albedo except alkaline surfaces with their dark look due to organic matter. Landscapes with a high salt content in soils own a high dynamic and the inherent variability makes an assessment difficult. If moisture is available biological soil crusts (BSC) could appear in hypersaline soils where other salt-intolerant vegetation is absent. On the other side salt-tolerant vegetation can mask the spectral features of saline areas.

Surface roughness in dry areas is a further major factor affecting soil reflectance and can be used as indicator to distinguish different surface conditions. Cierniewski and Karnielli (2002) separated typical drylands surfaces such as desert pavement, BSC, sand areas and playas with the help of bi-directional reflectance studies and their behavior to forward and backward scattering. Soil erosion as the next important issue is normally indicated by a loss of SOM and the loss of the upper soil. Constituents from deeper soil horizons like iron oxides and carbonate can appear at the surface.

The combination of all the above mentioned processes requires synoptic vistas over large regions with sufficient spatial and spectral resolution to quantify the different processes. A synoptic validation of plant and soil properties for the assessment and monitoring of DLDD is done by various bio-physiological indexes that are listed in the next section.

14.2.3   Bio-physiological Indexes for Assessment and Monitoring

A variety of spectral indexes was developed during last years taking into account the specific advantage of absorption characteristics of plants and soils and their appearance in spectral bands. Most important are the vegetation indexes that deliver information about vegetation cover and the "greenness" of an area. The vegetation indexes can be distinguished in pigment-based, foliar water-based and foliar chemistry-based indexes. Additionally we find soil adjusted vegetation indexes and soil indexes (Table 14.3). Table 14.4 summarizes a selection of vegetation indexes widely used in the assessment and monitoring of DLDD. Simple vegetation indexes (VIs) use the contrast between the red and NIR reflectance caused by healthy green vegetation. The measure gives evidence of vitality and amount of vegetation (biomass) on the ground. In drylands a correction of soil background is necessary to reduce data variance.

Pigment based indexes look at photosynthetic pigments such as chlorophyll,

Table 14.4 Bio-physical indicators derived from vegetation indexes (after Ustin et al., 2009).

Vegetation Indexes (Index short cut)	Formula	Explanation	Source
SR	L_{NIR}/L_R	Green vegetation cover; wavelengths depending on sensor	a
NDVI	$(L_{NIR}-L_R)/(L_{NIR}+L_R)$	Normalized differentiated green vegetation cover	a
NDVIa	$(L_{750}-L_{705})/(L_{750}+L_{705})$	Leaf chlorophyll content	b
SGR	$\sum L_{nn}=500$ to 599	Green vegetation cover	b
PRI	$(L_{531}-L_{570})/(L_{531}+L_{579})$	Light response of xanthophyll; efficiency of photosynthesis	c
RGR	$(L_{600-699})/(L_{500-599})$	Anthocyanins/chlorophyll ratio	b
NPCI	$(L_{680}-L_{430})/(L_{680}+L_{430})$	Total pigments/chlorophyll	d
SRPI	L_{430}/L_{680}	Carotenoid/chlorophyll α	e
NPQI	$(L_{415}-L_{435})/(L_{415}+L_{435})$	Chlorophyll degradation early stress indicator	f
SIPI	$(L_{800}-L_{445})/(L_{800}-L_{680})$	Carotenoid/chlorophyll α	a
Plant-Stress-1	L_{695}/L_{420}	Stress status in plants	g
Plant-Stress-2	L_{695}/L_{760}	Stress status in plant	f
Plant-Stress-3	L_{440}/L_{690}	Health index of vegetation chlorophyll fluorescence ratio	h
Plant-Stress-4	L_{440}/L_{740}		i
NDWI	$(L_{860}-L_{1240})/(L_{860}+L_{1240})$	Leaf water content	j
WBI	L_{900}/L_{970}		g
NDNI	$[\log(L_{1680}/L_{1510})]/[\log(1/L_{1680}L_{1510})]$	Foliar nitrogen concentration	g
NDLI	$[\log(L_{1680}/L_{1754})]/[\log(1/L_{1680}L_{1754})]$	Foliar lignin concentration	g
CAI	$0.5(L_{2020}+L_{2220})-L_{2100}$		k

Source: a: Tucker (1979); b: Fuentes et al. (2003); c: Gamon et al. (2003); d: Penuelas et al. (1995a); e: Penuelas et al. (1997b); f: Zarco-Tejada (1998); g: Serrano et al. (2002); h: Lichtenthaler et al. (1996); i: Gao (1996); j:Penuelas (1997b); k: Nagler et al. (2000).

SR: Simple ratio; NDVI: Normalized Difference Vegetation Index; NDVIa: modified NDVI; SGR: Summed green reflectance; PRI: Photochemical Reflectance Index; RGR: Red/Green ratio; NPCI: Normalized pigments; CRI: Chlorophyll ratio Index; SRPI: Simple ratio Pigment Index; NPQI: Normalized Difference Water Index; WBI: Water Band Index; NDNI: Normalized Difference Nitrogen Index; NDLI: Normalized Difference Lignin Index; CAI: Cellulose Absorption Index; L: Light with specific wavelength which is the dominant pigment of green vegetation. Apart from chlorophyll, a variety of other photo synthetically active pigments exist in plant leaves that regulate the entire photosynthetic process (e.g., carotenoids, xanthophylls). Some indexes like PRI focus on these specific pigments like xanthophylls which are controlling the light absorption in high radiation environments. The Foliarwater-indexes use the strong water absorption throughout the SWIR domain. Most of the small band indexes work on the 970 nm and 1,240 nm water absorption. Important approaches are the widely used broad band indexes based on Landsat bands 4, 5 and 7. The foliar-chemistry indexes usually focus on the nitrogen content in plants. Prominent examples are the normalized difference nitrogen index (NDVI) or the cellulose absorbance index (CAI). CAI measures the cellulose content of old plant matter and are useful for arid area assessment where green vegetation is mostly under 20 % cover and biomass is accumulated in non-decomposed litter.

Combining the set of economic and social indicators (from statistics and field surveys, household questionnaires) with the set of biophysical indicators results in an integrated set of desertification indicators. Using the terminology of the DPSIR framework, biophysical indicators measure status and changes in the states of soil and vegetation; economic indicators measure the impacts of this on income associated with crop yields; and social indicators measure the impacts on human welfare. A decline in soil fertility and vegetative cover lowers crop and livestock yields, and reduces human (and animal) health.

Until today, it is very difficult to map the above mentioned issues with moderate to coarse satellite data which normally offer broad band information. Only imaging spectroscopy and high spatial and spectral resolution sensors are able to derive this information. Latest sensor developments like AVIRIS (already existent) or EnMAP (Environmental Mapping and Analysis Program, on schedule) are hyper spectral satellite mission providing high-quality hyper spectral image data on a timely and frequent basis that can offer new insights into the assessment of DLDD. But for mapping huge areas like the DEA region, only medium to coarse resolution satellites offer long-term time series (over 20 years) that are a prerequisite for the monitoring of desertification processes. Available sensors and data over the DEA area are reviewed in section 14.3.

14.3 Review of Available Sensors and Data over DEA and Their Suitability for Detecting Desertification Indicators

This section tries to give a short review about existing observing systems and remote sensing data currently available for applications in desertification monitoring and new sensors available in the near future. Remote sensing provides the most feasible platform for spatially and temporally continuous observations of biophysical parameters at the scales from local to global. A choice of global observing systems is shortly listed (see Box 3) and sensors will be mentioned with respect to their suitability for detection of key indicators (link to Chapter 2 in this book) and their actual availability over DEA (Table 14.5).

Box 3: Global Environmental Observation coordination—in-situ and satellite remote sensing

---

Global Observation Systems include land, oceans and climate (GTOS, GOOS, GCOS, together labeled G3OS, see http://www.gosic.org/), guided through an Integrated Global Observing Strategy (IGOS) and supported by the IGOS Partnership (http://www.igospartners.org/).

Global Earth Observation initiatives:

- Committee on Earth Observation Satellites (CEOS, http://www.ceos.org/)
- United Nations Office of Outer Space Affairs (UNOOSA, http://www.unoosa. org/)
- Global Earth Observation System of Systems (GEOSS, http://www.epa.gov/ geoss/)

The measurement of the current status of key indicators (e.g., vegetation cover) belongs to the first step inside the DPSIR-framework (Fig. 14.1) and is essential for the entire subsequent monitoring starting after a first baseline survey. Assessment is the next activity that should be based on the outcome of the monitoring process. Monitoring vegetation cover as a key controlling variable of the hydrological cycle and soil stability discovers many associated ecosystem services. The underlying key vegetation process is net primary production (NPP) which can be continuously estimated from FAPAR and solar irradiance records. Another sensitive observation of living plant cover can be done by LAI estimations. Both measurements (FAPAR and LAI) are fundamental observations of the living plant cover and are recognized as "essential climate variables" (ECV). Additionally to NPP as a core ecosystem service, the human appropriation of NPP (HANPP) can be measured. HANPP provides the information about the carbon amount needed to produce food and fibre products for human consumption including organic matter that is lost during harvesting and production (Imhoff et al., 2004). Key indicators as mentioned above and more condensed indices are shown in Figure. 14.4. Most of them can be derived from already existing fundamental data sets.

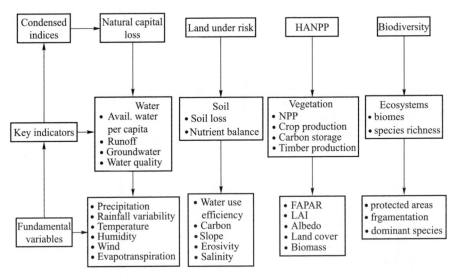

Fig. 14.4 Monitoring scheme for global coverage of key indicators for a Drylands East Asia Observing System (DEA-OS).

Most of the fundamental variables in Figure. 14.4 are measurable by remote sensing methods and can be converted to key indicators. In the following, we concentrate on the key indicator NPP as an example for deriving a global coverage over DEA that is best monitored by FAPAR and LAI estimations. LAI is a significant ecological attribute that controls vegetation photosynthetic activity and is widely used as input variable for land surface modeling of biosphere processes, and especially for predictions of photosynthetic primary production. The biophysical parameters LAI and FAPAR are also indispensable as input to environmental services that use these data, at the same time as other data types (in-situ, agrometeorological models, etc.) to produce environment monitoring indicators (water quality, drought or famine risks, desertification, deforestation/reforestation, etc.). LAI estimation from remote sensing data is done by the analysis of multispectral and multi-directional surface reflectance signatures of vegetation that performs photosynthesis. In general, two basic approaches are used to get LAI from surface reflectance (Kappas et al., 2012):
– Empirical or semi-empirical relationships between LAI and vegetation indices (i.e., NDVI, combination of surface reflectances) are used. The vege-

Table 14.5 Available global LAI products over the DEA region.

Sensor	Coverage	Project/Product	Spatial resolution	Temporal resolution	Temporal availability
AVHRR NOAA-9 and NOAA-11	global	ISLSCP	1°	monthly	1987 to 1988
AVHRR	global	Boston University	0.5°	monthly	07/1981 to 05/2001
AVHRR	global	Boston University	16-km	monthly	07/1981 to 05/2001
AVHRR	global	Ecoclimap	1-km	monthly	1992 to 1993 1997
VEGETATION	global	Cyclopes	1-km	10 days	1999 to 2003
VEGETATION	global	Geoland	0.5°	10 days	2002 to 2003
VEGETATION ATSR	global	Globcarbon	1-km/10-km/0.25°/0.5°	10 days	1998 to 2007
POLDER	global	Polder-1	6-km	10 days	1996 to 1997
POLDER	global	Polder-2	6-km	10 days	2003
MODIS TERRA/AQUA	global	MOD15A2	1-km	Daily and 8 days	2000 until present
MODIS TERRA/AQUA Combined	global	MOD15A3	1-km	4 days	July 2002 until present

NASA = National Aeronautics and Space Administration

AVHRR = Advanced Very High Resolution Radiometer

ISLSCP = International Land Surface Climatology Project

MODIS = Moderate Resolution Imaging Spectroradiometer

POLDER = POLarization and Directionality of the Earth's Reflectance

VEGETATION = Vegetation sensor aboard SPOT4 and SPOT5 satellites tation index (VI) is designed to maximize sensitivity to the vegetation characteristics while minimizing disturbing factors such as atmospheric noise, soil background or view-illumination geometry. These relationships between LAI and VI's are specifically calibrated for distinct vegetation types using either coexistent in situ LAI and reflectance measurements or simulations from canopy radiation models.

– Inversion of a radiative transfer model which models surface reflectance from canopy structural characteristics (including LAI), soil and leaf optical properties, and view-illumination geometry is used. Look Up Tables (LUT) and neural networks are the main inversion techniques deriving LAI from radiative transfer models. The expected range of the model parameters is either set up for each vegetation type (e.g., MODIS algorithm) or globally modeled (e.g., CYCLOPES algorithm).

Global LAI / FAPAR data sets are generally produced using various approaches and algorithms applied to many sensors data in the frame of specialized projects: CYCLOPES, GEOLAND, VGT4AFRICA, POLDER, AMMA and others. In general, for global and regional LAI products, we find three main sensors as data providers for LAI derivation over DEA: AVHRR, SPOT VEGETATION and MODIS.

The products in Table 14.5 are available on an operational basis and are restricted to a spatial resolution not higher than 1,000 m×1,000 m. The LAI products or other indicators from higher resolution sensors exist only on a local scale and only for short-time periods (sometimes only for one over flight).

The overview of available sensors points to a general problem of remotely sensed data for assessment and monitoring of DLDD. Either remote sensing offers coarse to medium spatial resolution with a high temporal resolution (two scenes per day) or we get high spatial resolution but only weak time series (often only a few satellite scenes for the same area over years and mostly not over the same seasonal period).

14.3.1   Short Outlook on Future Satellite Sensors over DEA

Most of the DEA area is captured by medium to high resolution sensors (MODIS, MERIS, Landsat, SPOT). The US Landsat program has ended with Landsat 7 and NASA has launched a new millennium program for next generation sensors. One of them was EO-1, which was flown in constellation mode with Landsat 7. EO-1 mission has also ended and the Landsat Data Continuity Mission (LDCM) was expected to be launched at end of 2012. LDCM will carry two sensors, the operational land imager (OLI) and thermal infrared sensor (TIRS). OLI and

TIRS will provide 15 m panchromatic and additionally ten-band multispectral data (5 bands in the optical domain with 30 m resolution, 3 bands in the NIR with a resolution of 30 m and 2 bands with 100 m resolution in the thermal IR. Apart from the huge satellites INSAT, RESOURCESAT and CARTOSAT, India will launch smaller satellites like the joint programs of SRMSat and SARAL. Pleiades-1A operated by Astrium is already launched and will be followed by SPOT6, Pleiades 1B and finally SPOT 7 (between 2012 and 2014). Pleiades is a component of the ORFEO program. Pleiades and SPOT will provide 2 cm to 50 cm products for high resolution analysis. NASA is also engaged with their follow up to the EOS missions (earth systematic missions—ESM) and many joint missions with NOAA. Latest example is the SUOMI NPP that offers a new 2012 "Blue Marble" in contrast to the first "Blue Marble" from 1972. Europe is considered with two programs, which have potential for the DEA area: GMES and Living Planet. The Living Planet initiative offers possibilities for operational services such as the earth explorer missions. GMES, the global monitoring for environment and security operates five Sentinel satellites, which have also high potential for operational use. Additionally the third generation of Meteosat satellites will provide on-going time series of the meteorological satellites. A challenging source for monitoring phenological development of plants is given by the already launched German RapidEye initiative. The RapidEye optical satellite system, which consists of five identical satellites, has a high potential for desertification case studies over DEA. It is designed to meet the following issues:

– A red-edge-band for vegetation analysis accompanied by four bands for blue, green, red and near-infrared.
– An improved radiometric resolution of 12 bit, which offers better classification results.
– A ground sampling size of 6.5 m to 5 m (orthorectified).
– An imaging capacity of 4.2 million km^2 per day.

Apart, these possibilities of RapidEye to monitor vegetation development, the number of bands in general will rise up to 20, which are comparable to hyper-spectral sensors (Thenkabail, 2012). For instance Sentinel 2 has a MSI sensor with 13 bands today. Commercial satellites like the DigitalGlobe WorldView 2 offer an eight band sensor with distinct information about red-edge and other important vegetation indicators. Furthermore an own chapter would be needed to tackle the group of available and future synthetic aperture radar (SAR). There are many SAR satellites on the way; one of them is the Sentinel-1 satellite. Many environmental satellites of the future include thermal scanners, optical and microwave radiometers, scatterometers and others. Representatives are Sentinel 4 and 5 from ESA and the NPOESS satellites from NASA. This short listing of available and future satellites mission's points up the emerging role of remote sensing for the establishment of a DEA Observation System.

The spatial, spectral and temporal requirements of remotely sensed observations for monitoring drylands are discussed by Ozdogan et al. in Chapter 15.

In the next section we look at a case study of a remote sensing approach for desertification assessment.

14.4 Remote Sensing Approach for Desertification Assessment in Central Asia: History, Current Research, and Perspectives—A Case Study

In the former Soviet Union and in its satellite countries (among others Mongolia), national-wide desertification assessment and control began in the early 1980s. Historically, the Central Asian republics were the regions mostly threatened by desertification and land degradation. Deserts of Central Asia extend from the eastern coast of the Caspian Sea to the piedmonts of the Tianshan and Altay mountains. The area of the deserts consists of more than 350 million hectares. Semi-deserts and other drylands areas cover the rest part of the territory. From this reason, main efforts in the Soviet desertification research were focused on this region. Leading specialists at the field of desert research formulated detailed desertification indicators and assessment criteria (Boyadzhiev, 1982; Kharin, 1983). On the basis of this approach, desertification maps for the Soviet Union with particular focus on Central Asia were prepared and published (Babaev et al., 1984). Soviet scientists also advised specialists in several African and Asian countries (Mongolia, Mali, Afghanistan, Lybia, Egypt, etc.) to prepare national-wide desertification maps (Kharin et al., 1992; Kharin, 1993).

In the post-Soviet Central Asia republics, the "classic" Soviet method (Boyadzhiev, 1982; Babaev et al., 1984) was further refined for assessment and monitoring of desertification at the national-wide and in several cases at local levels (Babaeva, 2008). One of the best examples for such applications is the desertification assessment for the territory of Turkmenistan carried out by the Desert Institute (Ashgabat, Turkmenistan) which had been the most advanced institution in the Soviet Union dealing with the problem of desertification (Babaev, 1999; Babaeva, 2008). This assessment generally corresponds to the Soviet assessments from the mid-1980s. The same methodology was used by the Desert Institute to prepare desertification maps of Mongolia and Mali (Kharin et al., 1992; Kharin, 1993).

In the first decade of the 21th century, a number of studies re-examined critically the Soviet desertification assessment system. In some cases, current assessments of desertification are not as pessimistic as the Soviet assessments. Thus, the extent of desertification in Kazakhstan's pasture land has been reported to be much lower than suggested in the Soviet literature. According to a study by Robinson et al. (2002), rangelands of Kazakhstan are in good condition. A study by Propastin et al. (2008) used NDVI from NOAA AVHRR to investigate climate- and human-induced degradation of vegetation cover in the formerly Soviet Central Asia. They adapted a modified rain use efficiency method suggested by Evans and Geerken (2004) and Wessels et al. (2004). Their approach bases on the assumption that the strength of the relationship between vegetation dynamics and precipitation remains nearly constant over time if no devastation in the ecosystem occurs. The strength of the relationship always decreases when processes of vegetation degradation take place. On contrary, during rehabilitation of the vegetation cover, the response of vegetation to precipitation increases (Fig. 14.5). This approach offers an attractive solution to the problem of desertification assessment and, before being applied to the whole territory of the formerly Soviet Central Asia, it had been proven in a case study at the local scale by Propastin and Kappas (2008). According to the results of the assessment, less than 6% of all vegetation trends in the Central Asian region can be subscribed to anthropogenic impact (Propastin et al., 2008). Moreover, most of the temporal trends in the vegetated area were positive except some well-known desertification hot spots such as the Aral Sea basin, some areas around the Caspian Sea, etc. (Fig. 14.5). The assessment studies by Robinson et al. (2002) and Propastin et al. (2008a) contradict with the assessments done before the collapse of the Soviet Union. Reasons for the contradiction are twofold.

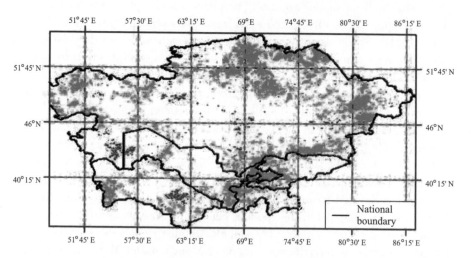

Fig. 14.5 Distribution of vegetation changes over the period 1982–2005 in the formerly Soviet Central Asia induced by human impact (from Propastin et al., 2008a).

On the one hand, Robinson et al. (2002) conclude that different results can be caused by the disparity in methodologies of desertification assessment in the Soviet system and in the West. This fact should be taken into account when comparing the two assessments. The FAO/UNEP-based Soviet desertification assessment system summarized by a data matrix with quantitative and qualitative evaluation criteria of desertification indicators (Table 14.6).

The columns of the matrix were classes of degree of desertification (slight, moderate, etc.). The elements of the matrix were the range of values of each variable corresponding to each degree of desertification status. The elements of the matrix were then integrated into an index corresponding to the aspects of desertification — present state (PS), desertification rate (DR), internal risk of desertification (ROD), influence of the natural environment (IA), and degree of anthropogenic impact (AI). After that, the aspects' values were summarized to the total risk of desertification (TRD) index. However, the FAO/UNEP's methodology has practical and logical problems concerning the number of implicit assumptions underlying the matrix and high labor-consumption which posed limitations to the frequency and/or the extent of assessments. The FAO/UNEP methodology was criticized to produce the unreal high estimation of world-wide desertification extent (70% of all drylands in the assessment from 1992; Veron et al., 2006). The Soviet methodology, being the product of the FAO/UNEP's methodology, should be contaminated by the similar problems. Therefore, the Soviet desertification assessment system may misjudge the degree and extent of desertification in Central Asian countries.

On the other hand, since independence, stock numbers in countries of the Central Asia have changed dramatically (for instance, in Kazakhstan from about 40 million in the late-1980s to about 12 million in the early-1990s). Such drastic decrease of anthropogenic impact on pasture land should lead to rapid regeneration of vegetation cover. Furthermore, a number of independent remote sensing studies confirmed a wide-area greening trends over the region, and particularly over steppes of Kazakhstan (DeBeurs and Henebry, 2004; Propastin et al., 2008a). Therefore, desertification status in the late Soviet era may not coincide with the post-Soviet era.

New perspectives in desertification assessment over the Central Asia region require satellite-derived biophysical indicators such as LAI and fPAR. Certainly, the LAI and fPAR products of MODIS are the best-known data sets which can be used for assessment of desertification. The mean problems of their use for desertification monitoring are the relatively short archive of these products (2000–date) and deficiency of validation in the Central Asia region. An alternative to the MODIS products is the use of NOAA AVHRR data which have much longer data archive (1979–date). However, the existing AVHRR-based LAI and fPAR product (Myneni et al., 1997) is also not validated in the Central Asia region and can be used only with caution.

Table 14.6 Criteria of vegetation cover degradation evaluation (Babaev et al., 1984; Babaev and Kharin, 1999).

Aspects	Criteria	Desertification Status			
		Slight	Moderate	Intensive	Severe
PS	State of vegetation cover	Climax changed communities	Long existing secondary communities	Short-living secondary communities	Almost default of vegetation cover
	Contemporary productivity (% of potential productivity)	> 90%	80%–90%	30%–60%	< 30%
DR	Decrease in biomass	< 10%	10%–25%	25%–50%	> 50%
	Annual increase in pastures degradation	< 2.5%	2.5%–5%	5%–7.5%	> 7.5%
	Annual decrease in pasture forage Ecosystems' stability	< 1%	1%–4%	4%–7%	> 7%
		stable ecosystems of clay, loamy and gravel desert	relatively stable ecosystems of forested deserts, and ecosystems developed on sandy soils	unstable ecosystems of mountain slopes, ecosystems of foothill loamy plains	unstable ecosystems of sand desert, ecosystems of steep stone slopes
ROD	Purposed new land cultivation (% yearly per project)	< 3%	3%–5%	5%–10%	> 10%

With regard to data lack in this region, the Department for Remote Sensing at the University of Goettingen developed a number of satellite-based region-specified LAI products (Propastin and Kappas, 2009a; Propastin and Kappas, 2009b; Propastin and Kappas, 2012) which can be used for detection and monitoring of desertification. Particular interesting for desertification monitoring applications is a newly developed AVHRR-based LAI product for the Republic of Kazakhstan (Propastin and Kappas, 2012; Fig. 14.6a). Extensive field measurements of vegetation structure in the key biomes in Kazakhstan provided parameters for calibration of the modeling algorithm. The validation of LAI estimates was carried out at numerous test sites in several biomes throughout the territory of Kazakhstan. The validation results revealed that differences in LAI between the AVHRR-based product and the field estimations are lower than 0.4LAI units in terms of root mean square error (RMSE).

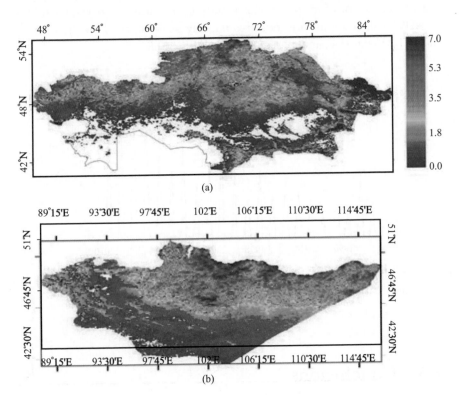

Fig. 14.6 Spatial distribution of satellite-derived leaf area index (LAI) over Kazakhstan (a) and Mongolia (b).

The Republic of Kazakhstan and Mongolia are the two countries in Central Asia with most similar climate conditions and vegetation composition. Taking into account these similarities, the LAI algorithm by Propastin and Kappas (2012) was employed to obtain a region-specific coarse-resolution LAI data set over Mongolia (Fig. 14.6b). The monthly LAI data set of Mongolia covers temporally the period 1982–2010 and has a spatial resolution of 8 km. Certainly, there is a need for further work in terms of extensive validation of the Mongolia LAI data set. Field data from this country would help to specify the algorithm to Mongolian conditions.

As it was discussed in section above, NDVI is an uncertain indicator for detecting degradation/rehabilitation of vegetation. Our experience in Central Asia shows that LAI is much more sensitive to change in vegetation conditions. Figure 14.7 demonstrates a temporal dynamics of LAI in comparison to NDVI at a test site in Kazakhstan, where strong rehabilitation of vegetation occurred during the period of about three decades. The rehabilitation of vegetation cover at this test site was proven in a previous study by Propastin and Kappas (2008). The NDVI value at this site indicates an only slight upward trend, while the trend in LAI over the same period is very considerable.

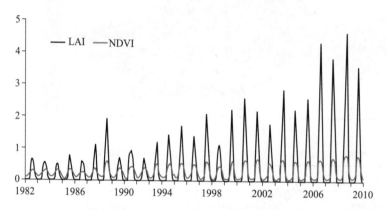

Fig. 14.7 Time series of monthly LAI in comparison to NDVI at a test site with strong rehabilitation of vegetation cover.

14.5 Conclusions

Monitoring and assessment of desertification over the DEA region is a challenging undertaking that needs integrative geospatial approaches. An integrative and spatially well-defined framework is needed to monitor and assess the interconnectedness between the main drivers, pressures and impacts on the landscape (e.g., DPSIR framework). The identified restrictions of existing observing systems over DEA contain:

– Mostly a sparse developed in-situ observation network exists to evaluate remote sensing products in order to characterize the status of DEA.
– A lot of environmental variables are operational derived from remote sensing, but many social or economic variables cannot be acquired by RS-techniques.
– General, a paucity of available data.
– High resolution observations and high spectral observations of satellites are infrequent or missing over the DEA area.
– Mismatch of historical context and long-term remote sensing time series of trends in vegetation cover occurs. Existing historical data archives are not linked to time series analysis for better interpretation.
– Integration of data from various remote sensing sensors and regional to local surveys into a sophisticated information processing system (Such as a GIS based DEA-OS) is not realized.

On the way towards a DEA Observation System (DEA-OS), we found a lot of constraints which call for urgent action:
– There are still inherent difficulties in defining and measuring important variables and indicators to represent land degradation and desertification within its biophysical and socio-economic aspects: Standardized methods (e.g., establishment of essential drylands variables) and their implementation at operational scale are missing.
– Decoupling of environmental signals in relation to short-term climate variance from long-term resource degradation is needed.
– A need to base monitoring and assessment on the understanding of the functioning of human-environmental systems: integrated monitoring means the contemporary monitoring of both biophysical and socio-economic variables as a baseline for assessment.
– Finally, the present assessment procedures lack behind the conceptual development.

References

Abraham, E., Montaña, E., and Torres, T.L. (2006). Desertificación e indicadores: posibilidades de medición integrada de fenómenos complejos. *Scripta Nova Revista Electrónica de Geografía y Ciencias Sociales*, 10, 214, CP1-U46.
Adeel, Z., Safriel, U., Niemeijer, D., White, R., de Kalbermatten, G., Glantz, M., Salem, B., Scholes, B., Niamir-Fuller, M., Ehui, S., and Yapi-Gnaore, V. (2005). *Ecosystems and Human Well-being: Desertification Synthesis, A Report of the Millennium Ecosystem Assessment*. World Resources Institute, Washington, DC.
Allen, W. A., Gausman, H. W., Richardson, A. J., and Thomas, J. R. (1969). Interaction of isotropic light with a compact plant leaf. *Journal of the Optical Society of America*, 59, 10, 1376–1379.

Allen, W. A., Gausman, H. W., and Richardson, A. J. (1970). Mean effective optical constants of cotton leaves. *Journal of the Optical Society of America*, 60, 4, 542–547.

Babaev, A. G., Zonn, I. S., and Orlovsky, N. G. (1984). *The USSR experience in desert reclamation and desertification control: The USSR national report.* Moscow, USSR State Committee for Science and Technology.

Babaev, A. G., and Kharin, N. G. (1999). The monitoring and forecast of desertification processes. In: Babaev, A. G. (Ed.). *Desert Problems and Desertification in Central Asia.* Berlin: Springer, 59–76.

Babaev, A. G. (1999). *Desert Problems and Desertification in Central Asia.* Berlin: Springer-Verlag.

Babaeva, T. A. (1999). The Mapping of Desertification Processes. In: Babaev, A. G. (Ed.). *Desert Problems and Desertification in Central Asia.* Berlin: Springer, 89–100.

Babaeva, T. A. (2008). The use of remote sensing methods for the cartography of desertification processes. *Problems of Desert Developments*, 3, 40–42.

Beatley, J. C. (1980). Fluctuations and stability in climax shrub and woodland vegetation of the mojave, great basin and transition deserts of Southern Nevada, Israel. *Journal of Botany* 28, 3–4, 149–168.

Berry, L., and Ford, R. B. (1977). Recommendations for a system to monitor critical indicators in areas prone to desertification. Massachusetts, Clark University.

Biard, F., and Baret, F. (1997). Crop residue estimation using multiband reflectance. *Remote Sensing of Environment*, 59, 530–536

Biodiversity Indicators Partnership. (2010). The CBD Indicator Suite. Available online: http://www. twentyten.net/language/en-us/indicators.

Bisaro, A., Kirk, M., Zimmermann, W., and Zdruli, P. (2011). Analysing new issues in desertification: Research trends and research needs. Final report of the IDEAS project to the German Federal Ministry of Education and Research (BMBF). Institute for Co-operation in Developing Countries, Marburg, Germany.

Boyadzhiev, T. G. (1982). Estimation and mapping of the desertification processes. *Problems of Desert Development*, 15, 3–12.

CBD. (2003). Report of the expert meeting on indicators of biological diversity including indicators for rapid assessment of inland water ecosystems. Convention on Biological Diversity, 10–14 November 2003, Montreal.

CBD. (2010). Framework for monitoring implementation of the achievement of the 2010 target and integration of targets into the thematic programmes of work. COP 8 Decision VIII/15. Available online: http://www.cbd.int/decision/cop/?id=11029.

Cherlet, M., Sommer, S. (2009). WAD implementation plan. Roadmap towards a new World Atlas on Desertification, Land degradation and Drought. Joint Research Centre, Italy. http://desert.jrc.ec.europa.eu/action/php/index.php?action=view&id=105.

Cierniewski, J., and Karnielli, A. (2002). Virtual surfaces simulating the bi-directional reflectance of semi-arid soils. *International Journal of Remote Sensing*, 23, 4019–4037.

CSFD-EDN. (2009). Le Comité Scientifique Français de la Désertification (CSFD)— European DesertNet (EDN) Indicators. Available online: http://www.european-desertnet.eu/cop9_prep_eu.php.

DeBeurs K. M., and Henebry, J. (2004). Land surface phenology, climatic variations, and institutional change: analysing agricultural land cover change in Kazakhstan. *Remote Sensing of Environment*, 89, 497–509.

Desert Institute. (1985). Map of anthropogenic desertification of arid territories of USSR. Scale 1 : 2,500,000. Ylum, Ashgabat.

DOE. (1996). Indicators of Sustainable Development for the United Kingdom. UK Department of the Environment. HMSO, London.

EEA (European Environment Agency). (2005). EEA Core set of indicators: Guide. EEA Technical Report No 1/2005. Luxembourg, 38. Available online: http://www.eea.europa.eu/publications/technical _report_2005_1.

Evans, J., and Geerken, R. (2004). Discrimination between climate-and humane-induced dryland degradation. *Journal of Arid Environment*, 57, 535–554.

FAO-LADA. (2009). Field manual for local level land degradation assessment in drylands. LADA-L Part 1: Methodological approach, planning and analysis. Rome, FAO, 76. Available online: http://www.fao.org/nr/lada/index.php?option=com_docman&task=doc_download&gid=231&lang=en.

Fuentes, D. A., Gamon, J. A., Qiu, H. L., Sims, D. A., and Roberts, D. A. (2001). Mapping Canadian boreal forests vegetation using pigment and water absorption features derived from the AVIRIS sensor. *Journal of Geophysical Research*, 106: 33565–33577.

Gallopin G. C. (1997). Indicators and their use: Information for decision-making. In: Moldan, B., and Bilharzia, S. (Eds.). *Report on the Project on Indicators of Sustainable Development*. Chichester: John Wiley & Sons, Inc, 13–27.

Gamon, J. A., Penuelas, J., and Field, C. B. (1992). A narrow-waveband spectral index that tracks diurnal changes in photosynthetic efficiency. *Remote Sensing of Environment*, 41, 35–44.

Gao, B.-C. (1996). NDWI—A normalized difference water index for remote sensing of vegetation liquid water from space. *Remote Sensing of Environment*, 58, 257–266.

Garnon, J. A., Serrano, L., and Surfus, J. S. (1997). The photochemical reflectance index: an optical indicator of photosynthetic radiation use efficiency across species, functional types, and nutrient levels. *Oecologica*, 112, 492–501

GCOS (Global Climate Observing System). (2010). Implementation Plan for the Global Observing System for Climate in Support of the UNFCCC (August 2010 Update) GCOS-138 (GTOS-184, GTOS-76, WMO-TD/No.1523. Geneva: WMO GCOS. Available Online: http://www.wmo.int/pages/prog/gcos/Publications/gcos-138.pdf

GEF (Global Environment Facility) KM: Land. (2010). Project Indicator Profiles for the GEF Land Degradation Focal Area. Final by the GEF MSP "Ensuring Impacts from SLM—Development of a Global Indicator System" (KM:Land Initiative). Hamilton Ontario: UNU-INWEH, 67. Available online:᾿ http://www.inweh.unu.edu/drylands/docs/KM-Land/KM-Land_Indicator_Profiles_Final.pdf.

Geist, H., and Lambin, E. F. (2004). Dynamic causal patterns of desertification. *BioScience*, 54, 9, 817–829.

Glenn, E. M., Stafford, S., and Squires, V. (1998). On our failure to control desertification: implications for global change issues, and a research agenda for the future. *Environmental Science and Policy*, 1, 71–78.

GOSIC (Global Observing Systems Information Center). (2010). GCOS Essential Climate Variables (ECV) Data Access Matrix. Available Online: http://gosic.org/ios/MATRICES/ECV/ecv-matrix.htm.

Grainger A. (2009). The role of science in implementing international environmental agreements: The case of desertification. *Land Degradation and Development*, 20, 4, 410–430.

Holling, C. S. (1973). Resilience and stability of ecological systems. *Annual Review of Ecology and Systematics*, 4, 1–23.

Imhoff, M. L., Bounoua, L., Ricketts, T., Loucks, C., Harris, R., and Lawrence, W. T. (2004). HANPP Collection, human appropriation of net primary productivity by country and product. Socioeconomic Data and Applications Center (SEDAC), Columbia University. http://sedac.ciesin.columbia.edu/es/hanpp.html.

Jacquemoud, S., and Baret, F. (1990). PROSPECT: A model of leaf properties spectra. *Remote Sensing of Environment*, 34, 75–91.

JRC. (2010). Development of a new "World Atlas on Desertification". Available online: http://edo.jrc.ec.europa.eu/php/index.php?action=view& id=105.

Kappas, M. W. (2009). Klimatologie. *Klimaforschung im 21. Jahrhundert— Herausforderungen für Natur- und Sozialwissenschaften*. Spektrum Akad. Verlag, Springer, 356.

Kappas, M. W., and Propastin, P. A. (2012). Review of available products of Leaf Area Index and their suitability over the formerly Soviet Central Asia. *Journal of Sensors*, 2012, 582159, doi:10.1155/2012/582159.

Kharin, N. G. (1983). Methodical principles of study and mapping desertification processes—on the example of arid areas of Turkmenistan. Ashgabat, Ylym.

Kharin, N. G. (1993). *Criteria and Methodology of Assessment of Desertification Processes in the Sahel*. Ashgabat, Ylym.

Kharin, N. G., et al. (1992). *Methodological Instructions on Study of Desertification Processes in Arid Territories (on Example of Mongolia)*. Ylum, Ashgabat.

Kharin, N. (2002). *Vegetation* degradation in Central Asia under the impact of human activities. Dordrecht: Kluwer Academic Publishers.

LADA. (2008). Land degradation assessment in drylands. Factsheet: assessing status, causes and impacts of land degradation, FAO, Rome, Italy.

Lichtenthaler, H. K., Lang, M., Sowinska, M., Heisel, F., Miehe, J. A. (1996). Detection of vegetation stress via a new high resolution fluoresence imaging system. *Journal of Plant Physiology*, 148: 350–382.

Liu, W., Baret, F., Gu, X., Tong, Q. Zheng, L., Zhang, B. (2002). Relating soil surface moisture to reflectance. *Remote Sensing of Environment*, 81:238–246.

Myneni, R. B., Nemani, R. R., and Running S. W. (1997). Estimation of global leaf area index and absorbed par using radiative transfer models. *IEEE Transactions on Geoscience and Remote Sensing*, 35, 1380–1393.

Nagler, P. L., Daughtry, C. S. T., and Goward, S. N. (2000). Plant litter an soil reflectance. *Remote Sensing of Environment*, 71, 207–215.

Niemeijer, D., and de Groot, R. S. (2008a). Framing environmental indicators: moving from causal chains to causal networks. *Environment, Development and Sustainability*, 10, 89–106.

OECD (Organisation for Economic Co-operation and Development). (1993). OECD Core Set of Indicators for Environmental Performance Reviews: A Synthesis Report by the Group on the State of the Environment. Paris: OECD Environment Monographs Report No. 83, 39.

Oldeman L. R., Hakkeling, R. T. A., and Sombroek, W. G. (1991). World Map of the Status of Human Induced Soil Degradation: An Explanatory Note, Global Assessment of Soil Degradation (GLASOD). International Soil Reference and Information Centre, United Nations Environment Programme, Food and Agriculture Organization, International Institute for Aerospace Survey and Earth Sciences, Wageningen, The Netherlands, 2nd Ed.

OSS. (2008). Long-term environmental monitoring in a circum-Saharan network: The roselt/OSS experience\OSS. synthesys collection No. 3. Tunis: Observatoire du Sahara et du Sahel (OSS). 96 pp. Available online: http://www.ossonline.org/index.php?option=com_content&task=view&id=600&Itemid=624&lang=en; http://www.wikiadapt.org/filestore//AMCEN/USBResources/ROSELT_OSS.pdf.

Penuelas, J., Baret, F., and Fillela, I. (1995a). Semi-empirical indexes to assess carotenoids/chlorophyll a ratio from leaf spectral reflectance. *Photosynthetica*, 31, 221–230.

Penuelas, J., Pinol, J., Oqaya, R., and Fillela, I. (1997b). Estimation of plant water concentration by the reflectance WaterIndex WI (R900/R970). *International Journal of Remote Sensing*, 18, 2869–2875.

Propastin, P., and Kappas, M. W. (2008b). Spatiotemporal drifts in AVHRR/NDVI-precipitation relationship and their linkage to land use change in Central Kazakhstan. *EARSEL eProceedings*, 7, 1, 30–45.

Propastin, P. A., and Kappas, M. W. (2012). Retrieval of coarse-resolution leaf area index over the Republic of Kazakhstan using NOAA AVHRR satellite data and ground measurements. *Remote Sensing*, 2012, 4, 1, 220–246.

Propastin, P. A., Kappas, M. W., and Muratova, N. R. (2008a). A remote sensing based monitoring system for discrimination between climate and human-induced vegetation change in Central Asia. *Management of Environmental Quality: An International Journal*, 19, 5, 579–596.

Propastin, P., and Kappas, M. W. (2009a). Mapping leaf area index in a semi-arid environment of Kazakhstan using fine-resolution satellite data and in situ measurements. *GIScience and Remote Sensing*, 46, 231–246.

Propastin, P., and Kappas, M. W. (2009b). Mapping leaf area index over semi-desert and steppe biomes in Kazakhstan using satellite imagery and ground measurements. *EARSEL eProceedings*, 8, 75–92.

Reining, P. (1978). *Handbook on Desertification Indicators*. Washington DC: American Association for the Advancement of Science.

Reynolds, J. F., Smith, D. M. S., Lambin, E. F., Turner, B. L., II, Mortimore, M., Batterbury, S. P. J., Downing, T. E., Dowlatabadi, H., Fernandez, R. J., Herrick, J. E., Huber-Sannwald, E., Jiang, H., Leemans, R., Lynam, T., Maestre, F. T., Ayarza, M., and Walker, B. (2007). Global desertification: Building a science for dryland development. *Science*, 316, 847–851.

Robinson, S., Millner-Gulland, E. L., and Alimaev, I. (2002). Rangeland degradation in Kazakhstan during the Soviet-era: Re-examining the evidence. *Journal of Arid*

Environments, 53, 419–439.

Rotondi, A., Rossi, F., Asunis, C., and Cesaraccio, C. (2003). Leaf xeromorphic adaptations of some plants of a coastal Mediterranean macchia ecosystem. *Journal of Mediterranean Ecology*, 4, 25–35.

Schilch, G., Bestelmeyer, B., Bunning, B., Critchley, W., Herrick, J., Kellner, K., Liniger, H.P., Nachtergaele, F., Ritsema, F., Schuster, B., Tabo, R., Van Lynden, G., and Winslow, G. (2011). Experiences in monitoring and assessment of sustainable land management. *Land Degradation and Development*, 22, 214–225.

Schlesinger, W. H., Reynolds, J. F., Cunningham, G. L., Huenneke, L. F., Jarrel, W. M., Virginia, R. A., and Whitford, W. G. (1990). Biological feedbacks in global desertification. *Science*, 247, 4946, 1043–1048.

Serrano, L., Penuels, L, and Ustin, S. L. (2002). Remote sensing of nitrogen and lignin in Mediterranean vegetation from AVIRIS data: Decomposing biochemical from structural signals. *Remote Sensing of Environment*, 81, 355–364.

Smeets, E., and Weterings, R. (1999). Environmental Indicators: Typology and Overview. European Environment Agency Report No. 25. European Environment Agency, Copenhagen. http://www.eea.europa.eu/ publications/TEC25.

Thenkabail, P. S., Lyon, J. G., and Huete, A. (Eds.) (2012). *Hyperspectral Remote Sensing of Vegetation*. CRC Press. Taylor and Francis.

Tucker, C. J. (1979). Red and photographic infrared linear combinations for monitoring vegetation. *Remote Sensing of Environment*, 8, 127–150.

UNCCD. (1994). United Nations Convention to Combat Desertification in countries experiencing serious drought and/or desertification, particularly in Africa. A/AC.241/27. UN General Assembly, New York.

UNCCD. (1997). Report of the conference of the parties on its first session, held in Rome from 29 September To 10 October 1997. Addendum. Part Two: Actions taken by the conference of the parties at its first session (ICCD/COP(1)/11/Add.1). Available online: http://www.unccd.int/cop/officialdocs/cop1/pdf/11add1eng.pdf.

UNCCD. (1998). Benchmarks and indicators report of the Ad Hoc Panel. ICCD/COP(2)/CST/3/Add.1 25 September 1998. Available online: http://www. unccd.int/cop/officialdocs/cop2/pdf/cst3add1eng.pdf.

UNCCD. (2009c). UNCCD 1st Scientific Conference: Synthesis and recommendations. Note by the secretariat. ICCD/COP(9)/CST/INF.3. Bonn: UN Convention to Combat Desertification. Available online: http://www.unccd.int/php/document2. php?ref=ICCD/COP%289%29/CST/INF.3.

Ustin, S. L., Palacios-Orueta, A., and Whiting, M. L. (2009). Remote Sensing based assessment of biophysical indicators for land degradation and desertification. In: Hill, J., Röder, A. (Eds.). *Recent Advances in Remote Sensing and Geoinformation Processing for Land Degradation Assessment. ISPRS book*, 8, 15–44.

Verón, S. R., Paruelo, J. M., and Oesterheld, M. (2006). Assessing desertification. *Journal of Arid Environments*, 66, 751–763.

Verstraete, M. M., Scholes, R. J., and Stafford Smith, M. (2009). Climate and desertification: Looking at an old problem through new lenses. *Frontiers of Ecology and Environment*, 7, 8, 421–428.

Verstraete, M. M., Hutchinson C. F., Grainger, A., Stafford Smith, M., Scholes, R. J., Reynolds, J. F., Barbosa, P., Léon, A., Mbow, C. (2011). Towards a global drylands observing system: Observational requirements and institutional solutions. *Land Degradation and Development*, 21:1–16.

Wessels K. J., Prince, S. D., Frost, P. E., and van Zyl, D. (2004). Assessing the effects of human-induced land degradation in the former homeland of nothern South Africa with a 1 km AVHRR NDVI Time-Series. *Remote Sensing Environments*, 91, 47–67.

Zarco-Tejada, P. J. (1998). Optical indexes as bioindicators of forest sustainability. Graduate programme in Earth and Space Science, Toronto, York University.

Zucca, C., and Biancalani, R. (2010). Guidelines for the use of the LADA set of indicators to respond to the needs of UNCCD reporting as described in Decision 17/COP9. Preliminary Draft Report Version 1.0—LADA Technical Report, 16.

Authors Information

Martin Kappas*, Pavel Propastin
Cartography, GIS and Remote Sensing (CGRS), Institute of Geography, Georg-August University of Goettingen, Germany
* Corresponding author

Chapter 15

The Effects of Spatial Resolution on Vegetation Area Estimates in the Lower Tarim River Basin, Northwestern China

Mutlu Ozdogan and Alishir Kurban

Summary: The fragile riparian ecosystems of the Tarim Basin in Northwestern China have been threatened by water shortages due to climate and land-use transformations in the form of irrigated agricultural expansion in upstream areas. In these riparian zones, remote sensing plays an important role to assess vegetation health and recovery following several interventions in the hydrology of the region, particularly for estimating the amount of vegetated areas as an indication of recovery. However, even with very accurate vegetation maps made from remote sensing, large errors in area estimates could occur because of the interaction between the size and the spatial distribution of vegetation communities and the spatial resolution of the observing sensor. These errors tend to be worse when the size and the extent of inter-connected vegetation communities are smaller than the size of the pixels in the image. To overcome these issues, our analysis suggests that 1) pixel thresholds defining class membership need to be related to the proportion of the area covered by riparian vegetation communities to get accurate estimates of vegetated areas; and 2) due to a large fraction of sparse vegetation cover, the use of high spatial resolution (less than 10 m) is recommended to monitor the changes in vegetation.

15.1 Introduction

Riparian vegetation communities in arid regions are in constant state of flux associated with the onset and decline of river flow at seasonal scales and with changes in climate at the decadal scales. This continuous change makes it important to monitor the area of the riparian vegetation communities on a repeated manner for ecological and local livelihood purposes. It is also important to assess the efficacy of restoration efforts in these delicate ecosystems as vegetation communities respond rapidly to water availability, but the level of success is hard to measure.

Changes in riparian vegetation communities associated with the changes in upstream water uses are perhaps best exemplified in the Tarim Basin, located in Northwestern China. As the largest closed inland basin in the world, the condition of vegetation in delicate riparian ecosystems of the lower reaches of the basin has been threatened by water diversions in the upper reaches, as well as by changes in climate (Chen et al., 2007; Kurban et al., 2010; Zhou and Xiao, 2010; Qi et al., 2012). However, the amount of changes and the extent and magnitude of recovery of vegetation following several water transfer schemes to restore the vegetation are not well known.

In the past few years, a number of studies investigated the results of the recovery efforts using remote sensing as an aid to measure the success of restoration efforts that result from water diversion schemes (Liu et al., 2007; Guli et al., 2009; Kurban et al., 2010; Duan et al., 2010). Remote sensing has been well suited for estimating the extent and the changes in the area of riparian vegetation communities in the basin due to synoptic coverage, availability of archival data to detect changes, and spectral bands that are suitable for distinguishing riparian vegetation from other land cover types. In this regard, a common approach has been to make a thematic map of vegetated areas and multiply the number pixels with the area of each pixel (Kurban et al., 2010; Duan et al., 2010). However, this approach may introduce additional errors into area estimation that stem from the interaction between the size and the spatial distribution of vegetation communities and the spatial resolution of the observing sensor. For example, when the spatial resolution of the sensor is larger than the isolated or narrowly interconnected vegetation communities, thematic classification and, by extension, area estimates become less reliable (Zhao et al., 2009). Also contributing to this problem is the presence of sparse vegetation that makes accurate recovery of fractions difficult, as there are strong heterogeneities in vegetation presence in riparian areas.

In this chapter, we investigated the influence of sensor spatial resolution, the size and spatial arrangement of riparian vegetation communities and vegetation defining thresholds on the accuracy of area estimates of these communities derived from remote sensing in the Tarim Basin. In particular, we investigated the ability of remote sensors at various spatial resolutions to estimate the area of riparian vegetation communities and how these area estimates would vary across spatial resolutions and image thresholds used to define vegetation presence. Based on our findings, we then related the overall proportion of a riparian landscape that is covered by vegetation to the accuracy of area estimates with remote sensing across different spatial resolutions.

15.2 Study Area

The study area is located along the lower reaches of the Tarim River in the Xinjiang Uygur Autonomous Region of China (Fig. 15.1). The Tarim River is the principal river system in the region and is recognized as the longest continental river in China. The riparian ecosystems of the river in the well-known "green corridor" of the lower reaches have been retreating constantly from the 1950s

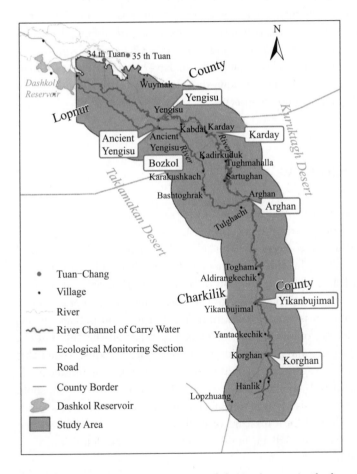

Fig. 15.1 The location and setting of the study area in the lower reaches of the Tarim Basin.

as a result of both agricultural development in the upper, middle and in some portions of the lower reaches and construction of the Dashkol reservoir in 1972. In 2000, the green corridor riparian ecosystems were temporarily re-linked with the original water sources by initiating an emergency ecological water transfusion project that continues today. As a result, portions of the vegetation communities have been slowly restored but more changes are expected (Kurban et al., 2010; Duan et al., 2010).

The study area is one of the extremely arid areas of China, with average annual precipitation reaching less than 50 mm but potential annual evaporation between 2,500 mm and 3,000 mm. Total annual solar radiation varies between 5,692 MJ m^{-2} and 6,360 MJ m^{-2}, with cumulative daylight hours ranging from 2,780 to 2,980. The annual accumulative temperature above 10°C exceed 4,200°C per year with the average diurnal temperature ranging from 13°C to 17°C.

The most dominant vegetation species in the lower reaches of the Tarim River include *Populus euphratica, Tamarix* spp., *Lycium ruthenicum, Karelinia caspica, Phragmites communis, Alhagi sparsifolia,* and *Glycyrrhiza inflate.* Desert covers the largest area in the lower Tarim River, with euphrate poplar forests, Tamarix bush, halophytic meadow, desert, saline alkali soil and water body being other dominant land cover types.

15.3   Methodology

From the perspective of treating vegetation as a subpixel proportion—defined as the fraction of a pixel occupied by vegetation—the estimated area of vegetation in a remotely sensed image corresponds to the number of pixels whose subpixel proportion exceeds a given threshold. In image data, the distribution of fraction of vegetated area within pixels is a function of both the spatial pattern of vegetation on the ground and resolving power of the observing sensor. For example, when the image resolution is smaller than individual vegetation patches, pixels tend to either completely contain vegetation or completely non-vegetated areas, resulting in a strongly bimodal distribution of subpixel proportions. When this occurs, the quality of the vegetation map and the quality of area estimates made from fractional vegetation maps are not particularly sensitive to the threshold used. In contrast, when pixels are larger than the vegetation patches in the landscape, many pixels will contain a mixture of both vegetated and non-vegetated areas and the area estimates will be highly dependent on the definition of an appropriate threshold.

As the distribution of subpixel proportions (or more accurately their probability density function) is central to the question of the effect of spatial resolution on area estimation, a robust approach to subpixel proportion estimates would be used to a statistical distribution as an alternative to pixel aggregation. As effectively shown by Key (1994) and Collins and Woodcock (1999), the beta probability distribution is particularly well suited for this task. The important qualities of the beta distribution are: 1) the probability distribution function of an arbitrary regionalized variable (i.e. arbitrary spatial resolution) is limited to the same closed interval $0 < x < 1$ as subpixel proportions; and 2) the parameters of the distribution are closely related to the mean and the variance of the distribution. Both Key (1994) and Collins and Woodcock (1999) suggested that with a constant mean, the variance of the beta distribution (and hence its shape) could be related to the size of the pixel relative to the size of the vegetated patches. Thus, if the variance of subpixel proportions at any arbitrary resolution is known, it may be used to parameterize a beta distribution to determine the influence of spatial resolution on vegetated area estimates.

At the heart of this method lies the variogram used as a way to estimate the variance of landscape vegetation cover over the image domain. Jupp et al. (1988, 1989) provided the method to estimate the variance of a variable regularized by an arbitrary resolution given the punctual variogram, and Atkinson and Curran (1995) as well as Collins and Woodcock (1999) provided a method for estimating the punctual variogram from the regularized observations. Once determined, the punctual variogram can be used to estimate the variance of subpixel proportions at different regularizing resolutions, allowing a beta distribution to be parameterized and hence making it an easy matter to determine the effects of sensor spatial resolution on vegetation area estimates in the riparian zone.

The principal source of data used in the analysis was a set of QuickBird images, acquired on July 5, 2005 and classified to extract vegetation/non-vegetation land cover information using a simple Soil-Adjusted Vegetation Index (SAVI) threshold approach (Huete, 1988). When compared with the ground truth data, the resulting vegetation/non-vegetation map was estimated to be over 95% accurate. In the next step, the binary vegetation mask image was divided into 100 equally spaced grids each of which was 100 pixels (60 m) in length on one side (Fig. 15.2). Next, a variogram for each of the 100 grid boxes was calculated from a random sample of approximately 10% of the image pixels, using a classical variogram estimator. We then estimated the punctual variograms from these regularized observations using the approach described above. Note that since the regularizing resolution was fine enough, the resulting variograms were treated as the underlying punctual variogram (e.g. Garrigues et al., 2007). Finally, the variance estimated from the punctual variogram was used to parameterize a beta distribution for subpixel proportions which made it possible to explore the sensitivity of vegetation area estimates to sensor spatial resolution as well as the thresholds used to define the vegetation category.

Fig. 15.2 The location of the grid boxes used in this study. The background image is acquired by the Quickbird sensor on July 5, 2005.

15.4   Results and Discussion

The first set of results concerns the performance of the beta model in estimating the distribution of subpixel proportions as a function of spatial resolution. Modeled cumulative probability distributions (CDF) of subpixel proportions at one of the Tarim sites across four different spatial resolutions are given in Figure 15.3. Each plot also includes a cumulative histogram of the image where the histogram has been scaled to have the same area as the beta CDF. Images at different resolutions were generated by degrading the original image by a squarewave filter. Theoretically, the histogram at each resolution should match the associated CDF. In general, the model seems to correctly approximate the probability at all pixel sizes, providing credibility to the beta approach. Similar behavior is observed at the other sites.

Given the distribution of subpixel proportions described by the beta probability density, vegetated area estimates can be defined as the probability that the subpixel vegetation proportion is greater than some threshold value, or graphically represented as the area under the beta PDF (beta Probability Distribution Function) curve to the right of any given threshold value along the abscissa. Using this definition, the influence of the selected threshold and the choice of

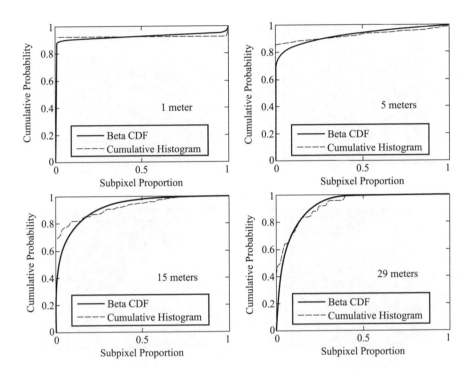

Fig. 15.3 Comparison of modeled cumulative probability distributions (CDF) of subpixel proportions to the cumulative histogram of the image across four different spatial resolution selections.

spatial resolution is further examined in Figure 15.4 across image samples with different true vegetation cover fractions. In each panel, the colors indicate the percentage of over (red tones) and under (blue tones) estimation of true vege-tated area given a threshold/resolution pair. In all panels, the colors have been adjusted so that the zone of no error is presented by the turquoise color. Sev-eral conclusions can be drawn from Figure. 15.4. First, the general structure of the resolution/threshold relation is similar across all panels—as the resolution coarsens, the selection of the class-defining threshold becomes stricter to get the true area fraction right. For example, at a fine, 1-m resolution, the chosen threshold does not matter and area estimates are close to the true area fraction (as indicated by the wide turquoise zone). However, as the resolution becomes coarse, the area estimates become increasing sensitive to the chosen threshold. Second, the relative proportions of over- and under-estimation of true vegetation area are sensitive to the amount of vegetation being observed in the landscape. When vegetation is sparse and disconnected on the ground, a large number of threshold/resolution pairs (from 30% to 100% threshold and from 5 m to 45 m

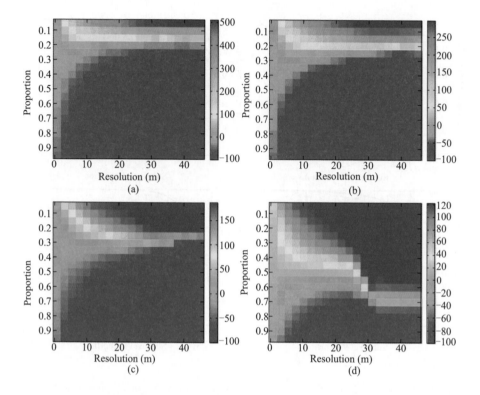

Fig. 15.4 Plots showing the relationship between arbitrary image resolution (X axis) and the threshold used to calculate vegetation area (Y axis) for images with four different sets of true vegetation fraction values. In each panel, the colors show over- (positive values) and under-estimation (negative values) of true vegetation fraction for the resolution-threshold combination. The true vegetation fraction values are 15% (a), 25% (b), 35% (c) and 45% (d).

resolutions) lead to under-estimation problems. This is not a surprising outcome as it has been known for a long time that one effect of coarsening spatial resolution is that small objects are consumed by averaging and hence using a threshold above the appropriate value leads to complete elimination of pixels, and by extension, under-estimation of areas. In other words, as the resolution increases, fewer numbers of increasingly mixed pixels contain such a large percentage of vegetated area. On the other hand, as the vegetation cover on the ground becomes more substantial (as exemplified by lower right panel in Fig. 15.4), the probability of under- or over-estimation of vegetation fractions become equally likely, leading to the possibility of errors canceling each other out. Third, the rate with which the vegetated area estimates become sensitive to the chosen threshold is also a function of the true area fraction on the ground. For example, for images with true vegetation area fraction of 15% or lower (upper left panel), spatial resolution of 1 m could support any threshold for an accurate area assessment. However, when the spatial resolution is increased to 10 m, the zone of no error (again indicated by the turquoise color) narrows to threshold values between 20% to 30%. When the spatial resolution is even coarser, say 40 m, then a strict threshold of 17% must be used for this cover fraction. This threshold is absolutely necessary to identify the correct vegetated area fraction and this critical threshold leads to the lowest deviation from the true area fraction. Increasing the threshold beyond this critical value would lead to decreasing numbers of pixels being identified as vegetated. This effect was also noted by Key (1994). In the other extreme case, when the true area fraction is 45% or higher (lower right panel), the zone of no error is larger, has less sensitivity to the chosen threshold, and is symmetric about the correct threshold. While it is harder to explain the sudden change in behavior at the 30 m resolution mark for this panel, it is likely that it is caused by the inexact nature of the beta approach for modeling subpixel vegetation fractions. Kurban et al. (2010) also reported similar findings.

For other true vegetation cover fraction values (as exemplified by upper right and lower left panels), the resolution/threshold pairs lead to over- or under-estimation behavior between these two extreme cases. While Figure 15.4 explains the relationship between class-defining thresholds, spatial resolution, and the amount of vegetation on the ground being observed by a sensor, the success with which to extract true vegetation area from remotely sensed observations ultimately depends on the abundance and the connectivity of vegetation on the ground. Obviously, when vegetation cover is sparse, the sensitivity to spatial resolution is increased and the thresholds become quite stringent. This finding then begs the question of how much of the area being observed is occupied by sparse, medium density, or abundant vegetation. Figure 15.5 displays the histogram distribution of mean vegetation cover for the 100 sample images used in this analysis. As can be seen from this histogram, the majority of samples have sparse vegetation (mean value of 11% cover). Since it is neither easy nor practical to choose stringent thresholds, one conclusion can be drawn from this analysis that in the lower Tarim basin, sensors with relative high (10 m or less) spatial resolution capabilities are required for accurate estimation of riparian vegetation area. While in some cases, it is possible to use sensors with coarser spatial resolution, especially in areas with abundant and inter-connected vegetation cover, these areas are a few and far in between. Alternatively, if high spatial resolution images are not available, it is possible to divide the study area into several parts and perform an analysis proposed here to determine the exact threshold values, and use these thresholds to estimate true vegetation areas. As shown earlier, it is likely that this analysis will result in several groups of thresholds, each of which is to be applied to areas with different on-the-ground vegetation abundance. Since the spatial resolution of the sensor is likely to be fixed for mostly

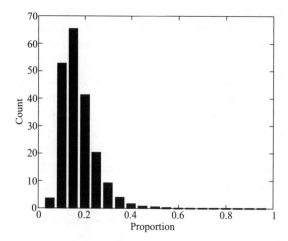

Fig. 15.5 Histogram distribution of true vegetation area in the image (here labeled as proportion) of all 100 × 100 pixel images. The data are log normally distributed.

practical reasons, this form of analysis, where variable rate thresholds are found and used, may lead to more accurate riparian area estimates than using a single global threshold value as previously used in this location (Jiaper et al., 2011).

15.5   Conclusions

In riparian vegetation zones of the lower Tarim Basin, remote sensing plays an important role to assess vegetation health and recovery following the several interventions in the hydrology of the region. Remote sensing is particularly helpful in estimating vegetated areas as one indication of recent recovery. However, even with very accurate vegetation maps of the area, large errors in area estimates could occur because of the interaction between the size and the spatial distribution of vegetation communities and the spatial resolution of the observing sensor.

These errors tend to be worse when the size and the extent of inter-connected vegetation communities are smaller than the size of the pixels in the image leading to the mixed pixel issue. In these situations, the magnitude of the problem also depends on the subpixel proportions used to define vegetation presence or absence and the proportion of vegetated areas in the window of analysis. As shown here, the use of the beta model for the distribution of subpixel proportions provides a powerful framework for studying problems of vegetation area estimation in the lower Tarim Basin. The practical findings of this study include 1) guidance on methods for selecting spatial resolutions of sensors for applications focused on riparian vegetation area estimation, and 2) guidance regarding the selection of thresholds in subpixel fractions used for defining what is "vegetated" in a thematic map. For example, to get accurate area estimates of vegetated areas in the lower Tarim Basin using remote sensing, thresholds defining class membership need to be related to the proportion of the area covered by riparian vegetation communities. However, due to fact that most of the area investigated here is occupied by sparse vegetation cover, our results suggest that the use of high spatial resolution (less than 10 m) is warranted. If the spatial resolution of the sensor is limited to more common medium scales such as those provided by Landsat or CBERS sensors, then it is recommended that a variable threshold strategy be employed, which can be guided by the beta model-based analysis described here.

Acknowledgements

This research was partially funded by NASA's Land Cover and Land Use Change (LCLUC) Program Grant number NNX09AI22G awarded to Dr. Ozdogan. Alishir Kurban acknowledges partial support from the Xinjiang Institute of Ecology and Geography as well as support by Natural Science Foundation of Xinjiang Uygur Autonomous Region of China, Grant number 2010211A57.

References

Atkinson, P. M., and Curran, P. J. (1995). Defining an optimal size of support for remote sensing investigation. *IEEE Transactions on Geoscience and Remote Sensing*, 33 (3), 768–776.

Chen, Y. J., Li, W. H., Chen, Y. N., Liu, J. Z., and He, B. (2007). Ecological effect of synthesized governing in Tarim River valley. *China Environ. Science*, 27(1), 24–28.

Collins, J. B., and Woodcock, C. E. (1999). Geostatistical estimation of resolution-dependent variance in remotely sensed images. *Photogrammetric Engineering and Remote Sensing*, 65, 41–50.

Duan, H., Kurban, A., Halik, U., Wang, S. Ablekim, A., and Barat, M. (2010). Study of the vegetation change based on temporal trajectory analysis using multi-temporal CBERS/CCD data in the lower reaches of the Tarim River. *Arid Land Geography*, 33 (2), 263–271. (in Chinese with English abstract).

Garrigues, S., Allard, D., and Baret, F. (2007) Using first- and second-order variograms for characterizing landscape spatial structures from remote sensing imagery. *IEEE*

Transactions on Geoscience and Remote Sensing, 45(6), 1823–1834.

Guli, J., Xi, C., Zhongguo, M., and Cun, C. (2009). Classification of sparse desert riparian forest in extreme arid region. *Journal of Desert Research*, 29, 1153–1161 (in Chinese).

Huete A. R. (1988). A Soil-adjusted vegetation Index (SAVI). *Remote Sensing of Environment*, 25(3), 295–309.

Jiapaer, G., Chen, X., and Bao, A. (2011). A comparison of methods for estimating fractional vegetation cover in arid regions. *Agricultural and Forest Meteorology*, 151, 1698–1710.

Jupp, D. L. B., Strahler, A. H., and Woodcock, C.E. (1988). Autocorrelation and regularization in digital images I —Basic theory. *IEEE Transactions on Geoscience and Remote Sensing*, 26(4), 463–473.

Jupp, D. L. B., Strahler, A. H., and Woodcock, C.E. (1989). Autocorrelation and regularization in digital images II —Simple image models. *IEEE Transactions on Geoscience and Remote Sensing*, 27(3), 247–258.

Key, J. (1994). The area coverage of geophysical fields as a function of sensor field-of-view. *Remote Sensing of Environment*, 48, 339–346.

Kurban, A., Ablikim, A., Halik, U., Hanming, D., Barat, M., and Mansagul, M. (2010). The monitoring of vegetation change process in lower reach of Tarim River. *Arid Land Research*, 27(3), 161–171.

Liu, H., Chen, Y. N., and Yang, X. M. (2007). Monitor of ecological response along lower reaches of Tarim River based on remote sensing. *Arid Land Geogr.*, 30(2), 204–208.

Qi, J., Chen, J., Wan, S., and Ai, L. (2012). Understanding the coupled natural and human systems in Dryland East Asia. *Environment Research Letter*, 7, 015202, doi:10.1088/1748-9326/7/1/015202.

Zhao, J., Xi, C., Bao, A., Zhang, C., and Shi, W. (2009). A method for choice of optimum scale on land use monitoring in Tarim River Basin. *Journal of Geographical Sciences*, 19, 340–350.

Zhou, H. R., and Xiao, D. N. (2010). Ecological function regionalization of fluvial corridor landscapes and measures for ecological regeneration in the middle and lower reaches of the Tarim River, Xinjiang of China. *Journal of Arid Land*, 2(2), 123–132.

Authors Information

Mutlu Ozdogan[1]*, Alishir Kurban[2]

1. Center for Sustainability and the Global Environment & Department of Forest and Wildlife Ecology, University of Wisconsin-Madison, Madison, WI 53703, USA
2. Xinjiang Institute for Ecology and Geography, Chinese Academy of Science, Urumqi, Xinjiang 830011, P.R. China
* Corresponding author

Chapter 16

New Ecology Education: Preparing Students for the Complex Human-Environmental Problems of Dryland East Asia

Jiansheng Ye, James F. Reynolds, Jeffrey E. Herrick, Julie A. Reynolds, Togtohyn Chuluun, Fengmin Li, and Ruijun Long

Summary: Present-day environmental problems of Dryland East Asia are serious, and future prospects look especially disconcerting owing to current trends in population growth and economic development. Land degradation and desertification, invasive species, biodiversity losses, toxic waste and air pollution, and water depletion are exacting serious economic losses, social conflicts and health costs. The list of stakeholders expected to resolve these problems include scientific researchers, government regulators, environmental engineers, business consortiums, resource managers and policy-makers. While all are crucial, in this chapter we focus on an often overlooked—but exceptionally important stakeholder—*students*. Given both the rapid rate and magnitude of change that have already occurred, it's not surprising that students often sense that the extent of future environmental problems are so overwhelming that there are no adequate means of fully understanding them. Consequently, educators have the task of instilling a sense of optimism that while the challenge is difficult, it is not impossible. We must assist students develop a suite of skills that will enable them to deal with the prodigious mix of societal and environmental problems that they stand to inherit. Towards this end, in this chapter we present our vision of a new ecology education course. The key topics in new ecology education emphasize interdisciplinary and multidisciplinary approaches; the role of strong conceptual frameworks; the importance of nonlinearities, thresholds and feedbacks in human-environmental systems; principles of both systems and resilience theory; and how short-term versus long-term solutions to any given problem may be quite different. Decision-making ultimately relies upon identifying and evaluating choices: thus the next generation of students must be effective communicators, problem-solvers, and systems thinkers.

16.1   Introduction

The various chapters of this book document some of the bewildering array of transformations and disruptions occurring throughout the Dryland East Asia (DEA) region. Key drivers of these changes include land use/land alterations, urbanization, industrialization and agriculture intensification, climate change, globalization of the economy, and the exponential growth of urban populations. These drivers are not independent but interact in innumerable ways. For example, Chen et al. (Chapter 1) describe how urbanization is intensifying throughout DEA as a result of the rapid transition from a traditional centralized economy to a modern market-based one; this is largely driven by the globalization of China's economy. In turn, this has contributed to a dramatic shift in the distribution of populations, from rural to urban centers. The paradox of urbanization is evident in Fan et al.'s (Chapter 5) analysis: although these dramatic changes have contributed to a robust economy, the long-term sustainability of this system is jeopardized by the by-products of this extraordinary growth. This is evident in Sun et al.'s (Chapter 8) analysis of the water resources of DEA. Water is naturally limited in this arid region so its future availability is closely tied to its judicious management and conservation. As a result of the aforementioned transformations and disturbances, there has been severe degradation of water quantity and quality as evidenced by shortages in drinking water, water pollution, the loss of wetlands and lakes, extensive soil erosion (both wind and water induced), depletion of river water, and salinization of soils and ground water. Liu and Yang (2012) provide a thorough analysis of some of the unintended environmental and socioeconomic consequences of China's efforts to manage its water resources.

Climate change is also an important driver of changes in DEA. Amongst the most important concerns, it threatens to exacerbate the problem of water resources. Qi et al. (Chapter 3) summarize patterns of significant temperature anomalies that have occurred during the past 100 years throughout this region. Although the consequences of these changes are not certain, the frequency of extreme events in DEA appear to be rising, which includes increases in temperature and precipitation variability, as well as increases in the duration of extreme events, e.g., drought and severe winter storms. In what well may be a cautionary tale, McMichael (2012) describes numerous examples over the past 12 millennia where climate changes led to destabilization of Chinese civilizations via food shortages, disease, and social unrest.

The DEA region faces a myriad of challenges in the near future. These issues must be addressed by concerned stakeholders, the usual list of which includes scientific researchers, local residents, government regulators, environmental engineers, business leaders, resource managers and policy-makers. While all of these participants are vital, in this chapter we focus on an often overlooked— but exceptionally important stakeholder—*students*. Given the state of current environmental concerns, it is not surprising that students often sense that these problems are so overwhelming and complex that there are no adequate means of fully understanding them. As educators, we have the task of instilling a sense of optimism that while the challenge is difficult, it is not impossible. Towards this end, over the past decade numerous educational organizations have pleaded that a "new ecology education" for students has been implemented that is multidisciplinary, deals with the inherent complexity and nonlinearity of human-environmental (H-E) systems, considers multiple spatiotemporal scales, and includes relevant aspects of economics, politics, and technology (Bybee, 2003). In this chapter we describe our vision of such a "new ecology education" course. The topics covered in our proposed the new ecology education course have been selected to engage students in thinking about ways to address the complex H-E problems of land degradation and desertification, which are major globally issues (Reynolds et al., 2007) and, specifically, in DEA (Yang et al., 2008). The individual topics covered in our the new ecology education are not new but collectively provide a roadmap for tackling the vexing, multidimensional problems that today's students are inheriting.

16.2   Description of New Ecology Education

Ultimately, given that the goal of society is to achieve sustainable resource use between humans and their environment, the new ecology education is based on a *multiple functions* approach. That is, managers and policy-makers must deal with conflicting goals (e.g., food production versus water conservation) by taking into account the plethora of linkages and feedbacks in coupled H-E systems (e.g., food, energy, water, biodiversity, quality of life) (Ayensu et al., 1999). Themes at the core of the multiple functional approach of the new ecology education are shown in Figure 16.1 and the topics covered are outlined in Table 16.1.

As depicted in Figure 16.1, the main objective of the new ecology education is to assist students to develop a problem-solving skillset that will better enable

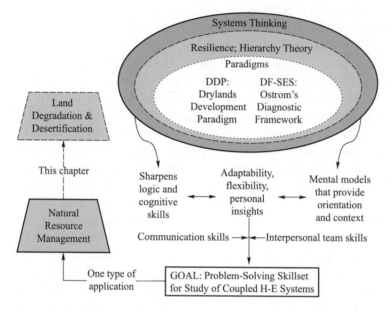

Fig. 16.1 Conceptual framework for New Ecology Education.

them to study complex H-E systems. One of the first important decisions in any study of H-E systems is selecting or developing a paradigm to frame the work. A paradigm refers to a suite of philosophical principles about the nature of the field of interest (for example, desertification), assumptions that tend to be shared by researchers working in this field, and methodological strategies linked to these assumptions (Maxwell, 2004). In the new ecology education, we use the philosophical principles of systems thinking, resilience and hierarchy theory (see Table 16.2 for definitions of key terms), which underpin the drylands development paradigm and the diagnostic framework for social-ecological systems (Fig. 16.1).

Since the study of H-E systems is multidisciplinary, communication skills and the ability to work across disciplines are important components of a strong problem-solving skillset. Hence, it is essential that students gain a set of skills that "predict outstanding manager or leader performance" in problem-solving (Boyatzis et al., 2002): this skillset (Fig. 16.1) includes 1) cognitive ability, such as systems thinking; 2) self-management or intrapersonal abilities, such as adaptability; and 3) interpersonal abilities. The approach used in the new ecology education emphasizes holistic and flexible thinking, sharpening of cognitive skills, and is intended to provide students with a platform that gives them confidence to pertinent questions and to proceed in the study of complex systems like DEA.

Table 16.1 List of the major topics covered in our proposed new ecology education course. Key terms are defined in Table 16.2.

Topic Title	Overview
1. What's Going On? (*Conceptual Models*)	Conceptual frameworks are invaluable tools for elucidating the boundaries of a problem, its component parts and key interactions.
2. Life is So Confusing! (*Nonlinearity*)	Nonlinearity exists at all levels of systems organization and is commonly manifested as synergies, feedbacks and thresholds. This makes predictions difficult if not impossible.
3. Everything is Connected to Everything Else (*Systems Thinking*)	Systems are composed of multiple components that interact for a common purpose. In her book *Thinking in Systems*, Meadows (2008) argues that viewing complex systems from a broad perspective, rather than focusing on specific, individual events, can help identify underlying causes of problems (at the scale of the 'big picture'). Even if it may appear that a transformation or dynamic change is a specific, isolated event, it usually is not: it is part of a larger system and taking a system view can help guide efforts to seek solutions.
4. Climbing Up-and-Down the Complexity Latter (*Hierarchy Theory*)	Hierarchy theory deals with scaled systems (O'Neill et al., 1986). Systems thinking seemingly creates a paradox: How are we supposed to study whole systems if we can't break them down into manageable parts? Hierarchy theory provides the answers.
5. What Does It Take to Change this System? (*Resilience*)	Holling's (1973) classic definition of resilience is the ability of a system to persist despite disturbances.
6. Coping with Land Degradation in Drylands (*Ecosystem Services*)	Desertification is the long-term failure to balance demand for and supply of ecosystem services in drylands (MA, 2005b). This definition provides a robust and operational way to quantify land degradation—and hence desertification.
7. Unraveling the Complexity of Coupled H-E Systems and Desertification (*The Drylands Development Paradigm*)	The Drylands Development Paradigm (DDP) is a framework to help understand and disentangle the complexity of land degradation in global drylands (Reynolds et al., 2007). It encompasses all of the previous topics and thus serves as a nice integration of knowledge with practical application to a serious problem in DEA.
8. Where Art, Science and Craft Meet (*Ostrom's Diagnostic Framework*)	Ostrom's diagnostic framework for analyzing the sustainability of coupled social-ecological systems is a detailed outline that identifies major subsystems of large complex social-ecological systems that are undergoing transformations (usually bad ones!) (Ostrom, 2009). Like DDP, it encompasses the previous topics.

Table 16.2 Definitions of some key concepts used in new ecology education.

Complex Adaptive Systems. A collection of elements or component parts that interact within and across multiple scales, react to both their environments and to each another, and exhibit emergent properties (Levin, 1998).

Dynamic Systems. Time-dependent processes that lead to changes in a system (Stahel, 2005). Examples include runoff from watershed, ecosystem carbon and nitrogen fluxes, and formation of the monsoon over DEA.

Emergent Properties. Refers to higher-level properties and behaviors that arise from the collective dynamics of a system's component parts (Levin, 1998). Importantly, these properties and behaviors cannot be identified solely based on the components that make up the whole.

Feedbacks. When a system is modified by changes in its own influence or size. There are two types: *positive* and *negative*. If the initial (direct) response is enhanced, the feedback is considered to be positive and destabilizing. If the initial (direct) response is decreased, the feedback is considered negative, which is stabilizing. Xue (2006) describes various types of land-surface simulations in global drylands that illustrate both types. Using a global circulation model (GCM), when dryland surface were saturated, this led to substantially higher evaporation, which led to higher precipitation, which in turn further enhance the evaporation, etc., producing a positive feedback. In instances of high surface albedo, this would lower net radiation and evaporation and, hence lower precipitation. However, this would also reduce cloud cover, enabling more solar radiation to reach the land surface, which could compensate for the net radiation loss and produce higher evaporation and precipitation: a negative (stabilizing) feedback.

Hierarchy Theory. A dialect of general systems theory that organizes elements of systems into groups (or levels) (Allen et al., 2009).

Propagation of Effects. An impact at one level in a system, even a very small one, may lead to larger changes as this impact moves up (or down) through a system. For example, Cury et al. (2008) described the propagation of impacts in a marine ecosystem food web. Climate change affected primary production (bottom of the food chain) and overfishing removed the top predators (top of the food chain). The impacts of both were propagated up and down the food chain, affecting all organisms.

Regime Shift. Abrupt changes between contrasting, persistent states (e.g., X, Z) of any complex system (deYoung et al., 2008). The loss of resilience of a system such that feedbacks, functions and structure of state X give way to new versions in state Z (Kinzig et al., 2006).

Resilience. The capacity of a system to absorb perturbations while retaining its structural and functional integrity (Walker and Salt, 2006).

(Continued)

Self-organization. A property of open complex systems that achieve order or structure "spontaneously". For example, as an ecosystem develops, relationships between biotic components develop, flows become modified, and the system eventually assumes shape through a process of self-organization (Levin, 1998). Self-organization has limits that are set by feedbacks of its component parts.

System Dynamics. A discipline that deals with modeling and simulation of dynamical systems (Richman, 1993). The focus is usually on feedback loops between stock and flow variables.

Thresholds or Tipping-Points. Critical values or set points in a system (Rial et al., 2004). When thresholds reached or surpassed, often result in major changes in the system, e.g., a regime shift (Groffman et al., 2006).

16.2.1   Topic 1: What's Going On? (Conceptual Models)

Robust conceptual models or frameworks are an important starting point in the study of complex H-E systems. Creating a conceptual model for a given research study on H-E systems is an iterative and creative process in which we identify the main things we want to study, e.g., variables, concepts and drivers that we think (at least initially) are most important, define some of the assumptions, set expectations (which are inevitably revised!), and apply key principles that support and inform the overall goals and objectives.

In this chapter we emphasize land degradation and desertification in DEA (as shown in Fig. 16.1). A conceptual model with regard to the dynamics of human activities and how these can strategically impact (positively or negatively) dryland development is given in Figure 16.2. Shown only this conceptual model, students immediately decipher many of the key structural and functional components of "what's going on" in coupled H-E systems in drylands and their consequences. Developments that lead to a downward spiral of land degradation and desertification are contrasted to developments that may led to a more sustainable balance between H-E components and improved human well-being, and political and economic stability (Fig. 16.2). We will return to this topic later in the chapter.

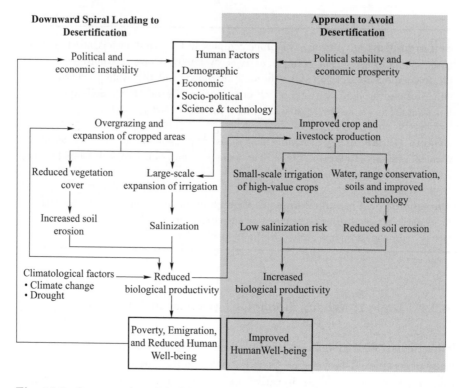

Fig. 16.2 Conceptual model of desertification showing dynamics of human activities and how these strategically impact dryland development.
Source: From Millennium Ecosystem Assessment (2005b).

16.2.2 Topic 2: Life Is So Confusing! (Nonlinearity)

Over 50 years ago, Ladis Kovak (1960) posited that nonlinearity was a major barrier to progress in the field of physics and that while it's an integral part of life, it remains elusive (Fig. 16.3). He wrote, "We have broken through the sonic barrier, we are well on our way to conquering the thermal barrier and we are now at the threshold of the nonlinear barrier. Of all three, the last seems the most insurmountable. Strange that these nonlinear phenomena that abound so widely in nature should be so intractable. It is almost as if Man is to be denied a complete knowledge of the universe unless he makes a superhuman effort to solve its nonlinearities". Since then, supercomputers have increased our ability to mathematically deal with nonlinearity but it seems that herculean efforts are still needed to identify its sources and consequences. We find most students are highly confident that they understand the concept of nonlinearity (e.g., Fig. 16.3) but when pressed for details, many find it difficult to explain. Given that it is such a crucial component of systems thinking and resilience (Table 16.1), it is a important subject to master.

Fig. 16.3 The theme of Kovak's (1960) essay "Life can be so nonlinear" is that nonlinearity is a part of everyone's daily life but it is much easier to observe than explain. He used two simple examples from a camping trip with his 9-year old son: the highly turbulent flow of water in a stream and the burning of wood in a campfire, where initially the fire burned quite slowly—occasionally flaring-up—then the flames changed color as it burned more intensely and eventually dissipated.

Nonlinearity exists when the relationship between two variables, X and Y, is not proportional. In linear systems they are proportional: that is, the effect of the action of combining two different inputs is merely the superposition of these inputs taken individually. This can be readily shown in terms of input (I)-response (R) actions (Fig. 16.4): if input I_i produces response R_i and input I_j produces response R_j then, if the system is linear, input I_i+I_j always produces response $R_i + R_j$. In a nonlinear system $I_i + I_j \neq R_i + R_j$, which reflects interactions and may produce dramatic new behavior quite unlike either I_i or I_j.

As shown in Figure 16.4 the response of linear system A to inputs is proportional (in fact, the frequency of an oscillatory response in a linear system is always equal to that of the input forcing). System B is also linear because its response to inputs I_i and I_j is additive (i.e., $R_i + R_j = I_i + I_j$). Lastly, in system C there is both a time lag and a disproportionate response to a square wave input signal whereas in system D exhibits response frequencies not present in the forcing inputs; hence both are nonlinear.

Generally speaking, there are two mechanisms that give rise to nonlinearity: extrinsic and intrinsic. Extrinsic mechanisms arise out of the direct response of variable Y to an external forcing factor X, where to a large extent X drives but is not affected by the value of Y, e.g., [X=precipitation, Y=crop yield] and

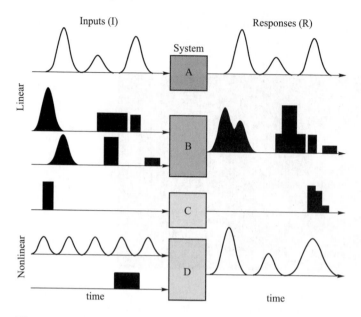

Fig. 16.4 Illustrations of linear and nonlinear systems using input (I) and response (R) actions depicted along a time line.

[X=central bank prime rates, Y=local cost of borrowing money]. In contrast, intrinsic mechanisms arise solely from the internal dynamics of the system itself, whereby the rate of change of a variable Y depends upon the value of Y, thus reflecting the existence of a feedback loop. Exponential population growth is an example, as is the tropical forest-global warming feedback loop described by Bonan (2008). Tropical forests are highly vulnerable to warmer, drier climate conditions and such conditions can exacerbate global warming whereby as tropical forests die, evaporative cooling decreases and more carbon dioxide is released, all of which lead to increased warming and more forest dieback (a positive feedback loop).

Both extrinsic and intrinsic mechanisms result in a diversity of behaviors and underlie the richness of nonlinear dynamics in H-E systems. They exist at all levels of systems organization and are commonly manifested as synergies, feedbacks, and thresholds (Harte, 1996) or self-organizing features of systems (see Table 16.3 for examples). *Synergies* arise when two or more processes interact in such a way that the outcome is greater than the sum of their separate effects (e.g., multiplicative rather than additive); *feedbacks* occur when a system or process is modified by changes in its own influence or size. If the initial (direct) response is enhanced, the feedback is considered to be positive and destabilizing; if decreased, the feedback is negative, which tends to be stabilizing; and *thresholds* occur where critical values or set points in the system are reached.

Table 16.3 Examples of synergism, feedbacks and thresholds mechanisms in H-E systems (Modified from Bradford and Reynolds, 2006).

Synergisms	Feedbacks	Thresholds
Vegetation Pattern: In arid ecosystems clumping or banding of vegetation can result in an overall increase of production and plant diversity due to the combined benefits of the redistribution of precipitation and nutrients into patches (Levin, 1998)	El Nino-Logging-Fires: Does selective logging in tropical rainforests lead to an increased susceptibility for fire? In the 1997–1998 Indonesian fires, forest fires primarily occurred in recently logged forests while primary forests were much less affected. These results support the hypothesis of positive feedback between logging and fire occurrence (Aguiar and Sala, 1999)	Plant Cover: Small changes in shrub/grass cover resulting from climate variability and grazing can lead to sudden increases in soil erosion (Siegert et al., 2001)
Climate Variation and Human-induced Changes: Combined, widespread and intense budworm outbreaks in southwestern forests of USA in the late 20th century (Breshears and Barnes, 1999)	Soil-Climate: Positive and negative feedbacks on methane consumption in montane soils by climate change (Swetnam and Lynch, 1993)	Habitat Fragmentation: There is a critical fragmentation in the landscape, beyond which grasshopper population abundance and persistence is seriously affected (Torn and Harte, 1996)
Climate-Ecosystem: Under projected scenarios of global change, modified ocean and atmospheric circulation will introduce exotic water- and air-borne propagules from neighboring continents, and resulting synergies of elevated temperature, UV radiation, CO_2, and precipitation will favor new trajectories of community development (With and Crist, 1995)	Economy-Water Resources: As the amount of irrigated land in SE Spain expands, the water demand is higher and, hence aquifer exploitation increases and piezometric levels decline. This increases water extraction costs, which affects profitability and slows down the expansion of irrigated land (Kennedy, 1995)	Management: How much and what type of clear-cutting is possible before an unacceptable threshold of public acceptance is reached? In a highly visible, balsam-fir landscape in Canada, when clear-cuts are in the form of a single patch, the acceptability threshold of user groups was 25% (of the visible landscape); a dispersed strategy reduces the negative visual impact and the acceptability threshold increases to 50% (Paquet and Belanger, 1997)
Insects-Fire-C Sequestration: Climate change can affect the frequency and intensity of pest outbreaks, which in turn can cause a considerable loss of wood, thereby affecting fire frequencies (McIntyre et al., 2000)	Economic Subsidy Positive Feedback Loop: The European Union hyped promotion of the Mediterranean diet and provided economic subsidies for the production of olive oil. This stimulated consumption and led a transformative growth of a traditional Mediterranean crop into an industrial cash crop based on irrigation, agrochemical inputs and mechanization. Feedback loops between subsidies, production and consumption (Scheidel and Krausmann, 2011)	Vegetation-Climate Feedbacks-Thresholds: Fragmented forests in Amazonia are more prone than intact forests to El Nino-induced droughts, increased fire, and positive feedbacks to regional climate, further reinforcing the fragmentation-drought-fire cycle. There is a critical "deforestation threshold" above which Amazonian rainforests can no longer be sustained (Laurance and Williamson, 2001)

16.2.3 Topic 3: Everything Is Connected to Everything Else (Systems Thinking)

In his highly influential book, *The Fifth Discipline*, Peter Senge (1990) contends that five scholarly subjects best enable us to deal with complex systems: mental models, shared vision, personal mastery, team learning and systems thinking. These subjects encourage innovative and adaptive human learning (note that all are represented in Fig. 16.1). The fifth discipline—systems thinking—is the logical glue that binds these together.

Systems thinking embraces holism (viewing the big picture!) and pluralism (getting everyone involved!), which counters strict reductionism [1] and dogmatism, respectively (Reynolds and Holwell, 2010). Hence, we introduce students to the work of Senge because 1) the "big picture" underlies the theme of NEE; and 2) we need a diversity of viewpoints, which involves identifying and including the input of relevant stakeholders (one process of achieving this is called scoping ; Costanza et al., 1997; Sandker et al., 2008). As Senge's argument goes, "a better appreciation of whole systems will lead to more appropriate actions."

A system is composed of multiple components, elements or parts that work together or interact for a common "purpose" (Forrester, 2007; Meadows, 2008). Purposes are emergent properties in that they represent more than the sum of the collection of individual parts. Examples of system purposes are soil carbon sequestration in a grassland ecosystem, providing electricity to a city through an electrical grid, the amount of water discharged from a watershed, the quality of medical care in a hospital, and milk production on a local dairy farm. Emergent properties exemplify nonlinearity so it follows that H-E systems are prototypical examples of complex adaptive systems (Table 16.2) (Levin, 1998). Why? Because their behavior emerges (i.e., self-organizes) from the nonlinear interactions of their component parts, which can lead to "historical dependency and multiple possible outcomes of dynamics" (Levin, 1998). Key elements of a systems thinker's toolbox include emergent properties, complex adaptive systems, chains of causality (feedbacks), self-organization, hierarchy theory, nonlinearity and thresholds (Table 16.2) (of course, these are not mutually exclusive; see Checkland, 1999; Meadows, 2008).

When confronted with a big complex problem, students have a natural tendency to deconstruct it into smaller parts, try to decipher how each part works, and then reassemble them in order to understand the big problem. Simon and Newall (as cited in Dale, 1970, 1973) described this as one of the basic modes of human problem-solving: i.e., take a big insoluble problem, repeatedly decom-

---

1 The point is that reductionism should not be the exclusive approach nor at the expense of more holistic views. Hence, we have argued for simultaneous "bottom-up" (reductionist) and "top-down" (holistic) approaches to problem-solving (following hierarchy theory, Reynolds et al., 1993; see Topic 5).

pose it into smaller and smaller subproblems until eventually each subproblem is (hopefully) soluble, and then sum the individual solutions to obtain a solution of the original problem [1] . Learning how to apply such a reductionist approach is a critical step as it requires students to identify the critical components of a problem. While necessary, it is not sufficient by itself to solve complex problems.

Since human learning tends to be highly compartmentalized, the value of systems thinking as a pedagogical tool in education has long been recognized (Betts, 1992). Systems thinking helps instill the sense of synthesizing individual parts (Hung, 2008). In medical schools, systems thinking has been proven an effective tool for enhancing problem-solving skills and clinical reasoning, whether the topic be biochemistry, sociology or anatomy (Rubin et al., 2012). It has been shown that nurses trained in the science of systems thinking develop superior skills when dealing with unstructured problem-solving, pattern recognition and uncertainties (Hodges, 2011).

A high profile application of systems thinking is from the discipline of Earth System Science (ESS), which evolved to illuminate complex relationships between sustainable resource use by humans and their global environment (Lawton, 2001; Rial et al., 2004; Schellnhuber, 1999). In NEE we adopt the simple ESS model of Schellnbuber (1999) to H-E systems of DEA to facilitate the discussion of complex systems. As shown in Figure 16.5, WS [DEA] represents the whole system of DEA in which people (H) interact with and are inseparable from the natural world (E). As the evidence from the various chapters in this

WS[DEA]=H[human domain], E[environment]

where

$H=(\alpha,\sigma)$

where α is the anthroposphere (the aggregate of human lives, values [culture], actions and products) and σ are protocols, laws, treaties and customs (local, regional, international) for land conservation, dealing with climate change, the preservation of biodiversity, etc. The components of σ are proposed by human societies in order to sustain the WS[DEA] for current and future generations

$E=(a, b, c, h, ...)$

where a=atmosphere, b=biosphere, c=cryosphere, h=hydrosphere,etc.

Fig. 16.5 A whole system (WS) model for H-E systems of DEA. Based on Schellnhuber (1999).

---

1 This should not be confused with system *decomposability* (see 16.2.4 Hierarchy Theory).

book, interactions within DEA encompass a broad interpretation of the mutual interactions between and among human activities and natural-world processes. Of course, as Schellnbuber (1999) observed, moving from a "broad interpretation to real world problems" leads to a plethora of challenges. The changes and transformations occurring in DEA are complex, occur locally and regionally, over short- and long-time periods, and are invariably nonlinear even when the stimuli or drivers themselves are continuous and gradual.

16.2.4 Topic 4: Climbing Up-and-Down the Complexity Ladder (Hierarchy Theory)

At this point in the course, students appreciate the value of systems thinking: it is unwise to choose some smaller component of a larger system for a detailed study with the goal of extrapolating these findings as representing the larger system. Inevitably, however, the following question is posed: "Since direct, manipulative, experimental studies of whole systems are generally impractical—and we're not to sum-up solutions obtained for smaller components if our domain of interest is the larger and whole system (e.g., DEA)—how on earth are we suppose to study whole systems?" In other words, many students sense that apparently they've been sold a paradox: they should take a systems approach and study whole systems, yet they can't break whole systems down into manageable parts for study. This seemingly paradoxical position is resolved by hierarchy theory, which comes to our rescue.

We return to Figure 16.5 where we noted that large systems like WS [DEA] can be subdivided in subsystems, i.e., H[human] and E[environment] domains. In turn, subsystem H was decomposed into other subsystems and subsystem E into subsystems $(a, b, c, h, \ldots)$ and so forth. This can be done repeatedly. Thus is the nature of complex systems: they are hierarchical—composed of interrelated subsystems, each of which includes other subsystems. How far we should decompose a system is of course a function of our interests and the spatiotemporal scales we wish to work with. In other words, each subsystem has characteristic rates of change, cycle times, response time, etc. For example, the social and environmental hierarchies in DEA are operating across a wide range of spatiotemporal scales: some things are happening at very high speeds and at small scales (e.g., the photosynthesis in a leaf) while others are occurring more slowly and at larger spatial scales (e.g., coal burning releases particulate matter into the atmosphere, which in the long run can lead to chronic respiratory ailments in humans).

What does this mean with regard to the aforementioned paradox? Does the fact we can identify subsystems means that we are able to study parts of the whole system as "independent" units? The answer is a qualified yes, although we caution that this entails assumptions and simplifications. Simon (1962) distinguished complex systems that are 1) decomposable, i.e., its subsystems do not interact; and 2) nearly decomposable, i.e., the interactions within components of subsystems are significantly stronger than those interactions between subsystems (in some instances, they may be weak but not negligible). Decomposable systems are rare in nature whereas nearly decomposable ones are common.

Each component of a hierarchy is called a holon: i.e., it is a whole that is composed of smaller parts, while at the same time it is part of some greater whole (Giampietro, 1994) [1] . In practice, this means that for a nearly decomposable system, e.g., WS [DEA] (Fig. 16.5), we can isolate a subsystem at level L in the hierarchy, study it and be safe in knowing that its dynamics are largely determined by the interaction of its component parts. But since the holon remains an integral part of a larger hierarchical system, higher level (L+1) subsystems exert constraints on L (boundary conditions) and lower level (L−1) subsystems provide initiating conditions (O'Neill et al., 1986).

Following Sumber (2002), a pastoral household in Inner Mongolia Autonomous Region (IM) of China could be holon (L). The mechanisms that regulate the daily dynamics of the household are determined by L−1 processes, which are the interacting and interdependent parts that make-up the holon: the grandparents, husband, wife, infant baby, teenage son, the felt tent with wooden frame they sleep in, and so forth. Also contributing to L−1 are work responsibilities of the men (e.g., herding, negotiating prices), women (raising children, making yogurt, cooking, etc.), and overall family life. Note that dynamical processes in L−1 are generally faster and operate at a smaller spatial extent than L. Constraints on L exist at level L+1, which operate at slower time scales and over larger distances. For instance, climate change, regional governmental regulations on allowing mineral mining in the pastoral grasslands, social programs and so forth constitute components of L+1.

Students often find the hierarchy theory to be a rich conceptual tool to help them navigate through complex systems and problems. We frequently hear the sentiment: "it always seems to be a question of what to include and what to exclude!" How true! This is where a paradigm such as DDP shown in Figure 16.1 comes in handy (discussed below).

---

1 We limit our discussion here. Technically, in a hierarchical system vertical coupling is defined as the interaction between different *levels* in a hierarchy whereas horizontal coupling is the interaction among *holons* that exist at the same level in a hierarchy. See Wu and David (2002) for details.

16.2.5 Topic 5: What Does It Take to Change This System? (Resilience)

Resilience "addresses the dynamics and development of complex social-ecological systems" (Folke et al., 2010). Brian Walker (interviewed by McDonald, 2007) identified the three main tenets of resilience, which are explored in detail in his book, *Resilience Thinking* (Walker and Salt, 2006):

- complex adaptive systems are self-organizing;
- systems are nonlinear, which leads to the potential for multiple basins of attraction and regime shifts; and
- systems go through adaptive cycles, which consists of a "repeated process of growth, conservation, collapse and re-organization"

Holling (1973) gave the classic definition of resilience that focuses the ability of a system to persist despite disturbances, i.e., the amount of change that a system can endure before it crosses a threshold and moves into an alternative state. Resilience is typically visualized using the metaphor of an landscape composed of hills, valleys and balls. As shown in Figure 16.6, balls are scattered at various locations in the landscape to represent the current location or state of a system; valleys represent "attractor states" and the degree of system resilience is represented as the size of the valley or basin of attraction: that is, the maximum perturbation that an system can absorb without shifting to an alternative state.

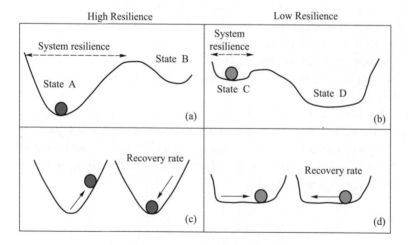

Fig. 16.6 System resilience. (a) State A can absorb a large disturbance before being nudged out of the valley, up over the steep hill, to state B. (b) Even a small perturbation can drive state C to D (low hill). (c) This system has a steep valley and thus a fast recovery rate. (d) Given the flat valley, this system will have a slower recovery rate. Modified from van Nes and Scheffer (2007).

Adaptability is defined by Walker et al. (2004) as "the capacity of actors in a system to influence resilience". Once a system is disturbed, its response represents the collective actions of its component parts (self-organization). Two examples are given, one of fire in a native rangeland ecosystem and the other of fire in a boreal forest managed by humans.

When a rangeland ecosystem experiences a fire, numerous changes occur (e.g., as described by Anderies et al., 2002 for Australian rangelands). Some are immediate while others occur over a much longer time span. Consider a case where the rangeland is dominated by grasses with a scattering of shrubs. Fire consumes the dead grass as fuel, which differentially kills shrubs, thus favoring grass reestablishment and growth. This affects nutrient cycling, belowground carbon dynamics, the microbial community, soil respiration, soil temperatures, and so on. Depending upon the way, these "actors" (in this case, ecosystem variables and associated processes) reorganize, the system may slowly (or rapidly) return to its condition prior to the fire, or by exceeding a threshold, move to a new state (e.g., grass-dominated). These dynamics are all part of the systems' adaptability.

Chapin et al. (2003) described many nuances of fire-human societal interactions in boreal forests in interior Alaska. In these systems human actors play a very important role in "managing" the threshold for system changes. Briefly, fire presents societal risks and benefits. With regard to risks, there is loss of property, lives, natural resources and risks to health (smoke inhalation). However, there are numerous benefits as well: following fires there is a high production of mushrooms and berries and an increase in moose and furbearing animal populations. Also, some indigenous residents rely almost exclusive on firefighting for their income. Hence, regime shifts from one type of forests to another due to fires are often managed by human interests, who are key actors that influence resilience.

The famous carved stone torsos (moai) of Rapa Nui (Easter Island) in the Pacific (Fig. 16.7) are symbolic of one of the most famous documented regime shifts of a coupled H-E system in history (Diamond, 1997). This example illustrates desired and undesired states of a system as well as the underlying mechanisms (some of the "actors") that led to these changes. Regime shifts occurred in both the human and environmental components of Rapa Nui, each to a less desirable state (as depicted in Fig. 16.6).

Although there is some debate as to the role of European settlers in its demise, an abbreviated version of the story of Easter Island is as follows (from Diamond, 1997; Rainbird, 2002; Walker and Meyers, 2004). When Easter Island was initially settled by humans around 800 A.D., it was lush with native flora and fauna. The human population flourished for centuries, reaching a high of about 10,000 individuals at one time. However, the beginning of the end began when islanders started a large-scale felling of the forests. The trees were used for

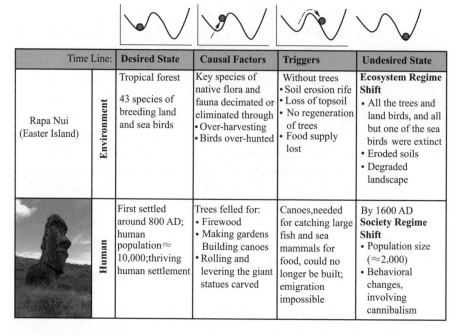

Time Line:		Desired State	Causal Factors	Triggers	Undesired State
Rapa Nui (Easter Island)	Environment	Tropical forest 43 species of breeding land and sea birds	Key species of native flora and fauna decimated or eliminated through • Over-harvesting • Birds over-hunted	Without trees • Soil erosion rife • Loss of topsoil • No regeneration of trees • Food supply lost	**Ecosystem Regime Shift** • All the trees and land birds, and all but one of the sea birds were extinct • Eroded soils • Degraded landscape
	Human	First settled around 800 AD; human population≈ 10,000;thriving human settlement	Trees felled for: • Firewood • Making gardens Building canoes • Rolling and levering the giant statues carved	Canoes,needed for catching large fish and sea mammals for food, could no longer be built; emigration impossible	By 1600 AD **Society Regime Shift** • Population size (≈2,000) • Behavioral changes, involving cannibalism

Fig. 16.7 Demise of the coupled H-E system of Easter Island shown as a time line. Both environmental and human systems move from a desired state to undesired one, driven by underlying causal factors that eventually trigger a regime shift.

firewood, building canoes, and levering the giant stones of the moai into place. Eventually, devoid of trees, there was extensive erosion, loss of fertile soils and the elimination of habitat for native plants and animals, which were a key constituent of the local's diet. Also, without trees, canoes could not be built, and thus fishing declined. It is estimated that by 1600 A.D. the ecosystem had undergone a regime shift and the human society, whose sustainability was tightly coupled to its environment, followed suite.

Much has been written on potential mechanisms and underlying drivers that can move a system to change from one equilibrium state to an alternative one. In general, regime shifts are caused by either of 1) catastrophic (or extreme) external perturbations (Laycock, 1991; Scheffer and Carpenter, 2003) or 2) gradual changes in internal controls and feedbacks (Folke et al., 2004; Levin, 1998). These causal factors are commensurate with the mechanisms that give rise to nonlinearity: extrinsic and intrinsic, respectively (see Topic 2). Easter Island appears to be an example of the gradual changes due to intrinsic nonlinear mechanisms.

Holling (1987) initially proposed the concept of adaptive cycles as a theory or metaphor to help explain the dynamics of ecological systems. It has also been applied to numerous case studies for H-E systems (e.g., Abel et al., 2006; Walker and Salt, 2006). An adaptive cycle consists of four phases: 1) "exploitation" or growth (the r phase); 2) "conservation" or consolidation (the K phase); 3) "collapse" or release (the Ω phase); and 4) reorganization (the α phase). In Table 16.4, we equate each phase to hypothetical events that may have occurred on Easter Island.

Table 16.4 The four phases of the adaptive cycle of H-E systems and activities typically associated with each (from Holling, 1973; Holling, 1987; Vang Rasmussen and Reenberg, 2012; Walker et al., 2006; Walker and Salt, 2006).

| Phase | Characteristics | Easter Island | |
		Human	Environment
r	"Exploitation" or growth: resources plentiful	Individuals or groups quickest to exploit will eventually dominate	Fast-growing plants/animals will eventually dominate
K	"Conservation" or consolidation: resources are "locked-up".	Customs, values, leadership structure, etc. dominate, making it difficult for new individuals or ideas to enact changes.	Mature ecosystems; sequester nitrogen; closed canopies limit light penetration; difficult for new colonizers to enter
	Likelihood of collapse increases→	Each system increasingly interconnected, less flexible and more vulnerable to external disturbances	
Ω	"Collapse" or release: Disturbances.	Loss of social capital (organizations, institutions, networks, norms, etc.)	Loss of natural capital (trees, soils, water, etc.)
α	Reorganization	New entitles can enter into the system. This is where innovation for new system processes and structures may occur via this new "window of opportunity". However, in some systems, such as the H-E Easter Island, both the H and E subsystems provide little capital to build upon	

The study of adaptive cycles is a valuable heuristic tool for the study of resilience and H-E dynamics: not because it is a straightforward recipe that unravels system complexity but, rather, because it doesn't always work in the implied linear model presented in Table 16.4 [1] . Vang Rasmussen and Reenberg (2012)

---

1 For example, in the spring of 2012, JFR and JH co-taught a version of NEE at Duke University and when students presented case studies of their on-going research, they reported the need to make major modifications to the adaptive cycle in order to better explain the dynamics of their particular H-E system. This is consistent with the findings of Vang Rasmussen and Reenberg (2012).

found that the adaptive cycle metaphor was "a simplification of more complex realities" when they applied it to land degradation and system collapse in Sahelian agro-pastoral systems. Nevertheless, as a conceptual model the adaptive cycle metaphor serves as an excellent launch pad for exploration and debate, which is a measure of its true value. Even for a novice, it is relatively easy to see characteristics of the recent dynamics of global financial markets mapped into the framework of the adaptive cycle: exploitation, locking-up of resources (increased vulnerability), collapse and then reorganization.

16.2.6 Topic 6: Coping with Land Degradation in Drylands (Ecosystem Services)

Ecosystem services are the benefits that people obtain from ecosystems. They represent the key links between human and environmental systems. In fact, the Millennium Ecosystem Assessment (MA, 2005b, Desertification Synthesis) defined desertification as the "long-term failure to balance demand for and supply of ecosystem services in drylands". This definition provides a robust and operational way to quantify land degradation—and hence desertification—in NEE. While most students are familiar with the concept, they have not considered it in the context of land degradation. We review the four broad types of ecosystem services defined by MA (2005a) and illustrate the links between these services, their economic value and human well-being in the context of land degradation and desertification (Table 16.5).

Assertions as to the "economic value" of each service are given in Table 16.5, although it remains an open question whether it is feasible to assign monetary or market values to them. Obviously, the underlying assumption is that if ecosystem services become more synchronous with market ideologies, decision-makers and stakeholders will work to safeguard nature. Considering the major changes occurring in the DEA region, this is a highly relevant topic. While there are many examples in the literature touting successful efforts to do this (e.g., Costanza et al., 1997; Liu et al., 2010; Liu and Costanza, 2010; Mäler et al., 2008; Pattanayak, 2004; Ronnback et al., 2007), it is a difficult task. Skourtos et al. (2010) described temporal differences in the reliability of economic evaluations; Peterson et al. (2010) argued that economic valuations of ecosystem services must be replaced with "multiple societal function systems", i.e., economical, educational, legal, political, religious, scientific and so forth, to be accepted in human societies; Potschin and Haines-Young (2011) suggested that political agendas drive this issue as much as scientific ones; and Spangenberg and Settele (2010) outlined the inherent difficulties in objectively assigning economic values to ecosystem services.

Table 16.5 Four broad categories of ecosystem services used by the Millennium Assessment (MA, 2005b). A general assessment of their economic value and application to desertification is also given (modified from Reynolds et al., 2009).

Service	Brief Explanation	Examples	Economic Value	Application to Desertification
Provisioning (or "goods")	Material items for direct or near-direct human use. Globally, often at the expense of the other types of services, there has been a trend to increase production of most provisioning services, largely due to the expansion and intensification of agriculture (2009).	Crops, forage, livestock, wild-caught fish or animals, fresh water, timber, fuel, fiber	Provisioning services are relatively easy to quantify and value, since formal or informal markets often exist, and where they do not, substitute values can be estimated.	Desertification is often a direct consequence of overuse of provisioning services, driven by complex external and internal factors such as population pressures and poverty. Examples of declining provisioning services in drylands include wild plants and animal products, fuelwood, genetic resources, clean air, and fresh water.
Regulating	Keep the flow of other ecosystem services within a desired range, and prevent ecosystem "disservices" (e.g., soybean production in Brazil at the expense of tropical forests, Fearnside, 2001). MA suggests that globally 70% of regulating services have been degraded. At a global scale, climate change can be seen as a breakdown of climate regulating services.	Pollination, climate regulation, flood attenuation, air and water quality maintenance, pest regulation	Drylands are inherently variable, so valuing these services is difficult (the value of regulating services is often delivered via other services). Nevertheless, an increase in certainty and a decrease in risk have economic values. The breakdown of regulating services can have dire social and environmental consequences.	Vegetation cover buffers both the hydrological and production systems. The weakening of regulating services can be slow and continuous, or irregular and only apparent during extreme events. For instance, catastrophic floods may be a combination of reduced infiltration, reduced slowing of overland flow due to a combination of soil compacting and the loss of ground cover coupled with an intense storm event.

(Continued)

Service	Brief Explanation	Examples	Economic Value	Application to Desertification
Cultural	Cultural services are invaluable to the functioning of societies. MA suggests there has been a rapid decline in many cultural services over the past century.	Recreation, aesthetic and artistic appreciation, educational and scientific benefits, spiritual inspiration, sense of place	People of all cultures value nature. Many of these services are readily quantified and valued, because well-established markets exist, such as for ecotourism. Others require more alternative approaches, such as hedonistic pricing, for example (i.e., increasing the value of a property when it has a nice view).	Empirical evidence suggests cultural services are readily traded for provisioning services in times of need, or simply because their economic value is not appreciated. For example, some dryland ranchers use excessive stocking rates to maximize short-term profit with the knowledge that it will lead to destructive feedbacks (erosion, loss of plant cover) to the very land they value (for example, agricultural practices can lead to loss of wildlife habitat, nutrient runoff, sedimentation of waterways, greenhouse gas emissions, and pesticide contamination of waterways, Power, 2010)
Supporting	Underlying ecosystem processes that allow provisioning, regulating and cultural services to be provided. Often constitute the slow variables (see Topic 7).	Net primary production, habitat for biodiversity, soil formation and nutrients cycling	Always delivered via provisioning, regulating and cultural services, and should be valued through those other services to avoid double counting	In desertification it is typically the reduction of supporting services that ultimately leads to the persistent decrease in the ability of the system to provide provisioning and regulatory services.

In spite of these and other shortcomings, the Millennium Ecosystem Assessment (MA, 2005a) lauded the critical role that valuation of ecosystem services has in sustainable development. As ecosystems progressively become more human-dominated, the services they provide will undoubtedly be viewed more in terms of their economic value (Costanza et al., 1997; Mäler et al., 2008; Palmer and Filoso, 2009). There is a rapidly growing field whereby ecosystem services are traded (Liu et al., 2010). The so-called market demand for these services is "driven by regulations requiring those seeking permits to mitigate or provide offsets for their environmental impacts" (Palmer and Filoso, 2009). This is a complex issue, evolving very rapidly, and is highly relevant to desertification. As reflected by the diversity of viewpoints in the literature, it has certain advantages and disadvantages. In NEE we have students read various papers that deal with this topic, albeit from somewhat differing perspectives and objectives. Two are described here.

Palmer and Filoso (2009) examined the new trend whereby the ecological restoration of ecosystem services (such as in a degraded rangeland) is used to support a growing environmental capital market, the goal of which is to create restoration-based credits that can be bought and sold. They strongly cautioned against this practice. Their argument is that restoring a system to its past state—which in the case of drylands may or may not be possible, depending upon the degree of degradation and whether or not vital thresholds have been surpassed (see discussions of this in Fernández et al., 2002; Stafford Smith and Reynolds, 2002)—implies that we're able to also reproduce a well-functioning community of organisms capable of producing the quality and quantity of ecological services it once did. They argued, "we must understand why and when restoration efforts fall short of recovering the full suite of ecosystem services, what can be done to improve restoration success, and why direct measurement of the biophysical processes that support ecosystem services is the only way to guarantee the future success of these markets. Without new science and an oversight framework to protect the ecosystem service assets on which people depend, markets could actually accelerate environmental degradation." In contrast, Mäler et al. (2008) offered an more optimistic approach whereby they argue ecosystem services can now more practically be included in the economic accounts of nations. Applying the concept of inclusive wealth [1], Mäler et al presented a standardized model for building a wealth-based accounting system and propose a step-by-step path, going from one ecosystem to another, arguing that recent advances in 1) valuation techniques, 2) survey techniques, and 3) dynamic modeling of ecosystems makes this feasible.

---

1 The sum of the different forms of capital: natural capital (e.g., the capacity of ecosystems to deliver services such as soil or water), social or human capital (skills or education) and manufactured or produced capital (buildings or roads) weighted by their contribution to human well-being. Based on Dasgupta (2004).

Of course, direct valuation approaches are typically driven by short-term human preferences and as the force of humanity increases on the planet, and ecosystem service valuation will need to switch from choosing among resources to valuing the avoidance of catastrophic ecosystem change (Limburg et al., 2002)! In fact, McCauley (2006) argued that there is scant evidence that market-based conservation works: "We will make more progress in the long run by appealing to people's hearts rather than to their wallets." Many cases of desertification attest to this.

In summary, the topic of ecosystem services is an excellent way to introduce students to land degradation and desertification, and vice versa. When presented with case studies of land degradation, it stimulates much debate and critical thinking.

16.2.7 Topic 7: Unraveling the Complexity of Coupled H-E Systems and Desertification (The Drylands Development Paradigm)

Reynolds et al. (2007) proposed the Dryland Development Paradigm (DDP) as a synthetic framework (or conceptual model, Topic 1) to help understand and unravel the complexity of land degradation in global drylands. In NEE, we show how many of the ideas covered thus far contributed to the derivation of DDP.

DDP consists of five principles (P1–P5, Table 16.6), which students immediately recognize as representative of both systems- and resilience-thinking. The following is a brief summary of its main points (see Reynolds et al., 2011; Reynolds et al., 2007). In drylands there is an exceptionally close dependency of human livelihoods (i.e., ecosystem services) on the environment and these relationships are always changing (P1). This is illustrated in Figure 16.8 where external drivers and internal functioning of each subsystem are depicted. There are critical linkages, created by human decision-making on the one hand (H→E) and the flow of ecosystem services on the other (E→H). As a result, ecosystem services that are important to local populations are changing and evolving over time (P1). This close dependency of livelihoods on the environment can impose a high cost if the H-E linkages become unbalanced or dysfunctional, which can happen if there is high variability in biophysical drivers and/or markets and policy decisions. This means that tracking changes are occurring, and their overall importance to the stability of the H-E balance is crucial but extremely difficult.

Ecosystem resilience is largely a function of "slow" variables, which tend to change very slowly, e.g., soils and long-lived organisms. For example, while the terrestrial primary production is dependent on both soil moisture and soil fertility, nutrients in the soil change very slowly over time, hence it is a slow variable. In contrast, the residence time of soil water changes rapidly and is therefore a fast variable (i.e., it is responding to noise driven by variability in the system). Slow variables are important because they actually control changes of

Table 16.6 A case study applying DDP to H-E systems in the Tuin and Baidrag river basins in Mongolia (based on Chuluun et al., 2012).

Dryland Development Paradigm (DDP)		Pastoral H-E Systems in the Tuin and Baidrag river basins in Mongolia	
Principles	Key Implications for Drylands	Human-Environmental Dynamics	Key Implications for Research, Management and Policy
P1: H-E systems are coupled, dynamic and co-adapting, so that their structure, function and interrelationships change over time.	Understanding issues of desertification and development always requires consideration of both H and E variables. The close dependency of most drylands livelihoods on the environment imposes a greater cost if the coupling becomes dysfunctional.	– In the past two decades significant changes in both H and E sub-systems have occurred: there has been intense warming and drought and a transition to a market economy. Hence, the coupled H-E pastoral systems have been heavily impacted, e.g., stocking rates of livestock has increased dramatically—mainly due to market demand for cashmere—leading to overgrazing.	– A comprehensive research is needed for understanding changes in resilience of pastoral systems to climate change and market forcing. – Management of pastoral H-E systems require strategies to cope with changing climate, markets and policies. – A win-win policy to increase both social and ecological resilience is needed.
P2: A limited suite of "slow" variables determine fundamental changes of H-E system dynamics.	A limited suite of critical processes and slow variables at any scale makes a complex problem more tractable. In contrast, identifying and monitoring "fast" variables masks long-term changes occurring in system.	– Global warming is reducing forage and water resources overall and seasonally. – Governing institutions (have not adapted rapidly enough to changing conditions).	– A decrease in available water resources (mainly due to global warming). – Spring season has become a bottleneck in short-grass steppe areas due to both increasing aridity and overgrazing. – Overgrazing has increased with privatization of livestock.

(Continued)

Dryland Development Paradigm (DDP)		Pastoral H-E Systems in the Tuin and Baidrag river basins in Mongolia	
Principles	Key Implications for Drylands	Human-Environmental Dynamics	Key Implications for Research, Management and Policy
P3: Thresholds in key slow variables define different states of H-E systems, often with different controlling processes.	Identifying thresholds and tipping points particularly matter in drylands because small changes in H-E feedbacks can produce highly variable outcomes. The cost of intervention rises non-linearly with increasing degradation.	– Slight changes in rainfall during the critical months of May through July results in large difference in grassland forage production. – Traditional modes of pastoral livelihoods and cultural traditions.	– Improved management in the remaining river basins and strengthening of one-river pastoral communities along these rivers are key to reduce vulnerability.
P4: Coupled H-E systems are hierarchical, nested and networked across multiple scales.	H-E dryland systems must be managed at the appropriate scale; cross-scale linkages are important, but are often remote and weak in drylands.	– Coupled hot ails embedded in streams; small river communities embedded in larger river basin systems.	– Integrated river basin H-E system management plans must be developed, which incorporate not only lower scales of coupled H-E systems, but address regional social-ecological systems.
P5: The maintenance of a body of up-to-date local traditional knowledge (LTK) is key to functional co-adaptation of H-E systems.	Hybrid LTK must be supported via preservation of existing LTK, and its use accelerated for both local management and regional policy.	– LTK, both traditional and scientific, is critical for adaptation.	– Diverse adaptive policies needed for different ecological-economic zones, which can only be achieved with input of local stakeholders. – Many development projects are maladaptive because of ignorance of traditional informal institutions, knowledge of rangeland management, and local cultural practices.

state, whilst fast variables usually reflect unimportant variability within states. Hence, DDP emphases the importance of slow or controlling variables in both H and E domains (P2, Table 16.6). Social resilience is controlled by either fast (fads or the introduction of new technologies, e.g., the iPad) or slow (cultural) variables (Walker et al., 2006).

Thresholds play an important role in H-E dynamics (P3, Table 16.6). Thresholds of slow variables are of most interest: if a threshold is crossed, this can lead to significant imbalances in the functioning of the system. Furthermore, the capacity of H-E systems to recover from the impacts of crossing undesirable thresholds is often slow (or irreversible, as for Easter Island).

The principles of DDP discussed thus far—slow and fast variables, thresholds and constant changes in the interactions and balance of H-E interactions—all depend upon the scale of interest. The definition of what constitutes a "slow" or "fast" variable is scale-dependent (P4, Table 16.6). What might be a slow variable at one scale may be a fast one at another. For example, the debt to equity ratio of a farm or grass basal area may be slow variables at a household/farm scale but fast ones when considered at a national scale where they are nested within other related, slower variables such as interest rates or land uses, respectively (Fernández et al., 2002). In managing H-E systems, such cross-scale linkages are important in decision-making. For example, rangeland pastoralists, livestock, wildlife, industry and governmental organizations interact at multiple levels, and scales and ignoring these scales can lead to "decision panaceas" that purport to solve problems, but instead, can create more problems than they originally attempted to resolve (examples given in Ostrom et al., 2007).

The circular loop in Figure 16.8 (H→E and E→H) is intended to show that links between H and E sub-systems are mediated in practice by human mental models and local traditional knowledge [1] (i.e., local traditional knowledge, LTK; P5). In some cases management and policy decisions could be improved substantially if LTK were taken into account. We give an example in Figure 16.9 where Han people immigrating into the Uxin banner (country-level division) in IM brought LTK with them, which led to changes in thinking of indigenous people. Of course, the acquisition of LTK is an ongoing, dynamic process and its use in management and policy requires social networks and institutional frameworks (Olsson et al., 2004). In NEE, students read Mazzocchi's (2006) critique of Western science and local traditional knowledge who posits an interesting dichotomy: while Western science favors more analytical and reductionist approaches to problem-solving, local traditional knowledge is based on more intuitive and holistic views, i.e., systems thinking! A selection of examples where DDP has been applied are given in Table 16.7.

---

[1] Connotes what indigenous people know. No universal definition exists and a wide variety of terms are used, including traditional ecological knowledge, local knowledge, indigenous knowledge, folk knowledge and tacit knowledge (Mazzocchi, 2006).

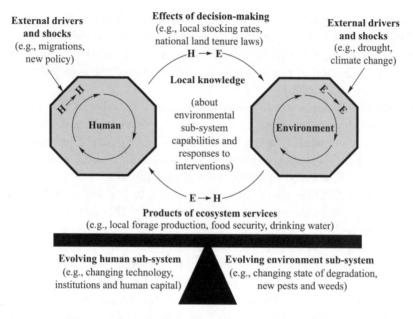

External drivers and shocks (e.g., migrations, new policy)

Effects of decision-making (e.g., local stocking rates, national land tenure laws)

H → E

External drivers and shocks (e.g., drought, climate change)

H → H

Human

Local knowledge (about environmental sub-system capabilities and responses to interventions)

E → E

Environment

E → H

Products of ecosystem services (e.g., local forage production, food security, drinking water)

Evolving human sub-system (e.g., changing technology, institutions and human capital)

Evolving environment sub-system (e.g., changing state of degradation, new pests and weeds)

Fig. 16.8 Schematic depicting interactions between human (H) and environmental (E) components. These systems co-evolve as balanced networks of feedbacks and interactions between H-E components in spite of constantly changing external drivers. Decision-making (H→E) and ecosystem services (E→H) are key linkages between components (moderated by an effective system of local and scientific knowledge; P5, Table 16.6). Historically, studies have tended to focus on each subsystem (i.e., H→H and E→E) at the expense of the linkages between them (Modified from Verstraete et al., 2009).

Fig. 16.9 Changing human-environmental relations in the Uxin banner in IM. See Jiang (2002) for narrative.

Table 16.7 Select examples of applications of the Drylands Development Paradigm (DDP).

Location	How DDP Used	Source
Honduras	To elucidate changing human-ecological relationships and drivers in the Quesungual agroforestry system	Ayarza et al. (2010)
Mexico	To analyze H-E dimensions of hydrology in a small catchment and village	Huber-Sannwald et al. (2006)
Australia	Framing the reanalysis of seven major degradation episodes over the past century in Australian grazed rangelands	Stafford Smith et al. (2007)
South Africa	Identify some of the H-E mechanisms (and management options available) in the stepwise degradation of landscapes driven mainly by overgrazing	Maestre et al. (2006)
Mongolia	To help understand social-ecological interactions in the Tuin and Baidrag river basins	Chuluun et al. (2012)
Mozambique, Zimbabwe	To determine what variables and processes should be part of a long-term monitoring program for land degradation	Lynam and Stafford Smith (2004)
South Africa	This paper considers the principles of DDP in relation to the South African housing policy. The authors argued that the South African low-income housing policy rarely considers how these basic principles are associated with the basic socio-economic realities in this country	Marais et al. (2010)
Global	The role that DDP can play as part of a global drylands observing system	Reynolds et al. (2011); Verstraete et al. (2009)
Global	In developing resilience-based approaches to ecosystem management, DDP is used to frame key factors that need to be considered in dryland biomes	Stafford Smith et al. (2009)
Mexico	To analyze the sustainability concept in Mexican Legislation	Pena et al. (2012)
Mexico	Globalization has resulted in a shift in smallholder livelihoods from mostly agricultural to increasingly wage-labor oriented. This affects land uses and landscape function. DDP is used to examine the origins, development and current states of farmer livelihoods and associated land use	Ribeiro Palacios et al. (2013)

16.2.8 Topic 8: Where Art, Science, and Craft Meet (Ostrom's Framework)

Elinor Ostrom proposed "a diagnostic framework for analyzing the sustainability of coupled social-ecological systems" (hereafter called DF-SES). Details of DF-SES are presented in Ostrom (2009, 2007) and only a brief overview is given here. A critique of DF-SES is a good way for students to gage their individual progress in acquiring the problem-solving skillset shown in Figure 16.1 that is needed to deal with complex H-E systems.

Ostrom, the first woman to win the Nobel Prize in Economics [1], was motivated to develop this framework because different scientific disciplines traditionally use disparate concepts and language and she believes that without "a common framework to organize findings, isolated knowledge does not cumulate." With regard to the inherent complexity in H-E systems:

"A core challenge in diagnosing why some SESs are sustainable whereas others collapse is the identification and analysis of relationships among multiple levels of these complex systems at different spatial and temporal scales. Understanding a complex whole requires knowledge about specific variables and how their component parts are related. Thus, we must learn how to dissect and harness complexity, rather than eliminate it from such systems." [2] (Ostrom, 2009)

Students recognize many of the principles and concepts covered in Topics 1–7.

There are four core systems in DF-SES (Fig. 16.10): 1) resource systems (e.g., a grassland, river basin); 2) resource units (quantity of water, wildlife in a grassland); 3) governance systems; and 4) users. Each core is made up of multiple variables (e.g., size of a resource system, mobility of a resource unit, level of governance (who's in charge? How are the laws made? How are they enforced?); and users (who are the stakeholders?). Each of these can, in turn, be further decomposed into deeper-level subsystems depending upon the problem. Note that social, economic and political settings and environmental/ecosystem factors are depicted as drivers and/or constraints in DF-SES. Interactions between the core subsystems and their outputs will play important roles as feedbacks that determine the rates, magnitudes and directions of responses.

For a specific SES problem, e.g., land degradation in IM, a unique version of the DF-SES model shown in Figure 16.9 would be created. This would be the starting point for a detailed qualitative and quantitative strategy for addressing this particular issue. Importantly, all the topics presented in NEE have a role in piecing together this unique DF-SES model. What are the key slow variables? What is the system-level question and what subsystems are needed to answer it? What are the key feedbacks? Are thresholds going to be important? With what are the strong H-E couplings that we must be concerned?

---

1 Ostrom (1933–2012). Indiana University's tribute page: http://elinorostrom.indiana.edu/.
2 Citations omitted.

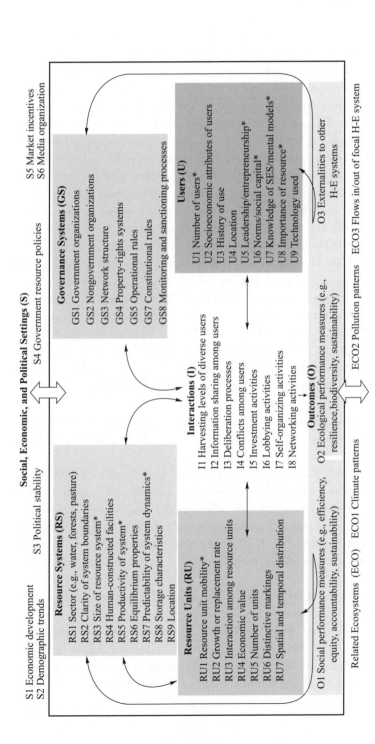

Fig. 16.10 Framework proposed by Elinor Ostrom for the study of complex social-ecological systems. Figure based on Ostrom. (2007, 2009).

* variables associated with self-organization.

16.3 Conclusions

Changes within DEA are remarkable in scope. The H and E subsystems and their interactions are constantly reorganizing and adapting (over time and in space), driven by both internal and external factors. This presents major social, political and environmental challenges to its residents (Chapter 1) and makes it critical that we train the next generation of students to effectively deal with such complexity. For decades the scientific community, especially in Western societies, have embraced and promoted the "balance of nature" paradigm (Wu and Loucks, 1995). In this view of nature, inputs are proportional to outputs, the whole is equal to the sum of the parts, and prediction is the product of careful planning. In this chapter we have presented key topics of a new ecology education course that can aid students in discovering for themselves that nature is not in balance! We are certain that future dynamics of DEA will not be forecasted from knowledge of the component parts examined in isolation.

We have found that students quickly embrace the idea that if policy and management decisions are based solely on linear rather than nonlinear thinking (Topic 2), the consequences can be disastrous. This is especially relevant for DEA where environmental problems are especially acute, and getting worse (Liu and Diamond, 2005). The list of H-E issues in DEA is lengthy, e.g., land degradation and desertification, air pollution, invasive species, biodiversity losses, depleted fisheries, toxic waste and water pollution, all of which are exacting serious economic losses, social conflicts and health costs (Liu and Diamond, 2005; Wang et al., 2007).

The challenge that all nations facing regarding both anthropogenic and natural H-E problems is nicely summarized by Holling et al. (1998; as quoted by Ostrom 2007):

"The answers are not simple...Characteristically, these problems tend to be systems problems, where aspects of behavior are complex and unpredictable and where causes, while at times simple (when finally understood), are always multiple. They are non-linear in nature, cross-scale in time and in space, and have an evolutionary character. This is true for both natural and social systems. In fact, they are one system, with critical feedbacks across temporal and spatial scales."

Putting the challenges of DEA (WS [DEA], Fig. 16.5) in a new ecology education context leads to the following observations:

- The scale of human activities in the WS [DEA] is historically unprecedented. The rapidly growing population, the constant introduction of new technologies, the extraordinary economic growth, and so forth clearly means that past experience is not a reliable guide to the future (Harte, 2002);

- The WS [DEA] is dominated by feedbacks, synergies, and tipping-points. Individual events or dynamical changes can exhibit a wide range of behaviors, including propagation, cumulative impacts, and synergistic interactions (just to name a few). These confound our intuition. Another basic tenet of systems thinking is that systems characteristically display counterintuitive behaviors (Meadows, 2008);

- Increasingly, we must rely upon models to tackle complex H-E problems (such as those outlined in this book for WS [DEA]). Oreskes et al (1994) argued that models are useful for guiding further studies but are not susceptible to proof per se. We agree but contend (Reynolds et al., 2001) that while we shouldn't take model predictions literally, we can take them seriously. This is especially true in terms of sensitivity analysis for exploring "what if" questions. This can help illuminate what aspects of a dynamical system are most in need of further study;

- The future state of the WS [DEA] is contingent on future, unknown human activity. As is the case in ESS, this seriously weakens our ability to test theory against phenomena not yet observed (Harte, 2002); and lastly,

- Historically, the disciplinary boundaries have been insular, which has impeded the study of coupled human-environment interactions. A major theme that has evolved over the past two decades is that environmental management and sustainability issues cannot be explained or solved by focusing on either the human or the natural (biophysical) elements of the system in isolation. Consequently, many of these barriers are being broken down and stimulating new interdisciplinary studies of H-E systems (Folke, 2006; Gunderson and Holling, 2002; Hussain and Doane, 1995; Lebel et al., 2006; Liu et al., 2007; Reynolds et al., 2007; Turner et al., 2007; Walker et al., 2006). The Drylands Development Paradigm and the Diagnostic Framework for Social-Ecological Systems are excellent examples of products of such collaborations.

The take-home message from NEE? Think critically, at multiple spatial and temporal scales, and from multiple perspectives.

Acknowledgements

Jiansheng Ye acknowledges support by the National Science Foundation of China, Grant #NSFC-31200373.

References

Abel, N., Cumming, D. H. M., and Anderies, J. M. (2006). Collapse and reorganization in social-ecological systems: questions, some ideas, and policy implications. *Ecology and Society*, 11, 17. http://www.ecologyandsociety.org/vol11/iss11/art17/.

Aguiar M. R., and Sala, O. E. (1999). Patch structure, dynamics and implications for the functioning of arid ecosystems. *Trends in Ecology and Evolution*, 14, 273–277.

Allen, T. F. H., Allen, P. C., and Wixon, D. L. (2009). Hierarchy theory in hydropedology. *Hydrology and Earth System Sciences Discussions*, 6, 2931–2959. http://www.hydrol-earth-syst-sci-discuss.net/2936/2931/2009/.

Anderies, J. M., Janssen, M. A., and Walker, B. H. (2002). Grazing management, resilience, and the dynamics of a fire-driven rangeland system. *Ecosystems*, 5, 23–44.

Ayarza, M., Huber-Sannwald, E., Herrick, J. E., Reynolds, J. F., García-Barrios, L., Welchez, L. A., et al. (2010). Changing human-ecological relationships and drivers using the Quesungual agroforestry system in western Honduras. *Renewable Agriculture and Food Systems*, 25, 219–227.

Ayensu, E., van R. Claasen, D., Collins, M., Dearing, A., Fresco, L., Gadgil, M., et al. (1999). International ecosystem assessment. *Science*, 286, 685–686.

Betts, F. (1992). How systems thinking applies to education. *Educational Leadership*, 50, 38–41.

Bonan, G. B. (2008). Forests and climate change: forcings, feedbacks, and the climate benefits of forests. *Science*, 320, 1444–1449.

Boyatzis, R. E., Stubbs, E. C., and Taylor S. N. (2002). Learning cognitive and emotional intelligence competencies through graduate management education. *Academy of Management Learning and Education*, 1, 150–162.

Bradford, M. A., and Reynolds, J. F. (2006). Scaling terrestrial biogeochemical processes: Contrasting intact and model experimental systems. In: Wu, J., Jones, B., Li, H., and Loucks, O. L. (Eds.). *Scaling and Uncertainty Analysis in Ecology: Methods and Applications*. Springer, Dordrecht, The Netherlands, 109–130.

Breshears, D. D., and Barnes, F. J. (1999). Interrelationships between plant functional types and soil moisture heterogeneity for semiarid landscapes within the grassland/forest continuum: A unified conceptual model. *Landscape Ecology*, 14, 465–478.

Bybee, R. W. (2003). Ecology education when no child is left behind. *Frontiers in Ecology and the Environment*, 1, 389–390.

Chapin, F. S., Rupp, T. S., Starfield, A. M., DeWilde, L. O., Zavaleta, E. S., Fresco, N., et al. (2003). Planning for resilience: Modeling change in human-fire interactions in the Alaskan boreal forest. *Frontiers in Ecology and the Environment*, 1, 255–261.

Checkland, P. B. (1999). *Systems Thinking, Systems Practice: Includes a 30-Year Retrospective*. John Wiley and Sons, Chichester.

Chuluun, T., Tserenchunt, B., Altanbagana, M., Davaanyam, S., and Stafford Smith, D. M. (2012). Dryland Development Paradigm application for the study of the Tuin and Baidrag River Basin social-ecological systems in Mongolia. *APN Science Bulletin*, 2, 49–54. Asia-Pacific Network for Global Change Research, http://www.apngcr.org/uploads/bulletin/ScienceBulletin_Issue42_March2012_web.pdf.

Costanza, R., d'Arge, R., de Groot, R., Farber, S., Grasso, M., Hannon, B., et al. (1997). The value of the world's ecosystem services and natural capital. *Nature*, 387, 253–260.

Cury, P. M., Shin, Y.-J., Planque, B., Durant, J. M., Fromentin, J.-M., Kramer-Schadt, S., et al. (2008). Ecosystem oceanography for global change in fisheries. *Trends in Ecology and Evolution*, 23, 338–346.

Dale M. (1970). Systems analysis and ecology. *Ecology*, 51, 2–16.

Dasgupta, P. (2004). *Human Well-Being and the Natural Environment*. Oxford University Press, Oxford, UK.

deYoung, B., Barange, M., Beaugrand, G., Harris, R., Perry, R. I., Scheffer, M., et al. (2008). Regime shifts in marine ecosystems: Detection, prediction and management. *Trends in Ecology and Evolution*, 23, 402–409.

Diamond, J. M. (1997). *Guns, Germs, and Steel: The Fates of Human Societies*. W.W. Norton, New York.

Fearnside, P. M. (2001). Soybean cultivation as a threat to the environment in Brazil. *Environmental Conservation*, 28, 23–38.

Fernández, R., Archer, E. R. M., Ash, A. J., Dowlatabadi, H., Hiernaux, P. H. Y., Reynolds, J. F., et al. (2002). Degradation and recovery in socio-ecological systems: a view from the household/farm level. In: Reynolds, J. F. and Stafford Smith, D. M. (Eds). *Global Desertification: Do Humans Cause Deserts?* Dahlem University Press, Berlin, 297–323.

Folke, C. (2006). Resilience: The emergence of a perspective for social-ecological systems analyses. *Global Environmental Change-Human and Policy Dimensions*, 16, 253–267.

Folke, C., Carpenter, S., Walker, B., Scheffer, M., Elmqvist, T., Gunderson, L., et al. (2004). Regime shifts, resilience, and biodiversity in ecosystem management. *Annual Review of Ecology Evolution and Systematics*, 35, 557–581.

Folke, C., Carpenter, S. R., Walker, B., Scheffer, M., Chapin, T., and Rockstrom, J. (2010). Resilience thinking: integrating resilience, adaptability and transformability. *Ecology and Society*, 15, 20. URL: http://www.ecologyandsociety.org/vol15/iss24/art20/.

Forrester, J. W. (2007). System dynamics—A personal view of the first fifty years. *System Dynamics Review*, 23, 345–358.

Giampietro, M. (1994). Using hierarchy theory to explore the concept of sustainable development. *Futures*, 26, 616–625.

Groffman, P. M., Baron, J. S., Blett, T., Gold, A. J., Goodman, I., Gunderson, L. H., et al. (2006). Ecological thresholds: The key to successful environmental management or an important concept with no practical application? *Ecosystems*, 9, 1–13.

Gunderson, L. H., and Holling, C. S. (2002). *Panarchy: Understanding Transformations in Human and Natural Systems*. Island Press, Washington, DC.

Harte, J. (1996). Feedbacks, thresholds and synergies in global change: Population as a dynamic factor. *Biodiversity and Conservation*, 5, 1069–1083.

Harte, J. (2002). Toward a synthesis of the Newtonian and Darwinian worldviews. *Physics Today*, 55, 29–34.

Hodges, H. F. (2011). Preparing new nurses with complexity science and problem-based learning. *Journal of Nursing Education*, 50, 7–13.

Holling, C., Berkes, F., and Folke, C. (1998). Science, sustainability and resource management. In: Berkes, F., and Folke, C. (Eds.). *Linking Social and Ecological Systems*. Cambridge Univ Press, Cambridge, UK, 342–362.

Holling, C. S. (1973). Resilience and stability of ecological systems. *Annual Review of Ecology and Systematics*, 4, 1–23.

Holling, C. S. (1987). Simplifying the complex: The paradigms of ecological function and structure. *European Journal of Operational Research*, 30, 139–146.

Huber-Sannwald, E., Maestre, F. T., Herrick, J. E., and Reynolds, J. F. (2006). Ecohydrological feedbacks and linkages associated with land degradation: A case study from Mexico. *Hydrological Processes*, 20, 3395–3411.

Hung, W. (2008). Enhancing systems-thinking skills with modelling. *British Journal of Educational Technology*, 39, 1099–1120.

Hussain, M. J., and Doane, D. L. (1995). Socioecological determinants of land degradation and rural poverty in Northeast Thailand. *Environmental Conservation*, 22, 44–50.

Jiang, H. (2002). Culture, ecology, and nature's changing balance: sandification on Mu Us Sand Land, Inner Mongolia, China. In: Reynolds, J. F., and Stafford Smith, D. M. (Eds.). *Global Desertification: Do Humans Cause Deserts?* Dahlem University Press, Berlin, 181–196.

Kennedy, A. D. (1995). Antarctic terrestrial ecosystem response to global environmental change. *Annual Review of Ecology and Systematics*, 26, 683–704.

Kinzig, A., Ryan, P., Etienne, M., Allison, H., Elmqvist, T., and Walker, B. H. (2006). Resilience and regime shifts: Assessing cascading effects. *Ecology and Society*, 20. URL: http://www.ecologyandsociety. org/vol11/iss11/art20/.

Kovach, L. D. (1960). Life can be so nonlinear. *American Scientist*, 48, 218–225.

Laurance, W. F., and Williamson, G. B. (2001). Positive feedbacks among forest fragmentation, drought, and climate change in the Amazon. *Conservation Biology*, 15, 1529–1535.

Lawton, J. H. (2001). Earth system science. *Science*, 292, 1965.

Laycock, W. A. (1991). Stable states and thresholds of range condition in North American rangelands: A viewpoint. *Journal of Range Management*, 44, 427–433.

Lebel, L., Anderies, J. M., Campbell, B., Folke, C., Hatfield-Dodds, S., Hughes, T. P., et al. (2006). Governance and the capacity to manage resilience in regional social-ecological systems. *Ecology and Society*, 11, 19. URL: http://www. ecologyandsociety.org/vol11/iss11/art19/.

Levin, S. A. (1998). Ecosystems and the biosphere as complex adaptive systems. *Ecosystems*, 1, 431–436.

Limburg, K. E., O'Neill, R. V., Costanza, R., and Farber, S. (2002). Complex systems and valuation. *Ecological Economics*, 41, 409–420.

Liu, J., Dietz, T., Carpenter, S. R., Alberti, M., Folke, C., Moran, E., et al. (2007). Complexity of coupled human and natural systems. *Science*, 317, 1513–1516.

Liu, J., and Yang, W. (2012). Water sustainability for China and beyond. *Science*, 337, 649–650.

Liu, J. G., and Diamond, J. (2005). China's environment in a globalizing world. *Nature*, 435, 1179–1186.

Liu, S., Costanza, R., Farber, S., and Troy, A. (2010). Valuing ecosystem services: Theory, practice, and the need for a transdisciplinary synthesis. *Ecological Economics Reviews*, 1185, 54–78.

Liu, S. A., and Costanza, R. (2010). Ecosystem services valuation in China. *Ecological Economics*, 69, 1387–1388.

Lynam, T., and Stafford Smith, D. M. (2004). Monitoring in a complex world—seeking slow variables, a scaled focus, and speedier learning. *African Journal of Range and Forage Science*, 21, 69–78.

Maestre, F. T., Reynolds, J. F., Huber-Sannwald, E., Herrick, J., and Stafford Smith, D. M. (2006). Understanding global desertification: Biophysical and socioeconomic dimensions of hydrology. In: D'Odorico, P. and Porporato, A. (Eds.). *Dryland Ecohydrology*. Kluwer Academic Publishers, Dordrecht, The Netherlands, 315–332.

Mäler, K.-G., Aniyar, S., and Jansson, Ä. (2008). Accounting for ecosystem services as a way to understand the requirements for sustainable development. *Proceedings of the National Academy of Sciences of the United States of America*, 105, 9501–9506.

Marais, L., Cloete, J., Matebesi, Z., Sigenu, K., and van Rooyen, D. (2010). Low-income housing policy in practice in arid and semi-arid South Africa. *Journal of Arid Environments*, 74, 1340–1344.

Maxwell, J. A. (2004). *Qualitative Research Design: An Interactive Approach* (2nd Ed). Sage Publications, Inc., Thousand Oaks, CA, USA.

Mazzocchi, F. (2006). Western science and traditional knowledge. *EMBO Reports*, 7, 463–466.

McCauley, D. J. (2006). Selling out on nature. *Nature*, 443, 27–28.

McDonald, T. (2007). Resilience thinking: Interview with Brian Walker. *Ecological Management and Restoration*, 8, 85–91.

McIntyre, S., MoIvor, J. G., and MacLeod, N.D. (2000). Principle for sustainable grazing in Eucalypt woodlands: landscape-scale indicators and the search for thresholds. In: Hal, P., Petrie, A., Moloney, D., and Sattler, P., (Eds). *Management for Sustainable Ecosystems*. Center for Conservation Biology, University of Queensland, Brisbane, 92–100.

McMichael, A. J. (2012). Insights from past millennia into climatic impacts on human health and survival. *Proceedings of the National Academy of Sciences of the United States of America*, 109, 4730–4737.

Meadows, D. H. (2008). *Thinking in Systems: A Primer*. Chelsea Green Publishing Company, White River Junction, VT.

Millennium Ecosystem Assessment. (2005a). Ecosystems and Human Well-Being: Current State and Trends. Findings of the Condition and Trends Working Group. Island Press, Washington DC.

Millennium Ecosystem Assessment. (2005b). Ecosystems and Human Well-being: Desertification Synthesis. World Resources Institute, Washington, DC.

O'Neill, R. V., DeAngelis, D. L., Waide, J. B., and Allen, T. F. H. (1986). *A Hierarchical Concept of Ecosystems*. Princeton University Press, Princeton.

Olsson, P., Folke, C., and Berkes, F. (2004). Adaptive comanagement for building resilience in social-ecological systems. *Environmental Management*, 34, 75–90.

Oreskes, N., Shrader-Frechette, K., and Belitz, K. (1994). Verification, validation, and confirmation of numerical models in the earth sciences. *Science*, 263, 641–646.

Ostrom, E. (2007). A diagnostic approach for going beyond panaceas. *Proceedings of the National Academy of Sciences*, 104, 15181–15187.

Ostrom, E. (2009). A general framework for analyzing sustainability of social-ecological systems. *Science*, 325, 419–422.

Ostrom, E., Janssen, M. A., and Anderies, J. M. (2007). Going beyond panaceas. *Proceedings of the National Academy of Sciences*, 104, 15176–15178.

Palmer, M. A., and Filoso, S. (2009). Restoration of ecosystem services for environmental markets. *Science*, 325, 575–576.

Paquet, J., and Belanger, L. (1997). Public acceptability thresholds of clearcutting to maintain visual quality of boreal balsam fir landscapes. *Forest Science*, 43, 46–55.

Pattanayak, S. K. (2004). Valuing watershed services: concepts and empirics from southeast Asia. *Agriculture Ecosystems and Environment*, 104, 171–184.

Pena, R. M. M., Huber-Sannwald, E., Moreno, J. T. A., Garbarino, M. C. C., and de Paz, F. P. (2012). Analysis of the sustainability concept in Mexican Legislation using the Drylands Development Paradigm. *Interciencia*, 37, 107–113.

Peterson, M. J., Hall, D. M., Feldpausch-Parker, A. M., and Peterson, T. R. (2010). Obscuring ecosystem function with application of the ecosystem services concept. *Conservation Biology*, 24, 113–119.

Potschin, M. B., and Haines-Young, R. H. (2011). Ecosystem services. *Progress in Physical Geography*, 35, 575–594.

Power, A. G. (2010). Ecosystem services and agriculture: Tradeoffs and synergies. *Philosophical Transactions of the Royal Society B: Biological Sciences*, 365, 2959–2971.

Rainbird, P. (2002). A message for our future? The Rapa Nui (Easter Island) ecodisaster and Pacific island environments. *World Archaeology*, 33, 436–451.

Reynolds, J. F., Bastin, G., Fernández, R. J., Garcia-Barrios, L., Grainger, A., Janssen, M. A., et al. (2009). Scientific concepts for an integrated analysis of desertification processes. In: Winslow, M., Sommer, S., Bigas, H., Martius, C., Vogt, J. R., Akhtar-Schuster, M., and Thomas, R. (Eds.). *Integrated Methods for Monitoring and Assessing Desertification/Land Degradation Processes and Drivers*. White Paper of Dryland Science for Development Consortium (DSD) Working Group 1 (Version 2) http://goo.gl/4zTIy. Prepared for UNCCD CST Scientific Conference 22 to 24 September 2009 Buenos Aires., Joint Research Centre, Ispra, Italy, 43–91.

Reynolds, J. F., Bugmann, H., and Pitelka, L. (2001). How much physiology is needed in forest gap models for simulating long-term vegetation response to global change? Limitations, potentials, and recommendations. *Climatic Change*, 51, 541–557.

Reynolds, J. F., Grainger, A., Stafford Smith, D. M., Bastin, G., Garcia-Barrios, L., Fernández, R.J., et al. (2011). Scientific concepts for an integrated analysis of desertification. *Land Degradation and Development*, 22, 166–183.

Reynolds, J. F., Hilbert, D. W., and Kemp, P. R. (1993). Scaling ecophysiology from the plant to the ecosystem: A conceptual framework. In: Ehleringer, J., and Field, C. (Eds.). *Scaling Processes Between Leaf and the Globe*. Academic Press, New York, 127–140.

Reynolds, J. F., Stafford Smith, D. M., Lambin, E. F., Turner, B. L., II, Mortimore, M., Batterbury, S. P. J., et al. (2007). Global desertification: Building a science for dryland development. *Science*, 316, 847–851.

Reynolds, M., and Holwell, S. (2010). Introducing systems approaches. In: Reynolds, M., and Holwell, S., (Eds.). *Systems Approaches to Managing Change: A Practical Guide*. The Open University. Published in Association with Springer-Verlag Limited, London, 1–23.

Rial, J. A., Pielke, R. A., Sr., Beniston, M., Claussen, M., Canadell, J., Cox, P., et al. (2004). Nonlinearities, feedbacks and critical thresholds within the Earth's climate system. *Climatic Change*, 65, 11–38.

Ribeiro Palacios, M., Huber-Sannwald, E., García Barrios, L., Peña de Paz, F., Carrera Hernández, J., and Galindo Mendoza, M. D. G. (2013). Landscape diversity in a rural territory: Emerging land use mosaics coupled to livelihood diversification. *Land Use Policy*, 30, 814–824.

Richman, B. (1993). Systems thinking: Critical thinking skills for the 1990s and beyond. *System Dynamics Review*, 9, 113–133.

Ronnback, P., Kautsky, N., Pihl, L., Troell, M., Soerqvist, T., and Wennhage, H. (2007). Ecosystem goods and services from Swedish coastal habitats: Identification, valuation, and implications of ecosystem shifts. *AMBIO*, 36, 534–544.

Rubin, D. M., Richards, C. L., Keene, P. A. C., Paiker, J. E., Gray, A. R. T., Herron, R. F. R., et al. (2012). System dynamics in medical education: A tool for life. *Advances in Health Sciences Education*, 17, 203–210.

Sandker, M., Campbell B., and Suwarno, A. (2008). What are participatory scoping models? *Ecology and Society*, 13, r2. http://www.ecologyandsociety.org/vol13/iss11/resp12/.

Scheffer, M., and Carpenter, S. R. (2003). Catastrophic regime shifts in ecosystems: linking theory to observation. *Trends in Ecology and Evolution*, 18, 648–656.

Scheidel, A., and Krausmann, F. (2011). Diet, trade and land use: a socio-ecological analysis of the transformation of the olive oil system. *Land Use Policy*, 28, 47–56.

Schellnhuber, H.-J. (1999). Earth system analysis and the second Copernican revolution. *Nature*, 402 (6761 Suppl S), C19–C23.

Senge, P. M. (1990). *The Fifth Discipline: The Art and Practice of the Learning Organization*. Doubleday, New York.

Siegert, F., Ruecker, G., Hinrichs, A., and Hoffmann, A. A. (2001). Increased damage from fires in logged forests during droughts caused by El Nino. *Science*, 6862, 437–440.

Simon, H. A. (1962). The architecture of complexity. *Proceedings of the American Philosophical Society*, 106, 467–482.

Simon H. A. (1973). The organization of complex systems. In: Pattee, H. H., (Ed.). *Hierarchy Theory: The Challenge of Complex Systems*. George Braziller, New York, 1–27.

Skourtos, M., Kontogianni, A., and Harrison, P. A. (2010). Reviewing the dynamics of economic values and preferences for ecosystem goods and services. *Biodiversity and Conservation*, 19, 2855–2872.

Spangenberg, J. H., and Settele, J. (2010). Precisely incorrect? Monetising the value of ecosystem services. *Ecological Complexity*, 7, 327–337.

Stafford Smith, D. M., Abel, N., Walker, B., and Chapin, F. S., III. (2009). Drylands: coping with uncertainty, thresholds, and changes in state. In: Chapin, F. S. III, Kofinas, G. P., and Folke, C. (Eds.). *Principles of Ecosystem Stewardship:*

Resilience-Based Natural Resource Management in a Changing World. Springer, New York, NY, 171–195.

Stafford Smith, D. M., McKeon, G. M., Watson, I. W., Henry, B. K., Stone, G. S., Hall, W. B., et al. (2007). Learning from episodes of degradation and recovery in variable Australian rangelands. *Proceedings of the National Academy of Sciences of the United States of America*, 104, 20690–20695.

Stafford Smith, D. M., and Reynolds, J. F. (2002). Desertification: A new paradigm for an old problem. In: Reynolds, J. F., and Stafford Smith, D. M. (Eds.). *Global Desertification: Do Humans Cause Deserts?* Dahlem Workshop Report 88, Dahlem University Press, Berlin, 403–424.

Stafford Smith, D. M., and Reynolds, J. F. (2003). The interactive role of human and environmental dimensions in the desertification debate. *Annals of Arid Zone*, 42, 255–270.

Stahel, A. W. (2005). Value from a complex dynamic system's perspective. *Ecological Economics*, 54, 370–381.

Sumber, D. (2002). As Mongolia shows, nomadic pastoralism and private land just don't mix. *The Economist*, December, http://www.economist.com/node/1487499.

Swetnam, T. W., and Lynch, A. M. (1993). Multicentury, regional-scale patterns of western spruce budworm outbreaks. *Ecological Monographs*, 63, 399–424.

Torn, M. S., and Harte, J. (1996). Methane consumption by montane soils: implications for positive and negative feedback with climatic change. *Biogeochemistry*, 32, 53–67.

Turner, B. L., II, Lambin, E. F., and Reenberg, A. (2007). Land change science special feature: the emergence of land change science for global environmental change and sustainability. *Proceedings of the National Academy of Sciences*, 104, 20666–20671.

van Nes, E. H., and Scheffer, M. (2007). Slow recovery from perturbations as a generic indicator of a nearby catastrophic shift. *American Naturalist*, 169, 738–747.

Vang Rasmussen, L., and Reenberg, A. (2012). Collapse and recovery in Sahelian agro-pastoral systems: rethinking trajectories of change. *Ecology and Society*, 17, 14. http://dx.doi.org/10.5751/ES-04614-170114.

Verstraete, M. M., Scholes, R. J., and Smith, M. S. (2009). Climate and desertification: Looking at an old problem through new lenses. *Frontiers in Ecology and the Environment*, doi:10.1890/080119.

Walker, B., Holling, C. S., Carpenter, S. R., and Kinzig, A. (2004). Resilience, adaptability and transformability in social-ecological systems. *Ecology and Society*, 9, 5. http://www.ecologyandsociety.org/ vol9/iss2/art5/.

Walker, B. H., Gunderson, L. H., Kinzig, A. P., Folke, C., Carpenter, S. R., and Schultz, L. (2006). A handful of heuristics and some propositions for understanding resilience in social-ecological systems. *Ecology and Society*, 11, 13. URL: http://www.ecologyandsociety.org/vol11/iss11/art13/.

Walker, B. H., and Meyers, J. A. (2004). Thresholds in ecological and social-ecological systems: a developing database. *Ecology and Society*, 9, 3. http://www. ecologyandsociety.org/vol9/iss2/art3.

Walker, B. H., and Salt, D. (2006). *Resilience Thinking: Sustaining Ecosystems and People in a Changing World.* Island Press, Washington, DC.

Wang, G., Innes, J., Lei, J., Dai, S., and Wu, S. (2007). China's forestry reforms.

Science, 318, 1556–1557.

With, K. A., and Crist, T. O. (1995). Critical thresholds in species' responses to landscape structure. *Ecology*, 76, 2446–2459.

Wu, J. G., and David, J. L. (2002). A spatially explicit hierarchical approach to modeling complex ecological systems: Theory and applications. *Ecological Modelling*, 153, 7–26.

Wu, J. G., and Loucks, O. L. (1995). From balance of nature to hierarchical patch dynamics: a paradigm shift in ecology. *Quarterly Review of Biology*, 70, 439–466.

Xue, Y. (2006). Interactions and feedbacks between climate and dryland vegetations. In: D'Odorico, P., and Porporato, A. (Eds.). *Dryland Ecohydrology*. Springer, Netherlands, 85–105.

Yang, X. H., Ci, L. J., and Zhang, X. S. (2008) Dryland characteristics and its optimized eco-productive paradigms for sustainable development in China. *Natural Resources Forum*, 32, 215–227.

Authors Information

Jiansheng Ye[1], James F. Reynolds[2,3,1*], Jeffrey E. Herrick[4,2], Julie A. Reynolds[3], Togtohyn Chuluun[5], Fengmin Li[1], Ruijun Long[6]

1. State Key Laboratory of Grassland and Agro-Ecosystems, Institute of Arid Agroecology, School of Life Sciences, Lanzhou University, Lanzhou 730000, P.R. China
2. Division of Environmental Science and Policy, Nicholas School of the Environment, Duke University, Durham, NC 27708–0328, USA
3. Department of Biology, Duke University, Durham, NC 27708–0338, USA
4. USDA-ARS, Jornada Experimental Range, MSC 3JER, Las Cruces, NM 88003–0003, USA
5. Dryland Sustainability Institute, Mongolia, P. O. Box 44/243, Partizan str. 31, Suhbaatar 5, Ulaanbaatar 14250, Mongolia
6. Engineering Research Centre for Arid Agriculture and Ecological Rehabilitation, Ministry of Education, Lanzhou University; Lanzhou 730000, P.R. China

* Corresponding author

Chapter 17

Grassland Degradation and Restoration in Inner Mongolia Autonomous Region of China from the 1950s to 2000s: Population, Policies and Profits

Liping Gao, Yaoqi Zhang, Guanghua Qiao, and Jiquan Chen

Summary: Grassland degradation is considered as both a local and global environmental problem as it affects not only hunters and herdsmen, whose livelihoods rely on healthy grasslands and wildlife, but also people who suffer from resultant hydrological disturbances, dust storms, and rising commodity prices. The increasing demand for both goods and ecosystem services from grasslands driven by increasing population, economic developments and urbanization have imposed threats but also provided opportunities for ecosystem restoration. This chapter uses Inner Mongolia Autonomous Region (IM) of China as an example to present the underlying forces for the grassland dynamics from three aspects—population, policies and profitability. Some policy implications and suggestions assisting the restoration of grasslands in IM are provided here.

17.1 Introduction

Grasslands play a unique role as they link agriculture, forestry, and environment and offer tangible solutions ranging from their contribution to food production, climate change mitigation, ecosystem health and resilience, biological diversity, and water cycles while serving as a basis of agricultural productivity and economic growth (Akiyama et al., 2007; Abberton, 2011). Grasslands are providing not only animal husbandry and biodiversity conservation, but also other kinds of benefits, for example, the non-agricultural amenities highly valued by rural society but not traded in markets. However, grassland degradation or the conversion of grasslands to croplands has adverse consequences for wildlife habitats and migration patterns, local water supplies, the amount of scenic lands, and local climate change (Conner et al., 2001; Wang et al., 2009).

Grassland degradation is serious in Northern China including Inner Mongolia Autonomous Region (IM) (Zhao et al., 2006; He et al., 2005; Ho and Azadi, 2010). Han et al. (2008) and Zhao et al. (2010) mentioned that grassland degradation is mainly caused by over-grazing and over-cultivation. Climate change exacerbates this problem (Han et al., 2008). Although the Chinese government has taken actions to address these severe problems through policy adjustments, restoration, poverty reduction projects, and other supports (Jiang, 2005), legislative protection is still not adequate to protect, restore, or develop grassland natural resources. Jiang (2006) believed that some effective measures taken for the sustainable management of grasslands have started to play a positive role in the restoration of grasslands in IM.

IM encompasses a core region of semi-arid climate but also includes areas with arid and semi-humid climates in the southwest and north, respectively. The semi-arid to arid areas in IM are expected to be most vulnerable to climate change (Ojima et al., 1998). The changes in temperature, precipitation and other related climate variables indicated that IM, as a region, has changed to a warmer and drier environment over the past 50 years, with the change rates being most significant during the last 30 years (Lu et al., 2009). Therefore, many researchers paid attention to grassland degradation and restoration from the perspective of environmental challenges such as water availability, variable precipitation, insect invasion, adequate pasture, and extreme winters or ecosystem (Jan and Frank, 1999; Su et al., 2005; Sternberg, 2008; Sandra et al., 2010; Wen et al., 2010).

Climate change is viewed as a potential factor for degradation. Grasslands and their ecosystems are sensitive to climate variation in IM (Xiao et al., 1995). In this context, the resulting meteorological changes and human activities are two main factors influencing grassland degradation and restoration (Li et al., 2000; Tian et al., 2011). The warming climate is also the main reason for the spread of pests and pathogens including the plague of locusts and the changing of the ecosystems of grasslands during recent years (Li et al., 2002; Chen and Gong, 2005; Bai et al., 2006). Decreasing precipitation in the long term for grasslands is observed to lead to grassland degradation (Li et al., 2002).

From Figure 17.1, we find that the temperature has increased in most regions of IM during the last fifty years; some areas increased about 2°C from the 1960s to 2000s and only a small part at the northeast decreased about 0.7°C during that time. However, precipitation has decreased in most regions with varying degrees; we see that most areas are classified as the range from −80 mm to −10 mm, indicating the dryer climate in IM during the last fifty years. The warmer

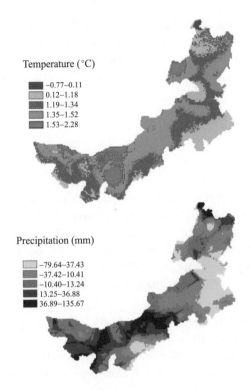

Temperature (°C)

■ -0.77-0.11
☐ 0.12-1.18
■ 1.19-1.34
■ 1.35-1.52
■ 1.53-2.28

Precipitation (mm)

☐ -79.64-37.43
■ -37.42-10.41
■ -10.40-13.24
■ 13.25-36.88
■ 36.89-135.67

Fig. 17.1 Change of precipitation and temperature between 1960s and 2000s in IM.
Data source: Tian et al. (2011).

and dryer climate exacerbates grassland degradation and is usually combined
with human activities such as over-grazing.

A number of ecological studies of grassland degradation in IM have been conducted (e.g., Li et al., 2000; Tong et al., 2004; Li et al., 2005; Su et al., 2005),
but investigations with adequate social-economic details are still scarce except
for some studies (e.g., Wang, 2004) that investigate the relationship between
grassland over-grazing and its impact on grassland degradation. In this chapter,
we will study the grassland management from the social and economic perspective. Some policy implications will also be explored and proposed to the local
or central governments and related agencies.

17.2 Population and Urbanization in IM

Human and livestock population growth are considered as the primary forces ex-
acerbating grassland resources (Meyer, 2006). The nomadic lifestyle and sparse

population in history keep the grassland in relatively good condition for thousands of years. The immigration from other regions brought in new technologies and the lifestyles had a significant impact on the environment. The population migration into the Mongolian Plateau was largely promoted by political and economic events and policies.

17.2.1 Population Evolution

During the 19th century, population pressure in the south led to a massive amount of Han Chinese farmers to migrate into the north in search of cultivation land. The migration was often promoted by government and military forces and particularly when natural disasters occurred (Sun, 2006) and the ecological migration was also enforced by the government (Ge, 2006; Wu, 2010). Since the foundation of the People's Republic of China in 1949, four distinct periods can be found in IM:

- 1949–1960: rapid population growth with the annual rate as high as 6.30% significantly contributed by migration from the south;
- 1960–1962: a large number of emigrants (1961 was the only year with negative population growth observed in the history of the region) due to the famine from natural disasters as well as policy failure;
- 1962–1973: fast population growth with an annual growth rate of 3.17% due to higher fertility as well as massive migrations of urban youth;
- From 1973: the speed of growth has been slowed due to family planning and more controlled migration.

The total population in IM had increased by about 257% from 5.6 million in 1947 to 20 million in 1985. The proportion of Han Chinese was increasing from 1947 to 1975, but decreasing from 1975 to 2005. Other minorities seem to have no change during this period. The change may be caused by a change in administrative territory. Some pastoral regions and agricultural and pastoral prefectures not previously in IM were included into IM in 1949, 1950, 1953, 1956, 1957, and 1979 by the central government. In contrast, a few prefectures in IM were relocated into the Heilongjiang, Jilin, Gansu, Liaoning provinces, and Ningxia Hui Autonomous Region in 1969. After the evolving population change of over one hundred years, Han Chinese constitutes a majority of the population, followed by the Mongolians (Table 17.1). The population is unevenly distributed, with most people concentrated in the agricultural belt south of the Daqing Mountain escarpment of the Mongolian Plateau and on the eastern slopes of the Da Hinggan Range.

Table 17.1 Ethnical population composition and change in Inner Mongolia (1,000 persons).

Year	Han	(%)	Mongolian	(%)	Other Minorities	(%)	Total
1947	4,696	83.6	83.2	14.8	89	1.6	5,617
1957	8,112	86.7	111.6	11.9	132	1.4	936
1965	11,294	87.1	144.5	11.1	225	1.7	12,964
1975	15,217	87.6	186.6	10.7	296	1.7	17,379
1985	16,862	83.6	274.7	13.6	550	2.7	20,159
1995	18,034	78.9	356.5	15.6	1,245	5.5	22,844
2005	18,538	77.7	412.7	17.3	1,199	5.0	23,864

Data sources: Inner Mongolia Statistic Yearbook (2010).

17.2.2 Population and Over-Grazing

There is a significant impact from population growth on grassland over-grazing. It is estimated that 1% increase of population will lead to a 0.88% increase of over-grazing of the grassland in IM (Wang, 2004). From 1947 to 2009, the total population rose from 8.5 million to 67.5 million—an increase of 694%; the agricultural population increased from about 4.27 million to 14.38 million. With the increasing population and economic growth, more livestock in pastoral areas are needed to meet the growing needs (Wei, 2006). The total number of livestock rose from 8.58 to 95.97 million from 1947 to 2009. Apparently, the livestock growth rate is much higher than the growth rate of population, leading to grassland degradation.

Figure 17.2 represents the overall population and livestock growth along the timeline. The fastest growth rate for both livestock and population is found from 1947 to 1965. Since then, the growth of livestock has been steady with a small fluctuation until the mid-1980s when economic reform began. Since the 1980s, the large fluctuation of livestock has been primarily caused by policies and market forces. Furthermore, after 2000, livestock increased sharply compared with the total and agricultural population growth.

Table 17.2 describes the decreasing grassland productivity associated with the pastoral population. Although the pastoral population has increased from 296,000 in the 1950s to 1.5 million in 2009, forage yield per hectare has decreased from 7.3 kg ha^{-1} in the 1950s to 1.3 kg ha^{-1} in 2009 and the total production of natural forage had decreased from 111.6 billion kg in the 1950s to 14.4 billion kg in 2009, leading to the storage of forage per capita decreasing from 377,000 kg to 9,600 kg. The increasing pastoral population and the decline of forage yield per

Table 17.2 Forage yield of natural pasture for pastoral population in IM.

Year	Forage yield per unit area (kg ha^{-1})	Total production of natural forage (10^9kg)	Pastoral population (10^3 person)	Storage of forage per capita (10^3kg)
1950s	7.3	111.6	296	377
1970s	4.2	63.6	969	65.6
1980s	2.9	40.9	1,838	22.3
1990s	2	28.9	1,912	15.1
2009	1.3	14.4	1,499	9.6

Reference: Modified from Meng and Qu (2011).

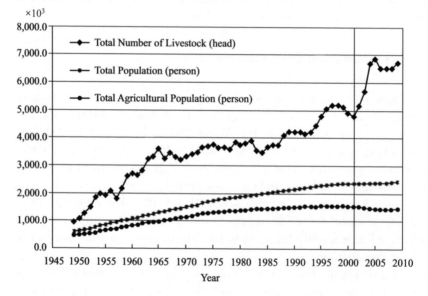

Fig. 17.2 Population and livestock in Inner Mongolia from 1947 to 2009.
Data source: Inner Mongolia Statistic Yearbook (2010) (data are taken at the end of year).

unit area and total production of natural forage suggest the increasing scarcity of the grassland resources and its productivity (Zhao et al., 2006).

17.2.3 Urbanization and Restoration

Urbanization is also considered an important factor influencing grassland. Increasing urban population suggests the rising living standard and demand for more resources and imposes pressure to the grassland. However, if more people move from the grassland, the land use pressure on the vulnerable desert steppe and desert might be released and ecological restoration would be accelerated. Although there are many problems and challenges, developed towns still provide herders and farmers with a great opportunity for an alternative livelihood from rural poor and release direct pressure on marginal land.

IM traditionally an agricultural and pastoral society, has become much more urbanized since the late 1990s, especially around the three major urban areas located in the center of the region such as Baotou, Hohhot, Jining, Chifeng, and Hailar (John et al., 2009). Currently, nearly half of the population in IM is classified as urban residents (see Fig. 17.2). Since the 1980s, urban residents keep the increasing trend, but the herdsmen and farmer population remains unchanged. Zhen et al. (2008) estimated that the urbanization level has increased from 26.4% in 1978 to 42.76% in 2000 and argued that the changes of the urbanization level are related to local economic development and that the urbanization level is sensitive to the growth of per capita GDP in IM.

IM is also well-known for its energy resources including coal, oil, natural gas, wind, and renewable energy. Urbanization is associated with a strong energy sector. IM has a proven coal reserve of 676.34 billion tons, ranking it first among all of the provinces in China. It also has a proven oil reserve of 700 million tons and a proven natural gas reserve of the Ordos Basin accounting for 40% of the nation's total reserve. More and more electricity has been delivered from IM to the eastern cities like Beijing and Shanghai (Li, 1999; Clark and Isherwood, 2010a). Since some related corresponding secondary and tertiary industry will be developed based on these natural resources, therefore more population will be attracted from pastoral or agricultural region to urban region as an effective measure to restore grassland.

The development of the energy industry plays a significant role in improving people's living standards and for energy requirements for the husbandry area (Li, 1999); however, some negative impacts have been observed such as degradation of environment and grassland that resulted from widespread mining sites (Chen et al., 2009; Clark and Isherwood, 2010a; Clark and Isherwood, 2010b; Borgford-Parnell, 2011). Overall, urbanization and economic development would have mixed impacts on the environment. The positive impacts should not be overlooked; for instance, the urbanization induced by ecological migration will contribute to grassland restoration. Some cities are able to support grassland restoration since significant revenue may be generated from energy or other industries like Erdos, Baotou, Huhehaote, etc.

17.3 Policy, Laws and Regulation for Grassland

In China, policy, laws and regulation, especially property rights, have influential effects on the changes of grassland and pastoralists' behaviors (Wen et al., 2007). The impacts have been investigated by many studies from various aspects, e.g., regional policies and local practices in specified areas of IM between 1949–1976 and 1976–present eras (e.g., Jiang, 2005), post-reform decentralization, "ecological construction" by government (Jiang, 2006), and grassland tenure (Banks, 2003).

The most important one is property right arrangement of the grassland. Prior to the foundation of the IM in 1947, tribe heads, religious leaders and landlords held the dominant positions for grassland in IM. There are several types of ownership or the usage rights of the grasslands; for example: 1) tribe heads-owned grasslands in the name of the tribe or nation, 2) herd owners owned the usage right of grasslands and pays something to the tribe or nation, and 3) temples and temple residents took charge of the usage rights of the grasslands. Very often, the grasslands controlled by all of the above three types owners could be rented with each other. We can see that the property rights were very much in mixed state-owned, common resources and some kind of open access. The impacts on grasslands must be assessed in the context of scarcity and with other institutions.

Since the establishment of the People's Republic of China in 1949, some dramatic changes in policies have taken place and the most important one was in property rights, which are usually divided into democratic reform, cooperative period, the People's Commune period, Cultural Revolution, and the economic reform and market economy period:

Democratic reform (1948–1954): In 1953, animal husbandry was proposed as the main economic activity in the pastoral areas, including Inner Mongolia Autonomous Region, Suiyuan, Qinghai Province, and Xinjiang Uygur Autonomous Region. The animal husbandry development was incorporated with policies to support poor herdsmen, to coordinate among industry, agriculture and animal husbandry, and to promote trade in pastoral areas. Some specific measures of developing animal husbandry such as improving the quality of livestock, preventing and curing animal diseases and protecting and restoring grasslands with reasonable division had been proposed. All of these policies and support had far-lasting impacts on the land use changes, population settlements, and the employment of grasslands.

Cooperative period (1954–1958): During this period, public ownership was established with the usage rights of grasslands controlled by local counties, townships and villages, and grasslands used by cross-counties with winter transition, adjusting the usage rights of fixed grasslands and implementing rotational grazing based on cooperation. However, various private ownerships of livestock still largely remained.

People's Commune period (1958–1965): By the end of 1958, IM had widely implemented the People's commune and more than two thousand cooperatives were reorganized into 152 communes with several types of transferring livestock into a collective commune. In 1962, the Central Government started to protect grasslands and prohibit grassland reclamation and emphasized animal husbandry as the key economy in semi-pastoral and pastoral areas.

Cultural Revolution (1966–1978): During the early-middle period (1966 to 1972), most administrative agencies at all levels were paralyzed and all of the existing national policies (such as the grassland protection policies made in the early 1960s) were not implemented. It was started again to promote the transformation of pastoral areas into agricultural areas. A large area of grasslands was reclaimed and agricultural land was expanded aggressively. By the later period of the Cultural Revolution (after 1972), some policies and institutions were rectified and the situation was improved greatly through a series of restoration policies in the pastoral area, which included polices for closed access to grasslands that were open-access to some degree. The real significant changes took place after the Cultural Revolution. Since the late 1970s, IM implemented a series of economic reforms and several important policies (see Table 17.3).

Table 17.3 Laws and regulations related to grasslands in IM.

Year	Policies and Programs
1984	Regulations on Grassland Management for IM
1991	Regulations on Grassland Management for IM (amended)
1998	Regulations on Basic Grassland Protection for IM
	Detailed rules on Grassland Management for IM
1999	Methods of the transfer of grassland's contractual rights for IM
2000	Provisional Regulation on the Balance between Grass and Livestock for IM
2002	Guidelines on Strengthening Grassland Protection and Construction
2004	Regulations on Grassland Management for IM (amended)

Apparently, the impacts of the policies in grassland are mixed. Some policies have promoted over-grazing, like the tragedy of the commons described by Hardin (1968), particularly in the People's Commune system and in the Cultural Revolution. Su et al. (2005) argued that the governmental policies, particularly the property right changes, promote over-grazing, which is one of the main causes of desertification in IM.

However, in recent years, rangeland restoration has become the main goal of governmental policies in IM. The most important policies include rewarding to balanced/reduced grazing, non-grazing, or alternative production subsidies. Education and training of pastoralists for livelihood transformation was also provided. Property rights reform is one of the most important institutional changes: 1) the property rights of the livestock first, then the grassland, from centralization ownership and management to decentralized management and privatization since the late 1970s and 2) grassland protection (regulation) and restoration policies since the late 1990s. Significant positive impacts have been observed on the protection and restoration of the ecological environment of grasslands, the changes of animal husbandry sustainable development, and the increment of pastoralists' income.

The impacts of the policies are apparent. The substantial increase in livestock in the late 1980s was largely a result of livestock and grassland tenure reform, while the drop in livestock around 2000 was caused by a grassland restoration policy enacted in 1998–1999. The substantial livestock increase since 2004 was likely caused by growing demand driven by fast economic growth and market reform.

17.4   From Production to Profits

Animal husbandry, tourism and environmental service are considered three main benefits provided by grasslands in IM. Herdsmen and farmers rely on grasslands for livelihoods directly or indirectly. With more restrictions on grazing, government and local residents begin to develop tourism in grasslands to improve their living standard level. Additionally, some environmental service is provided at the same time by the grassland.

17.4.1   Animal Husbandry

Animal husbandry is the economic foundation of IM. Grassland forage is considered as an intermediate good whose demand is derived from the demand of the final outputs, such as livestock. There are few estimates of the total forage consumed by livestock from grasslands. Researchers have typically relied upon estimates of livestock numbers to examine the trend in the use of grazed forages. Grazing animals fed with forages include mainly sheep, goats, cattle, and camels. The amount of livestock is limited by economic and grassland management policy (Yeung and Shen, 2004).

Figure 17.3 presents the total number of large animals. Sheep and goats have experienced a great increase from 1947 to 2009, with a particularly sharp increase from 34 million in 2001 to 61 million in 2006 for sheep and from 20 million to 29 million for goats. Only cattle, sheep and goats show a great increase with the same trend of the total number of all animals during this period and there are no significant changes for the others.

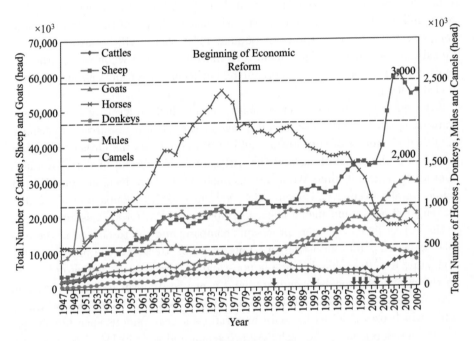

Fig. 17.3 Total number of livestock in the middle of the year in IM from 1947 to 2009. The bold arrows represent years of grassland laws and implementation from Table 17.3. Data Source: Inner Mongolia Statistic Yearbook (2010).

The amount of cattle has remained the same since 1947, which is largely due to grassland degradation, for there is not enough grass provided for cattle and comparative advantage, market demand, government restrictions, and so on (Qiao and Xue, 2011). The total number of large animals (donkeys, mules and camels) has remained at the same level from 1947 to 2009. There was a turning point in 1975 for the number of horses, which implies the transformation from a nomadic lifestyle to more settled lifestyle, resulting from economic growth, social development, environment change, and so on. IM has been a national cashmere-spinning base and its regional wool and milk products are very famous in China (Yeung and Shen, 2004).

Within the central planned economy, a significant amount of products were allocated to the growing demand nationwide. The growth and development of animal husbandry was guided by central planning with specific demands for the various products. The objectives of the planning economy are to maximize the productions to the social needs not only from local people but for the whole nation. There are many kinds of traditional foods including white foods, red foods, kumiss, tea, and flour in IM. Products made from the milk of cows, sheep, goats, camels, horses and mares are called white foods or milk foods. White is seen as a symbol of purity, luck and sublimity by Mongolians. They serve milk tea to guests to show their enthusiasm. People in the pasture seldom eat pork and mutton is the most popular meat there, which can be made as boiled mutton, roasted gigot, hand-torn mutton, roasted whole sheep, roasted mutton leg, roasted mutton chop, mutton barbecue, finger mutton, and instant-boiled mutton.

After entering into a market economy, the production levels are increasingly induced by the profits. Taking advantage of the natural resources, IM has established a number of corporations and products such as the Ords or Kingdeer brand of cashmere clothing and the Mengniu or Yili brand of dairy products that are famous in China. Wool and cashmere are two products in which IM has an advantage (Yeung and Shen, 2004; Nábrádi, 2007; Schönbach et al., 2009). Among 100 large- and medium-sized companies in IM, Ordos Cashmere, Ltd., is the largest listed cashmere processing company and the top brand in the textile clothes and furs industries of China in 2009. Recently, the new cashmere company, Kingdeer, has become famous and is named as a leading enterprise in the cashmere processing industry and a new state-level technical center in China. Yeung and Shen (2004) also mentioned that the Shiqi Business Suite, Ltd., which uses wool as its main material, is a very famous success example for the development of the cashmere processing industry in IM. Taking advantage of the quantity and quality of IM's livestock products, Inner Mongolia Yili, Mengniu Industry, Ltd., and Little Sheep Meat Co., Ltd., whose brands are well-known in the same industry in China (Yeung and Shen, 2004; Liu et al., 2011; Zhang et al., 2011; Yu et al., 2011).

17.4.2   Tourism Development

IM has the advantage in tourism development with rich natural resources and special and unique local culture. The beautiful and vast grasslands include the Xilamuren Grassland, Gegentala Grassland, and Huitengxile Grassland, which are all good places for a grassland experience. Mongolian ethnic culture and relics are the key tourist attractions in this region, which can be seen as benefits of environmental protection and restoration. The mushroom-like yurts, bright sky, fresh air, rolling grass, and the flocks and herds moving like white clouds on the remote grassland all contribute to make the scenery a very relaxing one. While visiting IM people can enjoy different activities such as Mongolian wrestling, horse and camel riding, rodeo competitions, archery, visiting traditional families, and enjoying the performances of Mongolian-style wrestling, horse racing and equestrian, and the beautiful Mongolian-style singing and dancing. The best time to visit the grassland is definitely during the traditional Mongolian Nadam Festival period when there is a better chance to both participate and feel the lively atmosphere of the grassland life.

Tourism in grasslands is a major part of the whole tertiary industry in IM since about seventy percent of its total area is covered by grassland. From Table 17.4, we can see that there are some grasslands that are really popular to tourists such as Huitengxile Grassland, Wulanbutong Grassland, Chilechuan Grassland, Gegentala Grassland, Xilamuren Grassland, and Bayinchanghuge Grassland,

Table 17.4 Basic conditions of the main grassland tourist attractions of IM in 2003.

Name of Tourist Grassland	Type	Rating	Location	TN
Huhenor Grassland	Meadow steppe	AA	Hulunbeir	26.9
Bayanhushuo Grassland	Meadow steppe	AA	Hulunbeir	11
Moergelehe Grassland	Meadow steppe	AA	Hulunbeir	13.4
Baiyinhada Grassland	Meadow steppe	–	Hulunbeir	–
Chalson Grassaland	Meadow steppe	AA	Hing'an League	25
Huitezhahanur Grassland	Meadow steppe	–	Tongliao	2.9
Huitengxile Grassland	Alpine meadow grassland	AA	Wulanchabu	560
Zhurihe Grassland	Steppe	AA	Tongliao	35
Bayantala Grassland	Steppe	–	Chifeng	2.9
Mastara Grassland	Steppe	AA	Chifeng	2.7
Gongger Grassland	Steppe	–	Chifeng	8.5
Wulanbutong Grassland	Steppe	–	Chifeng	130
Dalinuoer Grassland	Steppe	AAA	Chifeng	20
Jinlianchuan Grassland	Steppe	–	Xilin Gol League	26
Xiwuqi Nomadic Tribes	Steppe	AA	Xilin Gol League	33
Baiyinxile Grassland	Steppe	–	Xilin Gol League	34
Gongbaolige Grassaland	Steppe	–	Xilin Gol League	56
Dabuxiletu Grassland	Steppe	–	Xilin Gol League	5
Xiritala Grassland	Steppe	AA	Xilin Gol League	12
Gegenaobao Grassland	Steppe	AA	Xilin Gol League	9.8
Huitengxile Grassland	Steppe	–	Xilin Gol League	8.8
Honggeer Grassland	Steppe	–	Xilin Gol League	6.6
Chilechuan Grassland	Steppe	AAA	Hohhot	150
Saihantala Grassland	Desert steppe	A	Xilin Gol League	15
Xilamuren Grassland	Desert steppe	AAA	Baotou	180
Gegentala Grassland	Desert steppe	AAAA	Wulanchabu	210
Shanghaimiao Pature	Desert steppe	–	Ordos	16
Ordos Folk Culture Village	Desert steppe	–	Ordos	13
Bayinchanghuge Grassland	Desert steppe	AAAA	Ordos	130

Note: TN means total number of tourist received (thousands).
Reference: Liu (2010).

with different types and ratings, showing that there exists the potential development for grassland tourism in the near future. Tourism developed in IM will lead to more investment to the protection of grasslands for satisfying the needs of tourists at home and abroad.

17.4.3 Environmental Service

Grasslands provide not only animal husbandry or production inputs, but also other benefits such as environmental protection. The conservation of grasslands provides scenic viewing, recreation and tourism, erosion control, climate mitigation, and water and nutrient cycling. However, recently, with the degradation of grasslands, enormous pressure on natural resources rises and environmental quality is threatened. This has subsequently created pressure on the Chinese government to protect grasslands.

Increasing demand for environmental service may lead to the reform of grasslands, rural development, and environmental development (Hyberg and Pascoe, 1991). The concept of Payment for Environmental Services (PES) was introduced and accepted in China (Zheng and Zhang, 2006; Engel et al., 2008). The central and local governments make payment transfers to the main grasslands and poverty-stricken pastoral areas to coordinate the development and environment in the entire region and reduce poverty in some pastoral areas.

Several stages of compensation have been implemented. For example, pastoralists will get the compensation of 5 Yuan per mu (1 mu=1/15 ha) as the standard compensation if no grazing is conducted. The amount of compensation per person, per year is not less than 3,000 Yuan but does not exceed 5,000 Yuan, which will be implemented for a period of five years. Subsidies for fallow grazing will be provided, especially for good grasslands such as a meadow steppe or typical steppe. Pastoralists will get the subsidies of 0.5 Yuan per mu, per year and the amount of subsidy per person, per year is not less than 500 Yuan and does not exceed 1,000 Yuan. Recreation and tourism are also one aspect of the demand for environmental services. The beautiful grasslands and Mongolian ethnic culture and relics are key tourist attractions in this region, which can be seen as benefits of environmental protection.

17.5 Conclusions

The overall grassland degradation and restoration in IM is strongly related to the population change. Compared with the larger territory to the south, population pressure was historically low in the Mongolian Plateau. This is also due to the fact that the grassland carrying capacity under a given set of technologies determines its population density. The nomadic lifestyle reflects the impact of the carrying capacity as well as the adaptation strategy of the humans who live in this environment. Apart from the restricted food-providing capacity, other forces (e.g., natural disasters, wars, diseases) also often checked the population growth before it reached the carrying capacity in this region. The immigration from other regions brought in new technologies (farming) and lifestyles (such as permanent settlement) and significantly impacted the environment in the Mongolian Plateau. The population migration into the Mongolian Plateau was largely promoted by political and economic events and policies enforced by the governments.

Two periods in recent history have had significant impacts on the Mongolian grassland. The changes from subsistence herding and nomadic society to a planned economy from the 1950s to the 1980s in the first period and the market economy since the 1980s in the second period, without other supporting institutional arrangements, led to the deterioration of the grasslands.

In a subsistence herding society, the resources and the population check each other, keeping both the ecosystem and the population stable in the long term. In the planned economy, as implemented in IM since the 1950s, the role of the controlling humans and ecosystems on each other was broken. As witnessed in the general failure of planned economies, it is impossible to manage the ecosystems as well under this system. In a planned economy, there is no quick adaptation mechanism; while in the market economy, after the economic reforms, the objective is to maximize the livestock value if there is open access (like the 1980s in Mongolia), the grass value if there is open land (like the 1990s), or even the land value if there is private land (like in the 2000s). Such objectives would likely not be able to keep the ecosystems healthy, both in theory and in practice.

The failure of a planned economy and market economy to protect the grasslands does not suggest that we should return to the subsistence and nomadic society, which was sustainable but provided only a low level of well-being. The most important mechanism we need is to internalize the externalities of the environmental functions. The price of environmental services from the ecosystem will respond to the opportunity costs and benefits of the services. This is the most feasible way to provide the possibility of healthy coexisting dryland ecosystems and humans. Recent policies have been proposed and implemented to promote grassland restoration and economic development. The ecological compensation is fundamentally a market mechanism to develop the market between the grassland owners who provide the services and the benefit receivers in other regions. Some evidence suggests that grassland has been gradually restored to some extent during recent years.

Acknowledgements

Our study for this chapter has been partially supported by the LCLUC Program of NASA, the National Natural Science Foundation of China, the Chinese Academy of Sciences, and Henan University. We also thank two anonymous contributors of data, thoughtful discussion, and directions for our research.

References

Abberton, M., Conant, R., and Batello, C. (2011). Grassland carbon sequestration: Management, policy and economics. *Integrated Crop Management*, 11, 4–5.

Akiyama, T., and Kawamura, K. (2007). Grassland degradation in China: Methods of monitoring, management and restoration. *Japanese Society of Grassland Science*, 53, 1–17.

Bai, M. L., Hao, R. J., Di, R. Q., and Gao, J. G. (2006). Effects of climatic changes in eastern Inner Mongolia on ecoenvironmental evolution in last 54 years. *Meteorological Monthly*, 32, 31–36.

Banks, T. (2003). Property rights reform in rangeland China: Dilemmas on the road to the household ranch. *World Development*, 31, 2129–2142.

Borgford-Parnell, N. (2011). Synergies of scale: A vision of Mongolia and China's common energy future. *Energy Policy*, 39, 2764–2771.

Chen, S. H., and Gong, C. N. (2005). Features of climate change and its impacts on ecosystems of grassland in Inner Mongolia. *Chinese Journal of Agrometeorology*, 26, 246–249.

Chen, S., Chen, J., Lin, G., Zhang, W., Miao, H., Wei, L., Huang, J., and Han, X. (2009). Energy balance and partition in Inner Mongolia steppe ecosystems with different land use types. *Agricultural and Forest Meteorology*, 149, 1800–1809.

Clark, W. W., and Isherwood, W. (2010a). Inner Mongolia Autonomous Region (IMAR) energy base: Additional final report and recommendations. *Utilities Policy*, 18, 13–28.

Clark, W. W., and Isherwood, W. (2010b). Inner Mongolia must "leapfrog" the energy mistakes of the western developed nations. *Utilities Policy*, 18, 29–45.

Conner, R., Seidl, A., VanTassell, L., and Wilkins, N. (2001). US grasslands: Economic and biological Trends 30. Available at http://irnr.tamu.edu/pdf//grasslands_high.pdf.

Engel, S., Pagiola, S., and Wunder, S. (2008). Designing payments for environmental services in theory and practice: an overview of the issues. *Ecological Economics*, 65, 663–674.

Ge, G. G. W. (2006). Discussion on ecological migration policy in Inner Mongolia—taking Sunit Right Banner in Xilin Gol league for example. *Study and Exploration*, 3, 61–64.

Han, J., Zhang, Y., Wang, C., Bai, W., Wang, Y., Han, G., and Li, L. (2008). Range-land degradation and restoration management in China. *The Rangeland Journal*, 30, 233–239.

Hardin, G. (1968). The tragedy of the commons. *Science*, 162, 1243–1248.

He, C., Zhang, Q., Li, Y., Li, X., and Shi, P. (2005). Zoning grassland protection area using remote sensing and cellular automata modeling—A case study in Xilingol steppe grassland in Northern China. *Journal of Arid Environments*, 63, 814–826.

Ho, P., and Azadi, H. (2010). Rangeland degradation in North China: Perceptions of pastoralists. *Environmental Research*, 110, 302–307.

Hyberg, B., and Pascoe, S. (1991). Agriculture and environmental policy: Recent United States and Australian developments. *United States und Australian Developments*, 1, 114–123.

Jan, P. B., and Frank, B. (1999). Constraints in the restoration of ecological diversity in grassland and heathland communities. *Tree*, 14, 63–68.

Jiang, H. (2005). Grassland management and views of nature in China since 1949: Regional policies and local changes in Uxin Ju, Inner Mongolia. *Geoforum*, 36, 641–653.

Jiang, H. (2006). Decentralization, ecological construction, and the environment in post-reform China: Case study from Uxin Banner, Inner Mongolia. *World Development*, 34, 1907–1921.

John, R., Chen, J. Q., Lu, N., and Wilske, B. (2009). Land cover/land use change in semi-arid Inner Mongolia: 1992–2004. *Environmental Research Letters*, 4, 1–9.

Li, L. (1999). Renewable energy utilization in Inner Mongolia of China. *Renewable Energy*, 16, 1129–1132.

Li, F., Kang, L., Zhang, H., Zhao, L., Shirato, Y., and Taniyama, I. (2005). Changes in intensity of wind erosion at different stages of degradation development in grasslands of Inner Mongolia, China. *Journal of Arid Environments*, 62, 567–585.

Li, Q.F., Li, F.S., and Wu, L. (2002). A primary analysis on climatic change and grassland degradation in Inner Mongolia. *Agricultural Research in the Arid Areas*, 20, 98–102.

Li, S., Harazono, Y., Oikawa, T., Zhao, H., He, Z., and Chang, X. (2000). Grassland desertification by grazing and the resulting micrometeorological changes in Inner Mongolia. *Agricultural and Forest Meteorology*, 102, 125–137.

Liu, J. Q. (2010). The grassland ecotourism development in Inner Mongolia. *Journal of Arid Land Resources and Environment*, 24, 140–144.

Liu, G., Griffiths, M. W., Wu, P., Wang, H., Zhang, X., and Li, P. (2011). Enterococcus faecium LM-2, a multi-bacteriocinogenic strain naturally occurring in "Byaslag", a traditional cheese of Inner Mongolia in China. *Food Control*, 22, 283–289.

Lu, N., Wilske, B., Ni, J., John, R., and Chen, J. (2009). Climate change in Inner Mongolia from 1955 to 2005: Trends at regional, biome and local scales. *Environmental Research Letter*, 4, 1–6.

Meng, S., and Qu, F. (2011). Economic situation and development research of grassland husbandry in Inner Mongolia. http://nmgshkxy.nmgnews.com.cn/system/2011/04/21/010582887.shtml.

Meyer, N. (2006). Desertification and restoration of grasslands in Inner Mongolia. *Journal of Forestry*, 6, 328–331.

Nábrádi, A. (2007). The economic value of grassland products. *APSTRACT: Applied Studies in Agribusiness and Commerce*, 1, 1.

Ojima, D. S., Xiao, X., Chuluun, T., and Zhang, X. (1998). Asian grassland biogeochemistry: Factors affecting past and future dynamics of Asian grasslands. In: Galloway, J., and Melillo, J. M., (Eds.). *Asian Change in the Context of Global Climate Change*. Cambridge University Press, Cambridge, UK, 128–144.

Qiao, G., and Xue, Q. (2011). Understanding of several issues on the management system innovation in pastoral areas in Inner Mongolia. *Northern Economy*, 6, 34–36. (in Chinese)

Sandra, U., Li, F., Zhen, L., and Cao, X. (2010). Payments for grassland ecosystem services: A comparison of two examples in China and Germany. *Journal of Resources and Ecology*, 1, 319–330.

Schönbach, P., Wan, H., Schiborra, A., Gierus, M., Bai, Y., Müller, K., Glindemann, T., Wang, C., Susenbeth, A., and Taube, F. (2009). Short-term management and stocking rate effects of grazing sheep on herbage quality and productivity of Inner Mongolia steppe. *Crop and Pasture Science*, 60, 963–974.

Sternberg, T. (2008). Environmental challenges in Mongolia's dryland pastoral landscape. *Journal of Arid Environments*, 72, 1294–1304.

Su, Y., Li, Y., Cui, J., and Zhao, W. (2005). Influences of continuous grazing and livestock exclusion on soil properties in a degraded sandy grassland, Inner Mongolia, Northern China. *Catena*, 59, 267–278.

Sun, X. (2006). Analysis of pastoral population migration in Inner Mongolia. *Northern Economy*, 2, 23–26.

Tian, H., Melillo, J., Lu, C., Kicklighter, D., Liu, M., Ren, W., Xu, X., Chen, G., Zhang, C., Pan, S., Liu, J., and Running, S. (2011). Contribution of multiple global change factors to terrestrial carbon balance in China. *Global Biogeochemical Cycles*, 25, 1–16.

Tong, C., Wu, J., Yong, S., Yang, J., and Yong, W. (2004). A landscape-scale assessment of steppe degradation in the Xilin River Basin, Inner Mongolia, China. *Journal of Arid Environments*, 59, 133–149.

Wang, Y. (2004). A study on grassland degradation and sustainable development of pastoral livestock industry in Inner Mongolia (dissertation). Inner Mongolia Agricultural University.

Wang, Z., Song, K., Zhang, B., Liu, D., Ren, C., Luo, L., Yang, T., Huang, N., Hu, L., Yang, H., and Liu, Z. (2009). Shrinkage and fragmentation of grasslands in the West Songnen Plain, China. *Agriculture, Ecosystems and Environment*, 129, 315–324.

Wei, S. (2006). Study on effect and problem of implementing "Returning Grazing-Growing" project in Inner Mongolia (dissertation). Inner Mongolia Agriculture University.

Wen, J., Saleem, H. A., and Qian, Z. (2007). Property rights and grassland degradation: A study of the Xilingol pasture, Inner Mongolia, China. *Journal of Environmental Management*, 85, 461–470.

Wen, L., Dong, S., Zhu, L., Li, X., Shi, J., Wang, Y., and Ma, Y. (2010). The construction of grassland degradation index for alpine meadow in Qinghai-Tibetan plateau. *Procedia Environmental Sciences*, 2, 1966–1969.

Wu, R. T. T. G. (2010). *Research on Inner Mongolia ecological migration—taking valliage Orug, town Sanggen Dalai, Blue Banner (dissertation).* Inner Mongolia Normal University Press, China.

Xiao, X., Ojima, D. S., Parton, W. J., Chen, Z., and Chen, D. (1995). Sensitivity of Inner Mongolia grasslands to climate change. *Jounrnal of Biogeography*, 22, 643–648.

Yeung, Y., and Shen, J. (2004). *Developing China's west: A critical path to balanced national development.* The Chinese University Press, China.

Yu, J., Wang, W., Menghe, B. L. G., Jiri, M. T., Wang, H., Liu, W., Bao, Q., Lu, Q., Zhang, J., Wang, F., Xu, H., Sun, T., and Zhang, H. (2011). Diversity of lactic acid bacteria associated with traditional fermented dairy products in Mongolia. *Journal of Dairy Science*, 94, 3229–3241.

Zhang, J., Liu, W., Sun, Z., Bao, Q., Wang, F., Yu, J., Chen, W., and Zhang, H. (2011). Diversity of lactic acid bacteria and yeasts in traditional sourdoughs collected from western region in Inner Mongolia of China. *Food Control*, 22, 767–774.

Zhao, M., Han, G., and Mei, H. (2006). Situations of grasslands in Inner Mongolia. *Bulletin of the Faculty of Agriculture, Niigata University*, 58, 129–132.

Zhao, Y., Peth, S., Horn, R., Krümmelbein, J. L., Ketzer, B., Gao, Y., Doerner, J., Bernhofer, C., and Peng, X. (2010). Modeling grazing effects on coupled water and heat fluxes in Inner Mongolia grassland. *Soil and Tillage Research*, 109, 75–86.

Zhen, L., Yang, Y., and Liu, Y. (2008). Difference among the growth of GDP and urbanization of the provinces and the cities in West China since the reform and opening-up China population. *Resources and Environment*, 18, 19–26.

Zheng, H., and Zhang, L. (2006). Chinese practices of ecological compensation and payments for ecological and environmental services and its policies in River Basins. http://siteresources.worldbank.org/INTEAPREGTOPENVIRONMENT/Resources/ReportPESreviewChinesepracticeCAASFinalENFINAL.pdf.

Authors Information

Liping Gao[1], Yaoqi Zhang[1]*, Guanghua Qiao[2], Jiquan Chen[3,4]
1. School of Forestry & Wildlife Sciences, Auburn University, AL 36849-5418, USA
2. College of Economics and Management, Inner Mongolia Agricultural University, Huhhot 010019, P.R. China
3. Landscape Ecology and Ecosystem Science (LEES) Lab, Department of Environmental Sciences, University of Toledo, Toledo, OH 43606-3390, USA
4. Institute of Botany, Chinese Academy of Sciences, Beijing 100093, P.R. China
* Corresponding author

Chapter 18

Sustainable Governance of the Mongolian Grasslands: Comparing Ecological and Social-Institutional Changes in the Context of Climate Change in Mongolia and Inner Mongolia Autonomous Region, China

Jun Wang, Daniel G. Brown, and Arun Agrawal

Summary: As relatively intact terrestrial ecosystems, the Mongolian grasslands in Mongolia and the Inner Mongolia Autonomous Region (IM) of China play a significant role in sequestrating carbon dioxide, conserving biodiversity, and providing livelihood benefits to local herders. However, over the past 50 years, a number of processes have conspired to undermine grassland ecosystem services. This paper focuses on human dimensions of grassland degradation on the Mongolian Plateau since the early 1960s. Mongolia and IM share similar ecological gradients of climate, vegetation and soils, and have undergone significant social-institutional and ecological transformations: from collective to market economies, increasing market integration, and climate variations and change that affect vegetation productivity and human livelihoods. However, the two regions are different in their demographic, ethnic, cultural, economic, and political contexts. Moreover, their governments have different approaches to grassland management. These features of the two regions make comparative analysis interesting and causal inference meaningful for enhancing understanding of sustainable governance and social-ecological dynamics in grassland ecosystems. In this chapter, we first review the literature on models and frameworks for studying grassland dynamics, which were developed by ecologists and institutional analysts. Then, we adopt a hybrid state-market-community framework to analyze the dynamics of social-ecological systems in Mongolian grasslands over the past 50 years based on grassland, socioeconomic, and climate data. We end the chapter with a discussion of strategies for sustainable governance of the Mongolian grasslands in the contexts of climate change and increasing market integration.

18.1 Introduction

Grasslands occupy about 50% of the earth's terrestrial surface (and 38% of the Asian continent) and are generally characterized by single-stratum vegetation structures dominated by grasses and other herbaceous plants. They provide about 70% of the forage for domestic livestock globally (Brown et al., 2008). The Mongolian grasslands in Mongolia and Inner Mongolia Autonomous Region (IM), China constitute the dominant component of the Eurasian grasslands (Angerer et al., 2008). As relatively intact terrestrial ecosystems, they play a significant role in sequestrating carbon dioxide, conserving biodiversity, and providing the livelihood benefits to herders. For example, the Mongolian Plateau was estimated as a carbon sink of 0.03 Pg C yr^{-1} in the 1990s (Lu et al., 2009), compared with the intact tropical forests of 1.33 Pg C yr^{-1} in that period (Pan et al., 2011). The numbers of plant species in Mongolia and IM are roughly over 3,000 (MNET, 2009) and 2,100 (Xing, 2008). Grassland degradation involves the deterioration of social-ecological performances of these ecosystems, for example for livestock production, and is one of the major environmental problems worldwide. Recent studies show that grasslands in IM and Mongolia have degraded to varying degrees; the degradation status in IM is more serious than in Mongolia (Angerer et al., 2008; Jiang et al., 2006). Grassland degradation and rural poverty are twin problems; recent studies show that the major income sources for rural households in IM and Mongolia are still from livestock production (Olonbayar, 2010; Waldron et al., 2010). Herders in Mongolia rely more heavily on grasslands for their livelihoods than do the herders in IM; the livelihood strategies of herders are more diversified in IM (Zhen et al., 2010). Both Mongolia and IM have been transitioning from a centrally planned economy to a less regulated economy. As a corollary, herders have sought to increase their livelihood benefits by increasing livestock numbers, leading to over-stocking and grassland degradation in many parts of the region.

Scholars from multiple disciplines have contributed to a better understanding of the dynamics of social-ecological systems in the Mongolian grasslands. Increasing populations of humans and livestock, inefficient institutional arrangements for resource governance, distorted market incentives, reclamation of grasslands for grain production, urbanization, changing climate, and the increasing frequencies of climate hazards have all been identified as among the major drivers of grassland degradation (Angerer et al., 2008; Bijoor et al., 2006; Fernandez-Gimenez, 1997; Humphrey and Sneath, 1999; Jiang et al., 2006; Li et al, 2007; Neupert, 1999; Sneath, 1998; Zhang, 2007). However, most of the existing work tends to focus on one or two factors that cause grassland degradation and poverty, and provides solutions based on their identified factors. There has been little to no systematic analysis of how different factors and their interactions drive the dynamics of grassland social-ecological systems in the Central Asian region. However, the dramatic changes that the grasslands of IM and Mongolia have witnessed over the past half century necessitate a systematic investigation of the factors shaping grassland social and ecological dynamics to improve their understanding and sustainability.

In this chapter, we review the models and explanatory frameworks developed by grassland ecologists and institutional analysts and discuss the management and institutional strategies they offer. We bring together different types of evidence on changes of grassland quality and associated social-institutional processes in the context of climate change. We examine the available data in relation to different frameworks, and discuss an explanatory approach that considers state, market and community actors in relation to grassland dynamics and outcomes (Lemos and Agrawal, 2006). We discuss the feasible strategies for addressing grassland degradation, and societal adaptations to environmental change. We adopt an integrated and multiscale state-market-community framework for analyzing environmental problems associated with complex human and environment interactions. Linking historical social-institutional changes and dynamics of grassland productivity allows us to understand the dynamics of Mongolian grassland social-ecological systems over the past 50 years. Our integrated and multi-scalar approach considers as well the feedbacks and interactions between social, institutional, ecological and biophysical aspects of grassland systems, and leads to a more comprehensive consideration of alternative strategies to grassland management. Finally, we will draw conclusions about the dynamics and sustainability of grassland social-ecological systems on the Mongolian Plateau.

18.2   Explanatory Models of Grassland Dynamics

Broadly speaking, grassland ecologists have distinguished between two models of grassland dynamics: the equilibrium ecosystem model and the non-equilibrium ecosystem model. The equilibrium ecosystem model follows the Clementsian succession theory according to which natural vegetation in a given ecological site reaches a state of equilibrium over time, given climate and soil conditions (Zhang and Li, 2008). In equilibrium grazing systems, climate conditions are relatively constant with low interannual variability, enabling stable seasonal rhythms of vegetation growth across the years. In these zones, grazing intensity has a direct impact on grassland quality, and over-grazing leads to the deterioration of grassland quality. The preferred management recommendation is to stock grasslands at or below carrying capacity. This grazing model is still the dominant model used to make carrying capacity-based grassland management policies in China and Mongolia (Zhang, 2007; Olonbayar, 2010). The goal of these policies is to control the numbers of humans and livestock or ensure long-term exclusion of livestock grazing to allow grassland quality to recover and persist. However, this model has been criticized on the grounds that it ignores and at best simplifies spatial and temporal variability of precipitation and grassland productivity in grasslands. Because it does not take into account the extremely high levels of spatio-temporal variability characteristic of semiarid and arid ecological regions, prescriptions based on its assumptions, particularly those related to sedentarization of herders and animals, have also been viewed as faulty.

Over the past decades, a non-equilibrium approach to ecosystem functioning has been developed to explain grassland dynamics in the semiarid and arid regions. In non-equilibrium ecological landscapes, the high variability of climatic conditions is more important for the quality of grasslands than the livestock grazing intensity (Ellis and Swift, 1988; Oba et al., 2000). Predictions from non-equilibrium theories have been tested in the semi-arid and arid grassland regions of Mongolia and China and shown to better explain grassland dynamics (Fernandez-Gimenez, 1999; Ho, 2001; Zhang, 2007). In these regions, a simple carrying capacity value oversimplifies the dynamics of the environment. Livestock grazing needs to be organized according to variable precipitation patterns and forage availability, and these vary enormously across space and over years.

Another school of thought for governing grassland resources comes from neo-institutional economists, who focus on analyzing efficient institutional arrangements for sustainable use of natural resources. There are three main institutional frameworks for governing natural resources: privatization, state/public ownership, and community-based resource management. Traditionally, privatization and state control have been recognized as the two major solutions to solve problems of unsustainable harvesting of natural resources (Hardin, 1968). In the past decades, Ostrom and other institutional analysts have demonstrated self-organized collective action as an alternative approach to govern common pool natural resources (Agrawal, 2001; Ostrom, 1990; 2005; 2010). Because mobility is an essential characteristic of traditional herding strategies in semiarid and arid regions, cooperative use of grasslands by mobile herders can reduce the uncertainties caused by variations in precipitation and vegetation productivity in a given location, and reduce overall uncertainty (Agrawal 2001; Wilson and

Thompson, 1993). Studies have shown that large differences in levels of grassland degradation under a traditional, self-organized group property regime (i.e., Mongolia) versus national government management (i.e., China and Russia) on the Mongolian Plateau (Sneath, 1998; Humphrey and Sneath, 1999). Mongolia has allowed pastoralists to continue their traditional group-property institutions, which enable large-scale movements between seasonal pastures. China and Russia imposed agricultural collectives, which involve sedentarization and permanent settlements.

Besides pure state-, market-, or community-based governance strategies, Lemos and Agrawal (2006) proposed a governance framework that recognizes the importance of hybrid arrangements for sustainable environmental governance. Such hybrid arrangements connect the state, market, and local communities. The Lemos and Agrawal framework is particularly useful for dealing with the complex and multiscale environmental problems such as climate change and ecosystem degradation. State, community, and market actors have different strengths, and can play different roles in resource management in terms of institution building and implementation, collective action, and market incentives. Co-management links the state and local communities. Public-private partnerships link the state and markets, and private-social partnerships link markets and communities. For the dynamics of social-ecological systems in the Mongolian grasslands over the past 50 years, the national governments of Mongolia and China, local grazing communities, and local and international markets all have played significant roles. However, the importance of their roles has changed over time.

18.3   Analyses and Results

About 66% of the land in IM (0.78 million km^2) is classified as grasslands, a quarter of all Chinese grasslands (Zhang, 1992). Nearly 84% of the total territory in Mongolia (1.26 million km^2) is covered by grasslands (Angerer et al., 2008). Mongolia and IM share the similar ecological gradient of vegetation, which varies from forests to forest/meadow steppe, typical steppe, desert steppe, and desert (Fig. 18.1). Recent studies from China and Mongolia show that 90% of the total grasslands in IM and 78% of the grasslands in Mongolia have degraded to varying degrees (Erdenetuya, 2006; Ministry of Agriculture, China, 2007). Several large-scale field ecological surveys were conducted to assess grassland quality, measured by dry biomass, over the last 50 years (1961–2010). These field grassland surveys were based mainly on large geographic-scale field samplings, but the latter two times in IM were assisted by geospatial technologies. The overall grassland productivity in IM is higher than in Mongolia (Fig. 18.2). This

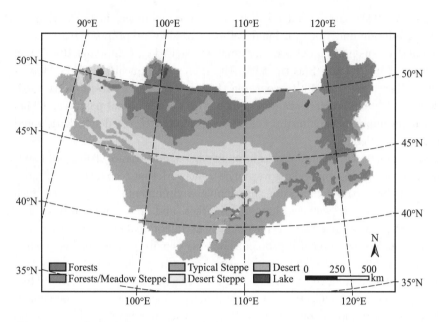

Fig. 18.1 Spatial distributions of the major vegetation types on the Mongolian Plateau.

Source: vegetation maps of IM and Mongolia were respectively provided by the Institute of Botany, China, and the Institute of Botany, Mongolia. They were made respectively in the 1990s and 1980s. The original scale of the two vegetation maps is 1:1,000,000.

is mainly caused by the climate constraints. IM is with warmer temperature and has more annual precipitation than Mongolia. In period 2 (1980–1985), the average grassland biomass in IM and Mongolia decreased to 57.1% and 75.9% of the value in period 1 (1961–1971), respectively (Fig. 18.2). By period 3, the average grassland biomass in the two regions decreased to 44.8% and 57.7% of period 1, respectively. The results of the most recent survey in IM show that the average grassland biomass increased slightly to 48.1% of period 1. The average biomass productivity still decreased in the last period in Mongolia. In addition, the ecological survey results of Mongolia also show that the average number of grass species per hectare decreased by periods 2 (24) and 3 (18) to 84.6% and 62.3% of period 1 (31), respectively (Olonbayar, 2010).

By the early 1960s, both IM and Mongolia had completed a dramatic social transformation from the traditional "communal" ownership into collective economies, begun in the late 1950s and early 1960s. They both experienced privatization in the middle and late 1980s, respectively. In IM after 2000, the Chinese national government has been making and implementing a range of policies to restore grassland quality. These policies are known as "Grain to Green" poli-

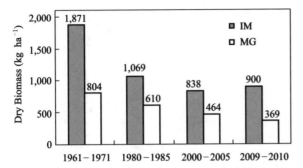

Fig. 18.2 Changes of the average grassland biomass of IM and Mongolia over the past 50 years.

Source: the biomass data of IM was provided by the Inner Mongolian Institute of Grassland Survey and Design (IMIGSD, 2011), the biomass data of Mongolia for the first three time periods was reconstructed from Olonbayar, 2010, and the biomass data for the last period of Mongolia was acquired from the Institute of Botany, Mongolia.

cies (Liu et al., 2008). Given these broad social-institutional changes, we divided the period into three sub-periods: collectivization (1961–1985), privatization (1986–2000), and recentralization (2000–present) periods. The recentralization period applies only to IM, China. Parallel with these economic changes, social-institutional changes have influenced the social organizations, culture, land-use behaviors of herders, and populations of human and livestock, which have consequently affected grassland quality and the livelihoods of herders in the two regions.

18.3.1 Collectivization of Pastures and Livestock

In the 1950s, pastures and livestock in IM and Mongolia were collectivized by a policy called "state purchase." Herders were responsible for selling livestock products to the state at below-market prices based on planned, rather than actual, numbers of livestock (Fernandez-Gimenez, 1997). In the early 1960s, all herders in IM and Mongolia were members of grazing collectives, and most of the livestock and pastures were collectively owned by the local grazing communities. Under the collective institutional arrangements, herders had little incentive to manage livestock well or increase livestock numbers. The total numbers of livestock and the herd compositions by livestock species in Mongolia (1961–1990) and IM (1961–1985) were fairly stable in the collective period (Fig. 18.3). In Mongolia, collectives, called *negdel*, played a central role in allocating pastures and campsites and directing seasonal movements that often respected pre-existing customary rights and were regulated and tightly controlled by *sums* (i.e., counties) and *Aimags* (i.e., provinces). Pastoral land-use practices

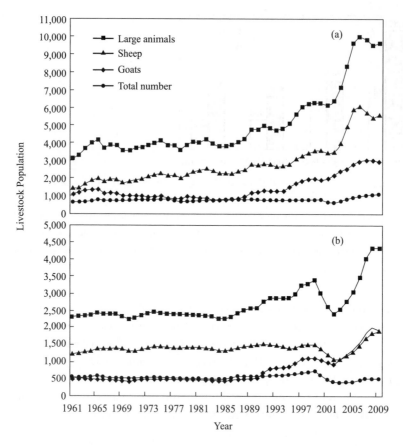

Fig. 18.3 Changes of livestock numbers in IM, China, (a) and Mongolia (b) (1961–2009) (Unit: 10,000).

Source: Annual census books of IM, China, and Mongolia (ACBIM, 2005, 2010; ACBM, 1990, 2010).

remained mobile and herding families were generally supported by deliveries of hay, and thus had little impact on grassland quality (Ojima and Chuluun, 2008). The collectives also engaged in veterinary services, producing livestock products, preventing livestock loss from natural hazards, and improving pasture quality through the development of water points at strategic locations. However, in this period, the overall herding radius decreased and herders were confined to smaller areas, thereby limiting access across broad ecological zones and reducing access to diverse forage resources used traditionally. Moreover, through the building of water facilities, winter shelters, and *sum* centers and the investments in "scientific" management of livestock, the nomadic pastoral economy was transforming into a sedentary and intensive one (Fernandez-Gimenez, 1997). In Mongolia, the conversion of grasslands for grain production started in the year 1959 and

1.34 million hectares of grasslands were converted to cropland prior to the early 1990s (Olonbayar, 2010). Although some grazing activities were sedentarized and some grassland was converted into cropland, the overall grassland quality in Mongolia did not degrade rapidly in the collective period (Fig. 18.2).

In IM, grazing collectives called production teams can migrate within their village boundaries seasonally and to other villages (or *sums*) in the years with natural disasters. Similar to Mongolia, grazing collectives were responsible for managing pastures and livestock production. In the collective period, human population in IM increased rapidly from around 12 million to 20 million (Fig. 18.4). The increased population was mainly from the migration of Han people from other provinces. The negative consequences of the "Great Leap Forward" (1957–1959) and the consecutive large-scale natural disasters (1960–1961) caused the "Great Famine" in the most of China. Population migration in this period was partially driven by the national policy for solving the starvation problem in China. Fertile grasslands were reclaimed for food production (Jiang, 2005). The "Grain First" policy implemented in the "Cultural Revolution" period (1966–1976) also caused large areas of grasslands to be converted to

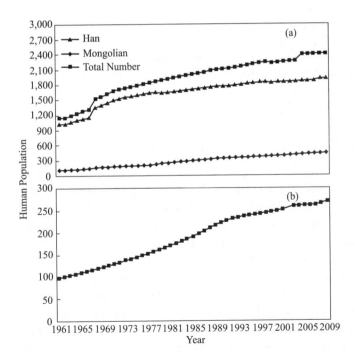

Fig. 18.4 Demographic changes in IM, China, (a) and Mongolia (b) (1961–2009) (Unit: 10,000).

Source: Annual census books of IM, China, and Mongolia (ACBIM, 2005, 2010; ACBM, 1990, 2010).

cropland (Jiang, 2005; Zhang, 2007). During the period 1949–1985, 9.2 million hectares of fertile grasslands were used for grain production, mainly corn and potatoes (Table 18.1). Conversion from grassland to cropland can easily destroy the thin surface soil layers and destabilizes underlying sandy layers. This can consequently cause desertification, leading to cropland abandonment in a few years. Some of the new migrants worked on grain production, and others migrated into pastoral areas to compete for pasture resources with local herders. Moreover, many coal and metal mining sites were built in IM in this period (Neupert, 1999). Due to the loss of fertile grasslands, overstocking and other intensive grassland-use behaviors (e.g., mining and collection of traditional herbal medicines), the average grassland biomass decreased rapidly from 1,871 kg ha^{-1} to 1,069 kg ha^{-1}, roughly in the corresponding period (Fig. 18.2).

Table 18.1 Amounts of grassland area reclaimed in IM, China (1949–2005) (Unit: 1,000,000 ha).

Period	Grain Production	Fodder Production	Other Uses
1949–1985	9.20	0.00	0.00
1985–2000	6.30	1.40	1.40
2000–2005	0.00	5.60	0.00
Total Area	15.50	7.00	1.40

Source: Inner Mongolian Institute of Grassland Survey and Design (IMIGSD, 2008).

18.3.2 Privatization and Market Incentives

In the middle of the 1980s, the Household Production Responsibility System (HPRS), also called the Double-Contract System, was introduced from the agricultural region of China to the pasture areas of IM. Livestock production was first contracted to herder households by local governments (1984–1988). Then, pastures were allocated to individual households (1989–1995). At the same time, China started its transition from the central planned economy to market economy. In Mongolia, the free-market reforms began with the first democratic elections in 1990. Privatization and market incentives stimulated herders to increase their livestock numbers in order to gain more benefits from livestock production. Sharp increases in all prices of livestock products in Mongolia during the latter half of the 2000s have similar trends with the increases of livestock numbers. The similar increasing trends between livestock numbers and the prices of livestock products are also seen in IM (Fig. 18.5). Compared with Mongolia, livestock production in IM is more connected to local and international markets, since

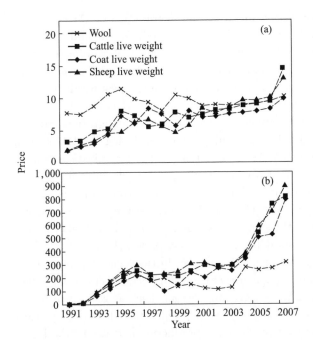

Fig. 18.5   Changes of the prices of livestock products in (a) IM (Unit: 1,000 Yuan/Tonne) and (b) Mongolia (Unit: 1,000 MNT/Tonne) (1991–2007). The historical prices from the Food and Agriculture Organization (FAO) were adjusted to constant 1991 currency.

Source: FAO price statistics database (FAO, 2011).

market economy is more developed in China than in Mongolia. Since the late 1980s and the early 1990s, the total number of livestock in IM and Mongolia increased rapidly (Fig. 18.3). For example, in 1990, Mongolia had 25.9 million domesticated animals. In 1998, this had grown to 32.9 million, an increase of 27%. Other studies also show that the high price of cashmere in international markets triggered the rapid growth of goats (Ojima and Chuluun, 2008). The species composition also changed since the early 1990s, and the number of goats increased more rapidly than other species in both IM and Mongolia (Fig. 18.3).

In IM, with pastures contracted to individual herder households, herders could not migrate over large areas after privatization. In this period, pastoralists were sedentarized, and migratory grazing was converted to year-round grazing on small pieces of contracted pastures. The leasing term of the contracted pastures was 30 years, and herders did not have the full ownership of the pastures, decreasing incentives to protect pastures (Humphrey and Sneath, 1999; Li et al., 2007). Contracting pastures to individual households destroyed the intact grassland ecosystems and traditional customs for pasture use, and conflicts over pasture use increased (Williams, 2002). The implementation of the HPRS has been recognized as a major reason for grassland degradation in IM (Li et al., 2007; Li and Huntsinger, 2011; Sneath, 1998; Zhang, 2007; Zhang and Li, 2008). Increased stocking rates and year-round grazing adversely affects pasture vegetation growth and regeneration and leads to deterioration of grasslands. In addition, the privatization period saw large areas of fertile pastures in IM converted for producing grain (6.3 million ha) and fodder (1.4 million ha) (Table 18.1). Human population also continued increasing due to immigration and natural growth (Fig. 18.4) and herd sizes steadily increased during the 1990s along with prices of livestock products. As more mining and other industries continued to compete with local herders for land the grasslands available for grazing decreased and grazing intensity increased. Fencing on contracted lands exacerbated the problem of reduced pasture area. The increases in grazing intensity likely explain the decreases in the average grassland biomass from 1,069 kg ha^{-1} to 838 kg ha^{-1}, roughly corresponding to this study period (Fig. 18.2).

In Mongolia, due to the lack of efficient resource institutions to govern grassland use, most grasslands became open-access resources. Levels of conflict over grassland use increased. Traditional grazing customs such as reciprocal use of grasslands in natural disaster years declined (Upton, 2009). Livestock privatization had a tremendous impact on livestock production and the marketing of livestock products. Herders became livestock owners and simultaneously lost the support of collectives (i.e., mainly the transportation support for seasonal and interannual migrations). Poor families who could not afford long-distance migrations migrated less frequently or became sedentary grazers around water points or fertile pastures. The numbers of water facilities and pasture reserves also decreased (Olonbayar, 2010). Data from the census books of Mongolia show that the area of cropland decreased 24.3% from 1995 to 2009 (ACBM, 2005, 2010). Cropland abandonment made lands prone to wind erosion. Roughly corresponding to this period, the average grassland biomass decreased from 610 kg ha^{-1} to 464 kg ha^{-1} (Fig. 18.2).

18.3.3 Recentralization of Grassland Management in IM, China

Since the year 2000, grassland management in IM, China, was recentralized to the national government. Therefore, we call this study period the "Recentralization Period." The national government has implemented several projects for ecological restoration and conservation in the pasture areas of IM, such as "Converting Pastures to Grasslands" and "Ecological Restoration of the Sandstorm Sources of Beijing-Tianjin-Tangshan." Most of the counties in IM are involved in these two projects. Under these policies, herders are subsidized in the forms of grain and money for grazing bans (i.e., all year round), grazing restrictions (i.e., on a seasonal basis), rotational grazing, migration out of pastures, pen-feeding livestock, and importing high value-added livestock. Due to grazing restrictions, pen-feeding of livestock has become popular in IM. This is one of the major reasons for the abrupt increase in total livestock numbers in IM after 2002 (Fig. 18.3). In 2011, the national government of China started a new ecological compensation and restoration project. Eight grassland provinces and autonomous regions, including IM, are involved in the project. This policy is based on the equilibrium ecosystem model of grassland dynamics and emphasizes reducing grazing intensity to keep the balance between grassland capacity and stocking rates. The social-ecological outcomes of the new policy are still to be assessed.

In the recentralization period, local herders in IM have been marginalized in the policy making and implementation processes, and many of the same problems associated with collectivization have become evident. Conflicts exist between market-oriented behaviors of local herders and the grassland conservation and restoration goals of the national government. For example, violations to policies of grazing restrictions and bans commonly exist in IM (Bijoor et al., 2006). High monitoring and implementation costs make these policies difficult to implement. Moreover, these polices have ignored the diversity of grassland ecosystems across ecological gradients. Additionally, due to pen-feeding, 5.6 million ha of grasslands were reclaimed for fodder production during 2000–2005 (Table 18.1). Recent studies show that the overall grassland degradation status did not get changed, although in some local areas, grassland quality has improved (Ministry of Agriculture, China, 2007).

18.3.4   Changing Roles of the State, Market and Community for Grassland Management

In the three study periods, state, market and community actors played significant roles in influencing grassland-use behaviors of herders, and their roles also changed over time. In the collective periods of Mongolia and IM, there was little market influence on grassland management and livestock production. The state and local grazing communities governed grassland resources and managed livestock production. After privatization, both Mongolia and IM have transformed from central planned economies towards free market economies. Livestock production by herders has become linked to fluctuations in global and local market demands. The roles of the state and local grazing communities have been deemphasized, especially in Mongolia. Traditional grazing customs have also not played a role in coordinating livestock grazing. In the recentralization period in China, grassland management was recentralized to the national government.

Though grassland-use behaviors of herders are still market-oriented, they are restricted by the new rules created by the state. Local communities no longer play important roles in governing grassland resources in the recentralization period.

18.3.5 Climate Variability and Change: History and Future

Over the past 50 years, the overall climate in IM and Mongolia became warmer and drier (Fig. 18.6). The increasing trends of annual mean temperature were significant in both IM and Mongolia ($r^2_{\text{IM}} = 0.57$, $p_{\text{IM}} < 0.01$; $r^2_{\text{Mongolia}} = 0.48$, $p_{\text{Mongolia}} < 0.01$). However, the decreasing trends of annual total precipitation were not significant in both IM and Mongolia ($r^2_{\text{IM}} = 0.02$, $p_{\text{IM}} = 0.37$; $r^2_{\text{Mongolia}} = 0.07$, $p_{\text{Mongolia}} = 0.05$). Other studies also showed that annual mean temperature increased about 2.1°C in Mongolia and about 2°C in IM; annual precipitation decreased about 7.0% in Mongolia (NCRM, 2009) and about 6.6% in IM (Ding and Chen, 2008). Drought increased significantly in Mongolia in the last 60 years, particularly in the last decade (NCRM, 2009). The worst droughts and Dzuds (i.e., heavy winter snowstorms) that Mongolia experienced recently were in the consecutive summers and winters of 1999, 2000, 2001 and 2002, which affected 50%–70% of the total territory. The substantial decline of livestock numbers between 1999 and 2002 (Fig. 18.3) was mainly caused by droughts and winter snowstorms in these years. About 35% (12 million) of the total number of livestock perished in the period. Recent studies show that in Mongolia, grassland productivity in areas in which grazing is not allowed has also decreased by 20%–30% in the past 40 years (Angerer et al., 2008). By statistical analyses of the climate data collected at national standard stations of Mongolia and IM over the past 50 years, we found that the interannual variability of precipitation in the growing season (i.e., from April to September) of most stations are over 0.35 (i.e., the coefficient of variance). Therefore, most parts of the Mongolian Plateau can be classified as non-equilibrium grassland ecosystems.

Future climate scenarios show that in the next 30 years, annual mean temperature will increase 0.4–1.6°C, especially in summer and autumn (0.8–1.6°C), and there is no apparent increase of annual precipitation on most parts of the Mongolian Plateau (Tang et al., 2008). IPCC AR4-A1B future climate scenarios of the Mongolia Plateau (mean projections of 21 models, Christensen et al., 2007) show that comparing the end of this century (2080–2099) with the end of last century (1980–1999), the average winter temperature will increase 3–5°C; the average summer temperature will increase 2.5–4°C; the average winter precipitation will increase 5%–30%; the average summer precipitation in most areas will increase 5%–15%, except in some western parts. Livelihoods of herders on the Mongolian Plateau will be more vulnerable to future adverse climate conditions.

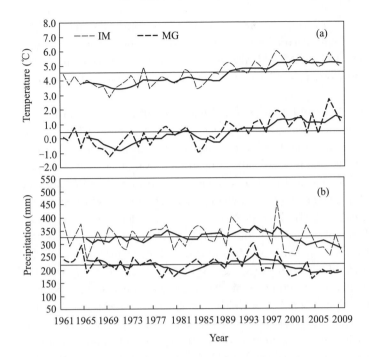

Fig. 18.6 The temporal variability of (a) annual mean temperature (Unit: °C) and (b) annual precipitation (Unit: mm) in IM and Mongolia with multi-year means and five-year moving averages (1961–2009).

Source: national standard climate stations of IM, China, and Mongolia (CIM, 2011; CM, 2011).

18.4   Discussion

Over the past 50 years, grassland quality on the Mongolian Plateau has been deteriorating, which has endangered the livelihoods of local herders. Future climate change and the increasing integration into world markets have the potential to exacerbate these problems. Therefore, simple solutions like those based on carrying-capacity are not sufficient for solving these complex and multiscale natural resource problems. An interdisciplinary framework that integrates social and ecological systems is needed to understand the dynamics of social-ecological systems in the Mongolian grasslands over the past 50 years, and to consider strategies for sustainable management in the future (Ostrom, 2009). In the context of warming and drying climate, social-institutional factors played significant roles in changing grassland-use behaviors of herders and grassland quality. These socioeconomic factors also interact with each other. The roles of the state, market and community in governing grassland resources in Mongolia and IM have changed over time. The above analyses show that none of the historical resource institutions implemented in IM and Mongolia (i.e., collectivization, privatization, and recentralization) was efficient for sustainable governance of grassland resources.

Grassland degradation and the increasing frequencies of climate hazards, such as drought and Dzud (i.e., heavy winter snowstorms that interact with summer droughts to endanger livestock), have endangered the livelihoods of herders. Since the middle 1990s, the poverty rate in pastoral areas of IM has increased. Grassland degradation, natural disasters, increasing costs of herding, and increasing competition in the livestock product markets were identified as the major reasons (Li et al., 2007; Zhang, 2007). In IM, fodder cost is the major household expenditure of herders (Li et al., 2007). Environmental problems have also made the poverty situation worse In Mongolia. For example, in 1998, the national poverty rate of Mongolia was slightly below 35%, and it increased to 36.1% in 2001–2002 as a consequence of the severe natural disasters between 1999 and 2002 (Olonbaya, 2010). Social-institutions also affect the adaptive capacity of herders to climate hazards. For example, studies show that the implementation of HPRS in IM, decreased the adaptive capacity (i.e., the ability to migrate to other places and to get help from other herders and/or the local governments in the natural disaster years) of herders to climate variability and change (Li and Huntsinger, 2011).

The high costs of privatization and the top-down hierarchy of state control render these approaches inefficient for governing grassland resources in the semiarid and arid regions. Grassland productivity and water resources are with high spatial and temporal variability in these regions, which makes demarcation of grassland resources very difficult. High monitoring costs make "command and control" an inefficient way for governing grasslands. The social-ecological performances (overall grassland degradation condition and rural poverty) of policies implemented in the recentralization period of China have demonstrated that state-control is inefficient. Community-based resource management (CBRM), which has cooperation and collective action at its core, has been recommended by scholars for solving grassland problems in the semiarid and arid regions of Mongolia and China (Angerer et al., 2008; Banks, 2001; 2003; Banks et al., 2003; Bijoor et al., 2006; Fernandez-Gimenez, 1997; Ho, 2001; Humphrey and Sneath, 1999; Li et al., 2007). Traditionally, herders on the Mongolian Plateau had a culture of reciprocal and exchange use of grasslands in natural disaster years, and the grazing boundaries and movement patterns were also flexible. These informal norms and rules enabled them to adapt to the spatial-temporal variability of climate and grassland productivity. However, social-institutional changes (i.e., collectivization and privatization) altered social organizations and the cooperative culture. For example, in Mongolia, the traditional grazing organizations, called khot ail and consisting of several households with clanship and/or kinship camping together, were replaced by grazing specialization groups, for example goat/sheep management groups, which were not family based. After privatization, due to market incentives and the lack of effective resource institutions to govern grassland resources, cooperative use of grasslands now become competitive, and the number of conflicts over grassland use increased (Upton, 2009). The broad social-institutional changes in IM were similar. Moreover, in IM, contracting grasslands and livestock production to herder households have caused social stratification and further incentivized competitions among herders (Williams, 2002). These changes make it difficult to consider recovering traditional customs in livestock grazing.

In order to avoid grassland degradation due to trampling from daily grazing and to make seasonal and interannual migrations possible, cooperative use of pastures is necessary. Cooperative organizations, such as pasture-use groups and water-facility-use groups, can help herders to improve their livelihoods and better adapt to future adverse climate conditions. The formation of collective action needs external drivers and internal coordination mechanisms (Ostrom, 2005) and effective decentralization requires the support from formal institutions (Ribot and Agrawal, 2006). In Mongolia and IM, support from the national governments can help the formation of cooperative organizations. For example, the national government of China has been providing subsidies for supporting herders to build cooperation organizations in order to increase their profits of livestock production in the market economy. A formal agricultural cooperative law was also implemented in the year 2007 to support the organization of agricultural cooperatives. For areas that are near the major or local markets, market-oriented cooperative organizations can be built, while areas distant from markets but with high frequencies of disasters might benefit from subsistence-oriented cooperative organizations. Where climate disasters happen with relatively high frequency, cooperation can be among neighbors or villages or counties, since in serious natural disaster years a large geographical area could be affected simultaneously.

Community-based resource management is not a panacea for reversing grassland degradation. High stocking rates caused by the increased human and livestock populations have reduced the feasibility of migration, especially in IM, and state-control of the overall grazing intensity of a large geographic area is still necessary. State-control policies need to be sensitive to spatial and temporal variations within the grassland ecosystems. Otherwise, those polices will not be effective and will lack the support from local herders. For example, annual precipitation in the eastern part of IM is fairly stable. Grazing intensity is the major cause for grassland degradation in those areas. Therefore, state grazing-control or privatization might be more effective than cooperative use in these areas, since cooperation and collective action involves lots of transaction costs, such as searching, negotiation, contracting, monitoring, and sanctions. Moreover, long-distance and frequent seasonal and interannual migrations are also not necessary in regions with stable precipitation and productivity.

Livelihood diversification has been promoted by the state as a major way to adapt to environmental change. For example, in order to reduce stocking rates in the grassland regions of China, the national government of China has been providing subsidies for herders to leave pastures and find jobs in cities. However, due to the lack of education and training, this policy has not worked well (Bijoor et al., 2006). Therefore, more institutional and government support may be needed in the future for herders to adapt their livelihoods to the changing climate and grassland services. Besides adjusting resource institutions and polices, improving grazing technologies is another solution. Indigenous knowledge (Fernandez-Gimenez, 2000) and recent research on grassland ecology and grassland use and management provide a broad knowledge base for technical solutions to reduce grassland degradation. Introducing new species with high productivity is an important approach for improving livestock production in the semiarid and arid regions. However, this strategy can increase the natural and economic risks of livestock production. Whether this strategy is feasible also depends on institutional supports, such as markets for livestock products, technology training, livestock insurance, and financial support.

18.5   Conclusions

Most areas of the grassland ecosystems on the Mongolian Plateau can be classified as non-equilibrium ecosystems. Institutions that govern grasslands should accommodate the characteristics of grasslands. The traditional nomadism was adapted to local climate conditions, and also preserved ecosystem functions of grasslands. However, in the past 50 years, the social-institutional changes have undermined the traditional resource institutions and replaced them with a series of alternative systems. Sustainability of the Mongolian grassland social-ecological systems has been affected as a result. A warmer and drier climate and the increasing frequencies of climate hazards have increased the vulnerability of the livelihoods of local herders on the Mongolian Plateau. Therefore, understanding these changes and providing feasible strategies to cope with the environmental problems are urgent. Numerous scholars from different disciplinary backgrounds have contributed to these topics. However, a systematic analysis is still missing. In this chapter, we adopted an integrated state-market-community model to analyze the dynamics and sustainability of the Mongolian grassland social-ecological systems. The results indicate that drivers from the human dimensions, such as institutional and policy changes and demographic change, play significant roles in changing grassland quality over the past half century. In this chapter, we propose cooperative use of grasslands to cope with future climate change and market fluctuations. In regions with high environmental variability, cooperation can pool climate risks over space and increase the predictability of precipitation and grassland productivity. With the increasing integration into world market, the market-oriented cooperative production can increase profits of livestock production. Diverse institutional arrangements and strategies are necessary to accommodate diverse ecosystem types and social situations across ecological gradients and social-political regions. In all, sustainable governance of grassland social-ecological systems on the Mongolian Plateau in the context of climate change need the integration and coordination of forces from the state, market, and local communities. Complex environmental problems need an integrated solution.

Acknowledgements

The work was conducted with financial support from the NASA Land-Cover/Land-Use Change Program (Grant No.NNX09AK87G). The authors would like to thank Dr. Yichun Xie from the Eastern Michigan University and Qi Xing from the Inner Mongolian Institute of Grassland Survey and Design, China, for data collection of this work.

References

Agrawal, A. (2001). Common property institutions and sustainable governance of resources. *World Development*, 29 (10), 1649–1672.

Angerer, B. J., Han, G., Fujisaki, I., and Havstad, K. (2008). Climate change and ecosystems of Asia with emphasis on Inner Mongolia and Mongolia. *Rangelands*, 6, 46–51.

ACBIM (2005, 2010). *Annual Census Book of Inner Mongolia*. Hohhot, Inner Mongolia, China: Inner Mongolia Press.

ACBM (1990, 2010). *Annual Census Book of Mongolia*. Ulaanbaatar, Mongolia: National Statistical Office of Mongolia.

Banks, T. (2001). Property rights and the Environment in pastoral China: Evidence from the field. *Development and Change*, 32, 717–740.

Banks, T. (2003). Property rights reform in rangeland China: Dilemmas on the road to the household ranch. *World Development*, 31 (12), 2129–2142.

Banks, T. Richard, C., Ping, L., and Yan, Z. (2003). Community-based grassland management in Western China. *Mountain Research and Development*, 23 (2), 132–140.

Bijoor, N., Li, W., Zhang, Q., and Huang, G. (2006). Small-scale co-management for the sustainable use of Xilingol Biosphere reserve, Inner Mongolia. *AMBIO*, 35 (1), 25–29.

Brown, J. R., and Thorpe, J. (2008). Climate change and rangelands: Responding rationality to uncertainty. *Rangelands*, 6, 3–6.

Christensen, J. H., Hewitson, B., Bucuioc, A., et al. (2007). Regional climate projections. In: *Climate Change 2007: IPCC Report*. Cambridge University Press, New York, USA, 847–887.

CIM (Climate dataset of Inner Mongolia). (2011) . Monthly mean climate dataset of Inner Mongolia (1961–2009). Inner Mongolia Meteorology Bureau. Hohhot, Inner Mongolia, China.

CM (Climate dataset of Mongolia). (2011). Monthly mean climate dataset of Mongolia (1961–2009). Mongolia Meteorology Bureau. Ulaanbaatar, Mongolia.

Ding, X., and Chen T. (2008). The annual variation characteristics of temperature and precipitation in Inner Mongolia in recent 50 years. *Inner Mongolia Meteorology*, 2, 17–19.

Ellis, J., and Swift, D. (1988). Stability of African pastoral ecosystems: Alternate paradigms and implications for development. *Journal of Range Management*, 41 (6), 450–459.

Erdenetuya, D. (2006). Assessment of pasture land condition by NDVI. In: *Proceedings of Theoretical and Practical Conference on Issues and Challenges of Pasture Management*. Ulaanbaatar, Mongolia.

Fernandez-Gimenez, M. (1997). Landscapes, livestock, and livelihoods: Social, ecological, and land-use change among the nomadic pastoralists of Mongolia. Ph.D. Dissertation. University of California, Berkeley.

Fernandez-Gimenez, M., and Allen-Diaz, B. (1999). Testing a non-equilibrium model of rangeland vegetation dynamics in Mongolia. *Journal of Applied Ecology*, 36, 871–885.

Fernandez-Gimenez, M. (2000). The role of Mongolian nomadic pastoralists' ecological knowledge in rangeland management. *Ecological Applications*, 10 (5), 1318–1326.

FAO (Food and Agriculture Organization). (2011). Price statistics database (FAOSTAT, PriceSTAT). Accessed October 20, 2011, http://faostat.fao.org/site/570/default.aspx#ancor.

Hardin, G. (1968). The tragedy of commons. *Science*, 162, 1243–1248.

Ho, P. (2001). Rangeland degradation in North China revisited? A preliminary statistical analysis to validate non-equilibrium range ecology. *The Journal of Development Studies*, 37 (3), 99–133.

Humphrey, C., and Sneath, D. (1999). *The end of nomadism? Society, state and the environment in Inner Asia*. Duke University Press.

IMIGSD (Inner Mongolian Institute of Grassland Survey and Design). (2008). Statistics of the areas of reclaimed grasslands in Inner Mongolia, China. Hohhot, Inner Mongolia, China.

IMIGSD (Inner Mongolian Institute of Grassland Survey and Design). (2011). Statistics of grassland quality change in Inner Mongolia, China. Hohhot, Inner Mongolia, China.

Jiang, H. (2005). Grassland management and views of natures in China since 1949:

Regional policies and local changes in Uxin Ju, Inner Mongolia. *Geoforum*, 36, 641–653.

Jiang, G., Han, X., and Wu, J. (2006). Restoration and management of the Inner Mongolia grassland require a sustainable strategy. *AMBIO*, 35 (5), 269–270.

Lemos, M., and Agrawal, A. (2006). Environmental governance. *Annual Review of Environment and Resources*, 31, 297–235.

Li, W., Ali, S., and Zhang, Q. (2007). Property rights and grassland degradation: A study of the Xilingol Pasture, Inner Mongolia, China. *Journal of Environmental Management*, 85, 461–470.

Li, W., and Huntsinger, L. (2011). China's grassland contract policy and its impacts on herder ability to benefit in Inner Mongolia: Tragic Feedbacks. *Ecology and Society*, 16 (2), 1.

Liu, J., Li, S., Ouyang, Z., Tam, C., and Chen, X. (2008). Ecological and socioeconomic effects of China's policies for ecosystem services. *Proceedings of the National Academy of Sciences*, 105 (28), 9477–9482.

Lu, Y., Zhuang, Q., Zhou, G., Sirlin, A., Mellio, J., and Kicklighter, D. (2009). Possible decline of the carbon sink in the Mongolian Plateau during the 21st century. *Environmental Research Letters*, doi: 10.1088/1748-9326/4/4/045023.

Ministry of Agriculture, China. (2006). National Rangeland Monitoring Report. Ministry of Agriculture, Beijing, China. 2007.

MNET (Ministry of Nature, Environment, and Tourism). (2009). *Mongolia's fourth national report on implementation of convention on biological diversity*. Government of Mongolia: Ulaanbaatar, Mongolia.

NCRM (National Climate Risk Management). (2009). Strategy and Action Plan of Mongolia. Mongolia.

Neupert, R. (1999). Population, nomadic-pastoralism and the environment in the Mongolian Plateau. *Population and Environment*, 20 (5), 413–441.

Oba, G., Stenseth, N. C., and Lusigi, W. J. (2000). New perspectives on sustainable grazing management in arid zones of Sub-Saharan Africa. *Bioscience*, 50 (1), 35–51.

Ojima, D., and Chuluun, T. (2008). Policy changes in Mongolia: implications for land use and landscapes. In: Galvin, K. A., Reid, R. S., Behnke, Jr., R. H., and Hobbs, N. T. (Eds.) *Fragmentation in semi-arid and arid landscapes: Consequences for human and natural systems*. Springer, The Netherlands, 179–193.

Olonbayar, M. (2010). Livelihood study of herders in Mongolia. Research Report, Mongolian Society for Range Management, Ulaanbaatar.

Ostrom, E. (1990). *Governing the Commons: The Evolution of Institutions for Collective Action*. Cambridge University Press, New York.

Ostrom, E. (2005). *Understanding Institutional Diversity*. Princeton University Press, Princeton, New Jersey.

Ostrom, E. (2009). A general framework for analyzing sustainability of socio-ecological systems. *Science*, 325 (24), 419–422.

Ostrom, E. (2010). Beyond markets and states: polycentric governance of complex economic systems. *American Economic Review*, 100, 641–672.

Pan, Y., Birdsey, R. A., Fang, J., Houghton, R., Kauppi, P. E., Kurz, W. A., Phillips, O. L., Shvidenko, A., Lewis, S. L., Canadell, J. G., Ciais, P., Jackson, R. B., Pacala, S. W., McGuire, A. D., Piao, S., Rautiainen, A., Sitich, S., and Hayes, D. (2011).

A large and persistent carbon sink in the world's forests. *Science*, 333, 988–993.

Ribot, J. C., and Agrawal, A. (2006). Recentralizing while decentralizing: how national governments reappropriate forest resources. *World Development*, 34 (11), 1864–1886.

Sneath, D. (1998). State policy and pasture degradation in Inner Asia. *Science*, 281, 1147–1148.

Tang, J., Chen, X., Zhao, M., and Su, B. (2008). Numerical simulations of regional climate change under IPCC A2 scenario in China. *Acta Meterologica Sinica*, 66 (1), 13–25.

Upton, C. (2009). "Custom" and contestation: Land reform in post-socialist Mongolia. *World Development*, 37 (8), 1400–1410.

Waldron, S., Brown, C., and Longworth, J. (2010). Grassland degradation and livelihoods in China's western pastoral region: A framework for understanding and refining China's recent policy responses. China. *Agricultural Economic Review*, 2 (3), 298–318.

Williams, D. (2002). *Beyond Great Walls: Environment, Identity, and Development on the Chinese Grasslands of Inner Mongolia*. Stanford University Press, Stanford, California.

Wilson, P. N., and Thompson, G. D. (1993). Common property and uncertainty: Compensating coalitions by Mexico's pastoral Ejidatarios. *Economic Development and Cultural Change*, 41 (2), 299–318.

Xing, Q., Wang, Q., and Zhang, D. (2008). *An Illustrated Handbook on Habitual Plant of Inner Mongolia Grassland*. Inner Mongolia People's Press, Hohhot, Inner Mongolia, China.

Zhang, Q. (2007). Impacts of double-contract responsibility system on rangeland and animal husbandry: A perspective of natural resource heterogeneity. Ph.D. Dissertation, Peking University, Beijing.

Zhang, Q., and Li, W. (2008). Policy analysis in grassland management of Xilingol prefecture, Inner Mongolia. In: Lee, C. and Schaaf, T. (Eds.). *The Future of Drylands*. Published joint by UNESO and Spring Press, 493–505.

Zhang, X. (1992). Northern China. In: National Research Council, Washington, D.C.(Ed). *Grasslands and Grassland Science in Northern China*. National Academy Press, 39–54.

Zhen, L., Ochirbat, B., Lv, Y., Wei, Y., Liu, X., Chen, J., Yao, Z., and Li, F. (2010). Comparing patterns of ecosystem service consumption and perceptions of range management between ethnic herders in Inner Mongolia and Mongolia. *Environmental Research Letters*, 5, 015001, 1–11.

Authors Information

Jun Wang*, Daniel G. Brown, Arun Agrawal,
School of Natural Resources and Environment, University of Michigan, Ann Arbor, MI 48109, USA
* Corresponding author

Chapter 19

Adaptive Management of Grazing Lands

Guodong Han, Tong Liu, Zhongwu Wang, Zhiguo Li, Mengli Zhao, Kris Havstad, Jianguo Wu, and David Kemp

Summary: Rangelands, the main land type used as grazing lands, occupy ~54% of the world's ice-free land surface, and grasslands dominate ~16% of all rangelands. China is the third largest country for rangeland resources in the world and has approximately 400 million ha rangeland, about 40% of China's land surface. These grazing lands are susceptible to severe degradation due to overexploitation, especially, overgrazing. This chapter provides an overview of the geographic distribution and management issues of these grazing lands, and a case study on adaptive management in an innovative grazing system in desert steppe of Inner Mongolia Autonomous Region (IM), China. We emphasize the importance of applying models and management demonstration related to stocking rate reduction, lambing time change and the use of warm shed based on household to prevent resource degradation. We discuss the interaction of ecological and economic benefits in the application of grazing systems for desert steppe areas. We provide evidence for the use of an innovative adaptive management practice based on development of a summer grazing system with low stocking rate and winter warm shed feeding.

19.1 Introduction

Adaptive management is an integrative approach that combines anticipation, implementation, monitoring and evaluation in order to improve ecosystem management based on continuous adjustment of management through a learning process. It is a tool that integrates research and development in a formal way to achieve better, applied outcomes (Salafsky et al., 2001). Lee (1993) noted that there were many uncertainties in the adaptive management process and the whole management cycle could be seen as a research experiment. Recently, this emerging adaptive management process is now described as "management by hypothesis", a process conducted in a very repeatable and scientific manner (Sayre et al., 2012). In adaptive management, the ecosystem managers need to identify objectives, design the experiment accordingly, collect and evaluate information during the whole cyclical process to explore alternative strategies to meet the objectives, predict possible outcomes according to current knowledge with efficient tools, implement better strategies, monitor the impact of management actions, and then make adjustments and improvements (Fig. 19.1). Simply, adaptive management is to "learn from practice". It requires clear management objectives to guide decisions on actions to be taken, and explicit assumptions of expected outcomes to which actual outcomes are to be compared. Research is required through each cycle of improvement to provide information needed to build adaptive management systems.

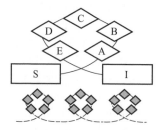

Fig. 19.1 Illustration of the adaptive management cycle (Salafsky et al., 2001). A—Design an explicit model of your system; B—Develop a management plan that maximizes results and learning; C—Develop a monitoring plan to test your assumptions; D—Implement management and monitoring plan; E—Analyze data and communicate results; S — Start: Clarify groups mission; I—Iterate: Use results and adapt and learn.

The overall objective of adaptive management of grazing lands is to achieve the sustainability of rangeland by improving management practices given environmental dynamics and uncertainties. Rangeland ecosystems are highly dynamic as they are constantly influenced by fluctuating environmental conditions in moisture and temperature limited climates and by changes in the ways livestock are managed. Changes in rangeland ecosystems are often nonlinear and unpredictable, somewhat chaotic and hence no single management solution exists. Rather there are typically ranges in values and general targets that can lead to better or worse system outcomes. Adaptive management is needed to maintain a balance between ecosystem capacities and human demands and to optimize the tradeoffs among integrated social, economic and ecological benefits. The core goals of adaptive management on grazing lands are to enhance ecosystem resilience through continuous adjustments in management actions and adaptations to more efficient management modes and strategies so that the system is sustained.

The main aspects of adaptive management of grazing lands are the needs to: 1) optimize livestock and forage production to improve the productive efficiency of animal husbandry; 2) adjust the management system on rangeland to build a management model that can sustain the rangeland and adapt to a variable environment; and 3) combine ecological, social and economic factors to improve the sustainability of grazing lands to support the desired provisions of ecosystem goods and services.

Simulating modeling is often considered as one of the more effective ways to examine ecosystem management strategies as part of building an adaptive management system. Models have utility, because there are typically too many combinations of factors to allow through comprehensive experimentation, especially considering the uncertainties of global climate change. For example, in 1995, the U.S. Department of the Interior's Fish and Wildlife Service (FWS) started implementing adaptive management in waterfowl conservation research sites within North America. A simulating model was developed to monitor the management processes. Through comparison between actual and simulated results, the optimized model was used to evaluate the effectiveness of current waterfowl management practices and to subsequently adjust management strategies accordingly. The procedure also could be started over again to re-optimize the model and management strategies. The goal in this case was to enable the survival of waterfowl species.

The purpose of this chapter is to describe the salient features of an adaptive management system that can be employed for management of livestock grazing systems within rangeland environments. These production systems and rangeland environments will be increasingly stressed in coming decades to supply not only food and fiber but also an array of ecosystem goods and services (Havstad et al., 2007). Given increasing climatic variations, these systems would benefit from implementation of adaptive management strategies. A specific case study based in IM is utilized to illustrate these salient features. Herders have developed skills over centuries that enable their households and livestock to survive, but the current high densities of both humans and livestock in these environments are threatening to result in significant degradation of these grasslands. There are limited opportunities livestock productivity to where household incomes increase, and also conserve grassland resources. Yet, our goal is to provide both economic and ecological viability in this system.

19.2　Distribution of Grazing Lands and Problems

Rangelands occupy ~54% of the world's ice-free land surface (Estell et al., 2012), and grasslands dominate ~16% of all rangelands (Fig. 19.2). Grasslands occur on all continents and are extremely important for extensive livestock production systems (FAO, 2009). Within that vast area, temperate grasslands form some of the largest groups of ecosystems including the Euro-Asia steppe, the Northern American prairie and the Pampas of Southern America. Unfortunately, grasslands are diminishing with the continued global expansion of woody dominated systems (Asner et al., 2004). China is the third largest country for range land resources in the world and has approximately 400 million ha grassland, less than that of Australia and Russia, which occupies ~40% of total China (Han and Gao, 2005). In recent years, under the dual pressure of climate change and human activity, due to unreasonable resource utilization and grassland mismanagement, grassland degradation has increased significantly and faster than previously imagined (Jiang et al., 2009; Hou, 2009; Tian and Wang, 2000), For example, research surveys have documented that 90% of total grassland area in China has degraded (Hou et al., 2011).

Grazing land
(Percent per gridcell)
100%

0

Fig. 19.2 Distribution of global grazing lands.
Source: http://www.uni-klu.ac.at/socec/in halt/1189.htm.

Within China, IM is rich in grassland resources. The total grassland area is around 86 million ha (Qiu et al., 2005), the second largest grassland region after Tibet. The grassland is classified as meadow steppe, typical steppe and desert steppe and span's from northeast to southwest across the region, along a gradient from east to west of declining rainfall. IM is typically open grasslands with dry, windy, and cold characteristics. The annual average air temperature varies from $-3°C$ to $9°C$, annual precipitation ranges from 450 mm in northeast to 150 mm in middle and west (Bai and Peng., 2000). So far, the more degraded grassland area occupies 25 million ha, which takes up 39% of total available grassland area. The areas of severe, moderate and light degradation are 4.4, 8.8 and 11.8 million ha, which comprises 17%, 35% and 47% of total degraded grassland area, respectively (Badaerhu et al., 2010).

Considering the causes of grassland degradation, human activities can not be underestimated, especially excessive livestock numbers. Lured by economic benefits, more and more herders have given up the ecological-friendly grazing regime which they have been using across generation for centuries, instead to pursue more income from grassland simply by increasing livestock numbers. Overgrazing not only result in poor animal conditions, which results in less economic return per head for herders, but also directly contributes to grassland degradation and can trigger cascading ecological disasters, such as sandstorms.

Grassland degradation has become very noticeable within the lifetime of older herders. This is associated with many social changes. The number of people and livestock eking out an existence on grassland has dramatically increased since 1950 (Kemp and Michalk, 2011a). The effect of these changes has been a decline in productivity of individual animals, shift in botanical composition to less desirable species, a decline in grassland production, and increase in soil erosion and dust storms.

19.3   Case Study and Adaptive Management in IM

A case study is presented here detailing the first phase of building an adaptive management system designed to improve herder household net incomes and to do that in ways, that provide opportunities for grasslands restoration. Our focus has been on analysis of the livestock production system given the significance of the production system on both grasslands conditions and household income. It is our premise that re-organising the livestock system can be done relatively quickly if we can justify both economic and ecological benefits. Implementing new conservation practices for grassland rehabilitation will take many years of research, though it is axiomatic that fewer livestock would result in increased standing biomass and vegetated ground cover and would be expected to improve overall grassland condition (Kemp and Michalk, 2007).

19.3.1   Study Site

Siziwang Banner (county) is located 150 km north of Hohhot, the capital city of IM. It lies in the north piedmont of Yin Mountain on the Mongolian Plateau.

The climate is characterized by windy spring, cold winter, and low annual precipitation (mostly in the form of summer rainfall). This region is classified as the desert steppe which is recognized as a typical zone of fragile ecology and an important ecosystem in Northern China. The local people mainly subsist on agriculture production including cropping and livestock. More than 90% of these grasslands are degraded in the Banner, which results in frequent sandstorms and other environmental problems due to the overexploitation of grassland resources primarily driven by livestock overgrazing.

19.3.2   The ACIAR-Model

A series of models (ACIAR Stage I, II, III) (Takahashi et al., 2011; Han et al. 2011; Wang et al., 2011) were built to analyse the livestock grassland production system in stages so that a strategy could then be developed. The data in the models were based on extensive surveys of households, through to intense monitoring of each animal on a farm (Kemp and Michalk., 2011b). From the survey farm, a "typical" farm was constructed. This was based on averages, modified where anomalies occurred, e.g., where one farm may have had crops and no others did then an average was problematic. The models were based on standard functions for animal nutrition (Freer et al., 2007) and used metabolisable energy (ME) as the basis for analysis. Within each model a financial analysis was done to identify the effects of management practices on net household income. In addition, field experiments done in the region were used to develop the functions for each model (Wang et al., 2011).

The Stage I model analysed feed supply and demand for all the animals on a farm on a monthly basis under steady state conditions. This model was transparent to the user and enabled all the primary data on animal numbers, live weight, physiological condition, etc. to be manually entered. This was done in order to calibrate the model to farm data and to build experience among a range of users about the underlying biological relationships. This model was used to resolve many of the basic aspects of the livestock production system that could be modified and to verify the data sets used in other models.

The Stage II model was a linear program, optimising model to resolve the optimal combination of factors that would improve household income, incorporating the real constraints that apply on farms. This enables direct estimates of the optimal stocking rates for a typical farm in a specified year.

The Stage III model was a dynamic model, designed to take the better solutions from the other two models and investigate in more detail their long-term impact on plant diversity and on soil erosion from wind. Plant diversity was analysed in terms of a simple functional group model that grouped species as desirable and less-desirable. Criteria could be explored such as the adjustment of stocking rates in relation to the herbage mass on the grassland.

19.3.3   Typical Farm

A typical farm is located in the Bayin Village in Chaganbulige Township, Siziwang Banner (Han et al., 2011). In 2005, 15 farmers were interviewed to collect data on biological, economic and social aspects of the livestock production system. More specific data related to livestock performance and seasonal changes in livestock performance were obtained from six farmers, and these surveys were utilized to construct a core database for a typical farm.

Survey results characterized that the net income is derived from gross income from lambs and young goats, wool, cashmere, old livestock sold for meat, dung and some minor goods. Raising sheep and goats for meat and fibre are the principal rural activities. Over 95% of the sheep are local Mongolian fat-tail sheep. The average livestock number is 270 heads on 520 ha grassland area. The main costs were feed supplements, veterinary treatments, grassland rental, transportation cost of both animals to market and delivery of supplement feeds, and labour. One of the major difficulties is providing enough feed from the farm. The dry environment means ground water is limited and local regulations limit the area of forage crops, typically maize, to a total of 0.67 ha Crop areas are limited in order to protect native grassland from conversion to cropland.

There are many aspects of the livestock production system that can be changed. The main options are discussed below in relation to the effects on net financial household income or their contribution to grassland rehabilitation. The underlying condition affecting livestock production is that feed supply only exceeds maintenance requirements for a few months in summer and for the rest of the year animals lose weight (Wang et al., 2011).

19.3.4   Economic Stocking Rate

The optimizing model (Stage II) was used to estimate the financially optimal stocking rate on the typical farm (Kemp and Michalk, 2007; Wang et al., 2011). These estimates assume that animals are fed to maintenance requirements and are kept in a warm shed in winter. These assumotions reflect the basic recommended changes for livestock production systems in this rangeland environment. In comparison with current conditions the financially optimal stocking rate is nearly half of the current rate (Fig. 19.3). Reducing the stocking rate to half

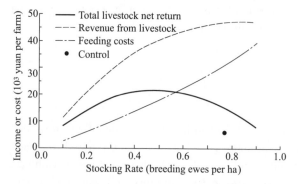

Fig. 19.3 Livestock production revenue and feed costs for the current meat production system in Siziwang Banner, IM, when animals are fed to maintenance requirements and kept through winter in a warm shed. The "control" data point is an estimate of current net income from livestock on farms in the same area, in which case animals graze outside all year, are not fed to maintenance requirements, and revenue and feed costs are less than apply in other calculations.

of the current rate effectively doubles the feed available per animal and that alone can increase animal productivity (Han et al., 2011), given animals are losing weight for nine months of the year. The lower stocking rate provides the opportunity through reduced grazing pressures to rehabilitate grasslands. An ecological ideal would be to restrict grazing of grasslands to the summer, when the herbage mass is above a critical threshold (which has not yet been determined but possibly of the order of 500 kg DM ha^{-1}) to reduce damage to the grassland. However, conservation practices that create management opportunities biologically and financially to limit grazing to summer only, at half the current stocking rates, needs to be developed.

Zhang et al. (2011) reported that the daily weight gain of individual sheep increased as stocking rates declined from heavy grazing, moderate grazing to light grazing. The lower stocking rate could reduce the pressure on grassland from grazing activity and provide time for recovery of grazed plants. Increased plant vigor would also carry over to the benefit of livestock in the following year.

19.3.5 Improved Feeding of Livestock during Winter and Spring

Feed supply is the main constraint on animal production and can be supplied from grasslands and/or from supplements. For Inner Mongolian grasslands, most supplements would need to be imported to the farm. To reduce grazing pressures on the grassland forage resources, an important adaptive management option is how long animals can be economically fed supplements through winter and spring to reduce the risk of damage to the grasslands through overgrazing, to maintain plant cover to ameliorate wind erosion, and maintain animal performance. The typical supplements used were maize grain, silage and straw, meadow hay, shrub stalks, stubble from millet, potatoes and other crops and purchased concentrates. It was apparent that herders focused primarily on quantity, with less commitment to feed quality and the pattern of feeding did not always aim to optimise animal performance. For a reasonable quality feed, sheep would require ∼1 kg per head per day, but current practice is at best to feed 0.1 kg and then animals graze the frozen, dead and sparse grassland (Han et al., 2011). It was difficult to obtain useful estimates of the prices of supplements as some come from non-market sources. The quantities and quality of what is available was difficult to estimate and hence optimal financial solutions were judged to be problematic when all possible supplements were considered. Sufficient data were obtained though to broadly estimate the likely benefits from improving the feeding of the better quality supplements through winter and spring. This was done using the Stage I model to investigate the effect of alternative feeding strategies on energy intake (Fig. 19.4) (Han et al., 2011).

The energy balance comparisons of grazing on grassland versus supplement feeding with maize hay, maize grain, and millet hay and concentrate (i.e., choosing the better quality supplements as the others would result in weight loss irrespective of the amount fed) show that feeding supplement of grass hay and millet hay or maize grain and concentrate are better than when the sheep only graze grassland. The amounts fed in these simulations approximate the rates that could result in better net financial returns from those feeds (done using simple gross margins in the models). It was uneconomic to feed at a level that completely satisfied animal demands and in consequence there was still a gap between actual ME demand and stimulated data from November to the following May, especially around lambing time in February and March. The better diet (A1, Fig. 19.4) had about twice the benefit through winter of only grazing the grassland, though it still did not satisfy all the animals' needs, especially around lambing times. The benefits would be expected to flow through to better live weight of adults and growth of lambs and kids that would have current and future life cycle benefits. Unfortunately, feeding more and better quality supplements from November through to May was only marginally financially beneficial at the prices used. Longer-term feed-forward effects on future production may achieve the required benefits and reduce grazing pressures on the grasslands. An increased demand for feeds could result in the medium-term in lower prices as more feed becomes available. Better quality and animals in better body conditions would generate higher market prices for animals further justifying better feeding strategies. These changes in feeding strategies could significantly affect animal performance and farms operations should implement these adaptive management practices.

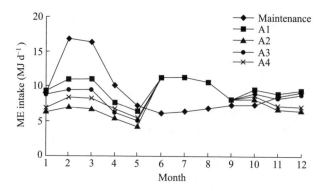

Fig. 19.4 The effect of different possible supplements on estimated metabolisable energy (ME) intake by livestock in Siziwang Banner, IM. Results derived from Stage I model. Maintenance—the energy required for maintenance at the same live weight; A1—actual energy intake of grazing all year with supplements (maize hay, maize grain, millet hay and concentrates) fed from October to the following May at the same live weight; A2—actual energy intake of grazing all year round on grasslands at the same live weight; A3—actual energy intake of grazing all year with supplements (maize hay and millet hay) fed from October to the following May at the same live weight; A4—the actual energy intake of grazing all year with supplements (maize grain and concentrate) fed from October to the following May at the same live weight.

19.3.6 Changing Lambing Time

Lambing (and kidding) time occurs from December to following April, with a peak in February; in the middle of a cold winter. Mating starts in September. The consequences of these practices are that the ewes underlying live weight declines up to and after lambing, the physiological stresses of pregnancy are considerable and lambs are typically small. Herders take the lambs off their mothers at birth, restrict their ability to get milk and start some hand feeding of concentrates from 7–10 days of age. Lamb growth rates are very poor and they only survive due to the care and attention of herders.

Shifting the lambing time to better align animal demand with the available feed supply from grasslands, especially at the lower stocking rates identified, would have the benefits of reducing the need for expensive supplements through winter and maybe reduce overall needs for them. The effect on the energy balance of lambing in April, compared to February (Fig. 19.5) (Han et al., 2011) showed the reduced energy intake and supplements fed through winter. April lambing did result in marginally higher energy intakes in summer, which would be from grassland. Changing lambing dates to April would need to consider sufficient supplements fed so that the pressure on grasslands was not increased.

The effects of changing lambing times were further evaluated at a range of stocking rates and included the more radical change of lambing in July when there is the best alignment between feed supply and animal demand (Fig. 19.6) (Han et al., 2011). This showed a marginally better net financial return from lambing in July, even though that was associated with a higher feed cost. Lambing in April was a less profitable activity. In these simulations, the animals were fed to maintenance requirements. At current stocking rates of ∼0.8 ewe ha^{-1},

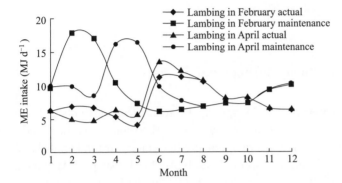

Fig. 19.5 The effect of lambing time on energy balance (ME=metabolisable energy) of ewes at Siziwang Banner, IM.

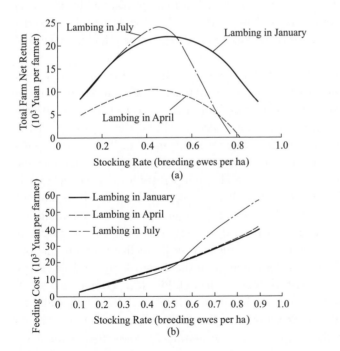

Fig. 19.6 Total farm net returns (a) and feeding costs (b) under different lambing times in Siziwang Banner, IM.

lambing in July would be effectively uneconomical. An important effect was that when the stocking rates for lambing in July were increased above the optimum, there was a very rapid decline in profitability due to the increased feed costs. That sensitivity would mean that herders who lamb in July would be more inclined to stay closer to the optimum stocking rates than would apply in other scenarios. Changing lambing dates needs to then take into account the optimal stocking rate as well as feeding strategy.

19.3.7 Use of Warm Sheds during Cold Seasons

Siziwang Banner is located on the Mongolian Plateau at an altitude of 1,450 m. Cold winters with strong winds are recognized as the typical weather condition along the Plateau. The average temperature in January around traditional lambing time is −15°C. Sheep lose approximately 9–17 MJ heat per day during winter when the temperature is lower than −5°C. This loss can exceed energy intake levels supplied from the best feed sources. However, sheep have traditionally been taken out to graze every day, and it is not possible to supply enough to eat to compensate for the energy expended in daily grazing activities. This situation is further compounded with snowfalls causing further restriction to the meagre grass resources. Under these conditions there can be a high mortality of livestock.

It has been recognised that "warm sheds" can help reduce heat loss from animals and compensate for the low energy intake. Warm sheds are built to face south, with a plastic or glass roof on half of the shed to trap heat. Where old sheds are suitable, they can be modified to achieve the objectives of the warm shed. Some sheds use heating stoves, which can be fuelled from methane digesters located in the shed that use waste from the livestock and households. Warm sheds typically achieve 10–11°C higher temperatures than the outside air and eliminate wind chill effects. There is still much for herders to learn about the effective use of warm sheds, but there is good acceptance of their value.

Warm sheds are being more widely used, but often without maximising their benefits through revising feeding strategies to optimise livestock production. Combining warm sheds with better nutrition of the livestock does enable energy requirements to be better satisfied (Stage I model, Fig. 19.7) (Han et al., 2011). The level of feeding used in these estimates was a level considered financially viable for herders, though the ideal would be to satisfy maintenance requirements and thereby minimise the weight loss. The marginally lower maintenance requirements through winter from pen feeding in a warm shed was because these simulations only used average climate data and not extreme events that occur at some stage each year.

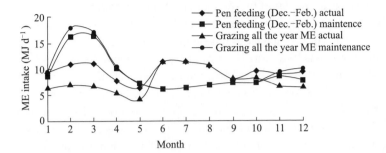

Fig. 19.7 Energy balances for grazing ewes all year versus pen feeding in warm sheds in winter in Siziwang Banner, IM (ME = metabolisable energy).

The Stage II optimizing model was used over a range of stocking rates to estimate the optimal strategy for the period of grazing by period for pen feeding in warm sheds (Fig. 19.8). Restricting grazing to June to October and pen feeding to maintenance (the better ecological strategy) for the rest of the year was most profitable at very low stocking rates, but the least profitable option overall. As grazing periods were extended the profitability increased, the optimal stocking rate did the same. Grazing for eight months from April through November and then pen feeding from December through following March had the best net financial returns. These returns were greater than from continuous grazing all year and were achieved at a lower stocking rate. These strategies depend upon the prices for livestock and for feed. Pen fed animals are likely to be larger and generate a higher price per kg as there is more meat per kg live weight, but insufficient data is available to model this effectively at this stage. The optimal

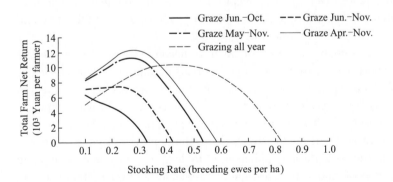

Fig. 19.8 Net financial returns from livestock at a range of stocking rates when animals graze all year and are fed supplements to maintenance requirements, or are grazed for part of the year and then pen fed for the remainder (Stage II model). Data for the typical farm, Siziwang Banner, IM.

least-cost ration that was calculated by the model involved feeding 1 kg hay and 0.2 kg concentrate per ewe per day. Future research should evaluate options for improving the unit price of the quantity and quality of feed used.

The consistent outcome is that restriction of grazing to when reasonable quality forage is available in the field, using a stocking rate that is half or less current rates and pen-feeding for as long as financially sensible would not only increase net financial returns from livestock, but also provide that opportunity for grasslands to rehabilitate. It would be important to update model estimates at least annually to adjust for variations in prices and further information becomes available on how the system functions.

19.4   Conclusions and Discussion

According to results from our case study in Siziwang Banner, implementation of grassland adaptive management option can play a significant role in improving grassland condition and livestock production. A principle for adaptive management option with both ecological and economical benefits is winter pen feeding. Results from the ACIAR-Model indicated that the most economic and effective strategy was to let livestock graze on the rangeland from April to November and have pen feeding during the rest of the year. The main practices include reducing stocking rate to a reasonable level of 0.3–0.5 ewe ha^{-1} in Siziwang. In addition, changing lambing time to April and July could be better to meet feed demand and minimize the gap between actual energy intake and the maintenance demand of livestock; building up the warm shed to reduce the energy loss of animals in winter. Supplemental feeds with application to this environment include high quality-oriented combinations, such as maize hay, maize grain, millet hay and concentrates from December to following March.

The vast desert steppe grasslands of IM have become degraded over the last century with sharply increased numbers of humans and animal. This has led to the need to find management strategies for the twin problems of increasing net financial returns from livestock to sustain households and to provide opportunities to rehabilitate the grasslands. The example outlined in this chapter has shown how an initial focus on the livestock production system using farm surveys to provide the basic data, supplemented by local grazing experiments and then using a series of models to investigate larger aspects of the system can lead to a set of initial strategies aimed at addressing these twin problems.

The need to focus on improving incomes as part of a program to rehabilitate grasslands is driven by the enormous difficulties that would arise if the land was to be abandoned in order to minimise grazing pressures, coupled to an

increasing demand for red meat as China's population becomes more affluent and
concurrently increases demands for meat protein. Reduced grazing pressures can
increase biodiversity of grasslands (Wang et al., 2011) though the rates of change
are likely to be slow. In the example outlined here it is evident that the market
can be an effective driver for initial changes in the livestock production system
leading to reduced stocking rates. It is financially viable to halve stocking rates
without decreasing net financial returns from livestock. This reduction would not
decrease the yield of meat, wool, milk per ha as productivity per animal increase
to compensate. That simple change is now being adopted by several hundred
herders in Siziwang Banner as an initial phase in improvements (Kemp and
Michalk, 2011). Animal culling practices that select the best animals to keep can
also improve animal efficiency per head. Further improvements in the livestock
production system would come from focusing on the most efficient enterprise,
e.g., wool vs. meat, changing lambing to better coincide with the pattern of
grassland growth, minimising the months that livestock graze the grassland,
using warm sheds to reduce energy demand and feeding better quality rations.
Each of these management options can be implemented in a staged sequence to
minimise transition costs providing additional economic incentives for adoption
of these more ecologically effective practices.

While these changes are in a direction that can lead to grassland improvement, it is not certain at this stage if the rate of change would be sufficient. A
faster rate of change may be desired. This could mean that stocking rates for
instance, need to be reduced to 20% of current rates to effect a rapid change.
The gap between a 50% reduction and an e.g., 80% "ideal" reduction could be
supported by government payments for improving ecosystem services. Further
modelling would be needed to resolve how this is best identified, implemented
and monitored.

The work reported here only applies to the initial phase of reorganising the
livestock production system to improve incomes and rehabilitate grasslands. As
each change in farm practice is made, other issues will arise that require further
research to build the tools needed to resolve the optimal solutions. It is not
possible in an adaptive management program to foresee all the issues that will
arise, though some are obvious. First, grassland improvement needs to be done
at an appropriate scale. With vast ecosystems such as the desert steppe, its
integrity depends upon improvements across large areas. Resolving these issues
will require trans- and inter-disciplinary studies, based on adequate databases
of the underlying resources. Farms need to be coordinated in their responses to
improvement. Second, ecosystems services need to be better understood, particularly if part of the adaptive management program involves government payments for those services. Research is needed on how ecosystem services change
under different management strategies. Third, grassland livestock systems are
subject to the vagaries of climate and adaptive management strategies need to

be developed that have inbuilt mechanisms to adjust practices with changing conditions. One option for grasslands is to chose a common factor that aligns with many aspects of the ecosystem and to manage for that factor; grassland herbage mass has been proposed as a useful criterion that is easy to monitor (Kemp and Michalk, 2011b). This may prove to be one of the key variables used to evaluate adaptive management practices to determine if the extent of system changes are adequate, if they should be increased or if the system state is above desired goals. A case for the later is if reduced stocking rates enabled grassland production to double then it may be realistic to allow some small increases in animal numbers so that household incomes could rise.

Adaptive management has been applied around the world in forestry, fishery, watershed and rangeland systems. Simulation models have been broadly used in ecosystem management. China has a huge area of grasslands which are of ecological, social and economical importance. As an effective approach to dealing with environmental uncertainties, implementation of adaptive management practices established through cooperative research among herders and scientists has great potential. Several areas need more research in the future. First, grassland adaptive management research should be carried out at appropriate scales. Integrating the adaptive management to household ranches is an effective way to solve the problems of production system in grazing lands, such as, overgrazing and grassland degradation. Second, quantifying rangeland ecosystem services and mapping them spatially in a region are important in future research. Databases on meteorology, hydrology, environment, and related socioeconomic factors should be established to facilitate more comprehensive and systematic interdisciplinary studies. Third, climate change, carbon sequestration, emission reduction, biodiversity and food security should also be evaluated as possible ecosystem goods and services that can be provided through adaptive management of rangelands.

Acknowledgements

This chapter is based on the thinking developed in many projects and especially in a coordination program funded by the Ministry of Agriculture of the People's Republic of China (201003019, 200903060), the Australian Centre for International Agricultural Research, the Australian Department of Agriculture, Fisheries & Forestry, the Australian Greenhouse Office, the Ministry of Science and Technology of the People's Republic of China (2012BAD13B02), Inner Mongolia Committee of Science and Technology (20091403), and Inner Mongolia Agricultural University (NDTD2010-5). There have been many people and students involved in this project since 2000 and we thank them all. Thanks to Drs. Jiquan Chen and Shiqiang Wan for the opportunity to present this work to a wider audience in the Workshop on Dry lands in Kaifeng in 2011.

References

Asner, G. P., Elmore, A. J., Olander, L. P., Martin, R. E., and Harris, A. T. (2004). Grazing systems, ecosystem responses, and global change. *Annual Review of Environment and Resources*, 29, 261–299.

Badaerhu, Z. H. (2010). Inner Mongolia grassland degradation and control. *Animal Husbandry and Feed Science*, 31, 6–7, 258–261.

Bai, K., and Peng, X. (2000). Current situation and countermeasure of sustainable utilization of grassland resources in Inner Mongolia. *Journal of China Agricultural Resources and Regional Planning*, 21, 6, 40–44.

Estell, R. E., Havstad, K. M., Cibils, A. F., Fredrickson, E. L., Anderson, D. M., Schrader, S., and James, D. K. (2013). Increasing shrub use by livestock in a world with less grass. *Rangeland Ecology and Management*, 65, 553–562.

FAO. (2009). The state of food and agriculture. Livestock in the balance. Rome, Italy.

Freer, M., Dove, H., and Nolan, J. V. (2007). *Nutrient Requirements of Domesticated Ruminants*. CSIRO Publishing, Melbourne.

Han, G., Li, N., Zhao, M., Zhang, M., Wang, Z., Li, Z., Bai, W., Randall, J., David, K., Taro, T., and David, M. (2011). Changing livestock numbers and farm management to improve the livelihood of farmers and rehabilitate grassland in desert steppe: A case study in Siziwang Banner, Inner Mongolia Autonomous Region. In: Kemp, D. R., and Michalk, D. L. (Eds.). *Development of Sustainable Livestock Systems on Grasslands in North-Western China. ACIAR Proceedings*, 134, 80–95.

Han, Y., and Gao, J. (2005). An analysis of main ecological problems of grasslands and relevant countermeasures in China. *Research of Environmental Sciences*, 18, 3, 60–62.

Havstad, K. M., Peters, D. P. C., Skaggs, R., Brown, J., Bestlemeyer, B., Fredrickson, E., Herrick, J. E., and Wright, J. (2007). Ecological services to and from rangelands of the United States. *Ecological Economics*, 64, 261–268.

Hou, X. (2009). Research progress and extension effects of grassland protection and construction techniques in China. *Chinese Journal of Grassland*, 31, 1, 4–12.

Hou, X., Yin, Y., and Ding, Y. (2011). An overview and prospect of grassland adaptive management in China. *Acta Prataculturae Sinica*, 20, 2, 262–269.

Jiang, X., Yue, J., Zhang, W., and Liu, B. (2009). Biodiversity, ecosystem functioning and spatio-temporal scales. *Acta Prataculturae Sinica*, 18, 1, 219–225.

Kemp, D. R., and D. L. Michalk (2007). Towards sustainable grassland and livestock management. *Journal of Agricultural Science*, 145,543-564.

Kemp, D. R., and Michalk, D. L. (2011a). *Development of Sustainable Livestock Systems on Grasslands in North-Western China. ACIAR Proceedings*, 134, 189.

Kemp, D. R., and Michalk, D. L. (2011b). Livestock production styles and managing grassland ecosystems. In: Lemaire, G., Hodgson, J., and Chabbi, A. (Eds). *Grassland Ecosystems: Productivity and Environmental Issues, Chapter 16*. CABI, 53–62.

Lee, K. N. (1993). *Compass and Gyroscope: Integrating Science and Politics for the Environment*. Washington, DC: Island Press.

Qiu, S., Huang, J., and Liu, B. (2005). The grassland degradation and protection in Inner Mongolia. *Inner Mongolia Prataculture*, 17, 4, 11–13.

Salafsky, N., Mar goluis, R., and Redford, K. (2001). Adaptive management: A tool for conservation practitioners. Washington DC: Biodiversity Support Program, World Wildlife Fund, Inc.

Sayre, N. F., deBuys, W., Bestlemeyer, B., and Havstad, K. (2012). The range problem are a century of rangeland science: New research themes for altered landscapes. *Rangeland Ecology and Management*, 65, 6, 545–552.

Takahashi, T., Jones, R., and Kemp, D. R. (2011). Steady-state modelling—For better understanding of current livestock production systems and for exploration of optimal short-term strategies. In: Kemp, D. R., and Michalk, D. L. (Eds.). *Development of Sustainable Livestock Systems on Grasslands in North-Western China. ACIAR Proceedings*, 134, 26–35.

Tian, S., and Wang, X. (2000). Application of satellite remote sensing technique in land desertification investigating in Duolun County, the Inner Mongolia Autonomous Region. *Geoscience*, 14, 4, 459–464.

Wang, Z. W., Han, G. D., Jones, R., Kemp, D. R., Li, Z. G., Takahashi, T., and Zhao, M. L. (2011). What are the solutions for dust and biodiversity on China's grasslands? In: Kemp, D. R., and Michalk, D. L. (Eds). *Development of Sustainable Livestock Systems on Grasslands in North-Western China. ACIAR Proceedings*, 134, 128–138.

Wang, Z., Jiao, S., Han, G., Zhao, M., Willms, W. D., Hao, X., Wang, J., Din, H., and Havstad, K. M. (2011). Impact of stocking rate and rainfall on sheep performance in a desert steppe. *Rangeland Ecology and Management*, 64, 249–256.

Zhang, L., Han, G., Zhao, M., Jia, L., Li, Y., and Bai, W. (2011). Effects of different stocking rate on vegetation condition and sheep weight in Stipa breviflora desert steppe. *Journal of Inner Mongolia Agricultural University*, 32, 3, 120–124.

Author Information

Guodong Han[1]*, Tong Liu[1], Zhongwu Wang[1], Zhiguo Li[1], Mengli Zhao[1], Kris Havstad[2], Jianguo Wu[3], David Kemp[4]

1. Inner Mongolia Agricultural University, Hohhot 010018, P.R. China
2. USDA-ARS, Jornada Experimental Range, Las Cruces, NM 88003, USA
3. Arizona State University, Tempe, AZ 85287, USA
4. Charles Sturt University, Orange, NSW 2800, Australia
* Corresponding author

Summary Ⅲ: Solutions and Adaptations

Martin Kappas and Jiquan Chen

The purpose of this section is to provide the reader with sound concepts and technology necessary to design, build, implement, operate, and use comprehensive spatial resource management information for the management of the physical and human resources of the DEA region. The authors of these six chapters focused on the socioeconomic aspect of the DEA region with adaptive management and policy-making plans as the focal points — the key elements for developing solutions and adaptations to proceeding and future global change issues in DEA.We explore the status of physical and human resources, specifically pronouncing twoquestions: Is there a reason to be concerned? What is the nature of such a concern?

Starting with an overview of state-of-the-art methods for the monitoring and assessment of dryland ecosystems in Chapter 14 and scaling importance in Chapter 15, the reader gets technical challengesin applying remotely sensed methods and technologies in a spatial context that can be broadly applied in DEA and elsewhere. The competition for scarce resources in DEA is driving the need for better management information systems designed to provide decision support tools to resource managers. The central message is that the DEA region needs a comprehensive observation system (OS), which has been, until now, not available. One such tool is a spatial resource information system (DEA OS). This DEA OS could be built on existing technologies and data sets providing up-to-date spatially extensive yet consistent information on the aspects of the resources of interest to the managers (e.g., grasslands for range management). Following this broad claim,Chapter 15 comes up with the concrete problem in the observation of vegetation areas in the Tarim Basin (Northwest China). The case study focuses on remotely sensed approaches, which are often fraught with errors that stem from the interaction between the sizes and the spatial distributions of vegetation communities and the spatial resolution of the observing satellite sensor. A major problem appears when the spatial resolution of the sensor is larger than the isolated (or narrowly interconnected) vegetation communities, thematic classification, and by extension and area estimates become less reliable.

The following chapter by Reynolds and colleagues (Chapter 16) presented a very comprehensive, up-to-date review of coupled human and environmental systems using many relevant case examples in drylands. They argue strongly that "the challenges that must be addressed and the usual list of stakeholders with vested interests are scientific researchers, local inhabitants, businesses, resource managers, and policy-makers", and suggest that education of the genenral public holds a special need for the long-term solution. Popular concepts, such as systems thinking, resilience thinking, hierarchy theory, the Drylands Development Paradigm, and the Diagnostic Framework for Social-Ecological Systems, are well-integrated into the Ewecol Framework. These concepts are further demonstrated in Chapters 17–19 for the Mongolia Plateau from social economic, biophysical and management perspectives. Mongolia and IM share similar ecological gradients of climate, vegetation and soils, and have undergone significant social-institutional and ecological transformations: from collective to market economies, increasing market integration, and climate variations and changes that affect vegetation productivity and human livelihoods (Gao et al., Chapter 17). Grassland degradation, for example, is considered as both a local and global environmental problem as it affects not only hunters and herdsmen whose livelihoods rely on healthy grasslands and wildlife, but also people who suffer from resultant hydrological disturbances, dust storms, and rising commodity prices. In Chapter 18, Wang and Brown provide the reader with information about institutional, market, and ecological changes in the context of climate change in Mongolia and IM. Here, an emphasis on the role of institutional change is made clear through analysis of grassland degradation on the Mongolia Plateau since the early 1960s. Finally, Han et al. (Chapter 19 of this book) provide us case studies from IM by addressing "adaptive management", which is an integrative approach that combines anticipation, implementation, monitoring, and evaluation in order to improve ecosystem management based on continuous adjustment and learning process.

The section "Solutions and Adaptations" provides evidence that the sustainable development of the DEA region can be achieved through a nexus approach— an approach that integrates land management and government across sectors and scales. A future nexus approach can also support the transition of the DEA region to a more sustainable development that focuses on resource use efficiency and better policy coherence. Showing the rising interconnectedness across sectors, a cutback of negative social, economic, and environmental externalities could raise overall resource use efficiency and environmental system services, providing better future prospects for the people living in the DEA region.

Index